THE OMNI-DIRECTIONAL THREE-DIMENSIONAL VECTORING PAPER PRINTED OMNIBUS FOR BEWITCHED ANALYSIS A.K.A.

The Omni-Directional Three-Dimensional Vectoring Paper Printed Omnibus for Bewitched *Analysis a.k.a. The* Bewitched *History Book*
© 2012 David L. Pierce. All Rights Reserved.

No part of this book may be reproduced in any form or by any means, electronic, mechanical, digital, photocopying or recording, except for the inclusion in a review, without permission in writing from the publisher.

All photos are from the collection of the author unless otherwise noted.

Published in the USA by:
BearManor Media
PO Box 1129
Duncan, Oklahoma 73534-1129
www.bearmanormedia.com

ISBN 978-1-59393-691-4

Printed in the United States of America.
Book design by Brian Pearce | Red Jacket Press.

The Bewitched History Book
By David L. Pierce

Table of Contents

ACKNOWLEDGMENTS 9
PREFACE 13
INTRODUCTION 17

SEASON ONE

I, Darrin, Take This Witch, Samantha 21
Be It Ever So Mortgaged 25
Mother Meets What's-His-Name 28
Help, Help, Don't Save Me 31
Little Pitchers Have Big Fears 33
The Witches Are Out 35
The Girl Reporter 38
Witch or Wife 40
Just One Happy Family 42
It Takes One to Know One 45
And Something Makes Three 47
Love is Blind 50
Samantha Meets the Folks 52
A Vision of Sugar Plums 55
It's Magic 59
A is for Aardvark 61
The Cat's Meow 64
A Nice Little Dinner Party 66
Your Witch is Showing 68
Ling Ling 70
Eye of the Beholder 72
Red Light, Green Light 74
Which Witch is Which? 76
Pleasure O'Riley 78
Driving is the Only Way to Fly 81

There's No Witch Like an Old Witch 82
Open the Door, Witchcraft 85
Abner Kadabra 87
George the Warlock 90
That Was My Wife 93
Illegal Separation 96
A Change of Face 97
Remember the Main 100
Eat at Mario's 103
Cousin Edgar 106
It Shouldn't Happen to a Dog 108

SEASON TWO

Alias Darrin Stephens 117
A Very Special Delivery 119
We're in for a Bad Spell 121
My Grandson, the Warlock 124
The Joker is a Card 126
Take Two Aspirins and a Half a Pint of
    Porpoise Milk 128
Trick or Treat 132
The Very Informal Dress 134
…And Then I wrote 136
Junior Executive 138
Aunt Clara's Old Flame 141
A Strange Little Visitor 143
My Boss, the Teddy Bear 145
Speak the Truth 146
A Vision of Sugar Plums 148
The Magic Cabin 149

Maid to Order	152
And Then There Were Three	152
My Baby, the Tycoon	155
Samantha Meets the Folks	158
Fastest Gun on Madison Avenue	159
The Dancing Bear	161
Double Tate	162
Samantha the Dressmaker	163
The Horse's Mouth	165
Baby's First Paragraph	167
The Leprechaun	170
Double Split	171
Disappearing Samantha	172
Follow That Witch, Part One	174
Follow That Witch, Part Two	176
A Bum Rap	177
Divided He Stands	178
Man's Best Friend	180
The Catnapper	182
What Every Young Woman Should Know	184
The Girl with the Golden Nose	186
Prodigy	187

SEASON THREE

Nobody's Perfect	193
The Moment of Truth	195
Witches and Warlocks are my Favorite Things	197
Accidental Twins	199
A Most Unusual Wood Nymph	201
Endora Moves in for a Spell	204
Twitch or Treat	208
Dangerous Diaper Dan	210
The Short Happy Circuit of Aunt Clara	212
I'd Rather Twitch Than Fight	214
Oedipus Hex	216
Sam's Spooky Chair	219
My Friend Ben	221
Samantha for the Defense	223

A Gazebo Never Forgets	225
Soapbox Derby	229
Sam in the Moon	231
Ho Ho the Clown	233
Super Car	235
The Corn is as High as a Guernsey's Eye	237
The Trial and Error of Aunt Clara	239
Three Wishes	242
I Remember You…Sometimes	245
Art for Sam's Sake	246
Charlie Harper, Winner	248
Aunt Clara's Victoria Victory	250
The Crone of Cawdor	252
No More Mr. Nice Guy	255
It's Wishcraft	257
How to Fail in Business with All Kinds of Help	260
Bewitched, Bothered, and Infuriated	262
Nobody But a Frog Knows How to Live	265
There's Gold in Them Thar Pills	267

SEASON FOUR

Long Live the Queen	275
Toys in Babeland	277
Business, Italian Style	280
Double, Double, Toil and Trouble	282
Cheap, Cheap	285
No Zip in My Zap	286
Birdies, Bogeys, and Baxter	289
The Safe and Sane Halloween	290
Out of Synch, Out of Mind	293
That Was No Chick, That Was My Wife	295
Allergic to Macedonian Dodos	298
Samantha's Thanksgiving to Remember	302
Solid Gold Mother-in-Law	305
My, What Big Ears You Have	307
I Get Your Nanny, You Get My Goat	310

Humbug Not Spoken Here	312
Samantha's Da Vinci Dilemma	315
Once in a Vial	317
Snob in the Grass	320
If They Never Met	322
Hippie, Hippie, Hooray	326
A Prince of a Guy	329
McTavish	331
How Green Was My Grass	334
To Twitch or Not to Twitch	336
Playmates	339
Tabatha's Cranky Spell	340
I Confess	342
A Majority of Two	345
Samantha's Secret Saucer	347
The No-Harm Charm	350
Man of the Year	354
Splitsville	355

SEASON FIVE

Samantha's Wedding Present	361
Samantha Goes South for a Spell	363
Samantha on the Keyboard	366
Darrin, Gone and Forgotten	368
It's So Nice to Have a Spouse Around the House	373
Mirror, Mirror on the Wall	376
Samantha's French Pastry	379
Is It Magic or Imagination?	381
Samantha Fights City Hall	383
Samantha Loses Her Voice	386
I Don't Want to be a Toad, I Want to be a Butterfly	388
Weep No More, My Willow	392
Instant Courtesy	396
Samantha's Super Maid	398
Cousin Serena Strikes Again, Part One	400
Cousin Serena Strikes Again, Part Two	402
One Touch of Midas	404

Samantha the Bard	407
Samantha the Sculptress	408
Mrs. Stephens, Where Are You?	411
Marriage, Witches Style	413
Going Ape	416
Tabitha's Weekend	418
The Battle of Burning Oak	421
Samantha's Power Failure	423
Samantha Twitches for UNICEF	427
Daddy Does His Thing	429
Samantha's Good News	432
Samantha's Shopping Spree	434
Samantha and Darrin in Mexico City	437

SEASON SIX

Samantha and the Beanstalk	445
Samantha's Yoo-Hoo Maid	448
Samantha's Caesar Salad	451
Samantha's Curious Cravings	453
And Something Makes Four	456
Naming Samantha's Baby	458
To Trick or Treat or Not to Trick or Treat	460
A Bunny for Tabitha	463
Samantha's Secret Spell	465
Daddy Comes for a Visit	468
Darrin the Warlock	471
Samantha's Double Mother Trouble	473
You're So Agreeable	475
Santa Comes to Visit and Stays and Stays	478
Samantha's Better Halves	481
Samantha's Lost Weekend	483
The Phrase is Familiar	486
Samantha's Secret is Discovered	489
Tabitha's Very Own Samantha	492
Super Arthur	495
What Makes Darrin Run	497
Serena Stops the Show	500
Just a Kid Again	503

The Generation Zap 505
Okay, Who's the Wise Witch? 507
A Chance on Love 510
If the Shoe Pinches 513
Mona Sammy 515
Turn on the Old Charm 518
Make Love, Not Hate 521

SEASON SEVEN

To Go or Not to Go 531
Salem, Here We Come 534
The Salem Saga 537
Samantha's Hot Bedwarmer 540
Darrin on the Pedestal 543
Paul Revere Rides Again 547
Samantha's Bad Day in Salem 551
Samantha's Old Salem Trip 555
Samantha's Pet Warlock 558
Samantha's Old Man 561
The Corsican Cousins 565
Samantha's Magic Potion 567
Sisters at Heart 569
The Mother-in-Law of the Year 574
Mary the Good Fairy 576
The Good Fairy Strikes Again 579
The Return of Darrin the Bold 581
The House that Uncle Arthur Built 585
Samantha and the Troll 589
This Little Piggie 592
Mixed Doubles 595
Darrin Goes Ape 598
Money Happy Returns 602
Out of the Mouths of Babes 603
Samantha's Psychic Pslip 605
Samantha's Magic Mirror 609
Laugh, Clown, Laugh 611
Samantha and the Antique Doll 613

SEASON EIGHT

How Not to Lose Your Head to Henry VIII,
    Part One 621
How Not to Lose Your Head to Henry VIII,
    Part Two 624
Samantha and the Loch Ness
    Monster 626
Samantha's Not-So-Leaning Tower
    of Pisa 630
Bewitched, Bothered, and Baldoni 634
Paris, Witches Style 638
The Ghost Who Made a Spectre
    of Himself 642
TV or Not TV 645
A Plague on Maurice and
    Samantha 648
Hansel and Gretel in
    Samanthaland 652
The Warlock in the Gray Flannel
    Suit 655
The Eight Year Itch Witch 658
Three Men and a Witch on a Horse 661
Adam, Warlock or Washout 663
Samantha's Magic Sitter 667
Samantha is Earthbound 670
Serena's Richcraft 674
Samantha on Thin Ice 676
Serena's Youth Pill 679
Tabitha's First Day of School 682
George Washington Zapped Here,
    Part One 684
George Washington Zapped Here,
    Part Two 688
School Days, School Daze 691
A Good Turn Never Goes
    Unpunished 694
Samantha's Witchcraft Blows a Fuse 697
The Truth, Nothing But the Truth, So Help
    Me, Sam 702

AFTERWORD 709
INDEX 713

Acknowledgments

This book would not have come about without the help of many people whom I would like to thank.

First, I would like to thank my Heavenly Father for all the blessings he has given me, specifically for seeing fit to place me in circumstances as good as mine. I would like to thank my parents for always supporting me in everything I do. I would've said 'family' but my brothers have never supported my love for *Bewitched* so really, a big "NO THANKS…jerks." I'd like to thank my sister, Heather, for her support and consultation on areas of the book. I also want to thank my nephew, Mayson, for watching *Bewitched* with me even with your daddy telling you how uncool the show is.

To Elizabeth Montgomery, the lady who caught me in her spell portraying America's favorite witch, Samantha. To Agnes Moorehead (Endora), Marion Lorne (Aunt Clara), Alice Ghostley (Esmerelda), Maurice Evans (Maurice), Bernard Fox (Dr. Bombay) and Erin Murphy (Tabitha) for being the best spell casters in the entire cosmos. To Dick York and Dick Sargent (the Durwoods, I mean, Darrins) for being a necessary, but irritating, conflict. And also to Director/Producer William Asher, for all his great input into the series.

A special thanks to the writers of *Bewitched* from whose fertile minds these great episodes sprang forth. There are too many to list here. Just watch any episode and my thanks goes to that person(s) who are listed after 'written by.' Thanks should also go to the rest of the cast and crew for making this magic real.

I would also like to thank those people or companies who made it possible for me to watch the show: Screen Gems for producing the show, ABC-TV for taking the chance on a show that could've been risky for them but turned out to be a ratings winner, my local stations, KSTU Fox13 for carrying *Bewitched* during the daytime when I was younger and KJZZ-TV for carrying it when I was older, Nick-at-Nite for introducing me to the rarely seen first two seasons and later on the rest of the show and TV Land, TBS, WGN, Columbia House videos for releasing the uncut versions on tape, and Sony Home Entertainment for releasing all the seasons on DVD.

I would like to thank the following individuals for allowing me to watch *Bewitched* at their homes even if they didn't want to: Leatrice and Ray Reddington; Louise and Lenard Jones; Shelley Malmgren; Carol Thomas; Grandma Pierce; Kimberly Mutz; Michael and Michelle Cousins; my college roommates specifically Travis Riggs and Dale Stewart for allowing use of their TV and VCR, my current roommates Tracey Jones and Jennifer Rohn, and, of course, my family.

My appreciation also goes out to Victor Mascaro, webmaster of Vic's Bewitched Page, for providing a great *Bewitched* site and to his friend Scott Viets aka The Bewitched Critic who provided great critiques of the episodes (I truly wish he'd finish the rest). And a special thanks to the webmasters of *Harpiesbizarre.com*, Melanie Parker and Bob, and the people who post there. I love being able to discuss my favorite show with others; to Mark Simpson for providing me tapes of certain episodes, some photos for this book that I could've never got without his help, and for also carrying on the magic of *Bewitched* with the Fanfares that he puts so much work and effort into; to Herbie J Pilato (author of *Bewitched Forever*) for writing the *Bewitched* Bible. Without his book I would've been at a loss to find a listing for every *Bewitched* episode before the internet came around. Thanks to *www.bewitched.net* for providing access to the original filming schedules, to Joe Gardener for finding the summer re-run schedules, to Ian Wallis for helping with information from old TV Guides and to Ronny Green for having saved some of my earlier 40 Years Ago…posts which this book is based on. Also thanks to author Charles Tranberg for inspiring me with his work.

And a big hug to my *Bewitched* family, whom I won't name by name, but you know who you are. I treasure the emails, calls, and postcards that I receive from you. Your friendship is very special to me. I must thank Sharon Orazi by name, though, as it was her brilliant idea to start up *Bewitched* Club, where we would watch an episode and then discuss, like book club. From those discussions came my thoughts on each episode which I share in this book. Years ago we also put together every date we could find relating to the show, for which I'm truly grateful, as it was her idea. I would also like to thank her for the photos from her collection she offered.

I would like to thank Ben Ohmart and Bear Manor Media for making my dream come true!

Lastly, I would like to thank Paula Abdul, for suggesting that her fans write goals and work at them which inspired me to actually finish the book and submit it. You have always left me 'spellbound' and I love you much!

If I have forgotten anyone I sincerely apologize. Please know that it wasn't intentional.

Preface

I have always been a fan of *Bewitched*, the enchanting television sitcom about what happens when a regular mortal guy marries a beautiful witch. The show aired in syndication in the afternoons when I was growing up and I watched it with my mother when I came home from Kindergarten. I was captivated by the supernatural reality presented where I saw people and things disappear, objects float, and historical figures brought back to life. But most of all I was captivated by the gorgeous enchantress known as Samantha played by Elizabeth Montgomery. Liz was so classy, yet funny. And her features were so mesmerizing: her green eyes capped by pointy eyebrows, her cute nose which somehow she managed to wiggle in order for Samantha to perform magic, and her beautiful golden hair. She was perfect. And she definitely was the reason I watched day after day, though the magic happenings were a huge plus.

Bewitched was the avenue from where I learned about major historical figures like Queen Victoria, George Washington, Benjamin Franklin, and Napoleon Bonaparte. I would've never wanted to learn about history had it not been for the show, presenting in the space of less than a half hour, key points about these figures and the times they came from. It was thrilling to be in history classes when these people were brought up and to be able to say a little bit more about them than my fellow classmates who hadn't had the pleasure of "meeting" these characters via *Bewitched*. You can imagine my sheer delight and awe when, during American History, it was announced we'd be studying the Salem Witchcraft Trials! I knew about Salem from the handful of episodes where Samantha and Durwood traveled to Salem so Samantha could attend the Witches' Convention. They also happened to travel back in time to where the trials took place. Never in my wildest imagination would I have thought such a thing would take place in the real world — people actually accusing and believing in witches! Could it be that Samantha, Endora, and all the other wonderful witches from TV were actual people? Of course, I learned that the Salem Witch Trials were much darker than what I had seen on *Bewitched*. However, I wouldn't have wanted to learn about the trials had it not been for the show.

As I grew older I became fascinated by how the show was created, who the actors were, and wished that I had been a part of the generation that was introduced to *Bewitched* in primetime. TV has been a big part of my own life and there are quite a few times where certain episodes of *The Simpsons*, *The Cosby Show* or *Sesame Street* evoked a memory of something that happened the night those episodes aired. I wanted to know what it would've been like to have *Bewitched* be a new show with its episodes taking place while my life was taking place.

And so it was as the fortieth anniversary of the premiere of the pilot episode of *Bewitched*, September 17, 2004, came rolling up that I decided I would try to recreate that feeling of "newness" and watch each episode on its fortieth anniversary. At the time I was also a very active member of the discussion boards at *www.harpiesbizarre.com* and seeing that Sony (the company which owns *Bewitched*) wasn't really doing anything to celebrate the anniversary, I thought I would do so by recapping each episode with my thoughts about it and any trivia I had found for that particular episode. And so each week, on a *Bewitched* episode anniversary I would create a post titled "40 Years Ago…" and write about the episode as though we were all just watching it for the first time. The posts were quite popular with the members of the board (known as "Harpies") and I was quite pleased that they found them interesting.

As time went on I realized that many major events took place during the run of *Bewitched* such as the assassination of Martin Luther King, Jr., the landing on the moon, and the Vietnam War. All those events are still discussed nowadays and are still quite relevant. Even more uncanny were the similarities to events that were happening now such as sending troops to another country where we seemingly don't have a responsibility to be, the election of a new president amid the failure of the economy, and the tensions caused by the clash between certain belief systems and ideologies in relation to the gay community, much like what happened in relation to the black community in the 60s. I realized that I was learning more about history than I had known before. It was strange how even though the things that happened around *Bewitched* were so long ago, they still had a part in shaping our world and helping us to understand it.

With the suggestion of my fellow Harpies, I decided that my posts were more significant than what I had thought, and that having them part of the ever-changing Internet wasn't the place to keep them, that a book would be a better idea.

The majority of the entries for each episode are pretty much word for word copies of what I originally posted on each episode's fortieth anniversary. Unfortunately, with the first two seasons or more, I didn't have the forethought to keep a hard copy of those posts and so I had to recreate them.

The intent of this book is to bring the magic of *Bewitched* to a bigger audience than just *Bewitched* fans but also to bring the magic and wonder of the world that was happening around *Bewitched* to those fans, like me, that weren't around to experience it all, so that we can see that even though we think we may have it tough, it's always been that way, but yet humankind still manages to make it without using witchcraft, like Samantha would try to do. Of course, it wouldn't always work, but at least we could see that someone so powerful was trying to get along the "hard way."

The episodes are described as they played out, followed by my review and any trivia known about the episode. Important world events that happened during the week are also discussed including important happenings in music and television. The book is intended to not really be read straight through, but more like an event calendar, but the choice is yours.

Introduction

America in the mid-60s was less than the idyllic image set up by the television programs of the day. For one, there were many riots throughout the South spurred by tensions from the bigotry seen from white people towards black people. The Reverend Martin Luther King Jr. was a proactive champion of peace and equality and would stand up for the rights of all men, but unfortunately, his words would sometimes hit deaf ears and hard hearts and the violence seen against so many people because of the color of their skin continued. An attempt to calm the trouble between the races was made by President Lyndon Johnson when he signed into act the Civil Rights Law of 1964 which abolished segregation. Unfortunately, just because a law was signed it still didn't ease much of the tension.

America's heart was also healing from the devastation caused on November 22, 1963 when President John F Kennedy Jr. was assassinated which symbolically, but quite literally, brought to an end the optimism exuded from his administration, a time known as "Camelot," a name meant to evoke the romantic images of King Arthur's kingdom.

And also continuing from the late 50s was the war in Vietnam which the U.S. supported with many troops, a war which many couldn't say why we were fighting, we just were.

But all wasn't so bleak, as it was around this time that America first heard the rocking tunes of the Beatles, which forever changed the face of music and brought a sense of fun and frivolity to the country. Amazingly enough, the Beatles occupied the top four spots on the charts for the first part of 1964.

And the sense of hope was still milling about via the space program at NASA, where the scientists, technicians, and astronauts kept vigilant work to bring to pass President Kennedy's promise that an American would land on the moon by the decade's end. It was in 1964 that Ford introduced the Mustang for the first time, a car which still captures the attention of the motoring public today.

Also in August 1964 one of the most magical movies of all time was released by Walt Disney: *Mary Poppins* starring newcomer Julie Andrews and TV favorite Dick Van Dyke from, of course, *The Dick Van Dyke Show*. The movie went on to win five Academy Awards and was the first Disney film to be nominated for Best Picture.

Speaking of Dick Van Dyke, to give you a picture of what was currently on TV when *Bewitched* popped in, his show was number three the previous year with *The Beverly Hillbillies* and *Bonanza* occupying the first two slots, respectively, and *Petticoat Junction* and *The Andy Griffith Show* rounding out the top five spots. The only real fantasy program on at the time was *My Favorite Martian*, which was the number ten show.

Keeping all that in mind, and realizing that all summer long ABC-TV had run brief commercials touting their newest program about a girl witch who marries an unsuspecting mortal boy we arrive at that most magical evening of Thursday, September 17, 1964...

Elizabeth Montgomery and Agnes Moorehead in a promo photo advertising ABC's Bewitched.

Season 1

SEPTEMBER 17, 1964

It was on this night at 9:30 PM EST that ABC aired Episode 1: "I, Darrin, Take This Witch, Samantha" brought to us by the Quaker Oats company, forever changing our lives.

Just like a fairy-tale *Bewitched* opened with the line, "Once upon a time…" accompanied by the scene of a beautiful young blonde woman

Endora ignores Samantha's pleas as she zaps Durwood to the hotel lobby.

walking confidently down a city street. She begins to enter a turnstile door to a building but her efforts are hampered by that of a "red-blooded American boy" who, for whatever reason, whether he didn't see her, or he *did* see her, enters the same section of the turnstile door causing them a bit of awkwardness. The door happens to be to a department store and they seem to bump into each other at every corner of the store. And so, like the narrator tells us, "…they decide they'd better talk this over before they get into an accident." In a matter of seconds for us viewers, this girl and boy go on many dates, all of which were mainly just smooching, and before you know it they are engaged, married, and on their "…typical honeymoon, in a typical bridal suite except…that this girl is a WITCH!" 'Witch' is where we see the beautiful girl motion towards a hairbrush across the room that immediately flies to her hand! AWESOME!

It's here we meet the girl's mother, a formidable looking, but beautiful, woman who in a flash of light appears in the honeymoon suite wondering where her witch-daughter has been. The girl tells her she's now married, but that doesn't seem to faze the mother who insists that her daughter fly away with her. Of course, that's ridiculous, and the girl says so and even goes so far to tell her mother that she's married a human man, not a male witch! Thinking that he's just a mere annoyance, Mother suggests that they just have him trip on a rug and break an arm or something, but the girl is insistent that she loves him and is not going to do him any harm. Mother has other ideas and tells Samantha, her daughter, that she'll take care of him as he's about to enter the bedroom. With a wave of her hand Samantha's husband suddenly finds himself in the lobby of the hotel! Thinking it must be the champagne he asks the desk clerk for the key to his room. Samantha is very annoyed with her mother and with the wiggle of her nose, something truly magical in and of itself, she incants some strange words which seemingly infer that she is trying to get her mother to disappear. But it doesn't work and by this time the boy has returned to the suite. With another pitch of magic, Mother sends him back down to the lobby. She also finds that Samantha hasn't told him about her witchly ways, but the girl assures her mother that she is going to tell him as soon as Mother leaves, which she does.

Samantha's bewildered husband makes his way back to the room where she greets him at the door of the bedroom. Forgetting all the confusion of the night, he goes to commence his honeymoon but surprisingly she stops him and closes the bedroom door telling him she wants to talk! He becomes even more flabbergasted when she tells him that what she wants to talk about is the fact that she's a witch! He doesn't take her seriously thinking that the events of the day may have messed with her mind but soon finds that maybe his mind is being messed with when the table lighter suddenly sparks by itself, the ash tray moves to catch his ashes, and when he goes to get some fresh air, the window opens by itself! Thinking that a strong drink may cure his confusion, one suddenly pops into his hand and changes at his request. It suddenly dawns on him that his wife IS a witch! When he about faints, a chair zooms to catch him and Samantha runs to his side to comfort him. Darrin (the boy's name according to Samantha) tells her he hadn't figured on all this but she negates his fears (for the moment) by offering up her womanly charms.

The next day Darrin takes his troubles to the bar and tells his friend Dave that Samantha is a witch, but Dave is too interested in offering inane advice. Seeing as he didn't get help from his friend, Darrin takes his worries to the doctor who thinks that maybe the honeymoon was so stressful that Darrin is in need of a vacation. Not even the bartender will believe him. And so, after having had some time to think of how he wants to handle this different situation, Darrin tells a nervous Samantha that even though she's a witch, he loves her and can't give her up. She is overjoyed and tells him she'll give up her powers and live like he does, which pleases him very much as for some reason he thinks that being normal is the way to go.

Later on, Darrin finds out that his troubles aren't all taken care of when he gets back to the office, McMann and Tate, an advertising agency where apparently he's Vice President, to find that his girlfriend, who had gone on a long trip to Nassau when he met and married Samantha, has returned. Sheila (the girlfriend who obviously idolizes Jackie Kennedy) knows about the marriage and acts like she doesn't care. In fact, she invites him and Samantha to her house for a relaxed "…sitting on the floor…" kind of potluck. Darrin is impressed at the way she's taken the news and accepts the invitation.

The night of the potluck arrives and Samantha is nervous walking up to Sheila's door as she lives in a rather affluent house and Samantha is dressed so casually. Darrin assures her that Sheila had said it was casual but finds he is wrong when the door opens to show that all the guests, and Sheila, are dressed in fine dinner wear! Sheila is as cool as a viper and does everything in her power to make Samantha look dumb, especially when she has Samantha sit on the opposite end of the table than she and Darrin. Samantha also does everything in her power not to resort to using her magical powers to make Sheila look dumb, but finally can't take it anymore when Sheila insinuates that Samantha has had plastic surgery. With a swipe of her hand across her own hair, Samantha causes a lock of Sheila's to come flipping up in her face a couple times, then she makes Sheila's soup bowl move underneath her elbow and finally causes Sheila to sneeze, spraying the soup in another guest's face. In all the commotion, Samantha makes a maid's empty tray suddenly appear with food which spills all over Sheila, who tries to make a getaway from the table, when suddenly the zipper on her dress breaks. Darrin, trying to be a gentleman, tries to help Sheila but he gets an invisible kick in the rear thanks to Samantha's wiggling nose. For the final act in her revenge, Samantha blows a candle out causing a huge windstorm to burst through the door sweeping up Sheila's wig in its wake. Sheila, utterly embarrassed, runs up stairs leaving a group of confused guests but a serene Samantha who continues on with dinner.

Later, back at their apartment, Darrin confronts Samantha who tries to play around with him. She tells him that it was much harder to give up witchcraft than she thought it would be and again uses her womanly charms to persuade him to forget all about it. As he decides it's time to move their "discussion" to the bedroom, Samantha notices that the kitchen is a total disaster and tells him she'll be in after she cleans up. Realizing that she just promised to try harder at using no witchcraft, she also realizes that cleaning the mortal way will totally kill the mood that Darrin and she are in, and so with a wave of her arms, the kitchen suddenly becomes sparkling clean and Samantha leaves, saying out loud, "Maybe I can taper off."

This episode is FANTASTIC! AWESOME! If we were to use a scale to rate the episodes, with four stars being the best and no stars being the worst, this one would DEFINITELY get TEN stars! Just like Mary Poppins it is "practically perfect in every way." Elizabeth Montgomery is so beautiful and innocent throughout, Agnes Moorehead, in her brief scenes as Mother, is wonderfully dramatic and Dick York is perfect as the "red-blooded American boy." What's even greater about the episode is how it runs about twenty-five minutes but seems longer, and NOT in a bad way! Nancy Kovak as Sheila is a perfect foil for Samantha and it's totally awesome seeing her get her come-uppance.

I must make note of the fact that the director of this episode, William Asher, was best known for his work on *I Love Lucy* for some of the most favorite episodes like "The Chocolate Factory." He had also directed many other series but was also a movie director and in fact had directed the 1963 movie *Johnny Cool* which co-starred none other than Elizabeth Montgomery. Even greater, it was on that set that they met and fell in love and were married. Another notable tidbit about this episode is the fact that it went into production the day President Kennedy was assassinated. Liz and Bill Asher were friends with the Kennedys but felt it would be better to go on with work even on that sad terrible day.

Liz said that she wished her father, debonair actor Robert Montgomery, would've been the narrator for the first episode. However around this time he wasn't in the greatest of health.

Also debuting for the Fall 1964 season were *Gilligan's Island*, *The Addams Family* and *The Munsters*.

Here is one of my favorite lines:

SAMANTHA: *"Even witchcraft can't keep him out there all night. It's our honeymoon!"*

SEPTEMBER 24, 1964

It was on this night that ABC originally aired Episode #2: "Be It Ever So Mortgaged" presented by Chevrolet.

After Darrin has left for work, Samantha tries to make him a cake the mortal way but has no success especially with her mother babbling on about how Darrin has changed Samantha into someone hardly recognizable. Soon Darrin comes home and against Samantha's wishes her mother decides to stay to observe him closer, but inconspicuously. Samantha seems very self-conscious with the affectionate Darrin, seeing her mother popping up all over, but she soon gets over it when Darrin announces that he has a surprise for her: he's found a house for them and he wants to take her to see it to get her approval before they buy it. So they make plans to go see the house the next day.

The next day soon arrives and Mother shows up again still in a snit about Samantha having given up her life that once was "…in the sparkle of a star." Samantha tells her that she's moved on and wishes that she could be happier for her and invites her mother to come along with her to see the house.

Later on, Samantha and Mother stand in front of the newly built house, so new in fact that the lawn hasn't been laid yet. Mother decides they need to see how it looks with the lawn and flowers and trees and so she zaps them up. Unbeknownst to the two witches, they are being watched from across the street by a busy-body woman named Gladys who has been watching the progress of the house and is completely mystified by the sudden changes. She tries to get her husband, Abner, to confirm but he's too "busy" being retired. Samantha likes the way the house looks on the outside but zaps away the changes insisting that she and Darrin will make them on time, rather than witchcraft, and she and her mother enter the house. Of course, by this time Gladys has nagged Abner into looking out the window and he sees the house just as it was making him think that his wife is crazier than he thought.

In the house Samantha and her mother start zapping in furnishings and decorations to see how it will all look. Gladys decides to come and investigate the house closer and find out what the two women were up to and when she looks in the front window she sees all the décor and takes a second look to see it all gone again, she freaks out running back to the not-so-sympathetic arms of her husband.

After having a good look at the house, Samantha decides that she is pleased with the decision and asks her mother to stay to meet Dennis, er, Darrin but Mother won't have it as she is just in her carpet slippers and with that she pops out. Darrin is pleased that Samantha loves the house as much as he does and is intrigued when Samantha suggests that her mother is there and that they should meet. When they go back in the house Mother is no-where to be found. A knock at the door makes Darrin think they've locked Mother out and when he answers the door and sees an older female there, he believes his assumptions are correct

Endora sitting atop 1164 Morning Glory Circle. PHOTO COURTESY OF MARK SIMPSON.

and gives her a big hug. Of course, this female is Gladys, who again freaks out and runs home.

Later on, after purchasing this house located at 1164 Morning Glory Circle, Samantha tells Darrin that the woman he hugged was actually Gladys Kravitz from across the street and he chuckles about it pleased that they won't be considered stand-offish and he and his wife enter their new home. Unknown to them, Mother is resting on the roof and tells us, "Believe me, it'll never work."

I would definitely give this episode four stars. It's truly magical what with Samantha and her Mother (who hasn't been properly named yet, though she is listed in the credits as 'Endora') zapping in furniture and changing the yard, to Mother's speech about witches being "…quicksilver, a fleeting shadow, a distant sound…" Of course the main event here is the introduction of the house, a character in its own right, 1164 Morning Glory Circle. This home is one of the best known TV houses ever! The outside of it is located at what is now known as the Warner Bros. Studio Ranch in Burbank, CA but back when the episodes were being filmed it was known as the Columbia Lot. It is merely a façade, meaning there is nothing in the house but struts and beams. The interior of the house was shot in studio a couple blocks away. However, there is a real house located in Santa Monica, CA that is the basis for the design of the house that is flipped.

We also get to meet Abner and Gladys Kravitz played by George Tobias and Alice Pearce. Gladys is the ultimate in wacky neighbors that seem to live near everyone in TV Land.

There are two bloopers in this episode, the first being able to see the definitely pregnant Elizabeth Montgomery in full shot when she's in the kitchen watching the broom sweep up the cake crumbs. This is because right after the pilot was filmed Liz found that she was pregnant with her and Bill Asher's first child and so they were in a race to get some episodes shot before she had to leave on maternity. The other blooper is that when Gladys looks in the front window of the house, you can see one of the beams that is holding up the façade.

Three nights later on September 27, *Bewitched* fans were given a rare treat to see the cast in living "culluh" (how Liz pronounced 'color' in her later *Bewitched* promotions) when a five and a half minute long promotion for Chevrolet's car lineup for 1965 aired immediately following *Bonanza*. The commercial took place in Virginia City where *Bonanza* is set and the cast of both shows interacted along with Robert Vaughn from another Chevy sponsored show *The Man from U.N.C.L.E.* to show off the new vehicles.

OCTOBER 1, 1964

It was on this night that the episode entitled "Mother Meets What's-His-Name" was to air but for some reason lost to history, it was pre-empted and aired the following week when "It Shouldn't Happen to a Dog" was scheduled to air, making them episodes three and four, respectively. However, because in later schedule viewings it was noted that an episode didn't air this evening it was assumed that "It Shouldn't Happen to a Dog" aired, marking it erroneously as the third episode, when in fact it didn't air until the end of the season on June 10, 1965.

It was also on this day that former Berkley graduate student Jack Weinberg was arrested for refusing to show his I.D. to the campus police while sitting at a table designated for distributing materials promoting C.O.R.E. (Congress of Racial Equality), which was banned by the school. Before the police car in which he was detained could move, upwards of 3,000 students surrounded it protesting his arrest for nearly thirty-two hours beginning the Berkley Free Speech Movement which lasted that school year.

The day before Elizabeth Montgomery came in fourth place for Top Female New Face at the Golden Laurel Awards.

OCTOBER 8, 1964

It was on this night that Episode #3: "Mother Meets What's-His-Name" aired, presented by the Quaker Oats Company.

Samantha receives a surprise visit from the Morning Glory Circle Welcome Wagon Committee comprised of Shirley Clyde, June Foster, and Gladys Kravitz. They have brought a cake as a gift and relish being invited in so they can make an assessment of whether the new couple in the neighborhood meets their standards. June and Shirley's two young boys and an unknown neighbor boy also run in the house making themselves at home. Samantha is embarrassed that she hasn't unpacked any of her silver or linens yet, which seems to really please June Foster as Samantha seems very amateur at being a hostess. That is, until Samantha twitches up some fine silver and real bone china so they can have coffee with the cake.

Upstairs the boys have found a surprise visitor in the form of Samantha's mother. When they introduce themselves as an Indian, a Cowboy and his horse, she tells them she is a witch, which doesn't faze them at all and they begin rough housing again, even falling play-dead on Mother's lap, who is quite uncomfortable.

As the ladies discuss the activities they are involved in Shirley notices that the children are awfully quiet and when they go to investigate they find all three boys bound and gagged lying on Samantha's bed. June and Shirley chalk it up to the boy's rambunctiousness but Gladys realizes there is no way all three boys could be tied up, because who would tie up the third? Gladys decides to call Abner and tell him about the new strange

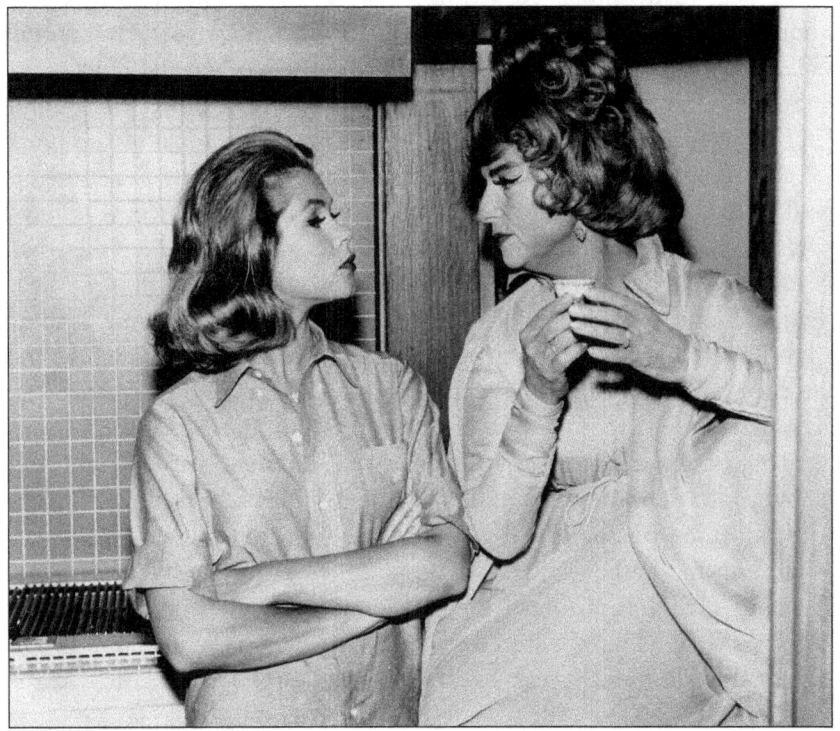

Samantha and Endora visit just before the women of the Morning Glory Circle Welcome Wagon arrive. PHOTO COURTESY OF MARK SIMPSON.

thing that has happened not realizing that the phone hasn't even been hooked up yet. Of course, Abner isn't attentive at all and finally Gladys hangs up on him just as there is a knock at the kitchen door. She answers letting the telephone repairman into hook up the telephones and doesn't realize the gravity of the situation until she leaves Samantha's, sick at the thought of having used an unhooked up telephone.

Later on Mother pops back in, disgusted at the behavior of the humans, but Samantha assures her Darrin isn't like that. She then suggests that maybe it's time that Mother and Darrin meet face to face. Endora agrees, promising not to do anything funny.

That night Darrin is nervous at the prospect of meeting his mother-in-law and is fearful of what she may look like considering he's never had a witch for a mother-in-law before. Samantha is incensed that he would think she would look anything out of the ordinary and just as they are about to get into an argument, the doorbell rings. Nervous, Darrin answers the door to find a regal looking woman at the door. Samantha introduces them, almost forgetting her husband's name and invites her mother in. Mother requests a very dry martini made with Italian gin, Spanish vermouth, and a Greek olive, but the Stephens don't have the ingredients so she just zaps one up. While visiting, Mother tells Dennis, er, Darrin that he may call her Endora (no last name, because he'd never be able to pronounce it). When Endora levitates a cigarette to her fingers and magically lights it, Durwood gets nervous. But Endora gets agitated when she sees Samantha lift an ashtray to her with her hand rather than levitating it to her. When she asks if Samantha has forgotten how, she is told that Durwood doesn't like her to do those things anymore. Endora is furious thinking that Durwood is trying to corrupt her daughter and he doesn't feel she should have any say as to what goes on in their house. Tempers flare to the point where Endora just about turns him into an artichoke but Samantha stops her. Not wanting to mess around with this hard headed mortal anymore, Endora goes to leave but tells him he'd better watch himself, because she'll be watching, and with a huge explosion she disappears in a puff of smoke. Durwood thinks maybe he should let up but Samantha tells him she made the decision to give up witchcraft. When he wonders what Samantha would've done had he been changed into an artichoke, she tells him she just would've turned herself into an artichoke too.

I think this episode should get four stars. It's brilliant through and through! My favorite scenes come from Gladys, especially when she's talking on the phone to Abner. And I love after she lets the telephone repair guy (which, by the way, is the first time a black person is shown on *Bewitched*) and she tells Samantha upon leaving, "I let in the repair man to hook up your telephone." And then, as she gets outside, she screams, "TO HOOK UP YOUR TELEPHONE?!!?"

I also like that, for the most part, Endora showed up willing to have a decent relationship with Donald (even if she couldn't remember his name) but because he has to be so pig-headed this wasn't to be possible for the rest of the series.

Samantha also tells us Endora's weight and height: "She's 5'4" and weighs 118 pounds." I wonder if those were Agnes Moorehead's real stats?

The scenes with the neighbors at first, along with the buying of 1164 in "Be It Ever So Mortgaged" were all part of the first episode script when Samantha was named Cassandra written by Sol Saks.

OCTOBER 15, 1964

It was on this night that ABC aired Episode #5: "Help, Help, Don't Save Me" as presented by Chevrolet.

Durwood has been assigned to the Caldwell Soup account and spends all night working on new ideas for the campaign. When Samantha sees them, she's impressed but realizes that maybe Durwood's groggy mind could use some help, so after reviewing them she adds a boost to each of the slogans, along with a little drawing for each. Durwood is thrilled, as Samantha's ideas are really great. However he begins thinking that maybe the reason they're so good is because she used witchcraft to come up with them. Samantha assures him they were really just her imagination but he doesn't believe her and he leaves for working believing she's lied to him.

At lunch with Mr. Caldwell, Durwood finds that the client is looking for something with a classic feel but also something with sex appeal (?!) and when he presents his original ideas to him, Mr. Caldwell flat out rejects him. He thinks about presenting Samantha's ideas but realizes he may just come to rely on her and her voodoo and doesn't do it.

That evening Samantha finishes making sure her apology dinner is going to look perfect, and that she looks stunning when Durwood comes home. Her plans are dashed when Durwood claims that he could feel Samantha invisibly prompting him to share her ideas. When she tells him she had been at home all day preparing for the evening, he again thinks she's lying. Having enough from him, she furiously runs up stairs into the bedroom slamming the door. He follows her and finds that the room is empty…or so he thinks as some suitcases come flying out of storage and begin packing themselves. He tries to stop Samantha but she won't and when the suitcases are packed they float out of the room, down stairs and out the front door into the night sky ignoring Durwood's pleading. Once he shuts the door Samantha appears outside followed by her mother. Samantha tells Endora that Durwood thinks she's a liar and Endora suggests they give it to him. Still madly in love with her husband, but hurt, Samantha declines and pops into her flying suit and with that disappears with her mother.

After a sleepless night Durwood is a mess at the office and his boss, Larry Tate, can see it. He tells him that they are going to lose the Caldwell

Campaign if Durwood can't come up with something quick. Durwood mentions that he has ideas that would cinch the campaign and shows Samantha's to Larry who is impressed and so he calls a meeting with Caldwell. Durwood is dejected "knowing" that it's witchcraft that will cinch the campaign and is blown away when Mr. Caldwell rejects those ideas too, saying they are too gimmicky! Realizing that he unjustly accused Samantha of using her magic he pardons himself and runs home where he throws his heartfelt apology to his wife out in the atmosphere. Samantha appears and tells him she accepts his apology and thinks it's silly that they let a can of soup ever come between them. Durwood realizes that she may have just spontaneously come up with a great slogan and rushes off to tell Mr. Caldwell and Larry.

A little while later, Durwood shows Samantha that her idea was a success and takes her out to the beach beneath a huge billboard of two people sitting across from each other that says, "The only thing that will ever come between us. Caldwell Soup."

I would give this two and a half stars and that's because Durwood is such a jerk and because Samantha is so willing to admit that she was wrong, when she wasn't. If Durwood really loved Samantha he would take her word that she hadn't used magic. He did make up for it at the end but only after someone else proved it to him.

I LOVE the scene with the packing suitcases, parts of which you can see shadows at the top of the screen of the poles used to fly the clothes around. And I also adore the scene outside when Samantha and Endora fade away. This is the first time we see Samantha in what she would later term to be her "flying suit."

Elizabeth Montgomery lent her drawing talents to this episode. You can see her drawing of a little elf briefly at first. Liz had wanted to be a Disney animator and was inspired to be an actor by watching *Snow White and the Seven Dwarfs* (1937).

This episode will later be remade in Season Eight as Episode #251: "A Good Turn Never Goes Unpunished."

The day before this episode aired Dr. Martin Luther King Jr. became the youngest recipient of the Nobel Peace Prize for his efforts in the fight against racial segregation through non-violent means.

OCTOBER 22, 1964

It was on this night that ABC aired Episode #6: "Little Pitchers Have Big Fears" sponsored by Quaker Oats.

Durwood is surprised when he finds that Samantha has developed a friendship with a boy who is very sheltered and coddled named Marshall Burns. His life is ruled by his overprotective mother who won't allow

Samantha gives encouragement to "Marshmallow" Burns. PHOTO COURTESY OF MARK SIMPSON.

him to play baseball as she thinks it's too dangerous. Sam feels Durwood should take Marshall to the baseball tryouts but he refuses as he feels that Mrs. Burns' wishes, no matter how insane, should be honored. Not wanting Marshall to miss out on being a kid, Samantha decides she'll take him.

The next day Samantha accompanies Marshall to the baseball tryouts and she sits next to her nervous neighbor Mrs. Kravitz who is there with her nephew Floyd. Mrs. Kravitz tells Samantha that she may as well go home because Marshall is so bad at baseball that everyone calls him "Marshmallow." Realizing that Marshall just hasn't had a chance she decides to ensure his place on the team by assisting his pitches with a few of her own. Marshall makes the team and is quite pleased.

That night when Samantha is telling Durwood all about the tryouts they hear the back gate open and when they go down to investigate they find Marshall, who has run away from home because his mother was banning him from playing ball. Durwood calls his mother who is furious that Samantha would harbor her runaway child and contribute to all the things that may hurt him. Durwood goes along with Mrs. Burns much to the surprise of Samantha until he mentions that of all the safeguards Mrs. Burns could enforce on Marshall, the best one would be to not have a bathroom in the house as it's so dangerous. Realizing that she's being made fun of, Mrs. Burns leaves.

The next day she calls again furious that Marshall may be over at the Stephens'. They haven't seen him and Samantha realizes that it's the season opener and that Marshall must've gone to the game. They talk Mrs. Burns into going with them and they head to the ballpark. Marshall is there just as Samantha suspected and Mrs. Burns demands that he come home with her. Coach Gribben won't hear of it as Marshall is such a great ball player, thanks to Samantha giving him a boost of confidence. Mrs. Burns relents and lets Marshall stay. With the score tied, Marshall is up to bat and hits a home run. Samantha thinks that maybe he won't make it around the bases to lead his team to victory but Durwood makes sure she can't wiggle her nose by kissing her and Marshall slides into home winning the game for his team! Mrs. Burns realizes that she has been preventing her child from having a happy childhood and she accepts Coach Gribben's offer to practice with her son.

I'd give this about two stars. It's cute enough but it just seems like not much happens.

Marshall is played by Jimmy Mathers, who is the younger brother of the Beaver, Jerry Mathers. They practically look like twins! And Mrs.

Burns is played by June Lockhart, better known to TV audiences as Timmy's mother from *Lassie*.

The Los Angeles Temple of the Church of Jesus Christ of Latter Day Saints can be seen off in the distance at the ballpark.

That same night *Bewitched* premiered in the UK. Two days before, it premiered in the Netherlands.

OCTOBER 29, 1964

It was on this night that ABC aired the first Halloween episode of *Bewitched*, #7: "The Witches Are Out" sponsored by Chevrolet.

Samantha's friends Mary, Bertha, and her bumbling Aunt Clara come to visit as they feel it's time that something be done about the horrible witch image of the old crone with the long hooked nose, blacked out teeth and warts that is propagated at this time of year and they felt that Samantha could help them.

Meanwhile, Durwood is unwillingly force-fed Halloween candy by new client Mr. Brinkman who tells him that he has the best idea for an advertising campaign for his candies and that would be an ugly old witch with blacked out teeth and warts!

Back at 1164 Bertha suggests that the fairy tales depicting witches as evil should be re-written. Samantha offers that Durwood might have ideas that may help them as he is in advertising. Just then he comes home and so as not to upset him the witches slip out through the living room wall, with the exception of poor Aunt Clara who simply bumps into it. She leaves out the back way. Durwood tells Samantha his day was rough and goes to work on the Brinkman Halloween candy campaign and comes up with an ugly old witch drawing. Just as he's finishing it up Samantha begins to tell him her idea about changing the witch image when she sees the drawing and is rightfully offended. She is furious when Durwood tells her that it's no big deal as nobody believes in witches anyway. Regardless, she feels he's being insensitive and tells him she's going to go hang by her feet in the attic and cackle at the moon. Before she can storm off Durwood rips up his picture and tells her he'll do something else for Mr. Brinkman.

The next day Mr. Brinkman is bewildered by the beautiful witch drawings Durwood has come up with including the explanation that the advertising should be different and that nobody really knows how witches look anyway, and if there are any, he wouldn't want to hurt their feelings. Brinkman thinks Durwood is nuts, and Larry even more so, when Durwood explains that he was going more for a Glinda the Good Witch of the North from *The Wizard of Oz* look. When Mr. Brinkman insists that he wants an ugly witch, Durwood refuses and so Larry fires him!

Samantha feels bad that she caused Durwood to lose his job and can't sleep thinking about it. She sneaks out of bed and calls on Bertha, Mary,

Samantha protests Mr. Brinkman's use of a stereotypical witch on his Halloween candy. PHOTO COURTESY OF MARK SIMPSON.

and Aunt Clara. She tells them that they should convince Mr. Brinkman that witches are good regular folk and suggests that they do a protest march in protest of using offensive witch pictures for his advertising. They zap up signs that say "Witches Are People Too" and "Brinkman Unfair to Witches" and "Coolidge for President" (that one was Aunt Clara's) and they fly off to Brinkman's.

Brinkman is awakened by his lights turning on and he sees Samantha sitting on his lamp and Mary and Bertha sitting on his canopy bed with Aunt Clara transfixed by his bedroom doorknob. Samantha explains their purpose for being there and demands that he change his advertising. Not believing what is going on he goes to call the police when the witches refuse to leave but Samantha changes his phone into a snake. When he goes to leave Samantha zaps him in front of a French firing squad after he blames his weird witch vision on French cooking, and just as he is about to be shot he confesses that he does believe in witches so she zaps him back. He still insists that he won't change the advertising, until the witches zaps his face into that of an ugly old witch. When he realizes that he is mistaken, he apologizes and Samantha and her friends leave and Mr. Brinkman's face changes back to normal. When he goes to leave his room he finds that his doorknob is missing!

The next day Mr. Brinkman tells Durwood that he can use his beautiful witch and explains that he had been robbed the night before of all the doorknobs in his house. Later, after the sales figures come in, they are phenomenal and Larry explains that they found that mainly fathers buy Halloween candy.

I would give this episode four stars. I think it's a brilliant idea to have the themes of racism addressed, but not in a direct way so as to keep with the lightness of the show. It's also the first episode with Aunt Clara, played masterfully by Marion Lorne, who in real life collected doorknobs. I love seeing Samantha sitting on top of the lamp. It's also worth noting that a spell ("Zolda Pranken Kopec Lum") is used to simply pour tea, when later something like that would be done with just a wave or twitch.

Bertha is played by Reta Shaw, who had just been seen in the smash hit *Mary Poppins* that summer. Mr. Brinkman is played by Shelley Berman, a famous comedian of the time.

This episode was the last to be filmed before Elizabeth Montgomery gave birth to her and William Asher's first child, William Asher Jr.

NOVEMBER 5, 1964

It was on this night that ABC originally aired Episode #8: "The Girl Reporter" sponsored by Quaker Oats.

A beautiful local junior college student named Liza Randall has decided to shadow Durwood at his job for the school paper. She comes to his home to interview him and it's obvious to Samantha that Liza has

Liza tries to clean up Durwood from the drink she spilled. PHOTO COURTESY OF MARK SIMPSON.

a crush on Durwood, based on a photo of him that was printed in the newspaper when he received an award. He makes plans to show Liza around the offices of McMann and Tate the next day. After Liza leaves Samantha is amused to find that Durwood can't see that Liza really likes him. He says that every girl likes an older mature man and when Samantha jokingly responds, "You certainly are that" he almost counters that at least he's not a witch but stops before it comes out. Of course, Samantha knows what he was going to say and pops out and back across the room a couple times before he slyly admits that she's an enchanting beautiful woman and she forgives him.

The next morning Liza shows up for their "date" wearing a sexy spaghetti strap dress and high heels causing a bit of concern for Samantha but she sees them off. Right after they leave a knock comes at the door and when Samantha answers she is greeted by a very tall robust young man who says that he is Liza's boyfriend "Monster" and that he had followed Liza to 1164 Morning Glory Circle when he became suspicious that she really wasn't going shopping with her mother like she said. He also informs Samantha that Durwood may not be physically well after they get home as Monster is going to rough him up! Not wanting Durwood to get hurt, she invites Monster in to alleviate his fears and offer him some food.

At the office Liza doesn't pay the least bit attention to Durwood's explanation of how the advertising world works and instead she prepares them a drink of gin and scotch. As she tries to make the moves on him, Durwood finally sees what is going on and tries to stop her and only manages to get the drinks spilled on him and her. When she tries to help him get cleaned up they tumble on the couch and are caught in a very compromising position just as Larry walks in with a client he was going to introduce to Durwood by surprise as they had seen Durwood's car outside. Larry avoids embarrassment for everyone by referring to Durwood by a different name and they leave as Durwood cuts his and Liza's meeting short.

Back at home, Samantha finds that Monster not only has a hearty appetite for food, (especially half banana cream, half apple pie) but he's got that hungry look for her! Before anything can go further, Durwood and Liza arrive and Samantha is shocked to smell alcohol on the both of them and she's not sure if she can believe Durwood's explanation. Liza is embarrassed and she and Monster leave with him furious at her until she insists that it was Durwood who made the moves on her. He turns back for the house and when he goes to punch Durwood, Samantha twitches up an invisible barrier which breaks Monster's hand. He tries again and is again met with the invisible resistance. Believing that Monster's hurt hands will hurt his football career, Liza goes to smack Durwood, who thinks that she'll meet the same barrier only to have her hand meet up with his face as she intended. When he looks to Samantha for an explanation, she looks pretty pleased with herself.

The next morning Durwood tells Samantha he knows she's still mad at him and when she nonchalantly asks why, he knocks on an invisible barrier she's put up around herself. He tells her there was nothing to be mad about and apologizes and she twitches the barrier away.

I love this episode and would definitely give it four stars. It seems like an episode that is rarely discussed but it has so much going for it! First of all, this is the first time in their marriage that another man has shown interest in Samantha. And it's really cute that Samantha twitches up the pies according to Monster's wishes only to end up with the impossible half banana cream/half apple pie. And the scene at first where no words are spoken is really cute when Samantha enlarges the sewing needle and still licks the enlarged string to get it to go through the eye of the needle, all without Durwood noticing. Samantha wears the same dress in this episode that she wore in last episode.

It was also this week, on November 3, that Lyndon B. Johnson was elected President of the United States having already been fulfilling the role for a little under a year due to the assassination of President Kennedy. He won the election with over sixty percent of the popular vote.

NOVEMBER 12, 1964

It was on this night that ABC originally aired Episode #9: "Witch or Wife" sponsored by Chevrolet.

Samantha spends her evenings having TV dinners in front of the TV and her days playing solitaire when Durwood is required to stay at the office for overtime while Larry is in Paris on business. Days pass without seeing her husband and thankfully the loneliness is broke up by a visit from her mother. Endora suggests that she and Samantha spend some time together. Surprisingly, Samantha agrees, though she says only for lunch. After vetoing the cozy Have-a-Snack, Endora suggests they have lunch in Paris. Samantha declines as she knows Durwood will be mad if she flies off, but then she admits that Durwood won't be home until very late. She relents and she and her mother fly off to Paris.

Mother and daughter have a divine lunch in Paris and when Samantha says she's got to get home Endora rebuffs with the fact that no woman would ever visit Paris without going to a fashion show. Feeling a bit nostalgic for her single carefree witch life, Samantha agrees to go.

While at the show, Samantha is horrified to see Larry and Louise Tate there and she tries to make a quiet retreat but not before Larry sees her and confronts her. She introduces her mother to the Tates and tells them that since Durwood was going to be working so much Endora offered to take her on a trip to Paris. The Tates suggest that they meet for dinner that night.

Samantha is quite distracted thinking of what Durwood will say when he finds out and she decides to pop home and call him so that he won't have any cause to wonder about what she's been doing. While she is gone Larry decides they should tell Durwood of their chance meeting and he asks for a phone to be brought to the table. When he calls Durwood's house Samantha answers the phone and quickly realizes she shouldn't

Samantha tries to hide her face from the Tates in Paris. PHOTO COURTESY OF MARK SIMPSON.

have and she hangs up and pops back to Paris. A confused Larry decides to try Durwood at the office and he tells him of the surprise meeting with Samantha and Endora just as Samantha gets back to the table. Nervously she picks up the phone to speak to her husband, and so the Tates won't be aware of the trouble she is going to be in, she pretends to have a happy conversation with him before hanging up.

Later that night when Durwood is finally at home drowning his sorrows, a penitent Samantha pops in wearing a gown she had picked up in Paris. She apologizes but drunk Durwood goes on about not wanting to be the one to clip the wings of an eagle that wants to fly. Realizing she isn't going to get anywhere with him, Samantha storms back to Paris.

The next day Larry shows up at the office early and tells Durwood that he's never seen a woman so depressed as Samantha was. Durwood realizes she truly was sorry and he decides to fly back to Paris to meet up with her.

Later, while in the middle of a dictation, Larry is interrupted by Samantha who was looking for Durwood. Larry tells her that Durwood is flying to France and a happy Samantha leaves on her own flight to find him. Endora accompanies her and Samantha flies down to peep through the window of one last flight and finds Durwood, who is sleeping. She knocks on the window and startles him before popping discreetly onto the plane to join him. They make up and continue on the flight to Paris.

I LOVE this episode! I think everyone looks so beautiful in it, and young! I like that we get to see the glimmer in Samantha's eye as she thinks back upon her life with Endora before she got married. I also like that she runs into the Tates in Paris and has to do some quick talking to explain it. That dress that she buys in Paris is gorgeous and I like the scene of her materializing at home and also when she dematerializes going back. Dick York looked very much like Jim Carrey when the wind was blowing in his face. Speaking of Jim Carrey, he was approached by Nora Ephron to play the part of Durwood/Jack in the big screen version of *Bewitched* but when he found out that it wasn't going to be a direct remake, he luckily backed out as the movie ended up being a big disappointment.

The flying scenes outside the airplane are awesome and I'm sure just like every other *Bewitched* fan I think of it when I'm flying on a plane.

Here are some of my favorite lines:

> SAMANTHA: *"Oh, if I walked in in a dress like that Durwood's eyes would fall right out of his head."*
> ENDORA: *"I doubt if Durwood would know a Dior form a gunny sack."*
>
> ENDORA *(on top of the plane with champagne in hand)*: *"It's the only way to fly!"*

NOVEMBER 19, 1964

It was on this night that ABC aired Episode #10: "Just One Happy Family" sponsored by Quaker Oats.

Endora covertly announces to Samantha that her father is coming for a visit and he knows that she's married. Samantha is delighted until it occurs to her that he doesn't know she is married to a mortal. She goes to see Durwood off to work and tells him about her father's visit. Durwood says he'll be happy to meet her father but Samantha explains that her father doesn't approve of mixed marriages and that her father will pulverize him when he finds out.

Later that night an anxious Samantha awaits her father's arrival with

Samantha is delighted at the beautiful gift her father has given her. PHOTO COURTESY OF MARK SIMPSON.

Endora. She decides she is going to stand up to him, until the doorbell rings. She hesitantly answers and finds her regal father, Maurice, standing at the door. After he dismisses his chauffeur with a wave of a hand he greets Samantha and his estranged wife with gifts. Samantha tells him that Durwood is away on business, though Maurice becomes suspicious when he sees a photo of Durwood in the army and wonders why a warlock would be in the army.

Meanwhile Durwood is trying to bide his time with Larry at a bar where he explains rather shakily that Samantha's father doesn't approve of mixed marriages. Finally he decides he's had enough of being an outsider to his own home and he goes to call Samantha in a phone booth to tell her he's coming home. Realizing that Durwood will not survive her father, she twitches the booth closed.

While Samantha has been preoccupied with Durwood, Maurice has found a birth certificate for Durwood not to mention pills in the medicine cabinet and now his suspicions are confirmed. Samantha finally relents and reveals that, yes, she has married a mortal. To say Maurice is furious is inadequate as thunder starts rolling and everything glass in the room begins to explode. Endora demands he stop but he's not about to listen

Maurice explains to his estranged wife Endora about what he did to a disagreeable little shop clerk in Zurich.

to her, she who let his daughter carry on with a mortal! She tells him that it happens in the best of families and as they are arguing Durwood, who had to have help breaking out of the phone booth, arrives at home and as he's jiggling the doorknob, Endora waves her hand so that when the door opens there is no one there. Maurice demands to know what she did with him but she stands firm though she suggests that Samantha bring in the "evening paper." Getting the hint, Samantha heads out doors with a furious Maurice who is incensed that she would be thinking about the paper at a time like this and he grabs it from her and tosses it into the fire! Horrified, Samantha reaches into the fire and retrieves her newspaper husband and zaps him back to human form. Beat and burned, Durwood confronts Maurice and tells him that no matter what he is going to always be with Samantha because he loves her. Maurice applauds his bravado but regrets having to obliterate him, which he does in a puff of smoke! Samantha is appalled and tries to get rid of her father by casting a spell at him. He finds it amusing but she seriously tells him that she never wants to see him again, that she loves Durwood. Endora, seeing her daughter's distress, threatens to move back in with Maurice if he doesn't bring Durwood back. Not wanting his jet set lifestyle cramped, Maurice agrees though he's not sure if he'll be able to bring Durwood back. With Samantha and Endora cheering him on, Maurice uses every energy in him to get Durwood back piece by piece until finally the fully reintegrated Durwood appears.

Later that night at dinner, Maurice is impressed with Durwood breaking out an old rare bottle of champagne which earlier Maurice couldn't produce. He tells Durwood that even with that it may take a few centuries for him to get to like Durwood. And with that he disappears.

I LOVE this episode! I love that we get to finally meet Samantha's father. I wish that Robert Montgomery, Elizabeth Montgomery's father, would've played the role, however I think Maurice Evans did a superb job and he and Liz have such great chemistry.

Liz looks particularly stunning in this episode. A still photo from this episode with Samantha, Durwood, and Endora graces the cover of the *Bewitched Fun and Activity Book* that was released in 1965 and proves that some of the colorizing on the DVDs was done wrong as Samantha's dress is teal but is colorized pink on the episode. Agnes Moorehead also wore that same outfit with a jacket when she first met Durwood and she also wore it to the premiere of *Mary Poppins* earlier that summer.

NOVEMBER 26, 1964

It was on this night, while we recovered from our Thanksgiving feast, that ABC aired Episode #11: "It Takes One to Know One" sponsored by Chevrolet.

Durwood is in a quandary about what to do about a model for the Miss Jasmine campaign when his thoughts are interrupted by a voluptuous beautiful sultress named Janine Fleur. He thinks she's perfect and so does Larry and they immediately set up a photo shoot. After working on the shoot for a couple hours, Durwood says they must break for lunch, especially since he has a lunch date with his wife. Dejected, Janine says that if she can't go to lunch with Durwood he better find another Miss Jasmine. Realizing he may not find another one in time, he reluctantly calls Samantha to cancel. Pleased, Endora pops in on Samantha as she hangs up the phone to gloat but Samantha tells her that it's for his work and to prove it she'll take Endora to the restaurant to prove that he's not there and she pops off with Endora close behind.

At the restaurant Samantha is shocked and depressed to find that Endora was right! Thinking that she has proved her point, Endora goes to order until she is interrupted by Samantha announcing that she thinks the woman is familiar. Endora tries to talk her out of confronting Durwood but Samantha does better than that and freezes everyone in the restaurant and walks over to the table where Durwood and Janine are. She recognizes that Janine is really the witch Sarah Baker, who admits that Endora had hired her to test Durwood's fidelity. Disgusted that Endora would stoop so low as to hire such a temptress as Sarah, she tells Sarah to stay away from Durwood and disappears. Realizing the gig is up and that she must back Samantha, Endora tells Sarah to honor Samantha's wishes and she disappears while reanimating the rest of the restaurant. When Durwood sees that time has passed faster than he had realized, he tells Sarah that they can meet later that night to discuss the campaign at her hotel. He also asks Larry to accompany him so he's not left alone with Sarah.

In Sarah's hotel room Durwood is all about business but Sarah is still set on fooling around with Durwood, so to get rid of their chaperone Sarah casts a sleeping spell on Larry. Before anything can happen, Samantha pops in and freezes Durwood. She tells Sarah that she totally trusts her husband but can't do so if Sarah is going to use magic. Sarah doesn't believe Durwood will remain faithful and she promises to not use magic. Samantha disappears and Sarah goes against her promise and throws a love potion on the fire causing Larry to want to sleep again and Durwood to make his move. Samantha, watching invisibly, twitches her nose and turns Durwood into a piranha, startling Sarah. Samantha pops in and tells Sarah she must put an end to all of it and she turns Durwood into a goldfish and puts him in a pitcher of water. Insinuating that there will be trouble if she has to pop back in, Samantha zaps Durwood back into himself, the pitcher into Sarah's hands, Larry awake, and she pops out. A confused and wet Durwood thinks that he got too frisky with Sarah and he decides they can discuss the campaign the next day. Sarah decides to accept Larry's advances until he freezes up, by magic, and Samantha pops in saying she is Louise's best friend and she zaps Larry into wanting to leave.

A little later, the Miss Jasmine campaign is a great success and when Samantha sees a model for one of the billboards with Sarah's face on it she twitches a funny face on it.

I would give this two and a half stars because I do not think Sarah is as beautiful and sexy as she's made out to be, all though I've seen the actress on *The Beverly Hillbillies* and she was quite beautiful. I suppose when compared to Liz, though, she would fall short. This is one of the first times that a sound effect didn't accompany a screen effect when Endora pops out of the restaurant. It also marks the first time Durwood is changed into an animal and surprisingly it's by Samantha's hand.

This episode was featured in the 1998 feature film *Crazy in Alabama* when the main character Lucile (Melanie Griffith) heads to California to become an actress and she lands the role of Lucile Fleur on this episode. The scene where she first enters the office is shown in the movie so we get to see Dick York for a little bit on the big screen. The confrontation at the restaurant is later acted out by stand-ins with a man playing Endora!

It was also this week that *Bewitched* made its first *TV Guide* cover with a still shot of Samantha from "Witch or Wife" when she is in Paris. This cover again proves that some of the colorization done in the late 90s was done wrong as her outfit is yellow but was colorized pink.

DECEMBER 3, 1964

It was on this night that ABC aired Episode #12: "And Something Makes Three" sponsored by Quaker Oats.

In the midst of a cleaning frenzy, Samantha is interrupted when the phone rings and on the other end is Louise Tate, the wife of Durwood's boss. She tells Samantha that she is at the corner filling station and would like to come over to talk. Hearing the nervousness in Louise's voice, Samantha agrees and once she hangs up she starts to straighten up, but realizing she'll never get the house cleaned before Louise arrives she lets out a magical exhale and at super-fast speed gets the house put together as well as herself together just as Louise arrives. Mrs. Tate is very distressed and seems to be saying that she's done with her marriage until she announces that after sixteen years of marriage, she and Larry are going to become first time parents! Samantha is thrilled and is delighted when Louise invites her to accompany her to the doctor for a checkup. She is surprised though when she finds that Louise hasn't told Larry yet as she is afraid of his reaction.

Downtown, Larry finds that he is going to have to go to the dentist for a cavity. After his appointment, he happens to see his wife and Samantha enter the office for Dr. Bricey, Obstetrician. Intrigued by why they are there, he goes to see what it's all about and overhears Samantha say that she can't wait to tell Durwood. Thrilled, Larry runs back to the McMann and Tate offices to share what he thinks is the impending news of Durwood's imminent fatherhood. Durwood, of course, is shocked and pleased at the idea of his first child. Larry tells him he should let Samantha break the news to him when she calls from the doctor's office to tell Durwood to invite Larry over so they can have dinner with the Tates that night where she intends to have Louise announce the baby news. As Larry and Durwood discuss the baby, Larry asks Durwood what he thinks it'll be which triggers the realization in Durwood that he may end up with a bouncing baby witch! He daydreams what it'd be like to have a little brood of witches and warlocks that invade his office on brooms as Samantha accompanies them on the way to the park. Durwood realizes that his wish for a witchcraft free existence will not happen with his offspring being witches and warlocks.

All dressed up for dinner, Samantha and Louise await the arrival of their husbands when Durwood and Larry show up with flowers for Samantha and they shower her with compliments and kisses. The men continue to ignore Louise for Samantha, which upsets Louise and just when Louise works up the courage to tell Larry about the baby, Samantha announces dinner is ready. As they sit at dinner, Samantha tells Louise she should tell them the news. Larry, not wanting Louise to ruin the surprise, kicks her under the table and he tells Louise that he knows that she was at Dr. Bricey's and in fact wants Samantha to tell Durwood. Perplexed, but pleased, Samantha tells Durwood about the Tate baby. Larry, thinking that Samantha just announced her own baby, gets up to congratulate the two of them until he realizes that the baby is his own. Surprisingly he is very pleased at the news and he showers his wife with kisses while Durwood and Samantha discuss the fact that it just wasn't their time yet.

I would give this episode three stars. I think it is really cute and fun. It seems that from here on out is where *Bewitched* really fell into the groove of everything working together. I can't put my finger on it but it just seems the previous episodes were all set up.

All though it's awesome to see Elizabeth Montgomery in a swimsuit for the first time it's tainted by that stupid swim cap. And it's also really weird that at first she dives in twice and then she's finished swimming. If you look close though you'll see that the Samantha that jumps in isn't Liz at all and most likely is Melody Thomas, Liz's stand in. And if you think about it, how would Mrs. Kravitz be able to see the swimming pool in

Samantha with her witch children as part of Durwood's day dream. PHOTO COURTESY OF MARK SIMPSON.

the backyard of 1164 when she was standing in her own front yard which faces Samantha's front yard? Of course, in reality, the pool at the Ranch faces the Kravitzes front yard with 1164 being down the street, across the street, and facing the side of the Kravitz's home.

I love Larry's reaction when he's so excited about Durwood and Samantha having a baby and he says, "No two people are dearer to me than Darrin and Louise!" And then the look of love and excitement on his face when he realizes that HE is going to be the papa is priceless.

I also think it's hysterical when he and Durwood first come home and he kisses Samantha on the forehead.

I do have to give the special effects crew major kudos for making all the kids fly. That must have been some feat! And speaking of the children, they are named Maurice, Endora, Samuel, Rebecca, and Julius. The first three make sense ('Samuel' being the male form of 'Samantha') and so does Rebecca as that was the name of Liz's maternal grandmother who she was very close with and the eventual name of her own daughter, but I wonder where they came up with Julius? It should also be noted that little Endora is played by Maureen McCormick, five years before she would become "Marcia, Marcia, Marcia" Brady on *the Brady Bunch*.

It was also on this night that police arrested eight hundred people at the University of California, Berkley for their peaceful sit-in against the punishment the Regents office had exercised on some students earlier in the year.

Three nights later on NBC, we were treated for the first time to the annual Christmas classic *Rudolph, the Red-Nosed Reindeer*, a one hour stop-motion animated special produced by Rankin-Bass.

DECEMBER 10, 1964

It was on this night that ABC aired Episode #13: "Love is Blind" which was sponsored by Chevrolet.

Samantha brings up her single friend Gertrude's situation with Durwood and suggests that he set his friend and co-worker Kermit up with her. Durwood thinks Kermit is way too busy with all the other women he has, not to mention he can't ever remember meeting Gertrude before so he's not sure how to describe her to Kermit. The next day at work Durwood is surprised that Kermit is willing to come over when he brings Gertrude up.

The night of the date arrives and all though she is very self-deprecating, Kermit is smitten with Gertrude. As the evening progresses Kermit asks for a unique drink that Durwood has never heard of before until, with a look from Samantha, Gertrude offers up the ingredients she didn't know. Kermit is smitten and Durwood is nervous thinking that Kermit is going to be set up with a witch! He tries to talk Kermit out of starting anything with Gertrude but Kermit dismisses him. Durwood pulls Samantha aside in the kitchen and requests that she tell him whether or not Gertrude is

Kermit (Adam West) joins Samantha, Durwood, and Susan (Chris Noel) for dinner. PHOTO COURTESY OF MARK SIMPSON.

a witch. Samantha thinks he's just being silly but then realizes that he's upset thinking Kermit is also going to get involved with a witch. Wanting to show her husband how ignorant he is being, she jokingly responds that all her friends are witches and they are just waiting for the right time to swoop down on Morning Glory Circle and claim it in the name of Beelzebub! She also zaps her roast out of the oven so she can season it to push it in his face that he happens to BE married to a witch.

A week or so goes by and Kermit and Gertrude spend every evening together. Durwood decides to break it up by calling up Susan, Kermit's last girlfriend, to invite her to dinner with him, Kermit, and Samantha. Knowing her husband is up to some shenanigans, Samantha invites Gertrude to show up to the restaurant.

At the restaurant, Susan shows up and she and Kermit reminisce about the great times they've had together. Seeing that Kermit may be forgetting Gertrude, Samantha twitches Susan into saying the truth, that she's not very impressed with Kermit at all. Susan leaves but has second thoughts until Samantha twitches her dress straps to break and her hair to come undone. Just then Gertrude shows up and Kermit is very pleased to see her. He excuses himself with her as he wants to ask her a question and when he returns, he's alone, saying that Gertrude is in the powder room, crying. Samantha is shocked until she finds out that it's because Kermit asked her to marry him and she accepted! Furious that Samantha used her magic to get Kermit and Gertrude together, not to mention he thinks that Gertrude is a witch, Darrin tells Kermit his thoughts on the matter. Of course, Kermit thinks he's being defamatory towards Gertrude and asks Durwood not to be so judgmental.

The wedding day arrives and in the middle of the ceremony Samantha freezes everyone to confirm to Durwood that the only reason Gertrude and Kermit are marrying is because of love and not witchcraft. Durwood tells her that he believes her and she restarts the wedding.

I would give this episode about two stars, if that. Gertrude, all though pretty, is very annoying. There is no way any man would be attracted to a girl who was always talking down about herself. And though I understand why she does it, I don't like that Samantha doesn't just come outright and tell Durwood that Gertrude isn't a witch. It also felt like the episode was supposed to be a setup for a great romance but it just seemed like a letdown.

Kermit was played by Adam West. This was one of his first television acting roles and two years later he would become quite famous for his portrayal of Batman, in the campy series that would also air on ABC.

DECEMBER 17, 1964

It was on this night that ABC aired Episode #14: "Samantha Meets the Folks" sponsored by Quaker Oats.

Aunt Clara unexpectedly drops in on Samantha taking her up on the offer to come visit any time as her collection of doorknobs just wasn't filling the void. All though pleased to see her aunt, Samantha is a bit nervous about having Aunt Clara stay as that evening Durwood's parents are coming to stay and it will be Samantha's first time meeting them. Aunt Clara says she'll leave but Samantha tells her that she'd rather have her stay as she is nervous to meet Durwood's parents and she'd like Durwood to meet her favorite aunt.

Durwood arrives with his parents, Frank and Phyllis Stephens, and everything seems to go well until Samantha and Phyllis are alone and Phyllis finds that Samantha doesn't believe herself to be a very good cook. Thinking that she can help Samantha with things she doesn't know about Durwood, she asks about Durwood's hives. Samantha tells her that she cured that when they realized he only gets them when he eats chicken cacciatore, something that Phyllis made all the time and was unaware was the cause of the hives. Phyllis suggests that Durwood loves a room with a lot of trinkets and she'll bring some for Samantha to decorate with until Durwood returns to the room. Phyllis tells him she was complimenting Samantha on her decorating and he responds he loves it because he hates a room to be cluttered up with ornaments. Before it can get anymore awkward, Phyllis mentions that she would like to meet some of Samantha's family and her wish comes true when Aunt Clara comes downstairs. Durwood is shocked and requests to speak to Samantha in the kitchen leaving Aunt Clara to visit with his parents. Samantha explained that Aunt Clara's visit was a surprise to her too. He's worried that his parents will find out that Aunt Clara is a witch but Samantha says there isn't any way that could happen. Meanwhile, Aunt Clara tells the elder Stephens all about her witchhood and how she's pleased that they have accepted Samantha's witchhood. They are very bewildered and even more so when Aunt Clara says she's going to go for a walk and she runs right into the living room wall and mentions how she used to be able to walk through them.

Wanting to help Samantha, who later on is emptying the ash trays in the living room, Aunt Clara enters the kitchen and tries to zap up coq au vin (a dish made with chicken) but she gets a live chicken at first. On second try she gets what she wants and she zaps up a pineapple upside down cake for dessert. At dinner, Samantha is shocked to find that the dinner is nothing like she made and she's quite embarrassed when she realizes that she had told Mrs. Stephens earlier that she didn't know how to make pineapple upside down cake. Durwood requests to speak to her after dinner and wants to know why she used magic to make dinner. Samantha denies it and says it must've been Aunt Clara trying to help. He says he'll have to talk to her about using witchcraft in his home and after dinner he finds her polishing her doorknobs. He tries to explain that his parents wouldn't understand about witchcraft but she acts like she doesn't understand until he leaves and she tells her doorknobs that they must leave.

He tells Samantha that he had a talk with her aunt but wasn't sure if she understood so Samantha goes to talk to her. Phyllis speaks to Durwood and tries to get him to admit that he's not happy in his marriage, which Frank disagrees with. Just then Samantha returns holding an umbrella and his furious with Durwood as Aunt Clara has left and she feels it's something he said to her. When he tries to calm her down she refuses telling him that he needs to accept her family just as he accepted her. Phyllis tries to interject but Frank stops her and Samantha admits that it was Aunt Clara that made the dinner and that she had wanted to impress Mrs. Stephens, but the truth is she's not good at housework or cleaning or anything else a housewife should do. Phyllis tells her she didn't want her to be perfect but she acted that way because she felt that she would be forgotten if she couldn't help Samantha with things. She also tells her that she knows that it is silly and she apologizes. Now that everyone is happy, Frank realizes that Aunt Clara is still missing and Samantha assures him that she is not because she asked her umbrella, who told her that Aunt Clara is at the bus station. Frank mentions that earlier Aunt Clara had told him they were witches and maybe she was right. Realizing that Frank thinks Aunt Clara was joking, Samantha tells him she is a witch.

After retrieving Aunt Clara, while they visit, Frank decides to do a magic card trick but Aunt Clara throws in some magic of her own and makes the card that he had Aunt Clara look at and put back in the deck, appear in his coat pocket. Aunt Clara decides to go on a walk and the elder Stephens decide to accompany her. Durwood tells Samantha that she needn't have worried about his parents visit, they loved her for herself and she takes that as a queue that he means her witchhood and she zaps all the mess from the evening away.

I would give this one four stars. It's so great to have Aunt Clara back in her second appearance. You can tell that Liz and Marion Lorne have a great rapport. And Robert F. Simon and Mabel Albertson are perfect in their roles. It's strange that this was the first time that they were meeting Samantha, however I guess since they did have to fly in, it makes sense.

I loved Aunt Clara's bag and umbrella arriving. Makes you wonder if they are really witches/warlocks that have been transformed and given to her to take care of.

That scene in the kitchen when Aunt Clara zaps up the chicken at first seems a bit scary if you think about it, as she zaps the chicken into the dish that utilizes chopped chicken. I can just imagine the witchcraft zooming through the pot tearing the feathers off the bird and cutting it up! Coq au vin will be mentioned many more times on the series.

Agnes Moorehead's big screen movie *Hush...Hush, Sweet Charlotte* starring Olivia DeHaviland, premiered two days before. Agnes was nominated for an Oscar for Best Actress in a Supporting Role and won the Golden Globe Award for Best Performance by an Actress in a Supporting Role for a Motion Picture. She came in second place for the Golden Laurel Award for Supporting Performance — Female.

DECEMBER 24, 1964

It was on this Christmas Eve, as we waited for Santa to bring us presents, that ABC gifted us with Episode #15: "A Vision of Sugar Plums," the first Christmas episode of the series, sponsored by Chevrolet.

It appears that the Morning Glory Circle community has decided to take part in a program with the Westridge Orphanage where families have an orphan stay with them for Christmas. Mrs. Kravitz is especially excited about this as she's never been a mother before, and though he doesn't want to admit it, Mr. Kravitz is excited too. They are assigned to Tommy, a nice bright eyed boy, and as they go to sign the paperwork, tough kid Michael comes up to start something with Tommy because Tommy believes in Santa Claus. Mrs. Grange, the orphanage director, breaks up the fight as Mrs. Kravitz tends to Tommy's bruises.

A little later Samantha and Durwood arrive to pick up their orphan, who turns out to be Michael. Durwood is apprehensive to take him home once he hears that Michael is a problem child but Samantha feels that they should give him a chance. She speaks to Michael and learns that he thinks Christmas is a lot of bunk and so is Santa. She tells him that he's wrong but he's still welcome to come to their home.

At 1164 as Durwood is getting Michael ready for bed, he tries to get him to lighten up about Christmas but it's no good: Michael is simply not a fan. Durwood and Samantha decide that maybe they can change his attitude by having him see "Santa Claus" delivering the presents. However Santa will be played by Durwood in a suit. Samantha goes upstairs to read to Michael, who falls asleep. A short while later Samantha hears pebbles being thrown at the window which is her sign that Durwood is ready. She begins reading the story very loudly to wake Michael and she acts like she didn't realize he had fallen asleep. She continues to read though they hear a commotion downstairs. She asks Michael to come help her investigate as Durwood had gone to the village for something.

When they arrive downstairs and turn on the light "Santa" turns around from delivering the presents and admits that he was caught but it doesn't matter as he goes to give Michael his present. Not one to be fooled, Michael calls Durwood out on his bluff and tells him that he's not a little kid anymore and he goes back upstairs. Deflated, Durwood gives up but Samantha says she'll talk with Michael. She finds out that his own father had dressed up like Santa and had told Michael that there really wasn't a Santa, that they were all kids' fathers stuffed with pillows dressed up. Samantha tells him that it's really not like that and she knows because she's met Santa Claus and has been to the house at the North Pole. Not believing her, Michael tells her nobody could get to the North Pole and Samantha tells him that she can because she is a witch. Now he really thinks she's flipped but she sees that he'll have to have some proof so with the wave of a hand and a twitch she suddenly appears in her flying suit. Michael is astonished but wonders where her black hat is. Annoyed that she's going to have to dress like the stereo type witch, she agrees, and with a sigh, a pointy black hat appears on the top of her head. As if all this weren't enough Michael wonders where her broom is and so she beckons towards the door and suddenly a broom comes dancing through until it stops at Samantha's foot. Delighted, Michael asks if she really rides it and she says she does and he can too and suggests that they fly up to the North Pole. Ecstatic, Michael agrees and starts to get on his robe when Durwood walks in flabbergasted at the sight of his wife dressed as a witch, especially in front of Michael. Samantha explains about their ride to see Santa Claus which stupefies Durwood as he didn't realize Santa was actually real! Samantha invites him along and, curious, he agrees.

Across the street, the Kravitzes and Tommy are singing Christmas carols and after they finish their last song Mrs. Kravitz says she's going to go do some dishes and then they'll go to bed. As she goes to retrieve a plate near the window something in the sky catches her eye, what looks like two adults and a child riding on a broom! She tells Tommy and Mr. Kravitz, who tries to cover up her hysteria by acting like she's acting like she's seen Santa and his reindeer and so he suggests they sing "Jingle Bells" to usher them in. Mrs. Kravitz tries to tell him that is not what she's seen but he won't listen.

A little while later, up North, Samantha and crew arrive at the snowy North Pole mere feet from the door to Santa's house. When they knock on the door a harried elf wants to know who's there and Samantha tells him to just tell Santa that Samantha is there and he'll know.

While they wait Durwood asks Samantha how long she's known Santa and she admits to a long time, however the way she says it seems to imply that it may actually be longer than Durwood realizes. They are ushered in and Michael is astounded by all the toys and the elves and then by the jolly Old Elf himself. Santa asks Michael to pick anything he would like from the tables and that maybe he would like to choose something for someone

Samantha, Durwood, and Michael wait at Santa's door. PHOTO COURTESY OF MARK SIMPSON.

he knows. He solemnly tells Michael that the beauty of Christmas isn't what we get but what we've seen with our hearts.

In the morning, Durwood wakes up on the couch with Michael sitting on his lap and he wonders if it just wasn't all a dream until he sees snow prints that he had tracked into the house. A little while later Michael goes over to the Kravitzes to give Tommy a truck he had picked up in the North Pole. Tommy is surprised but even more so when Michael tells him where he got it from and Gladys listens in. Realizing she can finally get Abner to believe her about what she saw last night she runs to get him. Meanwhile, Michael makes Tommy promise not to tell about the North Pole trip and he leaves. When Gladys gets back with Abner and sees that Michael is gone she tells Tommy to tell Abner what Michael had told him. He acts like he doesn't know what she's talking about and she's foiled again.

Over at 1164, while Michael and Durwood are playing with the new presents, Mrs. Grange shows up with the Johnsons, a couple who is going to adopt Michael. He gives Mr. Johnson a tool set and as he does he realizes what Santa said was true.

This episode definitely gets four stars! It is so sweet and filled with magic, both witchly and Christmas-y. I love the scene at first with Samantha bringing the tree home in her purse. I also love that we get to see Samantha dressed as the stereotype witch all though I prescribe to what Samantha and Endora say about witches, that they really don't dress like that. And seeing Durwood, Samantha, and Michael flying away on the broom is just awesome!

I also think that maybe the reason Gladys is such a snoop is that she's never had any children so she's never had anything to occupy her time.

It also feels like this episode was filmed quite earlier than the rest of the series, like in the 50s, and I think that's what also adds to its charm.

Michael is played by Billy Mumy, one of the 60s most famous child actors. He pretty much guest starred on about every show and was featured on *Lost in Space,* which would begin the next year.

Mr. Johnson is played by Bill Daily who would become known to TV audiences as Tony Nelson's best buddy Roger Healey on *I Dream of Jeannie* next season.

Santa is played by Cecil Kellaway. He played the father of witch Jennifer in the 1941 movie *I Married a Witch,* considered to be a precursor to *Bewitched.*

This episode also marks the first one NOT directed by William Asher. Instead it was directed by Alan Rafkin.

DECEMBER 31, 1964

For those of us that just wanted a quiet evening in to celebrate the New Year, ABC regaled us with a repeat of the first episode "I, Darrin, Take This Witch, Samantha" recut with Durwood and Samantha celebrating the New Year by thinking about the way they met and got married. This would be the first time *Bewitched* would air as a rerun.

It's also worth mentioning that sometime in 1964 the beloved children's classic *Charlie and the Chocolate Factory* by Roald Dahl was first published.

JANUARY 7, 1965

It was on this night that *Bewitched* returned with an all new episode, #16: "It's Magic," sponsored by Chevrolet on ABC.

Samantha is elected to be Entertainment Chairman for the Hospital Relief Fund by the women of the Morning Glory Circle Women's Committee by surprise when she goes to meet them for lunch. She finds she'll only have a budget of $50 but the women are confident she'll be able to pull it off. After they leave, Norman the waiter tells Samantha that he had overheard their conversation and he happens to know a magician who would perform for the $50 and he gives her his address.

She arrives at Zeno's, the magician, just as his business associate (and girlfriend) Roxie Ames is storming out because she's tired of him drinking away their funds and not landing any gigs. He's happy to help Samantha but she's not sure if he'll be able to do it as he continues to drink. She tells him that he'll be hired but only if he quits drinking. As he goes to raise a glass to that, she zaps in a couple of goldfish in his alcohol (hopefully also changing the vodka into water!). She zaps them away a moment later only to zap in a parrot and when he asks her if she sees it she zaps the parrot away. Nervous that he's gone too far, Zeno pours out his remaining alcohol.

Later at the Hospital Relief Fund Benefit where Zeno is to perform, Samantha finds that Zeno is nervous about performing, especially without Roxie. He admits that he's not a great magician and without Roxie to dress up the act, he won't perform. Samantha tells him that he's a wonderful magician but when he doubts that she knows what a great magician is, she tells him that her family does a little bit of magic and she ties his bowtie by just pulling on one end of it. Delighted, Zeno asks Samantha to fill in for Roxie and she reluctantly agrees.

Durwood and Mrs. Kravitz are surprised to see Samantha as Zeno's beautiful assistant and even more shocked as Zeno starts doing exceptionally wonderful tricks such as re-forming a cut rope and making multiple bunnies appear out of a top hat. If all that wasn't enough, Samantha twitches and all the bunnies jump backward back into the hat!

The next morning Durwood is upset that Samantha used her powers to help Zeno as he thought she had given up witchcraft. As they speak, the phone rings with Zeno on the other line. He has called to tell Samantha that he's been called in to be a last minute replacement on the television program *Variety Showcase* and he would like her to be his assistant again. She tells him she can't until he starts crying and she tells him she'll at least go to his rehearsal.

At the studio, Zeno tells Samantha that he feels it was because of her presence that he was so good at the Hospital Benefit and he asks her to stay for the show. She agrees seeing how important it is to him.

That night when the show goes on the air, the Kravitzes are in the audience as Gladys wants to prove that the reason Zeno is so good is that Samantha helped him. Before Zeno goes on, who should show up but Roxie who had heard that Zeno would be on TV. She tells him that she's going to go on tonight as his assistant. Once he goes on Roxie upstages him at every chance and his tricks do not go well at all. Zeno recognizes Roxie isn't there to really help him, and she admits that she wants to be seen on TV so she can be the *Variety Showcase* girl. When she goes off stage to retrieve a prop, she finds that Samantha has it and she tries to snatch it away dragging Samantha out on to the camera. Embarrassed and angry, Samantha causes Roxie's hand to become stuck in a fishbowl that she was supposed to show was empty. As Zeno tries to cover for her and move a table out of the way, he accidentally snags it on the back of her dress ripping it away. Roxie is so angry now she goes to throw the fishbowl at him, but Samantha throws a pitch of magic at her making Roxie disappear into a big puff of smoke! Seeing that the audience is really into it, Zeno gets more confident and continues with the show performing admirably. When he asks Samantha what happened to Roxie, she assures him that Roxie will be back. Durwood shows up and tells Samantha that Zeno has been renewed for the next thirteen weeks because his client, the sponsor, loved the act so much.

I would give this one three stars. It's an all right episode and really cute that Samantha would help out a magician with her magic. I like that the women of the Morning Glory Circle Welcome Wagon Committee are back. Unfortunately it's the last time we'll see the other two women.

The scene at Zeno's apartment is fun and the parrot popping out has always been one of my favorites as the sound matched up so well with the bird disappearing. However, on the DVDs, most likely because of what is known as a layer change, the scene is sullied because in the original, Samantha nods her head, and it switches back to Zeno and the parrot, and the bird disappears and Zeno turns to it. On the DVD Samantha nods her head, the scene switches to Zeno however the bird is already gone and the picture is paused for just a moment.

Samantha looked hot in that assistant's outfit and it's funny when Mrs. Kravitz tells Abner that she saw Samantha give Zeno a look and he says, "You should look so good!"

Three days before, President Johnson delivered his "Great Society" speech during his State of the Union Address. The Great Society was a set of domestic programs designed to eliminate poverty and racial injustice as well as help with medical, urban, education, and transportation problems.

JANUARY 14, 1965

It was on this night that ABC aired Episode #17: "A is for Aardvark" sponsored by Quaker Oats.

Thinking he's forgot to lock the back door, Durwood gets out of bed to do so only to trip down the stairs and sprain his ankle! What's worse is that Samantha remembers she already locked it.

The next morning, the laid up Durwood drives Samantha batty as she is constantly interrupted by him ringing a bell so that she can bring him something. She finally decides to save herself a trip upstairs when he flies a paper airplane note down to her to bring up another pencil so he can finish his crossword puzzle, so she flies a pencil up to him. Irritated that Samantha would resort to magic she tells him that she's getting tired of running up and downstairs for him constantly. She also suggests that she can get the house to cooperate with him whenever he asks for something. At first he's apprehensive but then when he sees how tired she is, he agrees. She tells him to ask for something to test it out and he asks for a banana. Happy that the house is going to help out, Samantha smiles waiting for a banana to come floating into the room but her smile fades as nothing happens. She goes downstairs to investigate and finds her mother sitting on the TV eating a banana. Endora admits that she saw it floating by but Samantha explains to her who it was really for. Amused, Endora tells her that her plan will backfire because every mortal will want more and more once they are given a little power. Samantha disagrees and sends another banana to Durwood.

Samantha and Durwood discuss his possibility to use magic. PHOTO COURTESY OF MARK SIMPSON.

Upstairs, Durwood tries out his new powers by opening and closing the window and then he decides to really try it out by ordering a ham sandwich and potato salad. In the kitchen Endora and Samantha continue their discussion when suddenly the refrigerator opens and the mustard, pickles, and various other condiments fly out to the counter where the ham lays a couple slices on some bread with lettuce. Samantha is pleased that Durwood is so open to using his powers but Endora insists it's all going to go to his head.

Later Samantha is a bit worried that maybe her mother was right when Durwood tells her that he's been thinking about how selfish he has been for making her give up her magic and that from now on they are going to have anything they want. She tells him that she's never been upset about giving up her powers and in fact had wanted to live as a mortal. He thinks she's just done that to please him and Endora pops in loving that she was right but also pleased at Darrin's new attitude. He tells the two his wishes for stuff that he's always wanted and when his list goes on and on, Samantha is shocked. He tells her that they should have everything they want and in fact he tells Samantha that she should zap up a fur coat for herself, one every bit as nice as Louise Tate's. He won't hear of it when she tells him that the only reason Louise has one is because they can afford it and so she begrudgingly zaps one up. Pleased with how everything is going Endora leaves.

The next day Samantha is shocked too when she comes in from shopping to find that Durwood has decided there is no point in working and has resigned from McMann and Tate! When she goes up stairs, Endora greets her to tell her she told her so but Samantha tells her that she's going to prove to Durwood that too much of a good thing is bad.

That evening when Durwood wants to know what's for dinner Samantha comes downstairs in a stunning white evening gown and tells him that she has decided that he's right, that they are going to live it up by having the best food, go on lots of vacations and get a bigger house with marble floors and sunken bathtubs, and sell their house which Durwood is surprised by as he always thought Samantha loved their house. A little sad, he goes to make plans to sell it. Samantha thinks her plan has failed as she hears a phone call come from the realtor to show the house. She hears the doorbell ring as she's upstairs packing and when she comes downstairs she sees that a package has been delivered. Durwood tries to hide it but she insists on seeing it and opens it to discover roses with a note from Durwood wishing her a Happy Sixth Month Anniversary. There is also a little box with the flowers that she opens to discover a watch with an engraving on it that says, "I love you every second." Samantha is overcome with emotion as she tells Durwood that she loves him and those gifts mean more to her than anything that she's ever had in her whole life. He tells her that he's been thinking about the fact that not working for anything anymore may lead to a dull life. She is pleased that he finally understands why she chose to give up her powers. He tells her that even though he feels like that now, it may be hard for him to not want powers again and so he requests that she turn back time a little to erase the memories of the past couple days. She agrees and turns time back to when he had flown the paper airplane down. However this time she just runs the pencil up to him thus averting the cooperating house conversation.

This episode is magnificent! Everything about it is perfect, and not just "practically perfect." It is such a powerful episode and so early in the series! But it wouldn't have worked better at any other time. Can you imagine this episode with Dick Sargent?

That scene in the kitchen with Endora and Samantha when Durwood's lunch is making itself was SO magical to me!

I noticed some weird things in this episode too. Durwood must be a real good paper airplane maker to make some of them fly from his bed at the far end of the bedroom, down the upstairs hall, TURN and fly downstairs. However, later on in the series ("Samantha's Super Maid") he mentions how he won a paper airplane making contest. Even then he wouldn't have been able to fly them the way he did.

I also noticed that in the sandwich making scene that another pickle seems to appear in the jar. What I think may have happened is that one was hiding behind the other and fell while they were setting up the next shots.

All in all, this episode gets ten stars from me. It's in my top episodes of all time and William Asher has said that it's the definitive *Bewitched* episode. It is also the first and last episode to be directed by a woman, Ida Lupino, who was a popular actress and director.

A publicity still taken during shooting of this episode was used on the cover of the *Bewitched* storybook from 1965. It's one of the rare times we get to see the cast in 'culluh!'

JANUARY 21, 1965

It was on this night that ABC aired Episode #18: "The Cat's Meow" sponsored by Chevrolet.

At the office, Durwood is being congratulated by Larry and Charlie Godfrey, the President of Countess Margaret's Cosmetics for his new ad campaign. However Mr. Godfrey dampens the mood when he reminds them that they must get approval from Margaret Marshall herself, known in the ad business as "the Iron Tigress" because of her aggressive nature. Just then she shows up and after reviewing the layouts she says that she'll need more time to decide. She says that she would like to make a few changes but she has to fly back to Chicago and insists that Durwood join her on her yacht. He hesitates as he doesn't want to break the plans he had with Samantha for their six month anniversary but Larry promises that he'll be there and reminds him, after Ms. Marshall and Mr. Godfrey leave, that the account could be up to a quarter million in billings annually.

At home Durwood breaks the bad news to Samantha and apologizes but he still gives her a present of a beautiful cat brooch. Samantha suggests that she could go with Durwood but realizing that he'll be able to get the account by letting Ms. Marshall flirt with him he tells her that wives and business don't mix. She suggests that she could change herself into a cat so no one would know she was there but he declines. So she requests that he tell Ms. Marshall to let him go early.

In Chicago, Durwood meets up with Ms. Marshall's captain, who is holding a Siamese cat, and he gets worried that maybe Samantha did turn herself into a cat to spy on him. He tries to call home to confirm that she's there but nobody answers because Samantha had stepped out to burn the trash.

Back on the yacht, Durwood sees that Ms. Marshall has dressed in a very tight dress and she fawns all over him. He becomes very nervous when he sees the cat watching him and he tries to bring the conversation to business. When Ms. Marshall suggests that they use a beautiful model rising from the sea for the campaign and that she may even model in something scant and sexy, he tells her he doesn't think it's a good idea so she goes to change to prove him wrong. He tries to catch the cat to have a conversation with his "wife" but it keeps running away causing him to think she's mad at him. As he searches behind the bar he comes face to face with a sexy pair of legs and realizes it's Ms. Marshall. She models for him and he hastily agrees with her causing her to suggest they move on to more recreational things and she kisses him! Durwood sees the cat run out of the room and he goes chasing after her. Out on the deck he comes across a pelican when he can't find the cat, and he thinks that maybe Samantha changed herself into the bird and as he tries to apologize to it, he hears the cat. He's also unaware that the Captain is watching him and he goes to discuss Durwood's odd behavior with Ms. Marshall. Durwood comes in and admits that he's been skittish because he's married and he should've told her but he was afraid she wouldn't want to listen to him if she knew. She dismisses him and tells him that the account is his because his ideas are so great and she requests that the Captain take them back to the shore so Durwood can go home.

At home Durwood walks in with the cat and is stunned to see Samantha sitting on the stairs waiting for him. He apologizes to her as he realizes she couldn't have been the cat and as they go upstairs to bed Samantha waits a little to say goodnight to her mother, who happens to be sitting outside in pelican form.

I would only give this one star and that is for Dick York's and the cat's performances. It is believed that this Siamese cat is actually Elizabeth Montgomery's own cat, Zip-Zip.

One reason I've never liked this episode is that Samantha is in it for so little. In fact, she never even shows up in the act after the middle break! I actually clocked all her screen time and estimate that she was only in this episode for just about seven minutes…that's much too little in my opinion. I ALWAYS avoid this episode when choosing one to watch.

I will say that I really like when Durwood comes home and Samantha says, "My, you're home early! I hope you haven't been fired." I always found it amusing and that scene at the end with the pelican and Samantha is cute, too.

This episode also marks the middle of the first season.

JANUARY 28, 1965

It was on this night that ABC aired Episode #19: "A Nice Little Dinner Party" sponsored by Quaker Oats.

Samantha tells Durwood one morning that she has invited his parents to a dinner party that evening at their house. When he asks if there will be anyone else at the dinner she carefully mentions that her mother will be there as well. Durwood is fearful for what may happen considering Endora is a witch but Samantha reminds him that they loved Aunt Clara and she is a witch.

That night Frank tries to prove to everyone else (but really himself) that being older doesn't mean you're done by naming off older people that accomplished much in their golden years. Just then Endora arrives and is all charm, especially towards Frank. He is smitten by her energy and mentions how Phyllis doesn't really like doing much anymore and that she doesn't even want to go to a musical he bought tickets for. Endora says she loves musicals and so Frank invites her to come along. Suddenly smitten with an impending headache, Phyllis says they have to leave. Realizing that Endora has created a rift between his parents and that his fears of having her come to dinner have come true, Durwood goes upstairs to sort through his anger and embarrassment.

That night Durwood is still mad but so is Samantha because all though she realizes her mother may have instigated it, Frank and his case of retarded adolescence only made things worse, and getting quite irritated with Durwood for always blaming her family she decides he'd better just sleep on the couch and zaps him down there.

The next morning Durwood goes to visit his parents to find that his father also slept on the couch because Phyllis, who claims not to be mad, is not speaking to him. Frank tells her that she is more than welcome to join him and Endora at the musical but she refuses.

Samantha also speaks with her mother and tells her that she must visit with Phyllis the next day and tell her that she has no designs on Frank but Endora thinks it's all ridiculous and mentions that none of this would've happened if Samantha had married one of the warlocks she had been going out with.

Frank and Endora go to the musical and the next day Durwood is surprised when his mother shows up at the office wanting to know the name of a good divorce lawyer as Frank never came home after the musical!

Across town Samantha finds Frank at the club and he tells her that when he arrived at home the previous evening he found he didn't have his house keys with him and when he knocked at the door Phyllis wouldn't answer so he came to stay the night at the club. He notices a beautiful scarf that Samantha has and tells her it reminds him of a time when he and Phyllis took his bright yellow roadster out to a place called Angel Falls and got caught in a rainstorm. Unable to put the top back up, they sat there in the pouring rain laughing their heads off, when for some strange reason he told her how lonely he was and she responded that he would never be lonely again and she wiped his face with a green silk scarf that she was wearing. He tells Samantha that it must be hard thinking of Phyllis as a young beautiful woman but Samantha tells him Phyllis is still beautiful and that he was reminded of what it was like to be young again by Endora's flirtation and that he could have the same thing with Phyllis. Deciding to help things along, Samantha decides to take Phyllis out for a day at the beauty parlor and to buy a new green silk scarf.

Meanwhile, Endora shows up at Phyllis' house to apologize but Phyllis tells her that there is no need to apologize as she realizes that Frank is over her. Endora pops over to Samantha's to tell her that the apology didn't work and that Phyllis is still feeling sorry for herself. Durwood decides to go talk to his mother when the phone rings. It's Frank who is at the airport getting ready to go on a world cruise after he finds that Phyllis had decided to board a train to Phoenix to stay with her mother. Durwood is panic stricken thinking his parents are truly going to divorce after forty years of marriage and he heads up to his room again to deal with his feelings. Samantha tells Endora that they must cast a spell to get Frank and Phyllis to meet up again, specifically in Angel Falls. Samantha focuses on the train and gets Phyllis to pull the emergency cord a couple times to stop the train while Endora turns the airplane around and the two end up in Angel Falls where a new train station and airport have popped up. Frank finds Phyllis at the train station and tells her that she looks beautiful and that he had somehow known he'd find her there. He tells her that he still loves her and that he hopes that she'll take him back.

A little later Durwood excitedly tells Samantha that his father had called and told him that he had reunited with Phyllis and that they were currently in Angel Falls where his dad had proposed to her in the middle of a thunderstorm. Realizing that she forgot the thunderstorm, Samantha quickly zaps one up to make things perfect for the new young lovers.

I'd give this one four stars. It's such a sweet realistic story about growing older and bored in a relationship and it's cool to see Durwood's parents meet Samantha's mother.

This is the first time we see Samantha zap Durwood out of bed to the couch but I don't like how it was done with the camera just speeding up. Endora also says her favorite colors are blue and white but we all know it's lavender and green.

It's funny when Phyllis puts the coffee pot in the fridge and Durwood tells her so and she says, "Oh, would you like another cup?" They continue speaking and then she says, "Now, would you like another cup of divorce?"

It was also during this week, on January 30, that the state funeral of Sir Winston Churchill took place and was the largest gathering of statesman in the world until the funeral of Pope John Paul II in 2005. Churchill had passed away on January 24.

FEBRUARY 4, 1965

It was on this night that ABC aired Episode #20: "Your Witch is Showing" sponsored by Chevrolet.

Durwood is in trouble with Endora when he refuses her invitation to attend Samantha's cousin Mario's wedding in Egypt. At the office, Larry suggests that Durwood may be in need of an assistant and implies that Durwood is getting older. Durwood is offended but relents and so Larry sends up the eager Gideon Whitzett just in time for a presentation for Wolfe Brothers Department Stores. The presentation goes horribly as Durwood suddenly gets the hiccups and Gideon implies he went to Yale, the same place Mr. Wolfe went to. Later on, while getting on the elevator with Gideon, Durwood, who has researched Gideon's credentials, confronts him about the fact that he never went to Yale. Gideon splits hairs saying that he never said it, but Mr. Wolfe seemed to believe it. Before the door closes, Gideon pushes the buttons to stop the door as he says he left something. As the elevator travels down it suddenly becomes stuck causing Durwood to miss another meeting with Mr. Wolfe and after getting out of the elevator he finds that Gideon made the presentation and happened to present his exact ideas which Durwood had just come up with the night before and never mentioned.

At home Durwood confronts Samantha and tells her about his day and how he feels that Endora has hired a warlock to drum him out of business. Samantha thinks it's ridiculous that he's blaming all his bad luck on witchcraft until he tells her about the campaign that Gideon couldn't have possibly known about. A little later, while Samantha is busy elsewhere and Durwood is brooding, Endora pops in from the wedding. Durwood confronts her and she promises she hasn't done anything though she agrees he must be a victim of witchcraft and tells him about a potion he can use to ward off witchcraft.

The next day there is yet another presentation with Wolfe Bros. and it still goes bad when Durwood can't seem to flip through the boards used for the presentation because they're stuck yet Gideon manages to breeze through them. The tension finally comes to a head when the model they were using to demonstrate the Wolfe Bros. new home furnishings catches on fire! While everyone is trying to get the fire out, Durwood sprays Gideon with the potion which turns out to be nothing more than an atomizer and Imodium water.

At home Durwood decides he must truly be under some sort of other curse and lays in bed when Samantha comes up to find his brief case as Gideon is coming over to get the layouts. When Gideon arrives, Samantha gushes over him and when he's not looking she decides to break through his fake charm and twitches a small truth spell on him. He admits that he's out for power and will go to any lengths to get it. She also twitches Durwood into feeling better and as she continues discussing with Gideon all the ways he's bested Durwood, Durwood comes sneaking down the stairs to listen. Samantha tries to get Gideon to admit he's a warlock but she realizes that he must not be and she shows him a bit of magic by lighting a lighter that wouldn't light. Gideon makes some suggestive remarks to Samantha but by then Durwood has arrived and Samantha gives him a little boost so that he lifts Gideon off his seat and he punches him out. Samantha and Durwood agree that Gideon was no warlock, just an unscrupulous go-getter.

I don't like this episode. I give it maybe a half star. The only part I like is when Endora is telling Samantha about the ingredients in the "potion" she gave Durwood and she laughs a little and then sighs…I think it's hilarious and I often use it in my own speech.

It seems like this is another episode that focuses all the screen time on Dick York and the office and I am watching *Bewitched* for witches.

Plus, Jonathan Daly that plays Gideon really grates my nerves. He shows up later as the store salesman that Cousin Henry turns into a mannequin ("Samantha's Shopping Spree") and I like him much better in that role. I was really surprised that Durwood knocked him out. That's the first time this season that he has belted someone. Gideon deserved it but it just seems so weird that it would come to that.

That sneezing part at the end kind of makes me sick because it sounds like she sprays which is what blows the candles out.

I also like at the beginning when Endora tells Durwood, "Oh yes! I have a message for you too, young man. You're in trouble!" and she pops out. That seems pretty scary! And then it turns out she doesn't even do anything to him, except give him the hiccups at the end. This is my least favorite episode of the first season. I hardly ever watch it.

FEBRUARY 11, 1965

It was on this night that ABC aired Episode #21: "Ling Ling" sponsored by Quaker Oats.

While lounging out in the backyard by the fence, Samantha discovers a beautiful Siamese cat. She also gets visited by Mrs. Kravitz who thinks the cat may have ate her canary Tweety, but luckily Samantha sees the bird up in a tree and twitches him to fly back to his cage.

Later on, Durwood tells Samantha that he's having a struggle at work trying to find the perfect model for the Jewel of the East campaign because the client, Mr. Pickering, is so picky. Samantha offers to help him but he refuses and leaves for work. As Samantha sits down for a cup of coffee, the cat suddenly jumps up on the table and Samantha realizes that the Siamese cat is from the Far East and could help Durwood out if she were human.

At the office, Larry is getting nervous that they may lose the Jewel of the East because they've gone through every model and he says that they may have to give up unless the perfect model walked in just then. And who should walk in but a beautiful Asian woman named Ling Ling who seemingly purrs as she talks. Larry and Durwood are blown away and immediately hire her and get to work photographing her. The photographer, Wally Ames, is definitely smitten by her. Durwood makes plans to have the Tates and Wally over for dinner and calls Samantha up to tell her the good news.

While all this has been going on at the office, Samantha has been visiting with Mrs. Kravitz who is very happy to have her bird back, though she says that Mr. Kravitz doesn't like Tweety. When the phone rings, Mrs. Kravitz excuses herself and Samantha is stunned to hear about everyone coming to dinner that evening, and with nothing in the refrigerator. Realizing the only way this dinner party will be a success is through witchcraft, Samantha justifies herself by saying that Durwood would understand and she sets to zapping up a gourmet meal. Just as she goes to thinking about what to have for dessert, Mrs. Kravitz returns to explain her comment about Mr. Kravitz hating Tweety. Samantha offers her a sardine hors d'oeuvres and Mrs. Kravitz is pleased until it dawns on her that there wasn't any food a moment ago. Samantha says she's a fast worker but Mrs. Kravitz knows there is something else afoot and she leaves again without finishing her sardine treat.

Soon the guests arrive and Samantha is stunned to see that Ling Ling is Wally's date! Knowing that she can't let Ling Ling lead Wally on, Samantha requests to speak to her in the kitchen after dinner. Ling Ling is content being a human girl and being fawned over by Wally. Just then Durwood enters and Ling Ling leaves and Samantha decides to tell him the truth. At first he thinks that Ling Ling has just been catty but then he slowly realizes that Samantha is being serious and he is upset until he realizes that he is going to have to make Wally fall out of love with Ling Ling. Samantha tells him she'll help and she serves Ling Ling a drink laced with catnip. When Wally and Ling Ling have a moment out on the patio alone, he tries to tell her his feelings but the catnip gets the best of her. He thinks she's getting sloshed and takes her drink away which upsets her and she claws his face and stalks out in a huff. The Tates and the Stephens console Wally who is upset that he is going to miss his bird watching date with Ling Ling.

Later that night Mrs. Kravitz decides that she should apologize to the cat with a saucer of milk for accusing her of molesting Tweety. Meanwhile, Samantha realizes that she forgot to turn Ling Ling back and when she goes searching she finds her lapping up milk at Mrs. Kravitz's and she zaps her back just as Mrs. Kravitz has seen the human Ling Ling lapping the milk.

I would give this one four stars. I think it's a great story and I love that the Siamese cat, which may be Zip Zip, Liz's cat, is used again.

I did notice that Mrs. Kravitz seems to live next door to Samantha rather than across the street, but it worked for the story.

I thought Liz was very beautiful in this one and so was Greta Chi (Ling Ling). I really liked the scene of Samantha zapping up all the food, though who would serve sardine appetizers? Bleh!

Three nights before, the Golden Globe Awards Ceremony took place. Elizabeth was nominated for Best TV Star — Female for *Bewitched* and Agnes Moorehead won for Best Performance by an Actress in a Supporting Role — Motion Picture for *Hush…Hush, Sweet Charlotte*.

FEBRUARY 18, 1965

It was on this night that ABC re-aired Episode #9: "Witch or Wife" which originally aired on November 9, 1964.

Three days before Canada officially inaugurated their new official red and white flag with the maple leaf design.

FEBRUARY 25, 1965

It was on this night that ABC aired Episode #22: "Eye of the Beholder" sponsored by Chevrolet.

Endora accompanies Durwood and Samantha for a day out antiquing. She becomes quite reflective seeing all the older objects and tries to remind Samantha of the good times they used to have except that she finds that Samantha is being flirty with Durwood. Irritated, she tries to remind Samantha that she shares in the memories too, but Samantha tells her that she's more interested in the present and future with Durwood. That gets Endora to thinking about the fact that Durwood hasn't realized yet that his wife is actually much older than him by a couple centuries and that he might not want to have a future with her if he were to find out, so she conjures up a picture of Samantha as "The Maid of Salem," dated 1682, and she levitates it to where Durwood will see it when Samantha has walked off to admire something. Endora's plan works as she sees the realization dawn on Durwood's face.

The next day, Durwood asks to speak to Samantha and he asks her when her birthday is. She's confused by this question as he knows it's June 6 but then he asks her how old she is and she tells him it doesn't matter. He tells her that he's worried about how she doesn't seem to age and especially what will happen when he gets older and gray and she's still young. She tries to soothe his worry by telling him that people will be impressed that he has the youngest wife on the block but that doesn't make him feel any better and when he receives no consolation from his friend Dave, his doctor, or the bar tender he goes to the park to sort out his feelings. While at the park he notices two squirrels up in a tree when suddenly he hears them talking and having a conversation just like he had with Samantha earlier. Of course, it's Endora up to her tricks again.

Later, Samantha notices the *Maid of Salem* portrait up in the closet and realizes where Durwood got all his insecurities about her age from and she calls on her mother. Endora pops in and admits that she conjured the picture but Samantha tells her it doesn't matter, that she was going to tell Durwood the truth anyway. Endora thinks he'll still not want to be with Samantha and she pops off telling her that she'll be waiting for her. Samantha decides that a nice candle lit dinner will be the best setting for their discussing her age but when he doesn't show up at his usual time after work she calls the office and is surprised to hear that Durwood left at his usual time. Right after she hangs up with Larry, the police call saying that they have found Durwood's car at the Westbridge Avenue Park and that it had been there all day. Samantha hangs up with them and pops down to the park, which is clear across town. She finds Durwood and he tells her that he just needed time to think, that he has decided he doesn't care how old she is and that he loves her no matter what. Just then the police come upon the couple kissing and ask if Durwood is Mr. Stephens and he admits that he is. They are disgusted at him cavorting with a woman in the park considering they just spoke to his wife who is clear across town.

This one would definitely get four stars. It hearkens back to the pilot episode with Durwood finding out a big secret about Samantha but looking past it because he loves her. I think it's odd that Endora zapped up the *Maid of Salem* painting with the year 1682 rather than 1692, the year the witch trials started in Salem.

Bewitched is still in it's infancy with Samantha calling on Endora by using a spell with Latin sounding words. However, I think it's cool and classy.

I love the magic done by Samantha of zapping the candles back up, into her coat and out. This is a testament to the effectiveness of the musical sound effects adding more punch to those scenes.

The fountain seen in the park is the very same fountain that was used in the opening of *Friends*. The tree where Endora hid to make the squirrels speak is the same one that Kasey Rogers (Louise Tate #2) sat under on a picnic bench to sign autographs at the 2005 *Bewitched* Fanfare for the small gathering there. It was such a hot day and Ms. Rogers had just had surgery for her throat cancer so it was very special that she would come to meet us.

MARCH 4, 1965

It was on this night that ABC aired Episode #23: "Red Light, Green Light" sponsored by Quaker Oats.

One morning Samantha happens to bump into Mr. Kravitz and Durwood's friend Dave at a busy intersection as they wait to cross the road, which happens to not have a traffic light. Mr. Kravitz says they'll never be able to cross as the traffic never stops. Dave decides to brave the traffic and goes out amongst the cars but being too scared for his safety, Samantha twitches and freezes everyone and then draws him back. An officer sees the commotion and asks what's going on. Samantha responds that they have been asking for a traffic signal for months. The officer tells her they should take it up with city hall. They decide to have a neighborhood meeting at Dave's house and later that night at the meeting decide they should have a sign ready advertising the rally for the next weekend and Samantha offers up Durwood's talents to create the sign. Mrs. Kravitz offers to make cookies and after they all leave, and just as they are about to walk into their house, Mrs. Kravitz decides to start on the cookies but she needs to borrow some cookie cutters from Samantha.

Meanwhile, Samantha discovers her mother and several different styles of traffic signals in her living room. Endora said she wanted to help her and that she can easily install it on the corner, Samantha just needs to choose one. Exasperated, Samantha tells her that she should put all the signals back. Unbeknownst to the two, Mrs. Kravitz has seen the signals and she hesitantly goes to knock on the door. Endora pops out with her traffic signals and shocks Mrs. Kravitz when she sees that the living room is bare.

Durwood starts work on the sign but just can't get into it until Samantha locks him in the den and tells him to whistle when he's done. Right after she leaves he whistles but she reminds him he must be done first! Before Samantha knows it the morning has arrived and she finds that Durwood has never come to bed. She goes to the den and finds Durwood sleeping on the couch but the sign is finished. Just then Dave shows up and is not quite as impressed as Durwood hoped as he suggests a few changes. Later on at the office Larry finds Durwood asleep at his desk and when he finds out why Durwood is so sleepy he suggests that Durwood and Samantha do what he and Louise did when they had the same traffic signal problem: move!

At the rally, the mayor tells the group that there just isn't a need for a traffic signal at the corner they requested. As they leave everyone freezes and Endora pops in and tells Samantha that the mayor isn't going anywhere and she pops out. Outside, Durwood and Samantha ask the mayor if they can have a ride home and he agrees only to find that his driver has the hood up. Samantha asks what is wrong and the driver tells her she wouldn't know. She twitches and tells him to try something which he says he already tried. Samantha suggests he try it again and it starts and so they leave. They happen to get to the problem intersection and Samantha makes it so that the horn on the car won't sound when the Mayor suggest that the driver honk his way through. After they've sat there for a while the Mayor suggests that the corner needs a traffic signal!

That night Samantha prepares for a celebration when she finds her mother in the living room with yet another traffic signal which she says would be nice as the guest of honor. Again Samantha refuses and is again unaware that Mrs. Kravitz is looking in. When Endora disappears with her "guest" Samantha answers the door to find that Mrs. Kravitz is prepared to find other guests there but there are none.

I really like this episode because it's just so odd. It seems like a pretty mortally themed episode yet there's a lot of witchcraft in it. I would give it three stars.

I would like to know if it's really that the community in Westport where they live is called Morning Glory Circle and it just so happens that Durwood and Samantha live on the street of the same name, possibly the first street in that neighborhood, hence giving the community the same name. Though I can't imagine that it would have a lot of traffic like was discussed.

This is the first time we've seen Dave outside of the bar and not interrupting Durwood. And the set for his home is the one which will be used next season for Tony's home on *I Dream of Jeannie*, but it has also been used before as the Kravitz's home, though the bar wasn't seen before.

I liked Samantha's reaction to Durwood's suggestion she fly across the street, even if he was joking. And I thought it was really cute how she would pop in and out of the room.

Gladys and Abner were really funny in this. My favorite is when she suggests they lie down in the middle of the street and Dave says that he doesn't think that's a good idea because they could get hurt. And Abner says, "Hurt? We could get killed!"

I also liked the snooping music in the background. It seemed different this time.

One of my favorite scenes is from the first when Endora snaps the ham cut. I always thought that was cool.

There is a goof where in one scene Endora is standing behind the couch and it cuts to Gladys snooping and then back to Endora who is in front of the couch and then back to Gladys and then Endora is back behind the couch.

Two days before, the blockbuster musical *The Sound of Music* opened at the Rivoli Theater in New York City. And that following Sunday the first of three marches from Selma to Montgomery in Alabama in support of civil rights to afford blacks the privilege to vote was cut short when police attacked some 600 marchers with billy clubs.

The next day the first American combat troops arrived in Vietnam comprised of 3500 U.S. Marines.

MARCH 11, 1965

It was on this night ABC aired Episode #24: "Which Witch is Which?" sponsored by Chevrolet.

Endora agrees to go shopping with her daughter as Samantha says that bargain hunting is a great thrill for mortal women. The department store is full of overzealous women fighting each other for the best deal and Samantha finds herself almost losing a dress to Mrs. Kravitz. She goes to introduce her mother to Mrs. Kravitz but can't find her anywhere. Mrs. Kravitz says she'll have to meet her another time and leaves. Meanwhile, Samantha's attention is called by her mother who points out a rather odd sign over in another area which says ninety percent off! The crazed crowd also hears this and runs off and Endora admits she did it to get out of the chaos. Samantha says they should go to the butcher as there is a sale on pork chops. Just then she remembers a dress fitting that she was supposed to go to upstairs and can't decide which one to go to. Endora offers to help by changing herself into Samantha for the dress fitting. Wanting to get both errands done Samantha reluctantly agrees.

Endora as "Samantha" goes upstairs to the dress fitting and bumps into a book signing by author Robert E. Frazer, a historical romance author whose latest book is about Helen of Troy. He is quite taken by "Samantha" especially when she mentions that she knows a lot about Helen. They make plans to go to dinner and "Samantha" goes to her dress fitting. After she leaves, Bob goes to make a phone call and wouldn't you know it, he's calling his good friend Durwood! Bob has just come into town and Durwood invites him over for dinner and tells him to bring the new girl he met.

Bob and "Samantha" have a great time together going to dance clubs and later on going to an amusement park. They spend every evening together and one day when Samantha goes to the department store where Bob is still signing his books he sees her and comes up and nibbles her ear. She is quite shocked and tells him she's married. Bob is quite confused.

When Samantha gets home she calls on her mother asking her if she may know anything about the strange man's advances on her realizing that Endora was playing her the other day. Endora says she did meet a man and that they have been going out and Samantha requests that she make a final date with the man to break it off so she doesn't have to fear that he may harass her again. Not wanting to be bothered, Endora suggests Samantha do it and just give a simple goodbye Bobby Frazer. Samantha is stopped in her tracks when she realizes that is the same name of Durwood's friend and demands that her mother make the date, explain that she has no designs on him and end it there. Endora reluctantly agrees.

At dinner that night, "Samantha" tells Bobby that she is married and it happens to be to Durwood. Bob can't believe it and feels that "Samantha" must not really be in love with Durwood and wants to hear her say it. Choking on the words, "Samantha" manages to spit them out.

The next day Durwood announces that Bob is going to come over for dinner and Samantha thinks all is well until Bob reveals "their" affair. Samantha pulls Durwood aside and explains what Endora had done and tells him that they may have to just tell Bob the truth. Just as Durwood is fumbling over his words, "Samantha" shows up and tells Bob that she didn't think to tell him that she was a twin, especially since she is the prettier one. With everyone relieved, Bob and "Samantha" leave for another night out and Durwood and Samantha get ready for bed.

I LOVE this episode and most definitely would give it four stars. I think it's lots of fun.

Elizabeth Montgomery does so well at playing Endora that at times I was thinking it was Agnes Moorehead just looking like Liz. She should've received an Emmy for this episode alone!

For some reason one of my favorite parts is when "Samantha" walks into the book area right past the book and then she stops and turns back with an, "Oh!" I just love how she says it.

My favorite part is when he tells her to say, "I love Darrin Stephens." It's so hilarious! I also like at the end when she tells Bob Frazer that "everyone can see I'm much prettier."

The costumer Vi Alford should've received one demerit for having the dress fitting be for a dress that Samantha has already worn several times this season!

And there is a blooper in this episode when "Samantha" and Bob are talking at the dress fitting about Helen of Troy. The scene is flipped so that "Samantha"'s hair part is on the other side and the words on the door behind her are backward.

This episode also had a commercial for Chevy Impala play where Endora and Samantha are waiting curbside for a car and an Impala pulls up and they get in much to the shock of the doorman who can see there is no driver. Both witches are also bewildered as neither of them own up to making the car drive by itself.

Two days before, in Alabama, a second attempt at a march from Selma to Montgomery is attempted with Reverend Martin Luther King Jr. heading it. They reach the place where "Bloody Sunday" occurred and hold a prayer service and then peacefully retreat due to a restraining order. Later that day white supremacists beat up Unitarian Universalist minister James J. Reeb, who is also white, in Selma. His injuries are so severe he would pass away the night that this episode aired.

MARCH 18, 1965

It was on this night that ABC aired Episode #25: "Pleasure O'Riley" sponsored by Quaker Oats.

At breakfast Durwood and Samantha hear a crash come from next door and Durwood races out to find that the moving man is caught under a dresser that had fallen as he was helping a new woman move in. Durwood helps him up and the woman is just so happy that Durwood was there to help. They formally introduce themselves and Durwood finds out that his new neighbor is named Pleasure O'Riley though she admits that's just a nickname as she couldn't pronounce her real first name of Priscilla when she was younger. She says that the name stuck and it's helped her to win a lot of beauty pageants for which she has a lot of trophies. She also says she moved to get away from her scary boyfriend Thor "Thunderbolt" Swenson of the Minnesota Manglers who had threatened to hurt her because he caught her with another man even though she had broken up with Thor. The moving man is ecstatic to hear of Pleasure's connection to Thor and she makes him promise not to tell anyone where she lives now. Samantha shows up to see where Durwood has run off to and can see that he's very taken by Pleasure but Samantha makes sure Pleasure knows he's hers.

Later that evening, Samantha has made a romantic dinner for her and her husband and everything is going great until they hear a crash coming from Pleasure's place again and Durwood runs to the rescue to find that Pleasure has fallen off a ladder with a box of trophies on her. She seems to be in a coma until she comes to and is happy to see Durwood and then mentions how happy she is to see Mrs. Stephens, to Durwood's shock, especially when Pleasure says Durwood was trying to help her with her bust…of her lips that she won in a contest. Seeing that she's OK, Durwood and Samantha go back home.

During the night Samantha is awoken by the sound of pebbles hitting the window and the frantic call of Pleasure for Durwood. Samantha wakes her husband and he goes to the window where Pleasure tells him that she's found out that the moving man couldn't keep his mouth shut and now Thor is coming to visit and she's scared. Durwood offers to come stay with her but Samantha says she'll go and Durwood can phone the police. Unbeknownst to everyone the Kravitzes have also heard all the commotion and look out their window to see what's going on.

Pleasure is beside herself and tries to pack up all her stuff, but Samantha tells her it would be better for her to go hide and Samantha will just answer the door. Thor soon comes pounding on the door and is shocked when Samantha opens it. He asks if there is a beautiful woman next door and when she coyly responds there is, he asks if she's been seen with another man and she lovingly admits she has and realizes her folly when Thor goes to pound the next door where Durwood is and possibly even pound him! Samantha chases after Thor and throws a pitch of magic towards the house. When the door opens Durwood has been transformed into an old woman who is furious to have been woken up, though Durwood is unaware of the change until Thor leaves and he checks a mirror. Samantha changes him back after a little chuckle. Meanwhile, Thor has gone across the street and pounds on the Kravitzes door and when Abner answers Thor asks if he has Pleasure in that house. Abner, thinking he means 'pleasure' says "not too often but occasionally" and Thor belts him one to the screams of Mrs. Kravitz.

The next morning the debacle is headline news in the *Morning Glory Gazette* and Samantha and Durwood find that the charges were dropped against Thor when he offered to pay for Abner's bridge work. As they discuss the events, Pleasure shows up saying that she has just got a modeling job for the city as Ms. Urban Renewal and they are even more shocked when Thor shows up to take Pleasure into the city as part of his compensation for the trouble he caused.

This one is brilliant! Four stars for everyone! Pleasure is just so ditsy and vampy that you have to love her especially when she slyly cuts at Samantha by referring to her only as Mrs. Stephens but Durwood as "Darrin."

The scene at the very first is cute with Samantha twitching the alarm clock back together but it makes no sense that Durwood would think it was Friday on Saturday if he had already done Friday. It would've made more sense to say that he thought it was Monday.

I love all the innuendos about Pleasure's legs and bust.

The Kravitzes were hysterical in this one and I love how Abner falls in love with Pleasure.

Samantha looked gorgeous throughout and I really liked that black dress with the white linings.

I love when Thor comes to the door and Samantha answers and tells him that a beautiful girl does live next door and when he asks, "The most beautiful girl in the world?" She gets embarrassed and says, "I wouldn't go that far." Her changing Durwood into Grandma is hysterical! Dick York did a fantastic job and I love it when later on Thor says "you sure look a lot like your grandma!"

Two days before this, police in Montgomery, Alabama again riot with over 1500 protesters and President Lyndon B. Johnson sends a bill to congress in reference to the recent goings on with the Voting march. This bill would eventually become the Voting Rights Act of 1965.

The night this episode aired Cosmonaut Aleksei Leonov becomes the first man to walk in space. A federal judge also rules that the Alabama protesters have a right to lawfully march.

MARCH 25, 1965

It was on this night that ABC aired Episode #26:"Driving is the Only Way to Fly" sponsored by Chevrolet (who else when it comes to driving?).

Durwood and Samantha begin her first driving lesson with Durwood as the instructor. Nervously, Samantha admits that "these newfangled gadgets" scare her and she becomes confused when Durwood teaches her the gear shift letters and she thinks that they have been mislabeled. Durwood starts getting irritated with her and becomes very belligerent when he feels that Samantha is not allowing herself to learn. However, she seems to be overly sensitive and tells him that his rudeness must be from the fact that he never loved her and she tells him that she is going to go into the 'H' for house!

Later on, Durwood calls from the office to apologize and make sure that Samantha feels comfortable taking driving instructions from a professional instructor. She confirms that she is and he calls the Reliable Driving School to confirm her appointment. The owner, Basil, assures him that the best instructor will be out. After he hangs up he bellows for Harold Harold (that is no mistake) to get in there. Harold is a big bundle of nerves and happens to be Basil's brother-in-law who bounces between his brother-in-laws for employment because he can't ever manage to maintain a job. Basil warns him that if he messes up he'll be finished and sends him out to Morning Glory Circle.

Samantha is surprised at how nervous Harold is but likes him and tells him that she's not scared to go driving with him as she's led a charmed life. When they get in the car and she says she is going to put the car into 'N' for neutral to start the car, she is delighted to hear that Harold thinks as she does, that it should be either 'S' or 'SC' for 'start car' and she tears off down the road. No matter how charmed her life may be Harold still manages to make her nervous when he says she is driving too far to the left, too far to the right and too far in the middle. But he about has a nervous breakdown when she drives into a parked moving van and back out and manages to make a U-turn on a crowded street and parallel parks in a very tight space. He asks how she managed to do all of that when Endora pops in to the back seat and says that maybe Samantha is a witch. Shocked that he's heard another voice, he asks who it may be and Endora responds that maybe it's another witch. When he goes to look in the backseat, she disappears. Looking back at Samantha he asks if she is a ventriloquist and she responds no and then he hears Endora tell Samantha that she's disgusted with her driving a car when she can fly and she becomes invisible again. Finally Mr. Harold cannot take it and he gets out of the car. He tells Samantha, who has also got out of the car, that he must've finally broke down and she tries to explain that he shouldn't be afraid but he says he is going to leave. When Endora asks what they should do with the car, he says to burn it and so she zaps it away in a puff of smoke. He runs away and Samantha demands that her mother bring the car back. She does so against her better judgment.

Later on Samantha and Durwood go to the driving school to see if Mr. Harold is OK and find that he is going to be fired for abandoning a student. Basil says he'll teach Samantha how to drive but Samantha refuses and asks for Mr. Harold. Basil refuses that until Samantha says she is going to take her husband's money elsewhere.

A couple weeks later Samantha tells Durwood that Mr. Harold is coming to take her for another lesson and that his confidence has boosted up after going to a basket weaving class with her and when Mr. Harold shows up Durwood sees that she is right and he asks to join them.

This is a classic in the truest sense of the word and gets four stars. Paul Lynde is HYSTERICAL! And because of this appearance on *Bewitched*, Elizabeth Montgomery and Bill Asher asked him to come back next season in the recurring role of Samantha's practical joking uncle Arthur.

It doesn't make sense that Samantha is learning to drive as she has been seen earlier in the season driving, but it's a cute episode. The driving scene is really funny when Harold yells "Selfish! Selfish!" And Endora's appearance is small but still fun.

The colorist for the episodes must've not seen still shots from the episode because they colored Samantha's ensemble blue when in reality it was red.

It was also on this day that Martin Luther King Jr. successfully ended the third march from Selma to Montgomery with 25,000 protesters. Unfortunately five days later there was a funeral for Detroit homemaker Viola Liuzzo who was shot to death by four Klansmen for driving back some civil rights protesters after the march.

APRIL 1, 1965

It was on this night that ABC aired Episode #27: "There's No Witch Like an Old Witch" sponsored by Quaker Oats.

Aunt Clara comes to visit when Bertha tells her that she'll need to stay behind from the conclave in Florida as her powers aren't too sharp. Samantha tells Clara that nobody's perfect and she's more than welcome to stay with her. Clara accepts and says they should just go on with their normal lives as if she's not even there and Samantha hesitantly agrees telling Clara that Durwood and she actually had plans to go to a play. Clara says she'll clean up the dinner and after Durwood and Samantha leave, Clara tries getting the dishes to fly into the kitchen but instead causes them to zoom up to the ceiling and break. After she cleans that mess up

Elizabeth Montgomery and Marion Lorne during filming of "There's No Witch Like an Old Witch." PHOTO COURTESY OF MARK SIMPSON.

she decides to do the dishes and casts a spell for suds, which works but only too well as the suds don't stop coming and eventually fill the whole house. Durwood and Samantha are shocked when they are greeted at the door by a mountain of suds and after it's cleaned up Clara feels that she's failed as a witch. Samantha tells her that she's just getting a little older and it's expected that her spells wouldn't work. Clara still feels bad and Samantha decides to invite her along with her and Durwood and their friends, the Caldwells, for a night out on the town.

When they arrive at the Caldwells, they find that their sitter got sick so Bea says they'll have to cancel. Not wanting the tickets to be wasted, Clara suggests she can babysit. Durwood isn't too sure about that but Clara assures him she'll be fine so they agree and leave her with Jimmy Caldwell. He is excited to show Clara all his toys and tells her that his toy dog doesn't like him much, but Clara says he's wrong and shows him by making the dog wag its tail! Jimmy is delighted and shows her his broken toy boat which she fixes and then she zaps him up a toy soldier. That night when he goes to bed she does one last trick of enlarging his pillow so that he'll sleep much better.

Soon the news gets out about how much Jimmy enjoyed Clara sitting with him and the neighborhood women call Samantha to see if Aunt Clara will sit for them. She is quite pleased as it looks as though Clara is over feeling sorry for herself.

While sitting with Louise and Gary Baine, Aunt Clara tells them about flying from country to country but that she's not able to make such long distance flights anymore. However when they ask her to show them how she can fly she tells them that she'll work on it and that the next time they'll fly with her from roof top to roof top. Their mother hears about it and fears that something dangerous may happen and can't believe that Clara has been telling the children that she is a witch. Wanting to warn all the other mothers, Mrs. Baine calls them. Later on Samantha receives a notification that Mrs. Baine is bringing charges against Clara, that she is an endangerment to the children, and has scheduled a hearing. Samantha is furious and they accompany Clara to the hearing where the Judge reviews the charge and then tells her that she shouldn't be telling the children she is a witch because witches are wicked old creatures. Offended, Clara tells him that's pure flummery and that witches are like anybody else except they are able to do extraordinary things. He asks to see some of those extraordinary things and she agrees and says she'll pull a rabbit out of her bag and instead pulls a birdcage with a parakeet out. She tries again and instead of a rabbit gets a poodle. She tries one last time and when she opens her bag, a lion roars. The judge is amused and asks that she babysit for his child as he sees she's no harm at all.

I would give this one four stars. Aunt Clara is such a sweet character and the story about her feeling worthless is very much a situation that we can all relate to as we get older. I love when she tries to do the dishes and they all zoom up to the ceiling and the soap bubbles filling the house is awesome! Marion Lorne was such a sport to do that.

Another reason I love this one is that Durwood, of his own volition, is nice to Aunt Clara and tells her how glad he is to see her. How could anyone not like her? And then to see all the fun things she did with the kids, it would've been awesome to have a babysitter like her.

I liked the "Winken Blinken" spell and I liked that essentially it was a math problem to get what you wanted. I also liked that you could tell Samantha knew the spells and was thinking Aunt Clara might, but then she winced whenever it came out wrong.

The scene at the end when Aunt Clara bumps into the wall and Samantha asks her if she is all right is the very same scene from "The Witches are Out." This is the third time this season that Samantha has worn that dress.

This is also one of the rare times that a character says the entire name of an episode that they are in.

It was also around this time that the first issue of the *Bewitched* comic book came out. And while we are speaking of memorabilia in 1965, there were several other items released including a *Fun & Activity Book*, a Story Book, a novel by Al Hine, a Samantha paper doll, two puzzles each including a poster of Elizabeth, a Samantha and Endora board game, a Stymie card game and most important, the Ideal Samantha doll. The original doll in the box has sold for over $2,000 on eBay and is quite rare!

APRIL 8, 1965

It was on this night that ABC aired Episode #28: "Open the Door, Witchcraft" sponsored by Chevrolet.

One night, Samantha arrives home just as the Kravitzes do and instead of getting out to open her garage door, Samantha decides to use her "automatic garage door opener" and twitches it open right in front of the Kravitzes. Gladys is shocked but Abner thinks that the Stephens must've purchased one of the new garage door openers they had seen at the store earlier and he tells Gladys he'll go ask them later that evening how they like it.

That night Samantha helps Durwood as he tries to pick out new fishing equipment for a trip he is going on and they are interrupted by Mr. Kravitz coming over to ask about their new garage door opener. Durwood is bewildered but slowly realizes that Mr. Kravitz must've seen Samantha use magic to open it. When Mr. Kravitz asks to see it, Durwood tells him that it'd be better to show him in the light of day and Mr. Kravitz leaves. Durwood dejectedly says he'll have to bypass on the fishing equipment so that he can go out and buy a new garage door opener.

The next day the garage door opener company installs the door and one of the workers mentions to his partner that one time he had set the frequency of the door opener to the same frequency as the airplane radios that flew overhead so that every time they flew over the garage door would open and close by itself. He laughs it off saying he'd never be able to do it again in a million years and they leave. Right after, a plane flies overhead and the door flies open! A little later Samantha comes out to retrieve the paper and sees that the door is open and thinks maybe she forgot to close it and closes it but after another plane flies again, she finds that it's open again. She realizes something weird must be going on and when her mother pops in she thinks that Endora may have been playing tricks but Endora says she'd be much more creative to pull another prank aside from opening and closing a garage door.

That evening, as Durwood and Samantha get ready for dinner with the Tates, Samantha tells Durwood about the strange events with the garage door and how it must be faulty so they can just return it, get their money back, tell the Kravitzes that they don't have one anymore and their problems will be solved! Durwood doesn't believe her and feels she was causing it to open and close by itself just so she could have some excuse to return it, and Samantha becomes furious. Durwood is furious too as he thinks she has tried to use witchcraft once again to get out of her problems and so she gives up and tells him that he can have it his way and that from now on, no matter what, she will not use witchcraft. He is pleased and they go to leave except that right after he opens the garage door a plane flies overhead and causes it to shut. He thinks Samantha is still mad and trying to get back at him but she insists it wasn't her. When he tries to open it again it won't open. Gladys, who had been spying on them, begins to get worried when she had seen that they were getting into their car, but hadn't opened the door yet so she insists that she and Abner go over to investigate.

In the garage Durwood demands that Samantha open it and she tells him that she had promised no more witchcraft and she was sticking to it. He decides that maybe the garage door opener just needs a rest, as though it were to get tired, and they sit there with Samantha fuming when suddenly the door opens. Durwood thinks that Samantha gave in and thanks her but she tells him that she's done with the stupid door, she zaps it closed and tells him that they will remain in there until he apologizes. He realizes with her being as mad as she is she must be telling the truth and apologizes and they kiss. Just then the door opens again with the Kravitzes peeking and Samantha is excited as it officially proves that she didn't twitch 'cause she couldn't as she was kissing. The Kravitzes are concerned but Durwood tells them that they fixed the door with a hairpin and that everything is OK and they leave.

The next day the garage door company comes out to fix the tuning and they mention that the Kravitzes have now bought one but that they need to adjust theirs and so have turned it off. Just then, Gladys pulls up and turns her head out to yell that they have got one too and she crashes into her door.

I would give this one two and a half stars. It's kind of like Endora said about Samantha's situation, the whole story is dull. Maybe back then it was more enjoyable as not a lot of people had garage door openers but nowadays you would be strange if you didn't have one!

I think Durwood is at his jerkiest here! Why wouldn't he believe his wife? That's why I have never really liked the Durwood character because he is so self-centered and egotistical to think that he is never wrong.

I did think Liz looked beautiful throughout.

And a major blooper is seen when the garage door opener is being installed. If you look to the left of Samantha inside the garage you'll see that there is a door that they could've just walked out of!

Three days before, the 37th Academy Awards took place with *Mary Poppins* taking home five trophies. The next day the 100th anniversary of the end of the Civil War was observed which will be the focal point of an episode on the next season of *Bewitched*

The night before, Agnes Moorehead guested on *Burke's Law* in "Who Killed Hamlet?"

APRIL 15, 1965

It was on this night that ABC aired Episode #29: "Abner Kadabra" sponsored by Quaker Oats.

When Gladys shows up to return a pan, she is delighted to hear from Durwood that Samantha may need help in redecorating until she walks in on Samantha waving her hands about to direct a couple of floating pictures. And with that Gladys faints.

A little later Mrs. Kravitz comes to and realizes she is in the Stephens house, but more importantly, that she had caught Samantha red-handed at her tricks. She tells Samantha that she knows what she is and that she thinks Samantha is from Venus. Insulted, Samantha tells her that's ridiculous and tries to talk Gladys out of spreading the news. Gladys tells her there is no use and that she can probably get confirmation of what is going on by going to tell a professor at the university who is an expert in extra-terrestrial beings. Not wanting her secret to go out, Samantha tells her that maybe it wasn't herself that was moving the pictures but Gladys that did it using ESP! Gladys is intrigued especially when Samantha tells her that she's been studying up on it and that she has learned that we have much more power in our minds than we realize. Over the top about her new found ability, Gladys agrees to try out a test where Samantha will write down a number and Mrs. Kravitz will guess. Samantha writes down "9" but Gladys tells her that it's "17" and so with a deft twitch Samantha changes it and Gladys is thrilled! Just then she feels that she's getting a message from Abner, that he needs her help, and she leaves.

When Durwood comes home, he sees Gladys out on her front lawn and says "hi" to her but gets no response and when he really looks at her he sees that she is holding the key to the sprinkler system, chanting "…water on…water on…" Thinking there must be something wrong, he goes over to investigate and Abner comes out to tell him that ever since Gladys' visit with Samantha she had got into her head that she had some special power. He tells Durwood that Gladys is now trying to prove her power by getting the water to come on by itself. Realizing that she must've saw Samantha at work with her witchcraft, Durwood hurries home and gets the explanation from Samantha. He tells her that she must go talk Mrs. Kravitz out of her delusion and reluctantly she goes when suddenly it starts raining and Gladys starts whooping and hollering as she believes her request for the water to come on has been answered by the rain. The rain continues and Gladys decides she'll try to turn it off and won't come in even after Samantha goes over to talk to her. Defeated, Samantha comes back but Durwood says she shouldn't give up, and as she leaves the rain stops cementing the end of any hope of talking Gladys out of her new attitude.

The next morning Gladys won't cook breakfast until she can get the stove to turn on by itself and Abner gets more irritated the longer Gladys stands there chanting "Stove on!" Samantha shows up and tells Gladys that she read up more on ESP and that it tends to fade away after a while but Gladys remains undeterred. Back at home, Samantha tells Durwood she has tried everything when Abner comes over and tells them that he's tired of all this, especially because the other neighbors are starting to talk. Samantha tells him that she has thought up of a cure: a séance! She says it will cure Gladys when suddenly Gladys calls up and says that she wants Abner to come home quickly as she is getting vibrations, which apparently she gets from chewing on the electric blanket, according to Abner. Durwood is confused about the séance solution but Samantha tells him that a séance is the way to go because she is going to scare Gladys out of her powers once and for all.

That night the Stephens join Abner in his living room with the lights low and a spooky type record playing on the turntable. They wait for Gladys to show up and just when they can't wait any longer Gladys shows up dressed like a fortune teller and tells everyone that they should hold hands and relax. She says that they are going to conjure up spirits and when she asks for a sign, Samantha twitches up some clinking chains and closing doors. Abner begins to get scared but Gladys is delighted. Frustrated, Samantha decides she should zap up a scary ghost and does only to find that her ghost happens to look like Gladys' uncle Harold. She goes on with it and has "Harold" tell Gladys that she must stop dabbling in stuff she doesn't understand. She refuses to listen and Abner is petrified at all the goings on, especially when the ghost disappears. He pleads for Gladys to stop but she tells him to dry up and Samantha takes that as her queue and zaps Abner into a pile of dust! She acts shocked and Gladys is even more so and when she almost breaks into tears and apologizes to Abner for turning him to dust, Samantha zaps him back causing Gladys to faint.

The next day Durwood is pleased that the ESP stuff is over with until Gladys and Abner show up to return the pot that Gladys had originally brought over. Samantha and Durwood tell them they are going to the movie and Abner suggests he and Gladys go too which causes Gladys to start talking about ESP again as she had been thinking about Abner asking her out.

I LOVE this episode! It's engaging throughout and Gladys really had a chance to shine here. I love that "I command you to stand back!" part. Another one I love is when she comes out in her fortune telling outfit and says, "I'm here, my son."

My favorite part is when she tells Abner to dry up. The look of "A-HA!" on Samantha's face is priceless not to mention they couldn't have picked a better sound effect for him changing to dust. I also like it when Samantha says, "Mrs. Kravitz! What have you done?!"

Alice Pearce's husband Paul Davis owned a framing store. I wonder if those pictures came from his store? It would make that first scene very sweet. That beginning scene was later re-done as the opening of the fourth season Christmas episode when Samantha is having Durwood help her decide where to put the Christmas tree.

Of course, the whole episode was later redone as the seventh season finale when Samantha convinces Mrs. Stephens that she's got the power... oh, that's another of my favorite lines from this episode.

> GLADYS: *"Abner, guess what I've got?"*
> ABNER: *"Heartburn?"*
> GLADYS: *"No, Abner, I've got the power!"*
> ABNER: *"Take some lemon juice and water, that should knock it out."*
> GLADYS: *"Not that kind of power..."*
> ABNER: *"Well, until you're over it I'll sleep in the den."*

Alice Pearce should've won her Emmy based on this episode alone.

I also wish I could find that music that they were playing during the séance. I think it's awesome!

It was on this day that Liz Montgomery celebrated her 32nd birthday.

APRIL 22, 1965

It was on this day that ABC aired Episode #30: "George the Warlock" sponsored by Chevrolet.

Durwood wakes up early and when he goes out to get the morning paper he is stunned by the sight of a beautiful young woman next door at Pleasure O'Riley's who is NOT Pleasure! She introduces herself to him as Danger O'Riley, Pleasure's baby sister and tells him that she's house sitting while Pleasure is on her honeymoon. Durwood is enchanted with her innocence, especially since she's so sexy, and when he goes to go back in the house, finds that the door had shut and locked behind him. Not wanting to disturb Samantha's sleep, he tries to open one of the windows but Danger tells him that she realizes she distracted him and to make up for it she'll have him over for breakfast of blueberry pancakes, which happens to be his favorite breakfast.

A little later Samantha is surprised to find her husband not in bed and when she goes down to make some coffee, sees through her kitchen window into Danger's kitchen window and finds her husband! She calls over to the other house and Durwood stumbles over his words and tells her he'll be home very quickly until the dishwasher starts rumbling and water starts pouring out. He tells Samantha he has to go quickly and hangs up on her so he can help clean up the mess. Samantha is furious and gets even more mad when Durwood seems to be taking his time. To bide her time on her "fun-filled" Sunday Durwood had promised her, Samantha starts playing solitaire and doesn't realize that her Queen of Spades happens to resemble her mother, and that's only on account of it IS her mother spying on her.

Endora is not at all happy about Samantha's mortal existence, especially being reduced to solitaire, and so she flies off to the pleasure palace of one of Samantha's old charming warlock boyfriend's, George, to talk him into charming Samantha back to the witch world. George tells Endora that Samantha won't be too keen on him as she's the only one to get away but Endora tells him that he should go in a different guise and suggests he use the one that inspired Edgar Allan Poe to write his most famous poem, *The Raven*. George thinks that's an absolutely wizard notion and transforms into the raven.

George flies down to 1164 Morning Glory Circle the next morning and waits for Durwood to leave, which he soon does to take Danger to a modeling engagement. Once Durwood has left George flies through the open kitchen window where Samantha has begun to do dishes and he transforms back into his handsome warlock form. Not at all impressed, Samantha tells him that he should leave as she's perfectly happy being married. He can see right through her emotions and tells her that she's more suited to being a witch and he zaps her into her flying suit. Samantha tells him that it doesn't matter what he does, she's deliriously happy with Durwood and changes back to her mortal clothes and shows him her wedding ring, which for some reason doesn't set too well with George and he disappears.

Downtown, Larry and Durwood are discussing the new Feathertouch Electric Typewriter campaign when Raven George swoops in and plugs in the model typewriter and begins typing on it. The men are impressed and decide that they must use the raven as the trademark for the account, and incorporate Edgar Allan Poe's *The Raven* into it. Larry tells Durwood he can keep the raven at home and so Durwood brings him home to a shocked Samantha who realizes that George is trying to wheedle his way into her life again. She hates to disappoint Durwood but she tells him that the raven isn't an ordinary bird, which he agrees with after having seen his tricks, but Samantha tells him that she used to date the bird and she zaps him out of the cage and into the living room in his human form. Durwood is shocked and dismayed when he realizes that he will need another bird. They suddenly hear Endora laughing and Durwood thinks he may be going crazy but Samantha tells him that her mother has been trying to break up their marriage. He calls for Endora to come and have it out with him and they argue until Samantha pleads for Endora to leave and take George with her. Endora, who has been insulted by Durwood, leaves without George. When Durwood threatens to throw him out, George turns Durwood into a penguin until Samantha asks him to turn her husband back. George complies and before he can do anything else, the doorbell rings and who should it be but Danger who has come looking for help as her oven door fell off when she opened it. George, who is smitten with Danger, tells her that he majored in oven doors at Oxford and he goes over to help her. When her back is turned, he zaps the door back to its proper place and she is instantly enchanted and invites him to dinner.

Durwood is nervous about Danger having a warlock to dinner but Samantha reminds him that at one point he had a witch for dinner. When he goes to say that he knew how to cope with the situation, Samantha is irritated thinking that he's insinuated that her heritage is a problem and she leaves him to eat dinner on his own in the dining room while she goes into the kitchen.

Over at Danger's, George tells Danger how beautiful she is and then tells her about being a warlock. She doesn't care as she says it's a free country and everyone is free to go to the church of their choice. Once she gets into the kitchen she pulls out the dictionary to see just exactly what a warlock is and George comes in and asks if she won't have anything to do with him now that she knows. She says she doesn't think it's a problem and he shows her some magic by zapping up a cigarette and they decide to go over to the Stephens to thank them for introducing them.

At 1164, Durwood is surprised to find that George already revealed himself to Danger and they celebrate the new relationship.

I would give this one four stars. I think it's awesome that we get a glimpse into Samantha's life before Durwood by meeting one of her warlock boyfriends, plus I love when Samantha gets mad at Durwood because Liz is so good at playing annoyed, but most importantly, Danger O'Riley is HOT! Out of all the women who have already thrown themselves at Durwood, she is definitely one that seems to be a true worry for Samantha. I also love that we find out that the raven from the poem is related to Samantha somehow. And how cool was it when the Raven whistled part of the theme song?!

There are several bloopers in this episode including the fact that with the way the house was built with the garage, there would be no way for a window to be over the kitchen sink because it would look straight into the garage. When Durwood is trying to get back into his house, at one point he's trying to get into the den window, the scene switches to Danger and then back to him and he's at the living room window. Another is that after Durwood leaves with Danger for her modeling engagement the camera blacks out for no apparent reason.

I am confused as to why the wedding ring is such a big deal to George. Is it just the fact that he is very much against marriage? This is the second time that we see Samantha in her flying suit and it is definitely black whereas the first time it's hard to tell what color it was. It also has a higher collar.

APRIL 29, 1965

It was on this night that ABC aired Episode #31: "That Was My Wife" sponsored by Quaker Oats.

After Samantha hears a radio commercial for a hair color treatment she decides to change her hair and after several colors and styles, she settles on a short brunette 'do when the doorbell rings and who should it be but Gladys Kravitz, who just moments before had seen Samantha checking herself in the mirror but between hairdos. Samantha tells her the hair is a wig and that she decided to mix things up a bit in preparation for a night at a hotel with Durwood, something they do every so often to keep the romance alive in their marriage. Gladys thinks this is great as Abner hasn't shown her any affection in a long time, aside from a not-very-warm handshake.

At the office, Larry asks Durwood to go with him for drinks but Durwood says he has other plans and is very elusive about it. Not having anything to do that evening Larry calls Louise to see what she would like to do but they decide they'll do their own thing: Larry will go see a ball game and Louise will go spend the evening with Samantha. As Larry leaves Durwood's office he hears the secretary confirming Durwood's reservation at the President Hotel and believes that Durwood has set up a romantic tryst with another woman.

Later that night, Durwood waits in the hotel lobby when a dark haired woman in a sultry voice asks him for a cigarette light. When he realizes that it's Samantha he's surprised but Samantha tells him she just wanted to surprise him. He tells her that all though it looks great, he wasn't tired of her usual look. As they go up to their room, Larry sees them as he's there to pick up his baseball tickets and as he sees that Durwood is with a brunette, he's sure that Durwood is fooling around.

Up in their room Samantha twitches her hair back and as they decide what to do for the evening (as though they would NEED to decide?!) Durwood realizes that he left his mystery novel at home. Samantha offers to pop home to get it and after a little hesitation, Durwood agrees to let her go. At home, just as she's picked up the book and ready to pop back, the doorbell rings and for some strange reason Samantha decides to answer it. It is Larry come looking for Louise, who he thought was going to hang out with Samantha. Samantha says she had been relaxing as Durwood had to work late but she was going to get dressed and go downtown to meet him for dinner. Larry realizes that Samantha may find out what Durwood is supposed to be up to and he races back to the hotel.

Back at the hotel, Durwood finishes his book and they are both surprised when there is a rapid knock at the door. When Larry announces that it's him, Samantha realizes there may be trouble if he sees her there so she pops out. Durwood is confused as to Samantha's actions and even more so at Larry's when he congratulates him on his carrying on with the brunette in the lobby. Durwood tries to tell him it was Samantha but Larry thinks Durwood is trying to cover up his affair. After Larry leaves Samantha pops back in and explains what happened but she says that maybe Larry will just forget about it.

That night, as Larry is ogling girls in the *Gals, Gals* magazine, Louise tells Larry it's disgusting that he has to look to other women for pleasure. He tells her that every man does but she cites Durwood as one that doesn't. Larry tells her not to be too sure about that but won't tell her why, until she nags him unmercifully and he admits what he had seen at the hotel. Louise is shocked and he makes her promise not to tell Samantha. She promises, but the next day she's immediately on the phone to talk to Durwood. She is furious with him and tells him to meet her at the lobby of the hotel so she can talk some sense into him. He agrees and Samantha tells him that he'll be able to clear his name so long as he tells Louise that he'll give up the "other" woman.

Durwood and Louise meet up and Larry ends up there as he hears from Samantha that Durwood is at the hotel. When he sees Durwood with the brunette he tries to listen in on their conversation and is horrified to find it's Louise.

The next day Larry loses control when he's around Durwood and socks him one in the eye and tells him that if he ever catches him around Louise again he'll be fired!

Samantha shows up with beef steak to put on Durwood's eye and she tells him that she'll just darken her hair again and have Larry and Louise catch them making out in his office. Louise shows up and Larry is very dejected but before they can get into a fight they hear a woman's giggling from the other room and run into Durwood's office to see him making out with the brunette. Just as they are about to lay into Durwood, Samantha turns around and they are both shocked but relieved.

I really like this one and would give it four stars. I think it has a cute premise and it's also what I view as the sealing deal on creating the character of Serena, the first part being Liz playing Endora in "Which Witch is Which?"

I do have to say Liz's hair looked really dumb at the first when she's coming down the stairs, and maybe it was done that way so that we could see why she'd want to try a new hairstyle.

I think this is the first time where the TV is not at the foot of the stairs but instead there is the stereo. I find it kind of odd.

That Civil War line is repeated by Sandra Gould's Gladys in "Weep No More My Willow" from the Fifth Season. I also think it's quite apropos that Abner is reading the book about the Civil War as it was the centennial anniversary of the end of the war.

I always thought it was a cop out that Abner says he's color blind when he could've seen the difference between dark and light.

I like that scene with Larry and Louise when he's reading the girly magazine, especially when she realizes he's not listening to her and she says, "We were overtaken by bandits, knocked unconscious and shipped to the Kasbah!" Larry: "That's nice, dear."

Another line I liked is when Durwood wonders if Samantha would know if he were cheating yet he never actually asks and she says, "Yes, I'd know." When he asks how, she says, "That's something for me to know and you'd had better not try and find out!" I wonder what she would do?

Durwood's mystery novel is titled *A Warrant to Kill*. I wonder if it's a real book?

I always found it ridiculous that Samantha answered the door when she popped home…and he even asks her why and she says, "The doorbell rang and I answered it." Almost like she'd been trained to do that.

I also like at the end when Louise asks Samantha if she can borrow "the wig" and Samantha says, "Oh I don't think so Louise, it's custom fit for my head." I like how she says "head."

Larry also punches Durwood. It seems like there was a lot of punching in the early episodes.

MAY 7, 1965

It was on this night that ABC aired Episode #32: "Illegal Separation" sponsored by Quaker Oats.

Just as Durwood is about to toast Samantha with a glass of champagne and a night of whispered sweet nothings, the resounding chime of the doorbell breaks the mood. To their shock, Abner Kravitz is standing there in his pajamas with news that he and Mrs. Kravitz have broken up after thirty years of marriage! He tells them they had a championship fight that started with a quarrel about where he should put his socks when they are folded. As the fight escalated, he left the house in a fit to go to his club to stay the night but realized he didn't have a club. When he tried to go back into his own house, he found he was locked out and Gladys wouldn't answer his cries. Samantha tells him that he can stay in their guest room overnight and when tempers subside in the morning he can make up with his wife.

The night is long as Abner snores really loud and just as Durwood is getting ready to go to the office, Mrs. Kravitz shows up. Durwood lets Samantha answer the door and she finds that Mrs. Kravitz has brought over Abner's clothes in a couple suitcases with a note that says "Farewell forever!" Samantha tries to talk Gladys into forgiving Abner, especially over a matter as silly as socks, but Gladys says it's more than that and she leaves. Durwood is shocked that Abner didn't leave with his wife and Abner comes down from the most restful sleep he's had in a long time. He also asks if they have orange juice for breakfast, which irritates Durwood. Samantha shows Abner the note and he is shocked…at Mrs. Kravitz's penmanship! He says that he has no intention of going back to his wife and takes his suitcases upstairs. Durwood asks that Samantha get rid of him before he comes back from work.

That afternoon when Durwood comes home he finds that he still has an unwelcome houseguest who has offered to cook dinner, involving Brussels sprouts. When he leaves to make dinner, Samantha admits she didn't have the heart to throw him out but Durwood says that she must get rid of him as she was the one who invited him to stay. So Samantha goes over to the Kravitzes and finds that Gladys has been sobbing over Abner. When Samantha tells her to just go over to her place and apologize to Abner, she adamantly refuses. Realizing that both parties are stubborn, Samantha comes up with a plan involving their mutual living room windows.

A little later, Samantha has set up a gin game between Durwood and Abner in front of the living room window with Abner able to look out. As they are playing Samantha mentions how she sees Gladys in a negligee and a new hairdo. Abner can't be bothered by such nonsense and Durwood mentions how great she looks too. Seeing what they are trying to do, Abner goes to the window and pulls down the blinds. Seeing that he won't give up on the game, Samantha twitches Durwood into winning.

The next morning Durwood is fit to be tied and even more so when Abner asks Samantha to do his laundry and mentions how Durwood had the morning paper yesterday. Samantha tells Durwood that it's no bother at all to do the laundry and Abner says he'll just go get his paper. When he arrives at the door Gladys opens it to reveal she is dressed like a geisha girl but he barely gives her a glance before he leaves.

That night Abner happens to not snore and as it's so quiet Durwood and Samantha can't sleep. She tells Durwood that she's been thinking that maybe she can give the Kravitzes a mutual dream about a time in their life before they were married when they were both blissfully happy, which Samantha has determined to be when Abner proposed. She goes to work casting her spell and the Kravitzes dream about when they were in a soda shop and Abner gave Gladys a diamond ring and professed his love. After she accepts, Samantha wakes them both up and she and Durwood run to the bedroom window to watch them reunite out in the street. Samantha makes it even more special by slowing them down like is done in the movies. The Kravitzes embrace each other out in the moonlit street and walk arm in arm back to their house.

I would give this one four stars. It presents a very real world situation with a dash of witchcraft. Plus it's sweet to learn about the Kravitzes early life. Alice Pearce and George Tobias are very funny in the malt shop scene.

Two days prior the first draft card burnings took place at the University of California, Berkley and a coffin was marched up to the draft board.

MAY 14, 1965

It was on this night that ABC aired Episode #33: "A Change of Face" sponsored by Chevrolet.

When Endora pops in on Durwood napping on the couch, she mentions how unsightly he is with his mouth is gaping open while he sleeps.

Samantha tells her that nobody looks good sleeping and besides, she didn't marry him for his good looks alone. Endora thinks Durwood doesn't look good at all and suggests that he may look better with curly hair and she zaps his hair into curls. Samantha gets into playing Mr. Potato Head with Durwood and zaps a pencil mustache on him. She likes it but not with the curly hair and straightens it out. Just then she hears the water bubbling for tea and goes to get it as the door rings. She asks Endora to answer it but Endora pops out. When the doorbell rings again, Durwood wakes up and answers the door to find Mrs. Kravitz asking if Mr. Stephens is there. When she realizes she is looking at Mr. Stephens she runs away screaming. He realizes she saw something on his face and when he goes to look in the mirror he about has a heart attack when he doesn't recognize the reflection and he bellows for Samantha who is shocked to hear that her husband is awake before she could put his face back the way it was. He demands to know what happened and for his old face back and she complies and tells him about her and Endora's conversation. He tells her that he thought she liked his face and she assures him she did, but that they were just playing around. He isn't too pleased to hear that and the next day at the office he can't stop looking at himself in the mirror. When Larry comes in to discuss one of the campaigns, Durwood surprises him by asking if Larry thinks he is attractive. Larry, befuddled, admits that Durwood isn't ugly but by no means is he the most handsome guy.

At 1164, Samantha receives a phone call from Larry who tells her about Durwood's weird behavior earlier. Feeling bad, Samantha tries to think of what to do when her mother pops in. When she tells her about Durwood feeling bad, Endora thinks that it's his own insecurities but Samantha assures her that it was because of what they had done. However she says she has come up with an idea and that is to have another woman hit on Durwood. Endora is disgusted to think of hitting on him but Samantha says she didn't want her to do it and shows her what she had in mind. With the wave of a hand, Samantha becomes a tall beautiful French woman and she pops on down to the bar. She finds Durwood and sits down next to him and tells him that she had been watching him and had wanted to talk to him. She says she is a sculptress and would like to do his head in clay as she could tell that he was a man of great character and that he has such great looks. She apologizes for being so direct but he tells her that he isn't embarrassed but that he feels she may be lonely as she is new in town. She says that they can get to know each other at her studio but he tells her that he is married. Michelle (Samantha's alias in her new guise) says that he must not have a good marriage if he was sitting at a bar alone and she tells him "Se la vie" and leaves. Joe, the bartender, is shocked that Durwood didn't take Michelle up on her proposition and tells Durwood, who has a knowing look, that he must have a fantastic wife and Durwood agrees.

When Samantha gets home Endora pops in impressed that Samantha thinks she has succeeded. She also thinks that Durwood won't tell her about the encounter but Samantha thinks otherwise. However at dinner, it seems that Endora is right as Durwood doesn't say one thing about Michelle because he knows what Samantha is up to.

The next day when Durwood asks for his secretary Ellen to come in to dictate he is shocked to find another secretary in her place, named Barbara. She tells him that Ellen went home sick from a sudden virus, which Durwood finds weird but Barbara says that type of thing happens and as the French say, "Se la vie!" Thinking that Barbara must be Samantha trying again to get Durwood to feel better about himself he starts to make the moves on her. Meanwhile, Samantha has come to see Durwood as she happened to be in town and she walks in on Durwood making out with Barbara! She is shocked but no more than Barbara who runs off. Durwood tells her that he thought she was Barbara and he's kind of pleased to see that she was jealous and then he admits that he knew about Michelle. He tells her that he thought she was playing dirty pool by trying to trick him, but she tells him that she knew he wouldn't take the bait.

I would give this one four stars. I think it's a very real situation that everyone goes through, and that is wondering if they really do have the looks to keep their significant other enticed. I liked Endora and Samantha playing around with Durwood's looks and it's funny when Durwood sees himself and yells, "I WANT MY OLD FACE BACK! I WANT MY OLD FACE BACK! I WANT MY OLD FACE BACK!"

This episode is also monumental in the fact that it's the first one with guest star Dick Wilson as the drunk and we see that his drunken stupor came originally from Samantha because it seemed he was holding his alcohol well until he met her.

This is yet another episode that hearkens back to the pilot as Durwood goes to get advice from Dave, the doctor, and Joe the bartender.

MAY 21, 1965

It was on this night that ABC aired Episode #34: "Remember the Main" sponsored by Quaker Oats.

Samantha decides to hold a political rally at her place to back City Councilman candidate Ed Wright when Shirley Foster, one of the women in the neighborhood, says that her husband doesn't like to have a crowded house when he comes home from work. Of course, Durwood

Samantha campaigns for Ed Wright for City Councilman.

isn't too thrilled when he finds his house crowded but Samantha tells him that it was he who told her she should get more involved with civic affairs. Ed goes on about his rival John C. Cavanaugh who currently holds the position and who has been involved in some rather shady dealings in the past including the water drain system that was put in with shoddy material. Durwood becomes interested and tells Ed he would like to be his campaign manager and that he can work up some posters for his campaign.

Mr. Cavanaugh hears that Mr. Wright is using the water drain system as his main attack point but he assures reporters that there is nothing to investigate and that the water drain system will outlast both he and Mr. Wright.

Later that night, Durwood and Samantha attend a rally for Mr. Wright out in the park where it seems to be going well when Mr. Wright announces that he is going to have a televised debate with Mr. Cavanaugh. All is great until some hoodlums throw some eggs and tomatoes at Mr. Wright. When they try again, Samantha twitches the food back in their face. Mr. Wright calls them out and tells them they can tell Mr. Cavanaugh that it'll take more than an omelet to get him to back down. Just then Durwood is handed the most recent paper which says that the governor has demanded a full investigation of the water drain system.

A couple weeks later at the televised debate, Mr. Cavanaugh seems to be a no show, and Durwood is sure that Ed will be a shoo-in. Ed addresses the TV audience and goes over a laundry list of the improprieties that Mr. Cavanaugh has. Just then Mr. Cavanaugh shows up and says that he will address all those things but he has brought a member of the governor's investigation team to address the audience. The investigator tells everyone that after a thorough check out the water drain system seems to be in tip top shape and should last for many years to come.

Durwood is furious that Samantha seemingly dragged him into the campaign and he's worried that he may be drummed out of the advertising business for slander against Mr. Cavanaugh. Samantha says that this happens to be the only thing that Mr. Cavanaugh has ever been involved in that has been honest and before Durwood can go on about it she puts him in "the deep freeze" and calls out to Endora to meet her downtown.

They end up in Mr. Cavanaugh's office and Samantha catches her mother up to speed and they go through his files and find that the water drain system is the only honest thing he's done. Samantha pops home and unfreezes Durwood. Endora however thinks there is a better way to handle things and she causes the water main to burst. Soon Mr. Kravitz shows up with news of the flood and Durwood is suspicious of how it happened and when he starts to accuse Samantha, Endora pops in to claim the glory. She says that she did it to get Durwood to quit raving at Samantha and that it would prove the investigation was wrong and it will cause them to re-evaluate the water drain as well as all of Mr. Cavanaugh's past dealings. Before he can argue, the phone rings and Ed tells Durwood just what Endora told him.

The elections come and go and Ed wins the election. He comes over to see Samantha and Durwood and Samantha introduces him to her mother. Ed says that he's come over to tell them that the investigation into Cavanaugh has come to a halt as Cavanaugh has disappeared. Durwood states that he would like to have him in the palm of a hand and with a deft look Endora makes it come true.

Like my friend Sharon once said of this episode, "I'd rather forget the main." It definitely gets one star. This episode is seriously SOOOOO boring! I felt very much like Samantha when she is sitting at the table with Durwood and Ed bored out of her mind and just wanting to go to sleep.

I thought the hats and sashes were kind of cute. I think they are a nice part of Americana. Did they still wear that stuff in the 60s?

Ed Mallory, who played Ed Wright, was married to actress Joyce Bullifant and they had a son together. They later divorced and after Elizabeth Montgomery and Bill Asher divorced Bill married Joyce and adopted Ed's son! How odd that he would allow his son to be adopted. By the way, I thought he was totally the wrong choice for this character. His voice seemed very monotone.

I also noticed that this episode began really weird in the fact that there was no music. It just starts with the phone ringing and an obviously pregnant Samantha answers the phone. I believe that scene must've been one of the last to be recorded for the first season as she wears that same outfit in "Cousin Edgar" and she looks different throughout the rest of the episode.

It's also funny that the neighbor lady who asked her to have the rally at 1164 is named Shirley Foster. The Morning Glory Circle Welcome Wagon committee neighbors from the beginning of the season and from "It's Magic" were named Shirley Clyde and June Foster.

Gladys and Abner were definitely under-utilized and used in the wrong way. I really doubt Abner would've been so civic minded to be on the flood watch. I think he would've been too worried about himself to go warn others.

One of my favorite lines is when Samantha and Durwood are arguing about the flood and how he thinks Samantha did it (of course!) and he says, "If you didn't, who did?" and Endora pops in "Good evening!"

DURWOOD: *"This doesn't concern you, Endora."*
ENDORA: *"Oh, I believe it does. Have you heard about the flood?"*

I just like how she says it.

It also seems in the black and white version that she is wearing little or no makeup in that scene but in the colorized she still has the harsh blue makeup.

I think that scene with Cavanaugh in Durwood's hand is so cheesy because they simply replay the audio from the debates but Dick York's expression is hilarious.

This episode is certainly towards the bottom of the list though it's no "Your Witch is Showing."

The dress that Samantha wears with the lining along the edges is the very same one that she is seen in on the cover of the Samantha paper dolls that were released in 1965. If you look at her in that photo you can see that Samantha wasn't colorized right as she has on blue eye shadow and red lipstick.

The next night the first ever skateboard championships were held and more protesters marched to the draft board at UC Berkley to burn more draft cards along with photos of President Lyndon Johnson.

MAY 28, 1965

It was on this night that ABC aired Episode #35: "Eat at Mario's" sponsored by Chevrolet.

Endora and Samantha have an absolutely divine lunch at a little Italian place named Mario's. Even Endora is impressed with her veal marsala and Samantha's fettuccine. When she tells the waiter to pay their compliments to the chef, they find out that the waiter is also the chef, the cashier and just happens to be Mario himself! The witches are flabbergasted that he doesn't have any help but he says that he doesn't have enough money to hire a staff and that's because pizza has become the Italian food of choice. He feels that his restaurant is going to fail because of this and, surprisingly, Endora feels bad for him. So does Samantha and she suggests that maybe Durwood could do advertising for Mario.

Later when Durwood arrives home from an exhausting day at the office, he tries to listen to Samantha's day but he keeps interrupting her telling about Linton Baldwin's new account, Perfect Pizza, the largest pizza chain on the west coast and now he wants to open up chains on the east coast and he wants McMann and Tate to handle the publicity. However, he is so picky about ad agencies he goes through them like "women go through dresses." Samantha is amazed at how Durwood's problem is so related to hers with Mario. Seeing that Durwood isn't in the mood to take on anymore work, Samantha decides to do the advertising herself and comes up with a very basic, but effective slogan—"Eat at Mario's" and with a twitch she zaps up a full page ad in the morning paper.

The next morning at breakfast she is pleased to see how great her full page ad came out in the paper. Durwood is also pleased to see how his quarter page ad for Perfect Pizza came out. When he sees Samantha's ad, he mentions how whoever did that must be nuts. When Samantha questions him about it, he realizes that Mario's is the restaurant Samantha was talking about the day before and she admits it saying she just wanted to help Mario by informing the public that Mario's exists. Durwood tells her that her little bit of magic is very harmful to the other advertisers and many more. She promises not to do it anymore and he forgives her though he says he's not happy that she was drumming up business for one of Perfect Pizza's competitors. Samantha assures him that Mario's isn't a competitor, as he doesn't serve pizza. He agrees that it won't be a big deal.

However, Mr. Baldwin thinks it's a very big deal especially since he didn't get a full page ad. Larry tries to tell him that they try to diverse the marketing rather than put all their eggs in one basket but Mr. Baldwin still isn't sold. Luckily an ad on a TV show for Perfect Pizza is about to air which grabs Mr. Baldwin's attention.

Across town, Samantha is about to turn on the TV to see the ad herself when Endora pops in saying how unimpressed with Samantha's ad she was as it was very ordinary and not even on the front page. The TV announcer starts to go into the Perfect Pizza ad but Endora has other ideas and zaps him into talking about Mario's. Back at McMann and Tate, Mr. Baldwin is furious and says he will sue the announcer, the TV station, and especially McMann and Tate and says that they definitely do not have the account anymore and that he is going to sign with Mario's agency. Durwood immediately gets on the phone with Samantha and when she tells him that Endora is responsible he threatens to kill her, though Endora says she'd just come back to haunt him. He gets so angry that he hangs up upsetting Samantha. Feeling bad for hurting her daughter, Endora tells her that she'll make things better by making "Mr. Pizza" change his mind and bets that Mr. Baldwin is at Mario's trying to discover who the ad agency is. They fly over there and find that Mr. Baldwin is there bugging Mario, who knows nothing of where the ads came from. Mr. Baldwin tells him that if he tells him who did it that he'll amalgamate him into his chain, but Mario says that pizza is an insult to humanity and orders Mr. Baldwin to leave. Samantha and Endora clap before they leave and soon Mr. Baldwin leaves.

Out on the street Samantha asks what they should do now and Endora says they'll do just what they did for Mario and advertise and with that she zaps sandwich signs on everyone. Samantha zaps up a huge billboard that Mr. Baldwin sees and is quite impressed with but not half as impressed when he sees a plane sky writing "Eat Perfect Pizza." Perplexed at how all this is happening, Mr. Baldwin heads to the park to take it all in. Endora and Samantha follow him and come upon an ice cream man who stops near Mr. Baldwin. When a little girl and boy come up to him, the witches make them ask for Perfect Pizza and if they can't have it they won't have anything. A dog comes up and Samantha makes it say the same thing. Astounded at the talking dog, Mr. Baldwin asks the women if they heard it and they say they did and that it must've been done by McMann and Tate.

Meanwhile, back at the office, Larry is very worried after seeing the sky writing and is surprised when Mr. Baldwin calls in and says he is impressed by Larry's plan of attack to get him by going forward with the advertising that he had seen. Larry is shocked, but pleased, and so is Durwood.

The next night Durwood, Samantha and Endora go to Mario's to celebrate and find the restaurant quite full. When they find they needed a reservation, they are deflated until Mario tells the maitre'd that there is always a seat for special friends.

I would give this one four stars. I think it's quite entertaining and I like to see Endora working with Durwood instead of against him. Mr. Baldwin is a perfect client what with his fervor for Perfect Pizza.

The talking dog is hysterical! And I like hearing all the kids say, "If I can't have Perfect Pizza, I don't want anything."

The scene with Endora and Samantha flying off is just reused from "Witch or Wife." It's funny how just in this first season they've reused scenes a couple times.

Three nights before this, sports history was made when Cassius Clay a.k.a. Muhammad Ali knocked out Sonny Liston in record time during their championship rematch.

JUNE 3, 1965

It was on this night that ABC aired the last filmed episode of the first season, Episode #36: "Cousin Edgar" sponsored by Quaker Oats.

During the middle of the night, Durwood lets out a loud sneeze waking up Samantha. Just before she goes back to bed she sees the familiar face of her cousin Edgar. In fact, that's the only part of the pointy-eared Edgar that she sees. The next morning she has breakfast with him after talking him into showing his entire self to her. He doesn't speak at all, but that's no matter to Samantha, as she is so glad to see Edgar, who happens to be an elf. Apparently Edgar was a great body guard for her when they were younger and then it dawns on her that she never saw him unless she was in trouble. When she asks him why he is there, he disappears.

Meanwhile, as Durwood tries to shave, the water suddenly turns itself off and he finds himself spraying the shaving cream all over and ends up with a few cuts. He chalks it up to being nervous about meeting with client Shelley Shoes who is also being courted by another agency. When he goes to drink his coffee he finds himself pouring it down his front and still chalks it up to being nervous.

Later, in the office, when Larry is yelling because he doesn't like Durwood's cutesy ideas for the campaign, the office door slyly opens and closes and suddenly Durwood finds himself being tickled by unseen hands and then when he sits down his chair tips him out. He realizes that it must be Endora teasing him but he dismisses it and tells Larry he has some other ideas and goes to draw them on a board with Larry looking on but then he loses control of his hand and draws all over Larry. When he tries to help Larry cleanup he suddenly gets Larry in a choke hold and they wrestle to the floor. Durwood is furious and calls Samantha to see why Endora is trying to make him look like an idiot and he demands that Samantha speak with her. Endora pops in and is absolutely confused by Samantha's accusation which leads Samantha to say that she has been trying not to upset Durwood even more than he already is, especially with Edgar in town. Endora realizes that Edgar is the culprit as he must see Samantha's mortal marriage as a blot on the family name. Samantha decides that she must get Edgar to stop by brewing up a potion to put him to sleep and she enlists Endora's help, who feels terrible about being so sneaky with Edgar.

Later on Samantha calls on Edgar and invites him for hot chocolate. Edgar is suspicious and when Samantha turns to get the cookies, he switches their mugs.

At Mr. Shelley's office, Durwood is a bundle of nerves looking around and under everything as they wait for Mr. Shelley. He's even more nervous when he finds that Mr. Froug, from the competing agency, is going to be in on the meeting to present his ideas as Mr. Shelley requested they both present at the same time. Froug shows up full of confidence and backhanded compliments. While the men are talking, the door opens and closes from an invisible visitor who happens to be Edgar. He ties Durwood's laces together causing him to trip and when Mr. Shelley comes in, Edgar causes Durwood to take Mr. Shelley's chair out from underneath him. Durwood finally has it and leaves.

When he arrives at home he finds Samantha fast asleep on the couch and he tells her that Endora has been at it again. Samantha can't focus on what he's saying and she immediately falls asleep.

At breakfast the next morning, Samantha tells Durwood it isn't Endora who has been causing all the trouble and tells Durwood about Cousin Edgar. Irritated that Edgar is trying to break up their marriage, Durwood threatens to punch him in the nose and immediately he spills coffee on himself. Having to leave for another meeting with Mr. Shelley, Durwood calls out to the air that he loves Samantha and wishes Edgar would see that and that he would stop making trouble or he requests that Samantha turn Edgar into a human. After Durwood leaves, Samantha asks Edgar to appear and she explains to him how much she loves Durwood and that she is not in any danger being married to Durwood. Suddenly Edgar fades out and Samantha feels defeated.

At the office, Durwood tells Larry that he's ready to make another presentation but Larry is not so certain that it's a good idea but Durwood says that he won't regret it. At the meeting Froug is there again and Durwood notices the door open and close and he realizes that Edgar must be in there. When Mr. Shelley arrives, Froug trips over his shoes which happen to be tied together. After he composes himself, Froug offers to show his ideas first. When he flips through his ads all of them have been changed to say things like "Shelley's Shoes are Corny" with caricatures of Mr. Shelley on them. Froug becomes as nervous as Durwood was and asks to be excused. Durwood goes up next and his ads have been changed to reflect the story of the elves and the shoemaker and Durwood realizes that Edgar is now on his side.

That night Durwood laughs at how much Mr. Shelley loved the sketches and he asks to thank Edgar. Samantha thinks Edgar is gone until they see his feet appear and then the rest of him. Edgar waves goodbye and Samantha and Durwood end the night with a kiss.

I would give this episode three stars. It would've got four but Edgar's fade-ins were so cheesy, especially that first one where his hand suddenly appears by his face to wave. It would've been cooler if his hand had just appeared separate from his face.

Dick York was superb in this episode and had quite a lot of funny scenes.

I also thought Elizabeth Montgomery was so cute when she was falling asleep.

And do you think maybe they were going to have Edgar be a recurring character?

It should be noted that Samantha wore that same circle-y top in "Remember the Main" but it was colorized blue.

This is also the first time that an episode has a scene filmed directly IN the bathroom.

JUNE 10, 1965

It was on this night that ABC finally aired what was supposed to be Episode #4: "It Shouldn't Happen to a Dog" that was originally supposed to air on October 8, 1964.

At McMann and Tate, Durwood gets into an awkward conversation with Mr. Barker about his baby food when Mr. Barker asks him if he's tasted his product, particularly strained bananas and buttered beet hearts, as he feels he can't really sell it if he doesn't know the product. Durwood also rejects Mr. Barker's ideas for labels and before he can present his own ideas, Mr. Barker tells him he'll discuss it with him that night at a dinner party at Durwood's.

At the party, Larry tries to see if Mr. Barker has made any decisions about Durwood's ideas but he's too busy making some decisions about Samantha, whom he is smitten by. Durwood finds out that Mr. Barker is impressed with Samantha and he tells her that having Mr. Barker happy has made him happy. Later on, as Samantha is cleaning things up out in the gazebo, Mr. Barker surprises her. When she suggests they go in, Mr. Barker forces himself on her and backs her into a corner. She warns him if he doesn't get control of himself, she's going to do something drastic. Of course, he doesn't take her seriously so in the mere twitch of her nose she transforms him into a shaggy little puppy. Just then Durwood comes out to see where Samantha has been and she tries to tell him about what she's done but he says they must get back to their guests.

At the end of the dinner, Mr. Barker's date leaves by herself when nobody can find him and Durwood puts the obnoxious dog outside for the night and suggests they'll try to find the owner in the morning. After a while the dog won't give up barking and when Durwood goes to see what his problem is Mr. Barker runs up to the bedroom to the arms of Samantha who is sitting on the bed. Durwood wonders how the dog came into the yard anyway and Samantha uses the opportunity to tell him that the dog is actually Mr. Barker. Stunned at this revelation,

Samantha fights off Mr. Barker's advances before turning him back into a dog. PHOTO COURTESY OF MARK SIMPSON.

Durwood tries to talk himself out of believing it but Samantha insists it's true. Realizing that his client is now a canine, Durwood gets furious with Samantha who tries to explain her actions, but he won't listen. When he tells Samantha that Mr. Barker is more important at the moment because he's a livelihood and she is just a wife, Samantha kicks him out of the bedroom.

A little later, while brooding over the night's events, Samantha is not surprised when her mother pops in to say "I told you so." While they talk they suddenly hear a cat yowling and Mr. Barker barking and when Samantha looks out the window, she sees that Mr. Barker is in a fight with a large cat. Not wanting to upset Durwood anymore, Samantha runs downstairs to break it up and finds that the gate is open so that Mr. Barker runs out with the cat close behind. She runs after them and ends up in an alley where Mr. Barker gets cornered on a garbage can. Before the cat can do anymore damage, Samantha twitches Mr. Barker back to human form. He is quite confused but then lets it pass when he tries to

Samantha casting a spell in a promo photo which was taken at the time "It Shouldn't Happen to a Dog" filmed.

make another pass at Samantha and so she changes him back to the dog just as two police officers pull up. Mr. Barker runs off and the officers detain her for running around in her nightgown and insist that she go back home and they will look for the dog.

At home, Durwood greets Samantha worried about where she was. She tells him that she had to chase after Mr. Barker and that she did change him back. Durwood tries to apologize but it isn't accepted and they go back to bed separately.

The next morning after Durwood has left for the office, Samantha gets a call that Mr. Barker was found and is now at the vets. When she goes to pick him up she finds that he has been given tetanus shots and a trim which makes him look like a poodle. She takes him down to McMann and Tate and transforms him there. Larry and Durwood walk into Larry's office where Mr. Barker is and are surprised to find that he now has very curly hair with a bow in it. He seems very distracted and he suggests maybe he had a bit too much to drink the night before. He also tells them that they can have his account but he would like to get another drink to help him clear his head. He goes into Durwood's office where Samantha is waiting and once again he can't keep from trying to make the moves on Samantha. Just as he's about to try and kiss her, Durwood walks in and knocks him out. Larry is shocked at Durwood knocking out a client and he tries to wake Mr. Barker. Seeing as there is nothing more that can be done, Durwood and Samantha leave.

The next day Mr. Barker shows up at Durwood's and apologizes and tells him there are no hard feelings and the account is his.

I would give this one three stars and that's because Samantha is practically attacked and put in a very uncomfortable situation. In fact, in the novelization by Al Hines that was released in 1964, this episode is part of it and Samantha says Mr. Barker tried to rape her!

Elizabeth Montgomery looks absolutely gorgeous throughout the whole episode and I love the nightgown she has, which pretty much looks like a dress. Those officers would be shocked to see what nightgowns consist of nowadays!

Had this episode aired when it was supposed to, it would've been the first time we meet Larry and Louise Tate. Mr. Barker also would have the distinction of being the first client.

The assistant director Marvin Miller told Herbie J Pilato (*Bewitched Forever*) that when they were filming this episode there was supposed to be a scene where the dog puts its paws on the hood of a car, which leads me to believe it was a bigger dog, but because the sun had been shining on it all day, the dog wouldn't touch it because it was hot.

I wonder if it was made known back in the original run that that was the last episode of the first season. Imagine having to wait the whole summer for new episodes!

Bewitched ended the season as the #2 show over all (NBC's *Bonanza* was #1). However the show was overlooked for any Emmy nominations.

ABC began airing reruns of the First Season during the summer. I present here the list of the rerun episodes which have been recently rediscovered via Joe Gardener using the archives of the *Los Angeles Times*, the *New York Times*, and the *Chicago Tribune*. The episode will be listed by number, name, and original airdate.

JUNE 17, 1965

Episode #6, "Little Pitchers Have Big Fears" *(October 22, 1964)*

The night before, a planned anti-war protest at the Pentagon turned into a teach-in, with the protesters distributing over 50,000 leaflets in and around the building.

JUNE 24, 1965

Episode #7, "The Witches Are Out" *(October 29, 1964)*

Three days later the big screen movie *Fluffy* starring Tony Randall premiered. It co-starred future Durwood, Dick Sargent.

JULY 1, 1965

Episode #8, "The Girl Reporter" *(November 5, 1964)*
Bewitched comic No. 2 was released this month.

JULY 8, 1965

Episode #18, "The Cat's Meow" *(January 21, 1965)*

JULY 15, 1965

Episode #10, "Just One Happy Family" *(November 19, 1964)*

The night before, the mortals started catching up with the witches when the U.S. spacecraft Mariner 4 passed by Mars taking photos, the first spacecraft to do so.

It was also that same day that Elizabeth made a brief un-credited cameo at the end of the big screen summer beach movie *How to Stuff a Wild Bikini* as a witch doctor's daughter. She even twitched her nose! This movie was directed by Bill Asher.

JULY 22, 1965

Episode #11, "It Takes One to Know One" *(November 25, 1964)*

Three days later, Bob Dylan drew ire for playing the electric guitar at the Newport Folk Festival.

JULY 29, 1965

Episode #26, "Driving is the Only Way to Fly" *(March 25, 1965)*

The prior day President Lyndon B. Johnson ordered an increase of U.S. troops in South Vietnam from 75,000 to 125,000 and to more than double the amount of men drafted per month from 17,000 to 35,000.

And on July 30, 1965 President Johnson signed into law the Social Security Act of 1965 creating both Medicare and Medicaid.

AUGUST 5, 1965

Episode #27, "There's No Witch Like an Old Witch" *(April 1, 1965)*

The next day President Johnson signed into law the Voting Rights Act of 1965 which made it unlawful to discriminate against anyone wishing to vote in any U.S. election.

AUGUST 12, 1965

Episode #21, "Ling Ling" *(February 11, 1965)*

The day before, the Watts Riots began in Los Angeles, sparked by police injustice towards blacks, as well as brutality against blacks, that had been happening for years.

On August 15, 1965 the Beatles performed the first ever stadium rock concert at Shea Stadium in New York.

AUGUST 19, 1965

Episode #33, "A Change of Face" *(May 13, 1965)*

AUGUST 26, 1965

Episode #17, "A is for Aardvark" *(January 14, 1965)*

Sometime in August, Liz and Dick York hosted ABC's Fall Preview as their *Bewitched* characters and Samantha suggested that she was going to deliver an heir on the air!

SEPTEMBER 2, 1965

Episode #29, "Abner Kadabra" *(April 15, 1965)*

Three days before, baseball history was made when player and manager Casey Stengel announced his retirement after fifty-five years. It was also today that Bob Dylan released his iconic album *Highway 61 Revisited* featuring the song "Like a Rolling Stone."

SEPTEMBER 9, 1965

Episode #24, "Which Witch is Which?" *(March 11, 1965)*

Three nights before, Agnes Moorehead was a guest on the talk show *Girl Talk*.

Stay tuned for an all new *Bewitched*, next week!

Season 2

SEPTEMBER 18, 1965

It was on this night that ABC aired the Second Season opener Episode #37: "Alias Darrin Stephens" sponsored by Quaker Oats.

Durwood and Samantha are going to dinner to celebrate their one year wedding anniversary when they hear a crash in the backyard and discover that Aunt Clara has crashed through the gazebo! After dusting her off, she tells them that she wanted to drop in to wish them a happy anniversary and give them gifts, which they find amongst the wreckage. They go inside and Samantha finds that she has been given a lovely apron and Durwood finds that he got a golf cap. Samantha goes to put the apron in the kitchen and Durwood finds that the golf cap is too small. Aunt Clara says she can fix it by a spell and begins to "Abba Dabba Dooba" all over the place when suddenly, in a puff of smoke, Durwood finds himself changed into a chimpanzee! Samantha is stunned when she comes back in the living room and worries when Aunt Clara can't seem to remember her spell. When Aunt Clara suggests Samantha reverse it, Samantha reminds her that she can't do it without knowing the original spell, and so being without a human husband, Samantha cancels their dinner reservation.

The next morning Durwood becomes offended when Samantha offers him a banana for breakfast. She calls the office to tell them that Durwood isn't feeling himself and that he won't be in. Just then Endora pops in recognizing Durwood immediately. Samantha feels that their problem amuses Endora, but she insists that she's just come to console as she loves Durwood very much. She also zaps up a little boys outfit so that Durwood can go out and play solidifying Samantha's suspicion that Endora finds the whole situation entertaining. Durwood gets offended and runs up to his room and Samantha asks Endora if she'll stay with Durwood while she runs out on an important errand. Endora agrees knowing she can get in some ribs at Durwood without being chided by Samantha.

A little later, Larry Tate shows up wanting to speak with Durwood, who he was told had laryngitis, but he says that Durwood should still be able to write. He has come to get some pointers on how to deal with a client. When Endora goes upstairs to tell him of the visitor, Durwood refuses to speak to Larry and runs out the window.

Across the street, Gladys Kravitz decides she wants to go deliver some of her ice box cookies to the Stephens and when she gets there, she can't help but look in the windows first in the hopes of catching something strange. She gets her wish when a chimpanzee in a suit and golf cap comes around the corner of the house frightening her. Intrigued at why a clothed chimpanzee is running around the neighborhood, she takes him home and as she gets a better look at him she realizes he looks very familiar. Abner suggests they call the zoo to come and get the chimp. The Municipal Zoo picks him up and puts him in a cage with three other chimps.

Meanwhile, Samantha arrives home and is surprised to find that Endora and Durwood are missing. However, Aunt Clara is there with one of her spell books, and tells Samantha that Endora went looking for Durwood but that she is on the job of finding a spell to reverse her monkey spell. Samantha is quite anxious as she tells Aunt Clara that she wants Durwood back so she can share some good news to him and she tells her that she's just found out she's going to have a baby! Aunt Clara is ecstatic and Samantha makes her promise not to tell Endora.

Samantha gets to work trying to find Durwood and finds that her husband is safe and sound locked in a cage at the zoo. She pops over to the zoo leaving Aunt Clara to continue looking for her spell. She finds Durwood sticking to himself and when she gives him a pad of paper and a pen to write with, he tells her that he feels fundamentally that there is a big difference between him and his cell mates. Just as Samantha goes to unlock the cage, Aunt Clara excitedly pops in having found the spell. She insists on casting it and when she throws out the magic words Durwood is changed to a seal! Samantha tells her she'll take over from there and she changes Durwood back into his regular form. The zoo keeper sees Durwood in the cage and threatens to call the authorities until Durwood gives him some cash. After sending Aunt Clara back home, Samantha sees that Durwood is absolutely furious and he tells her that he's had it. She tells him that she has something important to tell him before he makes any decisions, and she reveals that they are going to be parents. This immediately calms him down and he tells her that he'll try to be the best father there ever was. Before they go home, Durwood says goodbye to his chimp friends. It occurs to Durwood that as he's married to a witch their baby may be one as well but Samantha tells him it's possible it'll just be a mortal baby, but that they'll have to wait and see.

At home, they try to redo their anniversary celebration when Gladys Kravitz comes over wondering what happened to the chimp and she is startled to see Durwood in a tux and the golf cap that the chimp was wearing.

I would definitely give this four stars! What a perfect way to start off the new season. Everyone seems refreshed and it's so great to see Aunt Clara. Of course, Elizabeth Montgomery is obviously quite pregnant and it's kind of funny when she tells Aunt Clara, like it's a big secret. This episode finished filming May 20, 1965 when Liz was approximately four and a half months pregnant with her and Bill Asher's second child.

Endora is so funny in this episode! I love it when she pops in and immediately knows the chimp is Durwood. I love it when she says, "Come on, precious, try it on" about the play suit she zapped up. And then later, when she asks him to come downstairs "…so Mother Endora can comb you. You want to be a pretty chimp, don't you?"

Larry mentions to Endora how they met in Paris. I like it when the episodes refer to events that happened in previous episodes, like this reference to "Witch or Wife."

Three days before NBC premiered *Gidget* which was produced by Screen Gems. Gidget lived in the house next door to 1164 and she had an Ideal Samantha doll seen often sitting on the dresser in her room. Bill Asher directed many episodes.

That same day the big screen Patty Duke movie *Billie*, co-starring Dick Sargent, premiered. Two nights later NBC aired the first episode of their entry in the magic sitcom race, *I Dream of Jeannie* starring Barbara Eden and Larry Hagman about an astronaut who discovers a beautiful blonde genie in a bottle on a deserted island. Jeannie was a very worthy opponent to *Bewitched* and shared many similarities. Also that night *Get Smart* debuted on NBC.

SEPTEMBER 23, 1965

It was on this night that ABC aired Episode #38: "A Very Special Delivery" sponsored by Chevrolet.

Samantha worries about telling her mother of the impending birth while Durwood worries about Samantha being pregnant. He can't do enough for her even though she feels fine. At work, Larry notices how tired Durwood is and he tells him that he's read that women need to do stuff for themselves while pregnant so that they don't begin to rely on everyone. He also tells him that the baby will be stronger because of it and so Durwood promises that he won't lift another finger.

At home, Endora pops in furious about the baby as it means Samantha will be tied to Durwood indefinitely. Samantha is relieved that her mother somehow found out but she also knows that Endora is pleased that she is going to have a grandchild. Endora admits it but she also admits that Durwood should be hiring help for Samantha who assures her that Durwood can't do enough for her. Just then Durwood comes home and when Samantha asks him to lift a heavy pot for her and get some corn out of the bin, he suggests that she do it as exercise. Samantha is shocked but Endora is pleased that she was proven right. Furious at Durwood, Samantha leaves her mother and husband to talk about what just happened. Durwood tells Endora about what Larry told him and suggests that he knows every ache and pain Samantha is feeling. Realizing how ridiculous he is, Endora casts a small spell at a confused Durwood and she disappears telling him that he may not now know how she feels, but he soon will.

The next morning Durwood wakes up feeling a little sick and tired. He also finds that his clothes are fitting tighter and he tells Samantha that he feels like something crazy for breakfast. Samantha sees there is something off about Durwood but she shrugs it off and goes on with her morning.

At the office, Larry comes to get Durwood for a meeting and finds him crying in his office. When he suggests Durwood go home to rest up, Durwood is incensed and goes to the meeting, a lunch meeting where he insists on eating everyone's pickle. When the client, Mr. Martin, refuses to give his pickle up Durwood gets belligerent. Larry pulls him aside and tells him that as he's acting so strange he should go see a doctor.

So Durwood goes to the doctor and checks out fine until he tells him of his symptoms. The doctor thinks Durwood must be joking and suggests he sounds like a pregnant woman. This reminds Durwood of his conversation earlier with Endora and he realizes with horror that she may have actually made him pregnant…by witchcraft, of course!

Later on when Samantha calls to the office, she finds out that Durwood was complaining of things associated with pregnancy and that he had got in a fight over a pickle! She realizes her mother must be behind it and calls for her. Popping in from Rome, Endora tells her that Durwood will remain in that condition until he understands that being pregnant isn't all that easy and she pops off.

Meanwhile, Durwood has ended up at the bar sharing his new found condition with the ever non-listening Dave and then the bartender who tells him that he should be excited as he'll be the first man to pull it off! He then begins to imagine how it would be if he were to give birth and he realizes it just won't be kosher. When he awakes from his daydream he finds Samantha there and he decides to tell her but she assures him she all ready knows and that they are just symptoms which will soon go away and she takes him home.

The next morning Durwood returns to his old ways of spoiling Samantha and when she tries to assure him she feels OK he reminds her that he knows how she feels.

This one gets four stars! What a progressive idea it was for the mid 60s to have Durwood be having a baby! And Dick York was so funny, especially his rants about the pickle!

We have yet another shout out to the first episode with Durwood's visit to the doctor, speaking to Dave, and the bartender.

Here are some of my favorite lines:

DURWOOD: *"I already spoiled your figure, I might as well spoil the rest of you."*
DURWOOD: *"I demand your pickle!"*
DURWOOD: *"I don't know what's wrong. I just had to have his pickle!"*

SEPTEMBER 30, 1965

It was on this night that ABC aired Episode #39: "We're in For a Bad Spell" sponsored by Quaker Oats.

Durwood's old army bud, Adam Newlarkin, comes to stay with him while looking for a job. When Durwood asks why he would suddenly just move Adam says he doesn't know why, he just had a sudden urge to move though he was fairly settled in Salem, MA. At the mention of his hometown, Samantha's ears perk up and she asks about Salem saying she only knows of it by reputation. Immediately afterwards, Adam's tie falls in his soup. Durwood thinks it's Samantha trying to take out some hostility on him just because he's from Salem where they persecuted witches. When he pulls her aside to confront her she promises it's not her and when he starts yelling for Endora, Samantha assures him it's not her either as Endora is in the south of France. Just then Adam shrieks and when they reenter the dining room they find Adam covered in lettuce, which he says is from his salad attacking him.

The next morning, Aunt Clara drops in on Samantha after having been told about the strange occurrences surrounding Adam. She has brought her book that lists anyone who has had a spell on them. She confirms that Adam is in the book because of a curse put on one of his ancestors, a judge in old Salem who was also named Adam Newlarkin, who sentenced a witch named Zerelda to be dunked in the pond three times. She placed a curse on the judge and all his descendants that they would be accused of stealing money and have to face the same punishment. When Samantha tells Durwood, he doesn't believe it and says it could never happen as Adam would never be around money. That is until Adam comes home saying he just got hired on at a bank. Samantha says that Aunt Clara has gone back to her home to get a book of antidotes. Aunt Clara soon crashes in the fireplace and after she's been dusted off she finds the particular spell they need:

> Must kiss a spotted dog on the snout
> Then the spell will be partly out.
> Must be dunked in the water, one times three,
> But part of the spell still clings to thee.
> He must ride on a horse through the marketplace like Paul Revere,
> Yelling, "Witches are good! Witches are dear!"

The next morning Samantha suggests they have breakfast on the patio where a Dalmation is waiting for them. She tells Adam that they have a tradition of kissing the dog on the nose before eating breakfast and he refuses to do it until Durwood and Samantha do it. Seeing that his friends really do have this nutty tradition, he reluctantly kisses the dog and immediately hears a chime. Samantha tells him that it's from her musical toaster. She also tells him that Durwood has booked lunch at the Inn on the Terrace where there happens to be a pool.

At lunch, as Durwood and Adam are leaving, they walk by the pool and Durwood tells Adam that he can see something at the bottom of the pool. Adam says he can't see it, but Durwood tells him to look closer and as he bends closer Durwood pushes him in. Gasping for air and treading water, Adam asks Durwood for his help and when he's almost out, Durwood again pushes him in. When Durwood offers to help him out again, Adam refuses and after he's dried off he wants to know why Durwood would push him. Durwood denies it and excuses himself so he can call Samantha. He tells her that he just can't get Adam dunked again but Samantha reminds him it's the only way. When she tells Aunt Clara that Durwood may need help, she realizes she won't be able to get near Adam but maybe Aunt Clara can.

Back at the club, Durwood continues to apologize when suddenly they see an old woman who keeps dropping a big load of packages near the pool. Adam rushes to help her and she pushes him in. Of course, the old woman is Aunt Clara and when Adam resurfaces he hears the chimes again.

After getting dried off again, Adam gets back to work but finds that he's caught a terrible cold and Samantha insists that he come home. He tries to fight it but the bank manager tells him it would be best if he were to leave. They rush home as they must get him in his Paul Revere outfit with little time to spare. When he enters the house he sees Durwood in a Revolutionary War outfit and Aunt Clara dressed as Whistler's Mother. Samantha tells him they are going to a costume party and he is going as Paul Revere complete with horse. Adam thinks they are all nuts and demands why they are putting him through all this and they tell him it's to prevent a curse where he'd be accused of stealing money. He thinks that's ridiculous until he opens his briefcase and finds a ton of money. He insists the briefcase isn't his and wants to know how they knew this was going to happen and Samantha tells him that he is bewitched and has just a short time to become un-bewitched. Surprisingly he believes them as he was always told stories about witches and witchcraft and so he rushes to get into his costume and he rides off to the town square.

Meanwhile, the bank has found that a lot of money has gone missing and as they speak with the detective they hear a ruckus outside and see Adam riding up and down the square on a horse yelling, 'Witches are good, witches are dear!" The bank president suggests they check his place first.

When they arrive at 1164, Durwood, Aunt Clara, and Samantha try to stall the detective until Adam gets back. Just as Adam comes in, the chimes are heard confirming that the spell is lifted and when they open the briefcase the money is gone and Adam's things are back. The phone rings and it's the police station saying they caught another bank worker with $75,000 in his briefcase trying to board a plane to Rio and so Adam is free.

Later on as they are relaxing, Durwood asks if his name is in the *Book of Spellees* and Samantha tells him it is. When he asks what it says about him she tells him that it says he'll marry a witch and live happily ever after. Realizing that it can't be just that, Durwood questions the validity of what she said and she admits that's not what it said, however it's the truth.

I would give this one four stars! I think it's very witchy and fun and, of course, Aunt Clara is in it and she always raises the bar.

I like that we find out that there is a *Book of Spellees*. It makes you wonder who else was in the book and how many pages Durwood's entry was.

I love it when Adam comes into the Stephens' and Durwood and Aunt Clara in costume act like they don't know what's going on.

And, of course, this is one of the few times where the title of the show is used in the dialogue when Samantha says, "You're bewitched and you only have twenty minutes to get un-bewitched!"

The day before Agnes Moorehead received second place in the Golden Laurel award for Supporting Performance — Female for her role in *Hush, Hush…Sweet Charlotte*.

Five days before, the *Tom and Jerry* cartoon made its world broadcast debut on CBS.

And two days before, Fidel Castro announced anyone from Cuba could feel free to immigrate to the United States if they wanted.

OCTOBER 7, 1965

It was on this night that ABC aired Episode #40: "My Grandson, the Warlock" sponsored by Chevrolet.

During the middle of the night Durwood and Samantha are awoken by a call from Larry Tate who happens to be on the last day of a trip to London. Apparently their governess has taken ill and they would like Samantha to pick up their baby, Jonathan, to watch after him until they get home. Of course, Durwood agrees though he should've been shocked since this is the first we've heard of the Tate's having a baby! Across the street, the ever vigilant Mrs. Kravitz is watching and thinks that the Stephens are off to the hospital though Abner reminds her that Samantha is only three months along. A little while later, the Stephens return and Gladys's suspicions are confirmed when she sees Samantha carrying a baby into the house!

The next day as Durwood is leaving for work, Gladys runs across the street to congratulate him on the baby. Just thinking she's a little nutty, Durwood brushes it off and leaves. Right after he's gone another car, a vintage limo, pulls up, and a regal man steps out. She asks who it is and finds that he is Samantha's father, Maurice. She assumes he's there to see the new baby and he's shocked to hear that Samantha has had a baby. She shares in that shock as it only took three months but that surprises Maurice as he says it only took her mother twenty minutes to deliver Samantha! Confused by Maurice, Gladys runs back home.

Samantha is pleased to see her father and when he finds out that the baby isn't going to be taught in the ways of the warlock, he isn't pleased at all. When Samantha excuses herself to go warm a bottle, he goes up stairs and tells the baby Jonathan that they are going to go to the Warlock Club so that he can begin his training. Samantha comes up stairs and is horrified to find that not only is her father gone but the baby as well! Knowing that she's going to have to tell Durwood sooner or later, she calls him up and he is furious and comes home right away. Endora shows up and she and Samantha review where Maurice's favorite hangouts are and fly off to the corners of the Earth.

Meanwhile, in London, as the Tates are exiting their hotel, Louise sees Maurice walking down the street with her baby! Larry tells her she's just seeing things as their baby wouldn't be in London but she insists that it is him. Before she can run after Maurice, Larry grabs her so they can get in the cab. Maurice ends up at the Warlock Club on Wesley Street to show off his "grandson" but finds that the baby has no powers of witchcraft whatsoever! Nanny Witch confirms that he doesn't have any magical aptitude and Maurice becomes disenchanted.

The Tates arrive back in New York earlier than expected and so Durwood offers to pick them up as Jonathan is still nowhere to be found. He stalls them by opening the suitcases on the street, fumbling for his keys and acting like the car has problems. When Louise mentions that she thought she saw Jonathan in London, Durwood is excited and luckily Samantha pops in with a status report. When he tells her about what Louise said she realizes she should've looked in the Warlock Club first. However, when she gets there she is told that Maurice flew off in a fit of fury and frustration and so she pops home just as Durwood is getting there with the Tates. She twitches Louise into not caring about seeing her baby just as they hear Maurice fly in upstairs. She runs upstairs relieved to find Jonathan is safe and sound and she tells her father she'll speak to him later. Larry and Louise are ecstatic to see the baby (after Samantha removes the spell off Louise) and they leave.

When Maurice comes downstairs Samantha assures him that the baby wasn't hers at all and that she's not due for a while. Just then Gladys shows up with a present for the baby but Durwood, Samantha, and Maurice act as though they don't know what she's talking about and when she starts to get frazzled, Maurice leaves her with his huge martini and he walks out through the wall.

I'd give this one and a half stars because it just seems to be a mess of an episode. It really irritates me that Maurice doesn't realize that the baby is not Samantha's. You would've thought he would be able to tell that just by being a warlock not to mention her bigger size?! I also hate that he kidnaps Jonathan and Sam and Durwood simply assume that Maurice took him. What if the kid had actually been kidnapped by a criminal?

I do like the scenes at the Warlock Club. I especially like how they showed the kitty girl walking through the wall. The first time I saw it was really cool. I like that actress much better as the Kitty Girl rather than the girl she plays in "The Magic Cabin" later on this season.

I also thought it was horrible that when Gladys shows up at the end and they tell her that they haven't had a baby yet and she starts freaking out, why do they just stand there instead of saying, "Mrs. Kravitz, we were babysitting!" It seemed really mean.

I loved that line about Maurice having a thing for girls in bikinis. I thought it was funny. I also liked when Samantha popped in under the hood — that was a really cute scene. It should be noted that they were driving just across from 1164 even though they were supposed to be miles away.

Two days before (October 5, 1965), Robert Deverell Asher was born, the second child for William Asher and Elizabeth Montgomery.

Three days before Pope Paul VI made an historic visit to the United States to hold Mass at Yankee Stadium and he made a speech at the United Nations.

OCTOBER 14, 1965

It was on this night that ABC aired a pivotal episode in *Bewitched* history, #41: "The Joker is a Card" by Quaker Oats.

Endora pops in for dinner from Paris with a gift from Maxim's. She is also in a rather pleasant mood as she shockingly refers to Durwood as "Darrin!" However it was only in response to his calling her "mom" which she detests, and she promises to call him by his name if he promises never to call her "mom" again. When she goes to show them what she has brought from Maxim's, they are startled to find a toad. She says it had been a dessert and she has no idea how a frog got in there but Durwood thinks it's her weird sense of humor, especially when he goes to uncork the wine and finds that the cork is several inches long. It occurs to Samantha that these are practical jokes and there is only one person who relishes in that: Uncle Arthur! After looking everywhere for him, she realizes that the only place he could be is under the cover of the entree and when she lifts it up she finds his head there, which apparently he laughed off his body.

After dinner, as they are visiting, Arthur continues with his jokes and goes too far when he causes Endora's dessert to squirt in her eye. Durwood thinks it's hilarious which infuriates Endora causing her to zap his hair into that of a Beatle and she pops out. Arthur tells Durwood that he knows how he can help him combat Endora with witchcraft but

Durwood tells Arthur that he and Samantha have decided there will be no witchcraft in his house.

The next day at work, Arthur keeps pestering Durwood who refuses to give in all though he finds himself in very clumsy situations up to breaking his nose when trying to open a client's EZ-open door. At home, while nursing his broken nose, Arthur pops in offering one last time to teach him a spell that'll give him power over Endora. Durwood realizes he may be on to something and agrees.

In the den, Arthur begins to teach Durwood a spell that is in two parts, an incantation (written in long hand on scroll) and a cowbell and duckcall. Durwood thinks he must be joking but Arthur reminds him that as he's just a mortal, he needs sound effects to help him. He begins to read the spell — "yagazuzi yagazuzi yagazuzi zim" — as though he's at a funeral and Arthur tells him he must put some rhythm to it and he zaps in a xylophone and plinks out a tune. Still leery, Durwood tries it but then tells Arthur he's never seen Endora, Samantha or even Aunt Clara sing a spell but Arthur reminds him that they have the power whereas Durwood needs help. And so they continue their lesson.

Out in the living room, Samantha confronts Endora about Durwood's mishaps and she denies having involvement but tells Samantha that she's willing to forgive Durwood if he apologizes.

With the lesson over, Durwood goes to try it out however Arthur tells him he must not let Endora know what he's doing because she'll nullify it immediately. Armed with his cowbell and duckcall, Durwood goes out into the living room to confront Endora whom he tries to apologize to but when she zaps a chair out from underneath him, he's had enough and begins to shake the cowbell at her and blow the duckcall thinking it will scare her. She's not the least bit frightened but amused when he starts into the incantation telling her she's asked for it but Samantha is quite confused and Durwood is even more confused when she's still there. They hear laughter from the den and Samantha finds Arthur doubled over in laughter as Durwood fell for his joke as everyone knows you can't teach witchcraft to a mortal.

Endora, Durwood, and Samantha meet in the kitchen where Durwood threatens to kill Arthur but Samantha suggests they do something else to cure Arthur of his sick jokes.

Later on they ask to meet with Arthur and Durwood tells him he's decided he wasn't ready before but now he's built up his confidence. Arthur is shocked Durwood wants to make a fool of himself again but when they call for Endora, Durwood tells her he's taking another shot at her and goes again for the cowbell and duckcall when suddenly Endora changes into a parrot! Arthur is shocked beyond belief and actually quite scared as Durwood would be the only one to restore Endora and if he doesn't do it soon, Endora will remain a bird permanently! Durwood admits he doesn't know how to do it, but Arthur insists as Endora is his sister and he loves her. At that Endora returns to her human form and Arthur realizes he was had and he promises never to pull any pranks again.

The next evening Arthur pops in with gifts before he leaves and he gives Durwood a set of golf balls, Samantha an apron, and Endora a pair of opera glasses. When she puts them on and pulls them off they see that she now has two blackened out eyes and Arthur is in stitches saying he couldn't help himself. He promises to taper off and zaps away one of the black marks.

This one definitely gets four stars! It's absolutely hysterical and it is the first time we meet Uncle Arthur, a definite fan favorite. However it is Paul Lynde's second appearance as he appeared last season as Samantha's nervous driving instructor, Harold Harold in "Driving is the Only Way to Fly." It was after that appearance that he was asked to come back in a recurring role.

We find that he is Samantha's favorite uncle and that he taught her how to make her first pony when she was little. However, we never meet any other uncle so maybe he's her favorite on basis he's her only uncle. We also find that he is Endora's brother, one of the few times we are told exactly who of Samantha's relatives are related to who.

Dick York should've won an Emmy for this episode as his performance was hysterical!

The scene at first in the living room where Arthur speaks about hunting a lion in his pajamas was played during the big screen *Bewitched* (2005) movie when Jack is watching episodes. Jack also admits Uncle Arthur was his favorite character.

The next night, the first public burning of draft cards resulted in several arrests.

OCTOBER 21, 1965

It was on this night that ABC aired Episode #42: "Take Two Aspirins and a Half a Pint of Porpoise Milk" presented by Chevrolet.

While visiting with a client who is a botanist, Samantha becomes strangely ill when he shows she and Durwood the rare black Peruvian roses that took him nine years to cultivate. They cut the meeting short and go home where Samantha rests in bed and Durwood worries about her considering she's never been sick before. He goes to call the doctor again and leaves the tray of dinner he brought into her on the dresser. Not wanting to get out of bed as she was dizzy, Samantha twitches it to levitate to her though when it gets closes to the bed it teeters and crashes! Hearing the crash, Durwood comes rushing back in and Samantha suggests they may need to call a witch doctor!

Durwood worries and Samantha suggests that maybe the illness is due to her being pregnant but maybe she's just tired. He asks her to try out her powers again by opening up a window, but when she twitches it only breaks the window. He goes to call his doctor but Samantha reminds him that they can't explain that her witchcraft is out of whack, but he tells her he'll feel better if the doctor gives her the once over.

After the doctor leaves saying that he can't find anything wrong, Durwood asks her to try her powers out again by fixing the window but she only manages to turn it into a door! Just then Gladys Kravitz arrives with a bowl of chicken soup as she had seen the doctor but she's shocked when she sees the door where the window should be. The Stephens suggest that they are building a nursery and that they had to install the door first to get into the room to build it, which makes no sense as it would jut out over the front lawn (when in reality that window would actually face the backyard). Suddenly Gladys sees square green spots appear all over Samantha's face and she drops her soup and leaves screaming. Durwood is shocked too and as Endora isn't available Samantha calls for Aunt Clara.

When she pops in, she diagnoses Samantha with square green spots disease which usually happened to witches in Peru when the locals had come up with a breed of black rose that would cause them to lose their powers for a year and grow the spots unless cured within eight hours. Realizing that Samantha had been in contact with the rose, they press Aunt Clara for the cure and she tells Durwood he'll need to get four eye of newt, two bats wings, half a pint of porpoise milk, and an ostrich feather and she sends him to a local witch supply store so she can watch after Samantha.

Durwood finds himself in an old time goods shop which is filled with all sorts of weird items including the shop keeper who is using an old style telephone, which he says he's trying out to keep up with the times. He has all of the items with the exception of the ostrich feather which he says they've run out of. Knowing he's under a time constraint, Durwood worries where he'll get the feather.

Later on, he finds himself at the police station having attempted to steal an ostrich feather from a lady's hat. He had offered to pay her for it but she wouldn't give it up and so he tried to get it. The officer fines him $30 and lets him go.

When he gets back Aunt Clara decides she'll just conjure up an ostrich feather and when she begins to incant, Samantha realizes the spell isn't right and she's right as a whole ostrich appears!

After getting the feather and dematerializing the ostrich, Aunt Clara cooks up the potion and feeds it to Samantha. She tries to turn off a lamp with her powers but only succeeds in knocking it over and she questions Aunt Clara about the potion. As Aunt Clara reviews the ingredients, she realizes she missed one — four petals from a black Peruvian rose. Durwood realizes he'll have to steal them from the client and so he rushes over there and is almost out of the green house when the alarm goes off and he is sent to jail.

Back at home, Samantha and Aunt Clara worry as time is running out so Aunt Clara offers to go spring him from jail but only succeeds in switching herself with Durwood. They mix the petals in the potion and when Samantha drinks it her spots disappear. Not wanting to be charged with jail escape, Durwood requests that Samantha zap him back to jail.

The next morning Gladys drags Abner over to show him the square green spots on Samantha but when she answers the door they find that her face is clear and that she is feeling better. Realizing that she's left her soup bowl there, Gladys asks if she can retrieve it and she runs upstairs so she can investigate the strange door again. When she opens it and still sees it just leads to the outside she figures the Stephens are just nutty until she hears a knock at the door! Screaming she leaves and Abner suggests Gladys has an over active thyroid which Aunt Clara, who was knocking at the door and has just come downstairs, suggests she can cure.

The next day Durwood finds out that Mr. Norton, the client, is coming over after having agreed to drop the charges but Durwood is confused as to why. Samantha tells him she has everything under control and when Durwood goes to answer the door, Samantha twitches all the flowers in the backyard into black Peruvian roses which surprises Durwood and Mr. Norton. She tells Durwood she can only get sick from the roses one time and Mr. Norton is thrilled that as they took a cutting from his roses he can take one from theirs.

I would rate this at three stars. It's the first time Samantha is ill and we see that witches get ill in a different way from mortals. It's also quite sweet to see Durwood so concerned about Samantha, so much so that he lifts the ban on witchcraft to make sure that everything about Samantha in fine.

Aunt Clara is a treat and I love it when she says she hadn't ever known black Peruvian roses to cause pregnancy. Herbie J Pilato (*Bewitched Forever*) was told that Marion was so afraid of the ostrich that assistant director Marvin Miller was asked by William Asher to stand in between her and the bird and he was afraid because ostriches are known for their bad tempers.

This is also Maudie Prickett's first guest starring role of many on the series.

The next evening ABC aired *The Flintstones* Episode #146: "Samantha" guest starring Elizabeth Montgomery and Dick York voicing their prehistoric counterparts moving into the neighborhood where Samantha goes camping with the Flintstones and Rubbles.

As a *Flintstones* episode I think it works really well. It's very entertaining and really cool to see the two worlds combined. But, if this were strictly a *Bewitched* episode it would've been one of the worst! The reason I say that is I don't think we've EVER seen Samantha be so zap happy ever! She was twitching the toys on the shelf, twitching the kids clean — the one that bugged me the most was her zapping herself into the newly zapped up car. How LAZY! I also thought it strange, and very *Bewitched* movie like, that Wilma and Betty talk about how Samantha reminds them of the lady on that "nice witch sitcom."

I thought it a very sexist episode though. I mean, towards the end it starts to get to the point where it's made out that the women can and will do as much as the men, but then when Barney and Fred start mentioning how they want to do all sorts of things in the early morning, the girls say how they want to get back to home to gossip and cards!

I really like this cartoon version of Samantha better than the cartoon opening of OUR show. I also really like that they animated her heart necklace.

It should be noted that right after this episode aired the next one was where the Great Gazoo, the little green alien guy with special powers, aired and for the rest of the season he would pop up and "help" Fred out.

Oh, another thing about this one, why would Durwood schedule a boating trip right upon moving into a new neighborhood?!

Anyway, it's a very enjoyable one and I REALLY wish they would've included it as an extra on the Season Two *Bewitched* DVDs.

OCTOBER 28, 1965

It was on this night that ABC aired *Bewitched*'s second Halloween entry, Episode #43: "Trick or Treat" sponsored by Quaker Oats.

During the middle of the night before Halloween, Endora pops in discreetly on Samantha and wakes her up to encourage her to pack her bags so they can fly off in a couple hours. Samantha is confused and Endora reminds her that the black day of Halloween is upon them and she disappears.

The next morning Endora pops back in and finds that Samantha isn't going to leave with her to go to the sacred volcano, which she realized is where her mother wanted her to go to. She tells her mother that in fact she is going to be having a dinner party with the Tates and a client and Endora is incensed and appalled that Samantha is going to celebrate Halloween, especially with little kids running around with ugly witch faces, but Samantha tells her that's part of life when married to a mortal and that Durwood understands her problem. Just then the doorbell rings and Samantha finds that she's received a delivery which she believes is from Durwood showing how much he would like to make it up to her. However when she opens the box she finds some ugly witch pictures and broomsticks. Endora is pleased that her point was proven and Samantha calls Durwood to see what he was thinking. Confused, Durwood tells her he doesn't know anything about the witches hats. Larry, who is overhearing their conversation, admits he sent them as Mr. Rogers, the client who makes party decorations, had made them. Durwood tells Larry that they wouldn't be caught dead with witches hats for decorations as they find them obscene and he apologizes to Samantha. Wanting to know what Durwood said, Samantha tells Endora that they are going to discuss it later and Endora disappears.

At McMann and Tate, Durwood goes to make another phone call and finds that the receiver won't lift off the cradle and when he tries to pound it off only succeeds in dropping the phone just as Endora pops in admitting that she stopped all his calls for a few minutes. He tells her that he can't visit and tries to leave for a meeting but she slams his briefcase closed on him and plants his feet to the floor. She tells him that she has come to ask that he let Samantha go to the sacred volcano with her as it is a place they go to on Halloween. Durwood won't have any of it as it sounds too weird and witchy and she accuses him of being bigoted. She asks once more but he still refuses so she surprisingly relents and tells him he can have it his way and as she leaves she wishes him a good evening at his dinner party.

Later on that evening, Endora pops outside of 1164 as a group of trick-or-treaters is leaving and changes herself into a little gypsy girl. Durwood answers when she knocks and when she refuses the treats he's giving out she tells him she's going to have to trick him and she points her finger at him and mumbles something like 'Picket Ficket' and leaves. When Samantha sees him she's surprised to see that Durwood has a rather ragged beard growing not to mention thicker eyebrows and she asks what happened. He mentions the little gypsy girl and she realizes it has to be her mother and when she goes outside she finds the girl and tells her that she must come in. Endora tries to refuse but Samantha threatens to spank her. When they get inside Endora admits that pretty soon Durwood is going to become a "werewoof!"

The transformation begins happening pretty rapidly with fur growing on his hands and just as the company is arriving. Samantha puts Endora in the den to concentrate on remembering the spell and she answers the door as Durwood goes to shave. As the Tates and Rogers sit down, Samantha goes to check on Endora who can't remember the spell and Durwood comes out of the bathroom clean shaven though when he and Samantha return to the living room she notices that he's grown claws! He hurries back to the bathroom to shave again and trim his claws. When he's finished, he finds that it's futile as all the fur and his claws have grown back along with fangs! Larry gets quite suspicious of Sam and Durwood's behavior and he demands that Samantha get Durwood back in the living room. When she goes to retrieve him she finds him trying to climb out the den window and finds that her mother is nowhere to be seen.

Larry and Mr. Rogers go out on the patio to smoke and are startled by a noise which turns out to be the werewolf Durwood knocking things over. Durwood tries to smile it off but the men return to the living room to show the girls what they have found. By this time, Durwood is fully wolfman and Mr. Rogers couldn't be more pleased as he thinks it's such a great costume. Durwood says that the neighborhood kids love him to dress up like that but then he begins to growl and he attacks the furniture. Before he can do anymore damage, Samantha takes him upstairs where he insists she lock him in the closet so he won't harm anyone. She calls for her mother who pops in and Samantha tells her that she thinks it's unbelievable that Endora would act just like the stereotype witch image that she is so disdainful of, and especially towards Durwood who was willing to give them a chance. Seeing how hurt Samantha is, Endora relents and apologizes and changes Durwood back. When they realize that Endora never forgot the spell, Durwood gets angry and asks how she could've done that and she shows him by turning him back into a werewolf.

After tempers have subsided, Endora changes Durwood back and they return downstairs. As the Tates and Rogers leave, Mr. Rogers comments on how great a costume it is that Endora is wearing, which of course she is not wearing a costume, and so she zaps him with a tail as he leaves.

I would give this one four stars. It's very Halloween throughout and the opening scene is rather spooky. I also really like Endora's pop out when she drops the witch face.

In the last season Samantha mentioned that her mother flies to the south of France every year which must mean the sacred volcano is in France.

This is also Maureen McCormick's second and last appearance on *Bewitched* before she becomes everyone's favorite oldest sister "Marcia! Marcia! Marcia!" on *the Brady Bunch*.

This is also one of the rare times where a magic trick wasn't accompanied by a sound effect when Endora changes back from being a tree.

NOVEMBER 4, 1965

It was on this night that ABC aired Episode #44: "The Very Informal Dress" sponsored by Chevrolet.

Durwood is surprised to find Aunt Clara at his house when he returns from work early carrying a case of Mother Jenny's Jam which is produced by his client, Mr. Barlowe. As Mr. Barlowe is going to be leaving the next day, Larry has decided to have a little cocktail party to celebrate their getting the account. Samantha frets about not having anything to wear on such short notice, but Aunt Clara who has been listening in on their conversation, decides she can help and she zaps up a nice green outfit for Samantha. Durwood doesn't think she should wear anything zapped up by magic, but Samantha gives him a knowing look, that he should know things won't be happy if he hurts Aunt Clara's feelings, so he tells her that he'll look dumpy if he doesn't have a nice outfit. Taking that as a challenge, Aunt Clara zaps up a suit for him. Seeing as Aunt Clara is already there for a visit, Samantha asks if her aunt can accompany them to the party and Durwood concedes.

When they arrive to the office, they find that the only space to park close is occupied by a fire hydrant. Aunt Clara insists that she can help and she moves it to the next car in front of them. Just then a police officer comes up wondering why Durwood would park next to a hydrant but is confused when the hydrant isn't there and he leaves bewildered. Durwood wonders what will happen when the car that is now neighbors with the hydrant is discovered but Samantha assures him nothing will happen as it belongs to the police commissioner.

At the party they find that the refreshments are Mother Jenny's vegetable punch, which tastes terrible, and Aunt Clara takes it upon herself to make sure Mr. Barlowe knows so. Embarrassed, Durwood takes Aunt Clara away from Mr. Barlowe who starts up a conversation about himself with Samantha who gets totally bored until she discovers that one of her sleeves has disappeared! She tries to get Aunt Clara's attention while Mr. Barlowe isn't paying attention to anyone but himself but then her other sleeve disappears so before anymore of her dress disappears she zaps herself into another dress, confusing Mr. Barlowe who sees that her dress is now red instead of green. Samantha finally gets away from him and tells Durwood and Aunt Clara what has been happening and suggests Durwood better move the car in case the hydrant gets homesick. Mr. Barlowe asks if maybe Durwood can drive him to his hotel as he isn't feeling well and Aunt Clara requests to go home too as the vegetable punch as made her feel quite "healthy." When they get out to the car, they discover the hydrant has returned to its rightful place and suddenly Durwood's pants disappear! Mr. Barlowe is confused yet again and the police officer shows up wondering why Durwood is running around with his pants off. Aunt Clara tries to correct it but only manages to zap off all but his underclothes and so mayhem ensues as she tries to correct herself but only manages to switch clothes amongst the officer, Mr. Barlowe, and Durwood. The harried officer books Durwood into jail leaving Mr. Barlowe to hail a cab and Aunt Clara to zap the car into driving her home.

When Samantha realizes that Durwood hasn't come back for her, she gets worried and flies home where Aunt Clara tells her of Durwood's plight and how she has tried to help him in jail by zapping some clothes to him. Of course, Durwood's night is just terrible as he has to share a cell with a drunk who thinks Durwood can do magic just by snapping his fingers. When he tries to snap his own fingers Samantha pops in with a change of clothes for Durwood and when Montague, the drunk, starts going on about how he has zapped her up she puts him to sleep again.

The next morning Durwood faces the judge and is released when the officer's story and Montague's story make no sense especially since Durwood was thrown into jail in his underwear but came out fully clothed.

Durwood worries that he's been fired until Larry tells him that after he heard Mr. Barlowe's wild tale of the previous evening he decided he didn't want such a nut case's campaign.

I'd give this one three stars. It's a fun story and quite risqué for the time, what with everyone's clothes disappearing. But Mr. Barlowe is annoying. And since when does Samantha have to worry about what she is going to wear?

Aunt Clara is fun in this and we get to see that her magic really has gone amuck and it's fun to see her driving the car from the backseat.

Dick Wilson makes his second appearance as a drunk and gets named Montague.

Three days later, one of the most recognizable advertising characters made his doughy debut — the Pillsbury Dough Boy!

The next day the NBC daytime soap *Days of Our Lives* made its debut.

NOVEMBER 11, 1965

It was on this night that ABC aired Episode #45: "…And Then I Wrote" sponsored by Quaker Oats.

Dr. Passamore, chief psychiatrist of the Meadowbrook Rest Home, pays a visit to Durwood to ask if he can come up with some publicity for a celebration pageant marking the centennial of the end of the Civil War. However Durwood isn't home but Samantha feels that Durwood wouldn't mind being a part of it. She couldn't be more mistaken as Durwood is swamped at the office with work not to mention his limited knowledge of the Civil War. When the phone rings it's Dr. Passamore thanking Durwood for volunteering but then it's Durwood's turn to volunteer Samantha for a difficult task of writing a play about the Civil War!

Samantha is not pleased as she doesn't even know where to begin and when Endora shows up, she offers to be her secretary and begins to type for her until they discover she's not very accurate. The day wears on and Samantha finally churns out a script for the pageant which she gives Durwood to critique. He tells her that the characters are one dimensional and that she should think of them as real people.

The next day she tries again to write but just can't seem to come up with anything. Endora is shocked that Samantha is not finished writing but when Samantha tells her that she can't seem to make up any good characters, Endora suggests she visualize them just as Durwood had suggested and she leaves. Realizing that she may be on to something,

Samantha materializes her version of a Confederate officer named Captain Cochrane and his horse. Of course, Mrs. Kravitz is snooping at the time and is shocked to see the officer and his horse and she runs off. Samantha finds that Captain Cochrane is really pushy as to how she should write him so she returns him to her mind. Later on she materializes an American Indian which she felt could be sort of like a chorus, having no allegiance to either side of the war. She brings the Captain back to see how he measures up to the Indian and the Captain requests that she create a love interest for him. She agrees and zaps up a Northern girl named Violet which will cause part of the conflict in the story. Just then the doorbell rings and so Samantha zaps the characters away and finds Mrs. Kravitz there wanting to borrow a cup of sugar. When she goes to the kitchen to get it, the Indian and the girl reappear and tell Mrs. Kravitz that they are just figments of Samantha's imagination. Freaked out because she had seen them appear, Mrs. Kravitz bolts for her house just as Durwood shows up. The characters find Samantha in the kitchen and when she wonders why they are there, they say they don't know as she's the one that thought them up. Knowing that they can't just show up, Samantha asks how to get rid of them and the Indian suggests she make her mind blank and it works! They disappear. When she returns to the living room with Mrs. Kravitz's sugar she finds Durwood and when he goes to kiss her they all reappear. Samantha explains what's going on and when he kisses her they disappear. She realizes that when she kisses Durwood that's all she can think of.

The characters keep popping in every so often through the night and into the next day so Durwood suggests that Samantha quit the project but she feels that soon she'll have the play finished and then the characters will go away. They go to see Dr. Passamore to show him the posters for the play and find that Mrs. Kravitz has been there telling him her problems of seeing the characters. He tells her that she must tell herself that it's all in her mind and she leaves. As Durwood shows the doctor his posters Samantha begins thinking about the play and the characters appear much to the doctor's shock. Samantha and Durwood act as though nothing is happening and Dr. Passamore thanks them for their visit and they leave with the characters following behind.

At home Samantha chides the characters who admit that they have been trying to leave but they can't leave unless they have a plot to settle into. They tell her what should happen in the play and Samantha begins typing it out and when they get to the end of the story they disappear for good.

The play is a success, so much so that Samantha is asked to direct a vaudeville show for the Ladies League causing a vaudeville act to pop in!

I would give this one two and a half stars. I think Alice Pearce is hysterical, especially when she's trying to leave and can't get past Durwood. Also when Dr. Passamore asks her if she believes that the characters are all in her mind and she says, "no" followed quickly by "yes."

I don't like that a Caucasian played the Indian when Samantha is supposed to be a non-stereotypical thinking person. I did like Captain Cochrane though and I think it is HIGH-sterical when the vaudeville singers pop in at the end!

Endora wasn't used much at all which seems to be something that would happen in later seasons. But I do like her quote, "Write mortal, think witch."

Two days before, the Eastern Seaboard experienced a total blackout lasting in some parts up to thirteen and a half hours. It was chalked up to human error but *Bewitched* fans would find out the "real" reason next season in "The Short Happy Circuit of Aunt Clara."

NOVEMBER 18, 1965

It was on this night that ABC aired Episode #46: "Junior Executive" sponsored by Chevrolet.

Samantha finds Durwood sleeping at his drawing table after a long night of trying to come up with a campaign to sell a model boat. Not wanting to wake him up, Samantha is startled when her mother pops in and makes a snide remark about him playing with toys like a little boy. That gets Samantha to thinking about how she has never seen pictures of Durwood as a boy and she wonders what he looked like. Endora suggests they find out and she changes him into a ten-year old boy! All though she's not happy about this change, it does bring a smile to Samantha's face to see him sleeping peacefully but that's shattered when Endora opens the shutters waking Durwood who doesn't realize he's now a young boy until he goes to shave and finds he can't see himself too well in the bathroom mirror.

Later on, after Samantha has pleaded with her mother to change him back, Durwood is furious and starts to take his frustration out on Samantha until he realizes that it's not her fault. He apologizes telling her he's on edge about not being able to come up with a good campaign for the model ships.

After he leaves for work Endora pops in surprised at Durwood's lack of humor and when Samantha mentions how he had referred to her as "an old witch with a sick sense of humor" she asks where he is and zaps a long distance youth spell on him turning him back into boy just as Larry enters with Mr. Harding, the producer of the toy ship. Larry is shocked and Mr. Harding thinks they are up to something especially when the young boy mentions how his mother-in-law has gone too far and he storms out. When his secretary won't call his wife for him he tries to find a dime to use the pay phone and calls home to tell Samantha what has happened. She remembers how Endora cast the spell and changes him back and tells him she'll explain when he gets home.

At home Samantha explains that Endora just likes to mess around and when she asks what he told Larry, Durwood says he couldn't find Larry or Mr. Harding. Just then Larry shows up and tells Durwood that having the kid show up was a stroke of genius as Mr. Harding loved him and liked the idea of having a kid give his opinion of the model ship. He tells him that they have another meeting with Harding the next morning and that the boy should be there. Durwood tries to explain that the boy isn't around anymore and Larry explains to him that if the boy doesn't show up, Durwood won't be seen around McMann and Tate anymore.

The next day Samantha accompanies Durwood to the office and changes him back to a little boy and drops him off around the corner from the office. As young Durwood walks down the street with the model he is confronted by two young boys who taunt him and start playing 'keep away' with the model. When Durwood exclaims his fear of them breaking it, the boys give up and tell him that he can have his crummy old model back. When he asks why they think it's crummy one of them mentions that he has one at home but doesn't like it and they run off to the park. Durwood runs after them and Samantha, who had decided to go shopping, sees them and goes after them.

In the park, Durwood pesters the boys who finally admit that the reason they don't like the toys is that they don't do anything which means that there was nothing wrong with the campaigns but the products themselves. He asks Samantha to change him back and he goes to the office. But when he tries to share his ideas with Larry and Mr. Harding they wonder where the boy is and won't continue without him. So Durwood goes back to his office where Samantha is waiting and has her change him back into the boy. When he returns to Larry's office, they want to know where Durwood is and so young Durwood goes back to get his old self. As he is talking to Samantha, Larry walks in wondering where Durwood is.

Samantha tells him that Durwood stepped out so he goes to find him and Samantha changes Durwood back into his adult self just as Larry walks back in with another question. He's startled to find Durwood in there and wonders where the boy is and is told he stepped out but Durwood promises that he'll be in with the boy in a moment. Wondering how that is going to happen, Samantha questions Durwood and he says that they will figuratively kill the boy and she changes him back.

In Larry's office Mr. Harding wonders what is taking so long when he is startled after he is shot by a stream of water and finds that it's coming from the boy who seems to have suddenly gone off his rocker. When they try to stop him, he runs into Durwood's office and Durwood immediately comes out and explains that the boy is highly strung because he's so smart and that Mr. Harding shouldn't place his faith in a young boy, which Harding agrees with.

After the meeting, Durwood and Samantha return to the park as Durwood feels that he should repay the boys who had helped him. Samantha tells them that she'd like to repay them for being so nice and asks them what they would like and zaps up big kites to grant their wish.

I would give this one maybe a two and a half to three stars. One thing that has always bugged me about this episode is the sound effect they use when Durwood is being changed…it's too loud and it just sounds way off from the other sound effects.

It was good having Billy Mumy play young Durwood. It seemed like he took the role quite seriously.

I did find it VERY interesting that Endora said, "You'd better start praying for a girl, Samantha." It's just a very little clue into the fact that Endora had faith in a being higher than herself.

I always laugh at when Young Durwood is squirting Larry and the client in the face and then when one of them gives him back the gun, he says, "Thank you!" It's so funny because there he is being so disrespectful shooting them yet he has enough manners to say, "Thank you!" Another laugh is when he is on the phone with Sam and she says, "Your voice sounds funny." And he responds, "That's because it hasn't changed yet." The look he gives that snoopy lady is priceless!

This is the third time that Endora gets Darrin's name right. The first was in "A is for Aardvark" and the second was just a few episodes ago in "The Joker is a Card."

The park scenes were shot at the Warner Brothers Ranch and the fountain is the same one used in the opening titles of *Friends*.

NOVEMBER 25, 1965

It was on this night that ABC aired Episode #47: "Aunt Clara's Old Flame" sponsored by Quaker Oats.

Endora pops in one morning to tell Samantha that Aunt Clara seems to be getting worse in her old age as she can't even maintain altitude while flying and that while in England she waltzed into a convention with a doorknob that she had stolen from Buckingham Palace! Just then Aunt Clara arrives, after having bumped into the outside wall a couple times, to say that she wants to hide out as her old beau Hedley Partridge is in town. Samantha doesn't understand why she wants to hide out but before she explains herself, Clara suggests that Endora go haunt a house and with that Endora pops out. To allay Samantha's confusion, Aunt Clara explains that she is embarrassed to see Hedley as her powers aren't what they used to be.

Meanwhile, across the street, Gladys had seen Aunt Clara bumping into the wall several times until the last time she had seen her pass right through the wall but can't get Abner to believe her.

A little later Endora pops back in with the news that she has invited Hedley over for a dinner to get him reacquainted with Clara not to mention it will be good to have someone to watch over her with her spells not working anymore. Before Samantha can protest, Endora pops out. Not wanting Hedley's visit to be a surprise, Samantha tells Clara who refuses at first but Samantha assures her that hiding out can't last forever and that if she doesn't want Hedley to know about her waning powers, he won't have to know.

That evening, Hedley arrives and finds that no one is at home until there is a knock at the door and when he answers he assumes it's the lady of the house, however it's Gladys Kravitz. He introduces himself and mentions how he's a warlock and that he doesn't care about her mixed marriage. She is quite confused and gets frightened when he shows her how he can make flowers dance in a vase. Just as she leaves screaming, Durwood comes home and sets Hedley straight and tells him that Samantha and Clara had gone out shopping but should be back soon.

Across the street Gladys looks up the meaning of "warlock" and tries to unfruitfully convince Abner of the presence of magic at the neighbor's house.

When Clara and Samantha return, Hedley seems to be still smitten by Clara and they instantly rekindle their old friendship. Samantha asks Durwood to keep an eye on them, especially to holler if Clara needs help. When Hedley zaps up a cigar he asks Clara to light it as it was something that she used to do for him. Clara gets nervous however Durwood calls for Samantha who twitches the table lighter up, much to Aunt Clara's surprise as she thinks she's doing it. When she asks him if he'd like an ashtray she points but Samantha twitches it to fly over. Seeing that things seem to be going well Durwood and Samantha leave the two senior lovers alone. While reminiscing, Hedley recalls when they used to turn themselves into doves in Barkley Square and Clara suggests they do it again. Hedley declines saying it's been a long time ago but Clara insists and casts a spell resulting in Hedley being turned into a baby elephant and herself missing her entire bottom half! Unbeknownst to all, Gladys is snooping about outside and freaks out when she sees the chaos in the living room. Durwood enters the living room and cries out for Samantha who comes running in. They tell Clara that Samantha had done all the magic earlier and as they try to figure out what to do they are startled by Mr. and Mrs. Kravitz who have come in saying that they knocked. Abner is surprised to see the elephant which Durwood explains is a model for his new campaign and Samantha takes it into the kitchen and reverses Aunt Clara's spell. Hedley says that he wants to talk to Clara, who tries to run away from him through the wall but she only bumps into it. He explains to her that she mustn't be embarrassed as his powers have failed too. Gladys asks how he could've made the flowers dance and he shows her the strings that he had attached to them, proving to Abner that there is an explanation for everything and they leave.

Samantha is pleased to see that everything has worked out with Clara and Hedley and it turns out Endora is too as she pops in to play violin music for the couple to dance by.

The next day Clara drops by again and mentions how she was so glad to see Hedley and that he had left to go out of town on business trip as he's in the magic supply business but he had left her with a great big doorknob, which she thinks is better than an engagement ring.

I would give this one two and a half stars. It's cute but too cute. I like that Abner finally witnesses a strange going on with the elephant and I also like that we get to learn a little more about Aunt Clara's past.

I love the conversation about Sorrinda Ethrington who nearly knocks herself silly walking into walls and we learn that there is an old witches home. Can you imagine what would be going on there?

I thought the effect of Aunt Clara's bottom half being missing was cool up until the point that Marion put her hands on the couch to steady herself and they disappeared too. And I didn't like that Samantha could reverse the spell that Aunt Clara had done especially since in "Alias Darrin Stephens" she mentions that she can't undo another witch's spell.

DECEMBER 2, 1965

It was on this night that ABC aired Episode #48: "A Strange Little Visitor" sponsored by Chevrolet.

While cleaning house Gladys notices a normal looking couple with a young boy walking up to the Stephens house and remarks how strange it is that normal people should be visiting the Stephens. The couple happens to be the Brockens, friends of Samantha's and their son Merle, who happens to be a young warlock in training. They have come to ask Samantha to take care of Merle while they go to a conclave. Samantha is hesitant to accept because Durwood has had such bad experiences with Samantha's relatives and friends. Mr. Brocken suggests that Merle can pass off as a mortal and so Samantha accepts and they leave through the roof. Just as Samantha goes to show Merle his room upstairs there is a knock at the door belonging to Mrs. Kravitz who has come over for a snoop, er, scoop of sugar. Samantha introduces Merle and Mrs. Kravitz asks to meet his parents and is shocked when she is told they already left, and through the roof at that, and so she leaves.

Across town at a bar, Durwood and Larry are discussing Louise's birthday the next evening. Larry shows Durwood a beautiful expensive necklace he bought for her and asks him to keep it at his house as Louise likes to snoop, and Durwood accepts. When he leaves he is unaware that a fellow who had sat next to him at the bar has followed him home.

Durwood is surprised by his house guest, whom Samantha says is a friend's child, but as Merle seems to be normal, he's OK with him staying. However, Merle proves his normalcy outside by changing a stick into a bird and blowing water out of his ears as he's bored considering he didn't bring any toys. Mrs. Kravitz sees him and tries to get him to confess to the weirdness at the Stephens but gets nowhere with him. Still bored, Merle goes back in and Durwood suggests he teach him how to play baseball. When they go outside Durwood is blown away by how fast and hard Merle pitches and bats even though he says he's never played the game before. Seeing that he's no match for Merle, Durwood goes back into the house. Merle decides to play some more and hits the ball through the Kravitz's window but fixes it before Gladys can show Abner.

At dinner later on, Merle refuses to eat the meatloaf that Samantha has made and when Durwood tells him he'll eat it or go without, Merle retreats to his room to study his book of *Elementary Spells and Incantations*. He tries out his magic by changing a hairbrush into a fire truck just as Durwood comes in to talk to him. He's suspicious of the fire truck thinking that Merle stole it from another kid's yard and when he tries to take it away Merle shocks him. When Samantha comes in wondering what's going on Merle explains what he has done. Durwood is shocked to find that Merle is a warlock and Samantha chides Merle for revealing himself and demands that he go downstairs to finish his meatloaf, which he immediately changes into a strawberry cake. However, before he can take a bite, Samantha twitches it back and reminds him that she is an older more experienced witch and makes him promise not to do anymore witchcraft.

During the night, the man from the bar tries to break in and is quite noisy about the whole affair. Durwood hears the commotion downstairs and goes to investigate and finds himself face to face with a gun and eventually gets tied up. The man demands to know where the necklace is and is scared when Merle shows up wondering what's going on. Durwood thinks he's home free as he can just have Merle zap the burglar but Merle reminds him that he had promised he wouldn't do any more magic and so he gets tied up too. The burglar asks Durwood just to give up the necklace as he needs it to get money for his kid's birthday. Durwood suggests he just take Merle's fire truck and the burglar agrees, but Merle protests and zaps the fire truck into turning on, startling the burglar who tries to shoot it but Merle makes water come out of the gun instead of bullets. He then makes the fire truck shoot water at the burglar and Samantha hears the commotion and comes downstairs and calls the police. They arrive and take the confused burglar away.

The next day Merle's parents come to get Merle and confuse Mrs. Kravitz even more when they disappear right before her turned back.

I'd give this one three stars. It's nice to see another witch family that isn't related to Samantha and it was fun seeing Merle learning how to use his powers.

His father was played by James Doohan who is best known to TV audiences as Scotty from *Star Trek*. How appropriate then that he should "beam up" when disappearing at first.

It's funny when Merle is sitting there stuffing his face with the chocolate cake and Samantha says, "It's too bad you don't like chocolate cake, Merle."

The scene with the burglar was weird as there was hardly any dialogue and it was corny that the little fire engine would scare him so much.

DECEMBER 9, 1965

It was on this night that ABC aired Episode #49: "My Boss, the Teddy Bear" sponsored by Quaker Oats.

Durwood is worried about the Harper Honey account as he can't seem to come up with a great campaign when Endora pops in to invite him and Samantha to her cousin Miranda's wedding. She tells Durwood he should be able to take a couple days off but he refuses as he has so much work to do. She suggests turning Larry into an inanimate object for a couple days but that puts Durwood over the edge and he demands that she leave Larry alone.

However, a little while later Endora pops in on Larry who is at a toy store shopping for a new teddy bear for Jonathan as his crumbled under all the affection. The bear is a specific one as it nods its head when you touch its paw and the store is all out. Larry is pleased to see Endora and she tells him of the wedding and asks him to allow Durwood to go to it and Larry agrees. When he leaves Endora zaps up the bear he wanted and pops into the office. She asks to leave the bear with Secretary Betty with a note to Mrs. Tate saying it was compliments of Endora and she pops out.

Later on when Durwood shows up to work, he notices the bear and jokes with Betty about her having to bring toys to work. She tells him that a red-headed woman named Endora had dropped him off for Mrs. Tate. Recalling his conversation with Endora earlier he is filled with horror and asks to keep the bear with him thinking it's Larry. He tries to assure "Larry" that everything will be all right and when he asks if "Larry" understands and the bear nods its head, he takes that as confirmation that his boss and friend is now a stuffed bear! Just then Mr. Harper arrives with a model for his campaign and he thinks Durwood has flipped his lid talking to the bear and insisting that he hold it close. The model Diane asks to hold the bear and she goes off to change into another outfit for the campaign photo shoot while Durwood discusses his attachment to the bear which he is horrified to find is in the dressing room with Diane and he demands she give him back. When she drops him on the floor Durwood nearly passes out thinking "Larry" will have a concussion but before he can do anything Mr. Harper demands Durwood forget about the bear before he has to forget about the campaign.

Awhile later Louise shows up to the office to tell Larry about finding a replacement teddy bear and sees the Larry Bear on Betty's desk. She is pleased that Endora would be so thoughtful and as she was going to have the one she found sent to their house she decides to take back Endora's bear.

When Durwood finds out Larry has gone back to Tippet's Toy Store he calls Samantha and asks her to meet him down there so she can help him find "Larry." They are disheartened to see that there is a whole wall of the same looking bear and even more disappointed when the toy store clerk tells them that all the bears nod. Realizing that they will need to investigate further, they purchase all twenty-four teddy bears and take them home. Soon Samantha finds one without "Made in Japan" on its rear and they deduce that it must be Larry. Just then Endora pops in and Durwood chews her out and demands she change Larry back. When she has had enough of his demands and insults she causes the teddy bear to explode and she pops out. Samantha and Durwood are horrified thinking that Larry has just been murdered and can't believe it when Louise walks in saying that she had knocked twice. She also mentions how she recognizes the bear and Durwood takes that to mean she can see Larry in it and so as he goes to tell her what happened who should walk in but Larry! Durwood and Samantha are relieved and Durwood apologizes to Endora the next day. Realizing that they have twenty-three teddy bears on their hands Durwood realizes that he can use them for the honey campaign and base it off the children's poem about the teddy bears picnic.

I would give this one four stars. I think it's fun throughout and it's a treat to see Endora interact with Larry and especially that Larry agreed to let Durwood go to the wedding. Dick York was hysterical in his interactions with the teddy bear!

It was also on this night that Christmas television history was made by the debut of *A Charlie Brown Christmas* which aired on CBS earlier that evening. It has been on every year since then and is the most successful of all the CBS Christmas specials.

DECEMBER 16, 1965

It was on this night that ABC aired Episode #50: "Speak the Truth" sponsored by Chevrolet.

One morning Durwood finds that Samantha looks so beautiful sleeping that he lets her sleep and makes his own breakfast and, get this, does the dishes! When he goes to leave, Samantha comes down stairs wiping the sleep out of her eyes and she apologizes for not getting up. He tells her he thinks she looked beautiful even though her hair is a mess and she's very sleepy looking. And with a kiss he leaves. Samantha goes to look at herself in the mirror wondering what in the world would possess

Durwood to say such nice things about her looks when Endora pops in the mirror telling her that she must be gullible to believe Durwood and that mortals lie every chance they get. Samantha disagrees saying that Durwood would never lie to her but Endora insists she's right and pops out to end up in Durwood's office as he hasn't arrived there yet. She calls upon Agatha, a witch shopkeeper, to appear and she does with a gift box. Apparently Endora had time to meet with Agatha to buy a little hand carved statue that, when around mortals, forces them to tell the truth, however it has no effect on witches. Endora is pleased and has Agatha write a note signing it from Durwood's world traveling uncle Herbert and they pop out just as Durwood comes in. He is intrigued by the gift and asks Betty to come in so he can find out about where it came from. The statue immediately starts working as Durwood comments on how great Ms. Thatcher looks in her dress, especially as it's so tight. At first she's offended until she comes close to the statue and then she admits that she wore it specifically for Durwood so he would notice that she's more than just a secretary. After she leaves Larry calls Durwood to see if he has started work on the Hotchkiss campaign but Durwood truthfully answers he hasn't been doing any work on it as he just isn't interested in it. Soon Larry shows up at the door wondering what is going on and finds that Durwood is very open about his feelings about how Larry runs things. When Larry gets close to the statue he admits that he wouldn't be able to get along without Durwood but he must act like he doesn't care so that the other admen won't think he's showing favoritism. As he leaves he reminds Durwood that he needs to work to keep his job.

Later on at home, Durwood finds Endora there and Samantha with rollers in her hair as she gets ready for a dinner party that night with the Hotchkisses and the Tates. He tells Samantha that it's very unattractive for her to be seen in curlers and she is a bit offended but no more so than when he tells her about how Betty looked. When he leaves the influence of the statue, he realizes what he said and tries to apologize. Luckily she accepts and before Endora leaves she mentions she'll be lonely for dinner so Samantha invites her to stay.

That night Endora zaps the statue around the room causing the Tates and the Hotchkisses to get into a fight with everyone else as the truth, the cold hard truth, comes out and years of resentment that Mrs. Hotchkiss has been carrying come to the top. Everyone gets so upset that the Stephens' guests leave.

The next morning Endora pops in and admits that the debacle of the previous evening was caused by the Truth God and Samantha is furious with her. She can't get into it with her as Larry has come knocking, furious with Durwood until he gets around the statue and admits that the Hotchkisses actually went back to their hotel and hashed through some old sore spots getting to a pleasant conclusion and that he actually really needs Durwood at the office.

I would give this four stars. It's brilliant that the inability of mortals to be perfectly honest is explored and I love that it's a little statue that causes it. This is also the first time that animations are obviously used (the real first time was in "Little Pitchers Have Big Fears" when the ball was speeding to home plate) and they are cute though it's confirmation as to how well just having the film cuts and music queues worked.

This is the first time that character actor Charles Lane makes an appearance. He is so good at it that he was invited back many times. Elizabeth Frazer, who played his wife, was in *Who's Been Sleeping in My Bed?* with Liz Montgomery. And Diana Chesney, who plays Agatha, would return in the Eighth Season as Aunt Enchantra in "Adam, Warlock or Washout."

Durwood's line about how tight Betty's dress was is hysterical! Especially when he tells Samantha about it later on and the look on his face when he realizes what he just said is priceless! It's also funny when he says, "She has nothing on you. I mean take her out of that dress and..." The look on Liz's face is priceless as well.

This is the first time that we see any of the characters floating when we see Endora outside floating and then she floats down to Earth. It was a really cool effect and something we'd see many times later on in the series.

The biggest piece of trivia about this episode is the fact that this episode would be remade almost word for word as the last episode of the series. And in turn, both would be remade on the big screen in Jim Carrey's *Liar, Liar* (1997) where a man is forced to tell the truth all the time. It's even a more eerie comparison when you realize that Jim Carrey was the man of choice to play Durwood in a big screen version of *Bewitched*, which he was asked to do but turned down when he heard that it wouldn't be a direct remake. Jim's secretary in the movie is named Samantha and the judge is Judge Stevens.

DECEMBER 23, 1965

It was on this night that ABC aired what really should've been the second Christmas episode of the series, Episode #51: "A Vision of Sugar Plums" sponsored by Quaker Oats, but really they didn't.

It starts out with a familiar scene of Samantha coming home from buying a Christmas tree by herself, and that's when we realize that we have seen it before and resign ourselves to the fact that ABC must've just pulled out last year's *Bewitched* Christmas episode, which isn't bad at all as it was an awesome episode. However, after the credits, it seems they realized their mistake as a new scene with Durwood coming down the stairs surprised that pregnant Samantha lugged the tree in by herself plays out. Before he can get mad at her she reminds him that it is Christmas though he admits that it won't feel like Christmas without having a kid in the house like they did last year, but she reminds him soon enough that they will have one. He shows her that they received a Christmas card from Michael, the orphan that stayed with them last year. He thanks them for having shown him the meaning of Christmas and it's then that they begin reminiscing about that Christmas via a re-airing of the rest of last year's episode. So all though, for the most part not a new episode, we still got a little new scene.

DECEMBER 30, 1965

It was on this night that ABC aired the last episode of 1965 with Episode #52: "The Magic Cabin" sponsored by Chevrolet.

For the past two weeks Durwood hasn't been able to come up with anything for the Kingsley Potato Chip account and is worried that he may not come up with anything especially when he starts coming up with slogans on the fly, something he is not very good at. Larry is worried that Durwood may be burnt out, as is Samantha and she suggests that he take some time off. Larry agrees and suggests that he take some time off by going up to Larry's cabin that happens to be up for sale. Durwood tries to resist, but Larry insists that he go or he'll be fired.

And so Durwood and Samantha go up to the rustic cabin and find that it's even more rustic than they anticipated as it seems to be falling apart. There are cobwebs over everything and the floor creaks as though it won't hold much longer. Durwood is furious at Larry for not telling them what dilapidated shape the cabin was in and Samantha suggests she can zap everything into perfect shape. Of course, Durwood won't have it until it starts raining and they discover multiple leaks in the roof. Samantha suggests they just go home but Durwood thinks they had better find out the road report. However they are reminded that Larry said there wasn't any phone so Durwood relents and let's Samantha zap up a phone. He finds that the roads turn to mud in a sun shower and so they are stuck. It's cold though and Durwood can see Samantha is chilly so he hesitatingly lets her zap up a fire. She also tells him that it's the perfect time for redecorating and she zaps a broken chair into a brand new one. When he tells her she shouldn't be doing things that way she agrees and zaps the whole place new. Seeing that his expectant wife is happy, he's happy and they settle in for a nice relaxing night.

The next day a young couple named Charles and Alice McBain show up to McMann and Tate inquiring about the cabin. Larry tells them that it's for sale for $5,000 but that it's run down and the deposit is $1,000. They want to go see it and Larry tells them that he has friends staying at it but that they shouldn't mind.

Up in the woods, Samantha and Durwood go outside to find that the weather has cleared up and so they go for a nice morning drive. A little while later the McBains show up and find the door unlocked so they let themselves in and are bowled over by how nice the cabin is, even more so that Larry was only asking for $5,000. They are sold and as they go to leave they are greeted by a surprised Durwood and Samantha. They explain that they are going to buy the place that day and leave to check out the grounds. Well this isn't good as they are paying for something that Larry didn't really have but Samantha tells Durwood that it should be OK as Larry won't have to know and the McBains seemed so happy. When the McBains come back they phone Larry and tell them they will buy it and he is surprised that they would go for it but then realizes he's even more surprised that they said they were calling from the cabin so he goes up to investigate.

Larry arrives at the cabin just as Durwood and Samantha are getting ready to leave and they panic realizing that Larry can't see the cabin in its refurbished state and so Samantha zaps it back and they accompany him in. He cannot believe the state of the cabin as it's worse than he remembered and he thinks maybe the McBains are swindlers who have found oil on the property. Just then Samantha sees that the McBains are coming up the drive and she runs out to greet them. They have returned because Alice couldn't believe that they found their dream home so they came back to make sure it was real. As they go in Samantha twitches and makes the half of the room behind Larry sparkling and new. As they discuss the purchase, Durwood and Samantha are shocked that Larry would charge $5,000 for the place and guilt him into selling it for the $1,000 deposit.

I LOVE this one, though I'd only give it two and a half stars and for the following reasons: 1) Alice McBain's voice is seriously

SOOOOOOOOOOO annoying! It's no wonder her husband heads straight for the bar when they get into the cabin and 2) all though I thought it was cool that half the room was broken down and the other half wasn't, there is NO way that either Larry or the McBains wouldn't have noticed the transition unless all three had tunnel vision, but that's a likely story.

I guess the reason I love this one so much, well the MAIN reason, is because it has the honor of being the first black and white episode of *Bewitched* I ever saw! Picture it: Rawlins, Wyoming 1991, the beginning of summer (is it a good Sofia (*The Golden Girls*) impression?). I'm staying with my cousins in their dad's trailer home while he works up there. They had cable and I had heard that Nickelodeon started a new thing called Nick-at-Nite where they showed old TV shows. See, at that time, my household didn't have cable so the only time we ever got to watch it was at other people's houses, which wasn't that often. I saw that *Bewitched* was listed in the *TV Guide* but I also noticed a strange notation by it that looked like this — b&w. I was pretty sure that meant black and white but, surely, they must be mistaken! *I've never seen a black and white episode of Bewitched*, is what I thought. I had to plead with my uncle Ray to let me watch it because it was on at 6:30 PM, the same time as his favorite show, *Jeopardy*. He finally relented. Well, I can't even express the sense of excitement I had when I saw the black and white opening to the show (remember how they used to play the cartoon opening first and then the episode?) and I noticed that it was a little different than what I was used to seeing because there were more stars in the sky and the buildings looked different and then in the kitchen there were cupboards and a door, things not seen in the color episodes. I remember being so confused by Samantha being SO BIG! Up to that time I had always thought the show was about Tabitha and that it just so happened that her mother was a witch as well, don't ask me why, but I didn't have anything to go by except in my mind the first episode was when Samantha discovers that Tabitha is a witch. I also wanted to know where Tabitha was and then it occurred to me that the reason Samantha was so big was because she was pregnant with Tabitha! Of course the next night was another BIG Samantha episode and I thought, *Man, I'll never be able to see when Tabitha is born* but luckily the following evening was Tabitha's birth and I couldn't have been more thrilled! Of course, this was all before Herbie J Pilato's *The Bewitched Book*, which was released like five months later and I was so thrilled to find that there were at least seventy more episodes I had never seen!

JANUARY 6, 1966

It was on this night that ABC aired Episode #53: "Maid to Order" sponsored by Quaker Oats.

Durwood decides that Samantha needs a maid to help her around the house while she's nearing the end of her pregnancy, so he has Samantha interview some prospective maids and she hires the klutzy but endearing Naomi. Samantha finds that Naomi is a terrible cook and helps her fix dinner by zapping her mistakes into great meals.

Later on Louise Tate finds that her maid, Esmeralda, has taken ill and asks if she could borrow Naomi's services for the evening. Durwood agrees to it and Naomi is thrilled as it will bring more money for her, which she is using to send her son through medical school.

Samantha finds out about Naomi helping the Tates and worries about how the evening will go, especially since it's for a client dinner, so she pops between her house and the Tate's and helps Naomi out just before Louise loses her cool with the messy kitchen.

Later on Samantha finds out that Naomi is a wiz at math and she asks Durwood if he couldn't find a job for her in the accounting department at McMann and Tate as Naomi is not maid material.

Naomi is played by Alice Ghostley in her first appearance on *Bewitched*. She will later return in Season Six as the witch-maid Esmeralda. It's funny that her character in this episode takes over for the Tate's maid Esmeralda.

I would give this one two and a half stars. I find it odd that Durwood would suggest hiring a maid considering he's so uptight about all the witchcraft going on in the house. Later when his mother wants Samantha to hire maid in "Samantha's Super Maid" he flips out for that very reason.

I noticed that usually on TV the second prospective maid, the beautiful blonde, her scene is always cut out. And that photo Samantha twitches up of a country bumpkin Durwood seems like it's a still from the beginning scenes of "Divided He Stands" which will air later this season

I also believe this is the first time the word "groovy" is spoken on *Bewitched*, first by the blonde maid and then by Samantha.

JANUARY 13, 1966

Tonight television history was made when the world's first possible witch baby was born on T.V. in *Bewitched* Episode #54: "And Then There Were Three" sponsored by Chevrolet.

As Samantha prepares to go to the hospital for the blessed event she receives a call from her long lost look-a-like cousin Serena who says she's come to visit because Westport is "the in place to be this time of year, darling." Durwood, meanwhile, is frantic about getting Samantha to the hospital in time so they can avoid naming the baby "Freeway, 'cause that's where it'll be born if we don't hurry!"

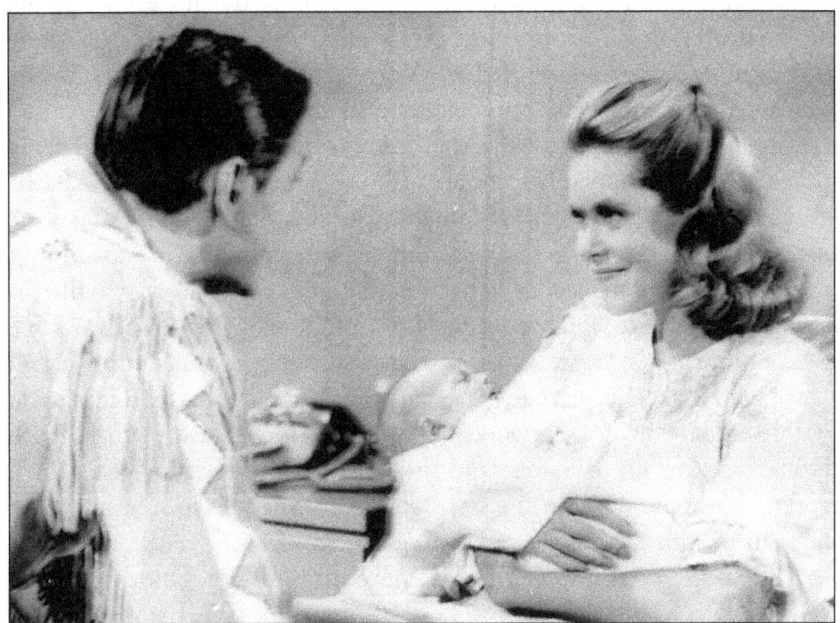

Durwood and Samantha marvel at being brand new parents to baby Tabatha.

While Durwood is nervously pacing the waiting room awaiting the news, Endora pops in. She has just been in the delivery room and announces that Samantha gave birth to a baby girl! And in a rare sweet moment Endora and her son-in-law embrace each other in tears.

He then gets to embrace his wife and look at the new baby for the first time. As they discuss names for the baby (luckily not Freeway) Samantha suggests Tabatha, a name Endora came up with. He's not too keen on the idea. And Nurse Kelton is not too keen on visitors so she kicks him out and takes the baby back to the nursery.

Later on as Endora and Durwood are admiring baby Tabatha in the nursery and commenting on whose side she takes after, Endora says in jest that she'll just make Tabatha older for a while so they can really see. Of course, he gets his pants in a knot at such a suggestion. Meanwhile,

Serena pops into Samantha's room and they renew acquaintances. She also zaps in a room full of flowers for Samantha, something Endora had done earlier but was reprimanded by Nurse Kelton as "too many flowers in the room take up all the oxygen." She also said she was going to bring a centaur as a play thing for the baby but Samantha suggests a rattle may be better so she goes off to the toy store.

Endora, by this point, has taken the baby out of the nursery for a walk as she was crying. Of course, she essentially had kidnapped her as none of the nurses were aware of this. When Durwood comes back to the nursery, he is understandably concerned that his child is missing. At this point Serena passes by and asks if he knows where the toy store is. Seeing that she looks remarkably like Samantha he assumes that she is Tabatha, all grown-up courtesy of Grandmama Endora. Serena doesn't take too nicely to his trying to get her back in the nursery and she zaps him in there instead with a pacifier in his mouth and goes on her way to the toy store. Embarrassed, Durwood runs out to follow Serena to the toy store.

At Tippet's Toy Store, Durwood finds not only Serena but his friend Dave who makes some suggestive comments about what he'd like to do with Serena causing Durwood to want to punch Dave in the mouth. Durwood runs up to Serena and insists she come back to the hospital and tells her she shouldn't be seen like she is. She tells him he shouldn't be seen like he is and zaps him into an Indian Chief's outfit. And with that she pops out. However Endora pops in wanting to know where he is and when he starts yelling at her about making Tabatha a grown up and demands that she take him to his daughter she zaps him back to the nursery.

When Durwood rushes down to Samantha's room, he finds her feeding the baby and he also sees Serena which confuses him. Sick of his badgering, Serena zaps him into ropes and she pops out. Endora shows up and after Samantha explains what happened, he apologizes and calls the baby Tabatha, much to the surprise of his wife and mother-in-law, and feels that it's a way to make up for accusing Endora of "growing" his child.

This episode is one of my most favorite. It's "practically perfect in every way," as Mary Poppins would say. And I also love that Serena finally enters the picture, even if she isn't in the incarnation that we usually think of her. It's also really odd that she would phone Samantha rather than just pop in. I wouldn't even think that Serena would know how to use a telephone.

Of course Eve Arden is brilliant in this episode and should've been asked to return for more episodes.

I really love Endora's line about how she doesn't mind if they don't name the baby Tabatha.

SAMANTHA: *"You don't?!"*
ENDORA: *"No, whatever you call her, I shall call her Tabatha!"*

That's my credo when it comes to discussing Durwood.

Speaking of the name of the baby, it was actually Elizabeth Montgomery that came up with the name. In an interview with Mike Connolly that would appear in the February 1967 *Screen Stories* she describes how she came up with it:

> *"The name was my idea," she explained. "I loved it, because it was so old-fashioned. I got it from one of the daughters of Edward Andrews, the actor. The two Andrews girls are named Tabitha and Abigail. Bill was surprised that I remembered their names, after meeting them only once. Now, really, isn't that just like a man—as though anyone could forget names like Tabitha and Abigail!"*

> *"Anyway, Tabitha is the name I picked for the daughter Dick York and I were supposed to have, when I was actually pregnant on the show, just like Lucy Ball was a few years before me, except that I had a son in real life when 'my time' came instead of a daughter. But, somehow or other, her name came out 'Tabatha' on the credit roll, and that's the way it's been ever since. Honestly, I shudder every time I see it. It's like a squeaky piece of chalk scratching on my nerves."*

I actually like it better with an 'A' and it will stay like that in the credits (and is seen that way in the mobile in Tabatha's crib in "The Safe and Sane Halloween") up until the Fifth Season episode "Samantha at the Keyboard."

It was also this week that *I Dream of Jeannie* history was made when NBC aired "The Richest Astronaut in the World" where Roger finds out that Jeannie is a genie.

JANUARY 20, 1966

It was on this night that ABC aired Episode #55: "My Baby, the Tycoon" sponsored by Quaker Oats.

In the middle of the night, Tabatha begins crying yet again and when Durwood finds that Samantha is too tired to get out of bed he bucks up to go get the baby her bottle. However, after he leaves Samantha groggily asks if she can use witchcraft to feed the baby as she has been up and down all night. In her sleep she hears Durwood give permission and so she twitches. Down stairs, right before he enters the kitchen, a bottle flies out of the refrigerator to land in the bottle warmer which plugs itself in. Durwood retrieves a bottle only to see the other one in the warmer all ready when suddenly a nipple materializes on it. After a moment the bottle begins to fly again through the dining room and up the stairs. Confused, and a bit intrigued, Durwood follows it straight to Tabatha's crib and her waiting mouth. It occurs to him that Tabatha is truly her mother's daughter and when he goes to tell Samantha she is shocked.

But the next morning she realizes that it was she that had done the magic as Tabatha is much too young to develop powers and Durwood apologizes to Tabatha for accusing her of being a witch. As he's getting ready to go to work, the Kravitzes come over with a present for Tabatha, a share of stock in Kapoopsie, I mean Poughkeepsie Woolens. Mr. Kravitz says that as the stock has never gone up or down in the twenty years that he's been a stockholder, he felt it was a sound investment.

Later, on Wallstreet, Gladys' cousin Julius Cushman, a stock broker who they bought the stock through, finds that Poughkeepsie Woolens suddenly jumped six points. When Durwood comes home he tells Samantha about it and accuses her of making it rise. She promises she didn't and clears Endora as she says that Endora would've just zapped up a couple million dollars cash. They go upstairs so Durwood can tell Tabatha about the news and when she smiles he takes it as a sign that she's pleased with herself and that maybe she is the one that caused it to rise. Samantha reminds him that Tabatha is much too young to do something like that. He thinks that there is still a possibility so he devises a test where he'll show her the stock page and whatever stock she points to, he'll buy and they'll see. Her finger lands on Nelson Aerodynamics and so he calls Mr. Cushman. Later on the stock rises by six points which Durwood takes as proof of Tabatha's greed and witchcraft. Samantha is frustrated with his lack of faith in his daughter. However she doesn't have an explanation.

The next day Julius calls Gladys and tells her that if she wants to make a lot of money, she'll get tips from Mr. Stephens as he seems to have an inside track to the market. She tells Abner they should go over to talk with him. He thinks that it's not worthy of his time but reluctantly goes over and tells Gladys to hold off on knocking until he verifies whether Durwood's car is in the garage. It's also at that time that Samantha is getting ready to give Tabatha a bath and she decides that she should bring up a baby doll that is downstairs, but as she has her arms full with Tabatha and the bathing supplies she twitches and flies the baby upstairs. Mrs. Kravitz, who is snooping, sees this and believes it's Tabatha. She tries to tell Abner but of course he won't believe her. Samantha overhears them and answers the door and advises them that Durwood is gone to work and that she was just on her way to bathe Tabatha. Mr. Kravitz asks if they can watch as they lead such dull lives and Samantha invites them in. After Samantha has gone upstairs Abner tells Gladys that the reason he asked is so he could show her that there is only one baby, a non-flier. Upstairs, while Samantha preps the bath, Gladys mentions the strangeness of the stock jumping and Samantha kids that maybe Tabatha told Durwood which one to buy. After she leaves to get water, Gladys decides to use Durwood's trick to ask Tabatha about which stock they should buy and Tabatha points to East South Dakota Petroleum. As they go to leave Samantha and Gladys run into each other at the door causing Gladys to fall down and the water spill…that is until Samantha does a quick twitch reversing the fall of both things. Gladys is freaked out and runs after Abner.

Later on, when Durwood comes home, he sees Abner nailing up a "Room for Rent" sign and when he asks about it Abner tells him how they sold all their stock to put it into East South Dakota Petroleum on a magical tip from Tabatha and it had immediately dropped twenty-one points causing them to lose their life savings. He runs home to tell Samantha and suggests that because the stock wasn't purchased in Tabatha's name, she caused it to go down. He calls Mr. Cushman to order one share of the Petroleum stock so that it was go back up. However he finds that it has already gone back up. Julius also tells Durwood that he found out about why the other stocks went up. Sheepish now that he's been proven wrong, he tell Samantha that the Petroleum went back up because of a false rumor about a new oil well failing to strike oil, and Poughkeepsie Woolens went up because of the discovery of a new synthetic fabric and Nelson Aerodynamics went up because of a new government contract. However it occurs to Durwood that maybe Tabatha knew about these things happening before hand but Samantha tells him that he's going to turn into a Gladys Kravitz if he doesn't quit accusing Tabatha, and he stops saying he's cured.

I would give this episode only one star. We've just had an historic event with the addition of Tabatha and we're given an episode dealing with something boring like the stock market. This would've worked better later on. However, I give the opening scene four stars! It's very awesome seeing the floating bottle, even if you can see the strings.

The bar is also missing from the dining room in this scene but appears there at the end of the episode.

This is also the first time we get to see the nursery. It seems to be a newly built room as it's never been shown before when guests have stayed.

Another reason it only gets one star is that Durwood seems intent on having Tabatha be a witch even when he's given proof positive and he never apologizes for accusing Samantha or Endora having fooling around with the stock market.

It's also quite apparent that Alice Pearce is sick as she seems very gaunt and drawn. When Gladys falls down it's clearly a stunt double.

According to *IMDB.com*, Heidi and Laura Gentry play Tabatha in this episode only. They were very cute!

Julius's last name is the same one as Liz's cousin Panda's last name — Cushman. Panda was Liz's look-a-like cousin and also considered an inspiration for Serena.

It was also today that future Durwood — Dick Sargent — appeared in the big screen classic *The Ghost and Mr. Chicken* starring Don Knotts along with several other *Bewitched* alumni including Reta Shaw, Lurene Tuttle, Charles Lane, Nydia Westerman, Jim Begg, Sandra Gould, Cliff Norton, Herbie Faye, J. Edward McKinley, Burt Mustin, Hope Summers and Dick Wilson, the most for any project outside of *Bewitched*. Joan Staley (Alma Parker) was in *Johnny Cool* with Liz as Suzy.

Dick Sargent also appeared on the TV series *Daniel Boone* in the episode entitled "The Deserter" tonight.

JANUARY 27, 1966

It was on this night that ABC aired a re-edited version of Episode #14: "Samantha Meets the Folks" but labeled it as Episode #56, sponsored by Chevrolet.

Tabatha receives her first letter in the mail from Durwood's parents announcing that they are going to visit in two weeks. Samantha remarks how it'll be fun to see them but Durwood says that depends as the last time they visited wasn't his idea of fun. Samantha tells him she had no idea that Aunt Clara was going to visit that same weekend and that it surprised her when Aunt Clara showed up in the fireplace. It's at this point the image fades to that time and the rest of the episode plays out like it originally had with Samantha meeting Durwood's parents.

Again, we are just introduced to Tabatha and get essentially a rerun! Not very impressive, especially since last week's episode was so boring.

There is an inconsistency with this episode as both Durwood and Samantha talk about how Durwood's parent's last visit was with Aunt Clara. However their last visit was in "A Nice Little Dinner Party" when Frank flirts with Endora.

This episode and the recut version of the Christmas episode were never shown on TV after their original airings until they were included on the Second Season DVDs.

FEBRUARY 2, 1966

It was on this night that ABC aired Episode #57: "Fastest Gun on Madison Avenue" sponsored by Quaker Oats.

When Samantha finds she is the first to arrive at Dundee's Bar to meet Durwood for what is supposed to be the finest dining in town, she waits at their table and soon becomes annoyed by a drunk trying to pick her up. Durwood shows up and tells the man to knock it off or else. The drunk thinks this is funny as Durwood is smaller and he grasps his nose between his fingers but soon receives a shock courtesy of Samantha's nose. When he goes to knock Durwood out, Durwood swings and misses by a mile but Samantha twitches again and knocks the drunk out. And wouldn't you know it, there are photographers in the bar who begin flashing their bulbs.

The next morning as Samantha prepares breakfast for Durwood she is horrified to find that the story on the front page of the paper is about Durwood knocking out heavy weight champ Joking Joe Kovack! She quickly folds the paper and tries to hide it when Durwood comes in. He is annoyed that Samantha had to be the one to beat up the bully and he asks her not to do it again and suggests that they forget about the whole thing. When he asks where the paper is, before she can say anything he sees the paper and Samantha quickly retreats just as he sees the front page and blows his top.

Across the street, Gladys Kravitz also loses her cool when she reads the headline which she shows to her husband finally getting him to believe that something unbelievable is happening across the street. When Durwood leaves for work, Abner runs across the street to get Durwood's autograph on the paper while he can still write as he believes Joe Kovack is going to want a rematch.

When Durwood arrives at work the elevator operator tells him that he better avoid Joe at all costs as he's been known to do some damage to his opponents. Durwood is a little shaken when he walks into his office and is startled to see Joe there along with his manager. He goes to put up his dukes, but the manager tells him to calm down, that Joe wants to apologize. They figure that nobody is going to want to pay to see Joe anymore, especially at his big match against Tommy Carter if a nobody like Durwood can knock Joe out. They've decided that they'll set up another meeting at Dundee's where Joe will apologize in public to Durwood, who should not accept, they get in another fight and Joe knocks him out, all for show though. Durwood won't agree to it but the manager reminds him he's really in no place to dicker.

Back at 1164, Samantha is painting a horse on Tabatha's crib when Gladys comes over and tells her that she thinks she should talk Durwood out of fighting again with Kovack. Samantha is surprised to hear this and when she calls to the office she hears that Durwood has gone to Dundee's again and so she leaves Tabatha with Gladys to go watch over Durwood.

At Dundee's, Joe and his manager show up and the staged apology seems to be going well, until Samantha shows up and sees that Durwood is about to get knocked out. She twitches Joe into throwing his punch at his manager. Confused, Durwood tries to go for Joe again but she twitches again and Durwood's fake punch knocks Kovack out again. Afterwards he tells Samantha what he was trying to do and again asks her to let him fight his own battles.

Later, Larry comes in to the office excited over Durwood's fight being front page news yet he's confused about how Durwood would've done it as they used to spar at the gym and Durwood wasn't very good. Offended, Durwood goes to a saloon to drown his sorrows. While there he is confronted by a dapper gentleman who recognizes him from the paper and asks him to punch him. Durwood refuses but when he tries to stand up he gets tangled in the bar stool and trips knocking the man over and out. The bartender is shocked as Durwood has just knocked out the heavy weight champ Tommy Carter! Sure that Samantha is there, Durwood calls out for her by yelling "Sam!" However, the bartender's name is Sam and Durwood thinks she's trying to hide. He tells her that he would like her to please leave. Of course, Sam is quite confused.

At home he finds that she really wasn't there and he tells her that he is going to avoid any more fights. That is until Larry shows up saying that Tommy Carter showed up looking for him. Instead Larry booked him for the Advertising Club's Charity Ball to box four rounds with Durwood. Samantha assures him that she'll be in his corner making him unbeatable.

I would give this one maybe one star. First of all, it's almost a direct remake of a *Dick Van Dyke Show* episode "Body and Sol" which aired the previous Thanksgiving week with Rob being thrown into the ring. Secondly, Tabatha has just been born and we only get the stock episode about her? No thanks. And third, it's just ridiculous that Durwood would get into this situation in the first place.

Durwood also tells Samantha that he goes to take her to the finest restaurant in town and yet they end up at a Bar?! In New York?! That first scene was filmed much earlier than the rest of the episode and I would think that Samantha would be smarter than to buy sixty cans of waxed beans.

Alice Pearce looks very ill and I hope that the box of weights was empty when she carried it and that she just did a good job of acting like it was heavy.

FEBRUARY 9, 1966

It was on this night that ABC aired Episode #58: "The Dancing Bear" sponsored by Chevrolet.

True to their letter, Durwood's parents come to visit Baby Tabatha for the first time and Endora decides to show up as well. She is 'bear'-ing a gift of a teddy bear for Tabatha which Durwood thinks may do something weird as he thinks it's made of magic. Endora insists it's not. However when she puts it back in the box, she levitates it and tells him the box is magic.

When Mr. and Mrs. Stephens arrive Mr. Stephens visits with Durwood while Samantha takes care of the baby. Still holding animosity from their last visit, Mrs. Stephens and Endora icily visit. It also turns out that they have brought the exact same teddy bear for Tabatha. Not to be one-upped by Samantha's mortal mother-in-law, Endora bewitches her bear into dancing any time Tabatha's name is mentioned. When Durwood and Samantha see this they try to hide the bear but Mrs. Stephens finds out and really feels that Samantha should've said something about Tabatha already having the bear. Of course, then she sees that Endora's bear dances. Frank, who is all about new inventions, is delighted and thinks he and his son will become millionaires marketing the bear, which Durwood said he had fitted with a mechanism.

Frank invites a toy manufacturer over to see the bear, and to dissuade him from wanting to take over the rights to the bear, Samantha twitches the new clown doll that Phyllis went out and bought into dancing as well. She also makes sure that both Grandmothers know that Tabatha won't be as unique any more if every child has a dancing clown and bear. The toy maker leaves and things are settled between the mothers-in-law.

I really liked this episode. I thought it was fun the rivalry being renewed between Phyllis and Endora. And Elizabeth Montgomery looked so GORGEOUS in this episode!

Endora mentions that Samantha's grandmother had flecks of gold in her eyes, pretty much the only time that she is mentioned in the series.

This is also the first time that Arthur Julian makes an appearance on *Bewitched*. He would later show up as the butcher that Mrs. Kravitz has the crush on and he would write the episode "Is It Magic or Imagination?."

A still color photo from this episode was used as the cover of the December 1966 comic book. This was the only time that an episode photo from the series was used as a cover for the comic books. It also shows us that the wallpaper out in the hall was red though Dynamics colorized it beige.

The only thing I didn't like about the episode was the fake baby crying. Or at least I hope it was fake, because it was REALLY annoying!

Three nights earlier *Mr. Ed* ended a five year run on CBS.

FEBRUARY 16, 1966

Tonight ABC aired the awesome Episode #59: "Double Tate" sponsored by Quaker Oats.

It happens to be Durwood's birthday and Endora decides to give him a gift. In fact it's a really good one as she gives, unbeknownst to him, three wishes. His first wish is wasted on making the elevator work faster and then he wishes a hot girl into a bikini. Before wasting the next wish on little trivial matters he finds that an important client, Mr. Turgeon, has arrived early to McMann & Tate and INSISTS on meeting with Tate only. It happens that Larry is stuck in Chicago in a fog. Durwood, in a moment of desperation, wishes that he could be Larry for just one day...and so it is!

Once he gets over the shock of finding that he's his own boss, he decides to go with it and appeases Mr. Turgeon. He is introduced to Turgeon's niece at a business dinner at a restaurant that Louise happens to be at. She immediately suspects Larry of cheating on her and makes him leave the niece so he can go straight home for being a bad boy!

At the Tate's, the Larry-ized Durwood phones Samantha and convinces her of who he really is. She immediately comes over and finds that she can't reverse the spell as Durwood put a time-lock on it making it last until midnight that night. Louise gets irritated that Samantha won't seem to leave and suggests that "Larry" go put his pajamas on to give Samantha the notion that they are getting ready for bed. Just when things couldn't get worse the real Larry arrives home and by some artful witchcraft Samantha makes sure he doesn't enter the house when he wanted to. Just as Louise and Larry-ized Durwood are kissing for the night (something Louise initiated) Durwood's wish ends and Larry walks in on them. Samantha twitches Louise asleep and tells Larry that Louise was sleep walking which sort of appeases him. And she makes Louise think she dreamed the whole night's events.

This is one of the better episodes of the second season. David White should've won an Emmy for this episode alone as he really made you believe he was Durwood.

This is the first episode Irwin Charone (Mr. Turgeon) appeared in on *Bewitched*. He played many different clients and he is my vote for the most annoying of the clients! There is just something about him that grates my nerves. Were it not for the fact that the premise of this episode is so cool I wouldn't ever watch it based on him being in it.

FEBRUARY 23, 1966

It was on this night that ABC aired Episode # 60: "Samantha the Dressmaker" sponsored by Quaker Oats.

The Stephens' are invited to a black tie affair at rich client J.T. Glendon's. Samantha decides to make herself a dress for it, but not by witchcraft. When her mortal efforts come out less than perfect, Endora whisks her off to Paris for some rest and during their trip they visit the show room of clothing designer Aubert. Back at home, seeing that her homespun creation isn't going to be done in time for the dinner, Samantha decides to just twitch up something she saw in Aubert's showroom for the dinner. Mrs. Glendon and Mr. Glendon's sister are quite impressed with Samantha's dress and ask her to make some for them for the unveiling of a new client's product line. Samantha, at Larry's insistence, agrees.

Mrs. Kravitz also happens to hear about this party and invites herself and requests that Samantha make her a dress as well. Samantha zaps up copies of the dresses she saw in Paris.

The night of the unveiling of the client's new product arrives and what do you know, the product is Aubert's new dress line! He faints when he sees his newest creations on the four American women. Later on he threatens to sue McMann & Tate. Samantha says she'll talk him out of it and pops over to his place. After chatting with him she finds that he's really mad that his creations didn't look good on the women and Samantha advises him that's because he didn't create them with a "real" American woman in mind. She tells him that if he'll come up with

Aubert (Dick Gautier) is shocked to see his new dress design on Samantha as he hasn't revealed it yet.

new designs she'll make them in time for another unveiling the following evening. And so everything turns out all right…even for Abner who gets to see his wife model and look quite stunning, really.

This is an all right episode. I really do like the scene when Endora freezes everyone in Aubert's salon and when they go to unfreeze them Endora moves Aubert's chair out from underneath him.

All though this isn't the last episode with Alice Pearce in it, it would be the last one to air while she was alive. How sad.

MARCH 3, 1966

It was on this night that ABC aired Episode #61: "The Horse's Mouth" sponsored by Chevrolet.

Samantha is shocked to hear a horse whinny come from the backyard and even more so to find there IS a horse in the backyard. Wanting to know where the horse is from, Samantha zaps her into human form and finds that her name is Dallyrand, a race horse who escaped from her trainer because he makes her throw races so her sister Adorable Diane can win. Dallyrand is jealous of her sister always getting the glory. She decided to take a couple days off from the races to calm down. When her trainer, Mr. Spindler, comes looking for her, Dallyrand is offended when he says that the missing horse isn't that great of a horse. Samantha assures him that she'll contact him if she sees the horse.

Just then Durwood comes home with his friend Gus Walters and Samantha introduces them to her new friend *Dolly* Rand. Durwood is confused about who Dolly is and suspects that Dolly is a witch but Samantha assures him she isn't. As they sit down to dinner, Gus tells them about his idea for a new office lamp that Durwood offered to advertise. However Gus doesn't have the money to put his idea into production. Dolly offers to take them to the race track as she knows which horses are the winners. Durwood isn't too keen on this though Gus says he's really got nothing to lose and everything to gain. It occurs to Durwood that Dolly is so keen to go to the tracks because she happens to be a horse and when he pulls Samantha aside she confirms it much to his displeasure considering that Gus is conversing with a horse. Samantha suggests it's a wonderful rare opportunity as there are few people that can say they had a genuine conversation with a horse not to mention Dolly is going to help Gus win money. He reluctantly agrees and they tell Gus they will meet him at the race the next day.

At the tracks, Dolly takes them down to the paddocks to talk to the horses to see who they think is going to win. Gus thinks it's amusing that Dolly talks to the horses but when he sees that her pick, Diamond Turkey, is favored to lose he begins to get nervous. Dolly assures Samantha and Durwood that Diamond Turkey will win because it's his birthday and the other horses are going to let him win. And she's right, he does win. When they go back down to the paddocks Dolly finds that Rompin' Roger is talking a strong race which he ends up losing, causing Gus to reconsider putting his faith in Dolly. On a return trip to the paddocks to give Rompin' Roger a piece of her mind, they come across Mr. Spindler, who is distraught that he hasn't found Dallyrand yet especially since he had to scratch Adorable Diane as she came up ill. Dolly gets excited and asks Samantha to return her to her horse form so that she can win the race as she feels so much better and Samantha complies.

Back in the stands they tell Gus to bet on Dallyrand based on Dolly saying that if there were any bet he should make it should be on her. Even though Dallyrand is favored to lose, he bets on her. His fears seem to be solid as she trails at first but at the last minute she picks up speed and wins.

This episode is horrible! Earlier this season I had said that the "Fastest Gun on Madison Avenue" was the worst of Season Two, but I'm changing my vote to this one, based on the corny horse jokes, the irritating actress who played Dolly, the even MORE irritating crunching sound effects used when she's eating, and the just lame storyline.

The actor that played Gus, Robert Sorrells, was sentenced to thirty-two years in prison in 2004 for having shot and killed a man in a drunken bar fight.

In the Eighth Season a remake of this episode happens in "Three Men and a Witch on a Horse," one of Liz Montgomery's favorite episodes according to Herbie J Pilato. And it is a much better episode even though it's an Eighth Season episode where generally the scripts weren't that great. But in that one the human form of the horse is a guy. And though she didn't mention this episode specifically, I'm sure it was a favorite as Liz loved horse racing as her Grandma Becca used to take her to the horse tracks to teach her math.

I also didn't like in this one how Dolly kicked that other horse. I'm sure that she didn't really kick him, but it sure looked like it, and it made me mad.

This episode also has the distinction of airing the same evening, March 3, 1966, that Alice Pearce died from cancer. In fact, according to *IMDB.com*, ABC interrupted this episode to announce her passing. And she was only seventy pounds at the time of her death. It's so sad. There are only two more episodes that feature Alice Pearce as Gladys, "Baby's First Paragraph" and "Prodigy."

I noticed that all though Liz looked really pretty her hair looked weird to me, as though it were longer or something.

MARCH 10, 1966

It was on this evening that ABC aired Episode #62: "Baby's First Paragraph" sponsored by Quaker Oats.

When her regular sitter gets sick at the last minute, Samantha finds herself relying on her mother to babysit. She's apprehensive as Endora has never been alone with Tabatha but Endora reminds Samantha that once upon a time Samantha was a baby herself. So Samantha consents and leaves.

A little while later, Gladys Kravitz comes knocking and when Endora tells her to come in, Gladys enters with a baby herself and is surprised that Samantha isn't there and even more so that she is meeting Endora for the first time. Gladys says the baby she has is her sister Edna's child Edgar who was born a week before Tabatha and that he is much more advanced than Tabatha because his father is a CPA, therefore Edgar is definitely more intelligent than Tabatha, whom she coos at suggesting that's all she would understand. Getting more irritated with Gladys, Endora causes her to feel a pin prick though she was nowhere near a pin. Gladys suggests that maybe Tabatha would like some milk as she's fussy but when she asks Endora to go get her some, Endora zaps Tabatha into saying she doesn't want any milk. Shocked out of her mind that young Tabatha spoke in a full sentence, Gladys runs back to her house to tell Abner all about it who, of course, doesn't believe her.

When Durwood comes home he is greeted by Gladys who congratulates him on Tabatha's big accomplishment. Confused, but also intrigued, by what Gladys has said, he goes inside to see if he can get his daughter to speak. Samantha thinks he's lost it until she reveals that Endora was babysitting and then it all makes sense. He hollers at Samantha until Endora pops back in and they get into it when he calls her a broom jockey. Before she can obliterate him, there is a ring at the door and he finds that Gladys is there with members of the press. He tries to tell them that his baby didn't talk and that his mother-in-law was playing a practical joke but as she's still mad at Durwood, Endora makes Tabatha talk again exciting the two reporters who take pictures and run back to the office. As her work there is done, Endora pops off too.

The next morning Tabatha is the head line on the *Daily Mail* newspaper and when Samantha tries to take her out for a walk she is hounded by the press. The phone never stops ringing with offers to be on TV shows like *The Hollywood Palace*. When Durwood gets home he tells her that he had to leave work early and sneak in the back way to avoid the press.

Endora is pleased with herself after aiding baby Tabatha (Julie Young) in speaking, courtesy of a deft spell.

Samantha tells him that she has an idea about how to put all this business to rest. However she'll need Endora to show up again and she won't.

Later on Endora does show up and Samantha shows her that all the focus Tabatha is getting is going to cause her own family never to be able to spend time with her again. Not wanting to not be a part of Tabatha's life, Endora asks what they can do and Samantha tells her her plan.

That night Samantha invites the original reporters and the Kravitzes over as she says she has an explanation for Tabatha talking. Endora tells them that she used to do a ventriloquism act in vaudeville and when Gladys came over bragging about Edgar she couldn't resist pulling a little prank. Gladys insists it wasn't done by throwing voices and when Endora tells them that it is merely throwing the voice to the back of the throat, she tells Gladys to try it. As Gladys argues her voice suddenly goes higher and Endora tells the press that anyone can do it and they are convinced and so a retraction is printed and all is back to normal.

I rather like this episode. I'd give it maybe two and a half to three stars. I think everybody is really funny in it and those storybook scenes with Endora and Tabatha are TOO cute! I really like Endora's line when she says, "WELL! Without so much as a 'by your leave' the two gluttons broke off a piece of her window ledge and ate it! Now what do you think of that?!"

I think Samantha being worried about Tabatha being a witch stems from the fact that she knows Durwood would flip out if she were and she doesn't want to have to worry about that possibility yet. Not to mention, she was probably thinking it was much too early in Tabatha's life for her to know levitation yet.

I like Gladys' reaction to Tabatha talking, how her last word is almost inaudible — "The baby talked!"

And speaking of Gladys, this is Alice Pearce's last episode to be filmed. It finished filming at the end of January and about six weeks later she passed away.

When Samantha freezes the members of the press, one of the lady reporters blinks. When Durwood goes out to get the paper, if you look inside the house there ISN'T an inside of the house, just a blank wall which is because they filmed that scene out at the studio lot.

I believe that the woman reporter is the same lady that did the voice of talking Tabatha. And that woman, June Foray, is also the voice of Rocky the Squirrel from *Rocky and Bullwinkle*.

The day before the U.S. announced a substantial increase in troops to Vietnam.

MARCH 17, 1966

It was on this night that ABC got into the St. Patrick's Day spirit and aired *Bewitched* Episode #63: "The Leprechaun" sponsored by Chevrolet.

Durwood finds that a visiting leprechaun, Brian O'Brian, oddly enough ISN'T one of Samantha's weirdo friends but one of his family's friends. Brian has come to reclaim his last pot of gold that he had hidden in a fireplace which was transported from Ireland to America by the wealthy Mr. Robinson. Without his pot o'gold Brian has no magic powers.

Durwood doesn't believe the story but then finds that Mr. Robinson's company doesn't do any advertising and would bring a great deal of revenue to McMann and Tate if he were to get the account. He goes to meet with him and sees that the fireplace was transported to America brick by brick with the original soot.

Later that night Brian breaks in and tries to reclaim the gold but is caught and thrown in jail. Samantha decides to break him free and help get his gold back. When she shows up at Mr. Robinson's with Brian he can't find his gold and Samantha thinks that maybe Durwood was right about Brian being a phony. Mr. Robinson happens in on them and tells them he does have a pot of gold. Brian reveals his leprechaunishness to Mr. Robinson who happens to believe him as his mother was Irish. Robinson agrees to give the pot of gold back but only if Brian agrees to be the symbol for his company in the advertising which he gives to McMann and Tate.

I didn't enjoy this one and like "Fastest Gun on Madison Avenue" and "The Horse's Mouth" it ranks amongst my least favorite of Season Two. I counted and the word "grand" was OVERUSED ten times in this episode. I would have to say the other leprechaun episode from Season Six is better than this one, though this did have some charm to it. However, why is a leprechaun as big as a normal man? And Samantha seems absolutely enthralled by Brian, to a fault.

It's also very corny, and most likely impossible, for Mr. Robinson to have been able to transport the fireplace across the ocean with the cobwebs and soot intact. I did like when Brian changed the big dogs into Chihuahuas.

Mr. Robinson was played by Parley Baer in his first of eight appearances on *Bewitched*. He would later voice Ernie, the Keebler Elf in the popular Keebler Cookie commercials.

Agnes Moorehead's movie *The Singing Nun* starring good friend Debbie Reynolds opened today in theaters.

The next evening *The Donna Reed Show* ended its eight year run on ABC.

MARCH 24, 1966

It was on this night that ABC aired Episode #64: "Double Split."

Samantha attends a function at a client's house with Durwood. He asks Sam to try to make friends with the client's snooty daughter, Miss Kabaker. When Miss Kabaker proves to be more of a "witch" than Samantha, the WITCH in Samantha comes out and she twitches a canapé in her face. At home Durwood is furious at his wife's apparent lack of self-control and they get into a huge fight. To make matters worse, at the office the next day Larry insults Samantha prompting Durwood to insult Louise all ending with Durwood quitting.

Meanwhile Samantha and Louise realize that Durwood and Larry's argument caused unnecessary words to be said in the heat of the moment and they discuss ways they can get their husbands to speak again. Durwood also lines up an interview with Ames Advertising which Samantha sabotages by having her husband revert to child talk with Mr. Ames. And he ends up spraying Mr. Ames with the fire extinguisher.

Well, he's had it with Samantha and her voodoo and when Durwood gets home she suggests he not stay there that evening. He goes to the club and at the same time Louise suggests to Larry that he stay the night at the same club. Samantha makes it so that both end up in the same room and in a very risqué-for-the-60s move, in the SAME BED! (Just think, not even Rob and Laura Petrie were ever in the same bed…well, maybe once). Larry and Durwood talk it over and realize that they have the best wives in the world and they go home to reconcile with their wives (who happened to be playing with an Ouija board).

I LOVE this episode! It's one of the better Sam-Durwood fight episodes, especially in the bed when it seems as though Samantha is using all the will-power she can muster not to blast him into smithereens.

Also Dick York has a visibly hard time keeping a straight face when he sprays the client.

Dan Tobin, who plays Mr. Ames, doesn't appear in the credits.

Julie Gregg, Ms. Kabaker, will return next season as Ms. Warbell in "The Crone of Cawdor," looking totally different than she does in this episode.

MARCH 31, 1966

It was on this night ABC preempted both *Bewitched* and *Peyton Place* to air a one hour color special entitled *This Proud Land*. According to the *Time Magazine* from January 28, 1966 ABC aired a special with this same name that night in January. It was hosted by Robert Preston and was a show about the Southwest with Greer Garson and Pamela Tiffin pointing out some of the sights. But *Bewitched* will return next week with a very spooky episode entitled "Disappearing Samantha" in which a witch hunter makes Samantha and her mother disappear against their will!

The night before, Dick Sargent appeared on *Bob Hope Presents the Chrysler Theater: Brilliant Benjamin Briggs*.

On April 4, 1966, Agnes Moorehead guested on Art Linkletter's *Hollywood Talent Scouts*.

APRIL 7, 1966

It was on this night that *Bewitched* returned after being pre-empted last week with an AWESOME episode, #65: "Disappearing Samantha" sponsored by Quaker Oats.

Durwood tries to attend a lecture given by one of McMann and Tate's new clients without inviting Samantha. And he has good cause: the client is Osgood Rightmire, a man whose career is to debunk the "myth" of witchcraft and anything associated with it. In fact, the reason he is associated with McMann and Tate is because he's written a new book about witchcraft which they will publicize. Anyway, Samantha finds out about what the lecture is and tells Durwood she wouldn't miss it for the world.

During the lecture Osgood makes several disparaging remarks about witches and those associated with them and finishes by saying that there is no such thing as witchcraft and if there is he offers himself up as a target for any witch in the audience. Samantha obliges by twitching him into a stumble which causes him to crash into his visual aids and the podium. He then asserts that it was just an unfortunate accident and then proceeds to say a spell which he says would cause any witch to disappear… and she does! Well, she becomes invisible against her will, anyhow. But not permanently: her visibility flickers on and off like a bad light bulb.

At home this continues and they consult with Endora who says that she needs to know what the spell is so that she can find one to reverse it.

Durwood goes to visit Osgood to get the spell but he won't give it up and tells him he must wait to see it in the upcoming book.

Endora decides that she'll force Osgood to come over and casts a spell on his car to make it drive to 1164 Morning Glory Circle. Osgood is accompanied by his "niece" Beverly, a woman much younger than he. Also at the Stephens' are Larry, Louise and a magazine publisher who is going to do an article about the book.

During the course of the evening Samantha and Endora's attempts to get the spell out of Osgood are futile. It also becomes apparent that the spell isn't necessary as Endora begins to 'flicker' in and out. They decide to test him to see if he is a warlock by giving him an 'Ordeal by Fire' which involves a lot of HOT sauces and peppers and a little bit of tomato juice. He fails the test which leads them to believe that he is wearing a charm or an amulet that has magic powers. They find that he is wearing a ring which he says never leaves his hand, until Endora zaps it off him in a shower of sparks. Once they get the ring, Samantha destroys it and twitches up a new one and they send Osgood and his "niece" on their way.

This marks Bernard Fox's first appearance on *Bewitched*. And because he was so well liked by Elizabeth Montgomery and Bill Asher they created the character of Dr. Bombay, the warlock doctor, for him so that he could come back. His first appearance as Dr. Bombay is at the end of the Third Season. This appearance is also Mr. Fox's favorite of his many appearances on *Bewitched*. A group of fans had the extreme rare pleasure of actually watching this episode with Mr. Fox and his family at the *Bewitched* Fanfare in Los Angeles in 2010 when Mr. Fox was honored with the Fan Appreciation Award for Favorite Recurring Character for Dr. Bombay. I presented him with the award as he is my favorite male character from the series. In his acceptance speech Mr. Fox shared memories of this episode including a very funny and risqué happening caused by his pants being much too big in the behind which caused the front to bunch up when he would sit down. He had a scene with Nina Wayne (Beverly) on the couch at 1164 and while they were waiting for their scene to be filmed he noticed her looking down at his crotch. Quite embarrassed but realizing there was no way to ignore the situation he broke into an Irish brogue and said to her, "Looks like the wee little fellow has taken a liking to you!"

Beverly Wilson was played by Nina Wayne. Her sister, Carol, will later appear on *Bewitched* as Bunny in the Sixth Season episode "A Bunny for Tabitha." They look and sound remarkably like one another though they are not twins.

This episode is one of the spookier episodes of the series. I remember when I first watched it I was totally astounded that a seemingly mere mortal would have that type of power, not only over Samantha but Endora too.

I also think it's funny when Durwood runs into invisible Samantha and says he must've hit some thick air. What sort of explanation is that? I would've just said I tripped on the carpet.

Of course Bernard Fox is brilliant in this! He plays smarmy very well and I love at the end when Samantha makes him walk into the wall.

I also think Samantha and Endora looked very beautiful in this episode, though the colorizers slopped the blue eye-shadow WAAAAAAAAAAAAY too thick on Endora, especially in that opening scene.

It's also funny when Osgood repeats the spell to make witches disappear and Larry says, "Must've not worked. Louise is still here." I also thought it strange that all though the people sitting behind them reacted a little to Samantha disappearing they didn't react big enough. I would've freaked out had I been them!

Speaking of Louise, this would be Irene Vernon's last episode as she says she quit to pursue a career in real estate.

I did think that Samantha's lower half disappearing was a little ridiculous considering she only does that the one time when they are walking from the car and the rest of the episode she full on disappears.

It's also weird that Endora mentions borrowing the books from Aunt Clara yet we won't see Aunt Clara until the second episode of the Third Season and by this time she hasn't been around for like ten or more episodes.

I also wonder what run-ins Samantha or her family or friends had with Osgood before, considering she knew about him or of him.

All in all, EXCELLENT episode!

I should also mention that there is a witch hunter in the movie *Bell, Book, and Candle* (1958) who gets the brunt of the witch's fury just like Osgood did. That movie is considered one of *Bewitched*'s "parents" along with *I Married a Witch* (1942).

APRIL 14, 1966

It was on this night that ABC aired the first two part episode of *Bewitched*, Episode #66: "Follow That Witch" part one.

As Durwood is handling the Robbins Baby Food account, Mr. Robbin's assistant hires a private detective — Charlie Leach by name — to look into Durwood's private life to make sure he is "Robbins Baby Food people." At first Mr. Leach doesn't find any dirt on Durwood but Mr. Barkley, the assistant, feels that more research should be done. Mr. Leach decides to speak with the neighbors around 1164 and ends up speaking to Harriet Kravitz, Abner's sister, who is house-sitting while Abner and Gladys are visiting Gladys' mother. Harriet has heard all the wild stories about the house across the street and relates them to Mr. Leach who is quite wary of this woman. He decides to investigate for himself and happens to see Samantha zap together a broken dish. He also catches her making Tabatha's baby carriage rock by itself and when he tries to figure it out Samantha makes the carriage jump on him.

He has an indomitable spirit and once again goes back to investigate but this time Samantha really lets him have it by zapping him to the top of a forty story building. Once Mr. Leach has recovered he decides that he does believe that Samantha is a witch and wants to use this to his advantage by getting her to zap up anything he wants if she doesn't want him spilling the beans on her.

Stay tuned next week for part two of "Follow that Witch!"

The character of Harriet Kravitz was originally intended as just temporary as everyone thought that Alice Pearce just needed some time off. Unfortunately she passed away a few weeks after this episode finished filming. I wish that Mary Grace Canfield (Harriet) had just been cast as the next Gladys as I thought she did a very good job in this role.

This episode and its second part are probably my favorites out of the Second Season. I think the story is very engaging and for this first part to end with Samantha seemingly caught between a rock and a hard place is awesome.

I also like the background music, especially the music used when Charlie is trying to leave the Kravitz's after Harriet tells him all about the flying babies and ostriches appearing in the living room.

When Mr. Barkley tells Charlie Leach that he'd like Stephens's wife shadowed and you hear the audience member exclaim, "Uh-oh!" that happens to be heard a lot on the canned laughter used on *I Love Lucy* where Bill Asher directed many famous episodes.

When Harriet mentions how Gladys said she saw the bottom half of her disappear, I just figured it was Harriet getting Gladys' stories mixed up considering Gladys saw the bottom half of Aunt Clara disappear. I think it's cooler now knowing that it was supposed to be a mention of Samantha from "Disappearing Samantha." And another mix-up that I think Harriet makes is when she says that Gladys saw an ostrich in the living room. The only time an ostrich was over there (that we saw anyway) was when Aunt Clara zapped one up in the Square Green Spots episode, but that was up in the bedroom. The flying baby was seen in "My Baby, the Tycoon."

This is the first of eight appearances by Steve Franken on the series. He joined the *Bewitched* Fanfare in 2008 as a featured guest where he did a Q&A session and posed for pics and signed autographs. He enjoyed his time so much that when he found that we were going to be having another Fanfare in 2010 he asked if we would mind if he came again. Of course, he was more than welcome.

APRIL 21, 1966

It was on this night that ABC aired Episode #67: "Follow That Witch" part two.

After being turned into a parrot, private investigator Charlie Leach requests that Samantha meet him at his apartment later that evening so that she can comply with his wishes for various riches. He promises to not even tell his wife about Samantha if she concedes to his demands.

Samantha shows up and complies with his demands in her own way: she zaps up a car in the middle of his fifth floor walk-up apartment (but later zaps it down to the street, something I wouldn't have done considering who I was dealing with). She also zaps up some new fancy duds for him, oversized at first, but then perfectly fit after he complains, and pulls a makeover on his apartment. She leaves asking him to never let her see or hear from him again.

Meanwhile, Durwood's secretary Betty advises him that one of her friends, who is a secretary for Little Fish Eyes a.k.a. Mr. Barkley, told her that Durwood's private life was being investigated…not only he but his wife! Durwood rushes home and learns from Samantha all about Mr. Leach and she explains she only gave into his demands to make sure that Durwood kept his job. Durwood explains that he does not like the under-handedness of the client in doing this so he and Samantha got to Mr. Robbin's office to resign from the account.

Of course, Mr. Robbins wasn't aware of his assistant hiring a private detective and with Samantha's help he confesses to his real plans, to take over the company from Mr. Robbins, who promptly fires him.

Back at home Durwood isn't feeling right about Mr. Leach getting away with blackmailing Samantha and so she says she'll go see him one more time, invisibly, to take back all that she had given him.

Over at Mr. Leach's he and his wife are grooving on all the new niceties until their furniture starts falling apart and a big rushing wind comes in and strips them of their clothes, all courtesy of invisible Samantha. Charlie knows it's Samantha and when he tries to drive over to her house she shrinks his car. He eventually arrives there and tells her that he'll still blow the whistle on her no matter what she does. Not to be pushed over again she zaps him straight to the middle of a bull fight in Old Mexico and Charlie swears that when he gets back to Nueva York he is "going to pay that witch lady a visit!"

This is the first time during the Second Season that we see Samantha in her flying suit. I LOVE these episodes! I would totally give this episode three and a half stars. It would've been four but the table breaking beforehand and Charlie's apartment not looking really ritzy is why I docked half a point.

I really like when Samantha gets cheeky with Mr. Barkley and corrects him by saying, "Sorceress. Why use the fancy names when the plain ones will do? I like the simple old term "witch"!" It makes me wonder if before her craze with mortals she used to tease them and was slipping back into that mode.

I also thought Elizabeth Montgomery looked BEAUTIFUL! I also like the lighting they did on her when she's in the apartment with Charmaine and Charlie.

The car being in the apartment is brilliant! But it makes me wonder if it had really happened, don't you think the floor would've caved in?

I really love when Samantha zaps Charlie to Mexico by saying, "As we say in Old Mexico…" and then she waves her hands like a Spanish dancer and snaps. His scenes coming back from Mexico were shot right behind the facade of 1164 and its neighbor. It still looks the same today, though, of course, the sign isn't there. And again, the music they play when Charlie is coming back from Mexico is my FAVORITE *Bewitched* background music so far.

Anyway, I LOVE this second part of this episode.

APRIL 28, 1966

It was on this night that ABC aired Episode #68: "A Bum Rap."

Durwood leaves for work saying that his Uncle Albert is coming to visit and asks Samantha to make sure Uncle Albert feels welcome when he arrives. Meanwhile, a couple of beggars, Mr. Horace Dillaway and Mr. William Dunn, former Vaudeville showmen, have shown up in Morning Glory Circle panhandling. Horace knocks at 1164 and Samantha just assumes that he is Uncle Albert and invites him in. During the day Durwood calls home and says he thinks it may be nice if Sam were to set out a picture of Uncle Albert that he had sent. When Samantha finds it, she realizes that she is not dealing with the real Uncle Albert, but as she's got to know him throughout the day she feels that she just can't throw him out. Durwood comes home and she convinces him to go along with it until the real Uncle Albert arrives. (Actually he had already arrived but Horace had answered the door and told him that the Stephens moved to Westport, which is one reason it's so hard to determine exactly where 1164 is).

William tells Horace that they are going to go through with their plan of robbing the house that night and Horace concedes until they are up the road a bit when he tells William that he just feels terrible about what they've done and he decides to break up their partnership. When Samantha and Durwood wake to find their house completely bare she magically suggests to William that he bring back all the goods. When he does return Samantha suggests that the two start up their act again.

I'd only give this episode one star because Tabatha is so cute! This episode gets my vote for "The Scariest Episode" out of the whole series simply for Samantha allowing Horace to be left alone with Tabatha, even if she did believe he was Durwood's uncle not to mention she just had Charlie Leach snooping around Tabatha's carriage and that didn't settle too well with her. I did find it cute when a close up of Tabatha is shown in the kitchen and she is giggling. It was precious!

I do like that we get to see 1164's living room sans furniture, something we rarely got to see.

There is also a little bit of a mystery about when this episode aired because some listings have it as Episode #68 and others as #69. The same goes for the next episode "Divided He Stands." However a *TV Guide* from Toronto for that week lists this episode so I'll stick with that.

Elizabeth Montgomery looked really beautiful!

I also really like it when Harriet says, "You're a BUM!"

MAY 5, 1966

It was on this night that ABC aired Episode #69: "Divided He Stands."

Durwood and Samantha's plans for a trip to Miami are thwarted when Larry requests that Durwood cancel it to help avoid the catastrophe of losing the Stern Chemical account after another executive on that account falls ill and can't finish his work on the campaign. Endora thinks it's because Durwood is such a stuff shirt he couldn't possibly have fun, but Samantha tells her that she's only seen one side of him, that Durwood has a fun and carefree side. When Samantha goes to unpack from the trip they never went on, Endora decides that rather than have Samantha be disappointed she'll make it so that Durwood can go and she pops into the den and with the wave of her arms she splits Durwood into two! One Durwood is all business and he remains in the den while the other bounds out of the den looking for his suntan oil. He tells Samantha that he's decided he doesn't care about the campaign and that he wants to spend his time with her living it up in Miami. She is confused at first but when she sees how enthusiastic and excited about the trip he is she goes upstairs to repack. A little later Fun Durwood asks where his book on surfing got to and Samantha remembers that she last saw it in the den so she goes into retrieve it but is startled to find Durwood in there! She asks him what he's doing and he reminds her that he's hard at work. As she realizes that she last saw him upstairs she asks when he saw her last and he tells her a little while ago when he had told her they had to stay home. It then dawns on her that there must be two of him and she leaves to call upon her mother. Endora pops in pleased with herself and she suggests that there really isn't anything wrong with Samantha going to Miami with Fun Durwood as she agrees that Durwood needed a vacation in the first place, plus Work Durwood can get the work done. Samantha agrees and she and Durwood, Fun version, fly off to Miami.

In Miami, Durwood cannot stop having fun. He wants to dance and swim and all the hotel guests love him. However, Samantha gets tired of him very quickly especially when he asks Samantha to twitch up some more ice for their party. She zaps everyone back to their rooms and tells him what her mother has been up to and calls for Endora to appear to confirm what she did. Realizing that Work Durwood must be driving Larry as crazy as she was feeling with Fun Durwood, she zaps to New York to the restaurant where Larry, Mr. Stern, and Work Durwood are and she asks to speak to him alone. His associates are relieved and before Durwood can protest anymore, she pops them back to Miami. Endora admits it'll be much harder to put them back together because they've both got to want it or they have to run into each other. Tricking them, Samantha offers to give each Durwood what he wants based on who reaches the door first. They both make a mad dash for the door and crash into each other becoming one again.

Back at home Samantha admits to Endora that she can't stand Durwood's work side, nor his fun side, but it's the whole Durwood she loves and that she would never want him to be anyone else.

This episode is DEFINITELY four star material! Dick York really should've got an Emmy for it. It's such a great idea because haven't there been times where you wish you could be two people to get more done?

I love when Samantha asks Fun Durwood (whoever thought we would say THAT?!) if he wants to get back to the party and he says, "Crazy!"

I wish when Samantha had popped out to go get Work Durwood that the scene had gone on longer to show Endora dancing with Fun Durwood! Wouldn't that have been awesome?!

Samantha is also very cute when she's answering Fun Durwood's questions about going to Miami. I love how excited she gets and how cute he is with her telling her that she's got the most beautiful green eyes and such! Sam is also cute when she's dancing.

Also of note is the fact that they use Jeannie's smoking-into-her-bottle sound effect for when Samantha reverses Durwood's dive.

And DAMMIT, Samantha should've been in a swimsuit! She very rarely ever was!

The opening scene was filmed most likely at the end of the last season as Samantha looks pregnant and if you listen closely you can hear the register of Agnes' voice lower from the rest of the episode. This is also the first time we see a character smoking a hookah. When Endora splits Durwood an animation of sparkles is used which is the third time animation was used for the effects.

Samantha utters the most ironic line of the series when she says that she wouldn't want Durwood to be anyone else. Of course, three years later he would be someone else when he's played by Dick Sargent. And speaking of Dick Sargent, the first episode he filmed was a remake of this episode, "Samantha's Better Halves."

This episode was also used as the basis for one of the skits on the 2002 NBC show *The Rerun Show* where comedic actors would do condensed versions of classic TV shows with a twist. In that version, the fun Durwood turned out to be a black man in the vein of Chris Rock.

MAY 12, 1966

It was on this night that ABC originally aired Episode #70: "Man's Best Friend."

Durwood has been keeping track of the days that Samantha has been witchcraft-free, as though she were trying to break a drug habit. She is at twenty-nine days without using her magic or having any of her witchy relatives/friends show up which has been easy as Endora is off skin-diving for a month. She is quite pleased with herself when out of the blue an obnoxious young warlock pops in. His name is Rodney and he's got a crush on Samantha and has had one since she used to babysit him (against her will). He insists that he wants her to join him and won't listen to her when she tells him she's married. She threatens him with telling his mother on him but when he finds out she can't use witchcraft he devises a plot to get her to use it thinking that Durwood won't want to be with her anymore.

Durwood comes home and says that they have a new guest, a dog he found outside. At first Samantha is in love with the dog until he starts eating her newly made chocolate cake and she realizes it's Rodney in disguise. She then tells her husband she doesn't want to keep the dog anymore but doesn't explain why. Rodney's plan is beginning to work. Later on he answers the door when Harriet Kravitz comes to call and tells her that he and Samantha are having a snort together. She tells Durwood about him and he questions Samantha about their guest. She tells him there wasn't anyone at their home but he insists there had to be if Harriet saw him. Samantha finally confesses that it was Rodney and that he had been bothering her and that he is really the dog. Durwood says he doesn't believe her and they argue with him ending up going to bed in the den at 8:30! Of course, Durwood had a master plan. Being the loving, devoted husband that he is, he believed Samantha and just wanted to catch Rodney changing back, which he does. He tells Samantha that Rodney's visit doesn't count and she almost makes the month mark until Durwood starts choking on a drink and she zaps up some water for him.

Rodney is played by Oscar-winner Richard Dreyfus in one of his first, if not THE first, TV roles.

This would also be the last time we see Harriet Kravitz.

I would only give this two stars. Rodney is really irritating and even more irritating is Durwood being so gung-ho about no witchcraft. Even at the end when he's choking on his drink he has to sputter out his disappointment about Samantha using magic to zap up water for him.

This would be remade into the Seventh Season's "Samantha's Pet Warlock."

It was also on this night that CBS aired the last episode of *The Munsters* after only two seasons, seventy episodes. However this would not be the last time we see the spooky family this year.

MAY 19, 1966

It was on this night ABC aired what was essentially the third, and last, part of the Charlie Leach episodes, Episode #71: "The Catnapper."

Just as he said in his last appearance, Charlie Leach, now back in New York, pays "that witch lady" a visit again and as he's snooping discovers that Samantha's mother is also a witch! He tells his wife, Charmaine, that now they will be able to really have all they want as he will get proof that Samantha and her mother are witches.

Meanwhile, Durwood is assigned to the United Cosmetics campaign and has to work with Toni Devlin, the head of the firm. When he takes her to lunch and Endora and Samantha see them, Endora insists that Durwood is having an affair. Samantha has faith that is not the case and tries to get Endora to see her point of view. When Toni comes over to the Stephenses to discuss the campaign Endora finds it to be too much and turns Toni into a cat! Of course, Charlie sees this and when nobody is looking catnaps Toni. He tells Samantha that he wants one million dollars in return for Toni. Samantha tells him that she isn't that powerful but she can give him something else: a money tree. It blooms $100 bills, ten each day. He says he'll return the cat the next day when he sees that the tree is blooming. Samantha says that's fine but she requests that he make sure to feed Toni at nine promptly. He agrees.

At nine Samantha turns Charlie into a mouse, which Toni the cat chases. Not wanting Charlie to really get hurt, Samantha changes him back and he promptly calls her. She tells him that she will change him into a mouse permanently unless he returns the cat. He complies with her request. But now, Endora is nowhere to be found to change Toni back and she is due for a meeting. Samantha flies around the world looking for her and finally finds her in Tibet meeting with the Lord High Lama. Meanwhile Durwood has brought the cat into the office in the hopes that she'll regain her human form in time for a meeting. He receives a phone call from Tibet and Endora changes Toni back over the phone.

Charlie, still thinking that he can use the money he had plucked off the tree finds that they have turned back to leaves. He vows he will get even with Samantha…but unfortunately this is the last we ever see of Charlie.

I give it three stars. It wasn't as good as Charlie Leach's previous appearances and all though I do think the majority of the flying sequence was CHEESY, I did like the thought of being able to see Samantha fly. The very first part where you can just see her upper half is way cool. And then did you notice "her" shadow over the Coliseum?

The beginning had no place in the episode and would've definitely worked better at the end. This is also the first time that we see Samantha in that white nightgown that's so sexy! I hated that she got out of bed to turn off the light. I either would've twitched it off or I would've pushed him 'til he awoke. Screw getting out of bed to turn off the light!

I believe the pompom belted other nightgown is really an aqua green. She wears it in "Sam's Spooky Chair" and in "I'd Rather Twitch than Fight."

I thought Toni Devlin was very beautiful, in fact one of the most beautiful female clients McMann and Tate ever had, but she was boring! I really liked that Durwood told her she was resistible, though why was he putting his arm around her?

I also thought it strange that both Endora and Samantha used wordless spells to change Toni and Charlie into animals but yet had to use words in order to change them back.

I really thought Charmaine was funny in this episode, aside from the weird cross-eyed "What have I done to deserve this?!" What was with that?

I liked that Samantha tricked Charlie into thinking she couldn't zap up a million dollars and instead gives him the money tree.

I wish Charlie would've popped back in every so often but I can see how it would get old after awhile. I mean, he threatens her with spilling her secret, she does something for him and then takes it back. And it was really odd that the very last scene was ONLY Charlie and Charmaine. I believe that's the first time only guest cast have been in that scene.

Three days before, the Beach Boys released their iconic album *Pet Sounds* which included such hits as "Sloop John B," "God Only Knows," and "Wouldn't It Be Nice."

That same day the Reverend Dr. Martin Luther King, Jr. made his first public speech about the Vietnam War.

On May 22, 1966 the Emmy Awards were presented with Alice Pearce winning for Outstanding Performance by an Actress in a Supporting Role in a Comedy and Bill Asher won for Outstanding Directorial Achievement in a Comedy. Liz actually presented the award for Alice Pearce to her husband Paul Davis. Elizabeth Montgomery was nominated for Outstanding Continued Performance by an Actress in a Leading Role in a Comedy but lost to Mary Tyler Moore who was on her way out from *the Dick Van Dyke Show*, Agnes Moorehead was nominated for Outstanding Performance by an Actress in a Supporting Role in a Comedy, and *Bewitched* was nominated for Outstanding Comedy Series but lost to *The Dick Van Dyke Show*.

MAY 26, 1966

It was on this night that ABC aired Episode #72: "What Every Young Man Should Know."

When Durwood catches Samantha using witchcraft to fix a broken statue that his Uncle Albert gave him he questions her promise "to love, honor, and no witchcraft." She tells him she just did it because she knew that he prized the gift from Uncle Albert, and besides, he knew she was a witch when he married her. Not quite, as Durwood reminds her, she didn't reveal her true identity until their honeymoon. When she asks him if he would've married her had he known beforehand he hesitates in saying yes which makes her question if maybe their marriage isn't as strong as she thinks.

Endora overhears their conversation and offers to send Samantha back in the past so that she could see what really would've happened had she told him she was a witch before their marriage. Samantha agrees only after Endora says Durwood won't remember the "new" past.

Samantha is sent back to a night where she was going to fix dinner for Durwood at his apartment, a night upon which he proposed. Originally she had planned on telling him then but she chickened out. In the new past she shows up to his apartment without the dinner items. As he is telling her how much he loves her she decides to tell him that she is a witch. He doesn't believe her until she twitches up a feast. She asks him if he cares that she's a witch and he says "no" but when she goes to hug him he freaks out and runs away. Endora, thinking that Samantha has her answer, brings Samantha back. Samantha is furious that he would be so chicken but she's also mad realizing now what she thought might be true: that their marriage really wasn't that strong. Durwood comes down the stairs when he hears all the commotion and she tells him what she has seen. When he asks what happened after he ran out in the past Samantha realizes she didn't see that far. He insists that he would've came back so Samantha requests that Endora send both of them back to see what happened after he ran out.

Back in the past Durwood realizes that he reacted harshly. He realizes that even though it is different being in love with a witch, that he IS in love. When Larry sees that he is so distraught he wants to know what is wrong and Durwood tells him he wouldn't believe him. Larry keeps pestering him and so when Durwood says that Samantha would tell him she was a witch if she were there Samantha shows up and does a disappearing act in front of Larry so that he knows Durwood is being honest. He also asks her if she could sway all the clients over to their agency and she tells him she could. She disappears when she's had enough but Durwood knows he hasn't had enough of her so, later, he calls Samantha to apologize. When she hangs up on him he thinks that he really has blown it until she pops in with a big hug and kiss for him. Just as he is about to propose Larry shows up and begins talking about how they are going to use Samantha to get financial gain. She is furious and hurt once again and at that point Samantha and Durwood return to the present. Endora thinks that now she has really proven that the mortal marriage was a sham but Durwood tells her that he would've never used Samantha's powers like that. She believes him but he also comments about how he might not have proposed had he met Endora beforehand.

So once more they are sent back and Durwood throws Larry out and goes to propose once more when Endora pops in. Samantha introduces them and Endora is disgusted by him and zaps him out of the room. He comes back and she once again zaps him further away. He still comes back and tells her that no matter what she does he will always come back, that he loves Samantha and NOTHING will keep him from her. Endora leaves and Durwood finally proposes.

Back in the present Endora realizes that there really is more to this marriage than meets the eye and she leaves.

This is one of my all-time favorite episodes as we are given insight into what Durwood and Sam's life was before the pilot episode. I do wish, though, that the makeup and hair department had tried harder to match Liz's makeup and hair from the first episode so it looked more like they really were in the past, but that is just a minor gripe.

I also didn't like that it's supposed to be Samantha going into the past but the way they filmed it, it was more like she didn't go anywhere but simply went there in her head, which may be what they wanted to convey but I always thought that she actually went to that alternate past.

I love Samantha showing her powers to Larry. I really like her clap to pop out. And I also like when she suggests that Larry is "bewitched" to meet her. That's the second time the word has been used on the series.

I believe it is the Truth god that she breaks. It's cool that they still had it though I thought Endora zapped it away at the end of its episode "Speak the Truth."

The day before, the famous Gateway Arch in St. Louis, MO was dedicated by Vice President Hubert Humphrey and U.S. Secretary of the Interior Stewart Udall.

JUNE 2, 1966

It was on this night that ABC aired Episode #73: "The Girl with the Golden Nose."

Durwood feels that he has a hit a plateau in his career and feels that were he to get the Waterhouse account, a really big client of McMann and Tate's, it would signify progress. But he has already been told that he won't be on that account and he shares his frustration with Samantha, who tries to remind him of all the success he's had so far, not only in his career but home life too, not to mention he's still young yet. After he leaves to get ready for work Louise Tate phones and tells Samantha that Larry changed his mind about the Waterhouse account and that Durwood will now be in charge of it. She requests that Samantha let Larry spring the news when Durwood arrives at the office.

When Durwood does arrive at the office he has worked himself up into a fine dither and demands that Larry give him the account. Larry agrees and Durwood is flabbergasted! He then thinks Samantha may have magicked Larry into making that decision and he is furious. When Waterhouse does arrive, Larry tells Durwood that Waterhouse is a conservative old school man which gives Durwood the idea to be totally obnoxious in an effort to lose the account, which he feels he got by witchcraft. Waterhouse tells Durwood that he doesn't like his personality or his style but he does like his ideas which further proves to Durwood that there is magic afoot.

After having a drink with his friend Dave he decides that maybe it's time to relinquish the ban on witchcraft, after all Samantha has been living Durwood's mortal life for the past two years, maybe it's time to live her way as a thank-you. Believing now that he has his wife's powers behind him he starts believing he is invincible especially when he feels that a rain storm will let up before he leaves for work (which it does) and when he correctly guesses that Secretary Betty's birthplace is actually different than what she has been told. When Larry tells Samantha that Durwood has gone off the deep-end, claiming that he can make the sun shine in the middle of the night she decides it's time to show him that she has nothing to do with this.

Durwood arrives home and finds his home transformed into "the Taj-mahal." Samantha tells him that it had been her plan to see how far she could go in using her magic to help him and when she saw that he was all right with it she decided that it was pointless to keep it hidden. As they talk she tells him that all the success he has ever had while they have been married has been due strictly to her. He knows that there are many times where the success he achieved was strictly due to his hard work and ideas. She then acknowledges that he is right and that she didn't have anything to do with his successes except supporting him in all he does. And at that she twitches the home back to its normal glory circle…oh…sorry.

I don't particularly care for this episode. It seems like we've seen this all pretty much before in "Help, Help, Don't Save Me" when he accuses her of using witchcraft for the ideas she gave him. You would've thought that he would remember that time, especially since it was such a big account.

I will say that this episode seems to look like it was part of the Third Season, what with Sam's hairdo, the nightgowns, and Endora floating in the living room. I think that's the first time we see her floating inside. Floating is something that will be seen more often in the seasons to come and it is a rather cool effect.

When they show Durwood sitting at the kitchen table behind him is supposed to be the corner where the stove cabinets and the sink cabinets meet but behind him it just shows the stove cabinet joining to a plain wall. And another one, though it was necessary for the shot, is at the first when Samantha is wearing the coat, they show a full body shot but in order to do that they had to take out the sink cabinets.

I think Samantha was pining over the coat because when she was living as a witch she had all the nicest clothes all the time. I think maybe she was getting "homesick" a little.

One of the other reasons I don't like this episode is I think Durwood's acting up in front of the client is SO annoying and embarrassing I can't hardly watch it. And I HATE how he says, "Brass tacks! Brass tacks!!"

This is also the last episode to be filmed for the Second Season, though not the last to be shown as the season finale will air next week. It is also the last episode to be filmed in black and white.

The day before CBS aired the last episode of *The Dick Van Dyke Show* after five seasons.

JUNE 9, 1966

Today ABC aired the Second Season finale of *Bewitched*, Episode #74: "Prodigy."

As Durwood and Samantha get ready to go over to the Kravitz's to watch Gladys' brother Louis play violin on television they discuss what a great occasion this is as Louis has been apprehensive about playing in public ever since his knickers fell to his knees at Carnegie Hall when he was just a child. They remember the last time Louis was in town when Samantha helped him to regain his confidence…

When Samantha was pregnant, Gladys had invited the Stephenses to meet her brother. Louis claimed to be staying with them until his next engagement but Abner thinks Louis is a moocher until Louis spontaneously begins to beautifully play the violin. Samantha is delighted and decides that he should play at the hospital benefit. Louis isn't too sure of that remembering his ordeal at Carnegie Hall but Samantha says that's a bunch of nonsense, that he'll do perfectly. She even offers their home for him to practice in when Abner tires of always hearing the violin now.

While watching him practice Louis decides the only way he can get out of it is to break his violin which he tries to do by slamming it on the stereo but Samantha twitches it to be indestructible…for that moment anyhow. Because a little later Abner comes over and accidentally sits on it and breaks it! No problem, however, as Samantha just twitches up a new Stradivarius violin. His nerves still get the best of him and he tries to leave town but Samantha uses her magic to bring him back and then she gives him a boost with her magic to play beautifully at the benefit.

Later on he is asked to perform on TV when what do you know, his knickers fall down!

I didn't think it was such a great episode. It was sort of boring to me but it was AWESOME seeing Alice Pearce again! It was sad and happy at the same time.

I really laughed hard the first time I saw Gladys tell Abner to hit her! Not that it's funny for a man to hit his wife, just the way she says it and seems to really want it!

When Samantha shows Durwood how magical it is to turn the lights on and off it made me think that the Ephron sisters may have got that bit in the *Bewitched* movie about the dimming lights from this episode. I actually really like that part in the movie.

I hated how the "pretty pony" was colored, it was all wrong! It will appear in the very next episode "Nobody's Perfect" which was filmed in 'culluh.'

This episode marks the last time we would see Alice Pearce as Gladys Kravitz as she had passed away in March. This episode had apparently been saved to air at the end of the season. I should like to think they would've prefaced the episode with an "In Memory of…" but I really don't know.

This also marks the last episode broadcast in black and white as by the next September all shows broadcast would be in glorious 'culluh!'

And it would also be the last time that Tabatha would be seen with brunette hair.

Bewitched ended this season at #7 in the ratings.

About a month previously, on May 12, *The Munsters* aired their last episode. Six days after this *Bewitched* episode aired a feature film about *The Munsters* entitled *Munster, Go Home* opened in U.S. theaters! This movie was highly publicized but failed to capture audiences.

This film gave audiences a chance to see the family in TECHNICOLOR and, to me, it proved that they were better in black and white.

It was also the appearance of a new actress for Marilyn, Debbie Watson. The producers of the film felt that Pat Priest, who was thirty at the time (but in no way looked it) was too old, so they recast the part with seventeen year old Debbie.

John Carradine plays Cruikshank, the butler. He wasn't in *Bewitched* but he did play Jed Carta in the episode of *Thriller* entitled "Masquerade" that Elizabeth Montgomery was in. On *The Munsters* TV series he also played Mr. Gateman, Herman's boss.

Bernard Fox plays Squire Moresby. Of course, he is best known to *Bewitched* audiences as Dr. Bombay.

Jeanne Arnold plays Grace, Freddie's sister. She will later play Mrs. Norton in *Bewitched* Episode #243: "Samantha's Magic Sitter" and Mrs. Hickman in Episode #248: "Tabitha's First Day of School."

Cliff Norton plays the drunk Herbert on the ship. He was seen earlier on *Bewitched* in Episode #16: "It's Magic" and will later make more appearances on *Bewitched*.

Diana Chesney plays Mrs. Moresby. She played Agatha in *Bewitched* Episode #50: "Speak the Truth" and will play Aunt Enchantra in Episode #242:"Adam, Warlock or Washout."

Arthur Malet plays Alfie. He will be seen on *Bewitched* next season in Episode #95: "The Trial and Error of Aunt Clara" as Judge Bean.

Henry Hunter has an uncredited role in the movie. He was seen as Durwood's Uncle Albert in Episode #68: "A Bum Raps" this past season.

Don Knight also has an uncredited role. He will play Durwood's Scottish cousin Robbie in Season Eight's "Samantha and the Loch Ness Monster."

Laurie Main also has an uncredited role. He was one of Agnes Moorehead's good friends and will show up on *Bewitched* in Season Four's "Samantha's Thanksgiving to Remember" as Francis, one of the judges. He also appears as the Guide in the Henry VIII episodes.

Wow, that's a lot of *Bewitched* ties!

I sometimes wish *Bewitched* had done a feature film during their heyday. The Salem Episodes alone would've made a great one.

The following is the summer re-run schedule. The episode will be listed by number, name, and original airdate.

JUNE 16, 1966

Episode #40: "My Grandson the Warlock" (October 7, 1965)

The day before, the cast and crew finished filming the first color episode "My Friend Ben" though it wouldn't be the first one to be shown in color.

JUNE 23, 1966

Episode #47: "Aunt Clara's Old Flame" (November 25, 1965)

JUNE 30, 1966

Episode #48: "A Strange Little Visitor" (December 2, 1965)

JULY 7, 1966

Episode #41: "The Joker is a Card" (October 14, 1965)

Two days before, Agnes Moorehead appeared on *Mr. Blackwell Presents*, a musical-variety fashion show.

JULY 14, 1966

Episode #42: "Take Two Aspirin and Half a Pint of Porpoise Milk" (October 21, 1965)

JULY 21, 1966

Episode #53: "Maid to Order" (January 6, 1966)

JULY 28, 1966

Episode #54: "And Then There Were Three" (January 13, 1966)

AUGUST 4, 1966

Episode #55: "My Baby the Tycoon" (January 20, 1966)

AUGUST 11, 1966

Episode #64: "Double Split" (March 24, 1966)

AUGUST 18, 1966

Episode #59: "Double Tate" (February 17, 1966)

The day before, the people of France were finally shown *Bewitched* in their native tongue. The show was re-dubbed in French and was called *Ma Sorciere Bien Aimee.*

AUGUST 25, 1966

Episode #58: "The Dancing Bear" (February 10, 1966)

SEPTEMBER 1, 1966

Episode #72: "What Every Young Man Should Know" (May 26, 1966)

SEPTEMBER 8, 1966

Episode #69: "Divided, He Falls" (May 5, 1966)

It was also on this night that Dick Sargent's new TV series *The Tammy Grimes Show* starring Tammy Grimes debuted. He played her twin brother and her character's name was Tamantha. Interestingly enough Tammy was the first choice to play Samantha but she turned it down. Tammy's show was cancelled after only four episodes.

Stay tuned for an all new *Bewitched*, next week, in 'culluh!'

Season 3

SEPTEMBER 15, 1966

On this night we all tuned into ABC, it was a Thursday at 9 PM, and saw what looked like an animated tie-dyed t-shirt with the words in a familiar font saying *"Bewitched* next in color." Of course, it wasn't a surprise as ABC had been advertising all summer long that our favorite show would be appearing in color for the Third Season, but still, the anticipation of seeing our favorite witchly family in color was almost comparable to Christmas Eve! And then it began after three long months...there was Elizabeth Montgomery looking as though she had spent her summer basking on the beaches in Mexico, with beach blonde hair feeding her newest in a line of baby actresses to play Tabatha, yet this baby really looked as if she could be Liz's daughter. And in comes Dick York looking like he may have joined Liz in the tan fest. But back to the episode itself... it was Episode #75: "Nobody's Perfect" kicking off the Third Season of *Bewitched*.

Samantha takes Tabatha to the doctor for a baby check-up only to find out that Tabatha is more perfect than she realized, for in the office as the doctor is telling an anxious Durwood over the phone that he has a perfectly normal baby daughter, Tabatha begins to levitate her toys and the doctor's stethoscope! At home Samantha worries how she is going to break the news to her uptight husband as he didn't take too kindly to the witchcraft when she revealed her own powers. Just then Endora pops in, and when Tabatha levitates a bottle, Endora is absolutely thrilled. Samantha tells Endora that Durwood doesn't know yet and that she wants to tell him but only when the time is right. When Durwood sees some toys floating around he blames Endora who really doesn't care as the joy of having a new witch in the family is just too much.

Later on Durwood invites a client over and when he sees Tabatha he insists that they use her face in a promotional campaign. Samantha doesn't want this at all as there is no telling when Tabatha will decide to use her new found powers. After a restless night she finally decides to tell her husband about their daughter only to find that he got up early and has taken Tabatha to the photographer's studio! She zaps up some clothes and pops over to the studio to find that Tabatha has been causing some trouble by levitating the prop toys driving the photographer nuts! Samantha retrieves Tabatha and they leave. Luckily the pictures turn out great as everyone thinks the pictures were set up to look like they included floating toys...but Durwood still doesn't know his daughter's secret!

I LOVE this episode! This, to me, and most likely 12,974,923,742,934 other people, is where *Bewitched* begins as the black and white first two seasons weren't shown in reruns until the late 80s on Nick-at-Nite.

Samantha has never looked better nor will she ever look better than she does in this season.

The sound effects seem to be much better than before, as are the visual effects. I always loved the scene where Endora is trying to teach Tabatha "Basic Topsy-Turvy."

Sam looked HOT HOT HOT in that nightie! I'm surprised they didn't have another kid until Adam!

I also thought the line about "no strings" was hilarious! Maybe they did that on purpose just to acknowledge that though they were good at special effects they weren't that good.

Besides the episodes now being filmed in 'culluh' there were a lot of other big changes on *Bewitched*. Baby Tabatha is now played by blonde twins Erin and Diane Murphy who happen to resemble Elizabeth quite a bit, Erin more so than the previous sets of twins. And what cute babies they are! And the entire house (or what we see in this episode) seems to have had an extreme makeover including a red brick fireplace replacing the white brick, new couch and chairs, a new painting over the fireplace where once hung a Picasso in the living room; the addition of the Rembrandt "Girl with Broom" painting in the entry hall and new wall paper; new brick in the kitchen instead of tile behind the stove and the window between the dining room and kitchen being enclosed; the dining room receiving a china hutch; and the bedroom getting rid of the closet behind the bed and the wall creating a little space between the closet and the bed!

Now all though this was the first episode to be shown this season, it wasn't the first to be filmed in color. That honor goes to the Ben Franklin episodes which will be shown later this season but which have been seen in the previews for the Third Season.

Here is my favorite line:

SAMANTHA: *"Tabatha! You twitched your nose! Just like mommy!"*

The cast and crew celebrated the new season that night at Chasen's Restaurant. Also the second out of four episodes of *The Tammy Grimes Show* aired tonight just before *Bewitched*.

The next night the Metropolitan Opera House opened at Lincoln Center Plaza in New York City with the world premiere of *Antony and Cleopatra* by Samuel Barber.

SEPTEMBER 22, 1966

It was on this night that ABC aired Episode #76: "The Moment of Truth," essentially the second part to last week's episode.

Samantha is still worrying about how to tell Durwood that their daughter is a witch and decides she'll tell him that night as they are celebrating their second wedding anniversary. Aunt Clara arrives to babysit and soon finds that her powers may be acting up as Tabatha's toys and pots and pans start floating around by themselves. Feeling bad, she decides to tell Samantha that she isn't feeling well. Samantha tells her that it's all right; they'll just celebrate at home and advises Aunt Clara to go home and rest. Samantha and Durwood decide to invite the Tates over to help celebrate which is good as it seems Larry has been dying to celebrate as evidenced by his continual drinking and a toast to "Happy Thursday!" When he spills some champagne he goes in the kitchen to get a towel and is attacked by a floating pan! Of course Tabatha wanted it and was levitating it up to her room. Samantha, Durwood, and Louise come in to see what's wrong and just chalk it up to Larry being plastered. As the Tates leave the kitchen the pan again begins to float and Samantha tells Durwood that it's just some of Aunt Clara's magic gone awry.

Back in the living room things go from bad to worse as Larry gets more drunk and starts extinguishing his cigarette on the end table where just moments before an ashtray had been (Tabatha floated it up to her room…and just what would she want with an ashtray??). Samantha goes to follow the floating objects and when Durwood sees a pan going up to the room he deftly tries to follow it without the Tates noticing. When he gets up to the room and sees that the pan is going straight for his baby and hears Samantha chiding her it dawns on him that it may not be Aunt Clara's errant witchcraft to blame. His daughter — like his wife — is a witch! Samantha confirms this with him with tears in her eyes as she knows how much it upsets him but she assures him that Tabatha doesn't know what she's doing yet with her newly discovered powers. They decide that rather than think on this new situation they MUST get the Tates out of the house before they discover Tabatha's secret. Of course, Larry doesn't want to go anywhere and not until they decide to tell him that he's sauced, and they'll prove it, will he leave. When he tries to walk a straight line as his last test Samantha twitches him into stumbling into Louise's arms. They finally leave and Samantha decides that she needs to tell Aunt Clara about Tabatha. Of course, Aunt Clara is thrilled and after giving a congratulatory bouquet of roses to Samantha leaves to spread the news, as Tabatha is the first witch of her generation in their family.

Durwood isn't too happy about all this but he tells Samantha later on that he's thought about it and it's been great living with one witch, it'll be more so with two witches in the family.

This episode, to me, is pure CLASSIC *Bewitched*. I would give it four stars.

I'm so glad Aunt Clara is back! We haven't seen her for a long time! Her last appearance was in January but that was in the redo of "Samantha Meets the Folks." Her last original appearance was in November (around Thanksgiving) in "Aunt Clara's Old Flame!" That's all right, though, as she makes up for it by appearing in over a third of the episodes this season.

The wires on the floating objects, specifically the pan, are clearly visible, especially when it lands in front of Tabatha in her highchair. I'm really surprised and impressed that Erin/Diane didn't play with the strings but really focused on what was floating. Another blooper is after Tabatha floats her pony over to herself in the chair, the scene cuts to Aunt Clara worrying about it and then they show Tabatha knock it on to the floor. The camera then cuts to Aunt Clara sitting down at the table near Tabatha and the pony is seen sitting on the counter near the window between the dining room and the kitchen. In the end scene when Durwood and Samantha are cleaning out Tabatha's crib from the toys and putting them in the playpen the pretty pony is dropped on the side closest to Sam. But when it floats out again it's a DIFFERENT pony coming from the other side! You can still see the one dropped in there.

Elizabeth Montgomery looked so beautiful in this episode, as did Kasey Rogers. This episode marks the first appearance of our beloved Kasey Rogers as Louise Tate (though it wasn't the first episode she filmed). She took over the role from Irene Vernon who had left the show allegedly to start up a real estate business. Out of all the cast switches on the series this is the only time that I actually liked the second person better than the first. Not that I didn't think Irene Vernon was good but Kasey seemed to bring more to the role and really seemed like the kind of wife Larry would've ended up with. Kasey's natural hair color is red but she was asked to wear a wig to match Ms. Vernon's raven hair. I thought her black hair looked authentic! And I do prefer her with the black hair.

I must make mention of how cute and sweet baby Erin Murphy was in this episode. What a sweet smile! And such sparkling eyes! You could also tell which twin was being used in each scene as Diane had shorter pixie like hair (quite similar to the Tabatha doll that was released earlier in the year by Ideal) and Erin's was longer and curly.

I also thought it sad how Durwood invited the Tates to their fiftieth wedding anniversary as pretty much if the character of Durwood's life was tied with Dick York's life, he wouldn't have made it to his thirtieth anniversary as he passed away in 1992.

One of the funniest bits of *Bewitched* is when Larry is trying to say "Chrysanthemum." One of my other favorite lines from this is when Larry is telling the joke and Louise interrupts him and Larry says, "Please Louise!"

The third episode of *The Tammy Grimes Show* co-starring Dick Sargent aired this night.

SEPTEMBER 29, 1966

It was on this night ABC aired Episode #77: "Witches and Warlocks are my Favorite Things," essentially the end of a three story arc about Tabatha's powers.

Endora advises Samantha that a Witches' Coven comprised of Samantha's aunts and Endora have been designated to test Tabatha's powers in order to certify her as a witch. Luckily Durwood has to work on a Saturday so their home is free for the testing.

Aunt Clara shows up via the chimney excited as ever that they will be testing a new witch. While waiting for her other aunts to arrive Samantha wonders if her father will show up and just then he does, much to Endora's distaste. He says that he won't stay long as he is on his way to see *Faust* in Vienna ("I always get a laugh out of that") not to mention that testing "is women's work!" But he gives Samantha a little whistle-like object that she can use to call him if needed. Aunt Enchantra and Aunt Hagatha arrive together (Aunt Clara: "How very sisterly!") via an old automobile and after popping out the mortal furniture in lieu of the testing equipment they are ready to begin. When Clara goes to zap the testing cape on Tabatha (who happens to be in the other room eating cookies) she mentions how she wishes Durwood could be there. So, of course, not giving full concentration to the task at hand the cape is zapped on Durwood who is in the middle of explaining a campaign to Larry, making him look rather foolish. Wondering what's going on at home, he decides to go there.

The coven tests Tabatha and Hagatha deems that Tabatha has proven herself to be a true and verified witch, much to the pleasure of all. As they sit and visit over a cup of tea, Endora, Enchantra, and Hagatha tell Samantha they've decided that Tabatha needs to leave her home to go to Hagatha's school to be taught how to use her powers in a proper setting. Samantha objects but Endora will hear none of it. At that moment

Durwood comes storming in wanting to know what's been happening. When he finds out, he is justifiably furious. The Coven (minus Aunt Clara who doesn't agree with the others), seeing that there is going to be hostility towards taking Tabatha, fix Samantha, Durwood, and Clara's feet to the floor, and so they won't have to hear their objections, change their voices to that of birds. Seeing that she was literally in a fix, Samantha uses the whistle to call her father who bursts in on the scene amid lightning and thunder. When he hears the plans of his wife and relations, he says no such thing will happen, that Tabatha will remain in her home and he zaps her to her room and demands that the Coven remove their spells, which they refuse to do. Endora and Hagatha protest much and Maurice will have none of it. When he has had enough he zaps the trio to the top of Mt. Everest and only brings them back when he can hear their anguished cries. They remove their spells and Maurice sends them on their way.

    This episode is a favorite of mine because it's so witchy! But, at the same time, the writers need to be spanked for making Endora such a meanie! It was totally out of character for her to want to literally kidnap Tabatha and call her own daughter "incompetent" in regards to raising Tabatha. If anything, Maurice should've been the one to kidnap since he's already good at doing that (referring to when he kidnapped Jonathan Tate last season in "My Grandson, the Warlock"). This is the first time we've seen Maurice since that episode and, surprisingly, we won't see him again until the end of the Fifth Season!

    This is also the first time we see an antique automobile drive into the living room. It's really a cool and funny visual pun but honestly, would witches really use an automobile to get around regardless of when it was made?

    It's also interesting to note that Reta Shaw plays Hagatha when previously she played a character named Bertha. I think they should've kept it that way.

    I also thought this episode has a very Harry Potter feel to it what with the floating candles and the references to a school of witchcraft.

    The floating ball would be seen again actually three more times (well four, if you count it's appearance in the Ben Franklin episode which was inexplicably deleted from the DVDs) in "The Trial and Error of Aunt Clara" and "Samantha's Power Failure" using the exact same opening in the bedroom with a variation in "The Trial and Error of Aunt Clara" of having Endora's voice say, "Follow me…follow me!" The last time it's seen is in "Turn on the Old Charm" from the Sixth Season.

One of my favorite quotes from this episode is from Maurice when he says to Hagatha, "One more word out of you, madame, and...!" Hagatha: "And what??!!" Plus Hagatha says her line with such distaste and disgust... it's hilarious!

Clara also says Enchantra's name as "Enchanta." I thought that was funny.

And if you notice, Marion Lorne accidentally hits Erin in the head but you can see her trying to make up for it.

It was also tonight that Dick Sargent's show *The Tammy Grimes Show* aired its fourth and final show.

Two nights after this, Elizabeth Montgomery would co-host *The Hollywood Palace* with Vic Damone. She would dance in a number set to the *Bewitched* theme where the words were sung and she also sang "Bewitched, Bothered and Bewildered," which Liz originally wanted to be used for the theme song. Paul Lynde also showed up and did some very funny skits with her.

OCTOBER 6, 1966

It was on this night ABC aired Episode #78: "Accidental Twins."

The Stephenses and the Tates are going to a play and Sam and Durwood have Aunt Clara babysit. As they are getting ready the Tates ask if it would be all right for Aunt Clara to watch their baby Jonathan as their sitter fell ill. Samantha agrees to it not knowing what else to say. She assures Durwood everything will be all right.

Everything does go well at first as Aunt Clara tells the children fairy tales. She then decides it would be fun to do a magic show. For her first trick, she'll produce a toy pony for Jonathan. In true Aunt Clara fashion a pony is not what she gets but instead loses her sleeves and gets a big stuffed giraffe and for her grand finale she ends up making a twin of Jonathan! In trying to put him back together, she finally gets a pony for him, and for his twin.

All night she tries getting him back together before the parents come home but instead gets herself a virtual FAO Schwartz in Tabatha's room. When the parents do come home, Samantha goes to get Jonathan and finds out what's going on. She decides to tell the Tates that Jonathan is sleeping and he can just stay the night. The Tates reluctantly agree.

In the morning Aunt Clara is still trying to get Jonathan back together but to no avail. Louise shows up saying she couldn't sleep without a baby in the house. Samantha assures Durwood that it won't do giving up one of the Jonathans to Louise as one of them is Aunt Clara's magic and they don't know which one is which. In an attempt to buy more time, Samantha reminds Louise that today is Jonathan's birthday and they had decided to throw a surprise party for him. Samantha zaps up party decorations out on the patio. While they are out there, Aunt Clara tries to sneak up stairs with the other Jonathan and as she is going up the doorbell rings. It's Larry! He decided to just pick Jonathan up for Louise. Samantha tells Larry about the party and zaps up decorations in the kitchen. Durwood, who was still outside with Louise, decides to move the party indoors to the kitchen but stops short when he sees Larry in the kitchen. He tells Louise that they are playing hide-n-go-seek with the babies. Samantha tells Larry the same thing and he goes to hide in the den closet.

After having a couple close calls, and finally getting both Jonathan's upstairs, Samantha pleads with Aunt Clara to remember the spell. Aunt Clara reveals that the same thing happened ten years ago and at that time she was able to remember the reversal spell. Samantha zaps up a youth potion and makes Aunt Clara ten years younger. She remembers the spell and puts the twins together again.

After all that trouble Larry reveals as he is leaving that he thinks Jonathan is such a great son he wished he had another!

This is the second time we've seen Jonathan on the show since he was kidnapped by Maurice last season. It also seems that he was never mentioned in the time between. It also seems that he isn't seen or heard of again until Season SEVEN when he shows up in "Mixed Doubles." That's too bad as he would've been a great playmate for Tabatha.

The twins who play Jonathan weren't credited and that is too bad. It would be interesting to know who they are.

David White's son was named Jonathan as well and I can't help but wonder if Larry's Jonathan acquired his name because of that. In the original script his name was supposed to be Timothy.

This episode was the third to be filmed in 'culluh' which means that it's the first episode OUR Kasey filmed!

There are many little bloopers in this episode including the whole house shaking when Aunt Clara bumps into the front door, the plant on the fridge changing, and when Aunt Clara enters Tabatha's bedroom the door, as seen from the hallway, opens to the right but when they show from inside the bedroom, it opens to the left. And that's another thing: Tabatha's bedroom is placed exactly where we have seen that the master bedroom is. I wonder why they didn't think about these type of things?

Probably 'cause they didn't think that the episodes would be seen but just once.

One of my favorite lines of all time comes from this episode and it's when Samantha is telling Durwood about the twins and then it cuts to the Tates in the living room and from off camera you can hear Durwood yell, "WHAT???!!!" It kills me every time!

I was quite impressed by how focused on the action the children were. What great baby actors!

I'm also inclined to think that this episode indirectly references "The Magic Cabin" episode. When Aunt Clara is looking through her spell book she only finds half the spell that she needs and Durwood says, "Isn't half a spell better than no spell?" Maybe he is remembering in the cabin episode at the end they run out of gas and as Samantha isn't supposed to be doing anymore witchcraft she offers to do just half a spell which gives them half a tank of gas. Of course Samantha tells him that this time it's no good because with only half a spell they still have two Jonathans.

OCTOBER 13, 1966

It was on this night ABC aired Episode #79: "A Most Unusual Wood Nymph."

Gerry O'Toole, a friend of Durwood's great-aunt Leticia (Durwood: "I didn't even know I had a great-aunt Leticia"), arrives from Ireland to stay with the Stephens until she can find a job. Samantha is not too pleased with this as Gerry is very beautiful and seems to be catching the eye of her husband. When they hear the baby cry, Gerry thinks it is a cat and freaks out saying that she detests cats. Samantha finds the amount of dislike towards cats very odd and soon finds that Gerry is even odder than she thought! It seems that Gerry is quite adept at weaving as she seamlessly fixes a hole in one of Durwood's sweaters. Thinking Gerry may be a witch Samantha questions her mother who helps Samantha understand that any being that is great at weaving and hates cats must be a wood nymph! And along with that it is well known that the only thing a wood nymph hates more than a cat is a WITCH!

Samantha confronts Gerry about her reason for being there. Gerry assures her that wood nymphs harbor no animosity towards witches anymore and the reason she is there to exact revenge on Durwood! Seems like in the 15th century Durwood's ancestor Durwood the Bold slew Rufus the Red, a friend to the wood nymphs and from that time forth the wood nymphs cursed Durwood the Bold and all his descendants. Samantha decides the only way to get her husband out of harm's way is to go back to stop the slewing, er, I mean slaying. Endora cautions her that doing something like that is the most dangerous of practices not to mention Samantha will be without her powers and will have only her wits to rely on. Samantha assures her mother that all she'll need is her wits and so Endora sends her back.

Agnes Moorehead and Kathleen Nolan share a moment between scenes in the kitchen, one place where Gerry and Endora are never seen in the episode.

Durwood the Bold is a very amorous and barbaric man and is canoodling with a maid when Samantha pops in. She catches his eye and he throws the maid down like a used banana peel and goes after Samantha. While he is trying to charm her, it is announced that there is a visitor to the castle who wants to lodge there on the grounds. Durwood the Bold requests the visitor to enter so they can talk. The visitor is Rufus the Red who requests that he and his men also be fed. Durwood the Bold says he'll feed them but only if they pay. Rufus refuses to pay and Durwood the Bold refuses to give, therefore, they declare a duel. Samantha sneaks off to Rufus' camp and finds him practicing his dueling on a melon and she takes his measurements, which she says is for his shroud, because as everyone knows Durwood the Bold has killed many, many men. Rufus begins to rethink the duel.

Meanwhile, Samantha goes back to Durwood the Bold and tells him that she overheard Rufus' men talking about all the men he has fought and killed on foot, over a hundred men that way and even more when he is on horseback. Durwood the Bold decides that he doesn't want to duel anymore but just then a message is sent that Rufus the Red has decided not to fight. Now that that situation is out of the way, Durwood the Bold sets his sights on Samantha again but she is zapped back to the 20th century before he can get too far.

Back in the present Samantha finds that Gerry has taken a page out of Durwood the Bold's book and is chasing Durwood until he falls. He then tells her that he has no interest in her, that he is very much in love with his wife. When Durwood goes to check on the baby, Samantha tells Gerry that she undid the murder of Rufus the Red. Gerry doesn't believe and Samantha tells Endora that Gerry wants proof so Endora obliges and zaps in Rufus the Red. Both are thrilled to see each other and pop off to the past.

I wanted to SMACK Gerry for using the word "darlin'" 239,482, 349,723,972,479 times! It was so irritating!

Rufus the Red was played by Michael Ansara, the then husband of *I Dream of Jeannie*'s Barbara Eden. I find it very unusual that with all that is said about Elizabeth Montgomery not liking *I Dream of Jeannie* that she would agree to have Michael Ansara on the show.

Henry Corden played Muldoon, the servant. He played Jeannie's father last season in "My Hero?" and would go on to replace Alan Reed as the voice of Fred Flintstone in all the incarnations of *The Flintstones* after the series.

The time travel dynamics in this episode have always bugged me as I am a HUGE *Back to the Future* fan and those movies thought out the implications of time travel to a T. First of all, if Rufus the Red were to continue living it's highly likely he might've had more descendants not to mention he probably would've killed more people as he seemed to be a warrior.

Secondly, the episode plays along like the present (1966) and the past (1472) run at the same rate meaning, Samantha seemed to be spending about an hour or two in the past and Durwood and Gerry were experiencing her being gone. Wouldn't Samantha have just returned to the present at practically the same instant as she left so that those in the present wouldn't notice her being gone?

Lastly, having Endora zap up Rufus in the present was dumb as that wouldn't be proof that he wasn't killed. That same argument could've been used with Ben Franklin, Queen Victoria, Napoleon, Caesar, and George Washington. What would've been better is to have had Gerry zapped back to the 15th century.

Another interesting thing is that here we have another case of a magical being involved in Durwood's history (the other time was with the Leprechaun from the episode of the same name last season). It would seem that Durwood was destined to be involved with magical beings which is funny 'cause he hates magic so much.

Regardless of that, this is a pretty enjoyable episode. Dick York is given time to shine playing a different character and he is hysterical! I did feel bad for him when he fell on the floor when Gerry was chasing him... hopefully it didn't hurt his back too bad.

Durwood the Bold will return in the Seventh Season, but this time played by Dick Sargent.

The music used for the writer and director credits is a jazzy theme used earlier on "The Moment of Truth" and would never be used again.

And aside from hearing her cry we do not see Tabatha, which is odd considering the whole summer promotion was about whether she would be a witch and all.

This episode was nominated for an American Cinema Editors (ACE) "Eddie" Award for Best Edited Television Program for Aaron Nibley.

OCTOBER 20, 1966

It was on this night ABC aired Episode #80: "Endora Moves in for a Spell."

Samantha sees that Oscar the Bear, which Endora gave Tabatha earlier this year, is dancing once more and begins to blame her mother when she finds out that it's actually due to Uncle Arthur's shenanigans. He's come to see Tabatha for the first time since she was born. As he stays for a couple days, it shows that he is really happy about the new little witch and he does all sorts of tricks for her including turning himself into a fifty foot balloon, walking on the ceiling, and taking her out for a ride in a stroller on a moving red carpet, which Gladys Kravitz sees.

Durwood has enough of this and tells Samantha he'd rather deal with Endora any day than put up with Arthur and his tricks. Endora pops in pleased with what Durwood said but disgusted that Arthur thinks he can take up all of Tabatha's attentions. She decides that she is going to show him who's boss and move into the neighborhood into a house on the corner so she can make sure he doesn't corrupt her granddaughter. The thing is, there isn't a house on the corner, it's just a vacant lot, until Endora waves her arms and up pops a mansion with a nicely manicured lawn! When Arthur sees this while out on his walk, he knows Endora is up to something and comes back and that's when the fireworks fly. They proceed to zap the house in and out and a puzzled Mrs. Kravitz knows this shouldn't be happening so she calls the police.

Meanwhile, Samantha and Durwood have been relegated to the kitchen where they can smell sulphur from Endora's acid comments. Samantha decides she has had enough and she tells her mother and uncle that she will not stand for it anymore, that it's her house and she and Durwood are in charge of their daughter. She also demands that they kiss and makeup. They do, sort of: they decide they will only see each other when invisible and promise to go their separate ways, divvying up the world (Endora gets top, of course!).

Outside, Gladys and the police have been looking to the house and the one officer finds that there really shouldn't be a house there. When Durwood sees that the house is still there Samantha tells him that she should be able to get rid of it now that Arthur and Endora are out of the way.

Later on at night Endora and Arthur pop into paintings down in the living room trying to out-sneak each other and Endora tells Arthur that she will not allow him to have free reign around Morning Glory Circle, especially with Halloween coming up!

I would give this two and a half stars and that's because everyone seems like they have PMS: Durwood's mad about the house, Endora's mad about Arthur, Arthur's mad about Endora, and Samantha's mad at everyone.

I really liked the effects in this one, especially the house disappearing and appearing even though you could tell it was just blue screen.

My favorite line from this is from Arthur when Endora pops in and Arthur says, "Endora! (speak of the devil) How are you?"

I also like it when Endora says, "You call yourself my brother?!" Uncle Arthur: "Only when I'm forced to, Endora! I deny it whenever possible!"

A blooper from this episode is that when Arthur returns from cake-walking Tabatha she is in a yellow coat and it's Diane he's holding. He hands her to Samantha and when it cuts back to her putting Tabatha in the playpen it's Erin with no coat but yet there was really not time for her to take it off unless she twitched it off. Another blooper was that the wall near the front window where the book cupboard usually stands now has portraits on it, except for in one scene where the book cupboard is back.

I always think of Endora's saying, "You are out of your ever-loving nefarious mind!" I've said that to some people. It's hilarious!

This is the first episode that Erin Murphy received screen credit for playing Tabatha, though her sister Diane shared the role.

This episode also marks the return of the Kravitzes, who haven't been seen since the end of last season, but with one glaring change and that is Mrs. Kravitz is now played by Sandra Gould. The original Gladys, Alice Pearce, passed away from cancer earlier in the year. It is a sad thing to see the character of Gladys not portrayed as just snoopy. Now it seems Gladys is bent on getting Samantha in trouble, though it's not quite apparent in this episode, however, it will become more so in future episodes. It should be noted that future *Bewitched* alumn Alice Ghostley was approached to take over the role of Gladys but she declined as she was a good friend of Alice Pearce's and didn't feel she could do that.

This episode also seems to go in a direction a lot of us 'techies' would like and that is the explanation, or almost explanation, of several particulars in the series that normally aren't alluded to including the fact that Endora and Arthur are siblings and that up until Arthur was born, Endora was an only child. Seeing as the other aunts seem to be as old as Endora or older, and definitely older than Arthur, this would indicate that the other Aunts are from Maurice's side or the possibility that they could be Endora's aunts.

Samantha says that Endora and Arthur have equal powers, which would explain why Arthur would be able to get rid of the house that was created by Endora's powers, though we have been told before that one witch can't undo another witch's spell. I personally don't think Arthur would be as strong as Endora, especially considering what he does in later episodes.

The last item that was almost explained is at the end when Samantha says she wants to wait until the police officer and Gladys get out of the house before she zaps it away. Durwood wonders why and Samantha tells him that they will disappear too. When he asks where she goes to explain and he stops her. I wish he hadn't. It would be interesting to have heard the explanation.

I find it strange that the "Girl with Broom" painting was replaced with another painting. What for? Couldn't Arthur have just popped into that one?

This episode also references Arthur's previous and first appearance in "The Joker is a Card" when he refers to Durwood as "my yagazuzy nephew-in-law" which refers to the bogus spell he taught Durwood.

Paul Smith appears for the first time as a cop, a role which he'll play at least seven more times on the series.

It should also be noted that this episode is essentially a remake of the First Season *I Dream of Jeannie* episode "What House Across the Street?" where Jeannie pops in THE SAME house across the street from Tony's as a place where she can have Roger meet her parents when she is dating him.

I also wanted to take a moment to discuss how *Bewitched* looked when it originally aired because, for the most part, none of us have seen a truly complete unedited episode, even on the DVDs.

During its original run *Bewitched* had several companies sponsor it and during the first three seasons it was Quaker Oats and Chevrolet. The show produced cartoon openings for each company utilizing their logos in the opening. They were used alternately each week. I'm not too certain on this part, but I believe that "Endora Moves in for a Spell" was sponsored by Chevrolet. Their logo would also be used in the end credits instead of the cartoon Samantha. So the show would've ran like this:

We would've seen a placard with "*Bewitched* Next in Color" in the *Bewitched* font in front of a background of red and blue changing colors and then the episode would start. When the credits came on, it began with the blue sky background but a big Chevy logo and the announcer saying "Chevrolet presents…"…the logo morphed into the moon and the opening cartoon ran just like we see it though the music was just slightly different with more bells and such. After the smoky credits fade we see cartoon Samantha and Durwood flying on Samantha's broom (which I think is WAY cool) and Samantha points changing the broom into the Chevy logo. The scene then is pushed up by film of a Chevy Camaro driving and the announcer says, "Camaro Pacesetter days means sure savings at your Chevrolet dealers." A commercial would play that was may be thirty seconds to a minute, most likely a car commercial, then it would come back to the "written by/directed by" credits and the episode would play. There would be another commercial break of no more than a minute or two, possibly two commercials, the show would return for the next act and then a close-up of the cartoon Samantha would be shown with the words *"Bewitched* will Be Right Back" and the witch would twitch. It would then go to another commercial and then return for the end scene. On this particular episode of *Bewitched* right after the last scene was shown another shot of the close-up of the cartoon Samantha appeared with the words "Next Week Endora's Halloween Party." We hear Elizabeth Montgomery say, "Please come. Incidentally it's "Twitch or Treat" and then she giggles in that way that only Liz can. After that the *Bewitched* logo appears on a bare blue background without any buildings and then the cartoon witch swoops in breaking the logo up flashing to another car commercial with the announcer saying "*Bewitched* has been brought to you by Chevrolet who reminds you that a spirited summer starts now with Camaro Pacesetter days at your local Chevrolet dealer." The end credits would then have shown with the Durwood and Samantha cartoon seen on the Chevy logo. The Screen Gems logo would've been shown and then the ABC logo.

It is unfortunate that the episodes on DVD cannot be restored like this as it makes watching the show a whole new fun experience.

You can learn more about the openings over at Vic's Bewitched Page including hearing them and seeing some of them.

Three days before was the premiere of *Hollywood Squares* with Agnes Moorehead being one of the first players. Game regular and center square Paul Lynde wouldn't make his debut on the show until next week.

The day before, Agnes came in third place for Supporting Performance — Female for *The Singing Nun* at the Golden Laurel Awards.

OCTOBER 27, 1966

It was on this night that ABC aired Episode #81: "Twitch or Treat," the series third Halloween episode.

It is Halloween night and Durwood wants to go to the movies. Samantha will have none of that. She feels they should celebrate Halloween properly by attending a party given by her mother in the house she zapped up last week! Durwood will have none of it worrying about what the neighbors will think. He demands that Endora get rid of the house once and for all before he returns from work…"or else!!"

Samantha confronts Endora who couldn't care less what "or else" is. She is also concerned at keeping Uncle Arthur out of the party, who just happens to pop in essentially inviting himself. When Samantha pleads with Endora to remove the house and have the party elsewhere Endora concedes and decides that she will have her party at 1164 Morning Glory Circle! With a wave of her hand she zaps up flowing sparkly curtains and a nice tinkling fountain.

The party begins and witches and warlocks from all over the world start flying in. Gladys sees all this and decides she had better get the town council in on it as you can never tell how wild the party will get.

Aside from a few minor interruptions from Councilman Green and his cohort, the party goes along splendidly. Durwood finds that EVERYONE is there including baseball great Willie Mays who happens to be a warlock (Samantha: "With the way he hits home runs, what else?"). Durwood also becomes the center of attention to Eva, a glamour-puss (literally) who had been Boris' date. When midnight arrives Durwood finds that Eva isn't all she seems as she turns back into her normal kitty self. Endora also decides to do her annual recitation of "Twas the Night Before Halloween." She doesn't get too far as Arthur keeps interrupting her with his witty jokes. Finally, seeing that she will get nowhere she replaces the statue in the fountain with Arthur and takes the party somewhere else.

At the end of the evening Durwood decides it was the most interesting Halloween party he has ever been too. Samantha promises that next Halloween they can spend Halloween with his family and Thanksgiving with hers.

This episode is rather strange in the fact that I LOVE it but if you really think about what we know of the characters up to this point, this episode makes no sense whatsoever.

First of all, we've come to believe that real witches don't really like Halloween because of the ugly masks and all which is why Endora would fly "to the south of France every year this time 'til it all blows over." And last year she wanted Samantha to go to the Sacred Volcano with her during Halloween, which we assume is in Southern France (a little while ago I found that there really is a volcano in Southern France). So the very fact that Endora is actually celebrating Halloween is strange indeed and mind-boggling in the fact that *1) she'd have it on Earth, 2) if on Earth, why not in Europe where she always goes* and *3) that she would actually choose to have it at Samantha's hum-drum mortal house!*

I thought the floating trays were really cool and wished I had enough money to have a set up like that where I'd hire puppeteers or theater kids to move the trays around from the balconies for a party I would throw.

I also thought seeing the council man and his friend go from the front of the house to the back was cool. I remember wanting to see a house that thin.

It's also rather creepy to me when Durwood goes chasing after Eva AFTER she's become a cat again!

The poem recitation is hilarious, especially seeing how much Uncle Arthur breaks himself up.

I really liked that it was shown that actual celebrities are witches/warlocks. And I always think it's funny how Willie says, "How doin'?"

And now for a very special Halloween treat! It was also tonight that CBS first aired *It's the Great Pumpkin, Charlie Brown*.

NOVEMBER 3, 1966

It was on this night ABC aired Episode #82: "Dangerous Diaper Dan."

The local diaper delivery man, known as Diaper Dan, gives Samantha a rattle for Tabatha which advertises his company. The rattle is more than it seems as it contains a bug device implanted in it so that McMann and Tate rival, A.J. Kimberly, can listen in on any campaign ideas that Durwood might spit out at home.

At this time McMann and Tate is handling the Wright Pen company who is also bandying with the Kimberly agency. When Durwood mentions one of his great ideas to Samantha who then unwittingly repeats it to Louise, the rattle picks it up and Kimberly presents practically the same idea before Durwood presents his. When this happens again Larry thinks that there is a leak within McMann and Tate and has everyone under suspicion.

Samantha believes she somehow may be responsible and tells that to Durwood who is furious with her and even more so with Endora whom he thinks has something to do with it. They quit speaking to each other, which doesn't bode well for Dan, so he sends Samantha flowers from Durwood and he sends Durwood a tie from Samantha. When they find that neither of them sent the gifts, Samantha thinks Endora may have done it but she denies it. Samantha calls the florist and finds that they came from Dan. It dawns on Samantha that Dan is in the neighborhood a lot and when she sees him outside she knows that something is afoot. She figures out that he bugged the rattle and she and her mother fix him with some good witchcraft to prevent him from escaping.

Durwood wins back the Kimberly Agency and Dan says that after his spooky experiences with his truck going haywire he is going to get some rest.

Dan is played by Marty Ingels who would later become Mr. Shirley Jones a.k.a. Mrs. Partridge of *The Partridge Family*, another Screen Gems show.

I have always found the pacing of this episode sluggish and disjointed and Endora seemed like she was bored to tears being there and what is she doing reading the mortal newspaper? As if she'd care what was going on in the mortal world.

I've always found Diaper Dan to be real creepy, almost pedophile creepy.

I noticed that in the course of what seemed like one day (based on Endora wearing that purple dress) Samantha changed outfits practically every scene!

I did like that we get to see Samantha let a mortal have it and when I was young I always liked the scene of the diapers flying out of the back and the tires popping. I did notice that a scene that was always cut out of the syndication prints is when Dan tries to throw the diapers back in and they just fly back out at him.

And is it my bad hearing or an edit on the DVDs, but I can't ever hear Samantha say, "pooh"…I see her lips move but I never hear it from her. But that is my favorite line from this episode.

The creepy baby's voice sounds like it was done by Agnes Moorehead.

One of A.J. Kimberly's men is the same actor who played Councilman Green's cohort in last week's episode!

There are certain lines and scenes from this particular episode that were used in one of the Third Season promos particularly when Sam says, "I have a good mind to go home to mother!" Durwood: "Why, your mother is always here!" And then they show Endora say, "I beg your pardon!" They also show when Endora is getting Tabatha to zap the plate of graham crackers over and Samantha says, "Mother I wish you wouldn't do that. Tabatha, mustn't twitch!"

All in all, this is one of my least favorites from the Third Season but definitely not the least favorite — that comes later.

Three nights later Agnes Moorehead would play the Red Queen in the TV movie *Alice Through the Looking Glass*, a role she took over from her friend Bette Davis who got sick.

NOVEMBER 10, 1966

It was on this night ABC aired Episode #83: "The Short Happy Circuit of Aunt Clara."

Samantha calls in Aunt Clara to babysit for them while they attend a dinner party at the Tate's with new client Mr. MacElroy of MacElroy shoes. Aunt Clara tries to sing to Tabatha but apparently singing isn't one of Aunt Clara's strong suits and Tabatha begins crying. Aunt Clara decides that maybe some piano music will soothe Tabatha so she goes downstairs next to the baby grand piano that has suddenly made its home in the living room of 1164 and tries to think of ways to get it up the stairs. She decides the best way would be to shrink it and carry it upstairs. On her way up the stairs she feels that the piano doesn't like being shrunk and it begins to grow until Clara is trapped on the stairs with the piano. In trying to return the piano to its "convenient" size, her errant magic causes the power along the entire Eastern Seaboard to go out!

Meanwhile, over at the Tate's, Durwood is striking out with Mr. MacElroy who isn't at all amused by the ideas Durwood is pitching and just when Durwood is going to present some better ideas, the power goes out.

Aunt Clara finally figures out how to get the piano back to its proper place but now she has the lights to contend with. Not knowing what to do she calls in her almost ex-boyfriend Ocky to help. He casts a spell with his hands raised and the lights turn back on, albeit only at 1164, and when he lowers his hands, the lights turn back off. Clara insists he keeps his hands raised and work on getting them to stay on without his hands.

Samantha calls home to see if everything is all right. Aunt Clara assures her it is as they have lights on. Larry overhears the conversation and decides they should move the meeting over there. Mrs. Kravitz also notices that the lights are on across the street, yet nowhere else, so she calls the power company to have them come out to investigate.

Before Samantha and company arrive back home, Aunt Clara sticks Ocky in the closet with the admonition to keep his hands up. When Samantha goes to put their coats in the closet, Clara casts a spell to get rid of Ocky which seems to have worked. The business meeting begins again with still more problems as the lights keep going out and the electric company arrives on a mission to turn the lights out as there is no explanation as to why they should be on. Mrs. Kravitz also sneaks in to see what she can find out and just as Mr. MacElroy is about to put a kibosh on the whole thing, Mrs. Kravitz is heard to scream. She had tried to hide in the closet but felt something in there besides coats. When Durwood goes to investigate, Ocky walks out of the closet and out the door. Well, his shoes do anyway, which causes Gladys to faint. Mr. MacElroy is enchanted by the walking shoes and decides that this is perfect for his campaign.

Aunt Clara figures out how to get the lights across the Eastern Seaboard back on and Durwood reads in the paper an explanation about a power influx which caused it, so he is satisfied that it wasn't magic induced. Samantha assures him that mortals always come up with rational explanations for things that witches do.

This episode is awesome in the fact that the writers did take a real life event of a huge power outage along the Eastern Seaboard a year earlier and explained it with magic.

This marks the first of two appearances by Ocky, Aunt Clara's boyfriend played by Reginald Owen who is famous from his appearances in *Mary Poppins* (1964) and later *Bedknobs and Broomsticks* (1971), both witchly movies.

This is also the second appearance of Arthur Julian as a client. He also wrote the Fifth Season episode "Is It Magic or Imagination?"

I have to say that Elizabeth Montgomery looks absolutely GORGEOUS throughout this episode. I love that orange dress she has on.

Marion Lorne is quite funny in this episode too. I love it when she tells Ocky that she hasn't called him in for anything "like that."

Ocky raising his hands to keep the lights on is very reminiscent of the Old Testament story about Moses from Exodus Chapter 17 where when Moses had his hands raised Israel would prevail in their fight against Amalek and when he would lower his hands Amalek would prevail. Eventually Aaron and Hur had to help Moses keep his hands raised.

This is also the first appearance of the piano in the living room. It will make its return in the Fourth Season and in the Fifth they have to rent a piano for piano lessons.

The sound of Jeannie smoking out of her bottle is used when Aunt Clara comes whooshing down the chimney and later, at the Tate's we see that they are eating in Jeannie and Tony's dining room.

Two days before, actor Ronald Reagan, a good friend of Agnes Moorehead's, became the governor of California.

The next day John Lennon would meet Yoko Ono at the Indica Gallery starting the beginning of the end of the Beatles.

NOVEMBER 17, 1966

It was on this night that ABC aired Ep. #84: "I'd Rather Twitch Than Fight."

Durwood gets his knickers in a knot when he finds that Samantha gave his hounds tooth sports coat with black and orange checks to the thrift shop. Samantha explains that she thought he didn't wear it anymore as it was so old. He tells her that she should've asked him about it before giving it away as it was his favorite sports coat not to mention the fact that he knows that she hated it. He blows his top like a little kid and goes on about how she shouldn't touch his stuff and storms out of the house.

He shares his concerns with Larry and admits that he shouldn't have lost his cool like he did. Larry tells him that it's because he doesn't know how to fight with his wife and explains that he and Louise have been seeing a psychiatrist, Dr. Kramer, who teaches couples how to fight. He then breaks down the different types of fights (YAAAWNNN!) and in the process tells Durwood that the jacket represented to Samantha Durwood's yearning to be free and single, which is why she got rid of it. Durwood decides he's right and goes out to buy Samantha a gift that will truly express how he feels about their marriage. Larry warns him to be careful in the gift he selects as he doesn't want to give Samantha the wrong impression.

Meanwhile, Louise has been visiting with Samantha and tells her that the jacket represented to Durwood his desire to be attractive and alluring to her and that by giving it away Samantha was showing him that she didn't find him that way anymore. They decide to go buy him another black and orange checked hounds tooth sports coat. At the clothing store, the clerk tells them that no one would be caught dead wearing something as old and horrible looking as that, today's gentleman is more sophisticated. Louise tells him that this is for yesterday's gentlemen and Samantha makes up a story about how they are shopping for a baron that is in town on vacation and they leave. They end up at the thrift shop where Samantha had originally given the coat and surprisingly it's still there, though the owner dyed it black as he felt that nobody would want to look like they were shopping at a thrift store. He sells it to Samantha for $5.00 (the cost of the dye job and the repairs) and she twitches it back to its former hounds tooth glory.

Durwood and Samantha exchange gifts and when both see what the other gave (Durwood had bought Samantha a gray bathrobe as he believed he wanted Samantha to convey the look that she is married) they are both disappointed. When Durwood asks Samantha to try the bathrobe on she says she'll wait a couple of decades. Durwood is incensed and tells her that he bought her something that expresses exactly how he feels about their marriage and she throws it down and goes to storm upstairs saying, "And you bought me a prison gown!" They argue again and Samantha reveals that she had to go to a lot of trouble to get his coat back to its former state including using a little witchcraft, which of course, puts Durwood over the top. He tells her that THAT is proof enough that she wishes she were single again. He goes to leave and she twitches him back in as no man of hers is going to walk out on her. He tells her again that she can't ever solve anything without using magic and when he goes to leave again she magically slams the door behind him.

Durwood spends a restless night at the office and he decides that maybe he and Samantha should see Dr. Kramer. Meanwhile, Samantha is feeling bad about the whole thing and tells Endora about it who thinks it's great that they are about to split up. Samantha tells her that they will not and that she thinks they should talk to Dr. Kramer. Endora is definitely against her daughter seeing a psychiatrist as they are anti-witch, telling people that witches are figments of their imagination. While Samantha calls Louise to get Dr. Kramer's number Endora goes upstairs to take care of Tabatha. She decides if Samantha insists on going to see a psychiatrist she may as well have the best and she zaps up Dr. Sigmund Freud, the original psychiatrist.

Dr. Freud listens to Samantha's problem but is stunned that she doesn't think her problem is the fact that she thinks she is a witch. He also thinks that the jacket represents nothing but bad taste. Durwood shows up with Dr. Kramer who falls in love with the jacket and Dr. Freud assures Samantha that there are just many people with bad taste. This doesn't settle well with Dr. Kramer who begins to argue with Dr. Freud and he wonders why Durwood didn't tell him they were consulting with anyone else. The doctors decide to settle this like men (with fists). Samantha and Durwood decide the only way to stop this is with witchcraft so Samantha zaps Dr. Kramer back to his place and has Endora zap Dr. Freud back to his. Samantha and Durwood apologize to one another and later on Samantha gives Durwood a nice smoking jacket which she says she got when she returned the hounds tooth and her bathrobe. She also apparently bought herself a nice nightgown and things are back to normal.

Norman Fell plays Dr. Freud and he would later go on to notoriety playing Mr. Roper on *Three's Company*.

I know this episode is a popular one among the *Bewitched* fans but I find it so dull, for the most part. All this talk about "amphigoric," "semi-amphigoric" just puts me right to sleep. But once Endora shows up then it gets much better.

I'd give it two and a half stars simply because this is one of the rare times where they show that Louise and Samantha are friends and for Samantha using her witchcraft in a defiant way.

My favorite parts out of this episode are the door slamming and that Samantha zapped Durwood back in the house after she yells, "Don't you DARE walk out on me!" I also really like it when she and Endora zap the psychiatrists back to their respective places.

I also don't like this episode as much 'cause I think Durwood is really rude to Samantha at the first.

Liz looks so beautiful throughout the entire episode.

Also, the sales lady Bridgette Hanley is/was married to E.W. Swackhamer, one of *Bewitched*'s directors.

Here's something interesting about Sigmund Freud: Jeannie popped him in on her show four days after this episode originally aired for her birthday party. Tony took him aside to discuss his problems with Jeannie. Of course, they didn't have the same actor as was on *Bewitched* but I found it "very interestink."

NOVEMBER 24, 1966

It was on this Thanksgiving night that ABC aired a non-Thanksgiving themed episode of *Bewitched*, Episode #85: "Oedipus Hex."

Endora pops in bored and decides to mess with Durwood by zapping up a bowl of popcorn which makes him totally care-free as he's leaving for work to meet an important client. Durwood tells Samantha that he's decided that he just needs to have a day to himself. Meanwhile, Samantha is going to have the women from a neighborhood committee over to discuss ways that they can raise money in order to save a neighborhood park. During the course of the day the milk man and the television repairman show up and fall under the spell of the lazy popcorn.

Larry is at his wit's end when he finds that Durwood isn't showing up to work and after he calls to Durwood's home and is chewed out by the milkman, he decides he had better run out there to drag Durwood into work. When he shows up, he blows his cool until he eats some of the popcorn. At this time the committee ladies begin showing up and Samantha asks Durwood to take his "friends" somewhere else so they move out to the patio.

When the new client, Mr. Parkinson, shows up to McMann and Tate and finds that his associates there are not to be found, he demands that they BE found! The secretary phones 1164 and Mr. Parkinson finds that Durwood and Larry seem to not give a hang for anything dealing with the matters at hand. Like Larry earlier, he blows his cool and races on out there.

Meanwhile, Samantha is beginning to get aggravated and embarrassed by the noise and rambunctiousness of Durwood's party as she is new to the committee comprised of rather snooty women, but she presses on. Endora, who has been hanging around invisibly, is obviously impressed by her new trick and has no intention of revealing the origin of Durwood's new attitude.

Mr. Parkinson arrives and practically bursts through the door disrupting the committee meeting and goes out to the patio to let the employees of McMann and Tate have it…that is until he gets some of that popcorn.

Samantha is about to lose her cool when the doorbell rings yet again and a police officer has shown up because someone (Mr. Parkinson) has parked halfway on the curb. He goes out to give Mr. Parkinson a ticket who then pawns it off on Larry who in turn gives it to Durwood as he's client relations. Durwood, in party mood, tears it up and throws it in the air as confetti. Just as the officer is really going to lay down the law Endora's popcorn lays it on him, and Durwood's party gets bigger.

Finally it has just become too much when the men come in wanting more sandwiches and popcorn. Samantha is confused as she doesn't remember setting out any popcorn until she puts two and two together and realizes that her mother has done it. The women of the committee have also decided that they are going to leave as nothing seems to be getting accomplished with all the noise and interruptions but Samantha decides to use the popcorn on them to get them to loosen up. In the meantime, Mr. Parkinson hears what the women were trying to do and decides that the raffle they had come up with will not bring in near enough money so he rallies the men to call all their contacts who can donate a lot and they get the money for the park. Samantha finally gets Endora to show up and remove her spell once she shows her how the popcorn has actually helped.

I LOVE this episode! It's definitely one of the funnier ones. In fact, my sister Heather and I one day watched it twice in a row (before the DVDs came out) 'cause it was so funny, especially that part about "Larry, could you take your high blood pressure somewhere else?"

I like that the spell was cast on the popcorn simply "out of sheer boredom, darling." Endora had popped in with nothing to do and when Samantha mentions that she would like Durwood to stay at home more Endora is then given the idea for something that she thinks will be entertaining, which is why she stuck around to watch it all. She was just simply bored and at that particular time couldn't think of something else to do.

I love it when they show the witches/warlocks floating in the air because I don't think I've ever seen the strings or the platform (well, once but that comes next season) so it makes the show all the more believable. I also liked the laughing sound accompanying Endora.

I also liked the New Yawk accented milk man and his attitude with Larry. I also laugh when he says, "Goo-bye!"

I cannot STAND the guy who plays the client yet here he is again and oddly enough will be back in about ten episodes to play the client in the "Super Car" episode.

I've always thought that Liz looked a great deal like older Erin Murphy, especially towards the end when Durwood leaves. And speaking of Liz looking like Erin, the Hallmark Christmas ornament of Samantha looks just like Erin Murphy. I also thought Liz showed off her brilliant comedic skills in this one when she was almost pushed over when the door opens again and Durwood comes back in and says, "I think I'll do this again another day" and he leaves and she crumbles to standing on her ankles and says, "I certainly hope not!"

The very end scene starts out with Melodie Thomas playing Samantha with her back to us, which I found very odd. It was such a short scene and Liz couldn't be there?

I also noticed that they are having their TV repaired yet it was just repaired two years ago BY SAMANTHA in "Just One Happy Family." What, her spell wore off? Or maybe she decided that she should probably have it fixed by a mortal just for appearances.

All in all, GREAT episode!

It was also on this day that the Beatles began recording what would become "Sgt. Pepper's Lonely Hearts Club Band."

Two nights later Agnes guest hosted *The Hollywood Palace*.

DECEMBER 1, 1966

It was on this night that ABC aired Episode #86: "Sam's Spooky Chair."

While shopping at an antique store Samantha finds a chair she really likes and ends up taking it home for $25.00 after the seller says he's been trying to get rid of it for a while as it is of poor workmanship. Oddly enough the chair kicks him, but he thinks that Samantha hit him with the chair. Unaware that she has bought a spooky chair Samantha takes it home quite pleased with herself.

When Durwood sees it he suggests they keep it in the den as it doesn't really match any of their other furniture, especially when he is going to have the Cosgroves (a client and his wife) and the Tates over for dinner. After dinner and retiring to the living room they find that the chair has ended up in the living room, though nobody moved it. Mrs. Cosgrove loves it and insists on buying it from Samantha, who reluctantly agrees, when she sees that not selling it to Mrs. Cosgrove could jeopardize the client relationship with McMann and Tate. When Durwood tries to take it out to their car he has much trouble as though the chair doesn't want to leave.

During the night Samantha wakes up when she hears the sound of someone tromping through the house and when Durwood won't wake up she goes to investigate. Downstairs she finds that the chair has made its way back to her house and it bows before her! "Say, you ARE a spooky chair!"

The next day Durwood and Larry are frantic as they cannot move things along with Mr. Cosgrove because his wife is so upset about the chair. Samantha discusses the chair with her mother who advises Samantha that it most likely is a witch/warlock who has transformed themselves because they didn't feel useful anymore. Samantha asks her to investigate to find out who it is and what the spell is to return him/her to their former state. Durwood comes home after Samantha tells him she knows what happened to the chair. It is obvious whoever the chair is they are not too fond of Durwood. At the same time Mr. Cosgrove shows up wanting to know where Samantha found the chair. Durwood tries to put the chair in the den closet but it absolutely refuses to go and puts up a fight which ends with it chasing Durwood out of the den. Mr. Cosgrove sees the chair and Samantha tells him that it is a copy of the other one. He says he doesn't care, he must have it as his wife is so upset about losing hers. Durwood and Samantha agree to it only after Mr. Cosgrove agrees that if he can take the chair than the negotiations with McMann and Tate can proceed that night.

That night at the Cosgrove's, the chair shows an obvious distaste for Mrs. Cosgrove who thinks her husband is trying to kill her when the chair pushes her out of it and crumples beneath her. When they go off in another room to argue, Larry, Louise, and Durwood follow to try to smooth things over. Meanwhile, Samantha takes the chair outside to the patio where Endora pops in with great news: she knows who the chair is! It happens to be one Clyde Farnsworth, a warlock who lived on the same street in Boston that Samantha and Endora did at the turn of the century. He had a mad crush on Samantha who didn't share the same feelings and when she rejected him he had Aunt Enchantra change him into a chair. Endora pops off so that Samantha can discuss with Clyde his irrational behavior. She explains that she liked him solely as a friend and she is very happy with her husband now. She changes him back to his warlock form and when he tells her he understands where she is coming from he also reveals that he has fallen in love with someone else, a lamp back at the shop where he came from, and where he intends to go back, as a chair. But before he leaves he zaps up a copy of his chair-self for Samantha to give to the Cosgrove's. She then explains that the chair had collapsible legs that weren't locked, which is why the chair crumpled. With the chair business behind them Mr. Cosgrove freely signs with McMann and Tate and all is right with the world.

I really like this one and would give it three stars. This episode is one of my favorites as the storyline really is kind of weird what with a haunted chair walking around and nobody knows who or what it is. I do have to say, though, that Clyde seems to be one of the wimpiest warlocks ever to want to be in Samantha's good graces. After the studly George, it's no wonder Samantha didn't want to give Clyde the time of day. It's odd because that same actor appears on *I Dream of Jeannie* later as an ice cream shoppe worker who talks to Dr. Bellows and he's much more animated.

I really like that green and yellow dress and the blue sparkly dress Samantha was wearing at dinner was pretty though I don't like it when she has her hair up like that. She's had it like that in "Mother Meets What's-His-Name" and "It Shouldn't Happen to a Dog."

I must say that the special effects people should've received great awards on animating the chair so well. I don't believe I saw any wires on it.

I really liked that Endora was just lying in the air. I know if I were a warlock I'd do that quite a bit.

Some of my favorite lines include when Mr. Cosgrove leaves with the chair after it has come back to the house and Durwood says, "Well, I guess he's going to sign" and Samantha replies, "If he lives."

I also love it when Endora pops in on the Cosgrove's balcony and she is trying to explain what she has found out about the chair and he keeps moving and Endora pauses and glaringly says, "Stop it!"

I wonder what happened to Louise after dinner? She really seemed to be underutilized in this episode.

Three nights later Agnes Moorehead received the B'Nai B'rith's Human Relations Award for her "personal and dedicated commitment to enhancing individual dignity and respect, promoting better intergroup understanding, and securing equal rights and opportunities for all, [which] have strengthened and enriched America's democratic heritage."

DECEMBER 8, 1966

It was on this night that ABC aired Episode #87: "My Friend Ben."

Aunt Clara pops in on Samantha trying to fix the cord on one of their lamps and suggests she'll call an electrician. Samantha declines and says that she'll just get Durwood to fix it and she goes to retrieve Tabatha to show her Aunt how much the baby has grown. Always helpful, Aunt Clara decides to cast a spell with a lot of "oomphs" and "amphs" and ends up getting the original electrician, Benjamin Franklin! When Samantha returns without Tabatha, who was sleeping, she is shocked to see Benjamin Franklin but not more than he is. She reveals that he is now in the 20th century because of witchcraft. Mr. Franklin is intrigued and wonders if any of his inventions made it through the years. She shows him the electric lamp and they discuss the library and other such things. Before they know it, Durwood returns from work and is more shocked than all of them to be meeting Benjamin Franklin in his living room! Samantha assures him that Aunt Clara will get Mr. Franklin back to his own time but in the mean time she feels it's a great opportunity to show him how his inventions have influenced the modern day. Just then Larry shows up to go over the new campaign for, wouldn't you know it, Franklin Electronics and thinks Durwood has been hiding his master plan to incorporate Benjamin Franklin. Durwood tries to deny it but Larry won't hear of it.

The next day Samantha, Aunt Clara, and Benjamin Franklin end up at the public library where a crowd gathers to hear Mr. Franklin speak. Everyone is enchanted by his wit and wisdom, especially after he embarrasses a hippie heckler. They end up at the fire department where a vintage fire engine sits. Samantha leaves the other two to go call Durwood and in the meantime Mr. Franklin manages to start the engine and crash it into a hydrant! Hearing the commotion, Samantha becomes concerned, even more so when Aunt Clara runs in bumbling and muddling up her words. When they go outside Samantha is shocked and decides to send Aunt Clara home so she can work on the spell to get Ben back home. A police officer tells Samantha that as she seems to know Mr. Franklin, they can take it downtown and tell it to the judge.

At court, the judge is not amused that Mr. Franklin insists that he is THE Benjamin Franklin and says that there will be an official hearing to see what the charges will be. The hearing is set for two weeks from then.

Not knowing what they are going to do, Durwood, Samantha, and Mr. Franklin arrive at home and as they are walking up to the house Mr. Franklin disappears! Aunt Clara comes running out of the house absolutely pleased with herself but Samantha and Durwood are sorely disappointed as they don't know what they'll do when Mr. Franklin doesn't show up.

Stay tuned next week for Part Two!

I used to LOVE this episode when I was a child but nowadays I'd only give it maybe two stars. And this is the first episode on the DVD releases that has unexplained edits that really detract from the viewing experience. It's un-frickin'-believeable that they would edit just a minor thing like the ball of light not to mention blanking out the screen at the end of the episode. On the Columbia House Video version of it the words "Part 2 Next Week" come up over the still frame of Sammy's face. Why the heck couldn't that have been on the DVD?! Not to mention the recap for the next episode is totally missing…it made me maddddddddd! This episode also features no laugh track, which though interesting to have an episode without one, it also makes it kind of awkward.

I really liked that this episode was informative about Benjamin Franklin, not to mention Fredd Wayne was so good as Franklin and obviously a great person to have as historical consultant. In fact, Mr. Wayne would end up reprising his role of Benjamin Franklin in 1969 on *Daniel Boone*, in 1982 on *Voyagers!*, and 1986 on *Simon & Simon*, as well as doing the audio recording of *The Autobiography of Benjamin Franklin*. I do have to say that I never knew all about Ben Franklin and fire engines and libraries until I watched *Bewitched* which then prompted me to look him up.

I really found Aunt Clara's befuddlement quite annoying as though Marion Lorne was trying too hard. I've never felt that with any of her other performances but this one just seemed like she was trying way too hard to have Clara stammer and all.

I found it weird that Durwood would be OK with them taking Ben out on the town. I would think that he wouldn't want Ben out in public at all!

The fireplace wall is in the same style as it was for the first two seasons though it has red brick instead of the white brick and I also noticed that the divider between the kitchen and dining room was the same as it was in the first two seasons with an opening between the ceiling and the top of the window. This episode and its second part were the first episodes to be filmed in color which means it was the first time Sandra Gould played Gladys Kravitz. I'm sure it was a daunting task for Sandra to know that she was taking over the role from someone they all loved. It makes me feel bad for her.

The hippie was played by Tim Rooney, son to film great Mickey Rooney.

DECEMBER 15, 1966

It was on this night that ABC aired part two of last week's episode, #87: "Samantha for the Defense."

At the office the next day, Durwood is horrified to find that Mr. Franklin's antics are the headlines of the papers. He is also not pleased when the District Attorney shows up, however he is quite amiable and tells Durwood that he feels that they'll be able to get the charges cleared as obviously whoever Mr. Franklin is can't be possessing all his faculties. Just as DA Hawkins goes to leave, Larry bursts in with the paper pleased at all the free advertising they have got. Thinking that this event has all been a ruse for gain, Mr. Hawkins tells Durwood that he intends to prosecute to the full extent of the law and that the hearing will be moved up to the day after tomorrow.

At home the press has gathered outside of 1164 where Samantha tries to get Aunt Clara to remember the spell to get Benjamin Franklin to return. Mrs. Kravitz sees all the hubbub and runs over to tell the reporters how she knows that witches live there and that the reason Mr. Franklin was there because of a spell that was cast and she proceeds to repeat the words she had heard Aunt Clara use originally when she was spying earlier. Samantha hears it and asks Aunt Clara about the part she hears and it begins to jog her memory. The doorbell rings and Samantha answers it with the reporters demanding to speak to Mr. Franklin. She tells them that he's not there and is embarrassed when the 14th President of the United States Franklin Pierce pops in behind her, due to Aunt Clara trying for Benjamin Franklin. The President soon disappears and Samantha assures the reporters that Mr. Franklin is not taking questions and she closes the door.

Samantha and her aunt are surprised when Durwood shows up from the kitchen saying he snuck in the back way. Before they can go any further Aunt Clara remembers the spell and Benjamin Franklin reappears not even aware that he had been gone. They apprise him of what has happened since he's been gone and Durwood worries that they are sunk, until Samantha suggests that she use a little magic to sway public opinion in favor of Mr. Franklin. She goes to work, first cancelling a high school assembly that was held in honor of an astronaut for one for Mr. Franklin to speak at. She also changes an anti-war rally into a pro-Franklin rally. Soon the whole town is a-buzz with Ben Franklin fever just in time for the hearing.

DA Hawkins tells the jury that he intends to prove that Mr. Franklin isn't who he says he is and that he destroyed public property. Mr. Franklin, who has decided to be his own defense, tells the jury that Mr. Hawkins also has the burden of proving that he isn't whom he says and he charms them again with his wit. Later the local librarian is called to the stand where she tells the jury that Mr. Franklin created quite a stir when he showed up to pay a library fine for a book that was over two hundred years old, one which he didn't have with him but which he said had been burdening his conscience for all that time. Mrs. Kravitz is asked up next just to identify who Mr. Franklin is and when she tries to tell the judge about all the magic that goes on, she is dismissed when Mr. Franklin declines to cross-examine her. Things don't get much better when Durwood is asked on the stand and admits that he believes that Mr. Franklin really is Benjamin Franklin. When the judge calls for a brief recess it occurs to Samantha that she can prove that Mr. Franklin destroyed his own property. She pops down to the fire engine and removes a plaque that bears the inscription "Ben Franklin Memorial Fire Engine." She asks to be called to the stand when she gets back and says that it would be ridiculous for Mr. Franklin to be accused of stealing his own property and submits the plaque into evidence. The DA isn't going to have any of it and goes to tell her that perjury is a punishable offense until she tells him to "hush up" under her breath and twitches his mouth closed while she explains that all Mr. Franklin has done in his time in their city is to remind them all of what great things Benjamin Franklin had done and what it means to be honest. She twitches the DA's mouth open and he tries to object but he's too late. The judge dismisses the charges and everyone is happy, except the embarrassed DA.

I noticed that this one was really lacking in reality because for one, why would a plaque saying that it was Ben Franklin Memorial Fire Engine be any sort of proof that the fire engine was his? Not to mention the fact that she stole it. And it was so stupid that she offered that just because Benjamin Franklin invented the first fire station or whatever that means that any fire engines created thereafter are his? That's like saying anything operated by electricity is his.

I really liked Samantha saying, "Oh hush up!" to the DA and zapping his mouth shut. It's totally something all of us would've done and even though she's promised no witchcraft to Durwood there is only so much a witch/warlock can take!

I also liked Ben Franklin's quote about optimists usually expect the best and therefore are let down when it doesn't happen…but if you expect the worst and something better happens you're delightfully surprised.

That part of Gladys on the stand saying, "But don't I get to tell you what I know about her?" was used in two of the commercials promoting the Third Season and the announcer responds, "No, Gladys, we'll let the folks find out for themselves on an all new season of *Bewitched* in color on ABC." I wish Sony would've included those as extras.

The world also lost a bit of magic when Walt Disney passed away at sixty-five years old that day. He was in the midst of producing *The Jungle Book*.

Three nights later the animated Christmas special *How the Grinch Stole Christmas* first aired on CBS, narrated by Boris Karloff.

DECEMBER 22, 1966

It was on this night that ABC aired Episode #89: "A Gazebo Never Forgets" a decidedly un-Christmas episode.

While gardening in the back, Samantha is startled when she hears a crash and finds that it's Aunt Clara who has crashed into the gazebo. After dusting her off, Samantha tells her that she's pleased she's there as Durwood has designated her to go apply for a loan so that they can tear down the gazebo to build a rumpus room. He would do it but he's in Boston on business.

Later on they go to take Tabatha for a stroll through the park and sit next to another mother with a baby who has a pink polka dotted stuffed elephant that Tabatha takes a liking to. When the mother steps away to get a drink at a fountain behind the bench, Tabatha twitches her nose and levitates the elephant to her. The mother is furious thinking Samantha was trying to steal the toy and she snatches it back and leaves.

After their embarrassing romp in the park, Samantha leaves Aunt Clara to babysit Tabatha while she goes to the bank to speak to the bank president Mr. Scranton about the loan. His loan officer, Mr. Hawkins, seems to be very opposed to giving anyone a loan and Mr. Scranton is too when he hears that Samantha wants it to get rid of her gazebo, a word which he's not familiar with. However, when he hears where Durwood works he perks up as his brother, the president of Super Soapy Soap, happens to be one of McMann and Tate's biggest clients and Samantha reveals that Durwood came up with their winning slogan. Mr. Scranton is all set for the loan but says that Mr. Hawkins must come out to their property as a formality to survey their property.

When Samantha arrives at home, she finds that Tabatha has been fussy as she wants the toy elephant. Samantha tells Aunt Clara that Tabatha can't have everything she wants and she goes to call Durwood about the great news. Meanwhile, Aunt Clara decides that she'll just zap up a toy elephant but instead ends up with a live pink polka dotted elephant! Samantha is shocked when she hears the elephant blow its trunk and she suggests Aunt Clara hurry and get rid of it as Mr. Hawkins is coming out to the house. Of course, Aunt Clara can't remember the spell and as she tries to remember it the elephant goes to the front window to stick its head out to eat some grass, just as Mr. Hawkins shows up. He is shocked at what he sees and runs back to Mr. Scranton to have him come take a look. When Mr. Scranton hears of the shenanigans at Durwood's he calls his brother to tell him that Durwood might not be stable and of course Larry soon hears. He calls Samantha to tell her that he is going to accompany Mr. Scranton and Mr. Hawkins to her house to make sure there is no funny business going on and if there is Durwood will be unemployed. Samantha tries to jog Aunt Clara's memory but finds that it's useless and she suggests they hide the elephant out on the patio during the bank's visit. Getting the elephant out there proves to be a chore but it's finally done and Samantha takes Tabatha upstairs to get her changed but soon hears the elephant coming back in. She figures out that the elephant wanted to be with Tabatha, something Aunt Clara already knew. She suggests that they hide the elephant in the den with Tabatha, when the doorbell rings and Aunt Clara says that she'll have to have the toy elephant from the park in order to get rid of the elephant. Samantha zaps her to the park in the hopes of meeting up with the lady with the toy and she zaps herself into a dress and zaps up appetizers out on the patio. Mr. Hawkins is sure the elephant has got to be out on the patio as the doors are closed but when they get out there he is proven wrong.

He knows the elephant is there and goes searching through the house while Larry and Mr. Scranton discuss the reliability of Mr. Hawkins. Soon Mr. Hawkins bursts into the den and is pleased that he was right and he runs to tell his boss. Samantha hurriedly removes Tabatha and the elephant to the kitchen before the men come back. They are about to leave but Mr. Hawkins asks them to give him one more chance and

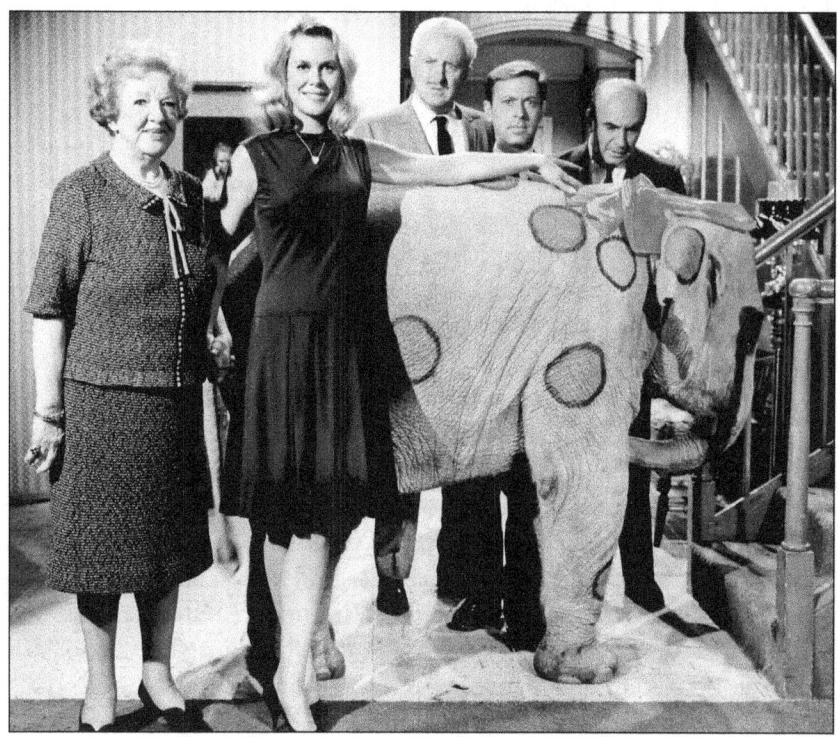

Aunt Clara, Samantha, Larry Tate, Mr. Hawkins (Steve Franken), and Mr. Scranton (Paul Reed) pose with the polka-dotted elephant in the foyer of 1164 Morning Glory Circle. Notice the black tape on the floor beneath the elephant that was used to mark where the actors should stand when filming.

they reluctantly agree and say they'll come running when he finds it. As he knows it can't go up the stairs he checks the kitchen and sees it and goes back to Mr. Scranton and Larry to tell them while Samantha sneaks the elephant and Tabatha back to the den so that the kitchen is clear when the men come in. Seeing that Mr. Hawkins is clearly delusional, Mr. Scranton and Larry leave. Mr. Hawkins is bewildered and as he goes to leave Tabatha comes running out of the den looking for her mommy. And soon the elephant busts through the painting in the hall, which Samantha suggests is Durwood's trophy elephant that he really should've shot first. The shot down Mr. Hawkins leaves just as Aunt Clara pops in with the toy elephant. After getting rid of the live elephant Samantha and Aunt Clara return to the park to return the toy, which Samantha wants to just zap back but Aunt Clara requests to do it to make up for the mess she causes and she needs up turning it into the live elephant once again!

I'd give this one about two stars. This episode has so many inconsistencies and all though I'm not a fan of Durwood, he is a necessary "evil." This is the first of thirteen episodes that Dick York would end up missing mainly due to complications he incurred while shooting the 1959 Gary Cooper movie *They Came to Cordura*. One scene required the men in the scene to lift a rail car off the tracks and they were supposed to set it down when the director yelled cut. Unfortunately Dick didn't hear and wrenched his spine when the others set it down. He went on pain pills and became addicted to them causing times where he just wasn't able to go into work and this was the first.

It really doesn't make sense that Aunt Clara would need the elephant toy to return the real elephant to wherever it came from not to mention Samantha's not even being able to zap it from room to room? I can understand not being able to zap it to Africa 'cause that's a long way but she really could've zapped it in close quarters. And that's another thing, was that pink polka dotted elephant REALLY from Africa? I don't believe so. I think, like the twin Jonathan, he was Aunt Clara's magic.

I really liked the bank manager, Paul Reed. I always think of him saying, "McMann and Tate? McMann and Tate!"

This was Steve Franken's third appearance. He was "Little Fisheyes" in the Charlie Leach episodes playing essentially the same role.

I always thought that the dig at the Nelsons was towards the *I Dream of Jeannie* people. What's even more interesting is that about three days before this episode aired the episode of *I Dream of Jeannie* titled "Jeannie Breaks the Bank" aired. In it, Tony and Roger want to go in on a boat together and Tony tries to take out a loan at the bank, essentially the same bank Samantha was at, at least it looks like it. He is denied at first because he has so little in assets so Jeannie blinks up $3,000,000.00 in his account.

I liked the scenes out in the park especially when the toy elephant floated. It seemed even more magical because they were outside with no overhead beams or ceiling where a prop man could be to hold the strings.

I always laugh when Sam and Clara are pushing the elephant out to the patio and Clara messes up the "Heave! Ho! Ho!" Samantha: "HEAVE! HO!"

I also noticed that Liz seems to shake her booty while walking up the stairs with Tabatha more so than normal as though she was trying to give the camera a show.

And what's with the elephant being able to burst through the "Girl with Broom" painting? That would mean that 1) the painting is an actual part of the wall and 2) the walls are literally paper thin. I did find it funny though when Sam was explaining to Steve Franken that Durwood was a hunter and it was his prize trophy and then she says, "I suppose he really should've shot it first."

I always wondered about the rumpus room too. Maybe they didn't get the loan because Hawkins' story about the pink elephant was verified seeing it as it showed up in the park near their house and of course you can't give a loan to people that would allow their pink polka dotted elephant to go roaming free.

All though this was the first season without a Christmas themed episode a Christmas tree was still seen in the living room of 1164 in a Public Service Announcement that Liz filmed touting giving Savings Bonds for Christmas. It was shown at movie-theaters and drive-ins.

DECEMBER 29, 1966

It was on this night that ABC aired Episode #90: "Soapbox Derby."

Samantha helps neighborhood boy Johnny Mills take his derby racer to the track to practice for the local races which in turn will give him a big chance to go to the National Derby Race in Akron, Ohio. It turns out Gladys Kravitz's nephew "Flash" is also competing and when she sees Samantha helping Johnny, she thinks she is also assisting him with magic. After the practices Johnny reveals that his father won't help him enter the races because he feels Johnny should focus more on school than the race. He asks Durwood and Samantha if they would act as his guardians for the race. They agree to but only after Samantha tries to ask Mr. Mills to do it himself.

Johnny ends up winning the race but Mrs. Kravitz wants a recall when she accuses Johnny of getting a supernatural assist from Samantha. The judges require Johnny's father to be there so Samantha pops over to his shop to persuade him to come over. He insists he has too much to do but Samantha uses her natural born talents to get most of the work done so he agrees to come over and vouch for his son. The judges side with Johnny and he goes off to Akron to compete where he ends up winning.

Elizabeth Montgomery, Agnes Moorehead and Dick York actually went to Ohio for the real Soap Box races in 1966 as *Bewitched* sponsor Chevrolet also sponsored the races. They were joined by *F-Troop*, another show from the 60s.

This is one of the episodes that also provides proof that maybe Samantha wasn't the Witch of Westport (the original title for the show) after all as Mills' Garage is located in Patterson, NY and that is stated on Johnny's racer.

I really like this episode and would give it three stars. In fact, many times it felt like it was becoming a drama what with Johnny's father giving that impassioned speech about how tough is life is.

I did like how most of the episode was shot outdoors, something which usually never took place.

I LOVED the scene at the garage with Samantha putting the wheels on the car and fixing the carburetor. I always remember seeing the hoses attach itself to the carburetor but I think that was just a made up memory as I just expected it to happen.

I also thought it was really cute when Johnny told Samantha that he felt that his father would have a hard time saying no to her. I kept thinking, "Man, how lucky is that kid to have been able to work with her?!"

I noticed there were a lot of close up shots of Samantha, something which seemed to only happen within the first season.

I hate that Sandra Gould turned Gladys into a meanie and this was definitely the worst of it. So I suppose it's good she got it out of her system in the beginning. I also wondered where Flash's parents were. And it's funny that Flash is Abner's nephew yet Abner doesn't even seem to care. Two of the racers names were announced as Bellows and Healey. Does that sound familiar anyone?

One thing I did notice that leaves me wondering "How did that happen" is that Samantha pops over to Mr. Mill's garage to talk him into coming over to the races and he agrees. Well, how did they get back over there? Wouldn't he wonder how she got there? I'm sure she must've said that Durwood dropped her off or something and then rode back to the races with Mr. Mills but it seemed like a good place to have put a joke about how she suddenly got there.

JANUARY 5, 1967

Tonight ABC aired the first new episode of 1967, #91: "Sam in the Moon."

Durwood gets irritated with Samantha's lack of interest in new pictures of the moon up close that NASA has been broadcasting. He's actually really irritated 'cause he is interested, it's just that she's vacuuming at the same time he's watching the pictures on TV and the vacuum scrambles the picture. When Samantha tells him she has more important things to do and besides, "I've seen the moon," he begins to wonder if she means up close.

Later Samantha is still doing what apparently is spring cleaning when Endora pops in and requests her company for a shopping spree. She tells Samantha that she'll let her clean the mortal way AFTER they go shopping and Samantha agrees though she is curious how they will go shopping if all the stores are closed as it is Sunday (how quaint!). Endora asks her just to follow and they end up in Japan where it isn't Sunday. They buy some marvelous warlock tea from a warlock member of the Japanese Chapter of witches and do some more shopping before returning.

Samantha begins to get back to her housework but decides it would be nice to spend the rest of the day with Durwood when he gets home so she has the vacuum do its job by itself while she goes upstairs to clean the attic. Durwood comes home a bit early and catches the vacuum. He begins questioning Samantha about what she has been doing in an attempt to get her to spill the beans about visiting the moon. She gets irritated and tells him she has been there and "one of these days" he will too. When he sees the warlock tea she tries to hide it from him and he suspects it may be moon dust so he takes it to the local druggist to have it analyzed. He then daydreams about what will happen if it is found out that his wife can just go to the moon with the snap of her fingers because it would save NASA tons of money, though he would get in trouble for having kept this secret for so long.

Samantha wakes him from his dream and the druggist calls saying that the warlock tea is nothing he has seen before and he's going to have his brother from Nassau look at it (though Durwood thinks he means NASA).

The brother does take a look at it and wants to know where Durwood got it from and when he comes over for more questioning Samantha twitches up a breeze which blows it all away.

Later, Samantha gazes out the window at the Lady in the Moon and Durwood still wants to know if she's been there…but she tells him that not all secrets should be shared.

This episode is really cute in the fact that it brings up the notion that your partner may have a life beyond what you know, and so what? As long as it's not anything horrible like being a murderer or something. You should be able to trust your mate.

It's also cute in the fact that it's two years before NASA actually does land on the moon. And a couple months before they do land on the moon, Endora is seen on the moon when she was chasing down Cousin Henry.

I really like this episode but I'd only give it three stars 'cause it seems like Durwood being mad over her having even been to the moon whether now or just recently is ridiculous! She's a witch for crying out loud! But I love Samantha being so passive about her having been to the moon. I also really liked the dream sequence and think it would've been HILARIOUS had they had Dr. Bellows and General Peterson in the dream sequence. Nowadays I think they would've done it as it seems that the networks really don't care about crossovers but back then I know it was a no-no.

I really liked it when they showed Samantha in the lineup and Durwood says, "I don't know her" and then Endora pops in and he says, "Her, I know!" And if those measurements on the wall were correct it would seem that Liz was about 5'6" or 7" and Agnes was just a little shorter.

I think the shot of the moon at the end is so beautiful and the shot of Liz is even more beautiful. It also makes me wonder why they didn't use this window as the one that Samantha and Durwood looked out of when Pleasure O'Riley showed up at night. They looked out the window that looks out over the backyard yet she was in the front yard.

I also like in that end scene that she says it's "The Lady in the Moon" and he actually questions it! I'm sure she would know out of anyone.

It always used to confuse me during the scene in Larry's den which is the Stephens's den even in the placement of the closet door and door to the outside! Why couldn't they have used another set?

The day before the Doors released their self-titled debut album.

Two days before, Jack Ruby, the man who murdered Lee Harvey Oswald, died.

And three days before, Elizabeth Montgomery co-hosted the Tournament of Roses Parade with Vin Scully. This event was promoted with a commercial where Liz is seen in the living room of 1164 with frequent guest star Dan Tobin narrating. Liz twitches and zaps Vin in to ask him to be her co-host.

JANUARY 12, 1967

It was on this night that ABC began airing *Bewitched* one half hour earlier at 8:30 PM EST with Episode #92: "Ho Ho the Clown."

Endora pops in to find that Tabatha and Samantha are going to be in the audience of the kid show *Ho Ho the Clown*, which happens to be Tabatha's favorite show. She decides to tag-a-long so she can see how inferior the other children are to her little Tabatha.

Meanwhile Durwood is watching the show as his client, the Solow Toy Company, is the sponsor and is responsible for getting the tickets for the show. He is shocked when Ho Ho goes to give away the prize of a Ho-Ho-Hope chest filled with toys from the client and he gives it to Tabatha who wasn't supposed to be in the drawing. Larry is furious but Durwood suggests that the program staff may have goofed; however he knows that Endora had something to do with it. Samantha tries to suggest the program staff goofed to allay his fears and as he had thought the same thing he goes along with it.

However the next day Ho Ho refuses to go on air unless the cute little doll from the day before that won the Ho-Ho-Hope Chest is in the audience. Larry tells Durwood that he needs to get Samantha and Tabatha back down to the studio ASAP or he will be fired, considering if Ho Ho doesn't go on there will be no show and no sponsor which means no client. Samantha realizes her mother put a spell on Ho Ho to fall in love with Tabatha and so she accompanies Durwood down to the studio where he watches from the control booth with Larry and Mr. Solow. When the camera starts rolling Ho Ho reveals that he is going to focus every show on Tabatha and make sure she wins the Ho-Ho-Hope Chest every show. Mr. Solow is furious and demands that they find out who the girl is.

Later on, sans makeup, Ho Ho shows up at Tabatha's house with balloons, a pony, and portrait saying he can't stand being away from her. Having had enough of this creepiness, Samantha takes the pony out back and calls for Endora to show up. She pops in from Mexico and agrees to remove the spell from Ho Ho and she pops off. Back in the house, Ho Ho is bewildered as to why he is there and before Samantha can explain, Larry and Mr. Solow show up as Mr. Solow figured out that Tabatha was Durwood's daughter. He also thinks that Ho Ho and Durwood were conspiring to put him out of business and so he cancels Ho Ho's show just as Larry fires Durwood. Not wanting things to get any worse Samantha freezes Ho Ho, Larry and Mr. Solow and tells Durwood that they must come up with an explanation for Ho Ho's behavior. She decides they'll say it was a publicity stunt for a new cute doll for the Solow Toy Company and she zaps up a doll that looks just like Tabatha. She zaps Ho Ho into believing he was all a part of it and then she unfreezes the men. She tells Mr. Solow what was happening and he loves the idea. On Larry's suggestion he decides to give each kids from the previous show a free Tabatha doll.

This episode is ho-ho-horrible! I'd only give it a half star. It's a horrible episode only for Joey Foreman (Ho Ho) but it was a good story line and it was good to see Dick Wilson sober.

Ho Ho is creepy and the lines about "cute little doll" and always saying "ho, ho, ho" are annoying! I also remember thinking that it was THE coolest thing when Samantha froze Ho Ho, Larry, and Mr. Solow, though in my head I thought she had actually stopped time throughout the whole world rather than just freezing them.

Before I knew what the real Tabatha doll looked like I always assumed it was the one they show in this episode. I thought that would've been a cool promotional item. So I was pretty disappointed when I found that the real Tabatha doll was made before this episode.

Here are some of my favorite lines:

> ENDORA: *"Care for a bite of taco, darling?"* (Just the way Agnes Moorehead says 'taco' is funny)
> ENDORA: *"Adios, muchacha!"*
> SAMANTHA: *"Olé…"*

A huge blooper occurs in this episode as the door to 1164 which is usually green is white.

Two days before segregationist Lester Maddox was sworn in as the Governor of Georgia.

Two days after the episode aired the "Human Be-in" took place in San Francisco's Golden Gate Park. It was a gathering of America's counterculture and became the origination of the word 'psychedelic' and also ended up making the Haight-Ashbury district the center of the counterculture as 20–30,000 young Americans looking for freedom of expression and love converged upon San Francisco. It was a precursor to what would be known as 'the Summer of Love.'

The day after the first Super Bowl took place at Los Angeles Memorial Coliseum between the Green Bay Packers and the Kansas City Chiefs, with the Packers winning 35-10.

JANUARY 19, 1967

It was on this night that ABC aired Episode #93: "Super Car."

After yet another encounter between Durwood and Endora that ends badly, Samantha suggests that if her mother were simply gracious to Durwood he would be nice back. Endora decides to test it out and sees Durwood engrossed in a magazine with a future looking car on the cover. He tells her it's the Reactor Mach II, which will be released sometime soon. She asks him if he'd like one and he says yes so she has him hold out his hand and she zaps in a set of keys which she says is to the car. When he looks out the window, he sees she is right! At the same time in Detroit, the manufacturers of the car who are testing it are horrified to see that the expensive car is missing from its locked and secure room.

Durwood is excited and takes Samantha out to see the car while Endora looks on. Samantha suggests he thank Endora but he's too impressed with the car to be bothered and so Endora pops off, offended. Durwood takes the car out for a spin and then tells Samantha he won't be able to keep it as it was created out of witchcraft which Samantha knows is not going to sit well with her mother.

Meanwhile, Larry is meeting with Mr. Sheldrake of Sheldrake Sausages who wants Larry to somehow incorporate the space age with his sausages. The phone rings with Durwood calling Larry about the car and he invites the two men out to see it. While Durwood waits for his business associates he still fawns over the car until he notices a manufacturer plate on the inside with a serial number and he realizes that the car must've really come from the manufacturer, meaning it was stolen! When he goes inside Endora has returned and he blows up at her. Not wanting to take any more of his guff, she says she's going to the Mardi Gras and pops off. Durwood becomes paranoid thinking that the police will be all over the missing car and about jumps out of his skin when the doorbell rings. However, it's just Larry and Mr. Sheldrake coming to look at the car. He tries to talk them out of it as he doesn't intend to keep it but they insist on seeing it. Samantha tells Durwood to let them go see it while she pops off to New Orleans to find her mother. Mr. Sheldrake is so impressed by the car, especially its space age look, he suggests that they use it for his ad campaign. Durwood refuses until Larry takes him out back to threaten him with firing if he doesn't allow it. Durwood relents and is sick when Mr. Sheldrake asks to take it for a spin. He reluctantly agrees and Larry goes back in the house to make a call. After Sheldrake leaves Endora and Samantha pop in covered in confetti and Endora agrees to get rid of it and as it's coming up the street she makes it disappear with

Sheldrake in it! Durwood is furious and as Endora doesn't seem to be able to please him she pops back to New Orleans. Just then Larry comes outside and Samantha doesn't understand why Durwood is worked up until he implies that Mr. Sheldrake took the car on a long journey.

Later Larry is shocked when Mr. Sheldrake doesn't come back and he apologizes to Durwood when Mr. Sheldrake calls from the airport and says that it's going to take him awhile to figure out what happened; however he was able to secure the rights for the car as he met the designers of the car.

I LOVE this episode! I love that Endora decided to finally give Durwood a chance and was doing something so nice for him. The only fly in the ointment is what an ass he is about not thanking her.

The Super Car was a prototype and had shown up in other TV shows of the time including *Batman*, as the Catwoman's Kitty Car complete with ears and tail. Durwood even refers to *Batman* when he says, "It makes the Bat-mobile look like a skateboard!" The magazine he first sees the car in would later show up on *The Flying Nun*. The car is now a part of a car museum in Oklahoma.

I also thought that when one of the workers (Dave Madden) is laughing about the squirrel dream HE sounded like a squirrel.

This is one of the first times that Samantha wears the same outfit for the entire episode. And apparently Tabatha is relegated to the nursery for the whole time as she is never seen though in the original script there was a scene where Samantha goes to check on her. Also, in the original script when Durwood asks Endora where the car came from she said "Where do you think it came from — heaven?" "Heaven" was changed to "the stork brought it?" I wonder if Agnes Moorehead, being very Bible oriented, objected to using the word "heaven" there. There were also scenes at Mardi Gras where Samantha is trying to find Endora that were cut.

They use the music from the Charlie Leach episodes whenever they show the car, which is one of my favorite pieces of music from the series.

Here are some of my favorite lines:

> DURWOOD: *"Honey, just because Larry gave me the day off in the middle of the week is no reason to get historical!"*
> SAMANTHA: *"Mother, Darrin's off today."*
> ENDORA: *"I think you're just noticing it for the first time!"*
> SHELDRAKE: *"Sheldrake's the name, sausage is my game."*

JANUARY 26, 1967

It was on this night that ABC aired Episode #94: "The Corn is as High as a Guernsey's Eye."

Aunt Clara drops in on Samantha to get comfort after having been told by Endora that she's an old cow and should be set out to pasture. Samantha suggests that she accompany her downtown to meet Durwood for lunch thinking it will make her feel better.

When they get to Durwood's building Samantha remembers she had told Durwood she was going to pick up his watch from the jewelers and she decides to pop over to the store to get it. She tells Aunt Clara she'll be right back and not to move.

At the same time, Larry is telling Durwood that they are about to lose the Morton Milk account as Durwood has taken too much time to come up with a campaign and that the Whittle Agency, in the same building, has been vying for the account, especially during National Milk Week where Mr. Morton is going to display his prize winning Guernsey cow, Ginger, in the lobby. The cow just so happens to be being delivered to the building just then; however, a policeman thinks something fishy is up and tries to get proof from the delivery man that he's waiting for a signature on it. Meanwhile, in boredom, Clara comes across the closed off display for the cow and goes inside to take a peek. It consists of a little farmhouse with a pail and a rocking chair which she sits down in and takes a nap. Samantha soon pops back in amid the skirmish going on about the cow and overhears the elevator operator saying what a strange day it's been with a fruitcake of an old lady talking to a plant one minute and a cow in the lobby the next. Remembering her conversation with Aunt Clara earlier Samantha assumes she took Endora seriously and turned herself into a cow! While the delivery man and the policeman argue Samantha pops the cow home with her. However, Louise is babysitting and when she hears Samantha talking to the cow she announces that she is going to come downstairs. As the cow won't go into the kitchen like Samantha asks, she zaps it in there just as Louise arrives wondering why Samantha is home. Sam says things went faster than expected and she hurriedly rushes Louise out with the wrong coat and zaps the cow back into the living room so she can talk "Aunt Clara" into changing herself back. She is shocked when Louise comes back in to return the coat and Samantha tells her that they are now into being thriftier so they've decided to milk their own cow. Again she ushers Louise out who thinks it's all a little strange and she rushes off to tell Larry.

Meanwhile Larry is ecstatic that the cow is missing because Mr. Morton is blaming Mr. Whittle for it and wants to put the entire city under arrest for cow-napping which means McMann and Tate may still have a chance at the campaign. Just then Samantha calls to tell Durwood where she and Aunt Clara are and Durwood tells her to try and get Aunt Clara back to normal and he goes down to the lobby to watch the war between Whittle and Morton.

In the lobby Durwood notices the closed off display and curiosity gets the better of him so he peeks in and about chokes when he sees Aunt Clara sleeping there. He suddenly realizes that the cow at his house is Morton's! So he rushes off to phone Samantha. Meanwhile, Larry is told that Louise is calling him and he goes to take the call at the phone next to Durwood. As Louise is telling him about the Stephens' cow, he also hears Durwood's conversation about the cow in the living room. When he gets off the phone he questions a nervous Durwood about it who suggests that their cow is a different one and they return to the lobby where Samantha discreetly pops in behind Durwood, having shrunk the cow to miniature and placed it in her purse. She decides that she'll enlarge it again on the elevator so that everyone will think the cow had just wandered into the elevator. As the elevator operator tries to regale Samantha with his stories of the women he sees she crouches down and pops out just as the cow returns to normal size causing him to faint. Mr. Morton is thrilled to find his cow again and even more impressed when he hears that Durwood has a cow and as a gift sends over a herd of cows to 1164!

I would give it at least two and a half stars but I did notice some discrepancies especially the fact that the cow wasn't supposed to be there until next week. I also hated the ending having all those cows herded into the backyard. Why not show what happens next? And, of course, if Gladys had been watching she would've called the Animal Control.

I did like Aunt Clara's reaction to the snoopy elevator operator: "Do you mind? This is private!"

I always liked when Samantha shrunk the cow. When I was little I really thought the mini-cow was real and I felt bad that it had to be placed in her purse.

But I was thinking about how Samantha, if she was thinking the cow was Aunt Clara, and was able to zap it, should've been able to zap the polka-dotted elephant from "A Gazebo Never Forgets." Therefore I decided the writers need to be smacked especially as those two episodes played within such a short time of each other.

I also thought it strange that Louise would leave a second time with the wrong jacket. You would've thought she would've said, "Hey, Samantha!

I need my coat! I don't give a flying rat's ass if you do have a cow, 'cause I'm gonna have one if I don't get my coat!"

There are two bloopers in this episode: when Sam knocks the lamp off of the table and it breaks, the table is still standing, but when we see her zap it back together again, the table is lying on the floor and straightens itself. Also, when Aunt Clara comes down the chimney, the set is almost entirely different than the previous shot of the smoke coming down the chimney. The plant is different, the pillow is different, the furniture has moved, etc.

The day after, a terrible fire claimed the lives of the Apollo I's flight crew — Gus Grissom, Edward Higgins White, and Roger Chaffee at NASA during a launchpad test. It was also on this day that the United States, Soviet Union, and United Kingdom signed the Outerspace Treaty which essentially said that no country would ever place nuclear weapons on the Moon or in the Earth's orbit, that no country would ever claim any planet as its own as they are the heritage of mankind. Space exploration was to be done for the good of humankind and not just a particular government.

FEBRUARY 2, 1967

It was on this night that ABC aired Episode #95: "The Trial and Error of Aunt Clara."

During the middle of the night Endora summons Samantha discreetly to tell her that Aunt Clara has finally messed things up so much that she (Endora), Hagatha, and Enchantra have decided that a trial should be held to see if Aunt Clara should be made earthbound! Clara has also chose Samantha to be her defense attorney and the trial is going to be held at 1164 in the morning and with that Endora pops out before Samantha can get any more information. She is startled by Durwood who wondered what she was doing and she decides to act like she was sleep walking and she goes upstairs.

The next morning after rushing Durwood off to work, Samantha finds Aunt Clara knocking at the cellar door. They sit down for some coffee and Clara tells her about her weekend with Endora and the aunts at Lady Montague's castle in Scotland which turned out to be a disaster as they went hunting and Clara shot one of Lady Montague's dogs as she didn't know they were hunting dogs. Just as she says that maybe she should be made earthbound, Endora pops in telling her Samantha knows all about the trial. Clara is relieved and decides to go rest before the trial but when

Endora tells her to pop into the den like a witch, she does; however her shoes are left behind. Realizing she has her work cut out for her Samantha begins to go to work immediately refreshing Clara's memory about how to perform basic spells such as levitating a pencil into a desk drawer. As Aunt Clara is concentrating, the doorbell rings so Samantha goes to answer it and finds Larry there who has come to retrieve a file Durwood left there in his rush to work. Before they can go into the den, Aunt Clara comes rushing out in a dither until Samantha finds that Clara is looking for the desk. They then notice it sitting at the top of the stairs with the drawers all out and everything scattered. Samantha tells Clara to work on getting the desk back to the den while she stalls Larry by taking him out on to the patio to discuss colleges for Tabatha. Clara soon does manage getting the desk back into the den and Larry goes to find the file but finds it difficult as nothing is filed correctly. As Samantha speaks with Aunt Clara, Endora pops in wondering if Samantha still wants to be Aunt Clara's defense and of course she does. Just then, to Samantha's horror, an old carriage car comes honking into the living room carrying Hagatha, Enchantra, and Judge Bean. She rushes off to make sure Larry goes out the back way, zaps herself into her flying suit and when she gets back to the living room finds that it's been transformed into a court room. The charges are read that Aunt Clara has repeatedly failed at the use of witchcraft and therefore should be made earthbound. Judge Bean says he could pass down a judgment then but Samantha tells him that wouldn't be fair and she asks that the charges be dismissed on the grounds of love. An annoyed Judge Bean denies the motion and asks for the trial to continue. Seeing that she's going to have to use a little trickery to make them think that Aunt Clara still has her powers, she asks Aunt Clara to make the judge's gavel fly to her and she twitches it to Clara, who is quite pleased with herself. Soon, Samantha hears Durwood's car pull up and when she goes to the window she finds that he has come home early to retrieve the correct file as Larry got the wrong one. Samantha locks him out and tells him she just waxed the front hall and that she'll get it for him. When she turns to go into the den she notices a palm tree now in her living room and finds that the prosecution had asked Clara to zap up something tropical in the way of a drink. She excuses herself and meets Durwood at the den window with a file and then she rushes off. When she comes back into the living room she finds a large stuffed polar bear, yet another attempt by Aunt Clara for a cool drink. Before she can say anything Durwood yells for her and she rushes off to find that he has crawled through the den window to get the file he wants as she gave him the wrong one. He tells her he knows why she doesn't want him in there and tells her she is having a meeting with the ladies of the bazar. She doesn't quite agree but rushes off only to find an Alaskan dog sled which was an attempt by Aunt Clara at Baked Alaska. Thinking that she can do some more tricks to make them think Aunt Clara is competent, Samantha tries to proceed but is shot down by Judge Bean who says that the overwhelming weight of the evidence is clear and at midnight Aunt Clara shall be made earthbound and no longer have place in the witch community.

Durwood finds that his desk is an absolute mess and yells for Samantha while he is coming into the living room. Seeing that things could get difficult for Samantha, Aunt Clara commands everyone to disappear and the courtroom returns to the living room furniture and the court participants all disappear in thunder and lightning. Durwood is confused as to what happened but Samantha explains it to him and she finds that Aunt Clara really thinks she did it. However, Clara tells her that it really was done by her as she didn't want Samantha to be in trouble.

I LOVE this episode and would give it four stars in a heartbeat! Aside from the different actresses playing Enchantra and Hagatha and the kitchen closet now being the cellar door, EVERYTHING about this episode is PERFECTION! Samantha looks so beautiful in this episode, the special effects are top notch, the whole idea that Aunt Clara may be earthbound and kicked out of her community is so touching and then her redeeming herself at the end, all excellent!

This is one of the episodes that I remember from my childhood and always thought it was spooky and cool at the same time. The lighting was fantastic and even though some of the camera angles were weird they worked too.

Now that I'm older I don't like that they are making Endora so mean but this is the fourth time she's been mean. The first was when she brought Hedley Partridge into town against Clara's wishes (in "Aunt Clara's Old Flame"), the second was at Tabatha's testing ("Witches and Warlock are My Favorite Things"), the third was just last episode, and now this. Last episode Clara said that Endora said she was an old cow and should be turned out to pasture! How cruel is that?! So I suppose if they were starting to go with the new mean Endora than this episode works.

I always felt that Endora's animosity towards Clara was due to the "fact" that Clara is Maurice's sister and that Maurice, out of great love for his sister, insisted that Endora invite her to join in on the activities she would have with Enchantra and Hagatha. I'm sure before Aunt Clara became so befuddled and all, Endora may have really enjoyed hanging around with her but as she became so sloppy in her spells Endora may have felt that would make her look bad not to mention her relationship with Maurice wasn't too stellar, therefore she would try anything to make sure she didn't have to be associated with them anymore.

I thought the funniest part of this episode is when Aunt Clara is telling Samantha about her weekend at Lady Montague's castle and proceeds to tell her she shot one of Lady Montague's dogs. I mean, it's sad but funny especially since Aunt Clara says, "She should've told me we were shooting birds." I agree! How are you supposed to know?

I also always think of Aunt Clara when at the end she says, "Well what did you expect with that magnificent piece of witchcraft I did?" I love the way she says it.

Also, this is the first time this season that we see the flying suit. It is one of my favorites, probably second favorite to the green bodied one that is seen in the Fifth Season on. And I love how they made it look like Elizabeth Montgomery really had it zapped it on as the cape flutters down in the air as though it had just fallen on her.

Anyway, I LOVE LOVE LOVE this episode! I could (and have) watched it over and over.

Three days later *the Smothers Brothers Comedy Hour* premiered on CBS.

FEBRUARY 9, 1967

It was on this night that ABC aired Episode #96: "Three Wishes."

Durwood is told that he will be attending a business meeting in Honolulu however Samantha isn't invited as the clients' wives aren't invited. Endora, who has popped in bored, thinks that Durwood is up to something and decides to give him three wishes without him knowing. Samantha brushes off her mother's suspicions even when Durwood calls from work to say that he doesn't have to go to Hawaii because he has been assigned to escort a swimsuit model named Buffy to a business luncheon and convention in Boston. Endora suggests that wish number one was used to wish himself out of the Hawaiian trip and wish number two was used to wish up the trip to Boston. Still not convinced that Durwood is using the wishes, especially when he tells her that he'll fly to Boston for the luncheon and then fly home for a late dinner with her, Samantha tells her mother that she still trusts him. However dinner time rolls around and Durwood is nowhere to be found and when he calls to tell Samantha that the airport has been fogged in, Endora tells her that it's the result of the last wish. Now doubts begin to creep in as what her mother is saying starts to make sense. The door rings with a Western Union messenger there for a message for Durwood and Endora suggests that any mortal woman would call her husband to tell him about the important message so she calls Durwood's hotel room and is shocked to hear Buffy's tired voice saying that Durwood isn't there right now and that she's too tired to talk and she hangs up on Samantha. And so it looks as though Endora is right.

The next day a grizzled Durwood comes in to find that Samantha will not give him the time of day as he tries to figure out why she's being so cold to him. When she still remains silent, but for the slamming of magazines down on the coffee table, he demands she tell him what's wrong. She snaps her fingers and disappears and when he hollers for her he hears her disembodied voice say that she's leaving him and going home to mother. He runs up to their room to find that she is packing invisibly and his efforts to stop her are fruitless as the suitcases float downstairs. He finally tells her that she should at least tell him why and the suitcases drop to the ground and in their midst Samantha pops in dressed in her flying suit. She tells him about the wishes and how he had used them. Durwood thinks this is all ridiculous and tells her that he actually slept all night and let Buffy have his room as the hotel ran out of rooms. And he also tells her that he can prove he didn't use them. For his first wish he demands that Endora pop in, which she does. Knowing that Endora would never do what Durwood asks Samantha realizes she may have been wrong. He then goes to wish that Endora would stay out of their lives forever but Samantha stops him and so he wishes Endora away for one week and she disappears. For his third wish he goes to wish away her flying suit but she tells him it's on the house and she pops back into her mortal clothes and apologizes to him.

Later that night, after Durwood takes a hot shower, he says how much he loved it and that he wishes he could take another and immediately disappears. Samantha realizes he never used his last wish but they have a little laugh over it.

I really like this episode and would give it three stars. It would get four but Durwood is such an ass in this one not to mention yet again they use a not-so-pretty girl to be the sexpot! Buffy looks so weird too, with or without those glasses she keeps putting on and off.

The scene with the floating suitcases was a direct remake of the same scene in Episode #5: "Help, Help, Don't Save Me." This is also the second time that Durwood has been given three wishes, the first time being in Season Two's "Double Tate."

I liked the scene at first as it was just another time of Endora popping in with nothing to do. And it seemed like the first thirty seconds were unnecessary showing Samantha flitting about the kitchen.

And what was with Endora's hair? That's the most outrageous style she's had yet! It totally looked like something the people on *Star Trek* would do to indicate that it's the future or that she's an alien.

I did find that boy staring at Durwood in the airport funny but weird. When I was younger I kept on thinking maybe he was Oliver Twist or something.

Something I really noticed is when Durwood is using up his wishes. If you look at Endora's face she has a look of abject horror on it when she believes he is going to wish her out of their lives forever! As though she really REALLY understood that had he said those words there would be no way to bypass it. And this would be per the rules established in the episode last season when Durwood wished he were Larry Tate for a day. And then when he was going to wish the flying suit away it seemed like Samantha was really abject to that as though the flying suit gave her more power and without it she would be lost.

Yet again Tabatha is nowhere to be seen.

I love episodes when Samantha gets mad, it's so hot!

Here are some of my favorite lines:

> SAMANTHA: *"I'm going home to mother!"*
> DURWOOD: *"Going home to mother? She's always here!"*

It was also on this night that Dick Sargent appeared on *Daniel Boone* in "When I Became a Man, I Put Away Childish Things."

The next evening Agnes Moorehead appeared on *Wild Wild West* in "Night of the Vicious Valentine." She would go on to win the Emmy for Outstanding Performance by an Actress in a Supporting Role in a Drama.

FEBRUARY 16, 1967

It was on this night that ABC aired Episode #97: "I Remember You… Sometimes" sponsored by Quaker Oats.

Durwood has a rather embarrassing run in with client Ed Pennybaker when he can't remember his name, made really embarrassing by the fact that Ed prides himself on his great memory, so Durwood brings home a book on how to improve your memory. Endora thinks this is laughable as she says mortals pride themselves on being able to forget because if they didn't they would be insufferable and to prove her point she casts a spell on his watch to give him perfect memory. Suddenly he remembers everything he knows about Mr. Pennybaker and his family and the next day at work Durwood redeems himself with Mr. Pennybaker when they start having a discussion about trivial things. However Durwood starts to irritate everyone when he insists that what he knows is more correct than what Ed knows. Thankfully Samantha and Louise show up so Louise can get money to go shopping and Samantha invites the Tates and Mr. Pennybaker and his wife for dinner. Before anyone can accept, Durwood says Larry actually said he would have the client over the next time based on a note he wrote on a client's file several months ago and to prove it he'll have Betty bring in the file. Samantha is totally embarrassed and says that there will be no discussing it, dinner will be at their home.

Dinner is insufferable when Ed and Durwood try to one up each other and Samantha realizes that this must be a spell on Durwood and so she excuses herself so she can call on her mother. Endora promises she didn't put a spell on Durwood and Samantha deduces it must be something that is on or around Durwood so she goes back into the living room where tempers are flaring. When Durwood's watch falls off he finds that he can't remember as much; however when Mrs. Pennybaker picks it up and she starts spouting off trivia, Samantha realizes the watch is the culprit and she takes it away. Mr. Pennybaker realizes he has been such a bore all this time and promises to keep his trivia to himself.

I think this episode is really boring though I do like it when Samantha gets mad at Durwood so I give it two and a half stars. When they do the close-ups on Samantha in the beginning, her hair is HUGE! The scenes with both her and Durwood shown, it's much lower, however, a bad hair day all around.

In wondering if the dates Durwood spouted off had any significance, we find that September 14, the day that Samantha last fixed blueberry pancakes, is the same day as *Bewitched* writer Ruth Brooks Flippen's birthday. It was also in 1948 that Agnes Moorehead's movie *Johnny Belinda* premiered. When Durwood was listing off some of the accounts where Betty had messed up, one of them is the Rohrbach account. That's the last name of the client in "Long Live the Queen" next season. He also mentions that Mr. Pennybaker's youngest is three year old Willie. Liz and Bill's son Willie was two and a half when this aired and would turn three in July.

The book Durwood has uses the same style cover with font and all as the cover of the book in *I Dream of Jeannie* when Jeannie writes a book about motherhood and uses Tony's name as the author. I almost thought it was the same book but I magnified the book in *Bewitched* and it does have the title Samantha reads out loud.

Dan Tobin was perfection for this role. He did seem like a know-it-all. He'll actually appear in another episode this season "Nobody But a Frog Knows How To Live" and was in Season Two's "Double Split."

Kasey Rogers was still able to fit into that green sweater dress she wears when her and Samantha show up to the office up to the end of her life.

This is another time where the effects crew tried animating magical stars to accompany the magic and for the most part it works as it really clued you into the fact that it was only the watch that had the spell on it.

The brown dress Samantha wears was the basis for the dress the TV Land Samantha statue in Salem, MA wears.

The day before Elizabeth Montgomery was nominated for Best TV Star — Female on the Golden Globes.

On Valentine's Day that week Aretha Franklin recorded "Respect" to be released in April.

FEBRUARY 23, 1967

It was on this night that ABC aired Episode #98: "Art for Sam's Sake" sponsored by Chevrolet.

Samantha is sketching out a painting of a still life when Endora pops in wondering why she's doing it the mortal way when she could just zap up a painting. Samantha says she thinks it's fun doing it the mortal way and that the painting is going to be part of a charity exhibit and may even win a prize. Not impressed, Endora tells her it better be spectacular so as not to disgrace the family name.

Later on Endora pops in again wanting to see the painting but Samantha tells her it's already down at the gallery at the university so Endora pops down to see it where she freezes a couple workers who try to stop her. When she sees Samantha's painting she is disgusted at how amateur it is and she switches it for a professional artist's, Henri Monchet, landscape and she switches his signature for Samantha's.

Meanwhile Durwood is working on a new perfume campaign for Mr. Cunningham who he is supposed to meet with the next day, when Larry tells him that Mr. Cunningham came in early and so they will meet with him that night. Durwood declines as he has to accompany Samantha to the exhibit but Larry says that's perfect as Mr. Cunningham is an art connoisseur.

At dinner Mr. Cunningham bores them with his art collecting knowledge and Samantha suggests he may not want to go to the amateur exhibit but he says he'll give it a shot. When they arrive at the exhibit they find that the Tates are there and they tell Samantha that her painting won first prize; however Samantha is shocked when the painting is unveiled and it is not her painting though it has her signature. Mr. Cunningham says that the painting is saying "I know you" to him and therefore he will bid on it. Samantha sneaks out to find her mother and Durwood and Mr. Cunningham get into a bidding war much to Larry's displeasure. When Samantha comes in she finds that Mr. Cunningham won it for $1,005!

They all go to Durwood's for appetizers and Samantha finds her mother and discovers who the real artist is. When she accuses Endora of stealing, Endora refutes by saying that the Henri Monchet will return to its rightful place at midnight, which it happens to be close to at that time. Endora also tells her Mr. Cunningham's perfume was terrible as she had smelled it earlier and so she went to Tibet and had a warlock whip her up a new perfume that is irresistible. Samantha realizes she can use the perfume to barter with Mr. Cunningham and so she puts some on and goes to serve the appetizers. Mr. Cunningham smells the perfume and insists he have the recipe. She says her mother created it and that she'll give it to him in exchange for the painting and he accepts. She also suggests he use "I Know You" as the label and he loves it! Samantha hurriedly has Durwood take the painting into the den but before he even gets there it disappears and Samantha's painting returns. When the Tates and Mr. Cunningham go to leave, Mr. Cunningham falls in love with her painting and she tells him he can have it.

I'd give this two and a half to three stars. Arthur Julian plays the client again for a second time this season (third overall) and he does a superb job. Really, nobody could've played it better than him. I love it when Samantha gets mad with him at dinner and Durwood has to calm her down.

I don't believe we've heard that music at the first before. It seemed a very lazy morning even though Samantha was painting and fixing breakfast. I thought that whole scene was really cool. We'll see the flipping pancakes trick again next season in "How Green Was My Grass."

It really was chintzy on the part of the director and the set decorators to use Sam and Durwood's bedroom as Larry and Louise's especially when it was used in a scene right after one in Sam and Durwood's bedroom at

1164! I don't understand why they couldn't use the bedroom set that they used in "Double Tate" where Durwood becomes Larry for a day.

The signature looked like Elizabeth Montgomery's. That's probably why the joke about it being Endora's handwriting is so funny.

My favorite line is when Endora tells Samantha, "Remember, anything less than a masterpiece will be a disgrace to the family name!"

It was nice to see Tabatha again. I almost forgot they had a daughter! And I liked that they just kept filming when she ran away. It made the show more realistic.

This is one of the rare times that *Bewitched* copied a prior *I Dream of Jeannie* episode. The Jeannie episode was from last season entitled "My Master, the Great Rembrandt" when Tony tries to paint a copy of a Rembrandt and Jeannie switches it out for a real Rembrandt.

MARCH 2, 1967

It was on this night that ABC aired Episode #99: "Charlie Harper, Winner."

Durwood's old college buddy, Charlie Harper, is coming into town to visit and Durwood isn't too excited as Charlie has always excelled at everything. Samantha tells him that Charlie can't be all that great but at dinner it seems that he is as his wife is beautiful, they are really rich and have triplets. At dinner Daphne, Charlie's wife, continually boasts of all Charlie's accomplishments. Eventually Charlie invites them for a getaway weekend right then and won't take no for an answer so after getting Endora to babysit they pack and leave in Charlie's limo.

At the resort Daphne continues her boastful ways though Samantha keeps her in check by twitching her into a few embarrassing predicaments. Soon Durwood finds out that Charlie wants to offer Durwood a job as President of a big advertising agency he bought. The job will require him to spend half a year in Europe every year but Durwood says that he couldn't leave Larry out in the cold like that. Meanwhile Daphne comes to offer Samantha something to wear for a formal dinner that night and also to tell her that they really do want to get Durwood out of his station in life. Samantha assures her Durwood is happy where he's at and when Daphne offers to get her some jewelry, Samantha decides to impress her and zaps up a jewelry box full of real diamonds. However, Daphne can't believe that Durwood could afford it and so when Daphne asks one more time if Samantha needs anything else Samantha does tell her she needs a hanger for a mink coat which she zaps up just then. Daphne is absolutely impressed but suddenly freezes surprising Samantha. Endora pops in disgusted at Samantha trying to impress Daphne by zapping up the fur coat. Samantha realizes she shouldn't have done it and so she says she'll get rid of it. When Endora pops out, Daphne unfreezes and Samantha tells her that she really doesn't like the coat and that she only accepted it because Durwood had it specially made for her from the pelts of identical twin minks.

Later on while getting ready for dinner Charlie comes calling and asks if he can buy the mink coat. Durwood is confused until he sees that Samantha knows what Charlie is talking about. Charlie offers thousands for it but Durwood refuses knowing the coat is a product of witchcraft and so Charlie leaves. Durwood is mad because he believes Samantha isn't happy with what he can give her and he leaves for the bar.

A little later Samantha meets Daphne near the bar and tells her that she wants her to just have the coat. Not believing it Daphne calls Charlie and Durwood in and tells them. Charlie says that Samantha can't give away something so valuable but with tears in her eyes she says you can when you value something a great deal more. Durwood realizes he is the one she values more and he embraces her.

Weeks later, a package arrives at 1164 which turns out to be the mink with a note from Daphne saying that she had to return it for reasons they would understand and Charlie signs it thanking them for giving him a new Daphne. Samantha immediately zaps it away and when Durwood asks her if she wanted to keep it, she responds that all though she could zap up mink coats all day long, she could never zap up another Durwood.

I love this episode as it's so real. I love that they made Durwood mad over what is possibly the REAL fact that he gets so uptight about witchcraft — that it makes him feel like a nothing compared to her, when in fact she would never think such a thing.

I found the whole scene with the darts weird as the camera rests solely on the dart board.

I love it when Samantha overhears Daphne talking about Durwood while she's playing table tennis and she twitches her lounge chair to collapse. The look on Daphne's face is priceless! And when she twitches the cards to flip out and Samantha tells Daphne, "They must've caught on your ring," Daphne does her own twitching! Well, it's her eyebrow twitching but it's hilarious!

Speaking of Daphne, Joanna Moore who played her, divorced Ryan O'Neal shortly after this episode finished filming. It's sad to think of what a troubled life she had.

I love it when Endora pops into the kitchen with her ice cream sundae and Samantha asks, "Mother what are you doing?" And Endora replied, "Being SICK!" And then I love it when Samantha says, "Mother, I hope you get FAT!" And Endora shrugs it off and keeps on eating.

Of course Samantha's line at the end about, "I could never zap up another Darrin Stephens" was unfortunately proven wrong in another two seasons.

This episode is #99 and I always felt it should've been #100. I guess back then they didn't celebrate those milestones as it didn't take that long to get there (whereas, today reaching #100 happens in like the fourth or fifth season).

MARCH 9, 1967

It was on this night that ABC aired a milestone episode of *Bewitched*, Episode #100: "Aunt Clara's Victoria Victory" sponsored by Chevrolet.

While Durwood is away on business in Chicago, Larry is left to deal with the incorrigible Mr. Morgan who lives his life as though he's in the Victorian age where the louder you speak the more right you are. Larry calls Samantha to see if Durwood has returned but Samantha says it'll be later that day. He also complains to Samantha about Mr. Morgan. After they hang up she tells the visiting Aunt Clara about Mr. Morgan which gets her to thinking about her time in Queen Victoria's court. Feeling homesick, Aunt Clara decides to travel back in time, however, in true Aunt Clara style, when the smoke clears from her spell she's still there. Soon, though, she and Samantha hear the tinkling of a bell coming from the living room and when Samantha looks in she finds it's from Queen Victoria herself seated in her throne! Aunt Clara suggests they run in to meet her and the Queen is appalled by Clara's limbs showing from her "short" dress and the fact that Samantha is dressed more like a nephew than a niece. The Queen suggests she knows where she is but she wants to know if Clara knows where Clara is and she is told she is in the 20th century.

Back at the office Mr. Morgan reviews Durwood's ideas, however, he wants to meet Durwood's wife as he judges a man by the wife he keeps.

Meanwhile, the Queen is being shown the wonders of the modern day via the television only to get upset by video of women in bikinis on the beach. She is so upset that she rushes the TV with her scepter and smashes it. To clear her mind she has Clara escort her into the kitchen where Samantha is going to follow, but the doorbell rings. She finds it's

Larry coming to ask if Mr. Morgan and he can drop by later as Morgan wants to meet Durwood's wife. Samantha says that's silly until Larry notices the throne and Samantha explains that her crazy aunt is visiting who thinks she is Queen Victoria. Soon Clara and the Queen come through the living room to go upstairs so the Queen may rest. Larry asks that the Queen be kept out of sight when he comes back.

Upstairs, as the Queen reads the newspaper, she realizes there is much to be fixed and it occurs to her that Providence must've brought her here to fix it. She quickly goes to work on coming up with some decrees.

Later, when Mr. Morgan and Larry are over, the Queen comes down to discuss with Clara the plan of attack on the world and Mr. Morgan is fascinated by the eccentric Queen Victoria and wishes to discuss how she runs her empire as well as how he runs his mattress factory empire. He soon irritates the Queen by sitting before she does and continuing to talk when she hasn't given him permission. After she's beaten him with her fan he tells her to shut up! This really irks Larry who has had enough and he tells Mr. Morgan to shut up, that he's tired of hearing his demands. Offended, Mr. Morgan leaves and says that his account is going with him. Realizing that he's lost out on a lot of money, Larry goes to lie down. Knowing that Durwood is the best man for the job, Samantha pops over to Mr. Morgan's hotel and put him in a sleep giving him a dream that he's Queen Victoria running his mattress factory empire just like a tyrant however he knows that tyrants always came to an end by being beheaded. He is startled awake and comes back over to 1164 to tell Larry that he can have the account. Larry is pleased but confused and leaves with Mr. Morgan.

Samantha then asks Aunt Clara to send Queen Victoria back but she doesn't want to go back as she's going to right the wrongs of the 20th century and, besides, Clara doesn't remember the spell. Samantha is done with this foolishness and zaps the Queen downstairs. She is truly shocked and Samantha reveals that she got there by witchcraft and that she and Clara are witches. Queen Victoria announces that had she known Clara was a witch in her own time she would've had her flogged. This jogs Clara's memory to the spell she needs to send her back but she ends up with Prince Albert instead!

I'd give it two and a half stars 'cause I think it's absolutely funny how self-absorbed the client and Queen Victoria are. My favorite scene is when Queen Victoria is hitting him on the head with her fan to punctuate her sentence! I laugh every time!

I always felt that most of Larry's lines really were Durwood's to begin with, especially when they are in the kitchen listening in on Mr. Morgan and Samantha tells Larry, "Weelll?!" That just seems like something she would say only to Durwood. This is the second episode of thirteen Dick York would miss.

I find it funny also when Aunt Clara and Queen Victoria walk over the broken glass from the TV and then Aunt Clara tries to act all prim and proper when she gets the newspaper from Larry but you can tell the crunching glass is disconcerting to her.

I also liked when Queen Victoria broke the TV but I do think that Samantha should've zapped it back together before she answered the door for Larry. That way she would've thought she was making things look normal but then would've realized that she forgot to zap away Queen Victoria's throne.

I also think it's hysterical when the client is dressed as Queen Victoria and he says, "If anyone talks back we let them have it with our fan!"

Regarding Larry saying that songwriters are missing the greatest song by putting music to the words "Shut Up," the Black Eyed Peas released a song titled "Shut Up" a couple years ago. It had a catchy beat but the lyrics are ridiculous.

I found it weird that Samantha would change herself into a Christmas tree to prove that she was a witch. I would've thought the simple act of disappearing would've done it. Maybe Samantha was just thinking ahead to Christmas as this episode aired in March. And as there wasn't a Christmas episode this season maybe everybody got to feeling sad and decided to show one, though there was one in "Accidental Twins."

MARCH 16, 1967

It was on this night that ABC aired Episode #101: "The Crone of Cawdor."

Durwood and Samantha are going to celebrate the third anniversary of their first meeting and set up a reservation at La Bella Donna's where they had their first date. However, when Durwood goes to go to work he is stopped in his driveway by a gorgeous woman who introduces herself as Terry Warbell, the daughter of Jay Warbell of the Warbell Dress account that Durwood is working on. She says that she had been given the assignment of working with McMann and Tate by her father and was staying nearby and thought that she and Durwood could drive into the city together. Durwood goes along with it as Endora is watching. She is quite suspicious and shows Samantha who says there is nothing to worry about because she trusts Durwood implicitly.

At the office, as Durwood tries to go over the campaign, Terry suggests that they go to lunch. Durwood declines as he has reservations with his wife at La Bella Donna and Terry says that he could break them for her account as she isn't in town for long. Durwood still hedges until Larry threatens him with his job and so he calls Samantha to tell her. She chalks it up to business but Endora is still suspicious and she suggests that Samantha pop downtown to check up on her husband. Samantha refuses and so Endora decides to do it herself.

In Durwood's office, Endora pops in invisible when Terry and Durwood are getting ready to go and when Betty, Durwood's secretary, asks Ms. Warbell if she thinks boots will be in style next season, Ms. Warbell naively responds that it depends on how Boots feels this season. Betty is confused, Endora is disgusted, and when Durwood reaches for some notes to take with them to lunch, she zaps them out of his pocket. He realizes that they are gone as they step out of his office so he excuses himself to go back to look for them. Just as he closes the door, Endora pops in looking like fashion designer Edith Head, claiming to be the copyrighter for Tate-McMann and asks Terry how she feels about the designs of Polyester and when Terry responds she's not familiar with her that's all the proof Endora needs to confirm her suspicions and she pops back to Samantha.

Meanwhile, at the Kravitzes, their boring afternoon is interrupted by a ring at the doorbell where Gladys discovers a rather old and confused lady who claims to be only twenty-four! Gladys thinks that she would have to be one of Samantha's people and she calls her. When Samantha answers and speaks to Gladys, she thinks maybe Endora was expecting someone who got lost and when she asks what the lady's name is, she responds, "Terry Warbell!" Endora suggests that Samantha pop over to the Kravitz's immediately and retrieve the old woman as there is definitely something going on. Samantha does pop over much to Gladys' shock and when she tries to get Abner to see Samantha and Terry pop back to 1164.

Endora questions the old woman who claims that she was driving down the street when she saw an old woman who needed help and the next thing she knew she was the old woman and the old woman was her and she didn't know where she was. As she thinks about it, Endora realizes this old woman must be the Crone of Cawdor, the subject of

Samantha's favorite bedtime story when she was young. When she asks Samantha to recall what happened in the rest of the story, she recites:

> *When the earth turns once around the sun,*
> *let the Crone go forth 'til the day is done.*
> *Another's form she'll take and her form leave,*
> *from six in the morn 'til six in the eve.*
> *And in this guise if she can secure*
> *a willing kiss from a mortal pure*
> *To her will pass the mortal's youth,*
> *to him will pass her age, forsooth!*

She realizes she must save Durwood from kissing who he thinks is Terry as she knows the Crone will be trying every trick in the book. After discovering Terry's address by popping in on Terry's father, she pops in on Durwood and Terry just before six o'clock. Durwood is furious and offended that Samantha would think he would try anything so he goes to kiss Terry but when he turns to do so she has turned back into the old woman and Durwood realizes Samantha was right. And with that he and Samantha pop back home where a confused Terry is sitting with Endora. They tell Terry that she had come over for drinks and had a little bit too much. Terry confirms that Durwood will be on the account but that she'll need to rest. And as their lunch plans were ruined, Samantha orders in from La Bella Donna and they celebrate the anniversary of their meeting just as they had planned.

I love this episode and give it four stars. It's creepy and witchy and fun all at the same time! Elizabeth Montgomery told Herbie J Pilato (*Bewitched Forever*) that this was one of her favorite episodes 'cause it was creepy. I did find Endora to be a little out of character what with her "mortal" hair and that ugly outfit she was wearing. I really don't think Endora would wear an outfit like that. It was TOO mortal. Not to mention, how would she know about baseball?! Though, that line was pretty funny.

This is the first time in about ten episodes that we see the Kravitzes. I found it funny when Mrs. Kravitz told Samantha that there was someone at her door who was "your kind of people." It was weird, though, that Samantha would think Endora would be meeting one of her friends at Morning Glory Circle. I also liked it when Endora called Mrs. Kravitz "loud mouth."

Dorothy Neumann, the Crone, appeared with Elizabeth Montgomery in the episode of *Thriller* titled "Masquerade."

This episode is generally believed to be around the time that Liz lost the original diamond heart necklace that William Asher had given her. You can see her at one point wearing a cut out heart necklace.

This is the first episode that Heather Woodruff (now Perry) filmed as Durwood's secretary Betty. I mention her as she will appear in one of the most memorable scenes in *Bewitched* history in a couple episodes.

Durwood and Samantha celebrate the third anniversary of their meeting which works perfectly if we are to believe that they met on September 17, 1964, the airdate of the pilot.

Two days before, the body of President John F. Kennedy was moved to its permanent resting place at Arlington National Cemetery.

MARCH 23, 1967

It was on this night that ABC aired Episode #102: "No More Mr. Nice Guy."

When Durwood discovers Endora trying to teach Tabatha how to pop out he grows furious that she's always at his house and using witchcraft when she knows witchcraft is strictly forbidden. He demands that she be gone by the time he get back from work and he slams out the door in yet another one of his snits. Endora is disgusted and says that he is very un-likeable but Samantha disagrees and says that he's very likeable, she's just never seen him that way but if she would try to get to know him, she would. Endora decides to show Samantha and Durwood how unlikeable he can be. She pops invisibly down to the office where Durwood is meeting with a new client Frank Eastwood, who is in charge of the PR for the mayor, and she casts a spell making everyone who comes in contact with Durwood hate him. Soon Mr. Eastwood thinks everything Durwood is saying is a jab at him or that he is being disagreeable and he leaves. Larry warns Durwood he better change his attitude and not offend the client but when a model for the Baldwin Blankets account comes in wearing just a nightie under her fur coat and thinks that he's trying to be insinuating about her, she stalks off in a huff. Durwood tries to plead his case to Larry, who admits that Durwood is usually very likeable, but when he hears that Mr. Baldwin has arrived to show off his new blanket, he warns Durwood not to offend him. Mr. Baldwin enters proud to show off one of his new blankets and when Durwood says that they could try the approach of how blankets gives you full protection, Baldwin takes it as though as he's insinuating his blankets are scary. He says that McMann and Tate are obviously not Baldwin Blanket people and he leaves. Confused at the sudden ill feelings toward Durwood, Larry suggests that maybe he see Bob Farnsworth, a psychiatrist friend. Durwood is offended and says he'll take his troubles to his bartender, Max.

At the bar the resident drunk takes an immediate dislike to Durwood which Max finds strange and he suggests that maybe Durwood has a complex and should see a psychiatrist.

At Bob's office, he suggests that Durwood is holding hostilities toward his wife for having dominance over him. However true that may be, Durwood denies it and while they speak, Samantha pops in on them, having been tipped off by Larry. When she's finally had enough of Bob accusing Durwood of being angry, she zaps Bob into deciding he should see his own psychiatrist. She reveals herself to Durwood and tells Durwood that she thinks he has a spell on him and that he needs to get back to the office and act as nice as he possibly can to win back Mr. Baldwin who had called to say he wanted to give them a second chance.

When he gets to the office, he's so nice it's ill-making, but Mr. Baldwin likes his ideas and has decided they can have the campaign, so long as he doesn't have to meet with Durwood anymore.

At home, Durwood yells at Samantha as Endora seemingly took the spell off before he met Baldwin so that he made a fool out of himself. Samantha reminds him that all that doesn't matter as she finds his charming *cough* personality and crooked smile endearing.

This isn't one of my favorites at all and really is second in line to being the worst of the Third Season just behind "Ho Ho the Clown." First of all, Durwood absolutely lost his cool when he walked in on Endora disappearing for Tabatha (and since when does Endora need a verbal spell to disappear? Not to mention if verbal spells give the spell a boost, Tabatha can't even speak well yet…). And then Endora's hate spell seemed to be a jumble of words and mismatched phrases such as "and with loathing treat." It just seems wrong.

Bob Farnsworth really bugged me with his tic — what was that all about? I believe this is the first time we've ever seen Samantha pop in invisibly sitting in the air. When she first pops in her cape falls down behind her however when the scene returns to her it's all tucked up behind her.

My favorite lines in this episode come from the client when he says, "I don't like the hard sell…my blankets are soft!" And also when Durwood has thrown out the security slogan and the client says, "It's scary!"

Other than that, I hardly ever watch this episode. I hate that everyone hates Durwood. I mean he's annoying, but he doesn't deserve all that.

This would be Heather Woodruff's second episode as Betty.

Three days later the Central Park Be-in took place in New York with some 10,000 people.

MARCH 30, 1967

It was on this day that ABC aired Episode #103: "It's Wishcraft."

Durwood is nervous when his parents say they are going to come and visit and Tabatha seems particularly interested in using her powers to levitate her toys around the house. He tells Samantha that he gives her permission to fight witchcraft with witchcraft while his parents are there. When he goes to leave for work, he suddenly finds himself up in Tabatha's room! Samantha is surprised that he is still there but he says he had left and in the middle of their conversation he disappears! She finds him in Tabatha's room again and she realizes that Tabatha has come into the stage of developing wishcraft, which is whatever she wishes for comes true, especially when she wants someone to be with her. She distracts Tabatha while Durwood leaves, but she realizes that keeping Tabatha in check may be harder than it looks.

Later, while Samantha is telling Tabatha that she mustn't twitch, Tabatha suddenly disappears! Samantha cannot believe that Tabatha has already learned how to pop out but when she goes in the living room she finds that Endora had zapped her in there. Relieved that she'll have help with Tabatha, Samantha tells her mother about Durwood's parents visit and asks her to stay. Endora agrees, though she's not too fond of Durwood's mother.

When the elder Stephenses arrive, things are instantly icy between Phyllis and Endora, though Frank and Endora have a great rapport. As Samantha goes to get some rolls she had made from Phyllis' recipe, the phone rings and Phyllis answers. It is Durwood and she asks him about Endora always seeming to be at the house, which he is surprised at and he requests to speak to Samantha. When she gets on the phone he begins blowing his stack about Endora but Samantha goes on with a fake pleasant conversation on her end of the phone so that his parents won't be aware that they are fighting. She tries to take the conversation to a private area of the room to tell him that he needs to calm down but Phyllis butts in and wants to know if they are having a fight. Samantha assures her everything is OK and when Phyllis says she is going to go see Tabatha, Samantha suggests Endora accompany her.

Later on, Phyllis shares her concern with everyone and she says that she thinks it's because Endora is always intruding and so they get into a catty fight. Samantha assures her that everything is OK and when she goes into the kitchen, Endora follows her seeing that Samantha is upset. She suggests that Durwood has made her cry but Samantha insists it was Endora. Not wanting to hear any more of it Endora pops out and casts a spell that involves buckets of water falling on Durwood's head for every tear Samantha has shed.

At the office, as Durwood is readying to go home, he is shocked when it starts pouring on him but not more than Betty is when she walks in. Durwood says it's a sudden cloud burst and promptly leaves.

Back at 1164 Samantha assures Phyllis that it was all a misunderstanding but Phyllis is still suspicious. When Samantha goes to make some tea Endora pops back in just as Durwood shows up at the kitchen window with the water still pouring. Samantha demands Endora turn it off and she reluctantly does so. Sopping wet, Durwood comes in and immediately starts yelling at Endora when suddenly he disappears and ends up in Tabatha's room because she wanted her daddy. Phyllis also hears him and just before she enters the kitchen, Endora disappears. Samantha tells her that it must've been Tabatha waking from her nap that she heard and Samantha goes up stairs where she finds Durwood. She tells him that he needs to be able to come into the house and show his parents that they aren't fighting when they hear Phyllis coming into the room. Durwood hides in the closet and Samantha shows Phyllis to Tabatha. They all hear Durwood sneeze and when Phyllis goes to check the closet Samantha zaps Durwood down to their room. She decides Tabatha will be OK for the moment while she goes to check on Durwood. She offers to dry him by magic but he declines, however when she suggests that she'll have to zap him downstairs when he's ready he realizes he'll have to allow that.

As Samantha gets downstairs, the doorbell rings bringing in Endora who immediately gets into it with Phyllis who accuses her of being mean to Durwood. Just as Phyllis is about to lecture Samantha, Sam sees Durwood at the top of the stairs and she zaps him outside. He soon bursts through the door jubilant as ever, even planting a kiss on Endora! Frank suggests that Phyllis is always seeing things that aren't there, though she says otherwise. This gives Samantha an idea of how to prove Phyllis was seeing things and she suggests she go fetch Tabatha. She pulls Endora aside and explains that they just need to do a little magical mischief to Phyllis while she's in the nursery and they make toys fly and Tabatha's crib move by itself. Phyllis realizes she must not be well and she apologizes.

I LOVE this episode and give it three and a half stars (it would be four but I HATE when the crib moves and throws Tabatha back)! After having not really seen a Tabatha-centered episode in a long time this one is a breath of fresh air and makes perfect sense that she would be developing her powers even more. I love that they call it "wishcraft," considering she's not a full grown witch yet.

I think Durwood gets mad at Sam for Tabatha's toys laying around only 'cause they were flying around and that's magic, her area of expertise and therefore she should be trying to manage it with her daughter.

The interactions between Endora, Frank, and Phyllis are hysterical. My favorite line comes from Endora when she says, "Durwood needs no criticism from me. What's wrong with him is for the whole world to see!" I also think it's hysterical when Endora rings the doorbell and Samantha answers it and Sam says under breath, "Oh Mother! Go away!"

The scene in the office when the buckets of water start falling on Durwood's head is hysterical! The look on Betty's face is priceless! Heather Woodruff joined us for the first time at the *Bewitched* Fanfare in 2008. She shared her memories from the set, particularly this scene which was filmed in one take. There was foam rubber on the floor to soak up the water and she said it was quite cold and sprayed everywhere. She also had to walk in high heels on it even though her feet are never shown. In speaking of Dick York, she became emotional as she said he was a sweet man and she could tell he was in a lot of pain. She also said one time when they were blocking scenes her stand-in wasn't there so she just offered to do it. Agnes Moorehead pulled her aside and in a very stern tone told her that if she ever wanted anyone to ever take her serious as an actress she wouldn't lower herself to do stand in work. In 2010 Betty was given the Fanfare Appreciation award.

But my all-time favorite part of this episode is when Durwood kisses Endora on the cheek! It was so unexpected and really quite daring of him!

Alice Pearce's widower Paul Davis directed this episode. I could (and have) watched this episode over and over.

It should also be noted that sometime in March that NBC's *Gunsmoke*, which was completing its Twelfth Season, was due to be cancelled, however many people, including members of Congress, protested and demanded that it be moved from its Saturday time slot to Mondays in the fall displacing *Gilligan's Island* which had been renewed for another season. *Gunsmoke* would actually end its series run in 1975, after an impressive twenty seasons!

APRIL 6, 1967

It was on this night that ABC aired Episode #104: "How to Fail in Business with All Kinds of Help."

Durwood feels that his ideas for a new campaign will warrant a bonus from Larry which means he and Samantha can finally take their trip to Bermuda. However, Endora thinks that the closest Samantha will ever get to Bermuda is an onion, and she suggests that the reason they can never go on trips is because Durwood needs help. Samantha assures her he doesn't need any help, but Endora reminds her that she should be living in the sparkle of the star and in the wind. Irritated by her mother's lack of confidence in Durwood, she tells her mother to blow. And she does!

Downtown, Larry is quite impressed with Durwood's ideas for Madame Marushka's Cosmetics and they go to show them to Mr. Wilkerson, Marushka's right hand man. Before they enter the room, Endora pops in and casts a spell on Mr. Wilkerson to only show Durwood attention, even though he is friends with Larry. The spell works as Wilkerson hardly acknowledges Larry and is quite impressed with the ideas however he says he must pass them by Madame Marushka who never leaves her "ivory tower."

At home, Durwood shares the great news with Samantha who mentions that she's glad her mother didn't meddle. That gets Durwood thinking that maybe she did meddle and while he is hollering Endora pops in to claim authorship of her work. Durwood tells her he definitely doesn't need her help and that he will take himself off the account.

At McMann and Tate, as Durwood is resigning from the account, Betty bursts in with the news that Madame Marush-KA has shown up to meet the man responsible for the ideas. She asks which of the men is "Steffans" and tells Durwood that she loves the ideas, however, she has a rule that she never works with someone whose name isn't a part of the company name and she insists that Larry add "Steffans" to the company name. Seeing how Marush-KA is always mispronouncing his name, like Endora, Durwood thinks that it must be Endora trying again to elevate his station and so he tells her he won't accept. Madame Marush-KA is furious, especially after he tells her to leave out the window and she storms out the door. Larry is sick and insists Durwood go home to rest while he tries to calm Madame Marush-KA.

When Durwood gets home he tells Samantha and Endora that he could see through Endora's disguise but they both don't know what he is talking about and Samantha assures him that her mother was with her all afternoon. As he realizes she is telling the truth, Larry calls to tell

Durwood he's fired. Endora feels somewhat responsible for this and won't abide her daughter and granddaughter not having someone to provide for them and she offers to cast a spell. Having had enough of spells, Durwood refuses saying he is going to make things right himself by going down to Madame Marush-KA's offices to apologize.

Durwood arrives at her salon just as she's throwing Larry out and he tries to get her to see the ads he came up with, especially his one with the tag "Don't play fair. Use Madame Marushka's Cosmetics." She insists she hates it and throws the ads on the floor and slams the door back into her office. Dejected, the men leave, not realizing that Samantha has popped into a picture in the office. She zaps the ads to herself and leaves.

While drowning their sorrows at a bar, Larry and Durwood see the layout on the back of the evening paper of one of the other patrons and are shocked thinking that someone has stolen their idea until they get to the office and find that Durwood's signatures are all over the release forms for newspaper ads, commercials, and billboards. Larry really thinks Durwood has flipped and sends him home so that he can sort everything out.

At home, Samantha admits she is the one that did it all to try and make amends but Durwood has had it and goes to leave just as Larry shows up, pleased as punch and offers Durwood his job back. As it turns out the orders from department stores for the Marush-KA line spiked after the ad in the paper. After Larry leaves, Durwood thanks Samantha though he still feels stupid that Samantha had to help him.

I really like this one and would give it three stars only because Durwood is too over-reactive in this episode. It seems like he got that way in the episode before last where everybody hated him. I don't like it.

I thought Tabatha was so cute when the wind was blowing and she sat there looking like she liked it.

I liked the scene of Samantha in the picture and found it cool that she didn't care about the secretary seeing the portfolio fly up in the air and obviously shrink into the picture.

I always thought the scene at the end with Durwood acting like he was turning the light off with magic was him making up for being such an ass about the witchcraft but it had nothing to do with the episode at all. And what was with him being able to unplug the lamp without her noticing? It seemed like he would've had to have really long arms to do so not to mention the fact that it's strange that the plug would be on his side of the bed. But I do remember when I was little I was as shocked as Samantha was at him being "able" to do witchcraft.

Two days earlier the Dr. Reverend Martin Luther King, Jr. publicly renounced the Vietnam War during a religious service in New York City. He would be martyred one year to the day later.

APRIL 13, 1967

It was on this night that ABC aired Episode #105: "Bewitched, Bothered and Infuriated."

Aunt Clara pops in on breakfast to find that Durwood hasn't left for work yet even though it's later in the morning. He says that Larry is gone away for the weekend and so he feels he can take his time. When Durwood offers her the morning paper, she insists she can zap up her own and she does; however, she finds it's for the next day. They discover that one of the major stories is that Larry Tate has broken his leg! Samantha is saddened to hear this, not only because he broke his leg, but because he was gone for the weekend for a second honeymoon with Louise. Aunt Clara suggests that she would send him a get well gift but it hasn't happened yet. This gives Durwood the idea that they can prevent it but Samantha reminds him that the Tates made sure nobody would know, however, he uncharacteristically suggests that she use her powers to find them so that they can prevent Larry from breaking his leg. Samantha warns him that it's dangerous to fool around with the future but he insists as Larry is his best friend, they owe it to him and so in a puff of smoke they disappear to the resort where the Tates are.

At the resort Durwood and Samantha pop in just as Larry and Louise are getting ready to go play badminton, which Durwood thinks is the perfect place to break a leg, and so they ambush the Tates who are shocked. Durwood acts like the Tates were the ones to surprise them and suggests that they have come there for work. Larry doesn't buy it and says that they had planned to be alone and they are still going to play badminton and they leave. Samantha suggests they leave but Durwood won't hear of it and they follow them out to the court. Surprised that the Stephens have the gall to follow them, Louise hits the birdie harder than she expected and as it flies off court it travels over a bench. Not paying attention, Larry goes to still hit and so Samantha twitches the bench out much to the astonishment of everyone. Irritated, Larry says they are going to the pool. Still not taking the hint, Durwood drags Sam to the pool where they see the Tates throwing a ball to one another around the pool and when Larry sees his soon-to-be-ex-friends show up he doesn't see a patch of water and goes to slip but

Samantha twitches him into doing a backflip. Seeing that Durwood is being so persistent, Louise mentions that maybe she and Larry should just go back to their room. Thinking that should be enough to convince Durwood to leave, Samantha says they should but Durwood refuses saying that most accidents happen indoors and he drags Samantha to the Tates patio. Samantha has had enough and pops home to check on Tabatha and Aunt Clara.

Meanwhile, Durwood sees Larry carrying Louise into the room about to crash into the coffee table he can't see so Durwood bursts through the sliding doors and grabs Louise while pushing the coffee table out of the way. Furious now, Larry demands that Durwood leave and he does.

Samantha soon pops back with the message that a meeting Durwood had at three tomorrow had been changed to two today and as it's close to two right then he requests Samantha zap him back to the office. Feeling bad about how they've been interrupting the Tate's vacation, she follows Larry to the sauna to apologize to him but he doesn't take too kindly to her and enters the sauna where she realizes he could slip and break his leg and so she zaps Durwood back into the sauna. Larry is irritated once again when he sees Durwood in there. Durwood apologizes and says to make it up they'll take them to dinner that night but Larry refuses.

As the Tates get ready for dinner they are shocked and truly irritated when Durwood and Samantha show up with a bottle of champagne as a makeup gift. Larry tells Durwood that all though it's nice, they do not want to have them as dinner companions or any part of this trip as they are trying to celebrate their honeymoon. Samantha tries to correct him by saying it is their second honeymoon but Louise says that it's their first as on their original, Larry broke his leg. Realizing that the paper was yet another of Aunt Clara's goofups, Samantha puts the Tates in the deep freeze and she zaps up the paper which is tomorrow's date, ten years ago. Samantha realizes the only way to remedy all the damage they've done is to send the Tates back to when they first arrived at the resort and so she zaps them back and she and Durwood run out to the patio just so she can make sure it worked. Everything is going fine until she notices that the champagne was left but it's too late. Larry reads the card attached and wonders how the Stephens knew where they were going but Louise insists it wasn't her and even says how fun it would've been to have them along. Before Durwood can say anything about staying, Samantha zaps them home.

This is one of my favorites from the Third Season. I would give it three stars.

It seems odd for Durwood to all of a sudden want Samantha to use her magic to prevent Larry from breaking his leg, but I think it also shows that he cares a lot about Larry as a friend.

I really liked all the magic in this one and I thought Samantha's spell made perfect sense. I don't think that type of spell would work looking for a witch/warlock but for mortals it would pin-point them perfectly. And it didn't make sense for Aunt Clara to use it — who or what was she looking for? They should've written in something about her using it to find one of her missing doorknobs or something and then still had her land in the closet because, of course, the spell wouldn't have worked for her.

Practically all the lines of the hotel manager are repeated later in "Samantha's French Pastry" by one of the television cameramen filming the commercial with Napoleon.

Also when Durwood, Larry, and Louise fall on the couch Durwood's leg is over Larry's knee but when they show the straight on shot, it is not.

I thought it was hilarious that Samantha would think of making herself invisible to go in the men's room. Of course, that is something everyone thinks of doing when pondering becoming invisible and it shows a little devilish streak in Samantha.

The part about this episode that drives me NUTS is when Louise finally tells them that they are there for their honeymoon and both Samantha and Durwood act all shocked and surprised that she didn't say "second honeymoon." Whether or not they were on the first, second, tenth, 295,724,623,456th honeymoon, they would STILL refer to it as "honeymoon" but yet Samantha acts like she just made the worst grammatical mistake!

One of my favorite lines comes from Louise when she says, "Larry, why don't we go up to our room for some alone time" or something like that. The look in her eyes was definitely "LET'S GET IT ON!" I also like that Larry actually treats Louise so well and even compliments her about her legs — so far in the series she's been the brunt of his criticisms.

Louise's sunglasses look like she bought them in the toy section of the grocery store!

All in all though, I like this episode.

This is the last time we see Aunt Clara for quite some time. She won't be seen until November in "Out of Synch, Out of Mind."

It was also on this day that Agnes Moorehead was designated Ambassador at Large by the city of Los Angeles for her charity work.

The following two days saw massive protests to the Vietnam War in San Francisco and New York City.

On April 15, 1967 NBC's *Flipper* aired its last episode. It began airing the same year as *Bewitched*. Elizabeth Montgomery also celebrated her 34th birthday.

APRIL 20, 1967

It was on this night that ABC re-aired Episode #84: "I'd Rather Twitch Than Fight" which originally aired on November 17, 1966.

APRIL 27, 1967

It was on this night that ABC aired Episode #106: "Nobody But a Frog Knows How to Live."

While taking Tabatha for a stroll through the park, Samantha is accosted by a fresh little man who seems to want more than he should, and so having had enough of him, Samantha zaps him into the nearby fountain. She is surprised when he is happy about it and even more so when he admits that he knows she's a witch! Leery of him, she asks how he knows that and he admits he knows because he is a frog! Still not really believing him, she tries to leave but he follows her home and requests that she turn him back into a frog which she can't do unless she knows when, where, why, and who turned him into a human not to mention that she can't undo another witch's hex. He can't believe it and won't give up so he sneaks into the back as Samantha takes Tabatha up to her room. When the phone rings, Fergus (the human frog) says he'll answer it shocking Samantha and Durwood, who is calling to ask about having dinner tonight with Larry, Louise, and Mr. Saunders of Saunders Soup. Samantha declines as she's not sure of how she'll get Fergus to leave, but as Mr. Saunders and Larry have walked into Durwood's office, he acts like she accepted and he hangs up with her. Meanwhile, Mrs. Kravitz comes knocking to warn Samantha of the prowler but she is surprised to see Fergus in the house. Samantha tells her that Fergus is a professor friend of Durwood's but Fergus denies it telling her that he is a frog and he's proud of it. Mrs. Kravitz thinks there must be something unusual going on and she runs back to tell Abner. Furious with Fergus, Samantha zaps him back to the park fountain and prepares for the dinner.

While she sets out the hors d'ouevers, Sam is startled by Fergus who has come back saying that she can't get rid of him that easily and that if she doesn't help him he'll tell the whole neighborhood about their resident witch. Before she can refute anymore Durwood and Mr. Saunders walk in followed closely by Larry and Louise. Just as Samantha is going to introduce Fergus, the Kravitzes barge in so that Gladys can show Abner the human frog. Samantha introduces Fergus as a professor who specializes in frogs and deflated, Gladys leaves with Abner. Mr. Saunders suggests they all have a drink so while Larry pours, Samantha pulls Durwood into the kitchen to explain about Fergus but they return to the living room in a hurry when they hear Fergus talking about frogs again. Samantha tries to steer the conversation towards Mr. Saunders soon-to-be-announced new flavor, which he decides to share: turtle soup. Fergus is horrified as some of his best friends are turtles and as he goes to fight with Mr. Saunders he makes Mr. Saunders spill his drink, so while everybody is focused on Mr. Saunders cleaning himself, Samantha twitches Fergus back to the park. Mr. Saunders decides it's time to call it a night and he and the Tates leave.

Soon Durwood finds that Fergus has come back to the patio and hears him talking to someone and sees that it's a frog he's had in his pocket. Samantha listens to him and finds that the frog is his girlfriend and that he's given up on trying to get Samantha to change him back. She invites him in and suggests that he can make his girlfriend, Phoebe, into a human. Fergus likes that idea until Phoebe is human, and a gorgeous one at that, but Fergus thinks she's horrible looking as she doesn't resemble her frog self at all. He mentions how he wishes he had never made a wish and when Samantha asks him to explain he says that he had made a wish to be human with a witch in the swamp who granted it. As it was his will that made the wish go into effect, Samantha says she can reverse it which delights Fergus and Phoebe.

I'd only give it two and a half stars. I find Fergus really irritating in the fact that he thinks EVERYBODY should realize that he's a frog. Why would he expect that considering he now looks like a human? But I do like the reverse story of a man wanting to become a frog again, instead of the usual frog wanting to be a man.

I also liked the filmed scenes out in the park. It gives the show more of a reality when it's filmed outside the studio.

And I swear they stopped the filming of Fergus flipping over into the fountain to switch out the actors, which doesn't make any sense. Of course, they would've had a stunt man to do the flip but they could've just had the stunt man fall in the water and then showed a close up of John Fiedler.

I also liked that Samantha wasn't going to take any of his crap and three times zapped him into the fountain.

That client is played by Dan Tobin who we saw just a couple episodes ago in "I Remember You…Sometimes". I find him really annoying. And who in their right mind would eat Turtle Soup?

I also really liked the spell to turn Phoebe and Fergus back and found it all really spooky.

My favorite part was the end of the episode when you can totally see that Sammy and Durwood have decided they are going to have a little fun upstairs.

One of my favorite lines comes from Fergus when he says, "Is this your husband? How come…did somebody put a curse on you?"

There is a fade out that happens when Samantha goes to the backdoor that is a blatant mistake on the part of the DVD makers because that fade-out is not in the episode that was released on VHS. It makes no sense that they would do that because there is nothing wrong with the few seconds of film that it covers.

I really think Sony did a bad job of putting together the Third Season. I know there are some studios that offer replacement discs when the customers complain but Sony isn't amongst their number.

It was also on this day that Agnes Moorehead appeared on the game show *Password* with Broadway actor Barry Nelson. She had been on all week and wore a diamond star brooch which she wore in many episodes of *Bewitched*. She left the brooch to Liz when she passed away.

MAY 4, 1967

It was on this night that ABC aired Episode #107: "There's Gold in Them Thar Pills," the Third Season finale of *Bewitched*.

Endora pops in on Samantha to pick her up to go on a shopping date that Samantha says she forgot about not to mention she can't go anyway as Durwood is sick with a cold. She asks her mother to stay while she goes to fetch him a hot water bottle, and though Endora agrees, she still insists that Samantha come shopping with her. As Samantha is leaving she tells her mother that there isn't any way she can go unless Durwood gets better in a hurry. Endora realizes that there is a way to get him better in a hurry and with a wave of her arms she zaps up the family warlock doctor, Dr. Bombay, who is irritated that Endora interrupted his bath not to mention the fact that he doesn't work on mortals. He keeps refusing to help until Endora threatens to replace him with Dr. Agraphor.

After giving Durwood the once over, he tells him to take a pill he has which will cure his cold instantly. Durwood is suspicious until he pops the pill and is immediately cured! Elated over his quick recovery, Durwood offers to pay the doctor but his offer is refused as Dr. Bombay says he has no need for money. Just then the doorbell rings and so Durwood goes to get it. Endora thanks Dr. Bombay, who zaps himself back into his bathrobe so that he can get back to his bath and he immediately pops out.

Meanwhile, Larry has arrived and is shocked that Durwood is out of bed as he had claimed to be laid up. Durwood tells him about the pills and offers him one as Larry has a cold too and after taking the pill, his cold disappears as well. When Durwood tells him that they came from Dr. Bombay, he goes to take him upstairs to meet with the doctor as there are millions to be made from these pills but Endora stalls them and says she'll go get Dr. Bombay. When she does zap him up, he's soaking wet wrapped in a towel since he was still taking a bath. He insists he get back as he likes to take long baths, however Endora reminds him that Dr. Agraphor takes short showers and so he relents.

Downstairs, he meets with the mortal men who tell him all about the money, which he is still disinterested in, but then Larry hits the right spot when he tells him that all the pill bottles will bear Dr. Bombay's name and face and so they begin to talk.

Later on, after Dr. Bombay has returned to his bath, Samantha returns and is shocked that Durwood is healthy so quickly. As he's leaving for the office with Larry, he mentions that he was seen by a Dr. Bombay. Samantha is appalled realizing that Dr. Bombay is a warlock and she immediately hollers for her mother. Furious that Durwood was given a pill most likely never tested on a mortal, Samantha says she is going to visit Dr. Bombay against her mother's warning, and when she pops to Dr. Bombay finds that he's STILL in his bath and she pops back.

Meanwhile, at the office, Larry and Durwood present the idea of Dr. Bombay's Cold Pills to pharmaceutical client Mr. Hornbeck, who is also a victim of the cold season. He thinks they are nuts until he takes one of the pills and finds that he is instantly cured and so they begin negotiations.

Out in the cosmos, Dr. Bombay has FINALLY finished his bath and is brewing up something in his office when Samantha pops in and asks if he knows of any side effects of the pills. He admits never having tried them out on mortals before so he doesn't know but offers her some of his brew, which happens to be chicken soup.

Back at the office, Samantha pops in to tell Durwood about Dr. Bombay and he is furious to say the least. His anger grows even further when suddenly his voice becomes high pitched, which apparently is the side-effect. Realizing that Larry is already in the midst of selling his part of the company and making other purchases and that he will soon hear the side effect, Durwood tries to decide what to do while Samantha pops back to Dr. Bombay for an antidote. She comes back with one, however when he takes it, it gets rid of his voice all together! Samantha tells Durwood she'll try to get another one from Dr. Bombay and pops out. Meanwhile, Mr. Hornbeck and Larry are waiting for Durwood who comes in and acts like he can't talk. Larry tells him he can definitely write and as they are talking, Larry's voice grows really high. Durwood writes him a note telling him that it's a side effect. Mr. Hornbeck feels that they are trying to get out of the deal by faking this side effect stuff until his voice grows high. Soon, Samantha shows up with what she says is champagne to celebrate the new business deal and she also says that it will cure their voices. After the men drink their voices come back but so do their colds. Mr. Hornbeck is furious and leaves.

Later, as Larry is practically accusing Durwood for all the bad luck he's had over the past three years, they are surprised by another visit from Hornbeck who says he wants to meet with Dr. Bombay again as there is another side effect, which he shows them by removing his hat revealing a thick head of hair where before he was bald!

I would give this three and a half stars simply for the fact of the whack on Durwood's back is disturbing to me considering Dick York had back problems. It makes me flinch every time I see it, but other than that, this episode is practically perfect in every way!

Bernard Fox is a genius and after watching this episode I am reminded why I chose to take on the screen name of Dr. Bombay when posting on the *Bewitched* sites. I find it so funny that they happen to be interrupting him when he is trying to take his bath. I also love it when Endora batts her eyes at him and says, "Pretty please?" and he responds, "Endora, there are many women who can get away with being coy. You, however, are not among their number."

I love that they show his laboratory! It was designed expertly and I always liked that the flame beneath the cauldron seemingly is coming from nowhere. This would be the only time we are ever shown his laboratory.

The best part is when Samantha is going to pop in on him and ask him about the pills he gave Durwood and Endora says, "Oh, I wouldn't do that if I were you!"

SAMANTHA: *"Well, you're NOT me and I'm going to!"*
ENDORA: *"Don't say I didn't warn you!"*

And right after we see Samantha pop off we hear her scream.

Dr. Bombay is not yet in his true persona. He is very much like Osgood Rightmeyer, the witch hunter from last season's "Disappearing Samantha" but I suppose that is what they had in mind when they brought Bernard Fox back, they loved his performance so much. It's also interesting that Endora is simply able to conjure him up, rather than holler for him. And it'll be awhile before we hear the familiar, "Calling Dr. Bombay! Calling Dr. Bombay! Emergency! Come right away!"

Another reason I give this only three and a half stars is the *I Dream of Jeannie*-style ending. The client now has hair and plans to market the product! What's next? Is the hair permanent? Are there are any more side effects?

Another favorite line is after Durwood loses his voice and he mouths, "I'll KILL HER!" I just love it when Samantha says, "Kill who?" His anger is misdirected.

And it is ridiculous that he'd be laid up with a cold, especially if Larry was at work with his flu!

Anyway, LOVE this episode and I love Dr. Bombay!

Three days earlier Elvis Presley and Priscilla Beaulieu were married in Las Vegas. That same day Agnes Moorehead co-hosted *The Mike Douglas Show* and would do so through the rest of the week.

The following is the summer re-run schedule. The episode will be listed by number, name, and original airdate.

MAY 11, 1967

Episode #79: "A Most Unusual Wood Nymph" (October 13, 1967)

Three days before, Agnes Moorehead was a guest on *Mr. Blackwell Presents*.

MAY 18, 1967

Episode #78: "Accidental Twins" (October 8, 1967)

It was also on this day that Tennessee Governor Ellington repealed what was known as the "Monkey Law" but officially called the Scopes Trial which had banned the teaching of evolution in public schools. In 1955, the play *Inherit the Wind* premiered that was based loosely on the trial. In 1960 Dick York would appear in the film version of the play starring Spencer Tracy.

Three days before, Elizabeth Montgomery appeared on her fourth *TV Guide* cover.

MAY 25, 1967

Episode #91: "Sam in the Moon" (January 5, 1967)

JUNE 1, 1967

Episode #90: "Soap Box Derby" (December 29, 1966)
The Beatles also released *Sgt. Pepper's Lonely Hearts Club Band* which remained number one throughout the Summer of Love.

JUNE 8, 1967

Episode #85: "Oedipus Hex" (November 24, 1966)

JUNE 15, 1967

Episode #92: "Ho Ho the Clown" (January 12, 1967)
Two days earlier Solicitor General Thurgood Marshall became the first black person nominated as a US Supreme Court Justice.

JUNE 22, 1967

Episode #93: "Super Car" (January 19, 1967)
The day after, thousands of anti-war protesters clashed with Los Angeles police while President Johnson attended a dinner at the Century Plaza Hotel. Two days later, 400 million viewers watched *Our World*, the first live, satellite televised international production where the Beatles debuted "All You Need is Love."

JUNE 29, 1967

Episode #98: "Art for Sam's Sake" (February 23, 1967)

JULY 6, 1967

Episode #87: "My Friend Ben, Part One" (December 8, 1966)

JULY 13, 1967

Episode #88: "Samantha for the Defense, Part Two" (December 15, 1966)
The day before, race riots broke out in Newark, New Jersey after a black cab driver was allegedly illegally driving around a police car and gunning it down the road. They would last for six days. On July 14, in nearby Plainfield, New Jersey, riots also broke out sparked by these riots.

JULY 20, 1967

Episode #83: "The Short Happy Circuit of Aunt Clara" (November 10, 1967)

The day before, race riots broke out in Minneapolis, MN at the Minneapolis Aquatenial celebration. It was stopped within hours, however, the next day even bigger riots broke out resulting in more fires, gun shots fired and two dozen wounded and 4.3 million dollars in damages.

Three days after the episode re-aired, the worst riots in US history broke out on 12th street in Detroit resulting in forty-three deaths, 342 injured and fourteen hundred buildings were burned.

JULY 27, 1967

Episode #102: "No More Mr. Nice Guy" (March 23, 1967)

Three days later the Milwaukee race riots broke out lasting until August 2 and caused the shutdown of the city on August 1 for ten days. Some "Summer of Love." However, the fact that shows like *Bewitched* were on the air showed what an important part of gaining some short term relief from all the destruction television was.

AUGUST 3, 1967

Episode #97: "I Remember You…Sometimes" (February 16, 1967)

Two days prior all the race rioting began to spill into Washington, D.C.

Two days after the re-airing of the episode, Pink Floyd released their debut album *The Piper at the Gates of Dawn* in the United Kingdom.

AUGUST 10, 1967

Episode #107: "There's Gold in Them Thar Pills" (May 4, 1967)

AUGUST 17, 1967

Episode #99: "Charlie Harper, Winner" (March 2, 1967)

AUGUST 24, 1967

Episode #104: "How to Fail in Business with All Kinds of Help" (April 6, 1967)

The next day the leader of the American Nazi party George Lincoln Rockwell was assassinated in Arlington, VA.

Three days prior ABC's daytime Gothic soap opera *Dark Shadows* began airing in 'culluh!'

AUGUST 31, 1967

Episode #103: "It's Wishcraft" (March 30, 1967)

The day before, Thurgood Marshall was confirmed as the first black justice of the United States Supreme Court.

Stay tuned next week for an all new *Bewitched*, in 'culluh!'

Season 4

SEPTEMBER 7, 1967

It was on this night (which would've been Thursday night at 8:30 Eastern/Pacific time) ABC aired the Fourth Season premiere of *Bewitched*, Episode #107: "Long Live the Queen" which prompted a collective cheer throughout *Bewitched* fan-dom, even more so when we settled down and actually watched the episode.

Endora pops in with a message from Ticheba, Queen of the Witches, which says she is going to pop in to visit Samantha. This is a big deal which Durwood, of course, doesn't understand. Before he can get anymore worked up about it Ticheba arrives, and after berating their humble home, advises all that she has decided to abdicate the throne and that Samantha has been chosen to take her place! Well, Samantha and Endora are beside themselves with joy as only a select few are ever chosen as Queen. But the joy is short-lived when Samantha says she can't accept the position as Durwood (who had left for work before Ticheba announced Samantha's imminent Queen-hood) will object, not to mention her responsibilities as a mother to Tabatha and her home, but mainly 'cause Durwood will explode when he finds out.

Just as Samantha says, Durwood does get all in a dither especially when he finds that his house has been transformed into a veritable Taj Mahal as Ticheba felt that a Queen should have more suitable living conditions. Samantha tells her husband that becoming Queen is what every witch mother dreams of for her child, just like every mortal father dreams that one day his son will become President. She also tells him that she can't decline, because once you're chosen, that's it…at least for a year. Durwood finally gives in realizing that there is no use in fighting.

And so, in a magical glen somewhere in the Cosmos, with her mother proudly looking on, Samantha receives the crown and tells her new subjects that she can only conduct business after midnight so as not to upset her husband.

The first night as Queen is rather busy as Ticheba, whose fuse was very short, transformed many of her subjects into various animals and objects, and they have all come to request their original form back from the new Queen. One of them, a raven, wakes Durwood up at 3 AM when the bird is trying to find the Queen. Durwood tells Samantha that this is unacceptable as he is going to meet with a multi-million dollar account the next day that could lead to a bonus and possibly even a partnership in the firm. Samantha dismisses the subjects and tells them that she will see them after 12 tomorrow.

The next day Durwood has Mr. Rohrbach over for cocktails in the afternoon and things seem to be going great until the raven flies into the living room, unsettling the client and Durwood. Turns out the raven thought that Samantha meant 12 noon, when she really meant midnight. As Durwood is trying to figure out what is going on, Mr. Rohrbach hears a knock at the door and answers only to find that a chair wants in to see how come it's taking so long. When the chair finds Samantha, Durwood, and the raven in the kitchen, Durwood realizes that Mr. Rohrbach must've witnessed the chair walking through and goes to check on him. Mr. Rohrbach says he doesn't want anything to do with anyone that has anything to do with the craziness he has witnessed and when he goes to leave he finds himself in the midst of even more transformees.

Durwood can't take any more of this and tells Samantha that he's going to wait out her year as Queen at Joe's Bar and Grill. At the bar he finds a drunk there who laments his life as he hasn't been home for such a long time that his own child and dog don't even recognize him. Durwood doesn't want that not to mention the fact that Joe tells him that even though every man's wife has problems, she also has more good points too, so he returns home.

Samantha is delighted and he tells her that he's decided that he needs to accept that being Queen is part of Samantha's world and he shouldn't be so uptight about it. As he kneels before his Queen she commands him to rise and flippantly states, "Rise, silly goose" which turns him into a goose!

LONG LIVE QUEEN SAMANTHA!!!

This episode is one of my favorites simply because everyone in it is so great! I also like that new sound effects are being employed. To me, the Fourth Season sound effects are the most real/believable.

I would like to give the reasoning behind Samantha being chosen at birth to be Queen and still having it stick after her mortal marriage. The witch community views mortals as literally "impudent nothings" as Enchantra said when they were testing Tabatha's powers in Season Three's "Witches and Warlocks Are My Favorite Things." Also, when Samantha tells Ticheba that she can't accept because Durwood will be furious, Ticheba just brushes that off saying, "We'll just turn him into something useful like a doormat." I also remember somewhere else in the series someone saying that her marriage to a mortal didn't count. So, this all means that as far as they were concerned, though it was embarrassing that Samantha married one, it was merely an eccentricity on her part.

I think the idea of her being chosen at birth is very reminiscent of other cultures choosing their leaders from birth. And if you're chosen, you're chosen and that's that! However the writers should have had Samantha decide to accept and use her new role as a way of getting the view on mortals changed. That would've been a great thing to see.

I thought it odd that Tabatha, Maurice, Aunt Clara, Uncle Arthur, and even Serena (though she had only appeared in one prior episode) weren't at the coronation. You would think that would've been the biggest event of the century!

I always liked the witches 'glen' with its trees and fog and colored background. I like it even more when they use it in the Salem episodes and the eerie music that it is played in the Seventh Season.

I thought Dick York was HILARIOUS in this episode especially when he realizes that Mr. Rohrbach saw a chair walk through the living room and he runs in there to see what else is going on and slides to a halt! I've noticed that any time J. Edward McKinley is the client almost every time he witnesses some sort of magic. This is his first appearance.

One of my favorite lines is from Endora when Durwood returns from the bar and she says, "Samantha. Bad news. He's back!"

It's interesting that Dick Wilson didn't play the drunk in the bar. The guy that did was good though and Dick Wilson is back in the next episode anyhow.

The moving walls are a cool effect but there is no way that the guest room is on the other side of that particular wall of the master bedroom.

Gilligan's Island ended three days earlier on September 4, 1967. New this season to TV and ABC was *The Flying Nun* which aired right before *Bewitched* on Thursday nights. After *Bewitched* was *That Girl*. Those three shows comprised ABC's Thursdays Girls evening.

SEPTEMBER 14, 1967

It was on this night that ABC aired Episode #109: "Toys in Babeland."

While babysitting Tabatha, Endora finds that there is a big to-do in her honor being held that day at the Taj Mahal. Endora tells the messenger that she won't be able to attend as she is baby-sitting but he offers the suggestion of using one of Tabatha's toys as a sitter. Endora enlarges a toy soldier who can only nod his head. She leaves him a bell to ring if there is trouble and flies off to her party. Tabatha decides she wants a drink but the soldier doesn't seem to understand so she copies her grandmama's spell and enlarges the doll in her playpen, who happens to understand her.

Meanwhile, at McMann and Tate, Larry finds that Durwood and Samantha have invited Bob Chase, a client, to dinner and have in fact had dinner with him before. Larry thinks that Durwood might be on the way to opening his own agency and so he invites himself over to dinner.

When Samantha and Durwood return home they find their house has turned into a party without them, the guests being all of Tabatha's toys brought to life! Samantha assures Durwood she can return them to their normal state but when she tries it doesn't work. Meanwhile, Durwood calls

Durwood and Samantha with the Toy Soldier (Jim Brooks) that Larry took to the bar.

Bob Chase and the Tates to cancel dinner. Larry thinks that Durwood really is trying to keep him out of his new business, so he drives over to see what's going on. As he's peeking through the window, the toy soldier looks out and sees him. Larry thinks that soldier is another worker from McMann and Tate that Durwood is trying to get to come over to "his" agency. Larry wants to talk the soldier out of it and offers to buy him a drink and they drive off. Samantha sees this and warns Durwood.

At the bar, Larry has become totally sloshed and is in despair thinking Durwood has turned against him. Samantha and Durwood pop in and while Durwood distracts Larry, Samantha (who found out the spell from Tabatha) shrinks the soldier back to his original size. Durwood assures Larry nothing was going on and that he's just had too much to drink when he sees that he has been speaking to a toy soldier all night.

Back at home, Tabatha has returned all the toys to their former states though now she is using her witchcraft to make her toy phone work.

David White named this episode as his favorite, specifically for his scene with the Toy Soldier.

I really don't like this episode that much. I maybe give it two stars if that, 'cause David White was so funny and Erin was so cute! Those toys are SCARY, especially that rag doll and the bear.

I hate how Endora, of all people, would leave Tabatha in the care of a toy soldier who can't even speak! He just nods his head and looks like he just did a line of coke (and not the good drink kind neither). And WHY is it that they can't talk?

Also, if there is a big "to-do" in Endora's honor why isn't Samantha invited?

My favorite part out of the whole episode is when Samantha is trying to change them back and she's telling all the toys to look at her and she looks at the monkey, who's just lounging there looking bored with the whole thing, "That goes for you too…Farley." Seems like Samantha's had a run in with the monkey before.

I also liked Larry's: "Well, well, well, if it isn't speak of the devil!"

This is also one of the first episodes that *Bewitched* starts getting into a rut with where Endora is shown at the very first and then not again the rest of the episode.

Samantha also wore that wild looking dress in the last episode and it seems to pop up in more episodes this season.

That Barbie-like doll looks like the Tammy doll from Ideal, the same company that made the Samantha doll.

I think it's way cute at the end when Tabatha says, "Daddy mad" and then "Daddy not mad anymore."

It's also notable that Samantha used a variation on the first spell she ever used on TV when trying to change the toys back.

Three nights later Jim Morrison and the Doors performed on *The Ed Sullivan Show* for the last time when Jim used the word "higher" in the song "Light My Fire" though he was specifically told not to by Mr. Sullivan who thought it referred to getting high on drugs.

The next day CBS aired the controversial day time soap *Love is a Many Splendored Thing* and would become the first soap opera to deal with an inter-racial relationship.

SEPTEMBER 21, 1967

It was on this night ABC aired Episode #110: "Business, Italian Style."

To appease the request of an Italian client's business partner, Larry says that Dino (aka Durwood) knows how to speak Italian fluently, though this isn't the case. When Dino and Larry have a moment to themselves, Larry covertly threatens Dino with the loss of his job if he doesn't learn Italian by the next day to impress Mr. Romani of Chef Romani foods.

Dino decides that there isn't anything keeping him from learning Italian but himself so he buys some Italian language lesson records (including one that teaches phrases for the bachelor in Italy). Endora is thrilled at the prospect of Dino learning Italian as that means that he'll be more inclined to travel to Italy with her, Samantha, and Tabatha to visit Prince Pepe and all the great sights of Italy. That is, until she comes to her senses (in her own mind) and realizes that it's Dino we're talking about and he'll never learn Italian and Samantha will be stuck in her stultifying suburban nightmare. Samantha tells her that she doesn't care to see Prince Pepe or attend an Italian opera and she is pleased with her living situation not to mention that she does believe Dino will learn Italian.

Endora decides to give him a hand when she secretly pops in on his lessons, which don't seem to be going too well, and she casts a spell on him that will make him speak Italian.

After staying up all night with his records, and with the boost of the spell, Dino is confident that he knows Italian and shows off for Samantha. She is favorably impressed until he starts speaking English with an Italian accent and soon thereafter speaks ONLY Italian! Of course, she knows her mother is behind this craziness but after all of Samantha's attempts to get her to come back to remove the spell, Endora remains elusive.

In the interim, Samantha tries to re-teach English to Dino so that he can at least get by a little in the meeting with Mr. Romani. During their lesson Larry shows up as he decided to save the Earth from the added exhaust fumes by picking Dino up for work. Samantha explains to Larry that Dino has utilized a total immersion technique for learning Italian. So immersed is he that he doesn't understand English anymore. Larry goes along with it and at Samantha's request leaves Dino at home so that he can "decompress" from his total immersion. Of course this was a ruse so that they could buy more time to find Endora. But time runs out and Dino leaves for the office.

Once there, he does impress Mr. Romani with his fluent Italian but soon irritates him by refusing to speak English.

Back at 1164, Samantha shouts out to her mother that Endora will be forbidden to ever set foot in the house again unless she appears at the count of three, no matter where she is. And where she is happens to be in her bath, which pops in with her. With a mere "cancel the spell" spell she tells Samantha that the spell is done with but Samantha isn't too sure about that and demands that Endora fly with her down to the office to make sure...once Endora is dressed that is.

Things couldn't be any worse at the office as the spell is wearing off but Dino is speaking with an Italian accent that upsets Mr. Romani as he believes Dino is making fun of him. Samantha and Endora pop in (invisibly, of course) and as Endora concentrates harder the spell finally leaves Dino back to his normal self. He explains that he was trying to show how nobody likes to be made fun of and that even though Chef Romani is an Italian product it should be marketed with a completely American sell. Mr. Romani is satisfied and later at dinner insists that Dino speak more Italian to him as he is homesick for Italy. Samantha obliges by twitching a little Italian language into her husband.

I would give this a three and a half star rating. Dick York named this episode as one of his favorites, specifically because he said it was so much fun saying, "I'm-a hoppy to a make-a your acquaintenence." And when he says that to Larry it's hysterical! I also liked it that he gradually slipped into the Italian rather than just all of a sudden being Italian.

Agnes Moorehead seemed like she was rather subdued in her makeup and hair for the first part of the episode when she wasn't in her flying suit. And I love it when Samantha tells her to "BUTT! OUT!"

There was a LOT of dubbing in this episode! And not very good dubbing at that! But it was done so Dick York and Liz could get their Italian lines perfect.

Of course, the highlight is Endora's bath scene. She is so funny when she says, "Come and do a little work on your mama's back!" and "Samantha, don't shout or I shall have to ask you to leave my bathroom!" The best is Samantha dropping the sponge in there and saying, "Mother! Get dressed!"

The male voice on the record sounds like it was done by the actor who played Mr. Arcani and the female voice sounded a lot like the lady who usually plays Betty.

It was odd that Louise wasn't to the dinner party at the end.

And, of course, where is Tabatha?

This also marks the first time this season that Samantha wears her flying suit.

SEPTEMBER 29, 1967

It was on this night that ABC aired Episode #111: "Double, Double, Toil and Trouble".

Durwood awakes in the middle of the night due to the not-so-dulcet sounds of a mandolin playing. He finds that a warlock dressed in minstrel clothing (who also looks like the possible father of Jimmy Fallon and Chris Kattan of *Saturday Night Live*) has decided to practice whilst he waits to enter the presence of the Queen, our beautiful Samantha. Durwood, with his panties in a knot, goes down to yell at Samantha advising her that he has to get up early for a meeting with a very big client and demands that she clear court. Samantha agrees but is not very happy as she thought the agreement was that she could conduct the Queen's business after midnight, which she was doing. Endora is not too pleased with this and tells the court, who returns after Samantha and Durwood go to bed, that she has a marvelously evil idea about how to get rid of Durwood.

The next day after Samantha goes to the church to help set up for a bazaar, Endora pops in and calls on Serena, Samantha's look-a-like brunette cousin to help her in her "evil" scheme which is that Serena will make herself look just like Samantha and tick Durwood off enough to make him leave.

Durwood, who has been at home fixing the broken railing in the gazebo, hears "Samantha" come home from the church and decides he wants a little, ahem, afternoon delight? When he asks Sam/Serena to come sit by him on the couch she tells him to come to her over by the television. He does but she immediately pops out to the landing on the stairs. Thinking she's playing a little game with him he still pursues her until she pops out to re-appear at the door. He realizes something else may be going on, that maybe she's still mad about him having her clear court. She tells him she is and that she's had it. When he tries to get close to her she bunches up the rug in the front hall making him trip.

Just at that time, Mrs. Kravitz comes over to snoop (under the guise of borrowing a cup of sugar) as she had seen Mrs. Stephens come home but without a car. When she asks about the car, Sam/Serena asks about the where-abouts of Mrs. Kravitz's shoes which she zaps out. Sam/Serena then goes to get the cup of sugar while Mrs. Kravitz tries to figure out what has just gone on. Sam/Serena returns with the cup of sugar and returns Mrs. Kravitz's shoes which causes her to drop the sugar and run. Sam/Serena zaps the broken cup and spilled sugar whole again and Durwood tries to figure out what's going on. She tells him that she's tired of the whole mortal game and tired of jumping whenever he barks, that she wants to be free as the wind. Just then he freezes and Endora pops in to remind Serena to stay on task and not be so dramatic. She unfreezes Durwood when she pops out and Sam/Serena tells him she's not going to discuss it anymore.

Durwood is now really worried and calls Larry over to ask his opinion. Larry thinks that he can talk to Samantha and find out what's going on. When Larry and Sam/Serena are alone she plants a big ol' kiss on him stunning him, even more so when she starts to flirt big time with him. Endora again has to remind Serena to stay on task and Larry decides to leave after being unfrozen.

Meanwhile, Mrs. Kravitz has gone to the church bazaar where she meets up with Samantha. She is not too pleased with how she thinks Samantha treated her earlier. When she returns home, she tells Abner how she saw Samantha at the bazaar and realizes that she forgot her cup of sugar, which she apparently really needed and she sends Abner to fetch it.

As one last attempt to get Durwood really freaked out, Serena, still looking like Sam, walks in dressed like a go-go girl and tells Durwood she wants to get out and boil. He thinks people will stare and he tells her to change and look more like a housewife. She obliges, but looking like a dumpy toothless housewife in curlers (though we should all be so lucky if our wives looked like her).

At that moment, Abner comes to retrieve the sugar and sees "Mrs. Stephens," prompting Durwood to escort him out of the house. Abner wonders how Mrs. Stephens made it home so fast from the bazaar which makes Durwood think that Samantha may not be Samantha.

When Samantha does return home, she comes bearing a gift of a lemon meringue pie which Durwood takes and plants in his wife's face, thinking it's Serena. Samantha is totally confused by this and zaps up a pie which she plants in his face and when he asks for another, she gladly obliges only for him to grab it out of her hands before she can plaster him with it. He chases her around the table, and in her fear of being hit again, she calls for her mother, who enters from the kitchen only to get hit HARD in the face with the pie! Durwood tells Endora that he's sorry but that he meant the pie for Serena, who then walks in. When he and Samantha realize what's been going on, Samantha decides to even things up by planting a pie in Serena's face.

I would totally give this four stars! I LOVE this episode! It's funny every time and it's so refreshing to see Serena, even if she isn't in her "normal" routine yet. This is the first time we've seen Serena in "cullah" as this is her second episode. She was first seen in Season Two's Episode #54: "And Then There Were Three."

My favorite line is when Durwood is speaking to Larry and he goes to the den door and calls for Samantha and we hear a totally disgusted Elizabeth Montgomery say, "WHAT IS IT?!" off camera.

I LOVE the theme music for Serena, that slinky sexy music.

I did wonder where Tabatha was this whole time especially with the minstrel playing so loud.

The pie fight is HILARIOUS, yet scary. When Endora gets hit with the pie it really looked like it hurt and you would think that she would've blasted Durwood into a million pieces for doing that. And poor Liz — her head looked like it was totally thrown back when she was hit in the face as Serena.

It seems that this episode always had TONS snipped out of it when played in syndication like when Serena (as Sam) goes to get Mrs. Kravitz's sugar and she speaks to Endora for a little bit in the kitchen, when Endora floats down from the ceiling telling the whole witchly crew that the job isn't done yet, and surprisingly that very last scene where Durwood LICKS Sam's face! How sexy was that?! Thank heaven for DVD!

This will be the last time that we see Samantha fulfilling her duties as Queen, though her Queen-ship is mentioned in a few more episodes later on.

OCTOBER 5, 1967

It was on this night ABC aired Episode #112: "Cheap, Cheap."

Samantha has a fur lined coat delivered to the house which she bought on sale, though it was still a lot of money. Durwood doesn't seem pleased about this and though he tells her she can keep the coat, she can see that it doesn't sit well with him so she offers to take it back.

Endora thinks that Durwood is being a cheapskate and can't afford the coat, even if it is "a ratty old coat." Samantha assures her that he isn't cheap, they just simply cannot afford something like that right now. Endora decides to really make Durwood cheap and just as he's about to tell Samantha, over the phone, Endora places the cheap spell on him. Well, it's enough to make even Ebenezer Scrooge look careless with his money as Durwood is unbearably thrifty, to the point of even writing down the mere pennies Larry owes him for taking a stick of gum and a cigarette.

It also happens that at this time McMann and Tate has a client of the same cheapness, Mr. Bigelow. Durwood and Bigelow gel really well when they discuss cost cutting measures that McMann and Tate can use for his campaign, which means less money for Larry. Durwood invites the Bigelows and the Tates to his house for what he believes will be an inexpensive dinner but Samantha won't have that, even though she said she was going to whip up some veal birds (ground up veal on a stick made to look like chicken legs).

During the course of the evening Samantha, who still hasn't been able to find Endora to remove the spell, decides foolishly to try and do so herself. But the spell bounces off Durwood and hits Mr. Bigelow now making him a big spender, much to the delight of Mrs. Bigelow. Endora finally pops in looking like she just escaped from her genie bottle and removes the spell from Durwood, who later on tells Samantha the reason he wanted her to take the coat back was that he had bought the same one as a surprise for her but wasn't able to tell her on account of Endora's spell.

This one is pretty lame and I would only give it one and a half stars. The only parts I like are Samantha running down the stairs to get the door and her black and white dress at the dinner party. It looked like a dress that women would wear nowadays and she looked pretty hot in it! I also liked Durwood pulling out that huge jug of wine! Just the way he did it was hilarious!

One of my favorite lines is from Endora when she pops in on Samantha after she's put the spell on Durwood: "Penny for your thoughts? And I know you can use the cash."

This is also another rare instance of animation being used to show that witchcraft is happening. It was kind of a cool effect. I just wonder if *Bewitched* had been filmed nowadays if they would've used more visual animations for the magic? Frankly, it seems more real without it.

OCTOBER 12, 1967

It was on this night ABC aired Episode #113: "No Zip in My Zap."

Durwood wakes Samantha up at 6:30 AM with breakfast in bed to tell her that he has landed a huge account which means he'll get a bonus which means they get to go on their cruise to Bermuda they've always wanted to do! Samantha is thrilled and very proud of Durwood as he leaves for the office. Tabatha comes in just then wanting to know if her daddy has left and Samantha says "yes" only for Tabatha to point out that Daddy left his briefcase. Samantha tries to stop him before he leaves but just misses him. As she turns from the window where she had been calling to him, she sees Tabatha tip the breakfast tray on to the floor where all the dishes break, much to Tabatha's delight but not so much to Samantha's delight. Samantha decides to twitch them back together but finds that her twitch won't do it, that for some reason she may need an incantation. When that doesn't work she realizes that something is quite wrong with her powers.

She decides to try her powers out downstairs by getting their apparently new piano to play and a table lighter to light, all of which fails. Through this, she has been calling out to her mother for help, but Endora doesn't seem to hear when she suddenly pops in with a toy giraffe. Samantha tells her she's glad she finally popped in but Endora says she never heard her and in fact she had come to see Tabatha. Samantha explains what's going on and shows her how her powers are kaput by trying to light a fire in the fireplace. When Endora sees that her daughter's powers are fizzled she suggests they contact Dr. Bombay and she conjures him up.

Dr. Bombay, who had just been at a great concert where Nero was fiddling whilst Rome was burning ("a reenactment, of course"), checks Samantha's throat and asks her to levitate, which of course she can't do, nor can she levitate the tongue depressor. Dr. Bombay concludes that Samantha's lack of power use has caused them to dam up and that when the dam bursts her magic will go haywire. The only cure for this is levitation and so he sets Samantha up in the air about six feet and tells Endora to call him if they need any more help. Samantha isn't at all pleased with this but Endora assures her that she will take care of Tabatha while Samantha is incapacitated.

Meanwhile, Durwood and Larry are on Cloud Nine (not literally) over landing the new account and Larry says that he'll write the check out for Durwood's bonus as soon as they get Niles-Munster, the client's lawyer to sign the contract. Durwood recalls that he knew a Mary Jane Niles-Munster in school, and when he rejected her she vowed to get him back. He wonders if this could be the same person. Larry assures him that Niles-Munster can't be a woman with such a high position but when he asks the secretary if Niles-Munster has called she says that she wasn't able to speak to her as SHE was under the hair dryer. Durwood's heart sinks as he knows Mary Jane is going to ruin his life by ruining this deal. He and Larry head over to her hotel to get the contracts signed while Larry tries to soothe Durwood's nerves.

When they get there, Mz. Niles-Munster requests Larry to come and speak with her alone, and while Durwood is alone, he phones home to make sure Samantha hasn't bought the tickets for Bermuda yet. She tells him she hasn't but before he can get anything else out Endora grabs the phone from Samantha and tells him he can't talk to her anymore because she is flying and she promptly hangs up telling Samantha that the less contact with mortals in her condition, the better. As Durwood contemplates what Endora meant, he sees a fly zooming around the room and immediately thinks that it is Samantha. He tries talking "her" into going home and leaving Mary Jane alone when Larry and Mary Jane walk in on his little talk. The neurotic Durwood thinks that Mary Jane doesn't recognize him because of a spell that Samantha the Fly put on her and he goes to drown his sorrows at the bar.

When he arrives home later that night, Samantha has her mother release her from her levitation so she can talk to him only to find that he is talking like he has a mouth full of olives, he is so drunk. He goes on about her flying around and fixing Mary Jane so she would forget her vendetta against him just so that Samantha can go on the cruise. Of course, Durwood wanted to go too, but he also wanted things to work out on their own, even if it meant Mary Jane not signing the agreements to satisfy her grudge. Samantha doesn't understand any of this and tells him that she couldn't have gone anywhere nor done any magic because of her power problem. When she asks for a wandering Durwood to come back he is immediately pulled back and she explains that the dam has burst and she has no control over her powers and tries to tell him how she tried out her powers earlier at which point the piano starts playing, the lighter lights, and the fire burns. Durwood is very upset by this and thinks she's lying to him which makes her upset so she tells him to go back to his bartender with his mouth full of olives, which he immediately does.

At the bar, Durwood decides he is going to confront Mary Jane about who he really is and leaves for her place only to find when he gets there that she knew who he was the whole time and that she was over her childhood grudge.

Durwood goes home to apologize to Samantha, who is still mad that he didn't believe her but more upset that he would think she turned herself into a fly of all things. She also has to continue levitating so they have to "make" up tomorrow.

I LOVE this episode though I would give it a three and a half star rating because the scenes with Larry and Durwood walking in and out of elevators is SOOO boring and the scenes with Mary Jane are boring too!

This marks Dr. Bombay's second appearance his first being last season's finale.

I think this episode makes total sense in regards to Samantha losing her powers. Well, not so much losing them as having them clog up for non-use. And levitating, in an odd way, does make sense.

I LOVE the sound effects in this episode and they seem to me to be the most "realistic" out of the whole series with the exception of Dr. Bombay's popping sound. The later "WHAAAMPPP" is more realistic to me.

The scene where Samantha says, "I've been powerless all day. I've been trying to get the lighter to light, the fire to burn and the piano to play..." and then they do is used in one of the Fourth Season promos.

I also like that "stick your tongue out" line and Endora's delivery of "Oh Samantha, REALLY!"

That dress that Samantha wears is really weird unless it's just some sort of house dress but even then, still weird.

Sometimes you can see the board Liz is laying on while she's supposed to be levitating which reminds me of an ironing board as it's covered in the same material as her dress.

I like that in this episode we learn about Durwood's previous life. Mary Jane sounded like a real bitch when they were young. And I thought it was funny when Durwood was asking about the boy they called Stinky and it turns out she married him.

Herbie J wrote in his book that the fly they used was a real fly that they pulled the wings off...eww!

OCTOBER 19, 1967

It was on this night ABC gave us what essentially amounted to a twenty-five minute sedative in the form of Episode #114: "Birdies, Bogeys, and Baxter."

In an attempt to reclaim his great golf playing skills from college in order to impress sporting goods client Mr. Baxter, Durwood has been getting up at the wee small hours to practice. Of course, he's pretty much useless any other time as he's so tired. When Endora hears what he's up to, she tells Samantha that once he were to achieve his great skills he'd simply want more, which Samantha disagrees with. Endora decides to prove she's right by casting a spell on him to give him back his college game…and that's about the only fun part of the episode as the rest is Durwood, Larry, and Mr. Baxter out on the golf course where Mrs. Baxter and Samantha later join them, not to play, but simply to watch. And it seems that Endora is right: now that Durwood is playing well again, he's become cocky. But so is Mr. Baxter who Mrs. Baxter wants to see brought down, so Samantha throws in a few spells of her own to let Durwood make impossible shots.

When he ends up winning it infuriates Mr. Baxter who is not going to hire McMann and Tate until his wife reminds him that it's her daddy's money that got him the company and he'd better hire them. Mr. Baxter concedes that he's learned that he really is a poor sport and his account is theirs.

This episode is SOOOOOOOO boring! It's golf. No matter if there is magic or what have you, it's golf and golf = boring. It's especially disheartening considering that up to this point this season all the episodes have been very entertaining. I haven't watched it in centuries because it IS so boring! It seriously was like they took the cast out for a game of golf and filmed and then some lame-brain thought, "Hey! Why don't we just film some scenes of Elizabeth Montgomery twitching and call it an episode!"

I do remember when I was little I LOVED Endora popping into the tree and the spell she wove only 'cause she mentioned "scale of fish" and the way she insinuated she had scales with the waving of her hands.

The tag scene is a semi-remake of the tag scene of "It Shouldn't Happen to a Dog" where Samantha is wrapped in Durwood's arms and he says he'll get his hat and she says, "No, don't you dare move. I'll get it." And she twitches and gets his hat and he says, "Samantha!" And she says, "So sue me! It was worth it." That coat she twitches on is the same new coat she just got in "Cheap, Cheap."

In Herbie J's book he mentions how they hired a professional golfer to come in to film scenes for Dick York but Dick turned out to be a better golfer.

Two days prior the Broadway hit *Hair* opened off-Broadway but would move to Broadway the following April. *Hair* was a rock musical from the counter-culture with long haired hippies which was quite controversial in its themes of drug use, anti-U.S. sentiments and a brief full nude scene.

The day after that Walt Disney's nineteenth full length animated feature *The Jungle Book* opened. It was the last movie Walt Disney himself had been part of before his death the preceding December.

Two days after the *Bewitched* episode aired, tens of thousands of Vietnam protestors descended on Washington, D.C.

OCTOBER 26, 1967

It was on this night ABC aired the fourth Halloween-themed episode of *Bewitched*, #115: "The Safe and Sane Halloween" totally making up for the bore-fest that was last week's episode.

On Halloween Eve, Durwood walks in on Samantha reading Tabatha a Halloween bedtime story involving a gremlin, a goblin, and a jack o'lantern which he worries might stimulate her witchy side, but Samantha assures him that it was just a mortal children's story and that there will be no harm. It seems, though, that this time is Durwood is actually right as after her mommy leaves, Tabatha zaps the characters out of the book to play games with her.

The next day the Gremlin, the Goblin, and the Jack O'Lantern keep out of sight up in Tabatha's room and that evening Samantha takes her out for her first time trick-or-treating, which also happens to be Samantha's first time trick-or-treating. Tabatha is dressed as a tiger/leopard in a costume Samantha made and is really cute. She also wants her daddy to come with but apparently Larry wanted to come over so Durwood waits for him. Just after Samantha and Tabatha leave the Gremlin, the Goblin, and the Jack O'Lantern decide they want to go too, so they jump out of Tabatha's room to join their new friend.

Samantha assumes that these creatures are just some of the neighborhood kids and welcomes them in their trick-or-treating. But soon things go downhill when the Gremlin zaps a beard onto nice Mrs. Robinson. Samantha assumes it was Tabatha's doing and reprimands her, but they continue on to a grumpy old man's house, whom the Gremlin doesn't take too kindly to, so he zaps open the slammed screen door and levitates his candy bowl into Tabatha's hands. Mortified, Samantha tells Tabatha's "friends" that Tabatha will no longer be trick-or-treating as she has to go home and immediately zaps herself and Tabatha into the nursery.

As she's getting ready to put Tabatha down for the night as punishment, she comes across the Halloween book where she sees that there are pictures missing. It dawns on Samantha that Tabatha's "friends" weren't neighborhood children but the characters from the book who are now loose in the neighborhood! When she tries to zap them back in the book, she finds she can't and realizes that she must get them back in the vicinity of the book and have Tabatha return them to their proper place, so she pops out to the neighborhood to find them.

Meanwhile, Gladys Kravitz has made a jack o'lantern costume for her nephew Tommy. He hates it and would rather be a monster, but Auntie Gladys assures him that the jack o'lantern costume is just great. She also tells him they are going to avoid the house across the street as she believes that Samantha is strange and might even possibly be a real witch! While Tommy and Gladys are out on the town, Tommy sees the Gremlin, the Goblin, and the Jack O'Lantern and decides to play a trick on his aunt by switching places with the "kid" whose costume resembles his. And so Gladys unwittingly goes trick-or-treating with a real spook!

Samantha finds the trio hiding in some bushes and zaps them all back to her house only to find it isn't going to be as easy as she thought when the Jack O'Lantern takes his head off to reveal that he's Tommy and he wants his aunt Gladys! And to add more trouble, Durwood, upon hearing that Samantha and Tabatha are back, wants to bring Larry and Louise up to show them Tabatha's costume before she goes to bed. The Tates say their good nights to Tabatha and Larry makes some jokes with the Gremlin, who is only in the mood to joke around and he zaps a furry tail onto Larry which Samantha immediately gets rid of. Durwood now knows that he's dealing with some other worldly beings rather than just some mortal trick-or-treaters when he gets a pair of donkey ears zapped on to him. Samantha apprises him of the situation and tells him that she needs to find the real Jack O'Lantern and get Tommy back to Gladys before Gladys finds out her nephew is missing…

…well, speaking of Gladys she and "Tommy" have gone home for the night when the Jack O'Lantern splattered a pie in Mrs. Robinson's face. As Gladys is reprimanding him, he rises and his pumpkin head detaches from his body and floats around the room. Just then, Samantha calls asking about Tommy, and Gladys knows that she has something to do with her freaked out nephew and while talking to Samantha, the Jack O'Lantern leaves out the window.

Tommy tells the Gremlin and the Goblin, who had all been left in the kitchen by Samantha with strict instructions to stay, that he just wants to go home, "I'm just a little kid!" So the Gremlin obliges him by turning him into a goat! Gladys arrives looking for Tommy and when she goes into the kitchen where she is told he is at, she finds a goat there calling out her name! She tells the other spooks to scat, which they immediately do. Samantha tries to capture them while Gladys tells the Tates about the goat. Larry goes to have a look and does indeed see a goat which means Gladys now has a witness to all the craziness she has witnessed over the years.

Samantha finally captures the Gremlin and the Goblin and she twitches Tommy back into his normal state. She then zaps herself and the spooks up to Tabatha's room where she explains that putting the characters back in the book will make Daddy happy so Tabatha obliges.

Meanwhile, Tommy finds his aunt Gladys and Larry tells all that he just said he saw a goat to make Gladys feel better. Just when Samantha thinks all is well, the Jack O'Lantern shows up but immediately disappears in front of Larry but it's all chalked up to the drinking going on and so things are back to as normal as they can be in a house of witches.

This episode is a lot of fun and one of my favorites from the Halloween episodes. I really like that it shows so many Trick-or-Treaters whereas all the previous years, except Season Two, didn't.

Erin was really cute in this episode especially when she was talking back, like when Samantha told her that if she put her friends back in the book she could play with them tomorrow and Tabatha says, "Play now!"

I really wish they would've included Endora! However, her being gone matches more with what Samantha said in the first Halloween episode, that Endora flies to the South of France around Halloween 'til it all blows over.

I really liked the sound effects in this one too, especially when Samantha zaps herself and all the spooks back home.

One more thing — Dick Sargent's Durwood also gets zapped with donkey ears in "If the Shoe Doesn't Fit," the leprechaun episode from the Sixth Season.

A funny blooper happens in this episode when Samantha walks into the living room with a drink in hand and as she takes a drink she practically spills the whole thing down her front but Elizabeth keeps on going! Another blooper is at the beginning when she is closing the book, you can see the characters are already missing.

Another cool thing is that Tabatha has the *Bewitched* Baby Bottle in her room that was available for purchase back in the 60s. That's kind of interesting as that would mean OUR show could be watched by Samantha and crew which would probably 'cause a meltdown in the universe!

Erin Murphy has home video shot by her parents the day that they were filming at the Ranch. It's too bad it couldn't be included on the DVDs.

It was also on this day that future Senator John McCain, who was a Navy pilot, was shot down over North Vietnam and kept as a POW.

Two nights previously, on NBC, *I Dream of Jeannie* fans were disappointed to find that their favorite show had been pre-empted for a televising of the Beatles' 1964 movie *A Hard Day's Night*.

NOVEMBER 2, 1967

It was on this night ABC aired Episode #116: "Out of Synch, Out of Mind."

Durwood's mommy, Phyllis, interrupts Durwood and Samantha's relaxing Sunday afternoon by showing up with suitcases in hand announcing that she is leaving Durwood's daddy, Frank! Apparently he was caught with something that looked suspiciously like lipstick on his collar though he claims it was from lingonberry pie, though lingonberries are out of season. Before they can apprise Samantha's relatives of their request to not pop in until further notice, Aunt Clara shows up. Samantha decides Durwood should show home movies to his mother to occupy her while they try to get his father to come pick her up.

Durwood's gone all high tech this time with the movies as he has SOUND that he can play with them, and hopefully synch the sound up with the picture which is a movie of Samantha and Tabatha singing "Old MacDonald Had a Farm." Of course, just because he wants it to work, it doesn't. Just then Frank calls looking for Phyllis and this upsets her as she says she doesn't want to talk to him though you can tell she really does. She decides to go lay down until Durwood can get the movie working properly. Aunt Clara says that she may be able to help with a spell, which she casts. And it does work until they find that it also has caused Samantha's voice to fall out of synch with her mouth in real life! Now they've got to worry about Phyllis finding out about this.

Aunt Clara goes off to retrieve Dr. Bombay to see if he can cure Samantha. Meanwhile, Durwood and Samantha decide to tell Phyllis that Samantha is sick. Phyllis, who believes she has nursing experience via her time pushing the book mobile at the hospital, says she can try to help Samantha, so she takes her into the bathroom to gargle some salt water and aspirin. When she sees that the gargle noise has come after Samantha finished gargling, she knows something is wrong. Just then Aunt Clara pops in with Dr. Bombay causing Phyllis to faint. Dr. Bombay thinks that Phyllis is the sick witch when he takes her temperature but after being advised he has the wrong patient he says that Phyllis isn't too warm for a mortal.

After examining Samantha, he decides to brew up a batch of Bombay's Super Cure-All, which he created to fix Aunt Clara's sloppy spells. After he administers the potion to Samantha, her voice and her mouth synch once more. Thinking everything is great, Samantha tries to focus on the problem with her parent in-laws again, but all is not right when green stripes start appearing on Samantha's face in front of Phyllis, who has had enough of all the craziness going on at her son's house. Just then she sees that Frank has pulled up to the house and she tries to tell him that strange things are going on.

Meanwhile, Dr. Bombay advises that the stripes will disappear soon, and they do. But then, Samantha's voice becomes out of synch again. Dr. Bombay then leaves just as Aunt Clara remembers her spell eraser, which fixes Samantha. When Phyllis tries to show Frank the stripes, she sees that they are gone and she decides that maybe she imagined the "lip stick" on his collar too and therefore she decides to return to her husband. And so everything ends happy…except that when Samantha's voice returned to normal, Durwood's was thrown out of whack!

I'd have to agree with the *Bewitched* Critic's rating of two stars, though I do enjoy Dr. Bombay's scenes a lot. The episode seems to just sort of mosey along, until he shows up.

This is Dr. Bombay's third appearance, and is it ever hilarious! He is slowly transforming into the Dr. Bombay we all know and love. My favorite part is when he rushes everyone out of the bathroom, including Samantha! And speaking of the bathroom, this is a rare instance where we get to see inside it and this time it's red instead of blue. I love it when Dr. Bombay appears and says that Phyllis is one sick witch and that she's burning up. And when they tell him that she isn't the one that is sick he says, "Well, she isn't too warm for a mortal." I also thought the effect of the fire burning under his cauldron was really cool and magical. Where is the flame coming from?

This episode also could be a premonition of things to come as we now have a different actor (Roy Roberts) playing Durwood's father, Frank. Maybe the switching in actors is a hereditary thing and that's why Durwood gets another actor down the line (wink).

This is the first time Samantha wears one of those groovy Gucci pant suits.

I had never heard of lingonberries before this episode. I wonder what they taste like? Probably pretty good for Frank to get them all over his collar.

I thought the home movie with Tabatha was really cute. It seemed like it was just Liz and little Erin Murphy just being themselves and they worked it into the episode.

One of my favorite lines is from Aunt Clara when she first appears and talks about how the chimney needs sweeping and then she says, "Boy, does that chimney need sweeping!"

It is rather odd that Dr. Bombay would be called in to cure one of Aunt Clara's spells. What's always puzzled me is that Aunt Clara has an apparently "cure-all" spell remover. Why don't they just write that one down and use it over and over when they are in a jam? Of course, that would get boring, but still...

I like that we find out that there is a cinder-path in front of Dr. Bombay's house.

The green stripes are really corny and I wish they wouldn't have done it. I'm okay with square green spots, but stripes are just too much. The mirror by the door just suddenly is there for this episode only. Usually if there is a mirror, it's hanging in the hall where now a door is.

Anyway, it's an enjoyable episode even if it is REALLY slow at first.

Also on this day, President Lyndon B. Johnson held a secret meeting with a group of prestigious leaders from around the country to discuss how they could get the American people to back the Vietnam War. They conclude that the citizens should only be given optimistic reports of the war. Yet, the next day, in the Battle of Dak To, heavy casualties were suffered on both sides.

NOVEMBER 9, 1967

It was on this night ABC aired Episode #117: "That Was No Chick, That Was My Wife."

Just as Durwood proclaims his weekend plans of doing nothing including not answering the phone or the door, Aunt Clara comes calling at their tree followed immediately by Larry at the door. The reason for Larry's visit is to tell Durwood and Samantha that he has planned a fantastic weekend for them in Chicago! They are not thrilled though and learn that the ulterior motive is to meet with client Mr. Springer before he officially comes into town next week to discuss renewing his Springer Pet Food account with McMann and Tate. Larry thinks Durwood and Samantha can soften him up at lunch with Mrs. Springer. When Aunt Clara offers to babysit, the deal is done and so the Stephens are off for a "fun" filled weekend in Chicago.

At the business luncheon the next day, things seem to be going swimmingly. The Springers are quite impressed with Durwood and his wife.

Back at home, Aunt Clara finds that apparently she was also going to be babysitting a monkey and is pleased when Samantha calls home to check on things so that Aunt Clara can ask what to feed the monkey. Of course, Samantha had no plans of having a monkey in the house and pops home to see what is going on. When she arrives, she sees that Tabatha has changed her toy monkey into a real one and though she is really pleased with how well her daughter can use her powers, she also realizes that her home is supposed to be witchcraft free, so she decides to go over things again with Aunt Clara. Just then, Louise Tate shows up to check on things at Larry's request. Aunt Clara quickly gets rid of her while Samantha hides, but Louise comes back realizing she hadn't been able to check on Tabatha. Of course, she sees Samantha and wonders why she isn't in Chicago. Samantha tells her that plans have changed. Louise decides to call Larry and see if he knew that Durwood was going to Chicago alone.

After briefing Aunt Clara, Samantha pops back to Chicago to find that Mr. Springer has decided to renew his contract and he is going to call Larry to tell him the good news and also tell him how much he and Mrs. Springer are enjoying the company of Mr. and Mrs. Stephens. Before Mr. Springer can get a word out edge-wise, Larry apologizes all over the place for Samantha not being there. Mr. Springer then believes that Durwood has had the colossal gall to bring some other woman to the luncheon and he tells the Stephens that he will not do business with any company that would hire people like Durwood.

Back at home, Durwood is distraught about what to do considering there really isn't any viable explanation for why Mrs. Tate saw Samantha at home when she was also in Chicago. Larry tells him that he was able to get the Springer account back but only on condition that Durwood never set foot in McMann and Tate again. He asks Durwood to come and clean out his desk the next morning before Mr. Springer gets there to sign the contracts. Samantha asks if she can go with him as she already has to be downtown to go shopping with Tabatha, and Durwood agrees saying he would enjoy her company in his last happy moments.

The next day they arrive and are greeted by Charlie the doorman, who addresses Samantha as Mrs. Stephens and talks about how beautiful Tabatha is. Watching all of this is Mr. Springer, who now finds that the woman he was introduced to in Chicago was really Mrs. Stephens. When Larry comes out to greet him, Mr. Springer is really confused as to why Larry would say Samantha was at home. Durwood and Samantha come up with an explanation that it was all a test to see if Mr. Springer was more interested in Durwood's personal life rather than how he did his work and Mr. Springer accepts that and renews his account.

Later on, Samantha invites Louise over just before she is on her way to the psychiatrist to explain the confusing situation. She asks her cousin Serena to pop in and look like her (well, even more than she does now) and they tell Louise that it was Serena she met the other day. When Louise asks why Serena didn't introduce herself, Serena responds, "You never asked." And so Louise cancels her psyche appointment and everything is well!

I really like this episode. I liked that it was a seemingly difficult situation to get out of with Louise having seen Samantha at home and the client believing Durwood's being gutsy by bringing another woman to the dinner.

Aunt Clara is hysterical in this episode! This is one of my favorite episodes of hers. My favorite line of hers is at the end when Samantha says, "Aunt Clara, I think I hear the baby crying." Aunt Clara: "Well, I don't hear any baby crying." And Samantha points up stairs and motions for her to get lost and she says, "Oh! OH! I think I hear the baby crying!"

I also like it when Samantha tells Louise that their sitter got sick and Aunt Clara starts her coughing attack. The monkey was really cute too.

I thought Samantha's hat was really beautiful and classy. I really liked her all white outfit.

This is the second episode Sara Seegar has been in (she was Mrs. Grange, the orphanage director in "A Vision of Sugar Plums") but the first time she has played a client's wife and is one of the actors that appeared most on *Bewitched*. This is Herb Voland's first episode and it seems he returns many more times, AND with Sara Seegar as his wife.

One of the bloopers in this episode is when they are out on the street in front of McMann and Tate you can see the mountains in the background which, of course, they are supposed to be in NYC so that doesn't make sense.

This episode is really special to me as it is the one I chose to watch when I had my first candlelight vigil for Elizabeth Montgomery a couple days after she died on May 18, 1995. I didn't have very many episodes on tape at the time, and most of them were at my Grandma's house where I was living. I had my candle light vigil at my mom's house that weekend and I was having it with my friend Janette, her friend Jenn, my cousin Pam, and my sister Heather. I wanted to watch an episode that showcased Liz's talents and I thought a Serena episode would do the trick as many, many people really believed Serena was played by a different actress. This was the only Serena episode I had at my mom's house which is a bummer because she was only in it at the end. So when I watch this episode I remember that night, which really helped me cope with Liz's death.

Two days prior, President Johnson signed the Public Broadcasting Act of 1967 which established the Corporation for Public Broadcasting.

NOVEMBER 16, 1967

It was on this night ABC aired a monumental episode of *Bewitched* in #118: "Allergic to Macedonian Dodo Birds," monumental in the fact that Endora, probably the most powerful witch in the cosmos, LOSES HER POWERS! Let me explain…

After Endora helps Tabatha finger paint by zapping her into painting an original Van Gogh, Durwood gets furious and demands she get rid of the painting. When she tries, nothing happens and so Samantha tries as they think there may be something wrong in the atmosphere. The paint disappears with no problem and Samantha wonders if her mother is not feeling well. Endora assures her that she is fine and that she must pop off to Monaco for a party, but when she tries to, nothing happens. Samantha tries popping out, and succeeds, and it becomes apparent that Endora has a pooped popper! This is most upsetting for the witches but Durwood couldn't be more pleased if he had won the lottery and makes sure everyone knows it by his snide comments.

Samantha suggests calling in a doctor but Endora insists that if she just rest overnight, she'll feel better the next day. Of course, this means that she is going to be resting at Durwood's house and he agrees that she may, but only for the night.

The next morning, Endora tests her powers by trying to levitate the morning paper to her hand but nothing happens. When the paper does start flying, it turns out it was at Tabatha's hand. Later at breakfast, Endora shuns the idea of cereal for breakfast and asks Samantha to twitch up her regular breakfast of fried ravens eggs but Durwood puts the kibosh on that. And when Samantha asks Endora to pour the coffee, she practically throws her back out doing it as "it's heavy." Samantha insists that she call in a doctor and conjures up the family warlock doctor, Dr. Bombay.

After giving Endora a thorough checkup, he deduces that she is suffering from an allergy to birds, and not just any bird, but the rare Macedonian Dodo Bird which is puzzling as they have been extinct for millions of years! He suggests this must be it and that it might've sneaked up on her from behind as she never noticed such a bird. He also says that as it's an allergy the victim's powers float off into limbo and float there unless by magnetic polarization those powers attach themselves to a witch/warlock whose own powers are dwindling. He says that it wouldn't be a stranger but would have to be a relative. He also says he can cure Endora instantly but they will first need to produce the tail feather from the dodo for the antidote as it provides the necessary anti-toxin. And with that he pops off.

Just as Samantha wonders aloud who could possibly be harboring her mother's powers, that person pops in and it turns out to be the obvious choice, Aunt Clara. She has arrived to show off her new powers, which she does by changing Endora into a goose, and after she changes her back, she zaps up a feast to celebrate.

Later on, Durwood finds himself alone with Endora, who is resting, out on the patio but she won't let him rest as she asks him, in a feeble voice, to straighten her pillow, wonders where Tabatha has been all morning and where her hot cocoa is that Samantha had promised. Durwood goes to check on the cocoa, which Samantha gives him as she tells him she must make a call. She calls for Aunt Clara who pops in from lunch in Holland. Samantha tells her she's pleased that Aunt Clara is so happy with her new found powers but she wants to talk about Endora's loss. Aunt Clara assures her she didn't steal Endora's powers, that she didn't know where they came from. Samantha is satisfied with that answer and Aunt Clara says she's going to go sailing and pops off. Not a second later Samantha hears a boat whistle and sees that their street has turned into a harbor, something Mrs. Kravitz also notices, and Samantha twitches the harbor and Aunt Clara away.

Samantha takes a drink out to Durwood and finds that Endora is still wondering why Tabatha is still up in her room. Durwood icily suggests that she may want privacy to which Endora responds, "He meant that as an insult! He HATES me!" Samantha tries to assure her that he doesn't but Endora goes on, "He does. He hates me. I shall have to live out my life in a CLIMATE of hatred!" When Durwood wonders if she might mean live out her life at his house, she confirms it saying that she isn't going to leave until she gets her powers back. He reminds them that he said for only one night and maybe Endora should be put into a senior citizens center. Samantha objects, reminding him that Endora is her mother, but he counters with the fact that he is her husband. Endora reminds him

The cause of Endora's power loss, a Macedonian Dodo bird, comes downstairs prompting Samantha to zap Dr. Bombay in.

that the marriage can be ended by a divorce. In his frustration, he decides to leave for the bar.

After being at the bar for a bit, Durwood suddenly disappears and finds himself back at home where Samantha suggests that they may find the reason why Endora's powers disappeared if they recreate the events of the previous morning because she doesn't think it could possibly be a Macedonian Dodo. That is, until they find one following Tabatha down the stairs! She tells them that she had zapped him up out of one of her coloring books and they deduce that she must have had him hidden in her closet, which is where Endora came into contact with him and he was also the reason she was up in her room so much. Samantha zaps in Dr. Bombay to apologize and he chases the bird until he soothes it enough for him to pluck a feather from its tail which he stirs the zapped up antidote with. Endora drinks it and tries to pop out and is successful. With that Dr. Bombay pops out and not a moment after, they hear a commotion on the roof and Aunt Clara calling for help. Samantha pops to the roof and finds that Aunt Clara was flying back from the yacht races when her powers went away and Samantha explains that they have returned to Endora.

Out of four stars I give this one ten! Frankly, it's my favorite out of the whole series. I laugh EVERY time I watch it, something which I cannot say for the other episodes, which some are still funny but I know the jokes already. For some reason the jokes in this one still seem fresh as the day they were originally broadcast.

I do have to say that the bird costume is ridiculous! Jim Henson, at that time, was already making big costume puppets such as the La-Choy Dragon that was used in many commercials. They should've hired him. Plus it looks nothing like what a Dodo Bird is said to have looked like, but on the other hand, it was from Tabatha's coloring book so maybe it was just a cartoon looking bird, which this one was, and then that makes total sense.

Agnes Moorehead should've been nominated on this episode alone for an Emmy! It's practically perfect in every way! The whole scene out on the patio is simply hysterical what with the "Durwood, help me!" Durwood: "I might help you if you used my correct name." Endora: "Oh…what was it?" Durwood: "DARRIN!" Endora: "Oh yeah, that's right…Dennis? Straighten my pillow." And of course, "He HATES me! I shall have to live out my life in a CLIMATE of hatred!" And then when she dabs her eyes with the quilt, oh man, Aggie is awesome!

Dr. Bombay is starting to come into his regular character with his lines like, "Samantha! You plucked me off me dolphin and I was winning the race!" I also like it when he is telling the group how Endora could've come in contact with a Macedonian Dodo and he says, "It could've sneaked up on her from be-haynd!"

Aunt Clara acquiring Endora's powers was brilliant and it was great to finally see Clara have her day by changing Endora into a goose. And, of course, how funny is it when she says, "I'm a swinger and I like to swing!" This episode could be used as a proof of Aunt Clara being a relative on Endora's side as she is the one that acquired Endora's powers.

This is the first time we see someone on the roof near the chimney, a scene we would see many more times, especially in the later seasons.

Anyway, LOVE this episode!

The next day, President Johnson told the nation that "We are inflicting greater losses than we are taking…we are making progress."

NOVEMBER 23, 1967

After we had gorged ourselves on as much turkey, stuffing, potatoes, and gravy, etc. that we could handle, we plopped ourselves onto the couch and tuned into ABC to watch how Samantha and company celebrate Thanksgiving courtesy of Episode #119: "Samantha's Thanksgiving to Remember."

Aunt Clara drops in on her niece and nephew-in-law unconsciously as apparently she hadn't intended on doing so, but as she talks in her sleep, well, there she was. Samantha was thrilled to have her favorite aunt join them for their Thanksgiving feast but, of course, Durwood wasn't. He had been planning on a nice quiet Thanksgiving with just the three of them, but Samantha tells him it'll be a nice quiet Thanksgiving with just the four of them.

While they wait for the turkey to finish cooking, Aunt Clara regales Tabatha with tales of the very first Thanksgiving considering she (Aunt Clara) was there. As she reminisces, she begins to be homesick for Plymouth and tells Samantha and Durwood that she has decided that she'll bow out of their invitation to Thanksgiving dinner so that she can go visit Plymouth. Durwood offers to buy her a plane ticket, but she tells him she can get there on her own power and begins to incant. At the same moment Mrs. Kravitz has come knocking on the kitchen door in the hopes of borrowing something but as nobody answers, she decides to let herself in. As she walks into the living room, unseen by the Stephens' and Aunt Clara, she finds that Aunt Clara is in the middle of a strange poem which ends in a huge explosion of smoke! And as the smoke clears, had she still been there, Mrs. Kravitz would've found that Samantha, Durwood, Tabatha, Aunt Clara, and herself were gone!

Back in 17th century Plymouth, all five 20th centuriers pop into a small cabin. Durwood thinks that Aunt Clara has simply zapped them all to Plymouth, but when he opens the door, he sees that she has also displaced them temporally. Mrs. Kravitz can't handle all that she has seen and immediately falls into a faint. Durwood, at his wit's end, worries about Samantha being in the 17th century when witch hunting was so prevalent, but Samantha assures him that they are in the early part of the 17th century and that the witch hunts didn't start until later. She also calms his fears of being discovered by zapping them all into 17th century clothing. And not a moment too soon as John Alden, one of the original pilgrims, comes calling to invite them to the Thanksgiving feast. Of course, they accept as who wouldn't?!

As they go out to see the town, they pass by a man named Phineas, who was carrying the turkey to the dinner table and Durwood startles him by saying, "Hey there! Everything OK?" Not exactly a proper 17th century greeting. Later at the dinner, Phineas reminds Durwood that his womenfolk are not to sit at the table with the men, that there are still many preparations to be done for the rest of the dinner and so Samantha, Aunt Clara, Tabatha, and Mrs. Kravitz go off to finish the chores.

While Durwood eats with the menfolk, Phineas remarks how he has not had such a good time since he attended the burning of a witch back in the old country. Durwood goes to warn Samantha that she must be extremely careful as he thinks Phineas may find out about her powers. Samantha assures him they will be all right and asks him to start a fire beneath one of the cauldrons they are using to cook. Durwood just so happens to have a match in his pocket, which he uses. This may not be such a big deal but as matches have not been invented yet AND Phineas was watching it becomes a big deal as Phineas cries, "Witch!" Of course, Mrs. Kravitz thinks he's talking about Samantha but Phineas corrects her when he says that it is Durwood who is the witch!

Durwood is put on trial with Miles Standish presiding. Phineas tells Durwood that he must confess to being a witch or he shall be burned and if he doesn't confess, he'll be burned for not confessing. John Alden, who is also part of the court, feels that there should be more proper evidence and that Durwood should be able to find someone to defend him, but Phineas says that no one but a witch would defend a witch.

Of course, that makes Samantha the logical choice. In her statement to the court, she remarks how Phineas has used Durwood's differing speech and mannerisms to bring up a charge of witchery, but that if they were to examine each other closely, they would find that everyone is different making no one safe from the accusation of witchery. She then asks Phineas to light the witches' stick a.k.a. the match (which Durwood had already lighted for the court to see that it was nothing to be afraid of). Phineas accepts, thinking that he won't be able to do it as Durwood said he wouldn't as it's already been lit, but by a deft twitch of the nose, Samantha lights it. Miles Standish tells Phineas that in light of the new evidence Phineas must either confess himself to be a witch or he need drop his charges against Durwood. It's at this time that Aunt Clara finally remembers the spell to get them home and they all arrive safely back.

Gladys, still in her pilgrim's outfit, now thinks she has the evidence to prove to Abner that she's not crazy but Samantha zaps her and everyone else back into their modern clothes and they proceed to have their nice quiet Thanksgiving with just the four of them.

I would give this a four star rating. This episode is really great in the fact that we are given a twist by DURWOOD being accused of being a witch and, realizing that back then it was very VERY difficult to prove your innocence but also knowing Samantha could've saved him with just a little twitch, it's satisfying that she didn't have to use magic. Well, okay, she did have to relight the "witches stick."

About Gladys and the "back" door: that door is on the same side of the house as the front door and as she's coming to borrow a cup of sugar, it makes sense that she would go to that door rather than the actual front door. It used to be hard for me to picture this until I saw the actual house and looked over the blue prints at *www.1164.com*, but if you try to forget about the window over the kitchen sink, it makes more sense. The kitchen sink and that wall with the washer and dryer share the same wall as the one side of the garage which means there couldn't have been a window there. The wall with the door that Gladys knocked on runs perpendicular to that.

I thought it was cool that Gladys was caught up in the trip too. She fainted and then woke thinking it was a dream and then she says THE funniest thing, "This dream is too much work!" I think this is the first time where we see Sandra Gould's Gladys acting more like Alice Pearce's Gladys would've.

I did think that Samantha's hair was too long and I really think it would've been up too. I also question how real it was to actually allow her to speak in court back then.

Herbie J actually watched this episode with Dick York as it was one of Dick's favorites, if not most favorite. How cool would that have been? When I asked Herbie J if he had watched any with Elizabeth Montgomery he said he was too scared to ask her because he didn't think she would've liked that at all. THAT would've been surreal.

I liked how when they returned to the present Durwood popped in like he was being dropped from somewhere.

All in all, it's a great episode worthy of watching any time!

I can't end without mentioning Samantha's shift in her clothing styles. That tie-dyed dress is groovtacular! She wears it in another episode later this season ("Tabatha's Cranky Spell") and again in Season Five's "Samantha the Sculptress." It seems that her clothes get more far out as the season progresses.

NOVEMBER 30, 1967

It was on this night ABC aired Episode #120: "Solid Gold Mother-in-Law."

Samantha comes home from shopping to find that she is now married to a pony! Of course, Tabatha loves it, or him shall we say, as the pony is her daddy courtesy of Grandmama. Apparently Durwood came home to find that Endora was babysitting and made remarks about her not knowing how to take care of Tabatha and accused Endora of riding him, so she decided to show him what it was like to really be ridden. As Samantha tries to soothe the pony Durwood, Endora gets disgusted at the sight and changes Durwood back to his normal form. Furious at always having to fight with Endora, Durwood says that he is leaving until Endora is out of his house. Endora decides that maybe it is time to do something nice for her son-in-law and so later on she decides to gift him with a framed portrait of herself which floats into his office. Durwood isn't at all impressed, especially when the picture has a living Endora in it that sticks her tongue out at him. When he tries to throw it away, the picture just floats back on to his desk and when he tries breaking it, he only succeeds in breaking his desk. He finally decides that burning it is the only solution so he takes it down to the furnace room and throws it in there.

Back in the office, he finds that Endora (and her picture) are not so easily thrown away as the picture has followed him back. Just at that time, Larry walks in with new client, Mr. Gregson, who is looking for a new ad agency to sell his home appliances. As they speak, he notices the picture of Endora and Durwood confesses that she is his mother-in-law. Mr. Gregson is quite impressed that someone would have a picture of their mother-in-law on their desk. He requests a meeting with Endora, as she must be quite impressive. Larry suggests that Mr. Gregson attend a dinner party at the Stephens that evening. Durwood says he didn't know about the party and Mr. Gregson says he'll just have to meet her another time and takes his leave. Larry is furious that Durwood didn't go along with the ruse and threatens to fire Durwood if he doesn't call Mr. Gregson up and invite him to dinner that night. So on threat of no job, he does. After Larry leaves, Durwood tells Endora that despite what she heard, she is not invited but she thanks him for the gracious invitation.

That night, Samantha assures him that Endora was probably playing around and most likely won't show up, when she does. Durwood agrees to let her stay if she promises no funny business and she gives her witches' honor. The Tates and Mr. Gregson show up and Endora plays it quite coy with Mr. Gregson, who is very impressed with her. During dinner, Endora acts as though she and Durwood are the best of friends which pleases Mr. Gregson, who is all about harmonious familial relationships. Larry tries to act like he is also best buds with his mother-in-law but as he continues his stories about her Louise can tell that he merely insulting her and so Louise kicks Larry and yells at him, only to go upstairs upset. Mr. Gregson tells Larry he obviously doesn't understand his image, yet Durwood does, which is why Mr. Gregson wants to set up Durwood with his own ad agency. In all the excitement Mr. Gregson gets a headache and leaves. Of course, Larry is quite upset with Durwood who he accuses of orchestrating the whole thing and so he and Louise leave.

The next day Durwood, who has been working all night on great ideas for Mr. Gregson, decides that Larry didn't mean anything about firing him and therefore he is going to say that the ideas were all Larry's so that Mr. Gregson will just stay with McMann and Tate. Just then the doorbell rings with a delivery man who is bringing Durwood's office furniture. Durwood decides that being nice to Larry is fruitless and he'll just go on with the plan to open his own agency. Samantha knows that all of this is happening in the heat of the moment and so she casts a spell over the lay-outs to contain Larry's signature.

Durwood goes to show his ideas to Mr. Gregson, who is impressed and he decides after all to go with McMann and Tate when he sees Larry's signature. Over at Larry's office, Larry is quite humbled by the gesture and tells Durwood he can have his job back and possibly in a few years maybe even make partner!

Endora has many funny lines in this episode, my favorite being "No one is as cuddly as Dar-Dar and I are." I also like it when she is telling Samantha why she changed Durwood into a pony, how "I made a few witty remarks…"
In regards to those sparklies on her face, what was that all about?
The client's name in the credits is listed as Mr. Hudson but throughout the episode he is called Mr. Gregson.
I always liked the floating picture. For some reason, I found it really spooky especially after it came back from the fire, which I always thought looked fake but I'm assuming they just filmed down in the studio's boiler room so it must have been real.
The day before, U.S. Secretary of Defense Robert McNamara resigned to become the President of the World Bank. His resignation was brought on by his anger over President Johnson's unwillingness to freeze troop levels, stop bombing North Vietnam and hand over ground fighting in South Vietnam.
Three days prior the Beatles released *Magical Mystery Tour* as a full album including songs such as "All You Need is Love," "Penny Lane," and "Hello, Goodbye."

DECEMBER 7, 1967

It was on this night ABC aired Episode #121: "My, What Big Ears You Have."
Dumbo and Samantha attend an antiGues show (according to the sign) where Samantha falls in love with a bentwood rocking chair, but unfortunately it's already been sold.
Later, the next morning, Endora pops in for her morning annoyance of Dumbo who receives a phone call from an unidentified woman. It turns out it's the sales lady from the antiGues show calling to tell him that the rocker has become available again. Dumbo acts very suspicious in taking the call in another room as he wants the rocker to be a surprise. Endora is sure he is fooling around and listens in on his call, via witchcraft, and comes in on the part of the conversation where Dumbo makes plans to meet the woman and even tells her that Samantha has no idea. This is all very disconcerting to Samantha, though she says she still trusts him.

When he re-enters the room, he makes a snide remark about his ears burning probably because Endora had been speaking about him which sparks an idea in Endora. She puts him in the "deep freeze" and tells Samantha that they'll now see if he's lying or not and proceeds to put a Pinocchio type spell on him, but instead of making his nose grow, his ears will! She reverses time a little and Dumbo re-enters the room where Samantha asks him who was on the phone. He tells her that it was just a secretary from McMann and Tate telling him about a meeting and right then his ears enlarge a little, and with that, he leaves to pick up the rocker leaving Samantha a little unsettled.

On the way out, Dumbo meets up with Mrs. Kravitz who can tell that his ears are bigger, but she just chalks it up to a haircut. He asks her if she wouldn't mind storing the chair at her place until he can give it to Samantha and she gladly accepts, jealous that a husband would do such a great thing for his wife. When she returns home, she complains to Abner, who is incensed as he had bought her a gift, a table saw. Of course, she's not impressed.

At the antiGues show at a hotel, Dumbo makes all the necessary arrangements and as he is about to leave he finds that another nosy neighbor, Hazel Carter, is there. He tries to avoid her but can't and when she sees that he had been conversing with the antiques dealer, she assumes he's cheating and decides to catch him in the act. She asks him who the woman was and he tells her she was simply a McMann and Tate client at which point his ears gain another size, shocking her. Now Dumbo knows something is going on as it seemed everyone was fascinated by his ears all day and when he sees what all the commotion was about, he knows his mother-in-law is up to something!

Hazel immediately runs to Samantha to tell her what she had seen and now Samantha is quite sure her mother may have been right. A little while later, Dumbo bursts into the door raving about his ears and Samantha explains she trusts him, despite her doubts, and asks him about his morning. He lies yet again in order to keep the chair a surprise. By now, Dumbo is rivaling his name sake in ear size.

Larry calls wondering where Dumbo is as they have a meeting with a client. Dumbo tries to feign illness but Larry insists he'll bring the client out. Samantha suggests Dumbo wearing a bee keeper's outfit as it's the only thing big enough to cover his ears and she zaps up a hive. Larry and the client arrive, perplexed at how Dumbo is dressed and even more so that he won't take the suit off, but the client loves the idea's Dumbo has come up with and they leave.

Samantha tells Dumbo that she really would like to know the truth and so he confesses about the chair. Samantha is pleased and feels foolish about not trusting him. Endora pops in sure that she has created enough distrust but when they explain about the chair she still doesn't believe and insists on seeing the chair and so Dumbo says he'll show her by taking her over to the Kravitz's.

While all this was going on, it turns out that the chair had been taken back by the table saw people when Abner decided to return it when he saw how displeased Gladys was. So when Dumbo unveils what he thinks is the chair, Endora is quite pleased that there is no chair, especially since Dumbo promised he would leave for a year if she were right. Abner hears the commotion out in the garage and tells them of the mistake and so Endora, defeated, undoes her spell and returns Dumbo's ears to normal.

I'd only give this one about two stars. I used to like it much more when I was younger but the more I think about it the more it just seems like a goofy episode. I get the feeling that the big ears thing was to poke fun at the fact that Dick York really did have big ears. I hope he was in on the joke. I'm wondering if they had originally written the episode to have his nose grow and then decided it would be funnier if his ears grew, which I do like that idea, I just can't help thinking it was at Dick York's expense.

And what WAS with Endora's hair? It looked worse here than it did in "Allergic to Macedonian Dodos" when it was supposed to look horrible!

I don't like that all of a sudden we've got Hazel, essentially another Mrs. Kravitz. If anything, they should've made Hazel the Kravitzes' daughter, who takes after her mother.

And another thing I don't like is at the end when he finally tells Samantha what is going on, and Endora pops in, she still insists that he's lying even though he tells her that he really did get a rocking chair AND his ears don't grow anymore. Why didn't Samantha just tell her, "Mother, wouldn't his ears be growing still if he was lying?" Instead, it seems that Samantha believes her mother. And then they do a little breaking and entering on the Kravitz property by opening their garage and going in. I would've felt better about it had the garage door just been open.

The part at the end was cute. I remember when I first saw it and saw those ears, like Samantha, I thought Endora had done something and I was so embarrassed by the makeup department as those ears looked so fake. Thank goodness they really were!

This episode seems to be one EVERYONE remembers.

DECEMBER 14, 1967

It was on this night ABC aired Episode #122: "I Get Your Nanny, You Get My Goat."

While getting ready for the Hunters Club Ball (which an important client happens to be chairman of), Durwood wonders who it is that Samantha got to babysit Tabatha. When she tells him that Endora wasn't available, he really wonders and she reveals that they have a new sitter who just happened to have been Samantha's nanny when she was little, which means she's a witch, which in turn means Durwood's feathers are ruffled. Samantha assures him Nanny Elspeth is "just plain folk" when she arrives a la Mary Poppins. Elspeth seems cheerful enough and remembers when Samantha skinned her knees up walking through walls and such, and then when she turns the spinach Tabatha was supposed to be eating into a sundae, Durwood really gets miffed even when he finds out it's Elspeth's special Spinach Sundae designed to trick kids into eating their spinach. He demands to speak to Samantha right then in the kitchen and that's when Endora pops in furious and offended that Samantha would replace her with Elspeth, someone whom she apparently doesn't like. Samantha tells her that she wasn't replacing her; it's just that Endora said she wasn't available. When Durwood makes a snide remark to her, she threatens to zip his lip but Elspeth stops her, noting that it's not very sporting of Endora to use witchcraft on a defenseless mortal. In a huff, Endora blows out of there and Durwood changes his mind about Elspeth, even after she pops up to the nursery with Tabatha.

Samantha and Durwood attend the ball and are having a marvelous time, so marvelous in fact that they decide to make out in the bushes, but Larry interrupts them saying that he was going to introduce Durwood to Roy Chappel, the client who's club was throwing the ball. Turns out Roy is a man's man and Larry knows he won't take too kindly to seeing Durwood be all makey-outy with his wife. When Larry goes back inside to get Roy, Endora pops in with a friend, Lord Clyde Montdrako, Elspeth's former employer, who is not pleased that Durwood has taken away his nanny. When Samantha objects to his wanting Elspeth to return, Lord Montdrako thinks Durwood isn't man enough to speak up for himself and to show that he isn't zaps a rose in his mouth which won't come out, and with that he and Endora disappear. Of course, Larry and Mr. Chappel come out just then and Mr. Chappel isn't at all impressed.

Back at home, Samantha tells Elspeth what went on and wonders why Elspeth didn't tell her that she was already employed. Elspeth tells her that Lord Montdrako was a crotchety old man whom she didn't care to work for anymore and she wouldn't go back to him.

When Durwood goes to the office the next day, Lord Montdrako pops in wondering if Durwood was man enough to send Elspeth back, but when Durwood mentions something about Samantha, Lord Montdrako takes it upon himself again to show Durwood for what a baby he is and zaps him into a Little Lord Fauntleroy outfit just as Larry is bringing Mr. Chappel back to show him a what a tough guy Durwood is. Mr. Chappel decides he cannot work with someone as flighty as Durwood.

After getting back home, Durwood is furious with Elspeth and fires her prompting Lord Montdrako to pop in to congratulate him, but when Elspeth still refuses to go Montdrako says that Durwood has no control over his house, that he's merely a reflection of man, and he makes it so by zapping Durwood into a mirror! And, with that, he pops off. Elspeth is beside herself for putting Durwood into such a situation and after Samantha calms her down finds that possibly the reason Lord Montdrako wants Elspeth back is because he is lonely. Samantha pops off to his castle and decides to make it a tourist attraction so Lord Montdrako will always have guests. He is delighted with the idea and decides he won't need Elspeth for company anymore and agrees to free Durwood of his mirror prison.

Back at home Elspeth has managed to convince Mr. Chappel that he shouldn't refuse to work with Durwood just because of the way he lives his life, but rather, he should listen to the great campaign ideas Durwood has, and thus everyone is happy.

Elspeth was to become a recurring character but for some reason never did, for which I'm grateful. I found her quite annoying. It is interesting that Hermione Baddeley, who played Elspeth, played Ellen the maid in Walt Disney's *Mary Poppins*, which also co-starred Reta Shaw a.k.a Aunt Bertha/Hagatha.

And speaking of Walt Disney, Lord Montdrako has always reminded me of him and I did think he made a good foil for Durwood.

I think the disdain Endora had for Elspeth should've been explained. It doesn't make any sense that Endora would've hired someone to take care of Samantha if she detested her. Maybe Maurice had a yen for Elspeth and he hired her!

I liked Durwood and Samantha being all kissy-kissy…it was cute!

I'd give it a two star rating only on the fact that Elspeth is so annoying! Especially when she is lamenting how Durwood is gone and is being so dramatic about it. I also thought Samantha acted way too excited about

Elspeth showing up, though, in a way, it was precious because it would seem that she must've had great times with Elspeth. What I also liked is when Elspeth was talking about how Samantha struggled with her magic when she was little, Durwood was actually smiling about it, as though he found enjoyment in thinking of his wife as a little witchlet. Normally, I would've thought he would've grimaced and complained through the whole thing. I also liked his face when Elspeth was saying "how nice it is."

When I first saw this episode I didn't have any idea that the tour guide Samantha zapped up was herself until the very end when it dawned on me that it was Elizabeth Montgomery! Now I can see why people never realized Clark Kent was Superman.

Agnes Moorehead guest starred on the short-lived series *Custer* in "Spirit Woman" that night. Robert F. Simon, Durwood's first dad, was a regular on the series and would explain his sudden inability to appear on *Bewitched*.

DECEMBER 21, 1967

It was on this night ABC regaled us with *Bewitched*'s version of *A Christmas Carol* by airing Episode #123: "Humbug Not Spoken Here."

Just before he is leaving for work on Christmas Eve, Samantha has Durwood stand in for the tree they are to put up that night as she wants to put it in a different place than they've always placed it. Finally having enough as he is going to be late, Durwood leaves promising not to buy the first tree he sees as Samantha tells him "last year's was a bit skimpy on one side." Still not knowing where she is going to place the tree, she decides to use a little magic to help her out and begins by replacing the TV with a beautifully decorated Christmas tree. Not impressed by that locale, she zaps it from corner to corner finally settling on where they had it last year (and the year before and the year before) and zaps it away with a satisfied expression of "Merry Christmas!"

At the office, Durwood walks in on his meeting with Larry and Mr. Mortimer of Mortimer Soups. Mr. Mortimer is all about the three Ps: Persistence, Prudence and Punctuality, and as Durwood has violated the last one, he sees no reason to continue the meeting even though Durwood offered up the excuse of holiday traffic. He advises that they will have a meeting at his house that evening at 6 o'clock promptly and he leaves. Durwood tries to get out of it by telling Larry he promised to help Samantha decorate the tree but Larry promises him the meeting will be short.

That night, the meeting seems to go on and on and Durwood has enough saying that he must get home for the Christmas tree decorating. Mr. Mortimer doesn't like that excuse as he doesn't like Christmas but Durwood doesn't care: sugar plums are more important to him than Mortimer Soups, and he leaves.

At home, he and Samantha decorate the tree when someone knocks at the door. Samantha answers it and finds Larry and Mr. Mortimer there. Larry says he felt they should move the meeting over to Durwood's but Durwood is adamant that he is done with business until after Christmas and when Mr. Mortimer threatens to leave McMann and Tate, it still doesn't work and Mr. Mortimer takes himself, and his account, home leaving Larry having a very blue Christmas.

As they get ready for bed that evening, Samantha ponders aloud about how Mr. Mortimer could hate Christmas so bad and is more than surprised at the thought that he may not even believe in Santa Claus! As Durwood drifts off to sleep, Samantha gets an idea of how she can help Mr. Mortimer see the joy of Christmas and she pops off.

Meanwhile, across town, Mr. Mortimer is woken by a cold breeze that blows his French doors open. As he shouts for his butler, Hawkins, to come close the door, the air immediately in front of the door becomes thick and forms into the form of Mrs. Stephens in a green dress with a cape covered in sparklies. She tells him not to think of her as Mrs. Stephens but as the Spirit of Christmas. He says it's all nonsense and gives her five seconds to leave, actually setting his alarm clock. She tells him the truth, that she is actually a witch and as the clock rings she gives it a zap and stops it. He still doesn't believe her and to prove it she zaps up her Christmas broom and tells him that she is going to take him on a long trip to give him his Christmas present and with that they end up in the starry night sky amid the falling snow on their way with Mr. Mortimer yelling the whole way.

The trip ends at the North Pole where Santa greets them at the door to his house where he was loading up his sleigh. Samantha tells Santa about the unbelieving Mr. Mortimer and Santa sees that Samantha would like a "convincing trip." Samantha and Mr. Mortimer help him until Santa sees Mr. Mortimer being rough with one of the presents, a Susie Bruisie doll that becomes black and blue when you hit it. Mr. Mortimer tells Santa he's had enough of all this nonsense and tries to uncover the fraud by pulling off Santa's beard, but, of course, it doesn't come off. After loading the sleigh, Samantha and Mr. Mortimer join Santa for his ride around the world delivering toys. Their last stop happens to be at Hawkins', the butler, house where Mr. Mortimer and Samantha peer through the window at Hawkins playing with his child and wife. Mr. Mortimer doesn't understand how they can be so happy when they are so poor but Samantha asks Mr. Mortimer if he's happy because he's rich. As Mr. Mortimer ponders that, he finds that they've arrived back at his house and Samantha and Santa Claus pop off leaving him out in the cold. Before he can even think about how he'll get into his house, he finds himself back in his bed.

Samantha pops in to her bedroom just as Durwood is waking up and she tells him to get ready in his Santa Claus suit for Tabatha while she makes breakfast.

Later, at the tree, Tabatha opens her presents with her mommy and Durwood as Santa comes bounding down the stairs with more. Of course, Tabatha knows it's her daddy. Larry shows up dressed as Santa but his plans are foiled as everyone knows who he is, except Tabatha who calls him "Daddy." An even bigger surprise shows up when Mr. Mortimer comes calling with a gift of Mortimer Instant Soups and an apology. Samantha invites him to stay and as she is cutting slices of 'yummy' fruitcake they hear a clatter on the roof and so she puts everyone in the "deep freeze." And who should come down the chimney but Santa Claus himself! He's brought the Susie Bruisie for Tabatha and Samantha gives him suntan lotion as a present, as she had mentioned before that he should take a vacation in Florida. She zaps him back up the chimney and unfreezes everyone. Mr. Mortimer notices the new doll Tabatha has and tells her all about it but he wonders how he knew all that as he thought his Christmas ride was merely a dream. Samantha gives him a cup of eggnog to reassure him and the gang enjoy their Christmas day.

I totally love this one and would probably say it's my most favorite of the Christmas episodes. I think the scene at first is brilliant and really magical…I love the sound effect of the tree popping out at the end and just the way Liz waves her arms. I also like that she looks so pleased with herself and says, "Merry Christmas!"

Charles Lane is my favorite of the actors that played clients. He reminds me so much of one of my bosses from when I was in college.

It always bugs me that they are doing all that decorating of the tree on Christmas Eve, though I realize in some countries that is the custom. Especially if Samantha insists on giving the tree "that delicate lacy look" by hanging the tinsel one strand at a time!

Have you ever noticed how the only times we ever see Samantha with a broom are during the Christmas episodes? Apparently this flying suit is the basis for that FAO Schwartz *Bewitched* doll that has the window box with the doors that was released in the 90s. And when you open those doors there are pictures from this episode inside.

I hate that they have a Susie Bruisie doll! It seems like a good way to teach kids about child abuse and HOW to do it. I can't help but think that maybe they were just trying to go for something like the Betsy Wetsy doll and that's all they could think of. I like when Samantha gets stern with Mr. Mortimer when they are packing the sleigh and she says, "Mr. Mortimer!" and then "You behave yourself!"

Tabatha was really cute in this episode especially when Durwood comes down dressed like Santa and she says, "Daddy!"

I've always thought that for the Christmas episodes they should've made a unique cartoon opening where they just add snow falling and snow resting on the roofs of the buildings and then when the cartoon witch is flying through the sky cartoon Santa comes riding by with his reindeer. Then when she stops and pulls off her hat to twitch it into a frying pan instead it turns into a Christmas ornament and she's standing in front of a Christmas tree with candles burning on it. She hangs the bulb, turns into the cat, and jumps into his arms and one of the candles falls on the tree and the whole thing goes up in smoke with "And Agnes Moorehead as Endora"…well, maybe not that last part, but you get the drift.

It was also on this day that Marion Lorne appeared in the big screen movie *The Graduate* which opened up in New York City. Alice Ghostley also appears in this movie in a brief scene with Marion, which seems to be an indirect passing of the torch considering in two seasons Alice would appear as the bumbling witch Esmeralda on *Bewitched*.

DECEMBER 28, 1967

It was on this night ABC aired the last episode of 1967 with Episode #124: "Samantha's Da Vinci Dilemma."

Whilst painting the trim on the outside of the house, Samantha is startled by Aunt Clara's crash landing and a little more surprised that Aunt Clara is wearing a chef's hat. Turns out Aunt Clara had just left the Witches' Annual Cookout where she had entered with her recipe for Pussy Willow Almandine but was disqualified. When Samantha tastes a sample she finds it was really fudge and suggests Aunt Clara reorganize her recipes. After getting her chef's hat fluffed by Samantha, Aunt Clara wonders why Samantha just doesn't wave on a coat or two of paint rather than doing it by hand. Samantha tells her it's more fun this way and leaves to answer the front doorbell. While she is gone, Aunt Clara decides to help her out by zapping in a painter and in true Aunt Clara style, she not only gets one, but by all accounts, gets the best — Leonardo Da Vinci!

Da Vinci is more than astonished at finding himself in the 20th century but is more than intrigued by all the gadgets he finds in Samantha's house. Samantha urges Aunt Clara to remember the spell to send him back before Durwood gets home and blows his stack. Of course, Aunt Clara has trouble remembering so Samantha figures as long as Da Vinci is going to be there awhile he should dress the part and she goes to fetch one of Durwood's suits. Aunt Clara is still surprised at Samantha's desire to do things "the hard way" and attempts to zap up one of Durwood's suits, but only succeeds in switching the clothing of the two men, much to Durwood's embarrassment and surprise considering he was just doing work at McMann and Tate to prepare to meet a new client, Mr. Pritchfield, who walks in with Larry Tate just as the clothes have changed. Mr. Pritchfield is quite amiable and in joking around with Durwood about his clothes decides that maybe this is for his campaign and rightly guesses that Durwood is dressed as Da Vinci and that the plan is to use the Mona Lisa in the campaign. Durwood assures him that last part is not it and excuses himself to go home.

At home, Durwood finds that the reason for the change of clothes was that Da Vinci is in his home all due to Aunt Clara's goofups, who was currently being bored to tears by Da Vinci's listing off of all his inventions. When Samantha and Durwood go to see if she has made any headway in remembering the spell they see that Aunt Clara is asleep and Da Vinci is gone. But when they wake her, they find that he hasn't returned to his own time but had left out the door. Samantha sends Aunt Clara to look for him at the park and she goes to the local art museum where she finds him causing a disturbance by chipping away at a big hunk of rock that apparently is finished modern work of art. When she gets the security guard to clear the crowd, she restores the work of art and pops home with Da Vinci.

Durwood advises that Larry and Mr. Pritchfield are on their way over to talk Durwood into going with the Mona Lisa idea. Samantha keeps Leonardo out of sight when they arrive and Mr. Pritchfield presents a work up of the Mona Lisa painting with a new toothy smile holding a bottle of the toothpaste Mr. Pritchfield sells. Durwood highly objects to defacing the Mona Lisa like that and refuses to have any part of it which in turn makes Mr. Pritchfield refuse his account with McMann and Tate. Just as he and Larry are about to leave, Samantha freezes them and tells Durwood that as they have one of the most creative minds in history in their house they should ask him for an idea on how to sell the toothpaste. He devises a selection of toothpastes of all different colors and tastes that come on a painter's pallet which is aimed at children. They just paint on the different colors and then rinse. Samantha unfreezes Larry and Mr. Pritchfield and Durwood presents the idea which Mr. Pritchfield loves and so the account is saved.

Meanwhile, Aunt Clara has remembered the spell to send Da Vinci back but not before he paints one of his greatest masterpieces, the Mona Clara.

Yeah, one and a half to two stars simply because I find Aunt Clara really funny here…well, just one line, when Leonardo is describing all his inventions and she tells him "Before we leave the Ps, let's discuss painting the house!" And because she is so disgusted with him and his total lack of attentiveness to the house.

One of the bloopers in this episode is when Leonardo is playing with the revolving door which is supposed to have glass panes you see his arm go through to the other side of one of the doors and he quickly retracts it.

Another one is when Da Vinci first pops in, the reddish light that was being cast on the smoke is still seen on his outstretched arm when most of the smoke has cleared.

I always liked the toothpaint idea. I always just thought the palette was just for display purposes and you could just buy each flavor/color separately. And when I was a child I always loved it when Samantha would freeze someone. I do have to admit the actor who played the client was perfect for this role with his huge teeth, but man, he's annoying!

JANUARY 4, 1968

It was on this night ABC aired Episode #125: "Once in a Vial."

Endora pops in from Paris with news for Samantha that she just ran into Rollo, the last warlock Samantha dated before meeting Durwood. Samantha's not the least bit interested as she says she enjoys her life with her mortal husband and she goes on with her cleaning. Endora decides that maybe if she were to bring Rollo to 1164, Samantha might see the error in her mortal loving ways.

Endora invites Samantha to lunch and just as they sit down, Rollo pops in, amorous as ever. Samantha will have none of it, so she pops home.

Endora follows her and guilts her into coming back to lunch by saying that Samantha must be way insecure about herself to not even have a simple lunch with Rollo. When they return to the restaurant, they find that Rollo is gone, but who should show up but Durwood and Mr. Callahan, a boisterous and rude perfume client. McMann and Tate is just about to start a campaign selling their new perfume, Autumn Flame, that Mr. Callahan says is for "the older babes," like Endora, who says she's not at all interested. Mr. Callahan will not take "no" for an answer and invites them all to dinner at his place that night where Endora can give him her final answer. Samantha tells him they can't as it will be impossible to find a sitter in such a short time so Mr. Callahan suggests they have dinner at her place. He also asks that the art director, Bill Walters, show up. Endora decides this will be a great time to get Rollo back in contact with Samantha and says she is going to invite him, too.

Endora finds Rollo lunching with another woman and finds that he isn't interested in getting Samantha back as he saw how unresponsive she was. Endora says that he had very little time to get back into Samantha's good graces and that he should think of something else besides his fatal charm and good looks to get her back. Of course, she is alluding to the love potion he happens to carry around with him and so he agrees.

That night, Mr. Callahan really works "Dora's" nerves over, and there is thick tension not only between Rollo and Durwood, but Mr. Walters and his wife. When Rollo sees that Samantha is still not interested in him, he decides to spike her martini with the love potion. Before she drinks it, she sets it down and Endora reaches for it thinking it's hers. Rollo tries to stop her but it's too late: she immediately falls head over heels in love with Mr. Callahan and coos and fawns over him to his surprise. Rollo tells Samantha what has happened and Samantha takes Durwood into the kitchen to explain. Meanwhile, Mr. Walters sees the effect the martini had on Endora and so he takes a sip and begins the same show of indulgent affection with his surprised wife, who tries to get away from him. When Mr. Walters comes after her, Samantha tells him it was quite rude to leave Endora and Mr. Callahan alone in the living room, but he tells her they left! Rollo also tells Samantha that the potion lasts one hour.

Turns out Endora has taken Mr. Callahan to a justice of the peace to tie the knot! The Justice tells them they need two witnesses and that his wife can fill in for one. Endora decides to zap up Rollo for the other witness. Knowing where Endora and Mr. Callahan are, Rollo pops home really quick to tell Samantha, who is in the midst of trying to help Durwood keep Mr. Walters from "attacking" his wife. Before she leaves with Rollo, she puts Durwood and the Walters in the 'deep freeze.'

At the Justice of the Peace, Samantha tries to convince Endora to not marry, but the potion is much too powerful and so the ceremony commences. Samantha twitches the Justice's glasses off but Endora reminds him that he must have it memorized after performing it so many times. He begins again but Samantha twitches him to forget. Endora, knowing that Samantha is impeding the wedding, zaps up a magnifying glass, but before they can commence again, she takes Samantha aside and reprimands her for being naughty at "her mama's wedding" and zaps her home.

With just a couple minutes left before the potion wears off, Samantha tries to pop back but finds that Endora has prevented that so she zaps in Mr. Callahan just as he is saying "I do." Shortly thereafter Rollo, Endora, and the Justice and his wife pop in courtesy of Endora. All the mortals are confused and Endora more so when the potion wears off. Samantha zaps Mr. Callahan back to his hotel and the Justice and his wife (with the help of Rollo) back to their place. Rollo takes Endora aside to explain what happened while Samantha reanimates Durwood and the Walters. Of course, Mr. Walters is back to his former ways and they leave in the normal "happy" state.

This episode is fairly new to me as I didn't see it until just a couple years ago and it's one of my favorites! Agnes Moorehead is so awesome in it! I'm glad they did this script because it gave her a chance to expand on the character. It's really funny seeing her fawn all over Mr. Callahan.

Up until the DVD I had no idea who Mr. and Mrs. Walters were because Bo requesting the art director (Mr. Walters) be there for dinner is always cut out. I think it would've been way more fun to have Larry and Louise there.

The sound effect used for the love spell is Jeannie's sister's blink.

I also liked all the popping in and out in this episode. It seems like that's what's going on the whole episode.

My favorite line is from Dumbo when he walks in and says, "Good morning! Good morning! Good-bye!"

On New Years' Day ABC began airing *Bewitched* during the daytime hours so on Thursdays you would've been able to see *Bewitched* twice in a day!

The next day Paul Lynde was a guest on *The Mike Douglas Show*.

JANUARY 11, 1968

It was on this night ABC aired Episode #126: "Snob in the Grass."

Samantha hasn't had dinner with Durwood for three nights in a row as he's been so busy working on the Webley Food account, which looks like McMann and Tate is going to lose. Durwood decides that he's had enough nights without his wife and calls her to tell her he'll be joining her for dinner as he's pretty much given up on Webley. Samantha is thrilled though Endora believes Durwood will find another excuse not to come home.

While Samantha is off buying a beautiful pork loin for dinner, Larry tells Durwood that since he doesn't really have to worry about Webley, he has found a different, much bigger, account for Durwood to sink his teeth into and that is the J.P. Sommers account. This doesn't set too well with Durwood as it turns out that Mr. Sommers' daughter happens to be the girl, Sheila, that Durwood was dating when he met and married Samantha. Larry knows this and thinks it perfect that Durwood and Sheila have a past because now there is an instant "in" with Mr. Sommers. And just to make sure, Larry sets up a dinner date with Mr. Sommers, Sheila, Durwood and himself for that night and upon threat of losing his job, makes Durwood call Samantha to cancel his dinner plans with her. Endora now "knows" she is right about his excuses but Samantha just chalks it up to more work.

Once Larry and Durwood arrive at the restaurant, they find that Sheila is alone and Larry makes himself scarce in the hopes that Durwood will play up to Sheila's advances. But he sticks to his guns and reminds her that he is married only to have the waitress slop his dinner on him. Before he can get mad about it, he sees that the waitress is actually his mother-in-law spying on him.

The next day at breakfast, Samantha is furious to know that dinner with her was cancelled for dinner with Sheila and without saying a word, makes Durwood quite aware of her unhappiness. Durwood tries to assure her that it was all Larry's idea and to make up for it, he is going to decline Sheila's invitation to a dinner party at her place. Samantha believes that Sheila would want Durwood to decline knowing that his wife made him do that, and Samantha won't have Sheila have the upper hand like that and so she tells him they will go. Durwood tells her it is a casual affair but Samantha remembers back to the last time Sheila invited them to a "casual affair," which turned out to be a formal dining disaster. Samantha decides that Sheila is just going to pull the same stunt again and so she puts on her fanciest dress and makes Durwood dress in a tux.

When they arrive at Sheila's, they find that it really was a casual dinner party and now they look ridiculously overdressed, which is just what Sheila wanted. The evening pretty much goes like the first time with Sheila making insinuating remarks about how Samantha is an outcast amongst their friends. Finally, Samantha has had enough and causes a fly to "bug" Sheila, later turning it into a bee. When the butler tries to swat it away, Samantha makes him grab onto Sheila's wig revealing her really blonde hair. Just when Sheila thinks things can't get worse, Samantha muddies up Sheila's dog who jumps on Sheila and when he goes to run off Samantha magically ties a loose thread from Sheila's sweater to the dog's collar causing the sweater to unravel before everyone's eyes and totally cause Sheila the utmost of embarrassments.

The next day, Durwood decides that maybe he should try again with Webley Foods as now they've obviously lost the Sommers account, but when he goes to find the Webley Foods layouts, they end up missing! Larry bursts in with news that he's pleased that Durwood was so forward thinking that he submitted the Webley layouts anyway, which Webley loved! Of course, Samantha really submitted them, but who has to know?

I LOVE this episode and it certainly is good that Sheila is back AND with the same actress! She really should've been back more often at least with Dick Sargent's Durwood just to help us really understand that he is supposed to be Durwood. It would've been fun to see Dick Sargent remake the first episode but, of course, nothing would compare with the first one.

I LOVE it when Endora appears as the waitress. When I first watched this episode it was hysterical seeing that the "clumsy" waitress was Endora. And I love the look on her face.

I also like that flashback. I did notice that they replaced the background music with the Fourth Season's music instead of what was originally on there. I also noticed that there were dresses in Samantha's closet that she has worn before. I like that they thought to really use her dresses, it makes the show more real.

It is also quite apparent with the scenes filmed in the kitchen that they were done at different times as both Samantha's and Endora's hair changes not to mention that where the washer and dryer are supposed to be is at first shown to be a plain flat wall! Also, the shadows behind Samantha slowly creep up more and more each time the camera comes back to her.

I did think it was cheesy when Sheila is spinning around when her sweater is unraveling. It was really cartoon like and more suited for *I Dream of Jeannie*.

Three days earlier, Dick Sargent guested on *The Rat Patrol* in the episode entitled "The Boomerang Raid."

The next day Agnes Moorehead was a guest on *The Mike Douglas Show*.

On January 10, Howard Smith passed away. He played C.L. Morton in Season Three's "The Corn is as High as a Guernsey's Eye."

JANUARY 18, 1968

On this night, it was sort of a bummer when we found that ABC was rerunning Episode #111: "Double, Double, Toil and Trouble"…sort of a bummer because that episode is really cool, but at the same time, not a new episode.

Three days later, one of the most publicized and controversial battles of the Vietnam War begins, the Battle of Khe Sahn.

JANUARY 25, 1968

It was on this night *Bewitched* returned with an all-new episode, #127: "If They Never Met", on ABC, and oh boy, was it good!

It seems that Durwood has finally had it with his mother-in-law after she buries him under a mountain of shaving cream, squirted all the toothpaste out of the tube at him, and placed a chicken in the sleeve of his coat. Of course, he deserved all this after he acted quite churlishly towards her for gifting Tabatha with a unicorn. As he and his chicken leave, he remarks how he can't take anymore of Endora's shenanigans only to find that his door has doubled itself, courtesy of her. Samantha pleads for her mother to try and make nice with Durwood but Endora says he was acting like a child and to emphasize her point zaps his car into a small child's car as the encore to all her tricks. Luckily for her (according to Durwood) he's late for work so he can't do anything about it.

Samantha tries to get her mother to see that all her tricks are unworthy of her but Endora doesn't see it that way, and in fact, tells her that the grand finale to all her tricks is the defanged cobra she left in his attaché case. And with that she pops off.

A little while later, Durwood comes exploding through the front door hollering for Samantha. Turns out that he just lost one of the biggest accounts — Prune Valley Retirement Village — that McMann and Tate has had in years due to the cobra that sprang from his attaché case in front of the client and all his associates causing everyone to faint, including Durwood. And after recovering from the shock, Larry fired Durwood. Samantha tells him that Endora promised to be good but he brings up the "fact" that there is a huge credibility gap when it comes to Endora's promises. Of course, he tells her this in his usual bull horn

Samantha and Endora zap themselves up to Durwood's office.

manner prompting Samantha to remind him that he's shouting at her but he finds no problem with it seeing as Endora is her mother and they hang together. As their fight escalates, Samantha throws out, "Maybe you'd be happier had you never met me" to which Durwood responds, "You said it, I didn't!" Almost immediately, he vanishes! Endora decided to give him his wish, even if Samantha was the one who had really said it, and has placed him exactly where he would've been had he never met Samantha. This doesn't sit well with Samantha at all and she pleads with her mother to bring him back as she says he loves her. Endora reminds Samantha of all that he has been through being married into a witch family and suggests that maybe Samantha take a peek at what his life would be like. Samantha agrees and pops into her flying suit to follow her mother through the winds of time to the now that would've been had Durwood never met Samantha.

In the alternate present, they end up outside McMann and Tate just as Durwood pulls up in a flashy Corvette which he has valet parking for. He mentions to the valet to bring it back around three so he can drive out to his boat, so obviously he's much richer without knowing Samantha. She thinks it's all to hide his unhappiness and they pop up to his office, which is much bigger and decorated with pictures from all his world travels and golf trophies. Just then, Larry walks in and congratulates him on signing up a new client. He then tells him that he was talking to McMann about making Durwood a partner soon. Just as it looks like it couldn't get any better, or worse depending on your point of view, Durwood's ex-girlfriend Sheila Sommers walks in and plants a huge kiss on him. Before Samantha can zap her into the cosmos, Endora reminds her that she isn't married to Durwood in this alternate reality and so Samantha backs off and listens to Durwood and Sheila's conversation. Apparently they are to be married in ten days but both seem to want to have it happen sooner. Samantha finds that Sheila's daddy is going to pay a ton of money for their wedding not to mention a really big honeymoon, which kind of irks Samantha as she only got to go to Atlantic City on hers. Sheila leaves requesting that Durwood not be late to a party that evening. Endora believes that seeing all this has proven that Durwood is happier without Samantha, but Samantha won't give up and says that she is going to go to the party that night.

Endora and Samantha pop in on the party which is being given by Sheila's daddy where he can gloat about how much he's spending on it. Durwood goes out to the patio for a smoke and Samantha and her mother follow him. Samantha wonders what he's thinking about and is surprised when he leaves the party. She follows him to a bar where he meets up with his old buddy Dave. Durwood expresses concern that maybe he's not in love with Sheila but also that he may not know what love is. Of course, Durwood might as well be talking to the wall as Dave still doesn't make a good listener but yet can dish out relationship advice. Durwood mentions to Al the bartender that maybe he's looking for magic and with that he decides to go back to the party. Samantha decides she has one last chance and bumps into him on his way out. He apologizes and buys her a drink and then tells her he must leave. And so, Samantha sees that her mother was right after all: Durwood must be happier without her if he didn't even stay, except that he comes back, apologizing for leaving and tells her that it may be the last time he can buy a drink for a beautiful girl before he gets married. They begin chatting and apparently Durwood sees that he really doesn't want to marry Sheila. He begs Samantha to stay at the bar while he goes back to Sheila's party to break off the marriage. Samantha is thrilled to know that Durwood really does love her and can't live without their marriage. In front of a very surprised Al, she pops back home.

Endora tells her she heard the whole thing, as sickening as it was, and she pops out and zaps Durwood back in where he picks up with the argument they were having but he ends it by saying that all though there were times that he wished he never met her there are more times where he realizes he couldn't live without her.

Later on, while looking through the help wanted ads, Larry shows up pleased as punch at Durwood's "instincts" by bringing in the cobra. Apparently, Leroy Wendle, the owner of Prune Valley, was indicted on a phony real estate scheme and so Durwood gets his job back.

Everything about this episode is PERFECTION! This is one of my top favorite episodes because of the fact that we get to see what would've happened had they never met.

I also like that it harkens back to previous episodes, like the pilot, but also Endora mentions when Durwood was changed into a monkey ("Alias Darrin Stephens") and a penguin ("George the Warlock") and a warthog (okay, this is where he wasn't actually changed into something but I LOVE when Endora says, "It's just that I thought about it so often").

I do find it weird that Sheila and Durwood are to be married FOUR years after the time when Durwood and Samantha would've been married. I think they should've just showed that Durwood did in fact marry Sheila but he had been miserable ever since because the magic/Samantha was missing.

I really like Samantha's flying suit and I did like the flying scenes.

I like that Dave was brought back and essentially didn't listen to Durwood like usual. The background music from "A is for Aardvark" when Durwood gives the watch to Samantha is used for the background music in this. I think it's the only time that they do use that music, which is good because it makes it more poignant.

I did notice that when Durwood goes to leave at the first, he opens the closet door while talking to Sam, the camera then cuts to her and then back to him and he opens the closet again as though he hadn't opened it in the first place.

I also think another reason why I regard this episode so highly is that it is the literal pinnacle of the series, meaning it is the halfway point being #127 and all so in that regard, it was like a very special episode at a perfect time. In another regard, it also means the gradual descent of the show into hum-drum-ness, even in the remaining episodes of this season, many of which are Durwood-less.

Clips from this episode were used in Fourth Season promos, specifically when Samantha says, "Maybe you'd be happier if you'd never met me, is that what you're trying to say?"

I also thought that Agnes Moorehead sounded like she was talking with a stuffed nose at first -it was weird — but all in all, I LOVE this episode!

Three days earlier NBC socked it to us by premiering *Rowan and Martin's Laugh-In*.

FEBRUARY 1, 1968

It was on this night ABC aired the groovtacular Episode #128: "Hippie, Hippie, Hooray."

While setting out Durwood's morning paper, Samantha notices her cousin Serena's face gracing the front page as part of an article about a riot at a love-in! Before Durwood can see who it is, Samantha twitches it away and waits for Durwood to leave before she twitches in her cousin. Serena looks quite different than the last time she showed up as she now has long blonde hair and apparently has embraced guitar playing. She is also not too pleased about being sprung from jail as she was having a perfectly groovy time leading her cell-mates in a love chant. Samantha tells her she'll have enough time to do that later once she figures out how to keep Durwood from finding out about Serena's new hippie ways, which Serena said she couldn't care less if he knew. Just then, Tabatha walks in and Serena tells her she'll play songs for her.

Across town, Larry Tate notices the picture in the paper and also the fact that the woman pictured looks very much like Samantha, so much so that he really believes it is her, especially when Louise admits to not having seen Samantha in a month. She makes him promise not to say anything to Durwood, and he doesn't, though he does invite himself and his wife to Durwood's place that night for a game of bridge so that he can see if Samantha is just her normal self.

When Durwood tells Samantha of Larry's request, Samantha is hesitant to have them come over, yet she won't tell Durwood. No matter, as he soon finds out when he hears the lucid tones of Serena's "lullaby" to Tabatha entitled "Rock-a-Bye Baby." When she has finished her jam session, he hollers for her to appear and demands to know what makes her think she could show up there when he's made it plain in the past that she wasn't welcomed there. She reveals that Samantha sprung her from jail and the pieces of the missing puzzle to that morning's paper and to Larry's strange request become clear. After dissing on Serena more, she warns him not to mess with her, but when he goes a step further, she pops out but only to the roof as she has plans to make his life a wreck.

The Tates arrive for the bridge game and as they are setting up Durwood suggests they watch the TV for their new Springer Pet Food commercial only for an interruption from the news about the disappearance of a hippie high priestess from the jail cell which is accompanied by video of Serena waving from the cop car. This only further cements in Larry's mind that it had to be Samantha as Durwood is acting so weird though Samantha is with them now looking as normal as can be.

The next day, Larry preps Durwood for his meeting with new client Mr. Giddings, a conservative man who is very old school. Larry tells Mr. Giddings that Durwood's wife bakes her own bread in their stone hearth and that Durwood was raised on a farm, which Durwood reluctantly agrees with. Just then the secretary announces that Mrs. Stephens is there, and as Durwood knows that he wasn't expecting Samantha to show up, he tells the secretary to tell Samantha he'll have to see her later. Mr. Giddings thinks that's quite rude and insists Samantha join them. Of course, who should walk in but Serena decked out in totally mod clothes with a skirt as high as…well, let's just say it's high. She flirts with all the men in the room, who (but for Durwood) believe she is Samantha, and insists that they join her at a beanery where they can listen to music. After giving Mr. Giddings a little taste of what it's like in her world, he leaves with Larry, quite flustered. Durwood goes to wring her neck but she tells him that she warned him and with that she pops out. Larry returns very shocked and upset because Mr. Giddings is upset but he is even more worried about the sudden change in Samantha. Durwood tries to convince him but Larry won't have any of it and Durwood tells him that he will prove that Samantha and Serena are two different people by having Larry and Louise over for dinner.

When he gets home, he finds that Samantha still can't find Serena but she tells him she may have a temporary fix to the situation and that is to change herself into Serena. The only problem with that is she cannot be both Serena and Samantha at the same time. Larry and Louise show up and Samantha, as Serena, puts on a great show including playing a gravy, er, groovy song called the "Iff'n Song." As the time to sit to dinner set for five arrives, Durwood yells out an apology to the cosmos. Meanwhile, Larry tells Louise that it's funny that Samantha and her cousin still haven't been seen in the same room all night and that when they do go to sit for dinner one of the women is going to come down with a fearful headache. And his premonition is right as Samantha and Durwood tell the Tates that Serena has come down with a headache but just then they hear a yawning from the staircase and Serena stating, "Serena's headache is all gone. I feel simply marvelous." And so the Tates see that Samantha is still herself and Serena really is Serena. Durwood is pleased and Serena announces to the happy gathering, "Love power conquers all."

This has always been a favorite because it's so funny plus it's cool to have Serena back. Too bad she won't be back until next season. It's also cooler now knowing that it was selected by Elizabeth Montgomery's family to play at the reception for her star ceremony in 2008. Anyway, my only gripe with the episode is the pacing seems weird like everyone (but Serena) is hesitant with what they want to say.

I wonder what happened to the guitar? I can't imagine they would've got rid of it or even painted it over. Speaking of guitars, Liz and Bill Asher's oldest son Billy would grow up to become a builder of guitars and owns his own shop called Asher Guitars.

Another minor gripe is the fact that Louise actually met Serena and saw her and Samantha together at the end of "That Was No Chick, That was My Wife" but it doesn't really seem like she brings it up, but then they are going to watch the Springer Pet Food commercial which was the account from that episode! Another episode mentioned is "Business, Italian Style" when Larry is telling Durwood that he needs him to act for the employer and he says, "Please don't tell me it's Italian, I've already done that." I like it when they refer back to episodes.

This is the second time that we see one of the witches pop on the roof to do a scene and did you notice it was snowy? The first was Aunt Clara and Samantha in "Allergic to Macedonian Dodos."

Here are some of my favorite lines:

> SERENA *(to Mr. Giddings):* *"Compliments will get you everywhere, you old charmer!"* I also like it when she is introduced to him and she says, "Giddings Tractors and His Psychedelic Six! Man, I play your records all the time!"
> SERENA *(to Durwood):* *"Cousin-in-law, when you use words like 'forbid' to me, smile!"*
> SAMANTHA/SERENA: *"Well, I guess I'll go put on a new face... pardon, Cotton Top."*

It's even funnier when you realize that it's actually Samantha saying it rather than Serena.

Elizabeth Montgomery appeared on the cover of *TV Guide* as Serena this week with an article by William Dozier about the beginnings of *Bewitched* and how it was just sold into syndication for $9,000,000, which I'm sure was a huge amount back then!

FEBRUARY 8, 1967

It was on this night ABC aired Episode #129: "A Prince of a Guy."

Tabatha wants to know what happens in *Sleeping Beauty* that her mother was reading her after the last line "...and they lived happily ever after." Samantha tells her she doesn't know and leaves her to go prepare for a dinner party involving the Tates and Durwood's cousin Helen and her boyfriend. Tabatha levitates the book to herself in the crib and twitches the Prince of the story into reality to ask him.

Meanwhile, Endora has popped in as she heard that Durwood is out of town and insists that Samantha and Tabatha join her on the Riveria but Samantha declines as she is having company over and suggests that Endora stay as well. The Tates arrive and as they all visit, Endora goes to check on Tabatha only to come back requesting Samantha come upstairs. As she goes, the doorbell rings and Larry answers it revealing cousin Helen and her boyfriend Ralph, whom Helen seems very enamored of.

Upstairs, Samantha discovers the Prince and tries to get Tabatha to get rid of him, but before she can, Helen wants to see Tabatha. Samantha thinks she can hide the Prince in the closet but Endora reminds her that the Prince cannot be kept within mere walls as he is a product of wishcraft and, therefore, has no substance, so Samantha zaps him into a suit just as Helen is entering. She becomes quite enchanted by the Prince totally forgetting not only Tabatha, but her boyfriend. They all go down stairs and Samantha introduces the Prince as her cousin Charlie. Louise is smitten by him too and she suggests they put on music to dance to but Helen takes the Prince out on the patio, and with that, Ralph leaves.

The next day, Larry returns with a brilliant idea, and that is to use Charlie as the spokesman for Abigail Adams Cosmetics. Samantha tries to dissuade him, but then Helen shows up, and as she goes looking for Charlie, Samantha follows her. When she can't find him, Endora says that Larry and Charlie left for the television studio and she reminds Samantha that this will be disastrous as Charlie cannot be photographed. Samantha flies down to the studio only to find she's too late…everyone has seen, or rather not seen, Charlie in the commercial, and they figure it's a technical glitch.

Back at home, as Helen waits, Ralph shows up to tell her she's the rudest girl he's ever met and it was a good thing he found out now as he was going to propose to her. That sparks Helen's interest again and they go to the patio to "discuss."

Samantha and Charlie come back and Endora tells Samantha that she's figured out why Tabatha can't get Charlie back in the book and that's because Charlie doesn't want to go. Samantha knows what will entice him as she realizes that at the point he was zapped out he hadn't seen Sleeping Beauty yet, so she zaps her in. Charlie is immediately smitten and agrees to go back after kissing Sleeping Beauty. Samantha zaps him back in his own clothes and Tabatha puts him back in the book while Samantha zaps Sleeping Beauty back.

Samantha goes to tell Helen about Charlie leaving but finds that Helen couldn't care less, she's got Ralph now.

This is the second, and last, time that we see one of Durwood's relatives in the series (other than his parents). The first was Uncle Albert from the Second Season's "A Bum Raps."

This is also the first non-Durwood episode of the Fourth Season but the third one so far that Dick York missed.

I don't care for this episode really. From this season it ranks as number two for being the worst in my book (no pun intended) (number one was "Birdies, Bogeys, and Baxter"). It just seems off to me and I really don't like Helen. I do like Samantha's black dress a lot, especially with her in it! She's really sexy!

At random times I think of Tabatha saying, "And THEN what happened?" with just her inflection. I think it's cute and it's a shame that she never got her question answered.

The scene where she floats the book over is used in the opening credits of *Tabitha*, our only 'real' indication that Lisa Hartman's character is the same one we saw on *Bewitched*.

Here's one of my favorite lines:

> ENDORA *(to the Prince):* "*Gads, you're gorgeous!*"

It was also on this day that a civil rights protest was convened at a white-only bowling alley in Orangeburg, NC. It was broken up by highway patrolmen and ended in the death of three college students.

FEBRUARY 15, 1968

It was on this night ABC aired Episode #130: "McTavish."

Aunt Clara arrives, via the refrigerator, from England (she had taken the P-P-Polar R-R-Route) to visit with Samantha. She tells her that she had been visiting Ocky, her boyfriend, who recently purchased a castle and opened it up as a hotel. The only problem is that there is a ghost named McTavish who is terrorizing the guests and won't leave. Aunt Clara felt that Samantha, being Queen of the Witches, might use the prestige of the crown to talk McTavish into leaving. Samantha declines the invitation as Durwood wouldn't take too kindly to her flying to England to deal with ghosts. Aunt Clara finagles her into doing it by confusing Samantha's offer to help her pop out with helping her get rid of the ghost. Samantha decides to help as Durwood is working late anyhow and getting rid of the ghost shouldn't take too long. She leaves Aunt Clara to babysit and pops off to Ocky's castle.

As luck would have it, Durwood's parents just so happen to be vacationing in Europe and have just arrived at Ocky's castle as well. Phyllis is unnerved by the ruckus the ghost is causing when Samantha tries to talk to him and when Phyllis goes out in the hall to check on things she sees Samantha! She tries to get Frank to see too, but by then Samantha has gone off to another part of the castle in search of McTavish.

Samantha finally corners McTavish in the library and he appears and tries to scare her by waving his sword at her and detaching his head from his body, but this doesn't faze Samantha in the least. Samantha tells him she understands why he is so cranky because the castle is cold and damp.

She tells him he could find much better places to haunt in Italy or France or even America where they have central heating and air conditioning. Just then Phyllis walks in on them and Samantha immediately pops out. McTavish, incensed that Phyllis didn't knock, disappears as well leaving her to faint into her husband's arms.

Meanwhile, back in the United States, Durwood has decided to go home early from working late but finds that only Aunt Clara is at home being confusing as ever talking about England and ghosts and Samantha going to get rid of the ghosts. Of course, he isn't pleased at all and after he sends Aunt Clara to go get her he drowns his sorrow in a drink or three. When he's nice and drunk, Samantha pops home surprised to see him there and she tries to explain but he is too busy feeling sorry for himself. She diverts him from his rant by remarking about the flowers he had brought home for her and they begin to kiss. Everything is great until Samantha opens her eyes to see that McTavish has materialized on their hearth! He decided to take her up on her offer to haunt an American home and has chosen hers and he will take no offer to leave.

The next day, Durwood leaves for work with the request that Samantha get rid of McTavish by the time he comes home. Easier said than done, especially when his parents call from the local airport as they have flown home so that Phyllis can prove that Samantha isn't there. When Durwood calls to tell Samantha this, she hears a rattling from the fridge and finds that it is Ocky, who has just arrived. He tells Samantha that he needs to get McTavish back as it turns out the guests really liked the castle being haunted. Samantha tells McTavish this but he doesn't care, he doesn't want to go back to the castle unless it has the moat removed and central heating and air conditioning installed. Ocky promises to do all this just as the doorbell rings. Samantha twitches the two of them back to England and answers the door to find her in-laws there. Phyllis sees that Samantha is at home and Samantha tells her that she was just spooked by the ghosts at the castle and was seeing things. Just then Aunt Clara arrives with a thank you package for Samantha, a portrait of McTavish from McTavish, which causes Phyllis to shriek and faint.

This episode was directed by Paul Davis, Alice Pearce's widower. It was his second, the first being last season's "It's Wishcraft."

It seems like forever since we've seen Aunt Clara and it was neat to throw a ghost into the mix. I always liked it when he detached his head from his body and he said, "Aren't you terrified by me horrible visage?"

I really don't enjoy Roy Roberts as Frank. It seems like he's acting too much rather than just BEING Frank.

This is the last appearance of Ocky. He first appeared last season in "The Short Happy Circuit of Aunt Clara" but I suppose that would happen considering this season is Aunt Clara's last.

Something I did find irritating is at the first when Samantha asks Aunt Clara why she just didn't come in through the door and Clara replies, "That would be like giving up the ghost." Instead of Samantha saying, "What do you mean by that" she says, "Ghost, huh?" Like she already knew Aunt Clara was going to be mentioning ghosts.

I also liked the entrance through the fridge and I think it's hysterical when Aunt Clara tells Durwood that Samantha is over in England and he responds, "ENGLAND?!" Aunt Clara: "Why yes, how did you know?"

I also like Aunt Clara's expression at the end after Phyllis screams at McTavish's portrait and she says, "Why I found him rather handsome." P.S. I wonder what happened to that painting. Even though it wasn't that great, I'd still want it.

FEBRUARY 22, 1968

Tonight *Bewitched* fans were let down when we discovered that ABC was airing a repeat of #110: "Business, Italian Style." This was the second time this year that a repeat has been shown. I believe this has to do something with Dick York's repeated absences. If you look at the original filming schedules, "Once in a Vial" completed filming on 11/9/67 and then there was a huge break in filming. The next episode to be completed was "Tabatha's Cranky Spell" on 12/4/67 and then "A Prince of a Guy" on 12/11/67, both non-Durwood episodes. There was another big break, partly due to the holidays, and then the next episode to be completed was yet another non-Durwood episode "Playmates" on 1/18/68. Dick York returned for the filming of "To Twitch or Not to Twitch" which finished on 2/5/68 but interestingly enough the next episode to be completed on the very next day was "A Majority of Two." I have the feeling that "A Majority of Two" originally did have Durwood in it but when Dick York couldn't make it in to work, it was shelved and all his lines were given to Larry. Of course, as episodes were filmed much earlier than actually aired ABC could shuffle them around so his absence wouldn't be that noticeable.

Three days previously, the children's program *Mr. Roger's Neighborhood* premiered on NET (which later became PBS).

FEBRUARY 29, 1968

Tonight, *Bewitched* returned with an all new episode on ABC with Episode #131: "How Green Was My Grass."

Just as Samantha is beginning to cook pancakes for breakfast, she is wanted on the phone, Tabatha is making a mess with her oatmeal, the gas man comes to the kitchen door, and the doorbell rings at the front of the house, all at the same time. A young man, who looks suspiciously like Merle (the young warlock Samantha babysat in Season Two's "A Strange Little Visitor"), is at the front door offering to mow the lawn and when Samantha consults with Durwood, he tells the young man that the lawn needs to be receded first. The young man tells him he can do it if he is only told how only for Durwood to respond that if he knew how he'd do it himself. Just as the young man tells him that he'll learn how, he also remarks how he smells something burning. Durwood tells him to come back later. Samantha realizes that she's forgotten about the pancakes, and just as Durwood goes running into the kitchen to do something about it, she twitches the pancakes back to their pre-burned state and flips them. Durwood is furious about this obvious use of witchcraft and accuses Samantha of using magic to get out of everything. As he leaves for work, he slams the door causing the nine in their house address (yes, I know, "A nine," you say? "There are only two ones, a six, and a four." Apparently writer Ed Jurist had missed all the other references to the address) to flip over becoming a six.

Shortly after Durwood storms out, Samantha takes Tabatha to the doctor and as they pull away, a van marked "Artificial Grass" pulls up and two men get out and approach the door. They remark about how the house owners said they would be home and they check their work order which said the house number was 162 and see that number on the house. They decide the owners will be home by the time they are finished and so they install the artificial grass.

Samantha is in such a rush to get home with Tabatha (apparently Tabatha didn't "go" at the doctor's office when she was told to) that she doesn't notice the new fake lawn. When Durwood arrives home, the paper boy, Tommy the orphan (from Season One's "A Vision of Sugar Plums"), shows up at the same time remarking on how great the new lawn looks. Durwood is even more furious now because he believes Samantha has done this to spite him. She doesn't understand what is going on and tells him she had nothing to do with it, but he won't believe her. He finally talks her into getting rid of it just before they go to bed and he tells her he forgives her but she is mad that he is forgiving her of something she didn't do and zaps him to the couch to sleep the night.

The next morning, the Artificial Grass men arrive realizing the mistake that has been made, but are flabbergasted to find the fake lawn gone. Durwood realizes that Samantha really wasn't at fault and tells the men if they come back later he'll have the fake lawn for them. He apologizes to Samantha who is still mad and won't bring back the lawn until Durwood mentions that she'll have to cut back on the household expenses to pay for the missing lawn. She agrees to bring it back but when she tries to, nothing happens. As they wonder what is preventing her from doing so, a flaming arrow lands at their feet with a note attached from Endora, who accepts responsibility for stopping Samantha's spell only because Durwood had been saying mean things about her (Endora).

A little while later, Mr. MacLane, the real resident of 162, shows up wondering where his lawn is as the Artificial Grass men told him of the mix up. Durwood tries to explain but Mr. MacLane thinks Durwood is trying to scam him and goes to punch him but Samantha magically blocks the punch. Mr. MacLane leaves and Durwood says that if Samantha can't get the fake lawn back at their house she should try zapping in one at Mr. MacLane's house. At first, she only changes the real grass to a 'beautiful' fake grass color but then she rewords her spell and the real fake grass arrives and everyone is happy.

I've always really liked this episode because it harkens back to the First Season where the story lines seemed to focus more on Samantha and Durwood and their neighbors rather than a new client. This is also one of the only episodes where we only have Elizabeth Montgomery, Dick York, and little Erin Murphy and none of the other regulars like Agnes Moorehead, Sandra Gould, or David White.

That whole address issue is REALLY irritating and Ed Jurist should've been properly smacked for such an error! 1164 would've worked just as well.

I love the spells Samantha uses in this one. They're really witchy!

I know I've never seen that porkchop scene before. It was AWESOME seeing it here for the first time on DVD!

Another boo-boo in this one is the fact that Samantha and Durwood go to the window in their bedroom that would face out back but we're lead to believe that they are looking out the front.

Of course, the Maclane's live in Major Nelson's house, one of the few times on *Bewitched* that we see that house. I also felt that Mr. Maclane's role could've been played by Don Rickles.

MARCH 7, 1968

Tonight *Bewitched* would not be seen so that ABC could bring us a special starring Debbie Reynolds, Agnes Moorehead's good friend, entitled...*And Debbie Makes Six*. It was an hour of comedy and music with Frank Gorshin, Bob Hope, Jim Nabors, Donald O'Connor, Nelson Riddle, and Bobby Durwood, er, I mean Darin (sorry...force of habit). This special was originally supposed to air on November 19, 1967, but because of a strike by the National Association of Broadcast Employees and Technician's against ABC, it was held off until tonight.

The night before, *Lost in Space* aired its last episode.

MARCH 14, 1968

Tonight *Bewitched* returned to ABC with an all new episode in Episode #132: "To Twitch or Not to Twitch."

Durwood has got his knickers in a knot (yet again) over something he caused! It turns out he made Samantha aware of a dress up dinner affair with the Tates and new client Mr. Sharp and his wife a mere hour or so before they were to leave and now he's mad because she's taking so long to get dressed. He doesn't want to hear her excuses and goes to pull the car out. Meanwhile, Samantha cannot find her hairbrush and decides to use a little speed up spell to help her in her search not to mention get ready. When she is just about finished getting ready Speedy Gonzales style, Durwood walks in and witnesses her and her finale of levitating her fur wrap to her shoulders. He makes a snarky comment about how they should've just pulled her broom out rather than the car. And so they leave with the weather matching Durwood's mood. He goes on and on about how everyone manages to get through their life without witchcraft and in the future he does not want, under any circumstances, for Samantha to use her witchcraft. Just as he is about to finish his point, he is interrupted by a tire blowing. As they sit in the silence broken only by the pounding rain he realizes the predicament he is in and tries asking sweetly for Samantha to fix the tire by magic. She retorts using his same speech about how everybody manages to get through their life without witchcraft and so will he. He gets fed up and goes out in the rain to fix the tire.

A while later, they show up very late to the Sharp's and Durwood is soaked to the bone. Mr. Sharp offers him one of his suits, which would be all well and good except that Mr. Sharp didn't have the good sense to be a few inches taller. And because Durwood is in such a frightful mood, he calls Mr. Sharp "shorty" after everyone laughs about the short suit on a tall guy resulting in he and Samantha leaving early.

At home, Durwood goes on and on about how the whole evening's disaster could've been avoided by Samantha fixing the tire. By this time she has had enough and tries to lighten the mood by quoting her version of Shakespeare's "To be or not to be.." speech, except she soliloquizes about twitching. Durwood is not amused, and to show it, comes back with a comment about her using Shakespeare most likely because she knew him personally on account of her being a very old witch. She responds that, in fact, she did know Shakespeare, who was more of a gentleman than her husband was being and for that matter, so was the woman-hating Blue Beard. When he wants to know just how well she knew Blue Beard, she's done with this ridiculous fight and tells him with storms in her eyes, "NOT as well as I knew Henry the Eighth!" And with that she slams her hairbrush down and disappears. Durwood, of course, is not finished with the fight and demands to know where she is and hears her call from the closet. When he opens the door, she storms out in her coat with suitcases in hand and advises him that she is going bowling. When he asks where she is really going, she tells him that she and Tabatha are going home to her mother's. Realizing that Endora most likely doesn't have a home as she is always either at their place or some exotic city around the world, he asks, "Just where does a witch go when she goes home to mother?" Samantha pops out leaving her voice trailing behind her, "That's for me to know and you to find out!" Durwood realizes now that she really means business especially when her portrait from the dresser disappears.

The next morning, Samantha still hasn't returned home and when he goes into the office, Durwood finds that she hasn't called either. Larry comes in upset about the previous evening but also relieved that Mr. Sharp has come in to make amends. He asks that the Stephens and the Tates have a redo of the previous evening but Durwood declines as he doesn't know where Samantha is, but of course he doesn't want to say that.

Up in the heavens, Samantha happens to be cloud sitting with her mother and Tabatha, who is being rocked to sleep in her own little cloud. Samantha is miserable and tells her mother that she regrets fighting with Durwood, but of course, Endora is not surprised and thinks that Samantha should just find a new husband. Down on Earth, Durwood comes home and calls out to Samantha that he is sorry for all the things he said and that he should realize how lucky he is to be married to such a beautiful witch. Samantha pops home and they have a joyous reunion on the stairs. Durwood tells her that he is going to take her out for a great dinner to make up. Just then, Larry shows up as Samantha goes upstairs to change and he tells Durwood he's shown up to make sure Durwood is going to show up at the Sharp's. Endora pops in, invisibly, and listens to all this and then pops upstairs to tell Samantha, who doesn't believe her until she magically amplifies the men's conversation. Samantha wonders why Durwood didn't tell her about this, and Endora leaves as he comes up the stairs. When Samantha asks him about it, he tells her that the only plans he has that evening are with her. She realizes that it may jeopardize the account so she casts a spell to have Larry call the house so that she'll answer and find out about the party, which she does. She tells Durwood that she's glad Larry called and they can celebrate another evening. As they go off to the Sharp's on a beautiful evening, everything seems perfect until the car runs out of gas but with a deft twitch of the nose Samantha zaps in a gas station.

I LOVE LOVE LOVE this episode! This is my favorite fight episode of *Bewitched* because it really seems like this is it. Everything about this episode is brilliant and is it just me or does it seem like it lasts longer than the normal twenty-five minutes, but in a good way?

I love it when Endora and Durwood are confronting each other on the stairs, so close you would think they were about to kiss! Samantha is brilliant throughout this whole episode. The delivery of all her lines is just superb especially "You are ONE step away from making Custer's last stand look like a love in." And it's kind of spooky when she slams the brush down and disappears because you KNOW she means business!

I also liked seeing Endora, Samantha, and Tabatha cloud-sitting.

Durwood coming home and talking to the air hoping Samantha will come back is a remake of the same scene from Episode#5: "Help, Help, Don't Save Me." The scene at the end is a bit of a remake of the same scene from "The Magic Cabin" though instead of just making a half a tank of gas, Samantha zaps in a full gas station.

It was also on this night that *Batman* aired its last episode.

Three nights before, *The Lucy Show* aired its last episode.

Two days later, the My Lai Massacre happened in Vietnam where upwards of five hundred unarmed civilians, mostly women and children were murdered by a unit of the U.S. Army. This wouldn't become public knowledge until November of 1969 and would raise anti-war sentiment. It was also on that night that Senator Robert Kennedy entered the Democratic Race for the U.S. Presidential nomination.

MARCH 21, 1968

It was on this night ABC aired Episode #133: "Playmates."

While Durwood is at work, his mother Phyllis shows up to visit with Samantha and Tabatha. She tells Samantha that she wants to introduce her to a friend of hers, Gretchen Millhowser, and her young son, Michael, so that Tabatha can have a playmate. Samantha is apprehensive about this knowing that Tabatha is just learning to use her powers and might make a show of it for Michael. She tries to get out of it but Phyllis will have none of that. And so they go to the Millhowser's for the afternoon.

Mrs. Millhowser is a mother who has learned her skills from many differing child psychologists and essentially believes in letting Michael have free reign of the house as she doesn't want to hinder his creative talents, which means that his toys are all over the house and he draws on the walls. Mrs. Stephens leaves the two women to get acquainted as she goes shopping.

Tabatha tries to play with Michael but he doesn't like sharing. But he's no match for Tabatha, for when he steals the sand shovel she was using, she just twitches it back to her hand, much to his astonishment. Then, she places him in a cage and when he begins screaming for his mother, Samantha arrives first and demands Tabatha release him, which she does. After the children have been somewhat pacified, Samantha and Gretchen go back in the house to talk some more. Meanwhile, in the backyard, Michael tells Tabatha he wishes he were a dog so he could bite her and when he wishes it again, so does she, and so Michael becomes a bulldog! When their mothers hear the barking, Samantha just believes it's the Millhowser's dog, but Gretchen tells her they haven't got a dog. When the dog runs in the house, Samantha gets a confession out of Tabatha and now she must get Michael the dog back in close proximity and have Tabatha change him back without Gretchen seeing. And who should show up but Mrs. Stephens. The dog manages to run away and Samantha finally captures him and brings him back, and while Mrs. Stephens and Gretchen are frantically searching for Michael, Tabatha changes him back. Michael tells his mother he was a bulldog but she doesn't believe him. Samantha advises her that maybe this is his way of crying out for some discipline and Gretchen realizes she may be right, so she demands Michael go clean up his toys so that he and Tabatha can have some milk and cookies. When he says 'no' she swats his behind and now he can tell his mother means business.

This is the fourth non-Durwood episode of the series, the second time this season.

This episode barely scrapes by with one star and that's for how cute Tabatha is and her line about how she has more fun with Grandma Endora. I also liked all the levitation going on.

I thought it was dumb at the end of the episode how Michael's mother suddenly decides she's going to be forceful and he minds her. It was too quick a change for him. But anyway, what a bummer that this episode was so pitiful compared to the one that preceded it.

Teddy Quinn will appear next year on *Bewitched* as the bully in the park that tells Tabitha she can't slide up a slide in "Samantha Fights City Hall." He also has his own blog website *http://www.tedquinn.com/*.

Four days later, Douglas Evans passed away. He played Mr. Foster in Season Two's "The Joker is a Card."

From March 19-23, a group of students at Howard University in Washington, D.C. shut it down with sit-ins and a takeover of the administration building in protests of the ROTC program and the Vietnam War as well as demand for a more Afro-centric curriculum.

MARCH 28, 1968

It was on this night ABC aired Episode #134: "Tabatha's Cranky Spell."

With Durwood away on a business trip in Chicago, Tabatha gives her mother a run for her money as she acts up by levitating her lamp off the dresser and zapping the shade onto her head as well as levitating her rocking horse all to avoid going to bed. Endora doesn't make any of this better by suggesting that with Durwood gone they should all fly to the Witches' Nursery School where Samantha learned to fly so that Tabatha can take lessons. Of course, Samantha will have none of that and Endora leaves in a huff. While trying to stop all the magic mayhem, the phone rings. Not wanting to leave Tabatha unattended, Samantha twitches Tabatha's play phone and answers. It's Louise Tate insisting that Samantha join them for dinner. Samantha tells her she can't find a sitter on such short notice but Louise has it all figured out: she'll just have her Aunt Harriet babysit, though Larry isn't too pleased about that as he thinks Aunt Harriet is a bit cracked. You see, Aunt Harriet is very much into the after-life and uses a crystal ball to try and contact spirits there.

Larry shows up with Aunt Harriet and threatens Samantha with Durwood's job if she doesn't come along. Apparently the Tates are having new client Mr. Baker and his wife over in an attempt to get Mr. Baker to realize that the packaging used for his product, which his uncle started over forty years ago, needs to be changed. Larry feels that if Mr. Baker gets bombarded by a woman's point of view from Louise, Samantha, and Mrs. Baker, he'll be more inclined to change the packaging. Samantha accepts the invitation and as they leave, Aunt Harriet mentions how she feels hot tonight and may even contact Mr. Henderson, a man she was engaged to for twenty years.

At the Tate's, Mr. Baker proves to be stubborn as he says he promised his Uncle Willie that he would never change the packaging, which Uncle Willie had designed himself.

Meanwhile, as Aunt Harriet tries to contact Mr. Henderson, Tabatha is still in a magic mood and decides that she wants her "horsey" to go for a walk and so she twitches the rocking horse to float downstairs and out the door. Harriet feels the cold breeze and feels it might be Mr. Henderson giving her a sign, though his heavy drinking during his life makes her think that he should be in a much warmer place. Now that the "horsey" is gone, Tabatha wants her ball, which is underneath the coffee table at Harriet's feet. Harriet asks Mr. Henderson to prove that he's there by knocking and when the ball floats up, it hits the bottom of the table. When Tabatha doesn't get her ball, she decides she wants the "horsey" back and calls for it and as it floats through the door, Harriet witnesses this and thinks it's another sign. She calls Louise to tell her the good news and when Samantha hears that something strange may be happening, she magically hangs up the call. Louise mentions that Harriet said something about a ghost, which perks up Mrs. Baker as she is very interested in ghosts. Samantha says she had better go home to make sure Tabatha is OK but Mrs. Baker insists that she would like the opportunity to possibly meet a ghost, and so the party follows Samantha home.

At 1164, they find Harriet trying to contact Mr. Henderson again and Mr. Baker is very annoyed with all this, especially his wife believing all this ghost nonsense. When Mr. Baker isn't looking, Mrs. Baker goes to search the house for a ghost and ends up in the kitchen where she witnesses the refrigerator door open and a bottle of milk pour itself into a glass which disappears when she tries to grab it. Of course, this was only because Tabatha wanted a drink. When she tells the others, Mr. Baker thinks it's all a ruse to try and get him to change the packaging as Mrs. Baker had mentioned trying to contact Uncle Willie to ask him about it.

Samantha decides the next day that she is going to save the account by having Mrs. Baker 'contact' Uncle Willie by taking the crystal ball over there, have Mrs. Baker try to conjure Uncle Willie and then change herself into Uncle Willie to tell her that the packaging does need to be changed. Everything goes according to plan until Samantha steps out onto the patio to change and finds herself facing the actual ghost of Uncle Willie! She changes herself back and finds that Uncle Willie has actually been haunting his nephew and niece-in-law but because of their not actually believing, he couldn't ever really contact them. He tells Samantha that he agrees that the packaging should be changed. He suggests that Samantha change herself back into him and with some golden nuggets of blackmail, convince Mr. Baker to change it.

Mr. Baker walks into the room and finds his wife conjuring and begins to yell at her when she shrieks and faints at seeing 'Uncle Willie.' Mr. Baker thinks it's Larry Tate trying to pull something on him but when Uncle Willie disappears he begins to believe especially when certain indiscretions that only he and his Uncle Willie would know are mentioned. He immediately calls Larry and acts like he made the decision himself and everyone is happy.

This is the third time this season that Dick York hasn't appeared in an episode, fifth time over all for the series. It seems to me that all of Samantha's lines at the first when Larry comes over were really meant for Durwood what with the "Next world?" "Crystal ball?"

This is also the second time Sarah Seegar plays a client's wife and it is her third appearance, her first being in "A Vision of Sugar Plums" as the orphanage director. I think it's so funny when she's watching the milk pour and she closes one of her eyes. I've always thought that pouring milk scene was really cool and I bet it took FOREVER to set it up just right.

Three days before, *The Monkees* ended its run.

And three days after, President Lyndon B. Johnson announced that he would not be seeking re-election.

APRIL 4, 1968

It was on this night ABC aired Episode #135: "I Confess."

As Samantha and Durwood wait for their car after dinner, Samantha remembers that she left her gloves at the table, apparently something she does a lot. She offers to retrieve them by witchcraft but Durwood tells her he'll go fetch them. While he is gone, Samantha is confronted by a frisky drunk looking for the Club Bimbo. As he makes his advances on Samantha, she warns him that he'll regret it. When he remarks that his spirit cannot be dampened, she says otherwise and zaps up a floating bucket of water that she pours on his head. Durwood walks out of the restaurant just as she zaps the bucket away just a little too late and so the conflict begins.

Durwood is miffed that Samantha always seems to resort to witchcraft to get out of her troubles not to mention that she always tries to hide it, from not only Durwood, but the rest of the world, which seems to be stressful to him and he suggests to relieve this stress that they tell the whole world her true identity! She cannot believe he would want to do that and as they get into bed, she puts him straightway to sleep and casts a dream control spell over him to show him what things would be like if they did reveal her secret.

The first part of the dream consists of their confronting Larry Tate. He first thinks that the Stephens' might be having marital problems but then switches to thinking that Samantha may be a man in woman's clothing, but after persistent remarks about Samantha being a witch, Larry asks her to prove it. She does by disappearing. When Larry looks for her, she appears behind him and he chalks it up to being done with mirrors. At that remark she zaps up two hand held mirrors. Flabbergasted, Larry tries to believe that maybe the mirrors were up her sleeve but Samantha changes them into two full length mirrors which he weakly tries to rationalize as the smaller ones being expandable. She zaps them away and Larry tries to gather his thoughts which end up being that with his brains and her voodoo they could take over the world, a dream Larry has had since he was a kid. Durwood and Samantha refuse to use her powers in such a manner and Larry promptly fires Durwood…

I interrupt this episode at a place where an actual interruption may have occurred that night when ABC news announced that the Reverend Dr. Martin Luther King Jr. had been killed in Memphis, Tennessee earlier that evening. Of course, Martin Luther King Jr. was, and is, considered the greatest leader of the Civil Rights Movement. America had been boiling over with high tensions with race riots for many years before now, but things really came to a boiling point with the murder of Dr. King. Most of the country would've turned to CBS to the beloved and trusted Walter Cronkite for information about this horrible circumstance.

I do not know if *Bewitched* resumed where it was interrupted or if this episode was reaired at another time. For our purposes here, I will continue the recap…

For the second part of the dream, Samantha tells Durwood that they tell the Kravitzes her secret. Surprisingly, Gladys says she doesn't believe her and Abner thinks that they may be on the *Candid Camera*, a TV show where people were put in embarrassing situations that were filmed for comedy purposes. When he tries to find the cameras, Samantha tells him she can zap one up and does. She immediately changes it to a chicken and then dematerializes that. Gladys admits she does believe her and that her earlier denial was her disbelief at Samantha confessing. But now both Kravitzes are scared that Samantha may want to abduct them like an alien might. Samantha assures her she is a good witch to which Durwood adds that her mother is the bad witch, and with that, they leave.

Samantha can see that these dreams are causing Durwood stress but they are not over. For the last part, she tells him that now because someone called the papers, the whole world knows that she is a witch and she shows them that they have lost their privacy as Mrs. Kravitz is giving lectures entitled "The Samantha Stephens I Have Known and Feared." Mr. Kravitz has set up bleachers so that people can view the house where the witch lives. When Durwood drives up from a hard day looking for work, he is mobbed and barely makes it into his house where he finds that Samantha has been on the phone all day denying requests for magic from everyone including Mickey Mantle. Tabatha is also distressed as her friends won't play with her anymore because her mommy won't give them all ponies. Just then a General Stanton and Agent W from the secret agency called the HHH arrive with the news that there have been demands that Samantha and her family be burned at the stake! They can avoid this burning if Samantha aids the government with her witchcraft in the defense area. Samantha refuses her using her powers like that but Durwood says she will when he sees that they might be viewed as anti-American if she doesn't. General Stanton says that they will be set up at a military installation somewhere out in the desert for protection and off they go. When they arrive at the installation Samantha and Tabatha are immediately whisked away for testing and Durwood can't take it anymore and cries to be let go.

In the waking world Samantha can see that the dream has gone far enough and she ends it and Durwood wakes up.

The next morning she tells him she has decided that she will tell the world her secret but he refuses saying that he has changed his mind because he slept on it.

This marks the return of Durwood after a two week absence.

David White surely is brilliant and it's hysterical every time he says, "I'm mad with power!!" I also think it's funny when they are saying that Samantha isn't a woman and he says, "Well, sir, that's a very nice outfit you've got on." I always thought the zapping in of the mirrors was cool and I give them kudos for not having any part of the studio show up in them.

I also like it when Abner says, "If you have to take one of us, take me!" By the way, when *Bewitched* aired on the Hallmark channel, they would cut out the WHOLE scene with the Kravitzes! Can you believe that?

Tabatha is also really cute what with her walking through the dining room and living room with her nose in the air because she's depressed. This also seems like the first time where Samantha doesn't have to go upstairs to get her or take her upstairs. Tabatha just does it by herself. Our little witch is growing up!

One of the bloopers from this episode is when Samantha, Durwood, and Tabatha pop out to go to the "concentration camp" you can see their shadows move across the floor.

The day before *Planet of the Apes* premiered. It co-starred Maurice Evans and would explain his absence this season.

APRIL 11, 1968

It was on this night ABC aired Episode #136: "A Majority of Two."

Durwood is gone yet again on another business trip and while he is gone Aunt Clara shows up to find solace as she has just broken up with her boyfriend Ocky.

Meanwhile, Larry shows up to check up on Samantha, or so he says. Really, he wants her to invite him and client Mr. Mishimoto to the house for an authentic Japanese dinner as Larry feels it will more fully persuade Mishimoto to come over to McMann and Tate. He tells Samantha that he phoned Mishimoto's secretary and found that his favorite dish is Hongai Wongurash and gives her a Japanese cookbook so she can find it.

Aunt Clara helps Samantha prepare the house but goes a little too far by preparing the coffee table as their dining table considering most Japanese dinner is served while sitting on the floor. She even zaps up a kimono to look the part. Samantha thinks this may be a bit much but Aunt Clara thinks she's thrilled with it and just as Samantha answers the doorbell, Aunt Clara zaps Samantha into a kimono as well. Samantha tells Larry and Mr. Mishimoto that she regularly wears one as she finds them so comfortable. Larry also informs Samantha that he found out that Mishimoto has a personal French chef to which Mishimoto adds that he travels so much he likes to experience different food. Samantha, who wasn't able to find Hongai Wongurash in the cookbook but fixed something else Japanese, explains that she felt that maybe having a Japanese dinner might make him feel more at home.

The night progresses beautifully even with Aunt Clara's strange sense of humor but this is OK because Mishimoto finds it charming, so much so that he asks her out on a date. She accepts and they begin going out all the time, allowing Mishimoto no time for Larry or the account. Larry threatens to get rid of Durwood's job if Samantha doesn't do something about Aunt Clara, so she magically sends a message to Ocky to have him apologize, knowing that Aunt Clara is really just looking for the attention she never got from him. Just as Aunt Clara is getting ready for another date Ocky calls and apologizes and asks her out, which she accepts. Things seem to be OK, except when Mishimoto finds out that Aunt Clara has stood him up, he's embarrassed and leaves saying that he will not do business with McMann and Tate and that he is taking the next flight back to Tokyo. Larry is confused but Samantha tells him that such embarrassment has caused Mishimoto to feel as though he has lost face. Samantha decides to head Mishimoto off at the airport and she tells him that she is actually on her way to find a job as Larry was mad at Samantha for her Aunt Clara embarrassing Mishimoto so much so that he fired Larry. Mishimoto cannot understand this as he feels that if anything Larry should be mad at him. Samantha then asks, while having her face disappear, why would Mishimoto be mad at Larry for something Aunt Clara did. Mishimoto is confused as Samantha literally losing her face and goes to leave and passes by a rather cute Japanese flight stewardess whom he looks over, but she is oblivious to him. Samantha sees this stewardess as a great opportunity and she reverses time a little but slows the stewardess down when time starts back up again so that she bumps into Mr. Mishimoto and they make a date to stay in the states.

Later on, Mr. Mishimoto and his new date arrive at Samantha's for a dinner party to sign the contracts with Larry. Samantha asks Mishimoto what Hongai Wongurash is as she could never find a recipe for it. At first confused, Mishimoto realizes that Samantha misunderstood his secretary and that in her broken English was trying to say "Hungarian Goulash."

I would give it a two star rating. I love any Aunt Clara episode, but it's just so painful with a Caucasian man playing an Asian.

I always liked Samantha's spell to get Ocky to call:

Hendrum Jendrum Wishing Weaver,
find for me the old deceiver,
on wings of night and wires of steel,
take my message to that heel!

It is kind of odd that she used the phone though...as if Ocky would have a phone...I wonder if originally they were going to have him show up but then they couldn't get Reginald Owen to come in.

I also think that this episode was originally written with Durwood being in it because it would seem that Larry coming over to discuss the client was meant for Durwood but they just had to give the lines to Samantha. This is the fourth episode this season that hasn't had Durwood in it, six overall for the series.

I also find it interesting that they didn't get a Japanese fellow to play Mishimoto when they got an Asian girl to play the stewardess and had an Asian girl play Ling Ling.

By the way, Richard Haydn, who plays Mishimoto, is the voice of the Caterpillar from Disney's *Alice in Wonderland* (1951). That is so cool!

It was also on this day that President Johnson signed the Civil Rights Act of 1968.

APRIL 18, 1968

It was on this night ABC aired Episode #137: "Samantha's Secret Saucer."

Samantha and Durwood go out for the evening leaving Tabatha in the care of Aunt Clara. Tabatha also has a new toy courtesy of her daddy, a UFO looking saucer that actually flies and a NASA space helmet. Aunt Clara tells Tabatha that she can take one more flight and then it's off to bed. Well, Tabatha navigates the saucer out the patio doors into the night sky. Not wanting to lose the toy, Aunt Clara casts a spell for its return but somehow manages to not only get it back but drastically enlarge it as well! Or so she thinks...after trying to shrink it, she decides to put Tabatha to bed and try later. Unbeknownst to her the huge saucer is actually a space craft containing aliens! It seems that her spell reached out into the universe and captured a craft from the planet Parenthia and its pilots Alpha and Orvis, who happen to look like dogs, who are quite bewildered as to how they managed to be flying one minute and grounded the next.

Samantha and Durwood return home and Aunt Clara tells Durwood that as much as he loved the saucer before he's going to love it even more now as there is so much more of it love, and she shows them the saucer. Of course, Durwood freaks out and Samantha calms him by saying after a good night's rest Aunt Clara will remember the spell to shrink it.

The next morning, Durwood is a wreck wondering if someone is going to question why he has such a great big saucer in the back yard and Aunt Clara hasn't even risen yet from her night's rest. Samantha assures him nobody is going to wonder. But this isn't so as Mrs. Kravitz happened to have heard something streaking to Earth last night in the neighborhood. She runs home to tell Abner who, of course, doesn't believe her and so she decides to get the Air Force involved. Surprisingly, they are more than willing to comply as they must investigate reports of an unidentified flying object and so they knock on the door of 1164. Durwood explains that it's a model for an ad campaign and this satisfies Colonel Burkett, though his colleague Captain Tugwell (who also happens to be his nephew) isn't so sure. But they and Mrs. Kravitz leave anyhow. Samantha says she'll go wake Aunt Clara, and as Durwood is leaving the patio, the doors of the ship open and the two dog aliens step out only to return screaming when they hear Durwood screaming.

Now things are really messed up, according to Durwood, as they have real live aliens in their backyard. Samantha feels that they could be nice aliens and might need some comfort being so far from home so she pops aboard to invite them to come out. At first Alpha and Orvis are surprised by how fast the Earthlings seem to move and are about to blast her with their N-guns but she promises that she is a good witch. They reveal to her that the N in N-guns stands for niceness so it wouldn't have hurt her at all. They come in to the kitchen where Samantha has made pancakes for breakfast.

Meanwhile, Captain Tugwell returns to Mrs. Kravitz house with the news that their radar screens did detect something streaking to the earth in that area last night so they go over to investigate further and see the aliens eating breakfast. He leaves Mrs. Kravitz to keep watch while he alerts his uncle and the rest of the air force.

When the aliens have finished their breakfast, Aunt Clara tells them all that she believes she has remembered the spell and so they go to leave but Mrs. Kravitz jumps out of hiding telling all in involved that they are going to be in tons of trouble for harboring aliens and lying to the air force. Alpha doesn't think this is so nice so he zaps her with his N-gun which immediately changes her demeanor and she goes off to pick flowers.

Colonel Burkett has shown up with MPs and Captain Tugwell goes to put everyone at 1164 under arrest just as Aunt Clara sends the flying saucer back off into space. When Colonel Burkett comes around and sees there is nothing and that Mrs. Kravitz is so nice now, he knows his nephew has cracked up and they leave Samantha giving her Aunt Clara a hug for a job well done.

Samantha pours coffee for alien Orvis (Steve Franken) as he shows her pictures of his family back on Parenthia.

Unfortunately, this would be the last time Aunt Clara appeared on *Bewitched* as Marion Lorne would pass away shortly after this episode aired. It's truly sad as Aunt Clara is one of the greatest characters from the show. I also think that this episode was not such a great one for her last one as the only thing that I like about this episode is that Aunt Clara is in it and Liz looks fantastic! But other than that, I would give this episode maybe half a star. It's so lame to have these types of aliens on the show. If anything, they should've made them a little scary, but a poodle dog alien? No thanks.

Steve Franken who played Orvis, the poodle dog alien, joined us at the 2008 and 2010 *Bewitched* Fanfares and related how any time Elizabeth Montgomery would run into him after that show she would tell him that whenever she saw a poodle she would think of him.

I like how Tabatha says, "It's STILL big!" when Aunt Clara is trying to make the UFO small.

A huge blooper in this is the fact that the kitchen window the officer and Gladys look through really wouldn't be there because that wall faces directly to the garage.

Marion was also nominated for the Emmy that year and received it posthumously a mere ten days after her death. It was accepted by Liz and I wish we could see the footage of that. It should've been included on the Fourth Season DVD.

APRIL 25, 1968

It was on this night ABC aired Episode #138: "The No-Harm Charm."

It seems that Durwood's dreams of becoming a full partner at McMann and Tate are about to come true as he has potentially brought in millions of dollars for the company from his brochure for Omega National Bank. But things go horribly awry when it is discovered that on the front page of the brochure Omega's assets are listed at "Over $100.00." Larry is furious and Durwood cannot understand or believe that he would make such a mistake especially since he went over everything in the brochure with a fine toothcomb. Believing he must really be ill, Larry suggests that Durwood take a lot of time off.

At home, Durwood is inconsolable and he comes to the conclusion that this mistake must've been caused by Endora. It's at this time that he decides he's tired of bucking all the spells thrown at him, therefore, he tells Samantha that she and her family are welcome to do any witchcraft they'd like, that prohibition has been repealed! Samantha cannot believe what she's hearing and knows that Durwood's problem wasn't caused by witchcraft and she tries to get him to see that there isn't always magic going on in their life. When she goes to show him the stew she's made for dinner, they find Uncle Arthur's head floating in the pot as he says he's a "stew" away. Of course, this only emphasizes Durwood's point of magic, magic everywhere and he goes off to bed.

Samantha isn't sure she should trust Uncle Arthur's idea to give Durwood confidence. PHOTO COURTESY OF SHARON ORAZI.

The next morning, Durwood doesn't come down for breakfast and when Samantha tries to get him out of bed, he won't budge, because he's simply given up. She tempts him with waffles, which seems to work except that he'd rather that she just twitched them up but she won't. She tells him that she finds it more fun to cook the mortal way and to take care of him and their daughter the mortal way, that if she didn't, she wouldn't stay around. She gives up on him and returns downstairs to find that she has two new guests for breakfast, Uncle Arthur and a cow. Apparently, the latter was zapped in because Tabatha wanted more milk. After Arthur zaps it away, Samantha explains about her troubles with Durwood and Arthur suggests that he'll have a talk with Durwood and he goes upstairs. He tells Durwood that he has a charm he can give him that will protect him from all harm and witchcraft. Of course, Durwood is leery but Arthur proves it to him by first shooting him with a gun. The bullets merely pass through him and then Arthur has him jump off a tall ladder and instead of falling swiftly to the ground he floats gently down. Durwood is now convinced and feels a renewed sense of power and invincibility until he trips over the bench at the end of the bed, which Arthur says happened because Durwood wasn't holding the charm. Durwood decides he is going to go into work and convince Larry that they can get the Omega account back.

Samantha doesn't believe what has happened but Arthur assures her he used psychology. He tells her that he gave Durwood the charm, which angers her as there is no such thing as a charm that protects from harm and witchcraft, but Arthur tells her that's the brilliancy of the plan. Durwood believes the charm is protecting him but really it's Durwood's belief in the protection that is doing it. Samantha knows this could get him into a lot of trouble and it almost does as they watch a car almost side swipe him when he's not paying attention backing out. Samantha suggests that she is going to follow her husband around invisibly to protect him because telling him the truth will only prove his point about witchcraft causing all his problems.

At the office, Larry is quite surprised by Durwood's appearance but Durwood tells him that the way they can get the account back is to play the mistake off as an intentional joke, because everyone knows a bank would have more than one hundred dollars. He tells Larry that he'll go and speak with Mr. Markham, the bank president and he'll get the account back. Meanwhile, Samantha has shown up invisible and Uncle Arthur soon joins her as he does feel responsible for what is going on. They follow Durwood to the bank where they watch Durwood finagle his way into Mr. Markham's office. Samantha is about to follow him, but Arthur tells her that she should let him on his own as it'll prove just how much Durwood can do on his own. Mr. Markham isn't the least bit happy at seeing Durwood and is even less enthusiastic about his proposal of the joke brochure. Just then, a courier arrives with a message for Mr. Markham which he says he must personally deliver. As Mr. Markham reads the note, he finds it's a demand for Mr. Markham to get his tellers to bring all the cash in the vaults to the office and the courier pulls out a gun! Durwood, thinking that the charm will protect him, tells the courier that he won't shoot the gun and asks him to set it down but the courier is insistent that he'll shoot. Durwood merely grabs the gun out of his hands and the police are called. Mr. Markham is impressed with Durwood's bravery and tells him that he'll come back to McMann and Tate though they will have to fix the error that happened.

At home, Durwood is happy but he does feel guilty that his heroics were seemingly achieved by magic and so he reveals to Samantha the charm. Samantha decides to tell him that the charm is in fact the filial off the top of the living room lamp. As the reality of the situation creeps up on Durwood, he faints and Arthur pops in to catch him before he hits the floor.

This is Uncle Arthur's first and only appearance this season. It's been since the beginning of the Third Season on the Halloween episode that we've seen him. It's also the first time that he's appeared without Endora, which I think shows, as this episode doesn't seem to be as funny without him sparring with her.

I think Uncle Arthur's painted on clown face was SCARY! If I had been Tabatha sitting there, I would've started crying.

I believe this is the first time we see any of the characters as see-through, an effect I really like. I was wondering why they weren't see-through when in the bank though.

This episode is also cool in the fact that it really brings the greatest reality of them all — DEATH — into play by the fact that Durwood could've been killed or even Mr. Markham could've been killed. And did you notice that when Arthur shoots Durwood you can see the hole from the bullets appear on the wall behind him? Also his pajama top has soot on it from where apparently the bullet went through him, yet after he has floated down from the ladder, the marks are gone.

From April 23-30 students at Columbia University in New York took over the administration building in protest to the Vietnam War.

MAY 2, 1968

It was on this night ABC aired Episode #139: "Man of the Year."

Durwood arrives home to find Samantha in a pretty dress with a homemade sign saying "Congratulations Advertising Man of the Year" and a bottle of chilled wine which is appropriate because Durwood was just nominated as one of the Huckster Club's Advertising Men of the Year, but in Samantha's eyes, he's THE man of the year. Endora pops in on the celebration claiming that this new accolade will go to Durwood's head, but Samantha says otherwise.

The next day, when Durwood arrives at work, Endora pops in and casts a spell, not on Durwood, but on everyone around him to absolutely LOVE anything he says including a simple "good morning" that Secretary Betty just loves. Durwood finds this odd but brushes it off when he finds that Larry is frantic as Mr. Slocum, a client, isn't pleased with how things are going with his campaign. Durwood tells Larry to let him have a go at him and so with apprehension, but also enthusiasm (due to the spell), Larry agrees. Durwood spouts out a rather bad idea for a new campaign that Mr. Slocum doesn't like until he gets near Durwood, and because of the spell, he's all for it. Larry is confused as to Mr. Slocum's change of heart, but when he speaks to Durwood, he oddly understands it.

Later, Mr. McMann requests Durwood's presence on his yacht to congratulate him personally for his being nominated as one of the Advertising Men of the Year. When he meets Durwood he sees something in him that outshines his partner Larry and he begins speaking to Durwood about making him a partner! Durwood is thrilled and it seems that Endora is right about him getting a big head.

Larry has a cocktail party that evening with other potential clients and Samantha is positively embarrassed at the dumb off-the-fly ideas Durwood spouts out that everyone seems to like. She realizes that Durwood must have a spell on him and she drags him out of the party and calls on her mother to remove the spell. Endora promises that there isn't a spell on Durwood but finally admits there is one around him. She takes the spell off and things seem to go downhill once Mr. Slocum and the others realize they agreed to dumb ideas. Samantha and Durwood don't feel this is fair to McMann and Tate to lose the accounts that were acquired through witchcraft so Samantha puts the spell back around Durwood temporarily.

This is the first time we have ever seen Mr. McMann, played here by Roland Winters. It seems that he is more than just a partner with Larry, or at least he seems to think so.

This episode is rather blah in my opinion just because it focuses too much on Durwood. I did it find dumb that Samantha would say, "What do I know about advertising?" when in fact she has practically done Durwood's job for him in about 3/4 of the episodes, but gives him all the glory.

I did like Mr. Angel listening to the ad Durwood had thought up of… it just seemed funny to me.

I also thought it kind of cool that Samantha took the spell off Durwood by grabbing it and pitching it. I'm sure that were it made today they would've actually shown the magic.

I also noticed that Samantha's hair seemed to be really big, like foreshadowing the awfulness of the end of next season, my vote for the worst Samantha hair (though the WORST Samantha hair is in Season Seven in "Money Happy Returns").

Two days before, the hippie musical *Hair* officially opened on Broadway.

MAY 9, 1968

It was on this night ABC reaired Episode #113: "No Zip in My Zap." It was also on this night that Marion Lorne, a.k.a. Aunt Clara, passed away. Phil Arnold, who played the Vendor in Season One's "Eat at Mario's," passed away as well. He was in Liz's first big screen movie *The Court Martial of Billy Mitchell*, and *The Conqueror* and *Meet Me in Las Vegas* with Agnes Moorehead, and *The Ghost and Mr. Chicken* with Dick Sargent.

The day before, the Bob Hope movie *The Private Navy of Sgt. O'Harrell* premiered. It co-starred Dick Sargent.

MAY 16, 1968

Tonight ABC aired the Fourth Season finale of *Bewitched* Episode #140: "Splitsville."

As Samantha is opening her bedroom window for some fresh air before she goes to bed, she notices Mrs. Kravitz out on the street in her robe with luggage, hitchhiking of all things! She tells Durwood that they should go see what the problem is. Durwood is apprehensive but this doesn't stop her.

Out on the darkened street, Samantha finds that after twenty-two years of marriage, Mrs. Kravitz is done and is on her way to Mexico to file for a quicky divorce! She's hitchhiking because Abner wouldn't let her use the phone to call a taxi as it's a toll call. Samantha offers Gladys their guest room as she doesn't want her to stay out all night in the cold. Gladys surprisingly accepts.

The next morning, the Stephenses find out what may have been the problem in the Kravitzes marriage, and that is Gladys who insists on everyone eating TOO healthy as she always has a glass of wheat germ oil for breakfast and thinks everyone else should too, as she "regards the human body as a furnace and everything we put into it as fuel." They find she repeats this mantra often and that Abner doesn't like hearing it. Neither does Durwood, who leaves for work with the request that Samantha get rid of Gladys by the time he gets back.

When he arrives back home, he sees that Mr. Kravitz is having the time of his life just mowing his lawn, which means that Mrs. Kravitz must still be at 1164. This is true as Gladys will have nothing to do with Abner. After an atrocious dinner of vegetable loaf and kumquat pudding that Gladys makes, Durwood insists that Samantha get Gladys out of the house. She tells him she'll do it the next day after she figures out how.

With the morning they find that Gladys is just too weird with her health rituals and Durwood has had enough. Samantha tells him that she has decided to use magic to get the Kravitzes back together and seeing that it may be the only alternative, Durwood agrees. Samantha has heard from Mrs. Kravitz that she thinks the local butcher looks like Henry Fonda, so Sam has decided to cast a mini-love spell on the butcher, Mr. Hogersdorf, to have him make the moves on Gladys in order to make Abner jealous.

Mr. Hogersdorf shows up with flowers that Samantha has zapped for him telling Gladys that he heard she was separated and wanted to give her the flowers to soothe her soul. She is quite smitten, but Durwood wonders how all this will rectify the situation if Abner isn't there. Samantha casts a spell to get him to drop what he's doing and come on over. When he shows up, he cannot believe Mr. Hogersdorf would be going for Gladys and Samantha tries to get him to see that's because he, Abner, wants Gladys for himself. He tells Gladys that he's tired of all her health kicks and her trying to force it on him but she tells him she has been doing it make herself better for her husband and also to help him out because she loves him. When he hears that, he tells Mr. Hogersdorf to leave else they will buy their chickens elsewhere, and the Kravitzes leave arm in arm.

This episode is a remake of the First Season's "Illegal Separation" where Abner leaves Gladys and ends up at the Stephenses.

Gladys' health kick just was so irritating to me, it's no wonder Abner is always irritated with her.

I did like that Samantha got another man interested in her to make Abner jealous…the mowing lawn scene was hilarious!

I also noticed that Sandra Gould looked really nice in that dress at the end and my favorite line is about her motive being love, mixed with a little hatred.

I also liked that she told him she was going to go back to her maiden name of Gruber. It's good that they remembered that's what it was as mentioned in "Illegal Separation."

Bewitched ended the season ranking #11 overall in the Nielsens, down three points from the previous season.

Three nights after this aired, the Emmys took place. According to the article that Adam Gerace wrote (with contributions from myself) on *HarpiesBizarre.com*, "the show's Fourth Season saw the series (producer: William Asher) and Montgomery again receive nominations. *Get Smart* won over *Bewitched*, *Family Affair*, *Hogan's Heroes*, and *The Lucy Show*, while Lucille Ball (in the final season of her series) won over Montgomery, Barbara Feldon (*Get Smart*), Paula Prentiss (*He & She*) and Marlo Thomas (*That Girl*). Dick York finally received a nomination for his work ("Outstanding Continued Performance by an Actor in a Leading Role in a Comedy Series"), although it was the star of the comedy series winner, Don Adams, who took home his second Emmy (other nominees were *Family Affair*'s Brian Keith and Sebastian Cabot and *He & She*'s Richard Benjamin). Moorehead was nominated in the supporting actress category (along with Marge Redmond of *The Flying Nun*, and Nita Talbot for an episode of *Hogan's Heroes*). This time it was Aunt Clara's creator, Marion Lorne who won. Again the award (bestowed on May 19) was bittersweet for *Bewitched*, with Lorne having passed away on May 9, 1968. It was Elizabeth Montgomery who accepted Lorne's award, saying "We owe her a big thanks for all the happiness she brought us" (*Delaware Daily County Times*, May 20, 1968, p. 2)."

The following is the summer re-run schedule. The episode will be listed by number, name, and original airdate.

MAY 23, 1968

Episode #117: "That Was No Chick, That Was My Wife" (November 9, 1967)

Three days before, Agnes Moorehead guested on *The Mike Douglas Show*.

MAY 30, 1968

Episode #112, "Cheap, Cheap" (October 5, 1967)

JUNE 6, 1968

Episode #121, "My, What Big Ears You Have" (December 7, 1967)

Two days before, *Bewitched* made its debut in West Germany known as *Verliebt in hiene Hexe*.

Early the day before, America was shocked when Presidential candidate Robert F. Kennedy was shot at the Ambassador Hotel in Los Angeles by Sirhan Sirhan after having delivered a victory speech for defeating Eugene McCarthy in the California Primaries. He would pass away today.

Two days later, James Earl Ray was arrested for the murder of Martin Luther King, Jr.

JUNE 13, 1968

Episode #114, "Birdies, Bogies and Baxter" (October 19, 1967)

JUNE 20, 1968

Episode #128, "Hippie Hippie Hooray" (February 1, 1968)

JUNE 27, 1968

Episode #120, "Solid Gold Mother-in-Law" (November 30, 1967)

JULY 4, 1968

It was on this night, when most of us were lighting of fireworks in honor of Independence Day, that ABC reaired Episode #131, "How Green Was My Grass" which originally aired on February 29, 1968.

JULY 11, 1968

Episode #126, "Snob in the Grass" (January 11, 1968)

JULY 18, 1968

Episode #132, "To Twitch or Not to Twitch" (March 14, 1968)

Three days before, ABC aired for the first time the day time soap *One Life to Live*.

JULY 25, 1968

Episode #127, "If They Never Met" (January 25, 1968)

AUGUST 1, 1968

Episode #125, "Once in a Vial" (January 4, 1968)

AUGUST 8, 1968

Episode #135, "I Confess" (April 4, 1968)
It was on this day the Republican National Convention in Miami, Florida, nominated Richard Nixon for President and Spiro Agnew for Vice President.

AUGUST 15, 1968

Episode #134, "Tabitha's Cranky Spell" (March 28, 1968)
Two days before, Agnes Moorehead guested on *The Steve Allen Show*.

AUGUST 22, 1968

Episode #139, "Man of the Year" (May 2, 1968)
The day before, the Medal of Honor was awarded posthumously to James Anderson, Jr., the first black U.S. Marine to receive the honor.

AUGUST 29, 1968

Episode #138, "The No-Harm Charm" (April 25, 1968)
The Democratic National Convention was held this week in Chicago where they nominated Hubert Humphrey for President and Edmund Muskie for Vice President. There were anti-war protests that became violent when the police became involved.

SEPTEMBER 5, 1968

Episode #137, "Samantha's Secret Saucer" (April 18, 1968)
Two days later, Mattel introduced Hot Wheels toy cars.

SEPTEMBER 12, 1968

Episode #111, "Double Double Toil and Trouble" (September 29, 1967. The first time it reaired was on January 18, 1968)
The day before, *The Young Runaways* premiered co-starring Dick Sargent.

SEPTEMBER 19, 1968

Episode #140, "Splitsville" (May 16, 1968)
The next day, CBS premiered *Hawaii 5-0*, which ran for twelve seasons.

Stay tuned next week for an all new episode of *Bewitched* in 'culluh!'

Season 5

SEPTEMBER 26, 1968

Tonight Chevrolet presented on ABC *Bewitched*'s Fifth Season premiere Episode #141: "Samantha's Wedding Present" in "culluh" at 8:30 P.M. Eastern Standard Time.

Endora pops in on Samantha (who has longer blonder hair, and is it me, or does she also have a tan?) who had been doing the dishes until Endora zapped them done. Samantha finds that Endora has just arrived from Paris with a wedding gift for her! Endora claims she wasn't sure the marriage would take and immediately zaps the gift out of the box and onto Samantha — a shimmering gold mini-dress with sparkling gold panty hose! Samantha loves it but gets nervous when she hears Durwood coming in. She tries to zap the present back in its box, but because of her infrequent use of witchcraft, she causes the box to encase her! Durwood is furious and even irritated with Endora for even bringing the gift which causes her to lose her patience with him accusing him of being "a small, small man!" And with that, she pops out in a gust of wind. Durwood thinks that's the end of it, but obviously it's not.

While dressing the next morning, Durwood finds that his shirt collars seemed stretched but he chalks that up to the dry cleaners. Later at the office, Larry notices that Durwood seems to be shorter even though they are supposed to be the same six foot one inch height. Larry thinks Durwood may be sick and suggests he go home. At first he fights to stay, but then as he notices his clothing getting bigger and bigger, Durwood agrees and races home hoping his feet will still touch the pedals!

Mrs. Kravitz watches from across the street as Durwood's car pulls in but a very short man exits it and enters the house. Of course, she is curious and demands that Abner accompany her to the Stephens's to find out what is going on. Meanwhile, Durwood is furious at what he knows is his mother-in-law's handiwork and Samantha is shocked to find that she is now married to a midget. She suggests that Durwood apologize to Endora for his earlier rudeness but he will hear none of it.

A little while later, Durwood has shrunk to a healthy height of about two inches with Endora no-where to be found. Mrs. Kravitz, in the meantime, has purchased a Great Dane thinking she'll be able to gain access to the Stephens's house if she claims to have lost her dog in their backyard, which she lets loose to go there. She and her husband knock at the front door to speak to Samantha about the apparently shrinking Durwood. The dog, on the other hand, finds the kitchen door open and finds mini-Durwood on the table trying to hide in a coffee mug, which he knocks to the floor. Shaken, Durwood makes a run for the outdoors to get away from the gaping jaws of the Dane.

Samantha agrees to help Mrs. Kravitz find her dog and when she goes to tell Durwood where she is going, she discovers she is now going to have to find him and even worse, that she might know where he is considering the Kravitz dog is in the kitchen licking its jowls!

Durwood hides in a pile of trash which the trash collectors gather and finds himself a little while later at the dumps. With the future looking grim, Durwood almost gives up hope until a bum named Frank O'Hara comes searching in the garbage and finds him, mistaking him for a leprechaun who must give him three wishes. Seeing that this may be his only way home, Durwood agrees but tells him he can only get his wishes if he takes him home. Mr. O'Hara obliges and finds Samantha has been missing her husband. Durwood suggests Samantha give Frank his wishes which consist of a new set of horned rim glasses, a new suit with a purple waistcoat, and a Shetland pony. With his wishes granted, Mr. O'Hara hands Durwood over to Samantha.

Durwood realizes that he was harsh with Endora and apologizes to her prompting her to return him to his normal size.

For me, this is just an "eh" episode, especially for a season opener. But it is interesting to note that this episode finished filming sixth out of the Fifth Season episodes. This season I'm going to take note of this as it is the most out of order in terms of when episodes were filmed and when they aired. Also, *I Dream of Jeannie* did the same type of story-line two seasons earlier not to mention CBS began airing four days earlier an entire series devoted to this same type of story-line with *Land of the Giants*. Speaking of series premiers, this month *Julia* on NBC, *Here's Lucy*, *The Doris Day Show*, *Hawaii 5-0*, and *60 Minutes* all on CBS, and *The Mod Squad* and *Here Come the Brides* on ABC all made their series debut.

We also see that over the summer, in addition to getting new plumbing installed like Samantha told Sheila they were going to do in Episode #126: "Snob in the Grass," the living room got new wall paper, which I totally don't like. I really liked the previous two seasons' wall-paper. There was also a closet installed in the wall across from the stairs. And where is Tabatha?

Sony did a good job fixing the HUGE tear in the film at the first of this episode just as the dishes are about to disappear. You can see it on the video version. But I will say that this episode was really jumpy, especially in the scenes with Durwood on the table. Did you also notice how at one point the mug looks like it's actually sitting on the pencil that's on the table? Shoddy work, in my opinion.

I LOVE Liz's new long blonde hair…too bad later in the season it goes darker again and way poofy. This season is my least favorite where her hair is concerned.

The beginning scene with the wind blowing the dishes all over and Durwood saying, "Just once I wish she'd leave the room in the normal way" is a clip used in the Fifth Season promo that Liz narrates. DARN Sony for not including that promo, though it was cool to have the clouded over Chevy logo WITH the proper credits! On the video it has the credits to "The No-Harm Charm" and it's just the regular witch.

I also wonder why the trash included doll furniture that didn't even seem as if it were broke!

OCTOBER 3, 1968

It was on this night that ABC aired Episode #142: "Samantha Goes South for a Spell."

Just as Samantha and Tabatha leave to go shopping, a new long and dark-locked Serena stealthily arrives with a raven on her shoulder who keeps cawing, "Let me out!" Serena finds Samantha's note to Durwood and decides she'll play a trick on him by pretending to be Samantha. She hides the talkative bird and changes herself into Samantha just as Durwood arrives downstairs in the kitchen. She immediately wraps her arms around him and gives him a huge kiss! And wouldn't you know it, Samantha walks in on this, having forgotten her shopping list, and stops her cousin's kissing game. Before she can reprimand Serena they all hear "let me out" coming from the closet and Serena unwillingly lets the bird out. Durwood leaves for his golf game so Samantha can sort things out with Serena who tells Samantha that the bird is really a warlock boyfriend of hers named Malcom who happened to omit the fact that he is married. So, of course, they are hiding out at 1164 from his wife. Before Samantha can object to this, they hear the noise of impending doom in the guise of Malcom's furious wife, Brunhilde. Malcom flies up to the rafters and Serena disappears as Samantha heads out to the patio to see what the cause of all this commotion is. In huge puffs of smoke, a plump evil looking witch appears mad as hell and out for revenge on the witch who stole her husband and assumes that Samantha is she. Samantha tries to explain who she is, but Brunhilde won't have it and freezes her. In her rants, she mentions how in the olden days they would've put the mistress away and then it occurs to Brunhilde that maybe this mistaken mistress should be sent to the good old days and sends her back one hundred years, and also a couple hundred miles as Samantha ends up in New Orleans circa 1868! Worse than that, she has no recollection of who she is!

While Brunhilde and Samantha's confrontation was ensuing, Serena was watching from the indoor staircase and before Brunhilde can tear

Samantha, now a Southern belle, doesn't remember who Durwood is, though he claims to be her husband.

apart the house, Serena releases Malcom from his fowl encasement. He claims that Serena put a spell on him against his will and Brunhilde forgives him and they leave.

Back in 1868, Samantha runs into Aunt Jenny who decides that she must take Samantha to her employer's plantation as she seems to be lost. Aunt Jenny's employer is the rogue Rance Butler who won't hear of taking in a stray, until he sees just how beauteous this stray is.

In the present (1968), Durwood has arrived home to find that his wife is now back in 1868 with no memory and Serena, after dissecting Brunhilde's spell, tells him that the only way Samantha can get her memory back and return is for her to receive a kiss from her true love. Which means Serena must send Durwood back to break the spell. He does so reluctantly with a photograph of his wife which he shows to the New Orleans townsfolk who had seen Samantha taken by Aunt Jenny.

When Durwood shows up at the Butler plantation claiming to be Samantha's husband, Aunt Jenny fears that her employer is going to commit bigamy causing her to lose her job, but Rance won't hear of it. He doesn't believe this stranger's claims, even more so when the stranger keeps calling the girl "Sam" and asks her to take off her dress to show off a mole in the middle of her back that only a husband would know of! Rance throws him out with instructions to never show his face again!

Later that evening, as Samantha is getting ready for bed, she wonders about the awkward stranger calling her "Sam" but then realizes he's got a weird name in "Darrin." After the house has become quiet, Durwood makes another attempt by climbing up, and falling off, the trellis but eventually he succeeds in entering Samantha's room. He covers her mouth startling her awake and tries to explain to her that it would be in her best interest not to scream. She agrees and proceeds to bite him causing him to scream. Both Rance and Aunt Jenny hear this and come running in. Rance immediately challenges Durwood to a duel, which becomes pretty violent ending in Durwood seemingly getting sliced, though Rance points out he merely tore his shirt. Before the fight can proceed, Samantha feels pity for Durwood and demands that Rance stop. She then gives Durwood a kiss and both disappear leaving Aunt Jenny and Rance quite bewildered.

The next day Durwood thinks he's had a dream about all this until he realizes that he has a bruise where he fell from the trellis and that the sabre duel seemed quite real and with that he faints.

Aunt Jenny was played by a pre-Weezy Jefferson Isabel Sanford and Rance was played by Jack Cassidy, father of Partridge family heart-throb David Cassidy. Both gave excellent performances here.

I would definitely give this one three and a half stars. It would've got more but here we are, the second episode into the season (and oddly enough the first one filmed and it should've been the first one aired), and NO TABATHA?! I always wondered where she was especially when we never saw her go out the door with Samantha.

This is one of my favorite Serena episodes. I like her long dark hair and I think she has a lot of great lines like "Exactly darling" and "You always make big deal out of nothing!"

Brunhilde was cool and they really should've had her come back. I can totally see a big fight between her and Endora.

I also thought it weird that Samantha was "in character" for 1868 New Orleans but Durwood wasn't. But Liz still did it perfectly and I found that she reminded me a lot of Carol Burnett in her delivery of some of her lines. I also like it when Rance tells her that the singers just love him and she looks puzzled and says, "Then why do they keep singing "Masses in the cold, cold ground"?"

I've also noticed that with this Fifth Season a lot of minor movements in all the characters are accompanied by some music or sound effect. I also love the pop in/out sound effect that accompanies Malcom when he is transformed and then when he and Brunhilde leave. It would later become Dr. Bombay's popping sound effect.

Of course, this episode was inspired by the 1939 multi-Oscar winning movie *Gone with the Wind*, which was re-released in the U.S. in October 1967 though the U.K. would get a re-release of the picture a couple weeks after this episode aired. And though Aunt Jenny was supposed to be the equivalent of Mammy, I think, and don't bet your plantation on this, that they costumed her more after Aunt Jemima of the syrup fame, which was owned by *Bewitched* sponsor Quaker Oats. I would bet that this episode was sponsored by Quaker Oats that evening but I couldn't find documentation to back this up.

Three nights previously, Vice President Hubert Humphrey's address to the Nation on Vietnam and American Foreign Policy aired on NBC as per the Papers of David C. Hoeh at Dartmouth College (Box 6, Folder 27). Per Dartmouth's website "in 1968, Hoeh was instrumental in persuading Eugene McCarthy to enter the New Hampshire Primary election, and became Chairman of the New Hampshire McCarthy For President Committee. As Chairman of the New Hampshire delegation at the Democratic National Convention in Chicago, Hoeh made national headlines by his arrest for trying to prove that the credentials machines used at the convention were fraudulent."

OCTOBER 10, 1968

It was on this night ABC aired Episode #143: "Samantha on the Keyboard."

Samantha and Durwood find that Endora has gifted their daughter, TabItha (They have a daughter? Where has she been?) with a BABY baby grand piano and has "taught" her how to play it. Durwood doesn't like her teaching methods and blows up accusing her of being worse than the Wicked Witch of the West! Endora is insulted to be compared to such an amateur and she leaves, taking her gift with her. Samantha tells Tabitha that they'll get her another piano and sends her off to her room while she tries to calm Durwood down. She assures him that Tabitha will learn to play the mortal way and he wonders if it can be done and challenges her to learn the mortal way. She accepts and they rent a piano for her new lessons but it begs the question as to what happened to the piano they used to have.

Anyway, Samantha's instructor arrives the next day for her first lesson. He's quite self-absorbed and snooty. Even his name, Johann Sebastian Monroe, sounds quite pretentious, and Samantha sees that her lessons may be more difficult than previously anticipated, especially when he condescendingly shows her where the black and the white keys are.

The next day, just before Mr. Monroe arrives for Samantha's next lesson, Tabitha is banging away on the keys causing Endora to help her play a little better with some magic. Mr. Monroe arrives and when he hears that the beautiful piano playing is coming from a four-year old girl, he is astonished and pleased believing he has found the world's next child prodigy! He insists that he begin coaching Tabitha and take her on a forty city tour in forty weeks. Samantha and Durwood are not pleased with this at all but it seems Mr. Monroe will not hear of anything else. They ask him to let them have the night to think it over and he accepts.

Samantha decides that maybe the way to get out of this is to find Mr. Monroe another piano child prodigy, one that truly knows how to play. Durwood agrees and so she casts a spell to find one and when she hears him playing, pops off to find him. She lands in a high school where she discovers young Matthew Williams, son of the school janitor, playing. He is playing on the school piano because his family is too poor to buy one. Samantha tells him that will all change once she gets him in touch with Mr. Monroe.

Almost immediately after she pops home, the doorbell rings and she opens it to discover Mr. Monroe with Maestro Farrinini, a world famous conductor and the object of Mr. Monroe's admiration. He has brought him over to hear Tabitha play. The Maestro is even more self-absorbed than Mr. Monroe and demands the child get on with it. Without Grandmama Endora's assistance, Tabitha bangs away on the piano frustrating the Maestro and totally embarrassing Mr. Monroe. Samantha tells Mr. Monroe that he shouldn't feel too bad, that she has found another prodigy for him. And after a couple weeks it turns out that Matthew was just what Mr. Monroe was looking for. It also turns out that Samantha could learn to play the piano mortal style and she shows off for Durwood only to be upstaged by her mother and Tabitha fiddling.

This is the first time in the series that Tabitha's name is spelled with an "I" in the ending credits. Elizabeth Montgomery most likely is the one that got this changed as she said in a 1967 Screen Stories magazine interview:

> "...Tabitha is the name I picked for the daughter Dick York and I were supposed to have...But, somehow or other, her name came out 'Tabatha' on the credit roll, and that's the way it's been ever since. Honestly, I shudder every time I see it. It's like a squeaky piece of chalk scratching on my nerves."

Gerald Edwards, who played Matthew, would later go on to play Weird Harold on Bill Cosby's *Fat Albert and the Cosby Kids*.

Jonathan Harris played Mr. Monroe. His series *Lost in Space* had just been cancelled this past March.

I'd rate this two stars but only because I really enjoy the piano playing and it seems that the witchcraft is virtually flawless. It doesn't seem that there are any jumps in the film when anyone pops in or out like there usually is.

It seems lame that they would have to rent a piano when every other time ("The Short Happy Circuit of Aunt Clara" and "No Zip in My Zap") they needed one it was just there by the window.

I thought the scene at the beginning with Durwood nibbling Samantha was really cute and sexy! It seems like they hadn't any scene like that since the First Season!

All though Jonathan Harris was perfect for this role, he is WAAAAAY too over the top and seems to not fit in on *Bewitched*.

I did think the ending scene with Endora and Tabitha was really cute. Looks like they had a lot of fun.

The next day NASA launched Apollo 7, the first manned Apollo flight with goals of the first live telecast from orbit and tests of the lunar docking maneuver.

OCTOBER 17, 1968

It was on this night ABC aired Episode #144: "Darrin, Gone and Forgotten" (I know. I said the same thing — "Who's Darrin?").

After cleaning up the evening dishes, Durwood and Samantha discuss settling down for a nice after dinner drink, which Durwood says he'll make while Samantha finishes up in the kitchen. When Samantha enters the dining area after Durwood not responding to her question, she finds that he is not there. When she calls after him and still gets no response, she fears he might actually have disappeared and calls the first person she can think of that would do such a thing to him — "Mother!"

Endora appears in a wetsuit as she was deep sea diving with world famous oceanographer Jacques Eve Cousteau and forgets her irritation when she hears that Durwood is gone! But she promises that it wasn't she

Samantha and Endora are startled by an evil laugh while trying to figure out where Durwood disappeared to.

that did it. Samantha wonders aloud who would do such a thing and is quite worried until she realizes it may be a prank of Uncle Arthur's. But before her worry goes away, it gets bigger when both she and Endora hear a rather nefarious laugh followed by an explosion of clouds revealing the perpetrator of Durwood's disappearance, the witch Carlotta. It seems that Endora knows Carlotta and apparently had made a pact with her at the beginning of the century ("Vanity prevents me from naming which") that Endora's first born daughter would be the bride of Carlotta's first born son when the planet Icarus passes between Pluto and Jupiter, and apparently that time has come. Samantha is furious realizing that her mother just put her in an arranged marriage, like something out of the Middle Ages, which Endora says is when she made the pact. Samantha refuses to oblige until Carlotta shows her where Durwood is, and that is running from bodiless wild animal voices in limbo. Samantha feels she has no other choice and dons her flying suit and pops off to Carlotta's heavenly home to meet her son, Juke.

Up in the clouds, Samantha finds that Juke's cloud room is decorated all over with pictures of herself. Carlotta introduces Samantha to Juke, who is an embarrassment of a warlock, dressing like Little Lord Fauntleroy and jumping at his mother's every command. Juke reveals that he didn't decorate his room himself but that his mother did it, and in fact he didn't want to marry Samantha. She tells him he should stand up to his mother and practices with him what he should say to her. When he finally does confront her, she gets furious with him and puts him back in his place. Samantha, at a loss for what to do, pops back to Earth.

After discussing her concerns with Endora, she decides maybe the best thing to do would be not to give in to Carlotta's threats. Immediately Carlotta announces her arrival by an earthquake and she arrives with Juke just as Endora pops out. Carlotta is furious with Samantha for leaving but Samantha tells her that she doesn't think Carlotta really means her threats of putting the bodies back on the voices of the animals chasing Durwood. Just as Carlotta is going to do it, Juke stops her and Samantha decides to act like she has given up on Durwood thinking that Juke will tell his mother that he doesn't want to marry Samantha. Juke goes along with it and Samantha shows Carlotta that she has no more say in what Juke does when she zaps him into some hippie clothes. Carlotta zaps him back into his regular clothes and the two witches keep switching him back and forth until he decides he's had enough! He's going to stay with what Samantha gave him and his mother doesn't have a say in it. He also says that he does want to marry Samantha, which surprises her. But she also sees that Carlotta still wants to control her son, even after he is married, but Samantha tells her that she will only be allowed to see her son on certain days and they will not live with her. Carlotta doesn't like this at all and cancels the marriage. Samantha also suggests that Carlotta give Juke more freedom if he lives with her, and Juke agrees and so the marriage is off. Carlotta tells Samantha she'll return Durwood once Juke comes back to her and she pops off. Juke thanks Samantha and pops out, a new warlock. Before Durwood comes back, Samantha races back to the kitchen.

Durwood pops in not realizing he has even been gone and he tells Samantha he's so glad they are going to have a nice quiet evening together.

A couple months later Endora arrives with a letter from Juke who just recently married. He wanted to thank Samantha for giving him the courage to stand up to his mother though by the sounds of it, he has married a girl just like her.

I LOVE this episode as it was totally weird that Durwood would just up and vanish without anyone, even Endora, knowing where he went.

I honestly do NOT believe that Endora was frightened or really believed that "zap for zap, Carlotta's unbeatable." I think that she merely said that to have Samantha believe it thus making it easier for Samantha to actually leave Durwood. Here is what I think happened between Carlotta and Endora at that party:

Carlotta and Endora were, once upon a time, real Best Friends Forever. Around the time of the party, Carlotta met Maurice and they began dating. Well, as the cosmos would have it, Carlotta introduced Maurice to her friend Endora and he fell instantly in love. Of course, this wasn't Endora's fault, but of course Carlotta wasn't too pleased. A little bit after this was the party Endora mentions and in the course of the evening Carlotta tells Endora she can have Maurice, as though Endora needed permission — keep in mind this is all to keep Carlotta happy — if Endora promises her first born daughter to Carlotta's first born son, a rather medieval arrangement, but under the influence of all that ambrosia, it would make sense. Endora, not really paying attention to Carlotta, or even dreaming that she was serious, agreed. Well, life went on, Endora and Maurice hooked up and had Samantha, Carlotta went on her way, met some wimpy warlock, had Juke but after all those centuries remembered the agreement from that party, and as Icarus doesn't pass between Jupiter and Mars very often and as mortal marriages don't count, she just waited for Icaraus and then came to collect.

In the episode we see that Endora is rather shocked at Carlotta showing up, probably 'cause she can't believe that Carlotta would actually take that agreement seriously, but then she realizes this just may be the circumstance to get Samantha out of the irreputable mortal marriage that she had promised Hepzibah and the Witches' Council she would break up, which is why she ACTS like she can't fight against Carlotta and help Samantha, but we all know that she could very well kick her ass without even smearing her eyeliner!

Anyway, this is the first time we see the green shimmery flying suit, which is my favorite!

I have to say that it seems that the pop outs and all were done EXTREMELY well, barely a film jump at all. I really like when Carlotta and Samantha are zapping Juke back and forth between outfits.

The cloud room was cool when I was little, but now-a-days is less than worthy of our show and were I to have tons of technical knowledge, I would replace them with real clouds and make it look like they really are in the sky. It's awesome that we can see that picture of Liz and her cousin Amanda "Panda" Cushman, who may have been the inspiration for Serena as they looked quite similar growing up. I wish we had a recent photo of her.

Oddly enough this episode was the second to finish filming, which I find odd because it's nowhere near all the episodes that Dick York will miss later on though he is barely in this episode.

And where the hell is Tabitha?!

Here are a few of my favorite lines:

> CARLOTTA: *"Endora, you're a sight for sore eyes!"*
> ENDORA: *"And you're a sight too…"*

Three days before, the U.S. Department of Defense announced that the Army and the Marines will send back about 24,000 on involuntary second tours to Vietnam.

Three days after the episode aired, former First Lady Jacqueline Kennedy married Greek shipping tycoon Aristotle Onassis on the Greek island of Skorpios. It was also on that day that Agnes Moorehead guested on *The John Gary Show*.

OCTOBER 24, 1968

It was on this night ABC aired Episode #145: "It's So Nice to Have a Spouse Around the House."

Endora pops in on Samantha during an earth-shattering mission — making Durwood breakfast — to give her a message from the Witches' Council. Samantha is requested to make an appearance in front of them considering she's only done so twice since she's been married. Before Samantha can truly object, Durwood walks in and rather than spoil his morning by seeing his mother-in-law, he opts to retrieve the morning paper. With him occupied, Samantha tells her mother that she has no intention of gracing the Council with her presence as she's too much to do around the house. And besides, Durwood would object anyhow. Endora warns her that they will be upset but Samantha doesn't care. That is, until she hears the low rumbling of thunder somehow not related to an impending rainstorm. Knowing that it's related to the Council, and most likely Durwood, she runs outside to find that she's now married to a bronze likeness of her husband, a hollow bronze likeness at that. Endora is tickled at the Council's move but Samantha asks her to go away so she can plan her next move. Endora obliges and Samantha decides to ask the noble eight members of the Witches' Council to release Durwood from his bronzing so she can ask him about going. The Witches' Council complies with her request but Durwood is a bit agitated knowing that something has just happened, but he's not sure what, though it involved his attracting little birds to his head. Samantha finally explains and asks him if she can go and he vehemently refuses her request stupidly telling her that first she's his wife, then she's a witch. Samantha accepts her defeat as she sees him leave to get ready for his golf game, which he did rather quickly considering Endora has popped back in.

Endora tells Samantha that she cannot NOT go to the Council, no matter what Durwood says. Samantha realizes that her mother is right and tries to think of a way out of it when it occurs to her that she can enlist Serena to cover for her by turning herself into Samantha and show up to the Council. Endora suggests that the Council would see right through the deception but Durwood wouldn't and so Samantha decides to ask Serena to take her place at home while she goes to the Council.

After contacting Serena, the care-free cousin shows up in the midst of meditations and isn't exactly thrilled at the idea, but agrees. Samantha pops off to the Council and right after, Tabitha shows up with some flowers that she had just picked for her mommy but sees that Auntie Serena is there looking like her mommy. Realizing this won't bode well for when Durwood comes back, Endora takes Tabitha to the zoo.

Meanwhile, Durwood's golf game doesn't go so well because he feels bad for the way he acted towards Samantha. Larry suggests that he take Samantha for a romantic weekend to make up and Durwood agrees.

Serena shows up in the midst of her meditations. If you look closely near the top of the photo, you can see the wires holding Elizabeth Montgomery up.

When he arrives home, he finds "Samantha" draped across the couch magically flipping the pages of a magazine while a duster dusts and the vacuum vacuums. When Serena notices that he's at home, she immediately zaps away all the magically moved items and apologizes. Durwood tells her that though he doesn't approve of witchcraft, he's gonna let it slide this time as he's sorry and wants to make up for his actions of earlier. He tells her that he wants to take her somewhere but he won't tell her where, though he seems rather excited, and frisky, about it. Serena cannot believe this and after he goes upstairs to pack, she hollers for Endora, who appears. When she tells Endora what he wants, her only suggestion is to go along with it, as that's what Samantha would do.

And so Durwood, his cousin-in-law in disguise, and Mother Nature head off for Moonthatch Inn, where Durwood and Samantha had spent their honeymoon. Serena tries to get him to turn back but he's a man on a mission. After he leaves her in the room so he can go get their luggage, she tries to come up with a way to get out of it by zapping up a "Closed for Business Sign" and a bed of nails on the bed, but she knows that both of those ideas are way too far out. When he returns, whistling the marriage march, and pulls out her sexy nightie she can't take it anymore and zaps away the bed. Durwood is irritated thinking Samantha is mad at him and not accepting of his apology. Serena tries to tell him that she's just embarrassed and would rather go home and so they do.

By this time, Samantha has returned from the Council and Endora tells her the whereabouts of her cousin. Samantha is horrified to think of what is going on until they hear the car pull up. Samantha pops out just as Serena and Durwood walk in, embarrassed by one another but also mad. Durwood goes upstairs to say "night night" to Tabitha and Serena begs Endora for Samantha's whereabouts. Samantha pops back in and Serena, after changing back into her flower child self, tells Samantha that the next time she needs a stand in to call a theatrical agent and with a click of her cymbals, pops out.

Upstairs, Tabitha asks Durwood if Auntie Serena brought her back anything. When he tells her Auntie Serena wasn't there, she tells him she was there this morning and he then realizes what has been happening all day.

As he and Samantha get ready for bed, he tells her that he is so tired from the "activities" at Moonthatch Inn and how wild he thought she was. Samantha is thunderstruck to think that her cousin let things go so far until Durwood asks her how things went at the Council. Then she realizes that he was just playing his own little deception and that he truly is sorry for having put them in the predicament in the first place.

This episode was the fifth to be filmed this season and also the fifth to be aired.

I think this episode is SOOOO funny and nerve-wracking thinking that Durwood might just bag Serena! Dick York is simply hysterical and I can't see how any of the cast kept a straight face during the filming of this episode.

I like it that Serena is slowly becoming her kooky self and I also enjoyed that line about "What should I do now, dust something?"

I also really liked Durwood's comment about how they'll be as free as the birds…and the bees.

It's quite obvious that Moonthatch Inn isn't the same place as the honeymoon suite in the first episode. Considering Samantha said in "If They Never Met" that their honeymoon was in Atlantic City, I would think that maybe Moonthatch Inn was some place closer to home where they stayed after Atlantic City just to extend the honeymoon a little longer.

This is the first time the Witches' Council is mentioned. And I think Samantha is alluding to her time as Queen at the end when she tells him at the end that she had promised that all Council meetings would take place in their house.

The day before, Elvis Presley's movie *Live a Little, Love a Little* premiered co-starring Dick Sargent.

OCTOBER 31, 1968

Bewitched fans were truly bummed out when we found that our show had been pre-empted, on Halloween of all days, in order for President Lyndon B. Johnson to announce a complete halt of U.S. bombing over North Vietnam in the hopes to restart peace talks. Keep in mind that Democratic Pres. Johnson's Vice President Hubert Humphrey was in the very last days of the Presidential Election running against Richard M. Nixon, so this bode well for the Democrats.

This would mark the first time in *Bewitched* history that there wasn't a Halloween episode. But this would've also been the first time that a *Bewitched* episode fell on Halloween and I'm sure we would've all been out Trick or Treating anyway, so really not a loss.

NOVEMBER 7, 1968

Tonight *Bewitched* returned on ABC after a week hiatus with Episode #146: "Mirror, Mirror on the Wall" sponsored by Kodak and their instamatic camera.

Durwood is worried that he's starting to show his age and might not be relevant to the youth of today, especially when trying to capture their attention in his advertising campaigns. Samantha assures him he's worried for nothing before he leaves for work but Endora, who pops in, thinks he's being quite vain. Completely disagreeing, Samantha assures her mother that Durwood doesn't have a vain bone in his body. Endora tells her she's not too sure of that and pops off.

A little while later, while Durwood is waiting at a red light, Endora invisibly pops in to the back seat and casts a spell on him making him super vain. Traffic backs up when Durwood finds that that he can't take his eyes off his reflection in the rear view mirror.

Meanwhile, Larry is meeting with the quite conservative Mr. Hascomb of Hascomb Drugs to discuss his campaign. Mr. Hascomb wants to stay with his quite old advertising but his wife thinks he should update it to fit in more with the modern society. Larry assures him that Durwood is a conservative man and he should fit right with Hascomb Drugs current style. Just as he finishes this statement who should breeze through the door but the NOT conservative, but very hippie mod, Durwood, who is wearing love beads and a turtleneck shirt beneath his suit coat. Larry is utterly shocked but not more than Mr. Hascomb who can't get over Durwood's fascination with his reflection. They decide they will meet later for cocktails so that Mr. Hascomb can think more on whether he'd like to continue his business with McMann and Tate. After Mr. Hascomb leaves, Larry threatens Durwood to not mess up the meeting.

Durwood leaves early and goes on a shopping spree buying even more hippie clothes and when Samantha sees what he has done, especially his fascination with mirrors, she knows her mother is up to no good. She tries to persuade him not to go to the meeting in his new clothes but he refuses. When Endora also refuses to appear and take the spell off, Samantha takes matters into her own hands and removes Durwood's beads as well as whipping up his regular suit. When he notices the changes he tries to look at his reflection in a pool at the restaurant and manages to fall in, embarrassing both himself and Larry.

A little while later, while Samantha is whipping up a cake, mortal style, she is suddenly surprised when she hears Durwood roar her name causing her to spray cake batter all over herself. When she greets him in the foyer, she sees that his clothes have become more outlandish and after magically cleaning herself up, she tries to clean him up, but he refuses. He also tells her that the meeting had been postponed to that evening at the Tate's and that he had bought even more clothes for it and he goes to change.

When he shows off his new outfit, Samantha is practically blinded by his fourteen karat gold lamé jacket and his new paste-on sideburns. Samantha knows that she is going to have to show him how ridiculous he is being by sparkling herself, so she zaps on a silver disc dress with feather boa, a very short silver dress.

They end up at the Tate's along with the Hascombs where Mrs. Has-

Samantha goes to zap on some glitz for herself after being blinded by Durwood's clothes.

comb has been trying to get her husband to see how old fashioned he is. She absolutely loves Durwood's youthful look and attitude and tells her husband that he should adopt some of Durwood's ways. Mr. Hascomb objects until she reminds him that she is the major stock-holder in the company and that Durwood should be the one to handle the account.

The next day, after Endora has taken the spell off, Durwood shows up dressed still like a hippie through no fault of Endora. It seems that everyone loved the new modern advertising from McMann and Tate so Larry wants Durwood to dress the part still.

As I mentioned above, this episode was sponsored by Kodak, a new sponsor to *Bewitched* this year. Before the end credits, a commercial starring Elizabeth Montgomery and Agnes Moorehead touting the Instamatic camera that is "easier to use than witchcraft" aired.

This episode was the seventh filmed but the sixth to air.

I LOVE THIS EPISODE! I would definitely give it four stars. Dick York is hysterical! I LOVE his facial expression when he walks into the office for the first time after the spell. And I really like that they play the music usually saved for Serena.

Now most of my stars though go to how HOT Liz is! And the thing is, she sparkles even when she's NOT wearing the sparkly dress.

William Asher makes a brief cameo as the irritated driver behind Durwood, which is funny because I noticed that DICK Michaels is actually the director of this episode! So then it makes me wonder if Bill Asher was just on set to make sure he was doing a good job considering it was only his third episode to direct.

My favorite line is from Samantha when she says, "If you can dare gold lamé, I can dare anything!"

Two nights before, Richard M. Nixon won the Presidential Election to become the thirty-seventh President of the United States of America in one of the most stressful years our country has ever seen.

NOVEMBER 14, 1968

It was on this night ABC aired Episode #147: "Samantha's French Pastry."

When Samantha opens her oven to check on her angel food cake, she finds her Uncle Arthur occupying the pan instead along with a hefty serving of his awful jokes. He says he's just come to visit but Samantha tells him tomorrow would be a better time as they are having the Tates over for dinner. She asks him to restore her cake and leaves the kitchen to attend to things in the dining room. Uncle Arthur thinks angel food cake is too cafeteria to serve and decides he'll zap up a nice French dessert, in the way of a napoleon. When he mis-rhymes a word in his incantation, he ends up with a napoleon all right, THE Napoleon, the Emperor of France from the 19th century! Of course, Durwood is upset and oddly seems surprised that this sort of thing could happen even though he's had Ben Franklin and Franklin Pierce in his home and has even traveled back to 17th century Plymouth not even a year before now! Samantha tries to act mad, but she seems to think it's funny, though she does tell Uncle Arthur he must get rid of Napoleon before the Tates get there.

Uncle Arthur tries to think of a spell and the arm gestures to accompany it but it doesn't work and wouldn't you know it, the Tates arrive! Durwood tells Arthur he's a failure as a warlock, insulting Arthur, who leaves. Samantha tries to get Napoleon to hide in a closet but he insists he won't, so Samantha tells him he can stay only if he promises not to reveal his true identity to the Tates. He promises and Samantha conjures up a modern day suit for him and passes him off as her cousin Henri from Paris.

During dinner Larry realizes that Henri seems familiar to him because he looks so much like Napoleon, which sparks the great idea for a commercial for Zoom detergent. He asks Henri to appear in the commercial, and he accepts seeing it as a way to conquer England, much to the chagrin of Durwood and Samantha.

The next day Henri is dressed as Napoleon and begins to shoot his first commercial for Zoom, but he is a terrible over-actor and Mr. Bradley, the chairman of the board for Zoom, thinks he's all wrong for the part. He tells Larry that he believes he will take his product elsewhere which causes Larry to get mad at Durwood for having the nerve to marry Samantha, who is Henri's cousin.

Back at home, Arthur shows up believing he has the correct way of sending Napoleon back and that is to do the spell backward. He tries it and it fails. Dejected, Samantha utters, "Oh bat wings and lizard tails" which happens to be the correct spell as Napoleon leaves in a puff of smoke.

It is sad that Uncle Arthur, who once upon a time could match his sister Endora in a house zapping contest ("Endora Moves in for a Spell"), has been reduced to not being able to reverse his own spell. And it's also a sad reminder that Aunt Clara won't ever be coming back.

That being said, Liz is gorgeous in this episode! And Uncle Arthur and Napoleon are very funny. One of my favorite lines is from Uncle Arthur to Nap: "Now stand up. All the way."

I also liked Samantha and Uncle Arthur's interactions. It seemed that Samantha, once upon a time, reveled in the practical joking when she starts to giggle at her Uncle's jokes, only to be immediately shot down by Durwood, who seems to be menstrual in this episode.

The camera man's lines are a repeat of the hotel manager's lines from the Third Season "Bewitched, Bothered and Infuriated."

By the way, David White was fifty-two when this episode was filmed though, as Larry, he says he is only forty-seven.

I also liked the client's comeback to Samantha when she said she uses Zoom all the time. "As you should" and it was funny.

Two years previous, *I Dream of Jeannie* had an episode all about Napoleon, though instead of him coming to the future Jeannie and Tony went to his time.

And yet again, where is Tabitha?

This episode was the seventh to air yet it was the ELEVENTH to film! As a matter of fact, the episode to finish filming just before it was #164: "The Battle of Burning Oak" which won't air until March!

Three nights later, NBC would cause one of the biggest blunders in broadcast history when they cut off the close game between the Oakland Raiders and New York Jets with 1:05 to go by airing the movie *Heidi*. When the game was interrupted the score was 32-29 but Oakland would score two late touchdowns to win the game 43-32. Fans were so outraged they flooded the NBC switchboards.

NOVEMBER 22, 1968

It was on this night ABC aired Episode #148: "Is It Magic or Imagination?"

While giving the house a thorough cleaning, Samantha receives a phone call from Durwood's mother who says she's at the corner drug store and would like to come for a visit. Samantha tells her to come on over but frets over the house being in such disarray. She decides that she will clean it by herself but gives herself a bit of a boost with a speed up spell so that she cleans everything in seconds flat. Durwood sees this and, of course, is furious but before he can get any angrier she explains that it was because of his mother coming to visit. He decides to duck out before she can see that he hasn't had a hair cut in two weeks.

Mrs. Stephens arrives and tells Samantha about a contest where the winner will receive an all-expense paid two-week trip to Tahiti for two. She feels that Samantha and Durwood are in need of a vacation and as her friend Miriam Rogers just won a trip, she's sure Samantha can too. The entrant must merely come up with a slogan for Tinker Bell Diapers. Samantha thinks about it for a moment and comes up with "Tinker Bell Diapers. It's time for a change." Mrs. Stephens loves it and she has Samantha submit it.

Weeks later, when Samantha is checking the mail in their HUGE mailbox, she finds that her slogan has won which means she and Durwood are off to Tahiti! Or so she thinks as she can't get his attention to tell him before he heads off for the office bubbling over with excitement at the big business he is going to drum up with Barton Industries.

Durwood's bubble is burst when Larry reveals to him that a mere housewife came up with a great slogan for one of Barton Industries products, Tinker Bell Diapers, and what's more that housewife happens to be Samantha! Thinking that Durwood is trying to ruin their business, Larry fires him. When Durwood arrives at home, he accuses Samantha of sabotage but she promises she didn't. When he still doesn't believe

Though this photo is from "Is It Magic or Imagination?," Durwood and Samantha never have a scene on the patio, which means this may have come from a cut scene.

her, she goes up to their room and locks the door. He tries to follow and bangs on the door only to find himself banging on nothing as she has zapped him downstairs.

Later on, Larry shows up to apologize to Durwood and offer him his job back, but more importantly, to offer Samantha a job with the company as he sees great potential in her as an addition to the company. Durwood is incensed that Larry's apology was insincere so he leaves to drown his sorrows at a bar. Samantha, of course, refuses to work for McMann and Tate and sets about trying to find Durwood. When she realizes where he may be, she zaps up a nanny sheepdog named Clarissa to tend to Tabitha, since apparently her mother and Aunt Hagatha aren't available, and pops off to the bar.

Durwood is none too happy to see her, not to mention sauced to the gills. When she asks him to come home with her, he refuses but she trumps him by intertwining her arms in his and zaps them both home. After he passes out, she zaps up a blanket to put on him and she goes to bed.

In the morning, Samantha sneaks downstairs and takes Durwood's ideas to Mr. Barton's where she leaves them on his desk. He loves the ideas and Larry calls up Durwood to tell him the great news. He also tells him that Samantha's Tinker Bell Diaper idea failed in a consumer analyzer test ran by a computer which means that Samantha really did just come up with the idea on her own.

I would only give this one and a half stars. It seems like Durwood is still PMS-ing like he was from last episode and Mrs. Stephens just bugs me!

The inclusion of Clarissa the dog is just so random. I wonder if she was supposed to be a recurring character. Her ears going up was ridiculous.

And why would Samantha sneak around Durwood to try and take his layouts to Barton when she could've just zapped them to her and then popped out?

All in all, a dull episode.

This episode was the ninth to be filmed, yet the eighth aired. As a matter of fact, "The Battle of Burning Oak" finished filming before it but will not air until later this season.

The next day the Beatles would release their self-titled album that would become known as the *White Album*.

NOVEMBER 28, 1968

Tonight, after we had stuffed ourselves to the gill on Thanksgiving delights, we settled in to watch TV, particularly ABC for *Bewitched*. We were kind of bummed out that we weren't given the Thanksgiving delight of a Thanksgiving themed episode like last season, but still delighted in Episode #149: "Samantha Fights City Hall."

While at Willow Street Park, after Samantha has chided Tabitha for sliding up a slide in front of a boy, Samantha and the other mothers there find that the park is going to be shut down so that the grounds may be used for a new shopping center. The head of the construction crew explains that H.B. Mosler, a descendant of the original owner of the park, had leased the land to the city for a $1.00 a year for many years but had somehow forgot to send the dollar in this year. The women are outraged that this park, the only one in the city, is going to be demolished. The foreman says to take it up with City Hall and Samantha says they will just as soon as she finds out how to do so.

Samantha tries to set up an appointment with the City Council but they are so booked up that it seems pointless. When she brings this up

Samantha and the neighborhood women protest Mr. Mosler's plans to get rid of the park. The woman behind Samantha is Bewitched hair-stylist Peanuts, who would often play extra roles.

to Durwood, he tells her that they should stand up for their rights. She takes it to mean they should organize a protest rally and so begins to make signs.

The next day, Samantha and the other ladies show up at the park blocking the bulldozers. No matter what the foreman says, the ladies will not back down and so he challenges them to try and stop him. As he begins to move the bulldozers forward, Samantha zaps a couple mechanical failures eventually ending in the machine spitting oil all over him. He relents but H.B. Mosler shows up and threatens the protestors with a court injunction that could have all of them thrown in jail if they obstruct the construction crew the next day, and he leaves.

It so happens that H.B. Mosler is also owner of the EZ Way Rent-a-Cars for which McMann and Tate, specifically Durwood, is in charge of their advertising. When Mosler tells Larry and Durwood of the reason for his tardiness for their meeting, Durwood's stomach turns realizing Samantha is the reason for this.

At home, Durwood tries to talk Samantha out of any further protests for the park which confuses her as he had been on her side before. He confesses that H.B. Mosler is a big account for them and that he is the owner of the Save Most market chain. Samantha is glad he told her as now she and her fellow protestors will not shop there. They continue to argue into the evening where Samantha finally has enough of his attitude and zaps him to the couch, sans blanket, to sleep for the night.

The next morning, Samantha and her group appear on the front page of the newspaper infuriating Larry as he knows Mosler will see that Durwood's wife is the instigator of the protests. Larry is right when Mosler calls up wanting an explanation. Durwood realizes that he should be supporting his wife rather than the company and goes down to the park to back her up.

At the park, Mosler tells Samantha that if she doesn't stop the protests her husband will be taken off his account. Durwood and Larry arrive at the park where Durwood advises that no matter what Mosler does, he is standing by his wife. Samantha asks Mosler what his grandfather, the original owner of the park, would think of his actions. Mosler says he doesn't care until the statue of his grandfather standing next to them starts chiding him courtesy of a deft twitch by Samantha. Mosler realizes that he has tarnished the Mosler name and that the children his grandfather thought about when giving the park to the city are still important. He then announces that he gives the park back to the city.

After three episodes, Tabitha is back! But a bit different as this episode is the only one out of the whole series where Tabitha is played solely by Diane Murphy. Erin was sick when the filming was going on.

I really like this episode and would give it three stars. I like that the majority of the action takes place outside. I also like that Samantha decided to fight City Hall even if she didn't know how to do it.

I've always liked it when she told Durwood that she was glad he told her who Harlan Mosler was so that she can tell her friends not to shop at his store.

This is the second and last episode that Teddy Quinn has appeared in. He was the boy at the slide and appeared last season as Michael Milhouser who Tabatha turned into a bulldog in "Playmates." Ted, as he goes by now, has a MySpace page at *www.myspace.com/tedquinn*. He is a musician now.

Mrs. Bentley is played by Barbara Perry a.k.a. Pickles Sorrell (one of them at least) from *The Dick Van Dyke Show*.

Dodo Denney plays Mrs. Gurney. She will go on to play Mrs. TeeVee from *Willy Wonka and the Chocolate Factory* (1971). She got her career start on a local Missouri program called *The Witching Hour* playing Marilyn the Witch!

This episode also has a bunch of cameos by the infamous hairdresser Peanuts! She is seen as one of the protestors and later as the secretary that lets Mr. Mosler into the office.

Samantha jokingly tells Durwood that she got a meeting with the City Council on Tuesday, April 15, 1997 at 2:30 PM. Of course, April 15 is Elizabeth Montgomery's birthday and that particular day would've been her 64th birthday. Unfortunately, she passed away a little under two years previously.

This episode was the tenth to be filmed but the ninth to be aired.

DECEMBER 5, 1968

It was on this night ABC aired Episode #150: "Samantha Loses Her Voice."

After showing Tabitha the wonders of a mortal-style talking doll, Samantha finds that her TV now has a cord just like the doll, so she pulls it and finds that her TV now talks too, saying, "How-a-bout-a-kiss, baby?" The voice is none other than the practical joking warlock Uncle Arthur and when he appears on screen she asks him what he's doing there. He responds, "You turn me on!" which is funny and creepy at the same time. Sammy replies, "You better get out of there or I'll turn you off" which is quite funny and not creepy at all. Uncle Arthur pops out of the TV and, after a few more jokes, announces that his visit is to bring a birthday present for Tabitha, which is strange as it isn't her birthday. When Samantha apprises him of that fact, he says he's aware of that but it is the poodle's birthday he's brought with him and just zapped up. Apparently he found it when it was raining cats and dogs and Samantha suggests it was because he stepped in a poodle! Yes, they are here all night, folks! Tip your waiters! Anyhow, the doorbell rings and Samantha answers it to find a distraught Louise Tate with suitcases in tow along with the declaration that her marriage to Larry is over! Samantha suggests Uncle Arthur give them some time alone and so he and his puppy retreat to the patio. After some questioning, Samantha discovers that Louise is upset because when she and Larry were going to play volleyball, and Larry was one of the captains, well, he didn't choose her for his team. Realizing how ridiculous this is, but seeing that Louise is genuinely upset, Samantha tries to console her but it just doesn't seem to be enough. Louise has made up her mind and decides that she would like to rest for a while at Samantha's.

Meanwhile, across town at a bar, Durwood hears the same story from Larry though he finds that Larry made the decision simply because he finds Louise to be a very poor volleyball player, and of course, he wanted to win.

Back at 1164, Uncle Arthur comes back in wanting to know if Samantha is going to keep the poodle or not as he has to leave to take part in the Ostrich Derby. Samantha would love to keep the poodle, but she says she must discuss it with Durwood first as she can't speak for him. Uncle Arthur suggests she can speak for Durwood and makes a slight gesture at her. When she goes to refute his claim, she finds that she now literally can speak for Durwood as Durwood's voice is coming out of her mouth! Arthur thinks it's hysterical but Samantha is furious!

Well, if Samantha has Durwood's voice it only makes sense that back at the bar, while in the midst of conversing with Larry, Durwood suddenly finds himself speaking like Samantha! And so he leaves. When he arrives home, he finds out the cause for all this madness and also finds that Arthur can't reverse the spell for some reason. When Louise hears Durwood, she thinks that Larry may have come with him and absolutely refuses to see him. Samantha assures her Larry isn't there but as luck would have it, he comes knocking. Knowing that he can't see the switched voice phenomena, they don't answer the door, but this doesn't stop Larry who opens the window. When he asks why Durwood wouldn't open the door, Durwood feigns laryngitis. Louise hears Larry and becomes upset all over again but when Samantha tries to calm her down, Larry hears Durwood's voice and becomes incensed that Durwood would lie to him. He leaves, breaking the window.

With everything in a mess, Samantha demands that Arthur correct the voice problem and he tries but only succeeds in switching his and Samantha's voices! With another attempt, he fixes it and pops off with his puppy. Louise comes downstairs wanting to speak to Samantha, who just about obliges until Durwood's voice starts coming out of her mouth again. Louise thinks that they are playing tricks on her to make fun of her and as she runs out of the house, Larry has come back. While he is getting the story from her, Uncle Arthur appears again and realizes that the reason the voices didn't stick to their proper place was he didn't use 'stick-em' and incants another spell fixing the voice problem. Yet, Samantha and Durwood, who had been holding hands as part of the spell, now can't take their hands apart. Being offended by Durwood blowing his stack, Arthur pops out again just as Larry and Louise come back in. Samantha tells Larry that all this confusion was to make Louise feel rejected thus forcing her to go back to Larry and they both buy that story and leave more in love than ever. Later on, Uncle Arthur reappears and unsticks the hands leaving his niece and nephew-in-law more in love than ever.

I do think this episode is extremely funny, but I wouldn't rank it very high and here's why: I think the whole thing with Louise is lame getting mad over a volleyball game, so mad that she wants a divorce?! To me, it seemed that she was harboring 'Aunt Flo' at her house like Durwood seems to have been doing this season and I just didn't like it. Also the fact that Arthur, who was able to match his sister Endora zap for zap in the house zapping contest ("Endora Moves in for a Spell"), AGAIN has made a boo-boo and can't seem to fix it. I did like that Sammy and Durwood's voices switched and I thought Dick York did a marvelous job with his dubbing but, er, well...Elizabeth Montgomery just sounded weird to me as though she were reading the lines for the first time and didn't know how to do it, which is funny because she did such a fantastic job doing the same thing on *The Flintstones*.

Aside from all that, Uncle Arthur is extremely hysterical in this episode and even though I've seen it 2,947,293,472,934,723,479 times, I STILL laugh at his jokes, especially about the poodle being trained to kill and his feet killing him.

Two nights previously on NBC, Elvis Presley made his comeback on what became known at the *'68 Comeback Special*. He hadn't had a #1 song since 1962.

DECEMBER 12, 1968

It was on this night ABC aired Episode #151: "I Don't Want to be a Toad, I Want to be a Butterfly," winning for the longest title of a *Bewitched* episode so far.

Mrs. Stephens shows up with an early birthday surprise for Tabitha, and, really, for Samantha and Durwood. She has decided that Tabitha should be enrolled in nursery school. Of course, Tabitha's parents don't like this idea at all considering she's much more talented, supernaturally, than the other children. But, Mrs. Stephens won't hear any arguments, and so the following day, she takes Tabitha, along with Samantha, to Delightful Day Nursery School where they meet the teacher, Mrs. Burch. Another girl, Amy Taylor, is also enrolling late and she and Tabitha quickly become good friends. Samantha asks if she may stay this first day but Mrs. Burch advises that Delightful Day wouldn't allow that and so Samantha decides to talk to Tabitha about all the things she shouldn't do as far as flying and magic goes, before she leaves. Mrs. Stephens thinks Samantha is being too clingy and suggests they go shopping to take her mind off Tabitha and Samantha apprehensively leaves.

While shopping, Samantha can't help but worry about what is going on back at the school and when the sales lady offers up five different dresses for her to try on, Samantha realizes she can utilize the time in the changing room to pop back over to the school to spy.

Meanwhile, Mrs. Burch's class has been playing musical chairs with Amy and Tabitha being the last two in play. Samantha peeks through the door just as the music stops with the chair seat being in front of Amy. Before she can sit, Tabitha manually twitches her nose and turns the chair towards her and sits, winning the game. Mrs. Burch is astonished at witnessing the movement of the chair but quickly forgets it when she spies Samantha spying. Samantha tells her she just hadn't left yet and grudgingly does leave.

At the dress shop, Mrs. Stephens finds that Samantha won't respond to her questions and so the saleslady peeks in to find that the dressing room is empty! Samantha pops in just as Mrs. Stephens peeks her head in. Wanting to buy more time, Samantha says she didn't care for any of the dresses and asks for ten more and once she's back in the dressing room, she pops back to the school.

With musical chairs being done, Mrs. Burch decides to play a forest game with the children and assigns Tabitha to be a bunny and Amy as a toad with a little boy next to her being a butterfly. Amy whines that she wants to be a butterfly but Mrs. Burch assures her that little girls that spill their juice at play time cannot be butterflies and before she can go on, she is drawn away to the ringing telephone. An upset Amy withdraws from the group to cry and Tabitha follows her to give comfort. She assures Amy that toads are all right too, but Amy insists that she wants to be the butterfly. Not wanting to see her friend cry anymore, Tabitha twitches her nose and grants Amy's wish only too well: Amy becomes a real butterfly! Pleased with her new ability to fly, she flutters into the face of Mrs.

Burch to show off and then flutters out the window. Mrs. Burch wonders where Amy has gone to and discounts Tabitha telling her that Amy is the butterfly. Samantha pops in outside the classroom window and finds that Mrs. Burch is frantically looking for Amy, who has seemingly disappeared. Realizing that Amy might've actually disappeared due to Tabitha, Samantha gets Tabitha's attention and finds out the truth. Tabitha also

Samantha is discovered in a neighbor's tree as she searches for Butterfly Amy.

tells Samantha that Amy is now resting in a tree across the street and, as that's too far for Tabitha to reverse her spell, Samantha pops up into the tree to try and catch Amy. The owner of the tree is surprised to find Samantha up in his tree talking to the butterfly, especially since they are so high up, but Samantha tells him that the butterfly has a nice reward out for its capture and so, as he goes to enter into his house to get some nets, Amy flies off and Samantha disappears as she tries to follow. Amy flies up to the beams of a building under construction to rest nearby some workers who have stopped for lunch. Samantha pops in shortly afterwards and captures Amy in her net and disappears, bewildering the construction workers.

Back at the school, Samantha finds that Mrs. Burch is in even more trouble as Amy's mother arrived early to pick her up and so she gets Tabitha to quickly change Amy back. Amy runs to her mother with her great tales of adventure as a butterfly and is quite happy. But Mrs. Burch is frazzled after her crazy day and as Samantha tells Durwood later that evening, Mrs. Burch closes the school for a very long sabbatical.

I don't know what it is about this episode, but it feels like a script better suited for the Eighth Season when nobody seemed to care, though I do enjoy it. I do like that they've focused on Tabitha, but if we remember, the show was supposed to be about Durwood and Samantha.

I thought the conversation between Samantha and Tabitha about her mortal grandparents being sick was funny! And that part about Frank being out of town on business seems to always be cut out of syndication. And what business is he out of town on? Trying to sell his "magic" vending machines?

I really like Maudie Prickett. She's PERFECTION as the teacher, so it's no wonder they have her back all the other times they needed a teacher. I found her teaching methods a bit questionable though I know they wrote her lines for laughs. What teacher would instill into the kids the fact that it's always better to win? And not allowing Amy to be a butterfly, which she so wants, just because she spilled her juice? Just give her a check by her name like they did with us in school.

I thought Amy's dress was WAAAYY too short and inappropriate.

And any time I enter a store dressing room or a public bathroom stall I always think of Samantha popping out of the dressing room she was in.

I found that scene at the first when Tabitha twitches the cake over only for Mrs. Stephens to wonder how it got there, ridiculous as there was enough time, and Mrs. Stephens not paying attention, for Samantha to have stood up and reached for it. What would've made more sense would be to have the cake sitting on Mrs. Stephens' right side and have it float behind her to Tabitha.

Erin Murphy said that this was her favorite episode. She also mentioned on *www.harpiesbizarre.com* that she was given the real Monarch butterfly as a pet but lost it when she went to show the pool man outside.

This episode was the eleventh to air in the Fifth Season but was the fourteenth to finish filming.

DECEMBER 19, 1968

Tonight ABC aired Episode #152: "Weep No More, My Willow" presented by Kodak.

Durwood and Samantha's breakfast is interrupted by a snooping Mrs. Kravitz who has shown up with a petition signed by many people in the Morning Glory Circle neighborhood. Said petition is for the immediate removal of the willow tree located at the residence of Durwood and Samantha Stephens, said tree being a menace to the community. Apparently this particular tree was given to Samantha as a Mother's Day present the day Tabitha was born but in the last while has grown quite ill and for whatever reason, maybe she's concerned with how the neighborhood looks, Mrs. Kravitz feels it should be immediately removed. Durwood shockingly agrees with their neighbor but finds that Samantha has grown quite attached to the tree and will not back down. As Durwood leaves for work, taking "hitch-hiker" HOT next door neighbor Elaine Hansen with him, Samantha ponders her options for keeping the tree.

Having mulled over, and exercised, all her options, it's become apparent that nothing will work except for a magical intervention. And who better to cure her sick tree than the family warlock doctor, Dr. Bombay, who she summons from his ostrich race in Sydney, Australia. After building up his ego, and after his examination of the ill tree, Dr. Bombay casts a spell with the added admonition to "water the patient daily, keep the neighborhood pets away, and pray!" Samantha feels that the tree is already beginning to look better and with that Dr. Bombay zonks away. As Samantha gazes at her saved tree, a slight breeze blows up and, for seemingly no reason at all, Samantha begins to tear up and cry, though she isn't sad at all. She then realizes that part of Dr. Bombay's incantation included the prompting, "…with every wayward breeze, that within your branches leap, you will weep and weep and weep." Needing to get the doctor back to fix his 'cure,' Samantha runs back in the house. Of course, this whole time, Mrs. Kravitz has been watching from across the street seeing everything from Durwood taking the beautiful girl to work to Dr. Bombay's disappearing and Samantha's crying. Confused, but concerned, she decides to investigate by offering a plate of brownies to Samantha, which she immediately takes over.

Samantha is furious with Durwood for agreeing with Mrs. Kravitz's attempt to get rid of their willow tree.

Mrs. Kravitz walks in on Samantha talking to the air, but crying. She feels that Samantha is having a break down over what must be her heart ache at Durwood cheating on her, especially since he was so blatant about it. Samantha assures her that everything is fine, that she's simply distraught about her willow tree. Mrs. Kravitz leaves, but calls Durwood up to chew him out for hurting Samantha so much. Larry, who had seen Durwood dropping Elaine off, also thinks that Durwood is cheating especially when he hears Samantha crying on the phone, so he decides to pay Samantha a visit to check up on things since Durwood won't admit to his affair.

Meanwhile, after countless combinations of words to find Dr. Bombay, he finally appears to Samantha where she shows him that something is terribly wrong with herself. He does another incantation commanding that laughter replace the weeping and then, just as Larry is coming down the street, he pops out. Samantha now laughs at every wayward breeze, which Larry takes to mean that she's trying to cover something up. He takes her inside to try and get something out of her, but she cannot stop laughing. Durwood shows up shocked at Larry being there but totally confused over his wife's uncontrollable laughter, which seems to be contagious.

Once the breeze has died down, and Larry has left, Samantha summons Dr. Bombay once more. He commands once more that the winds cure the willow tree while taking the laugh away from Sam. The laughter does stop and Dr. Bombay promises that the willow tree will soon be unrecognizable and with that he zonks away. Just then some men of the city have shown up to chop down the tree. Samantha tells them they can't and she will fight up to even the Supreme Court if there is just one ounce of sap running through it. The lumber jacks dismiss her threats and just as they are about to lay the first blow, the tree suddenly blooms to life and they make like a tree, and leave.

I LOVE this episode! I think practically everything is perfect about it, especially Liz. She's gorgeous, she's got her acting skills on, and I love that dress she's wearing. I do think that the crying does sound a little forced but it's still funny, especially when she tells Mrs. Kravitz "Thanks for the brownies." And when she's laughing through the crying on the phone with Durwood is also hysterical!

It's interesting to note that though this is the twelfth episode of Season Five, it was actually the third one filmed! No wonder everything is green and leafy in Morning Glory Circle 'ceptin' for that willow tree, even though this episode aired a week before Christmas.

I think if Samantha would've said that the tree was "my very own Mother's Day present the YEAR that Tabitha was born" it would've made much more sense. I also think that Gladys' petition should've said that it was an eye sore rather than a menace, but that's just piddly things.

Dr. Bombay is AWESOME here! He's finally getting into his own…I mean, he was awesome in his previous episodes, but it seems this is the episode that defines him. This is also the first time that he is conjured by use of incantations rather than just zapping him up with hand gestures. I think maybe he was tired of people popping him from his bath unexpectedly and made it so you literally have to call for him. I love the incantations Samantha uses especially that last one, "From Maine to California, Dr. Bombay, I warn ya!" But the first one is my favorite:

From Tripoli to Timbuktu,
I beg! I plead! I beseech of you!
A moment longer, do not stay,
come to me, come to me, Dr. Bombay!

And speaking of incantations, I think that the first one he uses for the willow is my all-time favorite spell from *Bewitched*. It's really pretty and every time I see a willow tree, whether ill or not, I recite:

Weeping Willow, black with blight,
I command with all my might,
let your sap run free and bright.
And, with every wayward breeze,
which within your branches leap,
you will weep and weep and weep!

The funniest line, though, is after he returns and he tells her that she must've got caught in the fall out and she says, "That's what I said." Dr. Bombay: "That's where I heard it." Even though they've used that line before on *Bewitched*, it's funnier here.

And after his second try at curing the tree, I giggle every time he says, "It has rather a nice lilt to it, don't you think?" And he looks all pleased with how great his spell is…man, HE'S THE COOLEST!

I also think that this episode has the SMOOTHEST pop outs ever witnessed on *Bewitched*. You'd be hard-pressed to tell that they even moved an inch. Plus, I LOVE the sound effect used for Dr. Bombay popping out or in.

And maybe one of THE coolest cameos ever was brought to my attention by Mark Simpson and that is the voice of Charlie the Lumber Jack is voiced by none other than William Asher! How cool!

I also noticed that the closeups of Liz and Dick York at the end were filmed in the studio whereas the far shots were out at the Ranch and they totally didn't match where they were standing in either shot.

Liz told Herbie J Pilato (*Bewitched Forever*) that this was one of her favorite episodes because of the difficulty in switching between crying and laughing. And Dick York told him that they filmed the last scene with Larry at the end of the day, which made it all the more crazy, and they were told to NOT laugh at something, which made them laugh even more, and you can tell that all their laughing is genuine. David White's laughing is hysterical! It's like he's going to quit breathing!

All in all, one of my most FAVORITE episodes of the whole series!

The next night, Agnes Moorehead guested on *The Don Rickles Show*.

DECEMBER 26, 1968

Tonight, we were all still groovin' on our Christmas presents but found there to be no Christmas present in the form of a Christmas-themed *Bewitched* episode when ABC aired Episode #153: "Instant Courtesy." Even worse, it wasn't much of a regular *Bewitched* episode!

While setting up to do some ironing in the morning, Samantha suddenly finds herself in rags, chains, and fetters courtesy of, you guessed it, Endora, who says if she's going to work like a slave, she might as well look like one. Of course, Durwood gets his giblets in an uproar and comments about how he would like it if Endora would show some courtesy now and then by giving notice that she's going to drop in instead of dropping in like a hurricane. Endora finds this funny as she thinks Durwood would make a fortune giving rudeness lessons. Not wanting to banter with her anymore, Durwood leaves for work. Samantha tries to get Endora to see that he is really a kind and courteous person except when she's around and before she can say more, Durwood calls for her. Endora decides she'll really show how courteous Durwood is by casting a spell on him making him overtly courteous.

At the office, Durwood can't open enough doors, hang enough coats, and give enough compliments, making everyone very uneasy at all this kindness. It also happens that the Adrienne Sebastian Cosmetic account, specifically Adrienne Sebastian and her advertising manager Mr. Traynor, are coming in to see if they would like to hire McMann and Tate. Larry feels that the hard sell is what is needed, but with Durwood being so overtly kind and considerate, it makes Mr. Traynor uneasy. Especially when Mr. Traynor goes to make a phone call which Durwood insists on dialing causing Larry to demand he hang up the phone which he does on Mr. Traynor's hand. Larry takes Durwood aside to find out what all this is about, but Durwood assures him that he's just being courteous and that he is going to find the soft campaign ideas they had to present to Mrs. Sebastian. Of course, Durwood gets side tracked helping out big haired Elaine Hansen a.k.a. Miss Springer, the secretary, which more than makes the decision for Mr. Traynor that McMann and Tate will not be handling the account and with that he and Mrs. Sebastian leave. Along with it, goes Durwood's job.

At home, Durwood tells Samantha he has lost his job because of Larry's apparent dislike of his new chivalrous attitude. Samantha sees straight through this to her mother's spell and tries to get Endora to remove it but merely receives a note by flaming arrow saying essentially that she won't. Meanwhile, Mrs. Sebastian drops by to tell Durwood that she really liked his ideas and feels that maybe he would do better in his agency and the Sebastian cosmetics account can be the first. She says they'll talk it over later. Samantha then decides that she must fix this situation somehow and casts a spell to get Larry to apologize. The spell works and Larry shows up to do it in person.

Before he gets there, however, Endora finally shows up saying she's bored with the whole situation (and quite frankly, so am I) and she "disappears [the] courtesy."

Right after Larry shows up, Mrs. Sebastian returns and believes that Larry firing Durwood was a clever gimmick to get her account and she cancels her offer. Durwood tells her that she can do what she feels best but he would like her to have the other ideas. She at first refuses but then accepts, with a deft twitch from Samantha.

Larry and Durwood are more than over joyed and drink it up with a toast to their friendship. And to make the evening better, Mrs. Sebastian calls up to say that she loved the ideas and would like to set up business at McMann and Tate!

Oh, this episode is DULL, DULL, DULL! And what is with having the majority of the first act without Endora (except for just a bit at the elevator) and NO SAMANTHA?! I'm watching *BeWITCHed* for witches not Durwood and his boss, though Dick York and David White are great actors.

But I thought the pacing in the episode was really sporadic and just felt jolty or something. I just don't enjoy this episode, and it's especially a letdown after that magnificent piece of work that was "Weep No More My Willow."

This episode, and many like it in the days and seasons to come, follow the old formula like is mentioned in a *Far Side* cartoon, and which every 'mortal' thinks EVERY *Bewitched* episode is like. In the cartoon, it shows the writer room at *Bewitched* and one of them says, "Hey, how's this? Endora puts some kind of spell on Darren (sp) and no one can figure out what the heck is going on, until Samantha catches on!"

This episode was filmed as the eighteenth of the season but aired thirteenth of the season. It was also the last episode to air in 1968.

And speaking of this irregular filming schedule, the last episode to finish filming in 1968 was #160: "Mrs. Stephens, Where Are You?" on 12/11/68. This is the first of six consecutive filmed episodes that Dick York is missing from. I will mention the others around the time of their anniversaries beginning next month.

Three nights previous, Apollo 8 became the first manned spacecraft to circle the moon with the actual going behind the moon happening on Christmas Eve. It was then that astronauts Jim Lovell, Frank Borman, and William A. Anders took turns reading from the Book of Genesis, which was broadcast to the Earth. This mission also is where one of the most famous, if not most famous, photos of the Earth was taken. The mission lasted from December 21-27, 1968. The astronauts landed in the Pacific Ocean and, in a bewitching coincidence, were picked up by the U.S.S. Yorktown.

JANUARY 2, 1969

It was on this night ABC aired the first *Bewitched* episode of 1969 with Episode #154: "Samantha's Super Maid."

The Stephenses are having a nice relaxing Sunday morning flying paper airplanes that Durwood has made, when the phone rings. Samantha answers and finds that her mother-in-law would like to come over for a little talk-talk a.k.a. snooping. Not thrilled with yet another unwelcome visit from Phyllis, Samantha tries to talk Durwood into staying home from his golf game, but as even he doesn't want to stay around for his mother, she's stuck.

Just before Phyllis arrives, Endora pops in from smoking a hookah with the Shah of Xanadu and delights in having a confrontation with Durwood's mother. Samantha asks her to "hide her hookah" and dress in something more appropriate just as Phyllis arrives. After a few catty remarks, Endora pops out practically in front of Phyllis. She shakes it off and tells Samantha that she has decided that Samantha should hire a maid so that it will give her more time to associate with the upper crust of the neighborhood, specifically Mrs. Endicott Otis, whom Phyllis feels could help Durwood rise up the ladder of success faster. Samantha isn't keen on this idea but can't talk Phyllis out of it, who admits that she already asked the employment agency to send over some applicants today. And with that, the first one arrives. Phyllis decides to make herself scarce as she doesn't want to interfere (groan!).

The first applicant is the formidable Mrs. Harper who has a list of demands as high as she is sharp, but when she finds out that there is a young child in the home, she flunks Samantha and leaves.

The next applicant is the very sweet, but odd, Amelia who finds everything rewarding and marvels at the comfortableness of Samantha's chair. Knowing that their household is not conducive to having any permanent unsuspecting mortals added to it, Samantha tries to dissuade the overly agreeable Amelia from accepting the job, but Amelia stays strong and decides she wants the job. Phyllis is thrilled and stays over to help Amelia prepare Durwood's favorite meal of Baked Alaska, asparagus with hollandaise sauce, and shepherd's pie but decides to leave once he arrives home so that Samantha can tell him the "good" news about their new maid. Of course, he's furious and they decide they must fire Amelia before she gets wind of any witchly activity. Both attempt to get rid of her but Amelia is so congenial and seems so happy they just can't do it.

Later on, Endora tells Samantha she should simply turn Amelia into a toad and put her out back, but Samantha would rather have a more constructive suggestion. Endora offers up a destructive one by creating a windstorm that absolutely messes up the house which she thinks will make Amelia definitely want to quit. Of course, Amelia is overwhelmed at the mess but doesn't let it faze her and gets to cleaning. Just then, Phyllis arrives with Leslie Otis to introduce her to Samantha and is shocked to find the house in such disarray. As they visit in the den, Samantha excuses herself and helps Amelia get the house cleaned in a flash. This impresses Mrs. Otis greatly who offers to hire Amelia for more money than what she is making with Samantha. Amelia refuses until Samantha twitches her into agreeing. And that is that.

One of my favorite scenes is the one at the first with Durwood teaching Tabitha how to fly the paper airplane. That scene alone is precious and goes to prove why Dick York was the best Durwood, in my opinion. And the scene later up in Tabitha's room was new to me so that was cool.

It's odd that Samantha says she's never seen a paper airplane before yet that was what Durwood used to send his messages to her in "A is for Aardvark" from the First Season.

I don't like the actress who plays Amelia. She's creepy to me what with seeming to be so, I don't know, out there, and what's with finding everything so rewarding?

Of course, this is a remake of Season Two's "Maid to Order," which itself was a remake of the *I Love Lucy* episode entitled "Lucy Hires a Maid" which was directed by William Asher, who oddly enough, did NOT direct this episode of *Bewitched*.

JANUARY 9, 1969

It was on this night ABC aired Episode #155: "Cousin Serena Strikes Again" part one.

Durwood and Samantha's slumber is disturbed by the not-so-dulcet sounds of a roaring motorcycle that not-so-oddly enough is coming from their living room! After putting their robes on they go downstairs to investigate and find that it's Serena taking her new bike out for a ride. Probably for the first time ever, Durwood gets justifiably mad at her for making such a ruckus during the night especially when they are going to be having high profile client Clio Vanita over for dinner. When Serena gets incensed at being asked to leave, she threatens to stay for breakfast, lunch, and dinner, dull as they may be. Samantha tries to talk her out of staying, especially for dinner because it may be dull, but Serena says she'll provide her own entertainment and zooms off on her bike.

Dinner arrives, but surprisingly Serena does not, which is good, because Durwood is a nervous wreck about having Miss Vanita to dinner. Soon enough, the Tates and Clio arrive and Samantha finds that Clio is less than likable as she is very forward with Durwood, not to mention very snobby.

Clio cannot be torn away from Durwood's side except for when she asks him to make her a very dry martini stirred with his so charming little finger. Samantha helps him and relays her distaste for the outrageous Clio. Just as Durwood is about to return to his guests with the drinks, Serena pops in behind him. Samantha tells Serena that though she is fond of her that she'd rather she be invisible if she is to stay to dinner.

In the living room, Durwood presents his ideas to Clio for her Vino Vanita wine but it doesn't go over too well. Clio says that Durwood is enough of a charmer and a bright man that if Larry's not too careful, she may steal him from his organization. Serena warns Samantha that if she's not too careful, Clio will steal him from her organization and with that pops out.

The Tates, Clio, Samantha, and Durwood sit for dinner and in the midst of it, Serena pops in, invisible, and begins to cause mischief by saying back handed comments about Clio making everyone think Samantha is saying them. After dinner, Clio requests Durwood show her the gazebo out back. While Samantha is clearing up, Serena appears and suggests that Samantha pop out to the patio to keep an eye on them, but Samantha promises she's not worried.

Out on the patio, Clio becomes very amorous and very touchy with Durwood, who is quite uncomfortable. Unbeknownst to the two of them, invisible Serena joins them just as Clio tries to wager her account with Durwood by suggesting that he should go back to Rome with her. If he doesn't, she will take her account with her. Durwood tries to decline but Clio just wants to kiss. He gets out of it by going to get another glass of wine and as she goes after him, Serena freezes her.

Larry sees Durwood alone and wants to know what's going on and when Durwood apprises him of the situation, Larry suggests he take Clio up on her offer to go to Rome. Durwood won't have any of it. Samantha hears them arguing and is surprised that Clio isn't with them, even more so that Durwood left her out on the patio. When she goes to retrieve Clio, she only finds Serena. When she asks where Clio is, Serena points up and Samantha sees a blonde monkey hanging on the awning! Serena explains that Clio was trying to make a monkey out of Samantha so Serena decided to do the literal same to Clio. Serena pops out just as Durwood comes out to the patio and before Samantha can explain about the new monkey, the Tates also come out. Samantha tells everyone that Clio is in the den resting as she had a terrible headache. The Tates say good night and leave but Durwood is confused as he never saw Clio go to the den. Samantha tells him that she actually kind of left and he accepts that thinking that she may have been offended by his rejecting her advances. He says they can tie the monkey up on the patio until the morning when they will investigate where the monkey came from. Before he can tie her up, Clio escapes and runs upstairs to the bedroom. They chase after her and Durwood thinks it's cute that she's settled on the bed. Samantha is not amused at all and is even more irritated when Durwood suggest she just sleep in the room. Not knowing what else to do Samantha reveals the true identity of the monkey and Durwood blows his top thinking Samantha did it. She explains that Serena did it.

As he proceeds to explain what he'd do to Serena if she were there, she appears and he demands that she change Clio back and then stay out of their lives forever. Serena tells him she'll comply with his last request and pops off. It's then that Durwood realizes he's just made a terrible mistake. Samantha tries to get Serena to come back, but she's very stubborn. As it's quite late, Samantha decides they just need to go to bed and hopefully by the morning Serena will have cooled off. Samantha goes to take Miss Vanita down to the patio to tie her up and…

Don't miss Part Two of "Cousin Serena Strikes Again," next week!

I'd have to give this episode a two star rating. My reasoning is that we've already had this client-turned-into-an-animal routine and I really wish that Nancy Kovak would've just been kept for Sheila. Heck, Sheila could've shown up again with a new blonde 'do and a sparkly dress and it would've worked just as well, if not better! I couldn't stand how Clio would always say a word in Italian and then follow it up with the English word.

Other than those gripes, I really like this episode because Serena is in it. I liked her leather jacket and the fact that she was riding a motorcycle and when she says, "Who were you expecting, Steve McQueen?" I also liked the special effect of having a see-through Serena.

I seem to remember when I was little that, at the end, when Samantha is talking to Clio in Italian, they had the English translation on the bottom of the screen but on the Columbia House tape and on the DVD it isn't there. And the *Bewitched* Collector says he hasn't seen it shown like that, so maybe I just dreamed it.

I also like on the DVD that the announcer voice telling us to stay tuned next week for the second part was included as it wasn't on the tape. How unfortunate that the color on the DVD is all messed up.

JANUARY 16, 1969

It was on this night ABC aired Episode #156: "Cousin Serena Strikes Again" part two.

Durwood dreams that super rich and sexy client Clio Vanita has dinner at his house with he, Samantha, and the Tates, where she proceeds to make her moves on him resulting in her turning into a monkey courtesy of Samantha's cousin Serena. When he wakes up, Samantha assures him it was in fact NOT a dream at all and that Clio the Chimp is tied up out on the patio.

During breakfast (which includes spaghetti for the Italian monkey), Durwood freaks out about what he's going to do about the upcoming meeting that he's supposed to have with Larry and Clio. Samantha tries to calm him by telling him that she's been trying to get in contact with Serena, but with no luck. Just then, Larry arrives wanting to find out what happened with Clio, whom Durwood had said he had taken home the previous night. Durwood tells him he'll tell him later, when Samantha and the chimp enter the room on their way to the patio. After Larry leaves, Samantha and Durwood hear the familiar voice of Serena coming from the kitchen announcing that she's back. Hurrying into the kitchen, they find sexy Serena seated on the table dressed like an Egyptian which she says was for a boat ride along the Nile. She says she's willing to change Clio back and when Durwood guides her out to the patio where Clio is supposed to be tied up, they find that she has slipped her rope! So, Samantha and Durwood head out into the neighborhood to find her.

After hours of searching, Samantha comes across a young boy who says that his friend had found Clio and taken her home. Samantha tells Durwood to head to the office and she'll go get Clio. Of course, it isn't that simple when Samantha finds that Clio had wrecked so much havoc on the boy's house that his mother gave the chimp to a pet store. Samantha races to the pet store and finds that Clio had just been sold to an organ grinder named Joe Scibetta. Samantha tries to buy Clio back from Joe but he won't have any of it as he's charmed by the blonde chimp. Before any further negotiations can happen, Clio slips her rope again and leads Samantha, Joe, and an angry cop on a chase. Giving up on doing things the mortal way, Samantha pops out and materializes ahead of the crew where she captures Clio and takes her into a department store ladies room with the cop following close behind. Before he can enter the ladies room, Samantha and the now human Clio emerge claiming no knowledge of the runaway chimp. He decides to go in after the chimp but is stopped by Serena, who wonders what he had in mind. Samantha thanks her cousin, who pops out.

Meanwhile, Durwood is trying to stall with Larry who is quite upset about the whereabouts of Clio as she is now two hours late to their meeting. Just as he is about to give up, Samantha shows up with Clio, who says she must've slept in due to a hangover from the Stephenses party the previous night. Samantha also says they were waiting for the models for the new ad campaign for Vanita Wine, which is Scibetta and his new monkey to be used with the slogan, "Don't monkey around with anything but the best. Drink Vino Vanita." Clio loves it which means so does Larry.

At home, Samantha and Durwood find Serena zapping up nursery rhymes for Tabitha. Of course, Durwood wants to give her a piece of his mind and assures Samantha he is going to be as gracious as he knows how which is telling Serena that the next time she stops by, don't. Serena tells him that if that's as gracious as he knows how to be she's going to show him how entertaining she can be and zaps up an elongated nose on him. Durwood is furious but can't apologize, leading Serena to pop off.

I'd give this one THREE stars for Liz in the Cleopatra outfit alone!

I thought it was fun having them chase Clio all over the neighborhood and especially that they got Bobo Lewis to show up. She's really funny.

And, of course, there is the infamous black lady that disappears with Samantha when she pops out, though you can really just see the back of her leg at the edge of the frame, it's more fun to think that she may be floating out in the cosmos somewheres.

I also like when the police officer is going to go in the ladies bathroom to find the monkey and Serena walks out and says, "Just what did you have in mind?!" Also in that scene, Peanuts (the hairdresser) is at the candy counter.

I love the scene at the end with Serena reading to Tabitha. The pop out of the chicken is flawless. I also love when Tabitha says, "I want to stay and hear you scream, Daddy," which is funny and sad if that's all Tabitha ever remembers about her daddy.

JANUARY 23, 1969

It was on this night ABC aired #157: "One Touch of Midas" sponsored by Chevrolet.

Durwood comes home with flowers for Samantha on the sixth anniversary of their first date. He plans to take her to the restaurant, Sorrento's, where they had that first date, to celebrate. When he leaves to go change, Endora pops in disgusted to find that Samantha is making Tabitha a dress, mortal style. She feels it's because Durwood is too poor to buy a dress. Samantha assures her that Durwood has given them everything they want and that they don't need absolutely everything. She then leaves to change and Endora starts scheming.

The next day at McMann and Tate, an odd looking gentleman with crazy white hair walks into the office carrying a fur covered doll with big ears. He tells Ms. Wilson, the secretary, that he is Professor McAllister and he would like to meet with Durwood about marketing the doll. Ms. Wilson is apprehensive at first but once she sees the doll, it seems to have a charming effect on her so much that she lets him into Durwood's office. The doll, which Prof. McAllister calls 'The Fuzz,' charms Durwood too, and so he agrees to go into business with the Professor and has Ms. Wilson call up Hanley's Department store to set up a display with the Fuzz. Durwood at first says that they'll need fifty dolls but the Professor insists that they should make five hundred.

Samantha gets the warm fuzzies with two of the Fuzz dolls.

The next day, Ms. Wilson tells Durwood that Hanley's sold out of the dolls in no time and that they want another five thousand! Durwood is really happy and decides to go buy his wife and daughter all the things he thinks they need including a chinchilla playsuit. Samantha is flabbergasted at all this and knows Endora is behind it but can't get her to admit it. It all becomes too much when Durwood talks about moving out of their house, and she confronts him. He tells her that he's always felt bad about not being able to get her anything she wanted, especially when she could do it herself but gave up her powers voluntarily. He requests that she just let him splurge this one time and she agrees until he goes on and on about all the extravagant things he's going to buy.

Samantha finally finds Endora and gets her to take the charm off the dolls and when they stop selling, Durwood realizes he went overboard and returns the gifts.

I've always found this episode confusing. I used to think Endora changed herself into Prof. McAllister and couldn't understand why she did, but then as I grew older I realized she must've enlisted his help. Then *www.HarpiesBizarre.com* came along with the script comparisons and we find that there was a cut scene where Endora conjures up McAllister and tells him of her scheme with the doll but she wants him to do it so she can truthfully say it wasn't her. It's odd that they didn't include it. But what's even odder is McAllister's weird hair.

It's really funny when Samantha tells Endora that Durwood is infatuated with a stupid doll and Endora says, "Oh my dear! What's her name?"

This episode is the beginning of the bad hair days Liz is going to have the rest of this season. I can't stand her poofy, long, untamed hair which is seen in the beginning scene of this episode. It seems that the rest of this episode was filmed earlier in the season 'cause her hair seems more tame and shorter.

I think the Fuzz is an attempt to capture the fascination the real world had with the Troll dolls of the time, you know, the ugly ones with the Muppety hair on top? In the late 60s they were the second highest selling doll in the U.S.

Cosmo, the hair dresser, was really Dick York's stylist. How sad that Peanuts never had a speaking role (on *Bewitched* anyway).

And how cool is it that Sony included the Chevy end credits on the DVD?! That only proves they know about them so then I wonder what the hell their excuse is for not including the sponsor end credits AND openings on ALL the episodes!

Three nights previously, *I Dream of Jeannie* was preempted on NBC so that they could show the inauguration of the 37th President of the United States, Richard Milhous Nixon with Spiro Agnew as Vice President.

Two days prior, Agnes Moorehead sang the song "You're Grown Up Now" on *That's Life*.

JANUARY 30, 1969

It was on this night we did see Episode #158: "Samantha the Bard" on ABC.

One morning just at dawn, and after a mild yawn,
Durwood noticed an oddity in the way Sam spoke
and thought it must be some cute joke.
For every time she spoke a word
it came out rhyming, which was quite absurd.
Sam promised she was not at play,
her rhyming was just happening that way.
And so when they were all at the breakfast table,
Sam called for Endora to show, when she was able.
Endora was puzzled, just like her kin, at the predicament Sam was in.
She decided to search for Dr. Bombay to cure her daughter right away.
Later on at McMann and Tate, Durwood found that his boss and mate
had scheduled a dinner without checking first
which would be troublesome now that Sam was cursed.
Just before dinner, while Sam was getting dressed,
Durwood was freaking out, simply a mess.
Endora popped in with Bombay's cure
which he said would make her speech pure.
Sam took a sip and drank it up,
and finding things right, she and Durwood left to sup.
At dinner things were great,
with the Durfees, the Stephenses, and Larry Tate.
But suddenly, to her chagrin, Samantha found herself rhyming again.
The cure Bombay had prescribed was not quite right,
and her incessant rhyming was killing the night.
Excusing herself so as not to bother,
Samantha popped home to talk to her mother.
She found that Bombay was currently hiking,
and without walking, jumping or biking,
she popped to his side to get another dose

of the cure for her rhyming, which sounded like prose.
Finding she was cured, this time for sure,
she popped back to dinner to comb the fur
of the riled Larry and the Durfees.
And she explained with the greatest of ease,
that she had rhymed all her words in order to show
that jingles are not the way the campaign should go.
Everyone was happy and they finished their dinner,
with Durwood once again coming out the winner.
That is, until the next day when Endora popped in,
rhyming like she was in a contest to win.
Durwood found it funny and started to gloat,
which led to her changing him into a billy goat!

Man, I didn't think I could do it! I don't mean to toot my own horn, but that was awesome!

I about spit out my food when I read the *Bewitched* Critic gave it three stars?! The only saving grace to it is the fact that Samantha looks great and Dr. Bombay is in it.

This is the first time the oft-heard "Calling Dr. Bombay! Calling Dr. Bombay! Emergency! Come right away!" is used. I thought the rhyming wasn't really irritating until about the third or fourth time she did it, especially when she said something about getting an answer "or my name's not Samansar." UGGGHH! And you could see that Liz didn't like saying it either.

It was three days prior that ABC sent out a notification that Dick York was leaving *Bewitched* after fulfilling his original five year contract. Jackie Cooper, west coast chief for programming at Screen Gems, stated that everyone "regretted Mr. York's decision to leave as he has contributed substantially to the series."

FEBRUARY 6, 1969

It was on this night ABC aired Episode #159: "Samantha the Sculptress."

Durwood blows his top when he sees Tabitha using witchcraft to model the clay Grandma Stephens gave her into replicas of her toys. As he goes on his tirade to Samantha about how he would like his daughter to simply use her hands, rather than her nose, he suddenly finds himself eating the daisies which were sitting on the coffee table. He and Samantha soon find, courtesy of a bouncing beach ball with writing on it, that

Endora had made him hunger for the flowers as punishment for going on about the mortal way. Samantha tells Durwood she'll learn how to sculpt by hand so she can teach Tabitha which insults Endora, who reluctantly lifts the hunger spell from Durwood.

The next day, Durwood and Larry meet with the "lush"-ious Walden R. Campbell of Campbell Sporting Goods, who insists they have a few,

Larry and Mr. Campbell (Cliff Norton) are confused by the spooky busts.
PHOTO COURTESY OF SHARON ORAZI.

or ten, drinks before discussing his campaign. After they have drunk the afternoon away, they make plans to have dinner at Durwood's that evening followed by more drinks and then the discussing of the campaign.

When a drunken Durwood arrives home, he finds that Samantha had been sculpting all day and in fact, she had made what she called a bust of Durwood, though it looked more like a model for one of Jim Henson's Muppets. Endora pops in and, of course, she and Durwood start bickering ending with Durwood making negative remarks about Endora's age. Not to be insulted by her son-in-law, nor embarrassed by her daughter's lack of artistic skill, she zaps the bust into a perfect likeness of Durwood but makes it so real, that it actually talks! Durwood sees this and is nervous about Larry and Mr. Campbell seeing it, not to mention it being a product of witchcraft. He tells Endora she needs to butt out and furthermore, that she isn't invited to that evening's dinner party which happens to be featuring Endora's favorite dish, coq-au-vin. Endora is incensed and pops out but Samantha knows that's not the last they'll hear of her.

When Larry arrives, Endora pops in the living room and brings the living bust with her. Larry is quite impressed with the work and Endora tells him that Samantha sculpted it and may have even done one of him, which she zaps up while they are eating dinner. Larry is quite impressed but unnerved when he sees the two busts speaking, but finds he isn't the only one who has seen it. Mr. Campbell also sees it though he won't admit it. Durwood is frantic now and suggests that they move their meeting to the den, but as they are going down the hall, Endora freezes them and zaps the busts into the den. When they arrive in the den and see the busts, Durwood says Samantha made a set for every room in the house. The men begin discussing the campaign but are constantly interrupted by the talking busts which finally spook Mr. Campbell out so much that he requests to sign the campaign ideas so that he can leave. He also vows to give up drinking and so, much to Endora's dismay, the evening is a success.

This episode is superb! And the eating daisies part is my UTTER FAVORITE! I have never laughed so hard in my whole life when I saw him eating those flowers and telling Samantha that's what he's doing like it's no big deal.

I liked that the drunkenness was the focus of this episode, as in every episode they drink but never seem to get drunk (very often, anyway). And at the end Mr. Campbell swears off drinking, which I liked.

I thought the fighting between Durwood and Endora seemed to be above their usual sparring...like there were new lines thrown out and the delivery of those lines.

And, I don't know if it's just a coincidence or not, but Stewie (the baby from *Family Guy*) has a purple octo-"fish" in his room and I can't help but think it's a shout out to *Bewitched*.

This will be the last episode we see with Durwood in it for over a month. As a matter of fact, beginning last December, Dick York missed the filming of all episodes up until the end of this month before his infamous collapse on the set of "Daddy Does His Thing," his last episode. This episode, however, finished filming 11/27/68.

Larry's bust is in the Hollywood Forever Cemetery in Los Angeles, now bronzed, and it resides with David White's ashes along with his son Jonathan's ashes.

On February 8, in the *TV Guide*, the Doan Report discussed the replacement of Dick York.

FEBRUARY 13, 1969

It was on this night ABC aired Episode #160: "Mrs. Stephens, Where Are You?"

Durwood calls from a Boston business trip to ask Samantha if she could air mail him some papers he left in the car. When she goes out to the car to retrieve them, she encounters kindly old neighbor Ms. Parsons trying to retrieve her cat, Victoria, who has climbed high in a tree on the 1164 property. Samantha helps her out by zapping Victoria down and while Ms. Parsons is overjoyed at the miraculous return of her cat, she is soon perplexed by the sudden appearance of Samantha's kooky cousin, Serena. When Ms. Parsons admits to having seen Serena appear out of nowhere, Serena asks if she would like to see it again and she pops out disturbing Ms. Parsons even further, who decides to go home with her kitty. Samantha is none-too-pleased with Serena, who had just popped in to visit, but Samantha tells her they'll visit after she gets back from mailing Durwood's papers. She also asks Serena to babysit Tabitha who is taking a nap. After zapping up a HUGE hourglass in which the sands fall up, Serena says goodbye to Samantha.

A little while later, Serena's lazy afternoon of babysitting is interrupted by a ring at the door. When she opens the door, she discovers Samantha's mother-in-law, Mrs. Stephens, who is under the impression that Samantha has cut her hair and dyed it. Serena clears up the confusion but is irritated when she finds that Mrs. Stephens would like to chat with her until Samantha gets back so she can find out more about Samantha's family. Mrs. Stephens proceeds to insult Endora and Uncle Arthur (whom she practically accused of being a toss-pot) and then really digs her claws in when she tells Serena that she feels that Samantha is raising Tabitha to be selfish. Having had enough of Mrs. Stephens catty remarks, Serena does what any ticked off witch would do and changes Mrs. Stephens into a cat! The confused kitty then runs out the patio doors. Serena decides that Samantha would much rather have her stay to watch Tabitha, than go chasing after Mrs. Stephens, and so she does stay.

Meanwhile, Mrs. Stephens is immediately chased by a dog into a tree in Ms. Parsons' yard. Hearing the commotion, Ms. Parsons, an avid cat lover, comes to Mrs. Stephens rescue. Samantha finally arrives at home and sees that someone has left a pair of gloves and a purse and Serena tells her it was Mrs. Stephens. Before Samantha can leave to return them, Serena advises her that Mrs. Stephens isn't at home because she happens to be a cat. Samantha is both furious and irritated when Serena admits she doesn't know exactly where Mrs. Stephens ran off to. She decides to go look for her and luckily Ms. Parsons hears her calling for Mrs. Stephens. She tells Samantha that she did find a cat earlier but, because she has so many, she's not sure exactly which one it is. Samantha distracts Ms. Parsons with a twitch induced back door bell ring and while she is gone, she casts a spell to turn all the cats but Mrs. Stephens into dogs. She retrieves Mrs. Stephens and changes the cats back and leaves.

When she returns home, she finds that Mr. Stephens has shown up to pick Phyllis up so she sends Serena outside with Mrs. Stephens to change her back. When they are all inside again Mrs. Stephens is confused as to what has happened during her afternoon, especially since she now has a new necklace consisting of a bell to warn the birds. Serena sums it up by saying how nice it is that Durwood has a tosspot on his side of the family.

This is one of my most favorite Serena episodes. I would totally give it three and a half stars. I would've gave it four but half is gone 'cause Durwood is gone, and even though he grates the nerves, he is a very important part of the show.

This is where Serena really becomes Serena as from here on out the character really doesn't change. And she looks HOT in that outfit! I'll bet DICK Michaels was just loving that he was directing this episode.

I thought Serena was a perfect match up against Mrs. Stephens. It was so good to finally see her get her just desserts.

There are tons of favorite lines in this one especially when Mrs. Stephens tells Serena about Maurice "we don't even know what he does." Serena: "Does? Nothing! He basks!"

Another favorite is when Serena is explaining why she changed Mrs. Stephens: "She practically had her claws in all of us, including dear Uncle Arthur whom she practically accused of being a toss pot. No, don't thank me, it was a pleasure!"

Ruth McDevitt was brilliant especially considering this is the same woman who, last season, played Ticheba in "Long Live the Queen"!

This episode was the twenty-second to be filmed for the Fifth Season but the twentieth aired. It is also the first episode this season without Dick York, seventh overall for the series.

FEBRUARY 20, 1969

It was on this night ABC aired Episode: #161: "Marriage, Witches Style."

While whipping up an Aunt Sue's Cake Mix cake, Samantha finds that one of her witchy relatives loves the cake as she sees a knife cut a slice, plate itself, and then float over to a kitchen chair. The invisible cake snatcher reveals herself to be none other than Serena, who just got back from a safari in Kenya and was on her way to Balmoral with Elizabeth and Philip and then to Athens for a yacht-christening. Samantha thinks it sounds fun but Serena surprisingly tells her she's bored with fun, that she wants to have an aching heart like Sammy must have with Durwood gone on yet another business trip. Samantha assures her she's not aching and is totally caught off guard when Serena says she's decided she is going to find herself a mortal and marry it! Being the only witch to have ever done so, and knowing the trials that come along with it, Samantha tells Serena she couldn't possibly but Serena will hear none of it. She asks Samantha where she should start and Samantha suggests a church picnic, the library and the Human Equation, a computer matchmaking service. Serena thinks it sounds groovy, as she's way into 'that science-fiction jazz.'

Samantha accompanies Serena to the Human Equation, which seems to be a successful business as the walls are adorned with many marriage photos. The enthusiastic owner, Mr. Beams, gives Serena an application and tells her the process that involves her information being fed into the computer and compared to the male clients where the best matches will be set up on a date. After filling out the application, Mr. Beams shows them that her information has been transferred to a data punch card and will be fed into the machine where all the male cards will also be fed and the ones that match hers will fall into her slot. After what seems an eternity of nothing falling into her slot, a solitary card finally ends up there. Mr. Beams is quite impressed as that has never happened before. He sets up a lunch date for Serena and her intended, a Mr. Franklyn Blodgett, at the Rotisserie where they can get to know one another better.

Later, at the Rotisserie, Franklyn shows up and Serena is smitten by his debonair good looks. He even knows her favorite wine before she even mentions it!

That night, Serena is giddy with love and tells Sammy that they could've eaten lunch right through dinner and that Franklyn has read books that haven't even been written yet! She also informs her cousin that she is going to use her house for their second date, a dinner, and asks her to go to a movie or something. Samantha suggests she'd better stick around to help with dinner but Serena insists she doesn't need any help and zaps up a chateaubriand, hearts of palm salad with vinaigrette, and pâté. It is immediately twitched away by Samantha, who reminds Serena that if she is going to marry a mortal she's got to learn how to cook like one. Serena wants to know what for, and Samantha tells her that mortal men like a woman who is helpless and so the more she acts like she can't do anything better than he, the more she'll endear herself to him. And so, Serena begrudgingly begins to cook.

Ironically, Franklyn happens to be a full-fledged warlock who is also looking for a mortal and, as he rides through the cosmos with his father on his way to Serena's, his father gives him practically the same advice that Samantha gave Serena, and that is mortal women find frailties in a man endearing. And so Franklyn pops out and appears at the door of 1164 with some beautiful flowers. But thinking they may be too perfect, he changes them to some wilted violets. Serena answers the door, looking wilted herself, and when Franklyn enters, he purposely trips.

The dinner is practically burned and tough, but they work through it, all the time both of them trying their very hardest to be clumsy, spilling the drinks and everything else, mentioning the fact that it's so human. At the end of the date, Franklyn asks if he can see her the next evening. Serena is ecstatic believing that Franklyn is going to propose. After he leaves, she gushes about him and her supposed impending proposal but Samantha reminds her that she must tell him she's a witch. Serena doesn't care about that now, she's going to be married!

The next night, Franklyn and Serena enjoy some drinks out on the patio where both struggle at finding the way to reveal their witchhood to each other. They move their discussion into the living room where the strained conversation finally hits its apex when Serena decides to just come right out and tell him. She tells him to look at her and not take his eyes off her when she proceeds to wave her arms wildly about and disappears! When she pops back in behind him, she thinks he's confused about the disappearance, so she tries it again. Franklyn is confused and when she thinks he's about to leave, she tries telling him that she's not a witch all the time, that most of the time she's a simple, helpless girl and she thought he'd understand. He tells her he does understand and with a snap, he pops out. When he pops back in, they both realize the humor of the situation — that both of them were looking for the same thing and were also worried about the same thing. Serena is happy that they won't have the usual adjustment period most people would have.

Franklyn says there would have to be some adjustments and proceeds to tell her that her wild way of flailing her arms about to disappear is considered rather gauche in the social circles in which he travels. Serena is a bit miffed but he tells her that he didn't intend to offend her but that he was just trying to show her that style and subtlety are preferred after he easily zaps up a champagne glass and a bottle of champagne and to end it all, with a mere look, pops the cork out of the bottle. He tells her that she looked like a demented windmill when waving her arms about. Serena has had it and tells him she can out-subtle him from now until doomsday and with a mere look, enlarges his full champagne glass and with the deft turn of her index finger, levitates it and tips its contents out all over him. Not reacting to his now doused state, Franklyn offers the laughing Serena some champagne which he makes spray out of the bottle. Of course, the both of them were too involved to notice Samantha come down the stairs and when Serena ducks, Samantha gets the champagne geyser. Seeing how mad Samantha is, Franklyn pops out and soon after, so does Serena.

The next day Serena, quite over Franklyn, is still on the hunt for a mortal and has dragged Samantha to yet another dating service. Samantha tries to tell her it'll be useless but Serena won't give up. Mr. Lovelace, the owner of that establishment, tells her he has found a man for her and before he can even say the name, Samantha tells him it's Franklyn Blodgett. But to her surprise it isn't, but a man with the very mortal sounding name of Ted Perkins. He says he'll call him to set up the date while Samantha and Serena wait in the outer office. But they peak their head in and witness a crown pop onto Mr. Lovelace's head after he asks Mr. Perkins to try and tone down his jokes.

This episode was the twenty-third to air but the twenty-first to finish filming for the Fifth Season. It is the second Durwood-less episode of the season, eighth overall for the series.

This episode is one of my ALL time favorites and even without Dick York, I give it four stars! It always makes me laugh and Serena in the sexy black feather dress is how I always picture her when thinking about her.

I thought the floating knife and cake were really cool special effects, even if you could see the wires.

This episode also seems to be quite risqué especially when Fergus, er, Mr. Beams says that "male card that matches your female card will drop into your little slot!" And then Serena: "Nothing is dropping into my slot!"

There are so many favorite lines from this but my favorite comes after the first date when Franklyn asks to see her the next evening:

> SERENA: *"Golly whiz! Two nights in a row?"* and *"Shall we say…eight o'clock?"*

The way Liz's face looks is priceless.

Did you notice when the champagne is poured on Franklyn his hair was all over his face when it happened, yet in the next scene, it had been slicked back?

I also like it when she says he's so hung up on the human race. "There are a lot of things, like birds…vegetables…*bees*. There are lots of other things!"

As I'm typing I'm thinking of more things I love in this episode and the scene where it begins with Serena saying, "I don't need any help" and then proceeds to zap up the dinner is way fun. I especially like when Samantha twitches it out and Serena says, "What's the matter? Chateaubriand too well done?"

Anyway, I LOVE THIS EPISODE!

The day before, Madge Blake passed away. She played Mary in Season One's "The Witches are Out."

FEBRUARY 27, 1969

It was on this night ABC aired Episode #162: "Going Ape."

Samantha and Tabitha are followed home from the park by a chimpanzee that had seen Samantha zap up roller skates on Tabitha's feet. Usually proficient in chimp, Samantha has a hard time understanding him to find out who he belongs to and so she zaps him into human form. The Man-Chimp tells her that he doesn't want to go back to the boy who owns him because he feels the boy only cares more about flying his kite than him and therefore won't tell her where he lives.

Meanwhile, at McMann and Tate, Larry is meeting with Evelyn Tucker, owner of Braun Cologne and her associate, Mr. Flynn, who has suggested they use more-than-half-naked male models that can pop their pectoral muscles in their television campaign. Of course, Larry is less than enthused when he sees that the half-naked models aren't female and suggests to Ms. Tucker that they wait for Durwood to come home from his Canadian business trip to hear his ideas. Ms. Tucker says she's tired of waiting for Durwood — who was arriving home that day — and so Larry offers that they go and wait for him at his house so that they can discuss the ideas.

Back at 1164, the Man-Chimp will not comply even with Samantha threatening to change him back into a chimp anyway. Endora shows up quite impressed with Samantha's new friend but that doesn't matter as Samantha goes ahead to change him back but is interrupted by Tabitha waking up from her nap. Right after she leaves, the doorbell rings and Endora answers it to find Larry, Ms. Tucker, and Mr. Flynn. She introduces the Man-Chimp as Durwood's cousin Harry Simian. Harry, who is doing all sorts of gymnastics on the swing set, fascinates Ms. Tucker. She says that she wants Harry to be the face of Braun Cologne. When Samantha comes downstairs from tending to Tabitha, she is shocked at the crowd in her living room, and even more so that Harry apparently has been given a job! She tries to refuse, but Larry tells her that if Harry doesn't show up for his first photo shoot the next day, that Durwood shouldn't bother to show up to work ever again.

After Larry and company leave, Durwood calls saying that his flight has been delayed which means it's up to Samantha to save the Braun campaign. Harry is excited at the prospect of working like a man but Samantha takes the opportunity to change him back until just before his photo shoot.

The next day, after Samantha has changed him, Harry goes in for his first photo shoot and impresses everybody, unfortunately. Larry tells Samantha that they want to hire Harry on permanently, but this doesn't please Harry at all who finds working much more difficult than just being fawned over as a chimp. Samantha tells him that he can get out of it by acting like he would naturally and so, at the next photo shoot, he bites people, swings from the rafters and causes general chaos. Ms. Tucker is furious and embarrassed until she hears the slogan that Samantha has come up with, "When your man uses Braun Cologne, there's no telling how wild he can get!" Of course, she says it was Durwood's idea and Evelyn loves it, on the condition that she never have to lay eyes on Harry again.

And so out of a job, Harry returns to being a chimp and finds his way back to his boy owner.

Danny Bonaduce makes the first of two pre-*Partridge Family* appearances on *Bewitched* as Harry's owner.

This episode was the twenty-fourth to air but the twenty-second to finish filming for the Fifth Season. It is the third Durwood-less episode of the season, ninth overall for the series. It should be noted that sometime during this last week in February the episode "Daddy Does His Thing" finished filming, which is the last episode that Dick York filmed before he collapsed on the set at the end of January and unfortunately would never return to the role of Darrin that he originated.

This is one of my least favorite episodes of the Fifth Season, though it isn't THE least favorite — that one hasn't happened yet.

It just seems that by this point everyone is like, "Where the hell is Durwood?" I mean, I've never liked Durwood but he is the added "evil" that makes the show have conflict and a good one at that: the beautiful enchanting Samantha for some reason falls in love with him, marries him and stays with him even if he blows up at every little piece of magic done. Liz seems bored to me and at this point every show in the 60s, including *Bewitched,* has done 293,472,397,423 monkey/chimp shows! Lou Antonio was a good choice for a human chimp, but it feels like I've seen this whole scenario too many times. It's also one of THE worst Samantha hair episodes! And it seems to just get worse from here through the rest of the season. And what is with that blue plaid vest? Bleh!

Three days earlier Elizabeth Montgomery was nominated for Best TV Star — Female for *Bewitched* at the Golden Globes.

MARCH 6, 1969

It was on this night ABC aired Episode #163: "Tabitha's Weekend."

After another un-welcomed visit by her mother-in-law, Samantha finds herself getting a visit from her father-in-law who had wanted to come visit without his wife. He tells Samantha that Phyllis feels Samantha is trying to keep Tabitha all to herself as she wouldn't let Phyllis take Tabitha to a museum, though she had heard that Endora had taken her to the zoo (if even Endora claimed that they had seen unicorns and dodo birds). Samantha tells him she just feels that Tabitha is too young for a museum, which Frank agrees with, but he says it would do Phyllis a lot of good if they could have Tabitha to their place for the weekend. Before Samantha can deny that request, Endora says it's a marvelous idea as it will give she and Samantha time to be together while Durwood is out on yet another business trip. Frank tells her that Phyllis will be over to pick Tabitha up in the afternoon.

Samantha, not wanting her in-laws to be alone with her witch-daughter, tells Endora that she is going to go along with Tabitha. When Phyllis does come to pick her up, she is surprised by Samantha wanting to tag along, but reluctantly agrees.

At the elder Stephens' home, Phyllis tells Tabitha she can do anything she would like while she is there and that she also has a surprise for her out on the patio. The surprise turns out to be a mynah bird named Black Bart that Phyllis has taught to say a couple of words. She leaves Tabitha with the bird while she goes to get cookies. Samantha, meanwhile, is trapped by Mr. Stephens, who is telling her all about an idea he has for a new invention. Tabitha gets bored of the bird saying very few words and twitches him into having a full vocabulary which causes Phyllis to get a sick headache. When she goes to tell Frank, Samantha realizes what must be going on and goes out to scold Tabitha, who changes the bird back to normal before her grandfather can see. Phyllis is upset that Frank won't believe her and even more upset when Samantha suggests that she and Tabitha are going to go home. And if it can't get any worse, Endora pops in causing Phyllis' sick headache to get even worse. She accuses Samantha of ambushing the weekend they were going to have which causes everyone to get in an uproar. When Samantha decides to leave, they find that Tabitha is no-where to be seen though she had just been there. They all decide to split up but Samantha tells her mother that she thinks Tabitha may have just disappeared. Endora suggests maybe not so much disappeared as changed herself into something small as she didn't want to be present for the adults fighting but at the same time, wanted to see them make fools of themselves just as Samantha had done when she was a little girl by changing herself into a postage stamp when Uncle Arthur and Maurice were fighting over who would take her to be presented at court.

Samantha and Endora look through the flower bowls and the desks, much to the bewilderment of Mr. and Mrs. Stephens, who had just looked in the yard. While they wonder where Tabitha could be, Samantha notices a raisin cookie on a nearby plate that smiles at her. Realizing it has to be Tabitha, Samantha sends Phyllis and Frank to the kitchen to get some sherry as they are all having a rough day. She tells Tabitha to change herself back and Endora does it just as Mr. and Mrs. Stephens are walking back in the room. Phyllis agrees that maybe this is not the weekend to spend with Tabitha and so the three witches return home.

I've always liked this episode 'cause the situation seemed so relatable to the real world. And even if Tabitha wasn't a witch, it still would've worked on the basis that Samantha, deep down inside, doesn't really care for her mother-in-law. It was quite obvious in this episode, what with her laughing at Endora's suggestion that she may take Phyllis with her the next time she goes to Monaco and lose her, and also when Samantha mimics Mrs. Stephens as they are leaving the house.

That vest outfit of Samantha's at the first is HIDEOUS!

I like that the familiarity that Frank and Endora established in the First Season is still there. And Frank's idea about the drink vending machine is something he told Endora about in Season Two's "The Dancing Bear."

I always liked the postage stamp story. I thought it was so funny and fun that Samantha would do that.

And the coolest part of this episode was seeing Tabitha as the cookie… that smiles! And I wonder what would've happened if someone had taken a bite out of her? I suppose she would've disappeared from their hand before that happened. And speaking of raisin cookies, I thought I would share a favorite recipe of my mother's. She found it when we were cleaning her mother's house after Grandma had passed away. It's entitled "Aunt Renee's Raisin Nut Nibbles" though nobody has any idea who Aunt Renee is. But these cookies are WAAAYYY GOOD! And they look just like the cookies Phyllis had made.

Aunt Renee's Raisin Nut Nibbles
1 cup water
2 cups raisins
1 tsp soda
1 cup shortening
2 cups sugar
1 tsp vanilla
3 eggs
4 cups sifted flour
1 tsp baking powder
1 tsp cinnamon
1/2 tsp nutmeg
1 tsp salt
1 cup chopped walnuts

Add water to raisins and boil five minutes. Cool. Stir in soda. Beat shortening and sugar until well blended. Add vanilla, eggs and raisin mixture. Sift flour with salt, baking powder and spices. Add to mixture and add walnuts. Place by tsp on ungreased cookie sheet. Bake at 425 degrees for ten to twelve minutes. Makes about 75–100 cookies (I don't know about that part, but it does make a lot).

Man, now I'm hungry!

We will never again see Phyllis and Frank with their original son Dick York. Turns out the last time that happened, with Phyllis anyway, was in "Samantha's Super Maid." The next time Phyllis shows up is in "Samantha and the Beanstalk," next season.

This episode was the twenty-third to air but the twenty-fifth to finish filming for the Fifth Season. It is the fourth Durwood-less episode of the season, tenth overall for the series.

MARCH 13, 1969

It was on this night ABC aired Episode #164: "The Battle of Burning Oak."

So apparently Samantha actually has a husband! His name is Durwood (or at least that's what everybody calls him) and he works for an advertising agency named McMann and Tate. One of their new clients is J. Earl Rockeford, a very wealthy and affluent businessman who one evening has dinner at the Stephens' with his wife and Mr. Tate to discuss his account. It also turns out that Mr. Rockeford is the chairman of the board of the Burning Oak Country Club and he offers Durwood a membership in the very exclusive club. Durwood declines the offer, much to the dismay and irritation of Mr. Rockeford, but even more so to Larry Tate, who knows that Mr. Rockeford may take his business elsewhere. And so the next day, Larry sends an apology to Mr. Rockeford from Durwood, and threatens Durwood with his job if he doesn't join the club. Durwood grudgingly accepts and he and Larry accept a golf date with Mr. Rockeford at the club.

Meanwhile, Mrs. Rockeford invites Samantha to the club that same afternoon so that she can meet the screening committee. Samantha finds it wrong that the club would even need a screening committee but she accepts the lunch offer in order to make Durwood look good. When Endora finds out that Samantha is going to be hobnobbing with a bunch of super snobs, she insists that Durwood will show his true snobbish colors, which Samantha refutes. To prove she's right, Endora puts a snob spell on Durwood before he leaves for the club.

While on the green, Durwood works his way into Mr. Rockeford's good graces by outsnobbing even Mr. Rockeford. In the club, Samantha is coolly grilled by the women of the screening committee who find her lack of socialite friends, and the fact that she does her own cleaning, very quaint to say the least. But on the other hand, Samantha is very upset by the club's rule of keeping out "undesirables," or what they say are anybody not pure-bred American. When she gets home, she finds that Durwood agrees and is shocked when she finds that he wants to have dinner at the club. She decides that she is going to prove to the club that there isn't any way any of them could possibly be "pure-bred" Americans and enlists Aunt Hagatha to look into their histories a couple generations.

At the club, the Rockefords and their friends, and especially Durwood, are unbearable in their disdain for the "outsiders." Before it all becomes too much, the whole lot suddenly freeze in a clap of thunder and a bolt of lightning — all but Samantha as she witnesses her mother pop in. Endora tells her that Aunt Hagatha apprised her of the situation and she found the information Samantha was looking for. She also agrees to take the spell off Durwood and does so before she leaves, reversing time just a little so that Samantha can have a running start in the conversation.

With time flowing freely now, Samantha interrupts the conversation about how to keep "undesirables" and "un-pure Americans" out of Burning Oak by bringing up the fact that the only true pure-bred Americans are the Native American Indians who could never be allowed in by the current standards. Then one by one she reveals that each of the club members has some sort of ethnic past that brought them to the country, especially Mr. Rockeford who prided himself on the fact that his ancestors came over on the Mayflower, though Samantha reveals that the relative was a horse-thief who stowed away, which meant he was illegally in the country. She also says that she and Durwood have decided to stay out of Burning Oak, which Durwood now agrees with, and she sums it up by saying that it's because she belongs to the greatest minority of them all — witches! And with that, they leave.

Though this was the twenty-fourth episode to air this season, it was only the eighth to be filmed! It was filmed just after "Mirror, Mirror on the Wall" and right before "Is It Magic or Imagination?" I just wonder why it was they kept it so long as Dick York didn't start missing episodes until later on in filming.

I really like this one and would give it three stars. It would've got four but they reused jokes like the Dr. Hafner one from the pilot and at the first when Endora says Samantha works like a slave, she might as well look like one. Other than that, everything is perfection!

I love Samantha's hair and I remember the first time I saw this episode when I was younger, I was thinking, "Oh good! Samantha's hair is going to go back to normal..." Too bad that wasn't true.

As the Mayflower is mentioned in this episode I thought I would mention that my ancestor William Pierce ended up being a captain of the ship after the original voyage and rumour hath it that he took it out to sea to pirate. Rumour also hath it that another relative, Captain John Pierce, actually owned the Mayflower which means we were NEVER in steerage.

Something quite interesting about Burning Oak (aside from the fact that it's Tony Nelson's house) is that in the original script it was called Burning Tree Country Club. There happens to be a real Burning Tree in Greenwich, Connecticut! Maybe they changed the name so as not to offend the super snobs at the real one.

I really liked Endora stopping time at the club and popping in in the flash of lightning. I also liked her spell to de-spell Durwood.

In the original script, there were many great things said and done that were left out. For example, Samantha originally spoke about not being ashamed of your background and how her people were from Salem and had to use witchcraft to avoid being burned at the stake. Her lines are too long to paste here, but it's a good read. The original script also spoke of how the help at Burning Oak was listening and agreeing. You can read these lines at *HarpiesBizarre.com*.

I also liked that we finally got to see Hagatha again, though it wasn't Reta Shaw. I liked this Hagatha.

And one last thing — Mr. Rockeford is played by Edward Andrews who had a daughter named Tabitha, which is where Liz said they got the name for Samantha's daughter.

Three nights previously, NBC aired Episode #108: "Jeannie for the Defense" of *I Dream of Jeannie* where local lawyer Mr. Cashman is played by none other than Durwood #2, Dick Sargent! How funny that this episode should air the same week that one of the last Dick York episodes of *Bewitched* should air, especially after four weeks of no-Dick York. I'm not sure if it was known yet that Dick Sargent would be taking over the role of Durwood, but still interesting none-the-less.

MARCH 20, 1969

It was on this night ABC aired Episode #165: "Samantha's Power Failure."

After what amounts to a really cool opening scene with the Witches' Council's voice being heard over a screen of dark ominous clouds announcing that they are done putting up with Samantha's mortal marriage, some of us more attentive viewers may have thought we were going to be treated to a reworking of the Aunt Clara-on-trial episode as we see the same ball of light that began that episode bouncing softly through the midnight air of the Stephens bedroom to wake her up. We began to wonder if maybe there had been a mix up at the station as to what episode was supposed to air, when suddenly the ball of light transforms not only into Endora, but changes the wallpaper and Samantha's hair all at the same time! It turns out it is a new episode with Endora informing Samantha that the Witches' Council isn't going to put up with a mortal in the mix anymore. Samantha, being the headstrong witch she is, acts like she doesn't care what they do until she finds out, after a bolt of lightning and crash of thunder, that They have just pulled the plug on her powers, when a lamp she tries to move with a nose twitch remains stationary. She was also told that Tabitha's powers would be revoked as well.

The next morning, thinking a good night's sleep would've calmed the Council, Samantha tries to move a flower pot but with no results. Endora pops in to try and make her daughter understand that she has no other choice but to give in to the Council's wishes. Samantha still refuses and before they can talk about anything more, Uncle Arthur pops up from the toaster, riding the morning's toast. Samantha is pleased to see him as he'll bring some ray of sunshine to her bleak morning, but before she can find the reason for his visit, the sound of cracking wood and a loud yell emanate from the living room. All three race in there to find Serena in a karate outfit standing by the now broken coffee table. Serena is quite pleased with herself as she has just earned her platinum belt in karate and wanted to show everyone. Even though she's impressed with her cousin's skills, Samantha requests Serena restore the table, which she does. Endora, irritated with all the interruptions, requests that Serena and Arthur leave but Arthur says he's too tired to leave and all he wants to do his rest his weary bones at which point he magically sheds his skin, muscles, and everything down to his weary bones and performs a rousing rendition of "Dry Bones." After his performance, Endora again requests that her brother and Serena leave as she wants to discuss important matters with Samantha. Arthur states that he and Serena know all about the loss of Samantha's powers, which is why they are there, to take a stand with her. Right after they've pledged their loyalty, a huge roll of thunder and lightning happen, which Endora knows is the Council's response to their stand: both Arthur and Serena have lost their powers too! Arthur proves this by trying to do his table cloth trick, which should find the table cloth slipping out from underneath a set table without disturbing the dishes, but he ends up breaking them and Serena about breaks her arm when she tries her karate again. Seeing that she won't be able to discuss the situation with Samantha, Endora gets fed up and leaves. Arthur tells Samantha that she shouldn't worry, that he and Serena will find jobs and function just like mortals.

Later in the afternoon, Serena finds an ad for an ice cream plant, no experience necessary, which sounds perfect for the two, and so Samantha

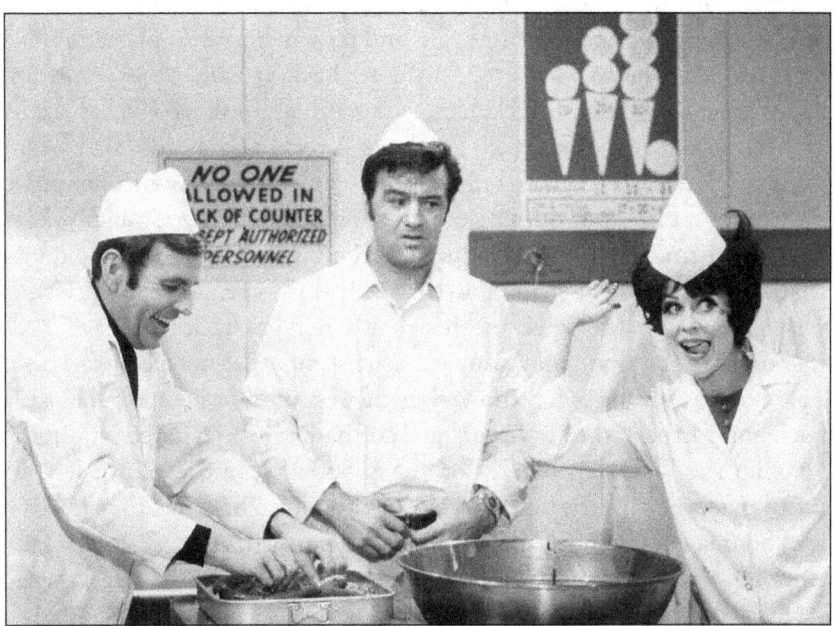

"Is my lipstick on straight," Serena asks, as she and Arthur ham it up for the ice cream customers under the stern watch of Buck (Ron Masak).

drives them there and drops them off. They meet the manager, Buck, who is quite smitten with Serena and is quite obvious about it. He tells them that they are going to work in the chocolate covered frozen banana division and he shows them, as though they are children, how they "take the banana like this, dip it in the chocolate, hand it to wise-guy, who rolls it in the nuts and sticks it in the tray." He tells them he'll come check in on them later and starts the conveyor belt. Things are going just swell, and it's even more fun as there is a window to the outside where the customers can see them. Arthur and Serena love the attention their getting until Buck comes in and sees how they seem to just be performing rather than working. He reprimands them and leaves, when the conveyor belt speeds up drastically. Serena can't handle the stress and tries to put the bananas anywhere she can, aside from the floor, which are dropping there anyway.

When the belt finally stops, the work floor is a chocolate nutty mess and Buck isn't pleased at all. He suggestively suggests that Serena take a break with him. Serena has had it and smashes a banana in his face, which busts her and Arthur up. Buck tries to keep his cool and when he tries to splash Serena with chocolate he misses and gets Arthur instead who returns the favor by a huge splashing of chocolate all over Buck. Serena and Arthur can't hardly stand up from laughing so hard, until Buck, in retaliation, tries to get Arthur again and only manages to plaster Serena.

Of course, the two are fired, and later back at Samantha's, fantasize about what they'll do to Buck once they get their powers back. Samantha isn't too sure that they ever will get their powers back because she doesn't want to give in to the Council. Endora comes to plead with her again. Samantha refuses, but does accept an audience with the Council where she tells them that they are acting just like the judges in Salem did and that even if they do keep her powers, she'll always be a witch. Once she's pleaded her case, the voice tells her that they'll get back to her.

So at dinner, Samantha can't eat as it seems that maybe she, Arthur, Serena, and Tabitha will be powerless the rest of their lives. As she paces back and forth, Arthur notices that Tabitha has just levitated a bottle of ketchup she had been asking for but nobody had retrieved for her. To prove that everything is fine now, he does his tablecloth trick to perfection and Serena karate chops the coffee table again with the greatest of ease. And just to make sure that her powers are back, Samantha reinserts the tablecloth underneath the dishes.

I LOVE this episode! It's always so funny even if I have watched it 947,234,972,349,828 times over…which is just about the exact number as it was one of the episodes I recorded as a child and would watch over and over.

Ron Masak (Buck) attended the 2010 *Bewitched* Fanfare where he mentioned that Liz was REALLY sick with the pregnancy when they filmed the ice cream plant scenes but he said she was a trooper and by watching the episode you would never tell she was sick. He also said the chocolate fight was filmed in one take! This episode finished filming in February which means Liz was about five months pregnant with Rebecca.

And speaking of filming, it was the twenty-sixth filmed, but the twenty-fifth aired. It was also the fifth Durwood-less episode of the season and the eleventh overall for the series. Dick York's brief appearance in bed at first doesn't count as that scene was filmed clear back in the Third Season.

Serena is my absolute favorite in this! Practically everything she says is hysterical! Especially at the plant when she says, "Is my lipstick on straight?" And, "Where'd everybody go?" I could go on but those are my two favorite. I also like her giggling at the people watching.

Uncle Arthur is really funny too even if practically every line he says are repeats of previous lines but, Paul Lynde makes it funny yet again.

Of course, I love that we get to see Sammy in her flying suit again and the scene in front of the Witches' Council is cool. I also liked that the episode started with them.

Endora seems different to me, like in the way she acts and her flying suit looks to be made out of thicker material…

Anyway, LOVE this episode and I think of it every time I'm at Disneyland because that's where they serve chocolate covered frozen bananas.

Of course, this episode is a remake of one of the most famous *I Love Lucy* episodes called "Lucy and the Chocolate Factory" which was the first episode of that show to be directed by William Asher, who also directed this episode.

MARCH 27, 1969

It was on this night ABC aired Episode #166: "Samantha Twitches for UNICEF."

Samantha is roped into working on the UNICEF campaign for the neighborhood committee, specifically given the job of trying to get a rich builder Mr. Haskell to make good on his $10,000 pledge. For some reason, Mr. Haskell has cut off all contact with the UNICEF committee and as Samantha did such a great job saving the park before, the committee feels that she's just the person to get him to pay.

Having been given Mr. Haskell's home address, Samantha finds that he is more than willing to let her in. His eagerness to meet with her turns out to be a case of mistaken identity as he thought she was his interior decorator. When he realizes his mistake, he asks her to leave. She tries to get him to pay the pledge but he won't do it. And it angers him that she won't leave so he practically throws her out and tells her that he never wants to see her face again.

As Mr. Haskell's day progresses, he finds that he does in fact see her face again everywhere he looks, from his chauffer to his secretary to his trophy moose-head! He decides it's finally time to see his psychiatrist again and when he explains how he has been seeing Samantha everywhere, the psychiatrist tells him she must be a manifestation of his anxieties as he is soon to be married. Samantha, who has been watching this session from atop the bookshelf, zaps the shrink into wanting a cigarette (even though he doesn't smoke), and after he leaves, Samantha pops into his place, mustache and all, telling him that his visions must be a manifestation of his conscience. Before she can go any further, Endora pops in telling her she's wasting her time. Mr. Haskell freaks out and leaves and Endora suggests that Samantha find his fiancé and see if she can find out why it is that Mr. Haskell refuses to pay on his pledge.

Samantha finds the girl, Lila Layton, who happens to be the former Maharanee of Ramipur, and a performer. Trying to play up to her sympathies for the underprivileged children of India, Samantha asks Lila to talk to Mr. Haskell but Lila refuses saying that Mr. Haskell is old enough to make his own decisions. Samantha feels that maybe the stuck up Lila, who is quite a bit younger than Mr. Haskell, may be the reason that he won't give the money. Leaving a bit deflated, Samantha meets up with her mother and they decide to have dinner in the same restaurant where Mr. Haskell and Lila are dining. Endora zaps in some truth salts to pour into Lila's soup and after it is eaten, Lila confesses that she is indeed using him for his money and that she has a boyfriend on the side. She leaves embarrassed and Samantha tries to get Mr. Haskell to see the error in his ways and get the money from him, but he refuses thinking she's still a figment of his imagination. But later on, the UNICEF committee receives his check.

I only give this one about one and a half stars. The demerits are for a lack of Durwood, Sam's HUGE hair, that moose head scene, and most importantly, though I know I'm supposed to have "suspension of disbelief," the fact that Samantha recognizes the need to help all those millions of kids that UNICEF helps, yet she is not using her witchcraft to do so?! Why doesn't she bypass the stupid committee and Mr. Haskell and just zap up all the clothing and food that the kids need? But then maybe there was a HUGE rule set out by the Witches' Council about helping mortals.

This is Bernie Kopell's first episode. He was well known for his portrayal of Siegfried on *Get Smart* that was still airing on NBC. As a matter of fact, he appeared on *Get Smart* that week in the first of a two-parter titled "The Not-So-Great Escape." As on *Get Smart*, here on *Bewitched* he's so funny! And I always laugh at that pencil line and also when he tells Mr. Haskell that they are going to play the word association game, but "please, no profanity."

I also like it when Samantha tells Endora, who has just interrupted her session with Mr. Haskell, "Mother, if you want an appointment just ask the nurse!"

The car scene was ridiculous in the fact that you could tell each woman was waiting for her turn to talk to Samantha rather than just leaving. And I'm assuming this episode was sponsored by Chevy?

Anyway, this episode is a big bummer after the brilliance of the last two episodes. This was the twenty-seventh episode filmed but the twenty-sixth to air. It was also the sixth Durwood-less episode of the season, the twelfth overall for the series.

Also this week, Liz was featured on the cover of the *TV Guide* with the accompanying article called "Husbands Beware" by Isaac Asimov.

Two days later, Dick Sargent guest starred on *Adam-12* in "Log 92: Tell Him He Pushed a Little Too Hard."

The day after the *Bewitched* episode aired Dwight D. Eisenhower, thirty-fourth President of the United States, passed away. During his tenure as President he oversaw the cease-fire of the Korean War and launched the Space Race and began the Interstate Highway System. His funeral was held on that following Monday evening being broadcast, causing the preemption of *I Dream of Jeannie*.

APRIL 3, 1969

It was on this night that ABC aired an episode of great significance in *Bewitched* history, Episode #167: "Daddy Does His Thing."

It's Durwood's birthday and he and Samantha have decided to have a nice quiet celebration at home in front of a roaring fireplace with some champagne. After he opens Samantha's gift of a watch, she tells him she has one more gift that's really for the both of them but before she can say what it is, she is interrupted by the first few bars of the French National Anthem causing Durwood to think she's given him the Eiffel Tower. Instead, the front wall suddenly opens up to a deep dark cavern out of which Samantha's father Maurice comes riding out in a fancy old car with driver onto the living room floor! Samantha is thrilled as it's been quite some time since she's seen her father. Durwood is less than thrilled but is taken back when Maurice, after dismissing his car and driver and restoring the wall, gifts him with a lighter that also has a perpetual calendar. And it does witchcraft. Durwood outright refuses the gift infuriating Maurice who tells Samantha that she has married a stubborn fool and that there is a jackass standing in her living room. Samantha disagrees, until she turns to look at Durwood, who has indeed become a mule! Before she can plead for her father to change him back, Maurice has disappeared in a cloud of smoke.

Samantha tries all evening to get her father to come back, but to no avail. Now that Durwood is a mule, he must sleep outside where Samantha points out that there is plenty of grass since he hadn't mowed the lawn. Unbeknownst to the two of them, Mrs. Kravitz sees from her window the mule and worries about it all night.

The next morning, as Samantha is fixing Durwood eggs benedict for breakfast, Mrs. Kravitz comes over highly concerned about the mule in the house. Samantha says he is their new pet and Tabitha tells Mrs. Kravitz that he's her daddy, which concerns Mrs. Kravitz even more and she runs off to tell her husband.

After breakfast, Samantha calls for Endora to ask her for help in finding Maurice. Endora suggests they try the south of France and so, leaving the mule-fied Durwood to tend Tabitha, they pop over to France. They find Maurice lunching with a beautiful woman he claims is his karate instructor. He reluctantly agrees to come back to turn Durwood back. When they get home, they find to Samantha's horror that Mrs. Kravitz had shown up with some men from the Animal Shelter who have taken Durwood into their custody. Samantha pops over to the shelter and brings Durwood back. Maurice tries to change him back, but after a few halfhearted attempts, and even the laying on of hands, nothing works. He decides they should find something the two of them can concentrate on and so he zaps up a chess board and they begin to play. When Samantha mentions something about Durwood's king, it stirs up a memory in Maurice about how a similar situation had happened before in King Arthur's court. He feels they should recreate the situation and asks Endora to leave as she hadn't been there at the time of Durwood's transformation. He then zaps the painting over the fireplace to show the events of the previous evening and reverses them causing Durwood to regain his human form.

This episode was the twenty-eighth to air but the twenty-seventh to be filmed. It finished filming on February 25, 1969 and it was the last episode Dick York filmed, though not the last to be aired with him in it. According to the man himself, in his published memoirs titled *The Seesaw Girl and Me*, Dick York says that he resigned. He collapsed on the set while filming this episode. But the way Dick York describes the episode it sounds like the script was supposed to follow what eventually became Episode #180: "Daddy Comes to Visit" and #181: "Darrin the Warlock" filmed with Dick Sargent. Dick York says that when he collapsed, he was sitting on scaffolding with Maurice Evans. The scene was supposed to be Durwood and Maurice floating in the air. He says he hadn't been feeling good anyway, and with all the light checks and stuff, it got him really sick and he passed out. In the hospital, Bill Asher came to visit and this is what Dick York wrote:

> *...Bill Asher comes to the hospital and he says, "What do you want to do, Dick? Do you want to quit?" I said, "If it's all right with you, Billy." He looked at me, and I guess he and Joey [Dick's wife] had talked, and I guess Bill knew when people had enough, and he said, "OK, kid, I'll tell 'em."*
>
> *And Bill Asher and I hugged for the first time.*

So I believe that he quit of his own free will, that he was man enough to realize that he was hindering the show by not being there all the time, though he did tell Herbie J Pilato (author of *Bewitched Forever*) that he had wanted the summer of '69 to rest up and he could've came back, but reading how his life went, there was no way he could've been back at full speed over just one summer.

I'd give it at least two and a half to three stars. It's a bitter sweet episode as you can totally tell Dick York is just wiped out and drained. I try not to think about this being the episode where he collapsed 'cause when I do, I get all emotional.

I've always enjoyed this episode probably 'cause they say "jackass" FIFTEEN times in one episode! Plus I think Maurice is hysterical, by himself and in his interactions with the jackass and Endora. This is the first time since Tabatha's powers were tested in the Third Season that we've seen him! Plus, Abner is really funny as well.

Luckily we have Maurice being funny what with his laying on of hands on the mule, 'Oh lowly beast of the field!...." And then Endora responding, "Hallelujah!"

I always liked the magical tunnel that appears on the wall of the living room. It really made the witch world seem other worldly.

Another favorite line is from Abner after Gladys tells him that the jackass is getting Eggs Benedict for breakfast. "Lucky jackass. All I get is lumpy oatmeal."

I'm mortified that Gladys didn't take Tabitha home with her. I wish that the writers had just had Tabitha say she hid from Mrs. Kravitz and the Animal Control and that she saw them leave a note on the TV or coffee table rather than having them give her the note.

Did you notice how the film is flipped when the jackass is shown in the kitchen? At one point the fridge is on his left side rather than the right which reminds me of another snafu that has happened this entire season and that is the brick wall seen outside the kitchen door. In "reality" were you to look out that door, you'd be looking down the driveway and across the street to Mrs. Kravitz's house but in REALITY, at the Ranch, you would see the corner of the park where the pool is located.

This episode also has the longest opening scene of any Dick York episode clocking in at exactly six minutes long! Usually they are around two or three minutes, sometimes even shorter. This opening is a quarter of the entire episode! But the longest *Bewitched* episode opening is yet to come…

APRIL 10, 1969

It was on this night ABC aired Episode #167: "Samantha's Good News."

Samantha's father, Maurice, pops in on her as she is cleaning up breakfast telling her that he had felt her special aura clear across the atmospheric continuum prompting him to make a visit. He also tells her that he has hired an assistant as he feels he is getting a bit forgetful in his old age. When he zaps up the assistant, Samantha is flabbergasted to find that her father now employs a very voluptuous sexpot named Abigail Beacham. Maurice insists he has only hired her based on her experience. Not wanting her father to forget her mother, Samantha insists he introduce Ms. Beacham to Endora and promptly calls for her. Endora is just as shocked as Samantha when she shows up, and to prove to Maurice that he hired Ms. Beacham based solely on her physical attributes, she turns the assistant into an old lady. Maurice changes her back, insulted by Endora's actions, but Endora will not stand for it and announces she is going straight to the Witches' Council for an ectoplasmic interlocutory, known in the mortal world as a divorce! Samantha is highly upset, but Maurice assures her that Endora is just making threats and requests that they have lunch.

Samantha treats her father and Ms. Beacham to lunch served mortal style of ham sandwiches, potato salad, and ice cream for dessert. Ms. Beacham isn't a fan and zaps up a huge meal. When she and Samantha get a moment together, Samantha finds that Ms. Beacham is very confident with her ways with older gentleman and pretty much admits that she and Maurice are together not for business purposes.

Once lunch is over, Samantha puts Tabitha down for a nap only to bump into Endora who has just returned. Endora admits she didn't go to the Witches' Council because she felt that's exactly what Maurice wanted. Samantha feels that there must be some way to get Maurice's eyes back on Endora, and what better way than to use the corny, but effective, old jealousy approach. She suggests that Endora find John Van Millwood, a warlock that used to compete with Maurice for Shakespeare's favor in his plays.

Later on Maurice and Ms. Beacham are still at Samantha's so Maurice could recite *Macbeth* to Tabitha, who is still napping, when Endora pops in with John Van Millwood. To everyone's surprise (but Ms. Beacham's), John takes to Ms. Beacham. Endora tells Maurice that she bumped into John and they had an intimate lunch together. Maurice and John argue over who was the better actor and finally Maurice, jealous as Samantha had predicted, loses it and tells Endora that as her husband he is insulted to the very marrow of his bones that she would choose such an untalented fraudulent colonial. Ms. Beacham tells the gathered crew that she is tired of all the bickering and that she is going to find another job. John suggests that he's looking for an assistant and they pop off. Endora and Maurice make up and then turn their attention to Samantha's glowing aura when they realize that it's because Samantha is pregnant! Samantha confirms it and calls Durwood at work to tell him.

I really like this episode as it is the only non-mortal episode in the whole series! That, and it's cool to have Maurice and Endora interacting with each other and, again, Maurice is quite funny.

With Maurice saying that he hasn't seen Endora in eighteen months, they should've used this as the season ender (especially because Samantha makes the birth announcement) or at least shown it before the previous episode.

One of my favorite lines of ALL time comes from this episode and that is when Maurice tells Endora that he is insulted to the very marrow of his bones! So dramatic! I also like it when he calls John Van Millwood "a ham from Down Under with an appalling speech impediment."

I also noticed that Samantha uses absolutely NO witchcraft whatsoever in this episode! There is only one other time that Samantha is truly witchcraft-free but that doesn't happen for quite a while.

I do not think that Ms. Beacham was as beautiful as Tabitha and Maurice thought, though she is a lot more beautiful than say Sarah Baker or Pleasure O'Riley. I could never understand why they got bleh-looking actresses to play the almost mistresses (with the exception of that hottie Danger O'Riley). And did you notice that Abigail is one of few witches, if any at all, that doesn't have a name that ends in "a"?

I also like when Endora asks about which side of the bed she's on 'cause it was so out of the blue. I also think it's hysterical when she says to Maurice "DON'T touch me!"

John Van Millwood was a perfect foil for Maurice. His name came from one of the horses at the tracks Liz would go to.

We also learn that Steve McQueen is in fact Dr. Bombay's nephew, which makes him a warlock! I always like it when real people are referenced as being from the witch world, like when they showed Willie Mays as a guest at Endora's Halloween party in Season Three's "Twitch or Treat."

Another favorite line comes from John when he asks Abigail, "Are you a thespian?" Abigail: "I beg your pardon?" How risqué!

Samantha's hair is absolutely the WORST in this episode! Could it get any bigger? I can't stand it. And the thing is, it's not big through the whole episode, just in certain close-ups. Frankly, my least favorite Samantha hair has been this latter end of the Fifth Season. It only gets better in the following seasons, with one episode having an exception which I won't mention now.

And, quite frankly, Samantha didn't even need to say she was pregnant, she definitely looked it in this episode. As a matter of fact, Liz was at least six months pregnant when this episode completed filming on March 4, 1969. Samantha, however, was only about three months pregnant if you base it on Adam being born on October 16, 1969, the airdate of "And Something Makes Four." This episode, however, was the twenty-ninth episode to finish filming, but the twenty-eighth to air. It is also the seventh Durwood-less episode of the season, thirteenth for the series.

APRIL 17, 1969

It was on this night ABC aired Episode #169: "Samantha's Shopping Spree."

Before going shopping with Tabitha, Samantha sees that her daughter has left her Jack-in-the-Box downstairs and when she goes to grab it, she about falls over as the box is stuck to the end table! Suddenly, the box pops open to reveal that the clown inside is now alive and laughing! Samantha thinks it's her practical joking Uncle Arthur but finds that underneath the clown suit is really her cousin Henry, also another practical joker. Henry zaps himself to normal size sans clown outfit and says that he just wanted to come and visit. He also tells Tabitha that he's brought her a present, which happens to be another Jack-in-the-Box but this time with a real talking clown. Samantha requests he zap it away and tells him she doesn't have time for a visit as she is taking Tabitha clothes shopping. Henry insists he come along, and before Samantha can protest, her mother shows up and insists that if Henry is going she is going. Realizing it's a losing battle, Samantha gives up and the whole crew leaves for Hinkley's Department Store.

At the store, they are immediately accosted by the eager new sales

Los Angeles Ram Jack Snow is confused when he pops into Hinkley's Department Store in New York. PHOTO COURTESY OF SHARON ORAZI

associate, Joseph Hinkley Jr., (who bears a striking resemblance to the eager, but ruthless, Gideon Whitzett who almost cost Durwood his job in Season One's "Your Witch is Showing") who happens to be the storeowner's son, on his first day. Samantha finds two dresses for Tabitha with Mr. Hinkley's help and she goes off to pay for them leaving Mr. Hinkley with Endora and Henry. He takes them over to the Men's Department as Henry said he was interested in a suit, but he slyly tells Endora he only wants to have some fun with the naïve salesman.

In the suit section, Mr. Hinkley tries his best to sell a suit, but Henry derides all the materials and colors and even rips a suitcoat in half, but restores it at Endora's demand. He finally decides he's had enough of Mr. Hinkley's pushing when Samantha comes back and sees that there is a bit of tension. When Samantha goes to thank Mr. Hinkley for his help, she finds he is gone but in his place is a mannequin that is quite similar. She realizes that Henry has done it and he admits it was because he was tired of Mr. Hinkley's pushiness. Samantha demands he change the salesman back, as does Endora, but Henry gets offended and pops off. Samantha and Endora find they can't change Mr. Hinkley back. Not wanting Tabitha to be in on all the magic goings-on, Samantha suggests Endora take Tabitha home while she figures out how to keep things under control at the store, especially since Mr. Hinkley's voice can be heard from the mannequin. And she requests that Endora get Aunt Hagatha to babysit while Endora search for Henry.

A little while later, Samantha sneaks into a dressing room to talk with Endora who hasn't been able to find Henry. Meanwhile, store workers begin gathering up the mannequins to get redressed and when Samantha emerges from the dressing room, she is shocked to find Mr. Hinkley gone. She finds from the cashier his whereabouts and goes off to search for him in the basement.

Endora, also on a search, finds Henry on the barren rock strewn landscape of the moon with a candle (he says he's moonlighting). He's still mad at his aunt and cousin and says he's going to sulk in a sulky and zaps one up and rides away.

Back in the basement, the workers get in a fight when they think the other is yelling at them, when it is really Mr. Hinkley yelling. Samantha discovers them and asks if she can buy the mannequin as she says it's her husband's exact size. They tell her that it's against the rules to sell them to customers and Samantha leaves. Just outside the door, she resorts to witchcraft by zapping Mr. Hinkley out to her and then she and he pop home.

At home, Endora has arrived from her moon trip with the bad news that Henry absolutely refuses to reverse his spell. She says it would help if one of them had seen the spell he had used and Tabitha pipes up saying she had and she shows them the hand gestures he used, which Endora recognizes as the Transcendental Triple. She releases Mr. Hinkley from his mannequinism but Samantha immediately freezes him and casts a spell on him that he won't remember any of what has gone on and they pop back to the store.

At the store, Mr. Hinkley Sr. has been looking everywhere for his son and is furious, but Samantha squelches his anger by telling him that his son had helped her in buying many things, which she proves by showing him a stack of boxed items on the counter that she had just twitched up.

This episode is my LEAST favorite out of Season Five because quite frankly, almost everything is wrong with it: Samantha's big hair is at its absolute worst, Durwood's missing AGAIN, and we have an imitation Uncle Arthur that is irritating as hell (and I like Steve Franken)! And Samantha even mentions how he is "not being original stealing Uncle Arthur's jokes." Then, if all that isn't enough, we have to deal with Gideon Whitzett again. Luckily, he's turned into a mannequin real quick. I don't know why he grates my nerves, but at the end, when he's helping Sam with the boxes, he drops them, and then she hands him one to help him pick up the rest and the dummy throws that one on the floor too!

And with all the shots of the real Earth that were available at the time, they give us that crude ball of clay which they had the nerve to even start off with a close-up on! But, with that being said, I really did like the idea of the scene being shot on the moon, cooler even still thinking about how the first men on the moon didn't arrive there until a couple months after this episode aired.

And the only line from this that I remember 'cause I just think it's funny the way Samantha says it is, "Mother, at a time like this you can't have Shakespeare!"

Did you notice Jack's box had *Wizard of Oz* cartoons all over it?

Anyway, bleh to this episode...

As I mentioned before, Durwood was missing from this episode. This phenomenon will never happen again as this is the last time Dick York would miss an episode. It was his eighth to miss this season and fourteenth overall for the series. It was also the last episode to be filmed for the Fifth Season, finishing on 3/11/69 as the thirtieth episode filmed but the twenty-ninth to air, which means the season finale is next week, so stay tuned!

APRIL 24, 1969

It was on this night ABC aired the season finale of *Bewitched*, Episode #170: "Samantha and Darrin in Mexico City." And unless you were one of the privileged few that could afford a subscription to *TV Guide*, you most likely were not aware of the significance of this episode.

Samantha and Durwood are bummed out when they find that Larry Tate has decided to take what was supposed to be their trip to Sexico Mity, I mean, Mexico City, to meet with the president of Bueno soft drink to pitch Durwood's ideas for introducing the Mexican soft drink to the American public. Not wanting to see her husband so upset by Larry's underhandedness, Samantha pops down, invisibly, to Mexico to look in on the meeting between Mr. Tate, Carlos Aragon, and Raul Garcia, president of Bueno. With a few deft zaps, Samantha makes Larry say some very embarrassing and rude things to the Mexican clients about the Mexican people causing them to rethink their dealings with McMann and Tate. Larry promises that he'll send down Durwood, who really knows his stuff and will be more "simpatico" to the Mexican people. After Samantha leaves, he also tells them that Durwood is quite fluent in Spanish, which Senor Garcia loves, as he thinks it will look good to the Spanish investors if the American client can speak to them in their own language.

At home, Durwood is thrilled to be given the opportunity but a little annoyed at Larry for promising his Spanish fluency. As he tries to learn as much Spanish as possible in the little time he has before flying, Endora pops in causing him to utilize his fluency in rudeness to her. After he and Samantha leave for Sexico Mity, er, Mexico City, Endora decides to repay him by casting a spell on him that should make it so that he does impress the client when he speaks Spanish causing his fears to vanish. But while he's practicing on the plane, he suddenly becomes invisible! Samantha pops home to find out what's going on, and Endora tells her of her little spell and that Durwood must be all fear if he vanished. She promises to reverse the spell once she has gotten over his rudeness. Samantha pops back to the plane with the bad news and when they land in Mexico, Durwood tries his best to avoid Spanish causing awkward moments with Larry, Mr. Aragon, and Mr. Garcia.

Later at their hotel (which was apparently designed by the same architects that designed Tony Nelson's house), Durwood finds that he now can speak Spanish without disappearing! But he does disappear when English falls from his lips. Samantha pops home again furious with Endora, who can't understand Samantha's plight as she did reverse her spell. She says she'll work on it again, and Samantha pops back. She decides that she'll throw in her own spells to make it so that when Durwood speaks to the investors, both American and Spanish, she'll make each group hear what language they understand all the while Durwood is just speaking Spanish. And to pay him back, she'll make Larry hear the whole thing in Spanish.

The presentation goes off beautifully after Samantha's nose gets quite a workout and Larry is utterly confused when he finds that apparently some of Durwood's speech was in English. Samantha decides that maybe Endora's spell will be lifted if Durwood just apologizes. He carefully throws an "I'm sorry" out to the atmosphere and finds that he is still visible and everyone is happy.

I really like this episode and would give it at least three stars. I love that Samantha finally gives Larry a kick in the pants for being so greedy and money grubbing. It seems that scene with her floating in the air at the meeting was always cut short in airings, maybe because Larry calls Mexico a backward country and calls them sleepy, which I thought was a strange thing for them to be offended about. I wonder if the line was originally "lazy" but they thought that might be going too far. Anyway, I LOVE seeing Samantha in her flying suit and Liz looked very gorgeous.

I also love it when Samantha pops out the first time from coming to ask Endora what she's done and she says, "Mother. You make a mockery of the word "mother"!" And then she gets that mean look on her face and pops out.

I must share with you an observation my friend Sharon made about this episode awhile back when we were discussing it because I've never laughed so hard! She said, "By the way, Liz herself had gotten a divorce just five and a half years previous from Gig Young…in Sexico Mity. No wonder she was so excited to go back there! She's gonna get a quickie divorce from Dick York and marry Dick Sargent, before the baby is even born!"

Sigh. Which brings us to the end of Dick York's five season tenure on *Bewitched*. At the end of January it was announced that he would not be returning to *Bewitched*. After having missed fourteen episodes for various reasons, he was let go or decided to quit depending on whose story you believe. And think about how hard it was on everyone on the cast and crew to have one of the main stars miss that many days of work. It had to be done. But the 156 episodes he was in are truly brilliant and Dick York will ALWAYS be Durwood, no, DARRIN in my book (no pun intended). You can just see how much he loved playing the role, how much he loved Liz, and his performances will always be remembered.

Now, of course, last week's episode was the last to be filmed for the season. This episode is listed as having finished filming on 9/19/68 as the thirteenth episode but the thirtieth to air, but I would say there were a few scenes that looked like they were filmed later based on Liz's WAY poofy hair and her different makeup.

It is interesting to note that the original scripts for this episode were quite different than what aired. One of the original titles was "Samantha and Darrin at the Olympic Games" and it involved Ocky! Remember him? Aunt Clara's beau with the "eyes like fishes, nose like dishes?" He is called in to babysit Tabitha and reads her a book about a kangaroo named Leaping Lena who is in training for the Olympics. He actually zaps her up and she ends up with Durwood and Samantha in Sexico Mity where they watch the Olympics. You can read more about the script changes on *HarpiesBizarre.com*.

Bewitched ended the season ranked as the #12 show overall, falling just one place from last season (the #1 show was *Rowan and Martin's Laugh-In* on NBC). The show also garnered three Emmy nominations for Outstanding Comedy Series (but lost to *Get Smart*), Outstanding Continued Performance by an Actress in a Leading Role in a Comedy Series for Elizabeth Montgomery (she lost to Hope Lange for *The Ghost and Mrs. Muir*), and Outstanding Continued Performance by an Actress in a Supporting Role in a Series for Agnes Moorehead (she lost to Susan Saint James for *The Name of the Game*).

It should be noted that last month, *Star Trek* ended its three season run on NBC but went on to become one of the most popular cult series ever.

Three days before, Dick Sargent guested on *The Outcasts* in "Give Me Tomorrow."

The following is the summer re-run schedule. The episode will be listed by number, name, and original airdate.

MAY 1, 1969

Episode #141: "Samantha's Wedding Present" (September 26, 1968)

MAY 8, 1969

Episode #150: "Samantha Loses Her Voice" (December 5, 1968)

MAY 15, 1969

Episode #142: "Samantha Goes South for a Spell" (October 3, 1968)
NASA launched the Apollo 10 mission on May 18, 1969.

MAY 22, 1969

Episode #151: "I Don't Want to be a Toad, I Want to be a Butterfly" (December 12, 1968)

MAY 29, 1969

Episode #143: "Samantha on the Keyboard" (October 10, 1968)

It was also this week that John Lennon and his wife Yoko Ono began their bed-in at the Queen Elizabeth Hotel in Montreal, Quebec on May 26 ending it on June 2. It was in this hotel room on June 1 that the song "Give Peace a Chance" was recorded along with Timothy Leary, Dick Smothers, Dick Gregory, and Al Capp, though Al didn't sing.

JUNE 5, 1969

Episode #146: "Mirror, Mirror on the Wall" (November 7, 1968.

Three days later the Emmy Awards took place with *Bewitched* nominated for Outstanding Comedy Series, Elizabeth Montgomery nominated for Outstanding Continued Performance by an Actress in a Leading Role in a Comedy Series, and Agnes Moorehead nominated for Outstanding Performance by an Actress in a Supporting Role in a Comedy Series.

JUNE 12, 1969

Episode #145: "It's So Nice to Have a Spouse Around the House" (October 24, 1968)

It was on June 17, 1969 that Elizabeth gave birth to her only daughter, Rebecca Elizabeth Asher, her third and final child and Erin and Diane Murphy celebrated their fifth birthday.

JUNE 19, 1969

Tonight we did see, a rerun of Episode #158: "Samantha the Bard" on ABC (originally broadcast January 30, 1969).

Screen icon Judy Garland died on June 22, 1969 of an accidental drug overdose.

JUNE 26, 1969

Episode #147: "Samantha's French Pastry" (November 14, 1968)

On June 28 police raided the Stonewall Inn in Greenwich Village and were met with retaliation from the gay community there who had finally had enough after years of persecution and brutality at the hands of the law marking the beginning of the gay rights movement. It's also the reason, or one of the reasons, why Gay Pride is celebrated in June, to mark the anniversary of that event.

JULY 3, 1969

Episode #154: "Samantha's Super Maid" (January 2, 1969)

It was also today that multi-talented musician, but heavy drug and alcohol user, Brian Jones of the Rolling Stones, was discovered at the bottom of his swimming pool, dead at the terribly young age of twenty-seven. He was credited for writing the jingle for a popular Rice Krispies ad in 1963.

JULY 10, 1969

Episode #155: "Cousin Serena Strikes Again" part one (January 9, 1969)

JULY 17, 1969

Episode #156: "Cousin Serena Strikes Again" part two (January 16, 1969)

Three nights later the mortals caught up with the witches when mortal astronauts Neil Armstrong and Buzz Aldrin (with Command Module Pilot Michael Collins orbiting above) became the first men to walk on the surface of the moon. We can be sure that Durwood was glued to the TV as the rest of the world was, most likely watching "the most trusted man in America," Walter Cronkite.

JULY 24, 1969

Episode #157: "One Touch of Midas" (January 23, 1969)

It was also tonight that the Apollo 11 astronauts, two of whom were the first men to walk on the moon, returned to Earth amid much celebration and were immediately put into isolation chambers.

JULY 31, 1969

Episode #166: "Samantha Twitches for UNICEF" (March 27, 1969)

AUGUST 7, 1969

Episode #159: "Samantha the Sculptress" (February 6, 1969)

This would be the last Dick York episode to air in ABC primetime as the rest of the summer they are all Durwood-less episodes.

It was also this week on August 9-10 that the gruesome and horrible Manson murders took place in Los Angeles. Amongst the victims was the beautiful actress Sharon Tate who was familiar to audiences from the movie *Valley of the Dolls*. She also played Janet Trego on *The Beverly Hillbillies*, Ms. Hathaway's secretary.

AUGUST 14, 1969

Episode #160: "Mrs. Stephens, Where Are You?" (February 13, 1969)

The night after this episode aired, the groove-tacular Woodstock Music and Arts Festival began in New York drawing a crowd of close to five hundred thousand people over the course of three days! Plus it is considered one of the greatest concerts ever what with great acts like Janis Joplin, Joan Baez, Santana, The Who, and Jimi Hendrix (just to name a few) that performed and gave some of the greatest performances of their lives. You can be sure that Serena was there. In fact, I wouldn't be surprised if sometime during the festival she didn't whip out her psychedelic guitar and drop a little "Iff'n Iff'n" on everyone. Peace and Love everyone!

AUGUST 21, 1969

Episode #169: "Samantha's Shopping Spree" (April 17, 1969)

AUGUST 28, 1969

Episode #162: "Going Ape" (February 27, 1969)

Two days prior, Bobby Byles who played Fred in Season Two's "And Then There Were Three," passed away.

It was also during this week that Elvis Presley staged his first comeback concert at the new International Hotel in Las Vegas after the huge success of his comeback TV special the previous year. The concert was a huge success and cemented Elvis' status as the King of Rock n' Roll.

SEPTEMBER 4, 1969

Episode #161: "Marriage, Witches Style" (February 20, 1969)

Also around this Labor Day weekend in 1969, ABC aired its Fall Preview. Lots of new shows were starting like *Room 222* and *The Brady Bunch*. What is interesting is when they get to the part about the returning shows there isn't the least bit mention of the impending Durwood-switch. However, *Bewitched* being a part of what was then the #2 day time programming is mentioned.

SEPTEMBER 11, 1969

Episode #167: "Samantha's Good News" (April 10, 1969)

It's very apropos that they aired this as the last summer re-run before the Sixth Season starts next week!

Season 6

SEPTEMBER 18, 1969

Tonight *Bewitched* fans across the U.S. switched to ABC at 8:30 PM EST in anticipation of the premiere of the Sixth Season Episode #171: "Samantha and the Beanstalk" after waiting four long months since the last new episode.

The familiar introduction by Elizabeth Montgomery invited us "to stay tuned for *Bewitched*, next, in culluh," the scene opened on the familiar backyard set where Samantha sat repainting Tabitha's old crib pondering on what boy's name they should use when the new baby arrives, and the scene switched to Durwood on the other side of the yard swinging his golf club...HOLD THE PHONE! A momentary lapse in breathing ran amongst all of us (well, at least those of us who didn't have subscriptions to *TV Guide*) when we realized that this guy that Samantha just called "Darrin" was not in fact "Darrin!" There may have been a brief moment of thinking, "Well, maybe Endora's changed out Durwood for another guy, most likely a warlock, in an effort to break up Samantha's marriage yet again but how weird that we weren't given that set up." And so we continued to watch, intrigued by this different guy that Samantha believed was her husband. Soon, Tabitha arrived out on the patio while they discussed baby boy names but by the look on her face, it seems she too recognized that something was amiss. And isn't that how it usually goes? The kids and the animals can see through the witchcraft? Tabitha tells her mother and whoever this new guy is that she thinks they'd most likely be happier with a baby boy and runs up to her room.

And that is when the credits started playing except they were NEW! I mean, it was still the cartoon night sky except now Elizabeth Montgomery's name filled the sky with the cartoon witch breaking through that, circling around and spelling out the name of the show and continuing on as normal except for when it got to the part about the kitchen. I don't know what the *Bewitched* writers were up to but the switching out Durwood for another guy seemed to have extended to the cartoon Durwood as well, as this definitely wasn't the original one though it was odd because the actor's first name was still "Dick" though the last name was changed to "Sargent." No, Dick York gone, really? NO! The credits continued on with the black smoke but there were more credits like "David White as Larry Tate" and "William Asher, producer." Our familiar show seemed to be a bit different, but it seemed to be good!

But back to the show...Tabitha moped in her room probably wondering what in the world happened to her daddy, when she realized she didn't want to mope by herself and decided that a good confidant would be Jack from the story *Jack in the Beanstalk* that lay open by her. With a finger-to-nose twitch, Jack suddenly appeared and Tabitha explained that her mommy and "daddy" would rather have a boy and she'd rather climb a beanstalk than stick around for the shenanigans going on. And with that, she zapped herself into the book.

Meanwhile, downstairs, Endora finally shows up and we thought we'd

Samantha meets the Giant's guard (Deacon Jones). PHOTO COURTESY OF SHARON ORAZI

get some answers about who this imposter Durwood is...except there was no mention of it! Instead, Mrs. Stephens arrives and Endora pops out. Well, surely Mrs. Stephens will know that her son is mis-placed but when Bizarro Durwood answers the door, she doesn't miss a beat by calling him "Darrin" and walks right in! Meanwhile, Samantha goes upstairs to check on Tabitha and finds that her daughter had been replaced with a little boy, and not just any boy, but Jack of Beanstalk fame! And things go from bad to worse when Bizarro Durwood shows up wanting to know who the boy is, and freaks out when he does! It's at this point we all realize that in fact this guy is not Bizarro Durwood, but in fact the REAL Durwood, that the episode isn't about Samantha's husband being switched, but about Tabitha running away into *Jack and the Beanstalk*. Really, no fond farewell for Dick York? No explanation? Well, anyhow...

After distracting Mrs. Stephens, Samantha tells Durwood the truth about Tabitha and pops into the book herself to go after her daughter, climbing the beanstalk herself even though she's pregnant.

At the top of the beanstalk, Samantha runs into the Giant's wife, who oddly enough is as tall as a normal person. The Giant's wife tells Samantha she'd better find Tabitha fast because her husband has a propensity for eating little children. And with that, Samantha heads for the castle.

During this time, Tabitha has made it to the castle, put the guard to sleep, and has found a way to rile up the Giant even more than he already was by showing him that no matter his size, he's no match for a ticked off little witch! When Samantha arrives, the Giant's guard ushers her in to find her "wicked little girl" who has zapped the hen that lays the golden eggs into laying real ones and charmed his magic harp into playing the Rolling Stones! Even worse, she has shrunk the Giant to being no bigger than a mouse! Samantha demands Tabitha restore order to the story and before anything else can go wrong, they pop home.

While Samantha and Tabitha have been gone, Mrs. Stephens has found her usual sick headache listening to Jack tell his adventures and before she can find out anything further about him, he disappears. And all is right with the Stephens family again…with the "minor" exception of the different Durwood.

Even with the switching of the Dicks, this episode definitely warrants four stars. It's very funny and it's great to see Tabitha coming into her own. I think the scenes between her and the Giant are SOOOO funny! Especially after Tabitha tells him that her mommy told her she's made of sugar and spice and everything nice and he says, "You're making my mouth water." I also like it when he tells her to get lost and she says, "I am lost!"

Samantha's hair, though long like the end of the last season, looks much more tame and beautiful.

I LOVE Bobo Lewis (the Giant's wife) especially when she says her husband was "Fee-Fi-Fo-Fumming all over the place." She should've been the replacement Mrs. Kravitz.

I noticed on the DVD that there were "new" scenes like when Endora pops out on the patio at the first and then says she has a pressing engagement with her tailor and pops out. I also don't ever remember seeing Samantha actually reach the top of the beanstalk and break off one of the leaves, which I think looks like Liz actually did on accident.

A minor boo-boo is the fact that when the Giant is resized, how does he get out of the dungeon? The door is much too small.

I also love the part about the Giant being cut down in his prime. If you notice Ronald Long in his other appearances on *Bewitched*, he is rather short in real life so it's funny that he would play the Giant.

And, it's worth mentioning that this was actually the third episode filmed.

The following Saturday morning *Scooby Doo, Where Are You?* and *The Archie Comedy Hour* debuted. Of course, *The Archie Comedy Hour* featured one Sabrina the Teenage Witch and launched the #1 song this week "Sugar Sugar."

Movie Stars magazine had a contest in the October issue to enter to win an apron worn by Liz Montgomery on the show if you could tell them which season was beginning this year out of the Fourth, Fifth, or Sixth Seasons. The winner was announced in the January 1970 issue as a Mrs. Jackie Alexander of San Bernardino, CA.

The entry form to win Liz's apron, alleged to be on the series.

SEPTEMBER 25, 1969

It was on this night ABC aired Episode #172: "Samantha's Yoo-Hoo Maid."

As Samantha is putting away groceries, Endora pops in and declares that she can no longer abide watching Samantha do all this work while expecting, therefore she has decided to hire a maid for her. Of course, this means a witch-maid, which Durwood is vehemently against. Endora tells him he needn't worry because this witch, Esmeralda, has lost most of her powers so there wouldn't be anything to worry about. Before either Durwood or Samantha can protest, Endora is saved by the ringing of the doorbell. When Samantha opens it, there seems to be no one there, until she hears a voice which apparently belongs to the invisible Esmeralda, whom Endora says fades when she is nervous. They invite her in and after she becomes visible, they speak with her about her background which included being nurse-maid to Henry VIII. Samantha decides that she could use the help and she persuades Durwood to allow Esmeralda to stay.

With that, Durwood retires to the study to work on an ad campaign but Endora casts a spell to get Larry to demand he come in so that she

Esmeralda holds the bouquet of flowers, invisibly, while Samantha kisses an irritated Durwood.

can tell Samantha a little more about Esmeralda. It turns out that fading isn't the only nervous tick she has nor is it the biggest, because every time she sneezes, she has what's termed "involuntary witchcraft" where something will happen without her control. Samantha is given a preview when she hears Esmeralda sneezing from upstairs followed immediately by all the living room furniture suddenly levitating. Samantha knows that this will not sit well with Durwood, who has found that Larry is bewildered by why he came in when they both agreed he was going to stay home and work on the ad campaign for Hampton Motors. Things get even dicier when Mr. Hampton shows up a day earlier than expected just to see how work on his campaign is going. Larry suggests that they go out to Durwood's place where all the layouts are.

Meanwhile, Esmeralda has been reading fairytales to Tabitha out on the patio and when she starts discussing having met a king one time, she sneezes and produces a unicorn! Samantha is beside herself, even more so when Durwood, Larry, and Mr. Hampton walk in. Getting no help from Endora, who has just popped off bored with all the happenings, Samantha zaps the patio doors closed buying herself some more time. Until Tabitha comes in wanting to show her Daddy (apparently Tabitha has accepted Dick Sargent as her daddy by now) the unicorn. When Larry and Mr. Hampton see it, Samantha suggests that the surprise has been spoiled and that it was actually all part of Durwood's idea for a new car called the Unicorn, "the car with the unique horn." Mr. Hampton is somewhat impressed but says he'd rather see what else is in store.

The next day, Durwood brings home flowers for Samantha from Mr. Hampton who wanted to thank her for her ideas. Samantha also tells Durwood that she has figured out how they can utilize Esmeralda the best and that is by having her be a "Yoo Hoo Maid," that is, any time she is needed Samantha will just "yoo hoo" for her.

I'd only give this episode maybe two stars, if that, and that's only on account of I think the floating furniture is one of the coolest, if not THE coolest special effects ever employed on *Bewitched*. It makes me nervous as I'll get out to hardly be able to see the strings, if any at all, when Samantha and Endora are floating, especially for Liz 'cause she's pregnant. I also find it funny when Mr. Hampton starts floating with Larry essentially in the room but can't really find the words to convey that he is.

But other than that, it is a rather dull episode because Esmeralda is such a dull and quite frankly, annoying, character. This in no way reflects how I feel about Alice Ghostley. It's too bad she didn't want to accept the role of Mrs. Kravitz when Alice Pearce passed away because I think she would've been perfect for that. I find Alice Ghostley's sneezing really irritating and fake. Of course, this is her second episode. She was first seen in Season Two's "Maid to Order" as a maid named Naomi who happened to be replacing the Tate's maid, Esmeralda.

I thought ALL the ideas for the campaign were lame, especially the Coyote and the Unicorn and how Liz could've agreed to having Samantha come up with that joke about "the car with the unique horn" is beyond me. That's so corny I could die!

It was also this week the big screen classic *Butch Cassidy and the Sundance Kid* starring Robert Redford and Paul Newman opened in the U.S. It's a great movie and by all means, if you've never seen it, you must go rent it. Five years later, Elizabeth Montgomery would play the wife of Sundance in a TV movie called *Mrs. Sundance* (1974) which is where she met her fourth and last husband, Robert Foxworth.

The day after the *Bewitched* episode aired, *The Brady Bunch* premiered on ABC as well as music saw the release of the Beatles' *Abbey Road* album over in the UK, being the last album the contentious band worked on together.

OCTOBER 2, 1969

It was on this night ABC aired Episode #173: "Samantha's Caesar Salad."

Samantha finds that she needs help fixing lunch for Durwood, who is coming home for it, so she "yoo-hoos" for her Yoo-Hoo maid Esmeralda to appear. After assuring the partially invisible Esmeralda that Durwood isn't home yet, Samantha delegates the making of a Caesar salad to her while she helps Tabitha change from her spilled milk clothes. Esmeralda finds that all though she said she knew how to make the salad, she really doesn't and decides she'll just zap one up! And she gets what she wants—a Caesar salad, minus the salad. The Roman Emperor is very confused as to what has happened and Samantha is beside herself when she finds out what Esmeralda has done. And when Durwood arrives home he, of course, blows his top. Samantha sets Esmeralda to remembering the spell to send him back while she tries to calm down her husband. In the meantime, Larry phones to say he is coming over with some great news for Durwood about an account they can land for Top Tiger cologne that isn't going so well. He tells Durwood that they will have a meeting with Evelyn Charday, the account owner, that evening and urges him to get cracking on a slogan.

In the kitchen, Samantha shows Caesar a history book with passages about his life and Caesar becomes incensed when he finds that he is listed as a dictator rather than the Emperor and demands that it be changed. Samantha leaves for a moment to find out if Larry is gone and while she is gone, Esmeralda stupidly urges Caesar to leave to find City Hall so he can do something about the misnomer he was given. When Samantha returns, she is truly annoyed with Esmeralda and runs off to find Caesar.

At City Hall, Caesar finds himself in the midst of an anti-war rally and demands that he be led to the Mayor's office. A police officer doesn't cotton to him and luckily Samantha shows up claiming that Caesar is a crazy relative that they let slip out of their watch. The officer releases Caesar into her custody and she takes him back home.

Larry's deadline arrives and Durwood has nothing and is even more under pressure when Larry says that he'll just bring Ms. Charday out to see his ideas. Esmeralda, in the meantime, has figured out the spell and with make-shift ingredients gets it to work, with the exception of Caesar not wanting to go back. Samantha decides they'll have to entice him and she zaps up Cleopatra just as Larry and Ms. Charday arrive. When

Samantha is pleased with her efforts to lure Caesar (Jay Robinson) back to the past using his lover Cleopatra (Elizabeth Thompson) as bait.

Durwood leads them into the den where Caesar and Cleopatra are, he is shocked and befuddled as to what to say, until Samantha suggests that the ancients are models for the new campaign slogan "Put a Tiger in Your Toga!" Durwood then thinks up of a campaign that would focus on the great romances of history and Ms. Charday loves it. After she and Larry leave, Esmeralda tries her spell again, and this time it works as both Caesar and Cleopatra leave.

I'd give this episode maybe a star. I didn't like it as much as the previous episode. Esmeralda seems to just be so dumb! Why would she let Caesar out the door thinking that would be a good solution to getting rid of him? And even more so, thinking Samantha and Durwood were going to like it? And she says that she knows how to make a Caesar Salad and then when she gets there acts like she has no idea where to even begin.

Also this same scenario with bringing someone from the past has already been done first with Ben Franklin ("My Friend Ben"), Queen Victoria ("Aunt Clara's Victoria Victory"), then with Leonardo Davinci ("Samantha's Da Vinci Dilemma"— there is even a similar scene of the switching of Durwood's suit for Leonardo's), and then just last season with Napoleon ("Samantha's French Pastry").

Tabitha spilling the milk was really dumb and they should've thought of a better way to have her do it rather than just clap her hands.

I did like Jay Robinson as Caesar and I liked the lady who played Evelyn Charday.

And did you notice that one of the hippie protesters is wearing a shirt that says "POT" on it?! SCANDALOUS! And what was with that woman's sign asking for someone to come home? I didn't get it.

Over all though, the episode was tedious.

OCTOBER 9, 1969

It was on this night ABC aired Episode: #174: "Samantha's Curious Cravings."

During Durwood's list of neighbors whom Samantha should call to take her to the hospital in the event that he's not home, she begins thinking of the chocolate cake they had earlier that evening, when suddenly a slice of it on a plate appears in her hand. She assures Durwood she didn't zap it up (because had she done so, she would've done it a la mode) and they leave it at that.

The next day, at Dr. Anton's office, Samantha tells him of her unusual cravings, which he tells her aren't so unusual for a pregnant woman, but as she thinks more about what sounds good to eat, a cantaloupe appears in her lap! The more she talks about the cravings, the more food just pops in, causing the doctor to be perplexed as well as Samantha, who is also satisfied. At home, Samantha tells Durwood of what has been happening, which worries him as they are to attend a cocktail party that evening and you can't very well have food popping in all the time, especially when a flaming shish kabob appears just as Larry arrives to discuss a new campaign. After he leaves, Dr. Bombay finally pops in from climbing the Matterhorn and after taking Samantha's pulse, and a few bad jokes, he blows a powder in her face for the cure. For the moment, it seems to have worked until Dr. Bombay leaves and Samantha starts craving a corned beef sandwich which doesn't appear...instead she disappears and reappears at the local deli!

After finishing her sandwich, Samantha pops home and Durwood cancels their appearance at the cocktail party where he was supposed to present his ideas for the new campaign, telling Larry that Samantha was beginning labor. At first, Samantha is appalled that he would lie but

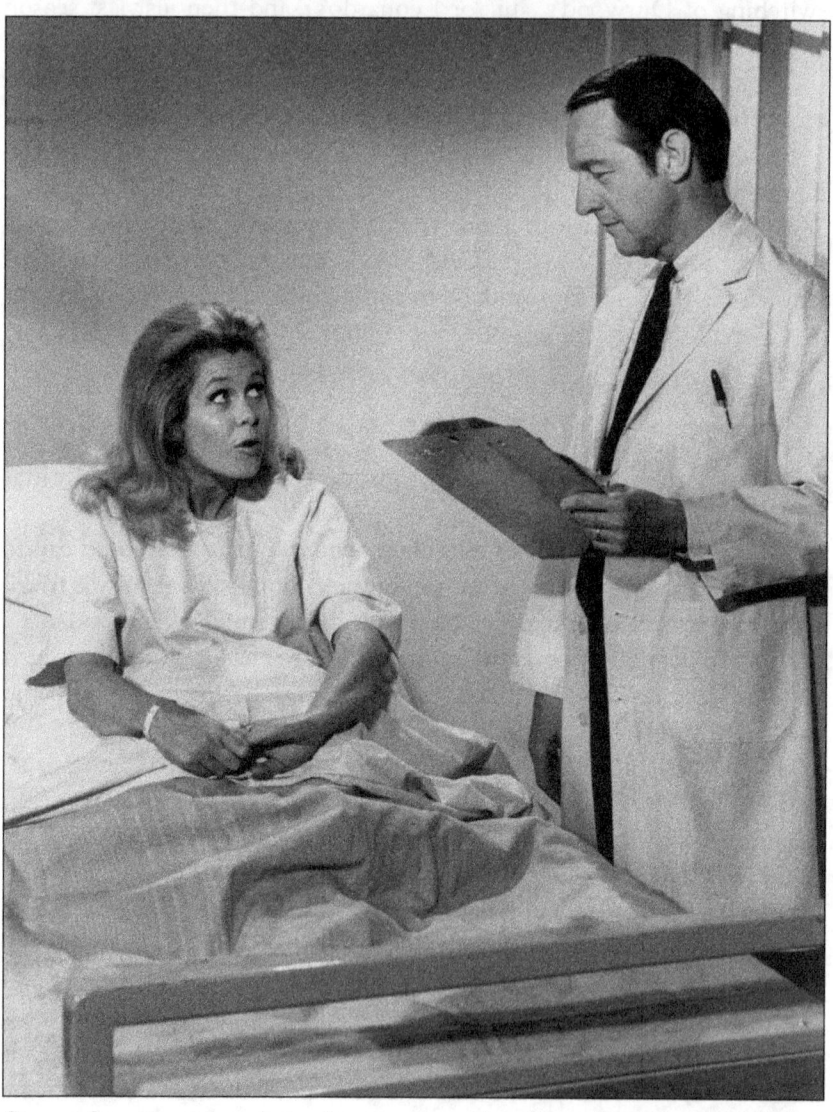

Samantha gets ready to hear the news from Dr. Anton (William Schallert).
PHOTO COURTESY OF SHARON ORAZI

decides differently when she begins feeling that maybe it is time for the baby to arrive.

On the way to the hospital, Durwood gets pulled over for speeding and is embarrassed when he tries to show the cop his pregnant wife, who isn't there as Samantha got a craving for hot dogs and popped into Shea Stadium. Once at the hospital, Samantha calls him from the stadium to assure him of her well-being and after watching a great play between the Dodgers and the Mets, she pops into the hospital and is admitted. While Dr. Anton is giving her a check, Durwood waits outside for Dr. Bombay to appear. When Dr. Bombay bursts into the room, Dr. Anton is a bit shocked that Samantha has another doctor on the case, but she assures him that Bombay is merely a family friend. Dr. Anton requests that Dr. Bombay wait outside but having no patience, or really patients, Dr. Bombay zaps Dr. Anton into another room and proceeds to blow more powder in Samantha's face while accompanying it with an incantation which cures her. When the bewildered Dr. Anton arrives back at Samantha's room, he announces that Samantha was merely having a false alarm.

Larry arrives excited to tell Durwood that as a gift to him, the client was awarding McMann and Tate his account in honor of the new baby. Of course, he is bummed out to find out that there is no baby, yet.

I would give this one three stars. It doesn't get four only on account of Liz's hair seems to be reverting back to end of Season Five and I HATE that!

I thought the premise of this episode was cute in that they take something everyone knows quite well—the strange cravings of a pregnant woman—and put the witchy twist on it. I wish I could get food to appear to me because that kebob DID look good! I thought it dumb that Durwood would still try to get her to get rid of it even though Larry had already seen it and had commented on it, but that's a very minor infraction on the part of this episode.

One of the neighbors on the list is the Cushmans which is in reference to Liz's relatives of the same name, Panda being one of them. Panda was her look-a-like cousin that is believed to be the inspiration for Serena.

Of course, the best part of the episode is Dr. Bombay in his first appearance this season! He's so funny, especially that part about wanting Durwood's soul. I also like when he does the incantation and just to make sure it rhymes adds, "Ho Ho Ho!" Liz's sneezing was cute, too.

I also liked Dick Sargent's take on the whole frazzled husband getting ready for the hospital. I thought it was really funny.

Didn't the hospital look quite real, as though they had really filmed in a hospital? I liked that part.

I also noticed that Durwood gets pulled over by the cop right in front of Pleasure O'Riley's house even though he supposedly had been driving for miles.

I also noticed Peanuts, the show's hair stylist, at the sandwich shop. And if you look closely you'll see a heart drawn on the wall by the pay phone Samantha uses which says EM + BA (Elizabeth Montgomery + Bill Asher).

All in all, a great episode! And thank goodness Esmeralda wasn't in it to mess it up!

OCTOBER 16, 1969

It was on this night *Bewitched* history was made when ABC aired Episode #175: "And Something Makes Four."

During the middle of the night (isn't that when it always happens), Samantha goes into labor and a frantic Durwood rushes her to the hospital where Samantha's father Maurice greets them. Samantha is taken to the delivery room while Durwood and Maurice uncomfortably wait together with another expectant father in the waiting room. Around 4:45 AM, the nurse comes to tell Durwood that Samantha has delivered a beautiful seven-pound baby boy! After showing Durwood the baby, she directs him to Samantha's room and tells him and Maurice that they'll be able to see the baby through the glass in the nursery. While Durwood goes to visit Samantha, Maurice goes to check on the baby and is appalled to find that the baby isn't in the front row. After the nurse refuses to move him, Maurice enchants the bassinette to move and then decides that everyone should be enchanted by his grandson and casts a spell upon him that whosoever looks upon him will straightway fall in love. His spell is a smashing success as everyone, including the other new parents, want nothing but to look at the Stephens baby.

While Durwood and Samantha are enjoying the glow of their new son, Larry arrives and falls in love with Baby Stephens and decides that he will be the new face of Berkley Baby Foods! When he tells Samantha and Durwood his idea, they are appalled but Larry won't hear of it and leaves to get a film crew. Samantha knows her father is behind this madness and when he pops in, he admits it. However he is immediately offended by Durwood demanding that the spell be removed, and he leaves. Endora pops in with her congratulations and accepts Samantha's request to find Maurice.

Meanwhile, the film crew has arrived and can't get through to see the baby for the crowd. Endora returns not having found Maurice and Samantha decides that she is going to blackmail her father by revealing to the Witches' Council her father's efforts in providing publicity for her son, the product of a mixed marriage which they frown upon, leading to his expulsion from the Warlock's Shakespearean Society! Maurice immediately pops in and removes his spell, well really altering his spell so that each parent will be in love with their own child. Larry is crestfallen when he finds that Durwood's boy isn't as enchanting as he once thought but all is not lost as Mr. Berkley has arrived and it just so happens that his grandson was born that evening too and he decides to use him for the campaign!

When Durwood and Samantha arrive back at home with the baby, Tabitha is excited to see her new brother. She asks if he'll be a warlock and just as Samantha tells her that they won't know for a while, a baby rattle appears out of mid-air and floats down to the baby. Everyone is shocked until Tabitha reveals that she conjured it as a being born present.

I'd give this episode about a two star rating and that's because I HATE that they had the whole story line with Larry trying to seal a business deal using the baby not to mention the fact that it's too coincidental that the client's daughter had her baby the same time. I also HATE Endora's hair! What is up with those curls on her forehead? Luckily those go away within a couple episodes.

What I DID like about it was the beginning scene and everything leading up to Larry showing up. Though not as sweet as when Tabitha was born, it was still nice. Bobo Lewis is funny and it's weird that they'd have her show up so soon after having been the Giant's wife but that is something they seem to do this season, which is to have the same actors over and over for the supporting roles. I also thought Samantha looked beautiful.

This episode marks the first appearance of Pat Priest a.k.a. Marilyn Munster out of three that she'll make, all in this season.

I like that we got to hear about when Samantha was born when Endora and Maurice fight over it.

It also would've been Alice Pearce's birthday who passed away three and half years earlier.

Also today, the NY Mets won their first World Series pennant against the heavily favored Baltimore Orioles, 4-1 and two nights later the Jackson 5 made their national TV debut on *The Hollywood Palace,* which was hosted by Elizabeth Montgomery three years earlier.

OCTOBER 23, 1969

It was on this night ABC aired Episode #176: "Naming Samantha's Baby."

Endora pops in to warn Durwood and Samantha of Maurice's impending visit, warning them because she knows how furious he'll be when he finds out that they are not naming the new baby boy after him. Samantha dismisses her, informing her that the baby shall carry Maurice's name as his middle name as they decided to name the baby Frank, after Durwood's father. Endora reminds Samantha that her father would never take second billing to anyone but Samantha believes things will be OK.

As if all this isn't enough, Durwood's parents are coming to visit for the first time and Durwood is nervous about having Maurice around but things seem to go fine as Maurice isn't there when his parents arrive. They are over-joyed to see the baby and present Samantha with a gift in honor of the birth — a little blue sweater. Phyllis, who is cattier than ever (must be residue from her last visit when Serena changed her into a cat), asks Endora what she brought for the baby. With a quick flick of the wrist, Endora zaps up a small bouquet of flowers and, while passing it over the baby, incants:

> *The gift of beauty I give to thee,*
> *sweet as this flower shall you be.*
> *Beauty is yours, in mind and sight,*
> *from baby's breath to the end of night.*

The elder Stephens are confused, but Samantha tells them it's an old family tradition, that Endora just hopes the baby will grow to love beautiful things. Just then a roll of thunder breaks the awkwardness signifying to Endora and Sam that Maurice is on the way, so Durwood rushes his parents out to the back to show them a tree he says he planted the day the baby was born. Maurice does arrive in his usual puff of smoke and he presents the child with a flower as well, accompanied by a different incantation:

> *Hear these words, O newborn child,*
> *on whom the universe has smiled.*
> *With this flower, I do shed,*
> *the gift of laughter on thy head.*

Mr. Stephens jokes around that it seems that Maurice and Endora want little Frank to grow up to be a florist. Maurice is furious when he hears that the baby is to be named Frank and proceeds to take his anger out on the various fragile items in the room. Samantha requests to speak to him in the den, and as they are speaking, Maurice decides that the baby's name problem should be discussed without the elder Stephens and he zaps Phyllis into wanting to leave. After they do, he suggests Endora leave as well, and after Samantha chides him for the spell he cast on Phyllis, he removes it, and they begin to head back. As Samantha, Durwood, and Maurice discuss the baby's name, Maurice suggests that "Frank" is not a suitable name for a warlock to which Durwood rudely responds that maybe they'll be lucky and the baby will be totally mortal and he tells Maurice it's none of his business. Maurice comes to the end of his rope when Samantha suggests that the reason he and Durwood fight is they are so much alike and he zaps Durwood into the hall mirror, where it just happens to be freezing cold.

Phyllis and Frank return and are perplexed by Durwood's image being in the mirror which Samantha explains is a new invention of her father's, the ability to project an image into any mirror. Frank, ever looking for new inventions, decides he would like to find out more about this and talk about investing in it with Maurice and so they retire to the patio where Maurice suggests that maybe having the baby named Frank isn't such a great idea as everyone will be inclined to call him "Little Frank." Frank agrees, as he was named after his father and was always called Little Frank. Meanwhile, Phyllis sees Durwood moving in the mirror and gets her usual sick headache forcing Frank to leave with her. Surprisingly, Maurice zaps Durwood out of the mirror at Samantha's request and they discuss the baby's name further with Sam suggesting that with a name like Maurice, he may be called "Maurie" by everyone. Maurice suggests that better not happen and Samantha counters with the fact that she really likes the name "Adam." Durwood says he doesn't like it, which, of course, means Maurice loves it and he deems that the baby will be named Adam (which also happens to be the name of Maurice's great grandfather) and he pops upstairs to see Adam. Of course, Durwood only said he hated it knowing what Maurice would do and so Tabitha now has a baby brother named Adam.

This episode is irritating for a couple reasons including, but not limited to, Phyllis being so mean, Durwood being mean, and Maurice's petulance about the whole name and the fact that it's taken them a week to name the baby! I've never heard of this before. I'm glad they didn't go with Frank Maurice but I do wonder where Adam came from as we know that Tabitha was the name of Edward Andrews' daughter and Liz really liked it.

The incantations were beautiful and I want to use them as part of a collage or something when I have children.

Dick York's Durwood was placed in a mirror in Season Four's "I Get Your Nanny, You Get My Goat." I like that they kept the idea that it's cold in the mirror world and I also liked Maurice's explanation of why: "Just luck!" I do find it irritating that they change *the Girl with the Broom* out on a whim. You would think they would have Samantha just mention how someone gave it to them as a congratulations present or at the very least that it needed to be hanging there because Phyllis gave it to them.

This episode seems to be slight remakes of "Just One Happy Family" and "A Nice Little Dinner Party" what with Frank trying to get everyone interested in his inventions.

Of course we get to see the palm trees of CT/NY when Frank and Phyllis are driving.

I always thought it was funny when Durwood said he liked the name Adam and Maurice mentions how that was the name of his great grandfather and Durwood says, "Your great grandfather was Adam?" Maurice: "Not THAT Adam!" The fact that Maurice Evans recites the lines emphasizing his name being pronounced "Mar-EECE" is funny in and of itself as Maurice Evans hated that pronunciation and used the "Morris" pronunciation.

One last irritating thing about this episode is how the elder Stephenses say how nice it is to see Maurice again when in fact this is the first time they have ever met.

Here are some of my favorite lines:

> MAURICE *(to Frank, about the name Frank):* "An appellation you have to share with the lowly hotdog."
> MAURICE: "Oh, you too, Endora. My cup r-r-r-unneth over!"

Around the time of this episode's filming, Liz filmed a public service announcement for Trick-or-Treat for UNICEF wearing the same dress she wears in this episode and I would assume it may have begun airing this week, however it may have begun airing at the beginning of October.

OCTOBER 30, 1969

It was on this night ABC aired the final Halloween-themed episode of *Bewitched*, #177: "To Trick or Treat or Not to Trick or Treat."

Endora pops in disgusted at Samantha's involvement with the local Trick-or-Treat for UNICEF campaign because Samantha is utilizing ugly witch masks and pointy black hats as some of the costumes for the kids, an image of witches that they have been fighting for centuries. Samantha assures her that since nobody believes in witches, it's not doing any harm. Ever suspicious, Endora believes that Durwood has put her up to it and when he hears the commotion, he tells Endora that it's every bit his family's right to participate in mortal Halloween traditions and that she shouldn't be sticking her pointy nose into everyone's business. Incensed, Endora storms out telling him that he'll regret his comment and he leaves for work thinking everything is fine…

…but it is not. While going over papers, Durwood feels what turns out to be a hairy wart on his chin and then notices that some of his teeth have become blacked out, just like the ugly witch masks Samantha was utilizing. Realizing that he'll need to get home, his efforts are thwarted by Larry, who has come in with the news that Mr. Bartenbach, of Bartenbach Beauty Products, is coming in to discuss his campaign. Durwood tries to hide his teeth and chin when speaking to Larry and Mr. Bartenbach, who is not impressed with the campaign. He tells Durwood he'll give him another chance and leaves. Durwood decides to leave just as his hat turns into a pointy black one and when he gets out to the car, his hair has grown long and scraggly.

Once at home, the transformation into an ugly old witch is complete. Durwood realizes that he did make a mistake in his hurtful comments to Endora as he realizes that the stereotype witch image really does not portray his mother-in-law nor his wife as they really are. He gives Endora an apology and, blown away, she accepts and changes him back. But then he blows it all by saying how it was fully within his province as head of the household to say whether or not his wife and daughter will go trick-or-treating and irritates Endora again so that she changes him back. Relegated to his new witchy form, Durwood retreats to the den to work on the campaign. Samantha realizes that Durwood will remain like that unless she stays home from trick-or-treating so she tells Endora she won't go and Endora changes her son-in-law back to his regular form.

At the office later on, Larry is furious with Durwood and explains that it's because Samantha quit the Trick-or-Treat for UNICEF committee which happened to be headed by Mr. Bartenbach's wife, who was upset at having nobody to help the kids in their efforts. Durwood runs home demanding that Samantha not fight his battles with her mother for him and demands that she go trick-or-treating. Endora is not happy about this at all and changes Durwood back into his witchy self and pops off.

Halloween night arrives and because of Durwood, in his "homemade" witch costume, their group collects the most donations in the history of UNICEF which pleases Mrs. Bartenbach very much, which in turn pleases her husband. Durwood tells him that he'll have new ideas for his campaign soon.

At home, Samantha requests the presence of her mother to show her that because of all the publicity Durwood got in his ugly witch guise, she is now doing what she was trying to stop, and that is to promote the visual of the ugly witch. Just then, the doorbell rings, which Durwood knows has to be Larry and Mr. Bartenbach, which is bad because he hasn't come up with any ideas for the campaign. Samantha tells him that he should use the image of Glinda, the Good Witch of the North from *The Wizard of Oz* to promote the beauty products and she zaps up her flying suit complete with a sparkly pointy black hat. Durwood agrees and just before he opens the door, Endora zaps him back to normal and she pops off. Durwood presents Samantha's idea to Mr. Bartenbach, who loves it and all is well.

I would give this one two stars. It is a remake of the first two Halloween episodes and even then they mess it up by having Durwood not know who Glinda is even though it was he who suggested it to Mr. Brinkman in the first Halloween episode!

For some reason I've always liked when Endora made the Princess Crown disappear. I liked it because she held it right up to the camera as though to show us she really can make things disappear even if you're looking at the object up close.

I also noticed that the magic seems seamless, especially when Durwood puts his hat on and it changes into the witch's hat.

I liked the trick-or-treating scene too. I just like seeing all the costumes and remembering how much fun it was to go trick-or-treating. And even though Durwood had on an authentic "costume," I highly doubt that would be reason enough to make everyone donate more to UNICEF. That was something that bugged me, too, is when Tabitha asks if she would get more candy if she were dressed like an ugly old witch and Samantha tells her "probably." Why?! That would be ridiculous for anyone to give the kids trick-or-treating more candy based on their costume.

And, sadly, Adam isn't seen nor even MENTIONED! You would've thought Liz being a mother, she would've said something about this.

I really think Liz looks beautiful (though I could do without the little curls underneath the sides of her hair) and THANKFULLY this is the last episode that Endora has those stupid curls on the top of her forehead. Whoever thought that looked good (Peanuts, anyone?) should be smacked, Agnes Moorehead included!

One of my last favorite parts was Samantha being in the flying suit. And I wish they would've just stuck with having her be invisible any time she's in it. It makes it seem more special but maybe the sparkly "dunce cap" negated the invisibility powers of the flying suit.

On October 29 the first message was sent over the beginnings of the internet known as ARPANET.

NOVEMBER 6, 1969

It was on this night ABC aired Episode #178: "A Bunny for Tabitha."

For some reason Durwood and Samantha are celebrating Tabitha's birthday in November rather than January when she was born and, in the midst of decorating, Uncle Arthur shows up when he's been shunned from a masked ball in Tasmania that the rest of the family is attending. Apparently, the Count was still sore at Arthur for nailing his shoes to the floor and giving him a hot foot. However, Arthur is there to help celebrate Tabitha's birthday and he zaps her up a wish box as a present. The wish box allows the user to wish for anything they would like and Tabitha uses hers to wish up a cottontail bunny. Arthur also offers to do a magic show for Tabitha's party. Durwood reluctantly agrees and Arthur sticks with mortal magic tricks except for when he zaps up his metal rings to the delight of the children.

During the party, Larry calls Durwood with the news that new client A.J. Sylvester has flown into town and is quite depressed over his recent breakup. Larry thinks discussing the ideas for the campaign will brighten his day, but Durwood refuses to come in as he is celebrating Tabitha's birthday.

Arthur tells the children that his next trick will be to produce a cottontail bunny behind a cloth. In the middle of doing the trick, Larry and Mr. Sylvester show up and witness Arthur conjuring up a bunny—a Playboy Bunny, which happens to be Tabitha's bunny in human form. Mr. Sylvester is quite impressed, not so much with the trick…well, maybe the trick, and he becomes quite familiar with Bunny, after Samantha zaps her into some rather well-tailored clothing. Arthur admits that his powers seem to be failing him so he can't change her back. Bunny and Mr. Sylvester retire to the patio while Larry tries to keep Durwood from disturbing them and Samantha gets Arthur to follow Bunny to return her back to her floppy eared self. However, Mr. Sylvester and Bunny have flown the coop to go get a drink at Mr. Sylvester's favorite hangout.

Samantha and Arthur pop over to the hangout to find them and witness a chance meeting between Mr. Sylvester and his ex-girlfriend, Anita. It seems that Mr. Sylvester may forget about Bunny until he tells Anita that he is quite involved with Bunny. Arthur grows tired of all the trivia and pops out. Samantha decides to invite Mr. Sylvester and Bunny back to her place for a vegetarian dinner in Bunny's honor and they accept.

Later at dinner, Mr. Sylvester announces that he and Bunny have become engaged and Samantha brings up their plans for a family. Bunny suggests she would like hundreds of children and when Mr. Sylvester brings up how he likes to hunt rabbits, the engagement is broken, much to the satisfaction of Durwood and Samantha.

The next day, Durwood comes home from the office with news that Sylvester got back with Anita and loved all Durwood's ideas. Just then, Arthur pops in with news that he had a complete checkup and a shot from Dr. Bombay and when he tries to put Bunny back to her original form, his magic spell is misconstrued by the powers that be to cause Bunny to split into six different versions of her sexy self!

I would give this one two and a half stars 'cause I thought it was funny, plus the anticipation of whether or not Bunny was going to come flying out of that dress was killing me! It's never been as clear as it is on the DVD just how TIGHT her dress was!

It's rather weird that Endora wasn't there for her only granddaughter's birthday party. And, for that matter, where were Adam and Jonathan and Louise Tate?!

I liked that Arthur didn't understand what the kids were so thrilled with when he made the rings appear and disappear.

I thought Samantha did a great job of decorating. Every shot of 1164 had some sort of balloons or streamer in it.

I wish that Liz's actual kids, Billy and Robert, would've been used in the scene, but maybe she didn't want to have them exposed to the world like that, though who would've known?

I love it when Bunny says, "Oh, I just love part-ies" and "I just love tricks" at the end.

It seems that some of Uncle Arthur's lines have been recycled from previous episodes, especially "In a battle of wits, you're unarmed" and "Been funnier if I had said it" That last one was said at least two times previous. The sad thing about Uncle Arthur is that he began the series as pretty much an equal to Endora and now has been reduced to flubbing up his magic.

A blooper is seen when small Uncle Arthur and Samantha are at the restaurant. Bunny goes to move her bangs and when her hand goes down it goes behind Samantha.

I also thought that freeze frame at the end of the teaser was weird but the episode seems to run at a regular length.

This episode was also used on *The Rerun Show* (2002) which aired on NBC where they took old scripts and reworked them as part of a sketch comedy.

This is also the second time that Bernie Kopell appears and it's the only time where he plays a part without an accent! I thought he was funny. It's also interesting that he was also still appearing as Siegfried over at *Get Smart* for their last season.

Speaking of *Get Smart*, it's worth mentioning that tomorrow the episode entitled "And Baby Makes Four" part one aired where Agent 99 gives birth to her twins. Had *Get Smart* not been cancelled after this season, David and Greg Lawrence were slated to play the twins and therefore would not have shown up as Adam.

Bunny is played by Carol Wayne, who's younger sister Nina appeared in Season Two's "Disappearing Samantha."

NOVEMBER 13, 1969

It was on this night ABC aired Episode #179: "Samantha's Secret Spell."

Durwood blows his cool once again when Endora pops in to invite Samantha to a masquerade ball for which she is dressing like the Knave of Hearts. After making a few uncalled for rude remarks, Durwood declares that Endora is no longer allowed in their house. Furious, Endora tells Samantha that Durwood is nothing more than a mouse and promises it will become true — PERMANENTLY — at midnight! Not wanting to be married to a mouse, Samantha seeks assistance from Postlethwaite, the witch apothecary to the cosmos who finds "a Spell to Prevent Subject from Being Changed Into a Mouse" in the BIG Book of Spells:

> *To void the spell the subject tries*
> *to touch a buffalo between the eyes.*
> *Next, while under water, he,*
> *must drink a potion given thee.*
> *To the last of the three, listen and hark,*
> *he must fly over water by day in the dark.*

He tells Samantha that it all must be done without witchcraft and the subject must not know what's being done. She'll know if it's worked because they'll hear the ringing of a bell after each step. Samantha is baffled at how she'll manage it but she requests he wrap up the spell and potion for her.

Meanwhile, at McMann and Tate, a rivalry is going on between them and Frazier and Colton, who are after the Illinois Meat Packers account. Durwood has come up with great ideas which Larry immediately locks up in a cabinet for which only he and Durwood have the key. Samantha and Tabitha show up at the office to persuade Durwood to go to the zoo with them so that Samantha can somehow get him to touch a buffalo for the first part of the spell. While they are visiting, fellow office worker Ralph Jackman enters the office wanting to borrow Durwood's key for the washroom. He is pleased to meet Durwood's wife as he had wanted to persuade Durwood to join the Loyal and Exalted Order of Buffalos. It dawns on Samantha that maybe Ralph will be a suitable substitute for the first part of the anti-spell and she covertly smudges some paint between his eyes telling him he has a smudge there. She talks Durwood into wiping it off and just as she thought, they hear a bell. Samantha tells Durwood she doesn't want to go to the zoo anymore and, in fact, she thinks he looks sick and talks Larry into thinking the same so that she can get her husband home in order to get him to drink the potion.

At home, she decides she'll have him take a bath and then, with the use of a funnel and a tube, she'll have him put his head under water and drink the potion. Realizing it's ridiculous, she plunges on trying to convince Durwood that he needs to take a bath, but he flatly refuses. However, he accepts her request to take medicine and she realizes she may be able to complete the second step of the spell by having him drink the potion while holding a glass of water over his head, and, it works!

Back at the office, Larry shows the security guard where the protected files are and informs him that there are only two keys, his and Durwood's, and when he opens the cabinet, the files on the Illinois Meat Packers account are gone!

With one more step to go, and the hardest one at that, Samantha decides to tell Durwood that they need to pick up Serena at the airport because the kooky cousin has decided to try flying mortal style. Durwood thinks it's strange considering the airport is so far away but Samantha mentions that there is a helicopter service that will take them from their town to the airport, knowing that it will have to fly over water at one point. He reluctantly agrees, and while they are flying, Samantha shows him a hat she has been knitting for him and has him try it on. However, she pulls it clear down over his face, putting him in the dark and a bell rings!

Once at the airport, they happen to bump into Ralph Jackman who says he's on his way to Chicago to visit his sister. When he leaves, he accidentally picks up Durwood's brief case. Larry and the security guard also show up, having been tipped off by Esmeralda that Durwood was headed to the airport, to head Durwood off, thinking he has stolen the campaign. When they open "his" briefcase, they find their suspicions are

Samantha is shocked to find a mouse in her kitchen, who she believes is Durwood.

confirmed until the security guard goes through it further and finds that Ralph's name is all over the papers inside.

Back at home, the witching hour has drawn nigh and Samantha is nervous for Endora's threat to change Durwood into a mouse. She has him hide in the kitchen and promptly at midnight Endora shows up. Samantha tries to persuade Endora to not cast her spell but Endora will hear none of it and casts a spell that the mortal within the house will change into a mouse. When she goes to the kitchen to check her work, she finds that it has worked and tells Samantha she'll change him back when he's learned his lesson, and she pops out. Samantha is shocked that the anti-spell didn't work, until she hears Durwood's voice and finds that the mouse is really Ralph Jackman, who had shown up to make amends.

I really like this episode because when I was younger I remember thinking there was no way Sam was going to be able to do the flying over water by day in the dark without witchcraft.

I also LOVE the scene at the Apothecary's. It's very witchy and spooky and it's funny when he slams the book on the desk and both he and Samantha do one swipe each of their hand to clear the dust at the same time!

It's unbelievable that Adam has not even been mentioned since his naming party. Well, I mean, I guess Durwood sort of mentions him in this when he asks Samantha what she and the kids will do if he is turned into a mouse. I remember when I was younger that I was totally shocked that there was a mouse in the kitchen. I thought, "Well, I guess her taking shortcuts like touching Mr. Jackman between the eyes just wasn't enough."

And, of course, that leads me to the very ending, the dreaded *I Dream of Jeannie* ending. So, how do they get Endora back when she's so pissed at Durwood to change Jackman back? And don't you think Larry would've had the police on Jackman's tail by this point?

Anyway, it is a fun episode and I do like the Apothecary, even when he does chase Samantha.

The day previous to this, TV history was made with the premiere of *Sesame Street* on the National Educational Television network, known today as the Public Broadcasting System, and it is still going strong! Millions of children have learned their ABCs and 123s from this great show which integrated learning with entertainment. One of the segments from the pilot episode centers on the letter W and Wanda the Witch.

NOVEMBER 20, 1969

It was on this night ABC aired Episode #180: "Daddy Comes For a Visit."

While making breakfast for Durwood, Samantha gets an unexpected visit from her father, Maurice, who has popped in to see how his new grandson is coming along. He has also brought a gift for Durwood in honor of the birth of Adam, a pocket watch that is water proof, anti-magnetic, has built in aircraft radar as well as being shock proof. Not only that, but Durwood will be able to perform witchcraft with it, which of course, he's not happy about at all. When he refuses it, Maurice turns him into a dog for being such a dog in the manger. After Samantha quotes Shakespeare about the quality of mercy that Maurice possesses, he relents and turns Durwood back into his human form. Maurice reminds

Durwood that Samantha has lived the mortal life for five long years so the least he could do is to live the witchly life for one short day. Realizing Maurice does have a point, Durwood accepts and goes to rush off to work to avoid traffic but Maurice reminds him he has the power of the watch which will zap him to work just like that with the added words "Zolda Pranken Kopec Lum." After saying the words, Durwood immediately shrinks away only to reappear at work without his shoes. So he uses the watch to zap up a pair of shoes.

Larry walks in mystified as to how Durwood got there so quickly when he just spoke to him on the phone. Caught red-handed, Durwood quickly comes up with a ruse about a gadget that he had hooked up to the office phones. Not wanting to hear the explanation, Larry bypasses that by reminding Durwood that there needs to be work done on the Bliss Pharmaceutical presentation, which Bliss Jr. is coming by to approve.

Later, during the Bliss meeting, when Durwood presents their idea for a new Bliss Cough Syrup bottle with the new campaign, it doesn't go over very well with Bliss Jr. who reminds them that they've used the same design since 1918, a design Bliss Sr. came up with. He's not sure that his father will like the new bottle design. Unbeknownst to the mortals, Maurice pops in invisible to check on how Durwood is doing. He overhears Bliss Jr. mention how he will present the ideas at a board meeting he is going to as well as decide if they may not want to go with Gilby and Associates and their idea. After Bliss Jr. leaves, and before Larry leaves, Larry mentions how he wishes they could sit in on the Board meeting. Maurice materializes after Larry leaves and suggest Durwood do go sit on the meeting. Durwood refuses but Maurice says they should speak about it over a Chinese lunch, which he zaps them to in Hong Kong.

In Hong Kong, Maurice tries to persuade Durwood to use the watch to go to the meeting and hypnotizes him into realizing what great power he now has. Durwood changes his mind and uses the watch to pop in on the meeting. Maurice joins him and they find that Bliss Sr. feels that no change would be necessary since they've been in business so long with their original bottle as well as campaign, which Gilby and Associates was going for. Durwood pops back to McMann and Tate but happens to pop in to Larry's office, where he explains that he has inside information about Bliss going with the rival agency. Larry tells him to start on new ideas and he will call Bliss Jr. to tell him that they've come up with another approach. It is then that Durwood realizes what power he does have and it makes him feel very good.

When Durwood returns home, he tells Samantha that he has realized that he's been keeping Samantha away from all that she deserves. He tells her that from now on things are going to be different…

Don't miss Part Two "Darrin the Warlock," next week on *Bewitched!*

This is one of my FAVORITE Dick Sargent episodes, if not THE favorite! Well, maybe not of all his seasons, but possibly for this season. I have the feeling this must've been one of the first ones I ever saw because I always remembered the scene of he and Maurice floating in the office and thinking that I wanted an office just like that because the decoration in it, especially that corner bookshelf, was so cool. And then when I'd see it on other episodes, I always would immediately think of this episode.

The "I'm a prisoner in an egg foo young factory" joke is so funny! Think of how strange that would be to crack an egg and find a message in it. And, what do you know, they actually DO have a baby boy! Adam is very cute in this episode and I do wish we knew who the babies were that played him in this season.

I always liked that Durwood was changed into a Rottweiler. I always felt it was the correct choice simply because everyone thinks they are so mean (when in reality they're not) kind of like Durwood.

That watch seemed like just a regular watch. How would it have been an airplane radar with just the simple face on it? That "Zolda Pranken Kopeck Lum" spell was used before by Bertha and Mary in "The Witches Are Out" to pour tea, but I like it better here especially when Maurice is repeating it at the Chinese restaurant and the waiter says, "Lum not here today." I think it's so funny and that part is ALWAYS cut out of the syndicated prints.

I love it when Durwood pops into Larry's office and tries to sneak out. It seems that in these later seasons Larry is given a lot more opportunity to witness the magic and wonder what's going on with Durwood.

The part with the "Sparkling Star speech" is cool though it kind of confuses me. Does it mean that Maurice put a spell on Durwood to WANT to do the witchcraft or was he simply just hypnotizing him?

I think the episode should've ended with Durwood saying he was going to take over the world.

Of course, this is the episode that Dick York was going to film when he collapsed because he talks about how he and Maurice Evans were on the scaffolding so they appeared to be floating.

It was also this week that Dave Thomas opened up his first Wendy's Old Fashioned Hamburgers restaurant in Columbus, Ohio. It was named after his daughter Melinda Lou "Wendy" Thomas.

Also, during this week, NASA launched the Apollo 12 to the moon marking the third and fourth men to walk on the moon, Charles Conrad and Alan Bean on November 19, 1969.

Two days before this episode, Agnes Moorehead appeared in her first TV movie *The Ballad of Andy Crocker*, which was supposed to be a pilot for a new series that was never sold.

NOVEMBER 27, 1969

It was on this night, as we recovered from the massive amounts of turkey, potatoes, and pie we had consumed, we let it all digest as we tuned into ABC to consume the second part of last week's episode, #181: "Darrin the Warlock."

For what amounts to the third time in a row, an episode begins with Samantha making eggs for breakfast only for the bowl to levitate out of the way causing her to break the egg on the counter. Maurice pops in wanting to know how Durwood has been since acquiring the magical watch. He also restores Samantha's egg as she tells him that Durwood hasn't even been fazed by the powers and that things are going to go back to normal. Maurice doesn't agree and tunes in the refrigerator to show her how easy it was to persuade him to use the magic. Samantha knows her father is right, especially when Durwood comes in and zaps up a gourmet breakfast served by beautiful girls.

After Durwood arrives at work, he tests out his powers by levitating a book which Larry happens to see. Durwood tells him that he's been reading about mind over matter and made Larry think he saw the book floating. Larry has entered to show Durwood a check written to him for $5,000 dated a year from today in case he lands the Bliss Pharmaceutical account. And speaking of Bliss, Senior calls to confirm their dinner appointment that night at Durwood's so they can go over the other ideas. Durwood is surprised by this news but Larry throws around his weight as boss and leaves saying he'll get the check redrawn for tomorrow. Knowing that Samantha will need some time to prepare dinner he pops home, right behind Samantha who was vacuuming, just about giving her whiplash as he startles her. He tells her about the dinner and also reveals how he found out Bliss's ideas. He also tells her that he's been converted to the witch way of life. But Samantha is disheartened, reminding him that she chose to live like a mortal when they got married because she loved it. He pays her no mind and pops back to work just as Larry is re-entering his office. Larry says after he left the first time, he came back in the office to find it empty and wanted to know how Durwood could've not been there. Durwood tells him it has to all do with the mind over matter business he had told him about earlier. He also tells him that his abilities are the reason he was able to find out that Bliss Sr. wanted to remain with his old advertising concepts and proves it to him by having Larry ask Secretary Betty what she had for breakfast by writing it down while Durwood stays in his office. Of course, Durwood materializes by Betty's desk, invisible, and watches what she writes and then pops back into his office so he can tell Larry everything she wrote. Larry is quite impressed and figures that he can use Durwood's powers with his genius to rule the world! He exclaims that he and Durwood will have the perfect partnership, a marvelous wedding. As he says these words, Durwood recognizes that his own marriage now could be at stake because he's gone so wild against all that they both believe.

Later on, Maurice pops back in to find a distraught Samantha. Durwood arrives at home and tells Samantha and Maurice that he has realized that he doesn't need magic to get ahead in life, he can do it on his own. Maurice disagrees, and later on at dinner he zaps the watch in front of Durwood when Mr. Bliss seems to not agree with anything Durwood presents. Durwood grasps the watch, but instead of using it, he stands up to Mr. Bliss informing him that his old ideas will not sell the product in the modern world. Mr. Bliss is impressed with Durwood's integrity but still doesn't agree with him and leaves with Larry, who has just fired Durwood. Maurice is ill over the fact that Durwood went against all his beliefs about mortals and, embarrassed, goes through his furniture breaking snits and pops off in a roar of wind and thunder.

The next morning, Larry shows up to congratulate Durwood for landing the Bliss account. Bliss Jr had called informing him that because Durwood showed that he cared more about the client than his own job, must have something and so they've signed with the agency. Larry gives Durwood his job back and just like Samantha had said at the beginning of the episode, things are back to normal.

All though I think this episode is great, it has all the boring parts of the first one. I did like seeing Durwood doing all that magic and it's just too bad he had to be such a dillweed about it when he came home. Rather than just say, "You know, I've thought about it and I just feel better about myself when I do things on my own," he had to act like a jerk about it.

This also marks Maurice's fourth and final appearance this season which is strange because he only makes one in the First, Second, and Third Seasons, none in the fourth, and two last season. He won't show up again until Season Eight! But I guess that's just as well, you can only watch him get mad and blow things up so many times.

I liked the sound effects used for Durwood popping in and out. To me, aside from the BARUMPH that usually accompanies Dr. Bombay, it is the most believable and realistic. I liked when he scared Samantha while she was vacuuming.

I thought Samantha looked real hot in that blue dress. I was glad it wasn't green as it seems that's all she wears this season.

My favorite line from this episode is when Maurice tells Durwood to "feed his face while I feast my eyes."

It was also this week that Barbara Eden appeared in her Jeannie bridal outfit on the cover of *TV Guide* in preparation for the big wedding next week!

Two days before, Agnes Moorehead appeared on *Lancer* in "A Person Unknown."

DECEMBER 4, 1969

It was on this night ABC aired Episode #182: "Samantha's Double Mother Trouble."

While having some mother-daughter time with Tabitha reading Mother Goose Nursery Rhymes, Samantha gets called away to take care of baby Adam when he starts crying. She "yoo-hoos" for Esmeralda to come finish reading to Tabitha while she runs to Adam. On the way the phone rings. Mrs. Stephens has called from the corner drugstore saying she needs to come over to talk to Samantha. Reluctantly, Samantha agrees.

Meanwhile, on the patio where Tabitha and Esmeralda are reading, Tabitha asks who Mother Goose is and in the midst of trying to think of an explanation, Esmeralda gets a sniffly nose and sneezes producing Mother Goose! Tabitha is ecstatic but Samantha isn't so much realizing that her mother-in-law will be over shortly not to mention an embarrassed Esmeralda has faded out leaving her reading glasses in mid-air. Fortunately, Esmeralda reaches from nowhere and retrieves her glasses, but Samantha still has a ditzy Mother Goose, who thinks Samantha's the Quite Contrary Mary, to contend with. Samantha leaves Mother

Goose to read to Tabitha as she answers the door where a groovtacular Mrs. Stephens greets her. Mrs. Stephens, now dressed like "a woman of tomorrow," has decided to leave Frank as she insists that he insists on living in the past. Mrs. Stephens tells Samantha that she'll need to stay with her and Durwood until she can find a place. She is also very complimentary of Esmeralda, who pops in to bask in the praise and to make up the guest room.

While Samantha visits with Mrs. Stephens, Mother Goose comes in from reading looking for some curds-n-whey for her and Little Miss Muffet a.k.a. Tabitha. Phyllis is shocked but Samantha introduces her as her aunt who's a little wacky, as wacky as witches. Before Phyllis can think more on the weirdness of the afternoon, Frank arrives looking for his wife. He claims to not know what she's mad about and it turns out that she took a comment about her new duds wrong. Phyllis snubs him and goes up stairs to have her sick headache and a little more of Uncle Arthur's re-assuring sherry. Just then Mother Goose returns from the kitchen and seems quite taken by Frank so she invites him out to the patio for more reading.

Well, if things could get worse, they do, because Durwood comes home from a cancelled game of golf and gets teed off even more when he finds out that his parents are there, his father specifically fraternizing with Mother Goose! Samantha tells him that they need to get his parents back together before Mother Goose fades out in front of them. She decides they can make Phyllis jealous by showing how affectionate Frank is towards Mother Goose. They go upstairs where Phyllis is resting and pique her curiosity by commenting on the reading party outside. When Phyllis looks outside, Samantha twitches Frank into inviting Mother Goose for a ride in his new carriage. Phyllis decides that Frank can have Mother Goose until she sees Mother Goose turn into a goose, courtesy of another sneeze from Esmeralda! Frank thinks Mother Goose is playing a prank on him and goes to look for her when he comes across Esmeralda's floating glasses and then sees the goose disappear. He quickly finds Phyllis, who is also bewildered by everything, and they make up and leave.

This marks the first, and only time that a main actor from the show directed an episode, and that, ahem, honor, went to David White. I choked when saying "honor" as, like my friend Sharon said, the writers "probably gave it to him because he was chomping at the bit to direct and nobody else wanted to touch this script with a 7,348,957,682,365,246,358,263,562,345 foot pole." AMEN!

Oh, this episode is PAINFUL! The *Bewitched* Critic gives it a bomb rating but I don't think that any episode of *Bewitched* is truly a bomb, but this one certainly does come close!

Samantha seems to be PMS-ing through this whole thing right from the very start. I was impressed with Durwood offering to help around the house instead of going golfing. He even offered three times and she tells him to just go and then icily says, after he leaves, "I hope the caddy snickers!" What the hell for?

Esmeralda is seriously still irritating but Mother Goose manages to come off even more irritating by being even MORE dumb than Esmeralda! I also hated that she thought everyone was one of her nursery rhymes. Her whole character didn't make sense as she admits to writing the rhymes but then thinks that they are real?! Truly, a shoddy script.

I did like Esmeralda's floating glasses (I hated them on her though… could they have been any bigger?). With the exception of the first fade-in, the special effects people did really well at making it believable. I always thought it was cool how Esmeralda's hand reached out of nowhere to pluck the glasses away from what we thought was just an invisible Esmeralda.

The only funny part is the goose hissing at the glasses and Frank being friends with it.

Mrs. Stephens is also another grating character but I think she shows up a couple more times this season. Sigh…

And for the first time so far this season, Dick Sargent was irritating to me, only because of his bugged out closed lip look when Samantha is trying to explain things to him in the den. It was overacting to the nth degree, but as it was only a small scene it's forgivable. That, and the fact that the rest of the episode pretty much sucked.

DECEMBER 11, 1969

It was on this night ABC aired Episode #183: "You're So Agreeable."

Durwood is pleased that Endora hasn't shown up for three days, eight hours, and forty-five minutes to inflict herself upon them. Samantha tells him that after all this time she had hoped they would grow to like each other. He tells her that what bugs him the most is that Endora just always shows up without notice when suddenly a note falls from the ceiling via a parachute announcing that Endora is arriving. Before she pops in, Samantha pleads with him to just be agreeable with her. When Endora does arrive, Durwood is overtly nice to her before he leaves for the office. Endora is quite suspicious of this drastic change in Durwood which Samantha explains is the fact that Durwood is so agreeable. Just then the doorbell rings, so Samantha leaves to answer it. Endora decides that she'll make Durwood truly agreeable by making it so that he agrees with absolutely everything!

When Durwood comes to see who was at the door, Samantha explains that Mrs. Kravitz was trying to get help in gathering signatures for a petition to upholster all the bus benches. Samantha told her that she would have to ask Durwood first. He says they'll discuss it later and as he leaves out the kitchen door to avoid Mrs. Kravitz, Endora freezes him and casts her agreeable spell upon him.

Once outside, Durwood runs into Mrs. Kravitz and agrees to gather signatures for the silly petition and he leaves for work.

At work, he presents his new ideas for Mr. Shotwell's campaign, which has been using the same advertising strategy for years. McMann and Tate were to come up with new ideas but in his quite agreeable state, Durwood agrees with everything Mr. Shotwell says as well as what Larry says confusing Mr. Shotwell who decides to take his business elsewhere. Larry is furious and suggests Durwood take a vacation for two years, without pay!

Back at home, Durwood tells Samantha of his plight and she suggests maybe it was time for a change. He agrees and mentions that he knows of an opening at Stone, Frazer, Moreheim, Cooper, Cooper and Washburn, one of the top outfits in the country. He thinks that Washburn would be the one to drop his name to in order to get into the company. Samantha silently agrees and tells Durwood she has some shopping to do and out of sight, she zaps into some clothes better suited for being downtown and pops to where Mr. Washburn is just as he is leaving to go to lunch. She twitches his secretary into telling him to enjoy his Darrin Stephens, er, lunch. Not thinking much of it, Washburn and his associate leave and Samantha follows them where she twitches the hostess and the waiter into saying Durwood's name at random spots. Washburn comes to the decision that he should hire Durwood, and with her work done, Samantha pops home. Durwood is ecstatic as Washburn has called to hire him as well as Mrs. Kravitz enlisting him to be the chairman of the Save the Starlings Committee. Realizing that Durwood wouldn't normally agree, she asks him how much Washburn is going to pay him and Durwood admits that it's a couple thousand less than what he's making now! Knowing that this could only be caused by her mother, Samantha hollers for her mother and demands she take the spell off. Endora freezes Durwood and rambles off the spell "lleps eht esrever" at which point she pops off as well as unfreezing Durwood. When Samantha asks Durwood how he's feeling, he practically bites her head off telling her it's none of her business and then demands a drink. Samantha is puzzled by the spell her mother just used and zaps the words up and when she views them from the other side, she sees that they spell "reverse the spell," meaning that Endora has made Durwood disagreeable. Just then, Larry shows up wanting Durwood to come back to work but only after he mentions that Mr. Shotwell decided he liked the ideas that Durwood haphazardly presented. Durwood refuses Larry's apology and Samantha can't take it anymore and freezes the both of them, hollering for her mother yet again. Endora shows up and truly removes the spell and pops out. After unfreezing Durwood and Larry, Samantha suggests that Larry was just welcoming Durwood back to the company, and Durwood agrees.

Later that night, Samantha and Durwood get ready to go out but their plans are shot when Mrs. Kravitz comes over wondering where Durwood is as he had promised to speak to the members of the Save the Starlings Committee. Realizing there is no way out, they forgo their evening so Durwood can make good on his word.

I would give this maybe one star. I used to love this one when I was younger because I LOVED the hanging "lleps eht esrever" sign. It reminded me of *Sesame Street* when they'd always have some sort of words in the air. I also thought it ingenious that Endora would use that spell but then it made me wonder why everybody didn't use it to reverse their spells, though it actually didn't make a great spell as it made Durwood do the exact opposite of the original spell. And now that I'm older, the backwards letters and putting "esrever" up top, is just plain dumb. Why would she have thought to do that? It would've made more sense to have block letters (though I liked that these were in the *Bewitched* font. I wonder if they just threw them away after?) and then as Samantha walked around them the individual letters would turn to show her what it really says and she could've figured out the order in which the words go.

Anyway, I really like Charles Lane. He's my favorite reused client and this is the first time we've seen him since the Fourth Season Christmas. And it is odd that they would use J. Edward McKinley no more than two episodes later. I wonder why?

Washburn's secretary seems cracked out! How did Luther James (the director) let her get away with reacting in such a weird way? And having Samantha zap everybody into hearing Durwood's name was just cheesy.

That scene at first with the floating plate is NEVER shown on TV. It was SOOO cool to see it on the DVDs but once you get over the awe of a "new" scene and watch it in context with the rest of the episode, it has no place in it. Durwood is UBER pissed over nothing and then when Samantha reassembles the plate she is standing there holding it, he walks in and not a second later the plate is nowhere to be seen, like she hadn't been cleaning off that top shelf.

And it seems that Gladys Kravitz has been relegated to just having petitions for everything. Seems like the last time I remember her on the show, she was passing around that petition to get rid of the Willow Tree! Though really she was in two episodes in between where there weren't any petitions ("Samantha the Bard" and "Daddy Does His Thing").

My favorite parts of the episode are when Durwood is leaving and goes to reach for his paper and Endora thinks he is going to kiss her. The other part is when Samantha has frozen Durwood and Endora pops in and Samantha says, "Take it off!" Endora: "In mixed company?" How risqué!

And one final thought, this episode is almost a *Far Side* script, you know where Endora puts a spell on Durwood and then disappears and Samantha has to figure out how to get rid of it. It's a sign of things to come.

DECEMBER 18, 1969

It was on this night ABC aired this season's Christmas episode, Episode #184: "Santa Comes to Visit and Stays and Stays," the first Christmas episode since 1967.

Tabitha comes home from playing with Sidney, dejected because he wouldn't believe her when she said there really is a Santa Claus because her mommy knows him and has been to the house at the North Pole. Samantha consoles her, reminding her that everybody is entitled to believe in what they want, even if what they believe may not be true. She also decides she is going to have Esmeralda come help for a couple days so Samantha can get some shopping done for Christmas.

Later on, while Esmeralda and Tabitha are eating lunch, Tabitha mentions how glad she is that Esmeralda will be there when Santa comes. That gets Esmeralda to thinking about how long it's been since she's seen him when suddenly she gets an itchy nose and sneezes conjuring up the jolly elf himself! Durwood is shocked that the real Santa is in his home but not more than Santa is at being whisked from the North Pole during his busy season. Not wanting everyone to be stressed out, Samantha suggests Durwood get ready for dinner so that Santa can relax and have more of a chance of fading back to the North Pole. Just then, Mrs. Kravitz comes knocking wondering if the Stephens are going to take part in the neighborhood Christmas decorating contest. Samantha gets rid of her but not before she sees Santa, thinking it's Durwood dressing up for Tabitha.

With no sign of fading, Santa gets pretty antsy as the evening wears on. To make matters worse, Larry shows up for a drink claiming that he's

Larry musters up some holiday cheer helping Samantha and Durwood to load Santa's sleigh.

trying to get away from the crass commercialism that seizes everyone during this so-called time of mirth. In reality, Louise (whom we haven't seen for quite some time, since Ms. Vanita was monkeying around to be exact) has been hounding him for a mink stole, which Larry isn't happy about. Samantha suggests Durwood get rid of Larry, which he stealthily does, after which Samantha decides to help Santa out by zapping up his elven workers so they can get everything done there.

The elves and Santa work all through the night at lightning speed making all the toys, much to the bewilderment of both Durwood and Mrs. Kravitz, who noticed a commotion going on during the wee hours at 1164.

The morning dawns and all of Santa's work is done. However, he has no way of delivering all the toys. Samantha decides to bring his sleigh and reindeer there so that he can be on his annual ride on time. With the newly arrived sleigh and reindeer, Mrs. Kravitz is quite impressed at their effort in decorating. Making sure no one is around, Samantha gives the OK for the elves to start loading the sleigh, which they do in no time flat. Of course, Mrs. Kravitz is watching and faints dead away. Just as Santa is about to leave, Larry pulls up for another visit. Durwood explains that he's hired Santa and his elves as part of their decoration so they can win the neighborhood contest.

After they've had a few drinks, Tabitha announces that Santa is leaving and Larry looks out to see the sleigh and reindeer ride off into the evening sky. Quite confused, Larry thinks about what he's seen and decides maybe Christmas is much more than just mink stoles, which he goes to buy Louise.

The next day, after having spent some time with Sidney, Tabitha tells her parents that her friend changed his mind about Santa after they got into another argument and Tabitha changed him into a mushroom! Durwood is about to get mad but Samantha reminds him that it's Christmas and should be a time of peace.

I've always enjoyed this episode though it's my least favorite out of all the Christmas episodes. I think it has a certain charm, though, brought on by the great opening shot with the tree and Samantha and the baby in the background, and then seeing actual reindeer out on the lawn topped off by the falling snow looking in on the living room from the patio window. I just wish they would've left Esmeralda out of it. I hadn't realized until lately just how irritating she is! I think it would've been better to have had Tabitha zap up Santa and then not be able to get him back cause she doesn't really want him to go back until Samantha or Santa gets her to understand how disappointed all the other children of the world will be if he isn't back to do his job.

I also wish they could've filmed at the Ranch in November or December when there were NO leaves on the trees or bushes and actual snow on the ground. It's actually quite surprising that the finished filming date for this was Halloween of that year. The trees look so GREEN!

I like the spell Samantha uses to bring the reindeer. I thought it was cute how they integrated a spell with "The Night Before Christmas" and that she mentioned the antennas.

I liked Larry in this probably because this is one of the rare occasions where he comes to visit just to visit and not to try and get Durwood to come to work or something. I wish Louise would've been in it. We haven't seen her since the middle of last season and WON'T see her for another five or so episodes!

I think Hallmark, or whoever does cards, should make *Bewitched* Christmas cards and the one that they make with sound, or ones that they make with sound, should have that greeting from the end of the episode with the music.

This episode also marks the last episode of the 1960s as next week's episode is a rerun. However the real last episode of the 60s is really "Serena Steals the Show" which finished filming this evening before the Christmas break.

DECEMBER 25, 1969

It was on this night ABC re-aired Episode #165: "Samantha's Power Failure" which originally aired on 3/20/69 but with Dick Sargent credits.

Two days before, Donald Foster passed away. He played Bob Frazer's father in Season One's "Which Witch is Which?"

JANUARY 1, 1970

It was on this night, while recovering from the reveries of the previous evening and welcoming in the brand new decade, we rested while ABC regaled us with a brand new episode of *Bewitched*, Episode #185: "Samantha's Better Halves."

Durwood and Samantha are preparing to leave to the Caribbean, their first vacation in five years. All though they are excited, Durwood is nervous that Larry is somehow going to foul things up and his intuition is right when Larry shows up with a portable bar as a going away present. However, he tells them that he's not excited to go to Chicago on a business trip that Durwood was supposed to go on, especially now that Louise is sick. Durwood stands firm and tells Larry that he is still going on his vacation. Defeated, Larry leaves. Durwood mentions how he wishes there were some way to be in two places at the same time and Samantha insists he keep that wish to himself as the walls, and her mother, have ears and may grant his wish like she did the last time he wished that. They then recall that right before Adam was born Durwood was to go on a business trip to Japan but was feeling guilty about leaving Samantha when she was so close to her due date. Endora offered to split him up but Samantha refused the offer, but when she was out on the patio playing with Tabitha, believing that Durwood had decided to go to Japan, Endora decides to honor Durwood's wish and she splits him into two separate beings, one being the work side of Durwood and the other being the caring doting Durwood.

Business Durwood leaves for Japan and Doting Durwood shocks Samantha when she comes back in, not only by his being there but by how much he insists on doing for her. Samantha finds out what Endora has done and is furious and demands her mother put the two back together. As Business Durwood is clear across the world, Endora starts to work putting them back together and only manages to switch the two Durwoods so that the Doting Durwood now ends up in Japan, confusing the client. With one more attempt, Endora finally manages to get them back together.

In the present, Durwood is finally satisfied with his decision to stick to going on the vacation when Larry returns hunched over as he says he's thrown out his back and now he will not be able to go on the Chicago trip. Quick thinking Samantha zaps up a vampire bat that comes swooping through the room causing Larry to straighten up to cover his head. Caught in his lie, Larry again leaves defeated and Durwood and Samantha race up stairs to pack.

I have to say that I found this episode pretty amusing. I'd give it two and a half stars. It would've got more but Dick York's version ("Divided He Stands") was infinitely better.

It seemed that Elizabeth Montgomery, Agnes Moorehead, and David White were really funny in this episode. My favorite line, which I had never seen before the DVD, was when freshly popped home Business Durwood is blah-blah-blahing and Samantha says, "Mother, will he remember any of this?" Endora: "No." Samantha: "QUIET!" It reminded me a lot of when Durwood in the Pie Fight episode calls out to Samantha (who is actually Serena) and she says from off camera, "What is it?!" Just the faces Samantha was giving either of her husbands was priceless.

I also love it when Endora cracks herself up by saying she may get 'spellbound.'

The funniest, though, is Larry coming back in holding his back. You just gotta love him for trying.

But, Dick Sargent in his first filmed scenes truly seems like he's trying to mimic Dick York instead of just be himself and he makes a lot of strange faces. And what the hell was up with the bat? They could've at least sped the film up. It looks just like they went pillaging through the old props from *The Munsters* and dusted off the Igor bat and used it.

If you think about it, the only "vacation" they've had is when Samantha went with Fun Durwood to Miami, but even then he wasn't himself and it didn't seem like much of a vacation for Samantha. And Sexico Mity doesn't count 'cause that was a business trip.

And how about we STILL have yet to see Louise? I wonder what Kasey was doing in that time?

I find it strange that the writers, producers, and director would've went ahead with this script with all those lines about just one Durwood. Maybe they realized it after they started filming and that's why they shelved it and reworked it to be a "remember when" episode.

And I noticed at the beginning, which by the way was SEVEN MINUTES long, probably the longest teaser in all of *Bewitched* history, that Samantha's hair goes from short to long depending on whether there is a close-up or not. I also think it may have been around the same time that the teaser and trailer scenes were shot that the Clairol commercial with Liz was shot, though she isn't wearing the same outfit.

JANUARY 8, 1970

It was on this night ABC aired Episode #186: "Samantha's Lost Weekend."

When Tabitha won't eat her HUGE lunch, Durwood gives her the option to go to her room, which she does. Then, after he and Samantha leave the kitchen to look for his golf glove, the visiting Esmeralda decides to take matters into her own hands and casts a spell on Tabitha's milk making "she who drinks this crave to eat." On her way up to Tabitha's room, she runs into Samantha who tells her that Tabitha cannot have anything to drink if she's not going to eat and drinks the milk herself. Immediately, she is starving and starts eating everything in the house. Esmeralda tries to remove the spell but it doesn't work, and at a loss, she pops over to the Apothecary's place to get an antidote.

Meanwhile, Samantha's eating fest is interrupted by Abner Kravitz who has come over on assignment from his wife to collect signatures for a petition to get the trash collection days changed. However, seeing that Samantha can't stop eating for a moment, he leaves in a befuddled haze. When Durwood comes back from golfing, Samantha tells him she thinks she may have a rare virus, more prevalent in warlocks, called Voracious Ravenousitis. Her calls to Dr. Bombay have gone unanswered on account of him being busy in his Saturday Water Buffalo Polo Game. She tells Durwood that as she's eaten everything in the house, she'll need to go to the store. Not wanting his sick wife to do so alone, he offers to drive her. Before they leave, she yoo-hoos for Esmeralda, who has still been waiting for the randy Apothecary to finish his antidote.

At the store, Samantha cannot help herself to all the food just lying on the shelves and in people's carts. After their disastrous market experience, they arrive home and Samantha tries Dr. Bombay once more. His new trained nurse pops in to explain that Dr. Bombay's water polo game has gone into triple overtime but tells them she'll notify the doctor that they called.

Abner interrupts Samantha's peanut butter and jelly sandwich-fest to ask her to sign a petition.

During the middle of the night, Durwood discovers Samantha down in the kitchen making a huge sandwich. Realizing she cannot go on like this, she puts in one more call to Dr. Bombay who pops in, excited to see what Samantha says is Voracious Ravenousitis, a malady he hasn't seen in centuries. He gives her a soundwave injection requesting that her disease be forthwith arrested, and with that, he leaves.

The next morning, her hunger finally satiated, Samantha greets Durwood and Tabitha who have awoke before she, only to find herself falling asleep standing up! However, she doesn't realize it when Durwood wakes her and immediately she falls asleep again. She suggests Durwood take Tabitha upstairs to get dressed while she calls for Dr. Bombay again. In the midst of doing so, she falls asleep again. Mr. Kravitz shows up again and sees her sleeping standing up in the kitchen. Taking a page from his wife's book, he barges in and tells Samantha that he's going to be very persistent about getting signatures, but is surprised when she falls asleep again.

Out in the cosmos, Esmeralda pops into the Apothecary's for the cure (which she gets in exchange for a kiss) and pops back to the Stephenses where she admits to what she has done. Since Samantha can't stay awake, she calls for Dr. Bombay to come remove his cure so that she can administer the real cure and everything is back to as normal as it can be at 1164.

I've always enjoyed this episode and would give it two and a half to three stars. It's almost like the "afterschool special" episode of *Bewitched* about eating disorders, but done in a magic fun way.

I actually didn't think Esmeralda was as dumb in this one. In fact, I found her rather funny what with her telling Postlethwaite that she's a young unmarried and that she's had tons of offers to go to the dance but then she pauses afterward like she's waiting for him to disagree with her.

I also enjoy every time the Apothercary is shown. His place is just so witchy and cool! Plus, I find it funny that he's so horny for being so old. I also like it like when he's chasing Esmeralda trying to convince her that while they wait for the shipment from Neptune they can fool around and then when he's out of breath, he says "Take five!"

Elizabeth Montgomery told Herbie J Pilato (*Bewitched Forever*) that this episode was one of her favorites, specifically the lettuce scene. And did you notice all the Quaker Oats stacked in the store?

Pat Priest's appearance is the first time we get to see one of Dr. Bombay's nurses, and she's hot! I love it when Durwood asks her if she knows how to cure what they think is Voracious Ravenousitis and she says "No." Samantha: "But I thought you said you were a trained nurse." Nurse: "I am, but that's not what I'm trained in." The look on Samantha's face, especially when she looks her up and down, is priceless! I also liked the very light *plink* when the Nurse popped in and out. This was Pat's second appearance.

Of course, Dr. Bombay is always awesome! I love it when he pops in and tells them he was in a conference and Samantha says, "We know. We saw her." And, for some reason, I always think of when Samantha tells him, "I think I have VorACIOUS Ravenousitis." I just like how she says it and the fact that the name is so descriptive. And then Dr. Bombay's response: "Really! I haven't seen a good case of Voracious Ravenousitis in centuries." I also like that he tells Durwood, "If you become a warlock, I'll become a mortal!"

The sleeping parts were very Velveeta and just Abner being in the episode without his wife was weird and a bit dumb. I can't see Abner, no matter how much his wife harps on him, actually going out to collect signatures for such a dumb petition. And, p.s., have you ever had garbage pickup twice a week?

It was also this week that the long running day time soap *All My Children* premiered on ABC.

Three nights earlier, Dick Sargent appeared on *Love, American Style* in "Love and the Fighting Couple."

JANUARY 15, 1970

It was on this night ABC aired Episode #187: "The Phrase is Familiar."

Samantha and Durwood have decided that maybe it's time to enroll Tabitha in kindergarten and Endora suggests that she be taught by Professor Poindexter Phipps, a warlock. Of course, Durwood won't hold with that at all until Professor Phipps promises to not teach witchcraft. As Durwood leaves for work, the Professor notices his campaign drawings and is not at all amused by the cliché phrases used. Endora isn't either until she finds out that if Durwood could think of more he would be more successful at his job thus providing a better life for Samantha and Tabitha.

Later, when Durwood is stepping out of the elevator Endora pops in freezing everyone and casts a spell on him making pretty much everything he says come out in cliché phrases. They arrive so often that it becomes irritating to hold a decent conversation so he races home realizing that he's the victim of yet another spell. Samantha demands Endora remove the spell which she does regretfully.

In the meantime, Professor Phipps has been teaching Tabitha about Charles Dickens and in the midst of talking about *Oliver Twist*, Tabitha inquires what the Artful Dodger looked like so Phipps zaps him up.

Just before Durwood is going to leave, Phipps comes out into the living room to ask for quiet and the Dodger follows him and steals Durwood's watch. Furious that Phipps used magic, Durwood demands that Samantha get rid of him and he leaves in huff. Furious over his reaction, Endora pops out and decides to put another spell on Durwood causing less clichés to pop out but when they do, he'll act them out.

Durwood shows up to a business lunch with Larry and H.P. Sommers to discuss Mr. Sommers' account and he finds himself losing his watch when he talks about time flying—his watch flies off his wrist! Mr. Sommers is all about the clichés but Durwood tries to talk him out of it only to end up embarrassing himself. He leaves the dinner table to call Samantha and struggles when he tells Samantha he's trying to get a grip of himself. Samantha promises to get her mother to undo her deed and Durwood runs home.

Not wanting to lose out on Mr. Sommers' business, Larry follows Durwood home with the client and when he won't answer the door, Larry

Elizabeth Montgomery and Agnes Moorehead play with the baby during breaks between filming. According to David Bloch-Mandel (Adam), the original babies that played Adam were girls!

proceeds to climb in the front window telling Mr. Sommers that they have an understanding that if Durwood doesn't answer the doorbell, Larry is supposed to climb in the window. During the conversation, Durwood mentions that if Mr. Sommers will play ball with him, he'll play ball with Mr. Sommers, when suddenly the two men appear in Mets uniforms! Samantha immediately freezes everyone and hollers for Endora, who appears and reluctantly removes the spell and returns their clothes to normal and then she pops out. Samantha unfreezes Durwood, who is worried about how they are going to explain the uniforms. Samantha tells him not to worry, just take Larry and Mr. Sommers' coats off while she fixes drinks. Afterwards, they rock them back and forth and bend them into sitting positions. She says that she'll unfreeze them and they'll carry on a conversation totally unrelated to what they were talking about and suggest that Mr. Sommers had already agreed to Durwood's new ideas. Samantha unfreezes them and they carry on the conversation with the two confused men and Sommers agrees that he had liked the idea not knowing what else to say.

Just as the two men are getting ready to leave, Phipps and the Dodger emerge from the den finished with Tabitha's lessons and Samantha introduces them. Durwood suggests that they leave through the door, as the Professor was going to pop out, and before they leave the Dodger manages to steal Mr. Sommers' cuff links.

I enjoy this episode about two and a half stars worth. It's one that I remember from when I was very young because I remember thinking there was no way that Samantha or Durwood would be able to explain the baseball uniforms. And I've always liked it when she froze people. I used to think she actually stopped all time, which I thought was way cooler than just simply freezing a few people.

In real time, the character of Tabitha should only be just four but they shot that all to hell in the Third Season when they mentioned in "Nobody's Perfect" about how she was over a year old, when in fact at that time she would've only been eight months old. So I think as the series went on they just figured everyone would just assume Tabitha is the same age as Erin, who was about five and ready to start kindergarten just like Samantha talks about, though it's dumb of her to just think about that in the middle of the school year.

I always like Tabitha zapping out the apples. I loved it when she would do magic and it seemed she hardly did. I also think it makes perfect sense for a little witch to be learning Charles Dickens considering Samantha spoke six languages right after she was born. I liked the Artful Dodger. I thought it funny when Samantha asks for her ring back and tells him he stole it and he says, "So I did. This hang nail catches on everyfing." Now that I'm older I find Professor Phipps pretty creepy and mean! He tells Samantha that he WILL continue to teach, as though she's in his house or something. Not to mention it's weird that everyone just leaves Tabitha alone with him. I know it's a sign of the times that I think like that, but it's still weird.

I always liked Dick Sargent's physical performance in this one, though I admit it's not as great as I used to think it was. And I don't believe I had ever seen that scene with the flying watch before, which I thought was cool.

I also don't think I'd ever seen that scene with Adam either. No wonder nobody ever knows that Tabitha has a younger brother! His scenes, no matter how brief, were always cut!

When Samantha froze Larry and Mr. Sommers, it would've made more sense for her to just zap their coats off and zap them into position on the couch but it was kind of funny seeing Durwood worrying about breaking them.

I also noticed for the first time all the snow out in the backyard and the frost on the living room windows and the bush up front covered for winter. Seems like they only ever had snow when it was a Christmas episode, so that was cool.

JANUARY 22, 1970

It was on this night ABC aired Episode #188: "Samantha's Secret is Discovered."

When Samantha comes home from a fruitful "month-after-Christmas" shopping spree, she finds her furnishings have been swapped out by her mother for rich, expensive, gaudy furniture which she had zapped in to make herself feel comfortable while babysitting. This does not set well with Samantha who happens to like her own furniture and she zaps hers back in. Endora insists Samantha is worth more than her shoddy furniture, which the Salvation Army wouldn't even pick up, and she zaps hers back in. After going back and forth between furniture styles, their argument is brought to a halt when they find that Durwood's mother, Phyllis, has entered the house and fainted from seeing the amazing sight of disappearing furniture.

After waking from her faint, Phyllis tells Samantha she must be losing her mind. Samantha tries to comfort her but Phyllis is certain she's finally lost it and she goes to rest. When Durwood comes home, Samantha informs him of his mother's condition but tries to soften the blow by telling him that now they won't have to hide her secret any longer. Just then Phyllis comes downstairs thinking she's heard Frank's voice. When she finds it's Durwood, she believes she's now hearing things. She tells Durwood that she's going to leave and fade into oblivion but Durwood decides to finally put her anxieties to rest and gives the floor to Samantha to tell the truth. They all sit down and Samantha tells her that she really did see the furniture change and it has to do with the fact that she's a witch. Phyllis doesn't believe her — just like Durwood didn't when she first told him — so she goes to prove it by doing practically the same trick she did when she revealed herself to Durwood by moving an ashtray. When Phyllis says it's done by mirrors, Samantha levitates a vase and drops it to the floor but then quickly reassembles it. Seeing that there couldn't be any other explanation, Phyllis feels relieved. Durwood is relieved too, but asks that Phyllis not spread the news. Just then the doorbell rings revealing that Frank has shown up. In the excitement of the moment, Phyllis tells Frank about Samantha's witchiness and goes to prove it to him by dropping the same vase on the floor so that Samantha can put it back together. Put in a corner, Samantha twitches to put it back together but nothing happens! Shocked, Samantha tries to do it again when Frank is irritated by the story, especially because Phyllis had thought she had been going crazy and now it looks like she is! She and Frank leave.

A little later, while trying to figure out what went wrong, Endora pops in advising that her powers were stopped by the Witches' Council because she was flaunting herself in front of mortals ("Durwood doesn't count"). Samantha goes to twitch the vase back and it does as she wishes. Endora tells her that she'll have to figure out another way of convincing Phyllis she's not crazy.

Across town, Phyllis tells her troubles to Dr. Rheinhouse, who cannot believe her fantastic tale about her daughter-in-law being a witch. He tells her that he doesn't think she's ill, he just recommends she keep taking her tranquilizers and start writing. However after he dismisses her, he tells Frank that she's seriously ill but he's not sure what's wrong with her, but suggests that he just love her and give her support while he sets up a couple physical exams for her. When Frank goes to leave, he finds that Phyllis has left, leaving him a note saying that she's gone for a rest.

Back at 1164, Frank shows the note to Durwood and Samantha. Not knowing where to start, Frank asks for suggestions and Samantha thinks that maybe Phyllis checked herself into a rest home so they begin to call every rest home in the phone book. Samantha decides to do things the faster way and she slips into the kitchen casting a spell to take her where Mrs. Stephens is.

She ends up at the Parkside Rest Home where Phyllis is and is able to look in on her invisibly while Phyllis discusses her recent arrival with resident Mrs. Quigley, who has a short term memory. Mrs. Quigley takes some of Phyllis' tranquilizers and Samantha decides to cause Mrs. Quigley to see some wild things like oranges falling off a tree and then falling back on to the tree. She also makes her see a male nurse turn into a donkey. When Phyllis tells her she doesn't see anything strange, Mrs. Quigley calls a doctor over. Samantha pops out but comes from around the corner surprising Phyllis. When Mrs. Quigley shows the pills she just took to the doctor, Samantha zaps the pills into hallucinogenics and the doctor shows Phyllis that all though the bottle was marked tranquilizers, they were the cause of her earlier visions and everything is back to the way it was.

I'd give this one three and a half stars and that's only because Samantha's hair is way high in some parts and looks ridiculous and the other part is, why wasn't she wearing her flying suit when she popped in on Mrs. Quigley and Mrs. Stephens? This is the third time where she is seen floating (after "No Zip in My Zap" when she was in therapy for losing her powers and "The No-Harm Charm" when she's with Uncle Arthur) in mortal clothes.

Anyway, I LOVE this episode, mainly for that beginning scene which doesn't make sense with Samantha being able to reverse Endora's spell, but boy is it cool! I think Endora zapped in the furniture just to irritate Durwood but Samantha happened to come home first. And I think Samantha was able to zap it out because Endora wasn't that adamant about keeping it, she probably just wanted to make sure Samantha could still do magic. I would love to know how they filmed that scene, whether they just filmed all the lines with the regular furniture all at the same time, and all the lines with the ritzy furniture all at the same time, and then just edited them together for the popping in and out, or whether they actually had the crew move in and out the furniture! I'm wagering on what I mentioned first, because if you really look Elizabeth Montgomery and Agnes Moorehead don't hold their poses too well.

I think it is so cool to finally have someone in Durwood's family get to know the secret. I found it amusing that the first trick Samantha performs for Mrs. Stephens is moving an ashtray, a slight variation on what she first did to prove herself to Durwood on their honeymoon. I also thought it was funny after Samantha can't do magic in front of Mr. Stephens and Endora tells her that her powers have been taken because she was flaunting them in front of mortals and then she gives a glance at Durwood and says, "Durwood doesn't count."

I've always liked the "Sloe ginn fizz" spell. And Liz ad libbed the line "Oh, that's terrible!"

I really enjoy Bernie Kopell. He has been on *Bewitched* A LOT this season, and he will be on until the end of the series.

One of my favorite lines is after Mrs. Stephens has awoken from her faint and is talking about, "What does one say when one thinks they're going crazy?" Endora: "How about bon voyage?"

I'm glad it was Mrs. Stephens that caught Endora and Samantha because had it been Mrs. Kravitz we would've had to have had another lame episode about a petition, and we've already had enough of those.

The rest home is simply Danger O'Riley's house dressed up. And Dr. Rheinhouse's office is Durwood's office with throw up on the walls. It's funny how much *Bewitched* reused sets and actors, but it still turned out awesome!

JANUARY 29, 1970

It was on this night ABC aired Episode #189: "Tabitha's Very Own Samantha."

Tabitha's wish to go to the play park with her mommy is shot down when she finds out that they can go but only after Samantha feeds Adam, gives him a bath, etc, etc. When she decides to settle on just having an ice cream cone, Samantha tells her she can have one but only after she's finished feeding Adam. Not wanting to wait, Tabitha twitches one up much to the dismay of her mommy and daddy, who invite her to go to her room. Once in her room, she decides to take matters into her own nose, er, hands and she wishes for her very own mommy that she won't have to share with anyone and immediately in pops an exact duplicate of Samantha. Exact in every way but one: she has no idea, nor does she care about Adam! Finally Tabitha can have her mommy all to herself.

Later on, Samantha hears a commotion in Tabitha's room as she's trying to lay Adam down for his nap and she goes to investigate. Tabitha claims to just be playing by herself but actually she and her Very Own Mommy were playing hide-n-seek. When Samantha asks her to play more quietly, she decides that they'll be very quiet if they aren't there and suggests to her Very Own Mommy that they go to the play park. TVOS (Tabitha's Very Own Samantha) thinks that's a great idea and they pop off to the play park where they ride every ride, eat every available food, and happen to bump into Mrs. Kravitz and her nephew, Seymour. Mrs. Kravitz is a bit put off by "Samantha" not acknowledging her and she's even more disturbed when "Samantha" acts like she doesn't know who Adam is. She rushes straight home to call Mr. Stephens, who is at work.

At McMann and Tate, Durwood has just found out that he is going to have the client, Mr. Nickerson and his wife, over for dinner for the second night in a row because Larry thinks since they enjoyed it so much the night before, Nickerson will be more willing to sign. When he hears from Mrs. Kravitz about her run in with "Samantha" and Tabitha, he calls home to speak to Samantha. She promises she hasn't left the house all day and that Tabitha has been playing in her room, but when she goes to check, she finds it empty! She suggests that maybe Serena has taken Tabitha to the play park and that she'll investigate further. When she "yoo-hoos" for Esmeralda, Aunt Hagatha pops in saying that Esmeralda is attending the Galactic Rejuvenation and Dinner Dance, so she's covering for her. With no more than a "watch Adam," Samantha pops off to the play park.

Tabitha and her Very Own Mommy having fun at the play park.

At the park, TVOS and Tabitha have just begun riding a miniature Ferris wheel and when Tabitha sees her Very Own Real Mommy she suggests that she and TVOS pop home, which they do at the top of the ride, almost causing the ride operator a heart attack. When Samantha asks him if he has seen a woman that looks like her, he's not very cooperative saying that he had seen someone like her and a little girl go up on his ride but not down. Not wanting to waste any time, Samantha pops home right in front of him.

Meanwhile, Mrs. Kravitz has come over to check on the baby and is greeted by TVOS, who still acts like she doesn't know who the baby is. Mrs. Kravitz calls Durwood again requesting that he come immediately because there is something definitely wrong with Samantha. When he arrives home, he finds TVOS in the kitchen making sundaes for Tabitha. He thinks it's Serena but TVOS admits she doesn't know who Serena is and she pops upstairs. When he goes to check what's up stairs, he finds Mrs. Kravitz nursing her sick headache and Samantha comes in and tells Mrs. Kravitz that the confusion was caused by her practical joking cousin.

That evening, Larry and the Nickersons show up and when Samantha goes to take the baby upstairs, TVOS zaps up her same clothes and comes downstairs to show off her perfect little angel Tabitha. After eating some hors d'oeuvres, Tabitha begins to feel sick because of all the treats from earlier. Just before she and TVOS go back upstairs, Samantha sees them and realizes that she's caught Serena and she goes to hide in Tabitha's room. When TVOS and Tabitha enter, Samantha demands an explanation from Serena but Tabitha insists it isn't Serena, and when Samantha takes a closer look she realizes Tabitha is right and she gets the true story from Tabitha. Samantha assures her that even though the baby is taking up her time, she still loves her and enforces some rules on her because of that love. Tabitha zaps away TVOS and she and her mommy share a tight hug.

I really like this one and would give it three and a half stars only 'cause Mrs. Kravitz having Seymour as a nephew is weird and dumb considering Tabitha just turned Sidney Kravitz into a mushroom at Christmas time not to mention the other nephews mentioned in "Soap Box Derby" and "Little Pitchers Have Big Fears."

Erin Murphy said that the reason she had the bandaid on her chin was because she got excited about having ice cream sundaes at her house and jumped up and down and apparently fell down.

I also liked Samantha's kind of messy hair so much better than the helmet head. And the ride pop out trick was cool! Mark Simpson a.k.a. The *Bewitched* Collector has mentioned that the park isn't there anymore.

Erin also mentioned how Liz just changed clothes in front of everyone when she had to pop in to the different dress.

I thought Adam was really cute in this episode. I'm glad they showed him a lot.

And I miss Serena! We haven't seen her since "Samantha's Power Failure." And the same goes for Louise, though it's been much longer since she's been on. I wonder what Kasey was doing at that time?

The *Bewitched* Baby Bottle is sitting on the nightstand by Tabitha's bed and it's quite possible that the coffee pot in her room is the *Bewitched* one though I didn't see the logo.

FEBRUARY 5, 1970

It was on this night ABC aired Episode #190: "Super Arthur."

Durwood is working hard on the Top Pop account on Sunday as they are going to approve the layouts the next day. Samantha suggests that he work out on the patio to get more sun and before she can interrupt his work more, he suggests she leave. Wondering what she meant by her comment about "more sun," he takes a look in the mirror only to find that his reflection has turned into Uncle Arthur, who has popped in out of sheer boredom. When Samantha reenters and requests he pop out, Arthur complies only to shatter the mirror on the way out. Thinking that maybe that mirror may have a curse on it, he decides to make sure everything is OK by popping into the hall mirror. When he pops out, the same thing happens — the mirror shatters. Samantha suggests they call Dr. Bombay but Arthur insists he's OK and pops up to the mirror in the upstairs hall, and before Samantha and Durwood can reach him to stop it, he's broken another mirror! Arthur decides he must be ill but may only need a rest, so he lies down for awhile.

A little later, when he's feeling better, Arthur sneaks downstairs and zaps up a floating pail of water over the kitchen door to catch whoever next comes out. Durwood does, but Arthur is deflated when the bucket doesn't spill. When he goes to check it out from underneath, the bucket turns dousing him. Samantha suggests Dr. Bombay again and, after drying off, Arthur agrees.

Dr. Bombay pops in thoroughly disgusted as his chess game was interrupted because someone got his king drunk. After checking Arthur's blood pressure (by plucking a hair he claims to be covered in dandruff), pulse, and hearing the symptoms, Dr. Bombay diagnoses him with Bombay Syndrome, so called after its world famous discoverer. He says it is caused by an allergy to horse feathers, which Arthur confirms would be the case as he just rode in the Winged Horse Derby only last week. Fortunately, Dr. Bombay has the cure in the form of a horse pill which he shoots into Arthur's mouth and with that, he pops back to his chess game.

Meanwhile, Larry has shown up to go over the layouts for Top Pop. He definitely isn't enthused by what Durwood has come up with. When he goes to leave to catch his plane to Chicago, he and Durwood find that there is a palm tree in the living room, which Arthur had zapped up to prove his powers were working because he was going to show Samantha how he could palm a half dollar. After the confused Larry leaves, Durwood is furious that Arthur is still there, and when he begins to complain, Samantha assures him that Arthur is feeling better and about to leave. Arthur confirms that he is feeling better, and in fact, he's feeling as frisky as a colt. Just then, he changes into a colt! Durwood can't take it anymore and decides to go shoot a bucket of balls at the driving range.

After he leaves, Samantha tries calling for Dr. Bombay but to no avail. Meanwhile, Arthur still has the problem of turning into anything he is thinking of, including the Devil, whom he was feeling like. Samantha suggests that they get his mind off himself by teaching him how to drive. He thinks that's silly as they know how to fly, but Samantha says it would be a good idea to brush up on his driving skills just in case he can't fly again. When they go to leave, Arthur pushes on the gas and about crashes into another car. They stop and frustrated, Arthur says he doesn't want to learn anymore, that he'd rather fly like Superman, and so he becomes the Man of Steel and begins to fly around the neighborhood! Soon the police see him and come over to investigate.

Back at the driving range, Larry has shown up surprised to see Durwood there, especially since he hadn't come up with an idea for Top Pop, and he tells him he'll escort him home to make sure he gets there. They arrive about the same time as the police and Samantha tells everyone that Arthur is in fact wearing a jet pack and is dressed like this as part of Durwood's campaign. Durwood hesitantly agrees, and tells Larry that the slogan for Top Pop is "Try Top Pop. It's groovy, man. It's tasty, man. It's super, man!" At first Larry doesn't buy this, but the police say they like it and Samantha adds that she thinks it's sensational, so Larry agrees. Super Arthur goes on one more flight before landing and after Larry leaves, Samantha tries to contact Dr. Bombay once more. He finally pops in and admits his cure did have that side effect and gives Arthur another pill to combat that, and Arthur is cured. Dr. Bombay pops off to his drunken chess game and when Durwood suggests that Arthur leave, Arthur says he'll vacate the premises and proceeds to zap out all the furniture. After having his laugh, he pops off and the furniture returns.

Don't get me wrong, I enjoy this episode but only about two and a half stars because it is so corny I could die!

I do like that Uncle Arthur has shown up again. Seems like he hasn't been around forever but it was just a couple months ago when he zapped up Bunny. And I always did like the breaking of the mirrors because it reminded me of *Alice Through the Looking Glass* for some reason. I always thought that Arthur broke the mirrors because coming through them his magic was faulty and he actually gained substance…well, you know what I mean…maybe…

I also thought it was hysterical when Samantha is talking to him, she turns around in shock and we see him in the CORNY devil costume, and she says, "What happened?!" Uncle Arthur: "Oh, I was just sitting here feeling like the Devil." I remember laughing so hard at that line when I was little. It's still funny but I HATE that costume! If anything, they should've put real looking horns pasted to his head and painted his skin red and put him in an all red suit. It could've had sequins on it still, but this was just like someone's Halloween costume their mother made them when they were in grade school!

The "floating" scenes are cool because you can't hardly see the wires, except maybe once, and Gladys doesn't see him flying because, did you see that there is a church just across the street instead of Gladys' house? She must've moved.

Of course, Dr. Bombay saves this episode. I love it when he grabs Arthur's ankle, Arthur moans, and Dr. Bombay says, "What's the matter?" Uncle Arthur: "A sprained ankle." Dr. Bombay drops the ankle. Uncle Arthur: "Make that a broken ankle." And then when he checks his blood pressure…Dr. Bombay: "Tsk, tsk, tsk..oh, my, my!" Uncle Arthur: "What is it?" Dr. Bombay: "I've never seen such a case of bad dandruff!" Uncle Arthur: "I know I have to put up with his malpractice, but must I put up with his bad jokes?"

Of course, this episode is the one Jack refers to in the *Bewitched* movie when he erroneously states that anytime that Uncle Arthur appeared on the show, he broke mirrors. This episode should've been included on the sampler episode DVD that came with the movie DVD instead of the first three episodes. And they also should've had the Aunt Clara episode where she knocked out power along the Eastern Seaboard so the mortals buying it would've been able to see the episodes that all the references in the movie came from.

FEBRUARY 12, 1970

It was on this night ABC aired Episode #191: "What Makes Darrin Run."

While in the midst of doing the household chores, Samantha finds that the dishwasher has sprung a leak, and as she mops it up, Endora pops in disgusted that Samantha has been reduced to the role of Cinderella. She feels it's all due to Durwood's lack of ambition that Samantha isn't living a better life, but Samantha argues that Durwood is very motivated and hard-working. Her point is shattered when her so-called ambitious husband shows up in his robe announcing that he's decided not to go into work until later, that he's going to play some golf during the morning. After he leaves to change and Samantha leaves to go do some laundry, Endora decides that she's going to give him a good dose of ambition.

Later on at McMann and Tate, Durwood finds Larry waiting for him trying to give him the Braddock Sports account as he feels that he's not connecting with Mr. Braddock on account of Braddock being younger and more athletic. Just then, an invisible Endora pops in and casts her ambition spell causing Durwood to suddenly accept the account he earlier refused on the condition he gets a big raise. Larry tells him that they'll be having lunch with Braddock later, so Durwood requests the files, both business and personal, on Braddock.

At lunch, Durwood shows up boasting of having been at the gym, and as he speaks to Braddock, they reminisce about their days running track in college as well as their own personal health beliefs, which Durwood claims to share with Braddock. He also makes Larry look like a fool, and when Larry leaves for a phone call, Braddock feels that all the work should be going to Durwood.

At home, Samantha tries to tell Durwood about her luncheon with Mrs. McMann and Mrs. Tate but Durwood interrupts her telling her about his impressing Braddock as well as his raise. He also mentions his plans to get promoted to a partner in the business just so that everything can be done to make him better. He suggests that they invite the McManns for dinner so that he can impress Mr. McMann so much so that he'd promote him which eventually would lead to him taking over the business. Samantha recognizes her mother's handiwork and when Endora shows up from her trip to Venus, she confesses she did it but won't remove the spell until Durwood is a multi-millionaire!

As they get ready for dinner, Samantha tries to tell Durwood of the spell, but he simply won't believe it. The McManns arrive and Durwood gets McMann to think about how old Larry is getting and how it may be time to have him retire. Samantha casts a spell to get the Tates to come over who arrive just as Mr. McMann has been convinced that Durwood is right. Before Mr. McMann can tell Larry of his plans for a shakeup in positions, Samantha twitches him into wanting more drinks but it seems he really wants to get it done and so she freezes everyone and calls for her mother. Endora shows up and complies with her request to get rid of the spell before she pops off to finish her Texan bronco busting. Samantha unfreezes Durwood and explains what was happening and tells him it's up to him to get out of it. When she unfreezes everyone else, Mr. McMann goes on about how it's time for young people to lead the way in advertising and before McMann can suggest that Durwood be the man for the job, Durwood interrupts with how much Larry is a very young thinker and that Larry is just the person to do the job. Confused, McMann thinks he may have had too many drinks and Samantha diverts his confusion to the great dinner she's made.

Durwood ends up impressing Braddock so much, without the help of the spell, that he gets a huge bonus allowing him and Samantha to leave on a cruise.

I'd give it two and a half stars. I thought it could've been a very real situation, even without the spell, 'cause it seems I've worked with "ambitious" people before that would do anything to rise to the top, including stab their friends in the back.

This is the second, and last time, we ever get to see Howard McMann, and he's even played by a different actor, Leon Ames, but I was glad to see that the character was still a drunk. The first time was in Season Four's "Man of the Year." I think he would've let Durwood talk him into changing up the business by virtue of his drunkeness. I'd really like to know how he became Chairman of the Board and why it is that all though Larry is a partner, it seems that Larry answers to McMann.

So after a year we FINALLY get to see Louise again, yet she's got RED hair! I think Kasey Rogers should've just dyed it because Louise just seems like she'd have black hair. But I do think the red hair matches her personality more.

I thought Samantha looked absolutely HOT in that black dress! And her hair, in the beginning, was really hot too.

Durwood asks Mr. Braddock if he attended Missouri U in '53. Way back in the Gideon Whitzett episode from Season One ("Your Witch is Showing"), Durwood mentions that he graduated from Missouri U in '50. Maybe Mr. Braddock went there for the full four years beginning in '50?

Also this week, *Bewitched* made its last *TV Guide* cover with an article entitled "Meet That Witch's New Husband." In it they interview Dick Sargent at his home where he has a luxurious garden that he's tended himself and he speaks a little about his past and mentions how during the summer he went all over the country promoting *Bewitched* in the hopes people would get used to seeing him. However one of the news articles that came out that summer was headlined with "Dick YORK Becomes Darrin."

FEBRUARY 19, 1970

It was on this night ABC laid on us two swinging mortal singers and some groovy tunes via Episode #192: "Serena Stops the Show."

After having been MIA for almost a year, Serena pops in on her cousin Samantha to give the great news that she's been elected Entertainment Chairman for the Cosmos Cotillion. Samantha, who was busy making beef stew for dinner that evening, tries to get Serena to leave before Durwood, who has just come home with Larry, finds out. The ever devious Serena says she wants to stay and say hello to her tall, dark, and mortal cousin-in-law and when she sees Larry, she begins flirting with him. Samantha and Serena find out that Durwood has got Breeze Shampoo to sponsor a music special featuring the happening and now musical group Boyce & Hart. He has brought home their most recent album for Samantha to listen to. The men retire to the den to iron out the details of the special and before Samantha can take a look at the album, Serena grabs it from her, enchanted by the band just from their photo. She decides to play the record her way by just floating it in the air and spinning it. Their groovy jam "I Wonder What She's Doin' Tonite" starts playing and the cousins start jamming until the attention deficit riddled Serena shuts the music off as she's just had a brilliant idea! She will hire Boyce & Hart to sing at the Cotillion! Samantha is totally opposed knowing that Serena usually gets Durwood into trouble, but Serena assures her nothing will happen and she pops off to find the group.

She finds them at their most recent venue having to bust through the throngs of crazed girls. She zaps her name onto the backstage pass list and meets with Boyce & Hart and their manager Chick Cashman, who insists his clients are booked now through 1976. He's irritated when he finds that Serena not only wants Boyce & Hart to play for her for nothing, but she wants them to sing a song she wrote. When he throws her out, Serena gets furious and she pops back to Samantha's interrupting the TV show they were watching. Serena thinks Durwood can exert influence over them and decides he'll be even more persuaded to do so after she plays her new song for him, entitled "I'll Blow You a Kiss in the Wind." Pleased with her impromptu performance, she soon becomes angered when Durwood tells her that it stunk! Before she can smash his head in with her guitar, Samantha zaps it away and requests to speak to Serena, alone. They zap into the kitchen and Samantha suggests that Serena go with a less popular (?!) group. Serena decides to take Sammy's advice and casts a spell to make Boyce & Hart very unpopular. The spell takes effect immediately and the crazed fans soon begin burning their albums and canceling their events.

The group is utterly shocked at their dive into obscurity, when who should show up but Serena asking if they might now be available. Mr. Cashman agrees to let the group play and, after a few practices on the piano of her song, Serena zaps herself and the boys to the out of this world Cotillion.

Meanwhile, Larry shows up mad that Durwood had hired the now hated group and after he leaves, Durwood demands that Samantha get

Sexy siren Serena enjoying the performance of Boyce & Hart at the Cosmos Cotillion.

Serena to reverse her spell, so she pops off to the Cotillion just as the group starts performing. Serena promises to reverse the spell once they finish singing and they are a smash! Wanting them to perform more, Samantha stops it, so Serena begrudgingly lifts her spell and sends them back to Earth with their memories wiped.

Boyce & Hart become more popular than ever and Durwood gets back in Larry's good graces.

I LOVE this episode! Quentin Tarantino also loves this episode and pretty much said it was the greatest moment in TV history when Serena is singing the song. He was going to use a clip of it in *Pulp Fiction* (1994) but I guess he couldn't get his hands on a decent copy. However, later on, when he hosted *SNL*, he sang the song.

It's such a tour de force performance by Liz who is credited as Pandora Spocks. You totally forget that it's her playing Serena, not to mention she sings! And she is HOT in every scene as Serena. I love those short skirts! And, what up with Melody, Liz's stand-in, showing her undies?! AWESOME! I think that she should've used the same guitar from "Hippie, Hippie, Hooray." I wonder what ever happened to it?

I love it when Serena first sees Larry and says, "Well, if it isn't little Peter Cottontop!"

I also love the floating ROTATING record! That was awesome!

One of the best parts, though, is the way Samantha dances…classic! And what's up with her plaid pants?!

Boyce & Hart are cool and I was so glad to find that they were a real band. I love their collection of greatest hits and I seriously love "I Wonder What She's Doing Tonite." They are also responsible for many of the Monkees songs, and Bobby Hart wrote the theme song to *Days of Our Lives*. He also joined us at the 2010 *Bewitched* Fanfare along with Art Metrano (Chick). Both had nothing but fond memories of their time on *Bewitched*. Unfortunately, Tommy Boyce committed suicide in 1994.

My favorite spells come from this episode too:

> *As the trumpets blare, let all ears smart,*
> *failures BOTH be Boyce & Hart!"*

I love it when she waves her arms and laughs and then pops out. And then:

Back from the cosmos to your planet,
your career's brightest since you began it!
Forget where you were, and what you did,
to keep my cousin from flipping her lid!

I could watch this episode pretty much every day...love it, love it, love it!

FEBRUARY 26, 1970

It was on this night ABC aired Episode # 193: "Just a Kid Again."

While shopping at Hanley's Department Store for a birthday present for Tabitha's friend, Emily, Samantha and Tabitha are assisted by store clerk Irving Bates who, as Dr. Bombay would put it, has a severe case of Peter Pan Syndrome. Irving shares his wish of being a child again with Tabitha, who is waiting while Samantha pays for the toy. Tabitha decides to help Irving out by granting his wish! And thus Mister Irving Bates becomes a nine-year old boy! Irving realizes this can't be good, and when he can't see Samantha or Tabitha around anymore, he finds Samantha's charge receipt with their address out in Westport on it. His troubles are far from over when he realizes that in his smaller state he isn't able to reach the gas pedal in his car and he is stopped by a cop who thinks he's playing around. After a minor skirmish with the cop, Irving hops into a cab out to Westport.

When he arrives at 1164, he shows Samantha his driver's license and to her shock, she realizes what Tabitha has done. Samantha insists Tabitha turn him back but when she tries, nothing happens. Samantha thinks that Tabitha isn't trying hard enough, but before she can try again, Samantha sees Irving lighting up a pipe. She tells him that it's not proper for a little boy to smoke, but he believes he's dreaming. Not knowing what else to do, she tells him about her and Tabitha's witchhood. Irving is still leery of her story but forgets about it when he realizes that he was supposed to be meeting his girlfriend Ruthie for lunch. He has Samantha call her, but Ruthie is quite suspicious thinking Irving has found another girl. Things get a little hairy when Durwood comes home from golfing. Samantha hides Irving in the kitchen with the request that he keep his real identity from Durwood. Irving becomes obstinate saying he doesn't want to, until Samantha shows him what will happen to him if he doesn't by blowing up the cookie jar. She immediately puts it back together before Durwood comes in, kidding around with the new little boy. He's shocked when Irving seems quite rude. Samantha sends Irving and Tabitha out to the patio. While pushing Tabitha in the swings, Irving decides that it may be nice to have a second chance at growing up and he tells Tabitha that he doesn't want to go back to being an adult. Tabitha agrees, thinking it'll be fun to have an older brother.

Meanwhile, Samantha tells Durwood that it's a possibility that Irving may be staying with them for awhile. Later on at lunch, Irving tells Durwood his true identity when Durwood keeps asking who he really is. Samantha tells him that they may need Dr. Bombay's help getting Irving to grow up again, and so she calls for him. Dr. Bombay arrives fresh from his Antarctic rounds where he was doing a nose job on a penguin, or so he says. Samantha shows him Irving and Irving's driver's license. Dr. Bombay suggests, after seeing the license picture, that Irving remain that age. After his kidding around, he casts a spell to get Irving fully grown, but it doesn't work. He requests a private consultation with Samantha where he tells her that most likely the reason Irving won't grow up is because he and Tabitha don't want him to. He tells Samantha she'll need to get Irving to want to grow up and with that, he leaves. Samantha decides the best way would be to take Irving to Ruthie so he can see what he's missing and they pop off to the travel agency where she works. They watch her from the corner and Samantha can tell her idea has worked as Irving is very much interested in Ruthie, until he speaks to her and he realizes she doesn't know who he is. Samantha furthers her plan by having Ruthie's boss chase after her. Irving can't take it, and starts to hit the boss until Samantha removes her spell and the boss stops his pursuit of Ruthie. The grateful Ruthie gives Irving a great big hug and with that, Samantha and Irving leave as Irving wants Tabitha to change him back.

At home, Irving explains to Tabitha, with the help of Durwood, that there are a lot of wishes made on the realization that they will never come true, but it's nice to dream. Irving asks Tabitha to change him back, and she complies, and Samantha zaps him to Ruthie.

I'd have to give this a two and a half star rating. It's totally a remake of "Junior Executive" but it's still fun, because Richard Powell, who plays little Irving, is just so good! And Dr. Bombay is hysterical!

I've always enjoyed this episode, especially the older I get and realize just how cool it would be to be made young again. I also always thought how weird it would be for Irving to know that there are witches in the world but apparently never tell anyone. That makes him and Michael the orphan ("A Vision of Sugarplums") the only other mortals that know about Samantha.

Did you notice Irving's tie? It was a map of the world. I found it a very odd tie for the 70s.

This is also one episode that provides proof that Samantha is actually "The Witch of Westport" the original title of the series.

Dr. Bombay is awesome, of course, and my favorite line is when he tells Durwood it would be a pleasure not to look at him.

I think it would've been hysterical if Irving would've returned to his adult form by the mere act of Ruthie pressing him to her chest! Of course, Ruthie is Marilyn Munster a.k.a. Pat Priest, in her third and final episode of *Bewitched*, all three appearances happening just this season!

And, honestly, who keeps pickled herring on tap?!

And last of all, Liz looked HOT in that brown dress! And kudos to her for not having it green!

MARCH 5, 1970

It was on this night ABC aired Episode #194: "The Generation Zap."

Durwood finds out that he is going to have a young college girl shadowing him right when he has a lot of work on his plate. Endora feels that Samantha is being too trusting having Durwood left alone with such a tempting temptation. She promises to butt out but, of course, does it her way. Endora enlists Serena, a champion at love spells, to ensure that the college girl will fall for Durwood.

At the office, Durwood meets the very sexy, but proper, Dusty Harrison, who happens to be the daughter of one of their clients. As he shows her his latest ideas for Hillgreen Coffee, he finds that he's not as impressive as he thought. Dusty tells him his ideas are just too cute. While they are speaking, Endora and Serena pop in invisibly, and at one point, Endora freezes them so that Serena can cast her love spell on Dusty. Endora reanimates them and Dusty is absolutely smitten. Once they verify that Dusty is going to try her hardest to seduce Durwood, they pop out. Durwood sees that something has changed and decides he won't be able to work with Dusty fawning all over him, so he sends her out to find a coffee pot with character for the new ads. Dusty enthusiastically accepts the assignment and leaves.

That evening, Dusty shows up with her hair all did and in a very SHORT skirt claiming that she's come to drop off the coffee pots she found as she missed Durwood at the office. Samantha is shocked by Dusty's lusty enthusiasm for Durwood and gets rid of her by announcing that dinner is ready. Dusty leaves and Durwood is shocked by Samantha not asking her to dinner. Amazingly, he doesn't acknowledge the big crush and Samantha tells him that he'll need to cut her shadowing short so as not to lead her on.

The next day, Durwood tells Dusty he thinks that she should shadow someone else, and she is crushed! She leaves in a fit and tells her daddy, who in turn tells Larry, causing everyone to be mad at Durwood. When Durwood tells Samantha about it, she thinks that maybe Dusty had been under a spell. Ruling out Endora, who had promised not to meddle, Samantha deduces that a love spell must've come from her cousin Serena, the love goddess. Durwood goes to straighten things out with Harrison and Larry, and Samantha tries to contact Serena, only to be given the message by butterfly that Serena is on Cloud Nine. She decides to confront her face to face and leaves for Cloud Nine. However, right after she leaves, Endora and Serena pop in, pleased with their little trick on Samantha and Serena zaps herself into looking like Samantha. Sam/Serena suggests to Durwood that he invite Harrison over to smooth things over because he'll see how happily married they are.

Harrison does come over and while speaking to Durwood, Sam/Serena flirts with Harrison and makes fun of Durwood. Harrison realizes that Durwood must be unstable and just when things couldn't get worse, Dusty shows up furious that her father is there. Dusty claims that she'll fight her own battles and she loves Durwood no matter what, even when he calls her a nincompoop. Harrison apologizes for Dusty's behavior, but Sam/Serena tells him it happens all the time and she suggests they go discuss it alone on the patio.

Samantha pops home, sees what's happening, and freezes Harrison. Serena tells her that it was just a test of infidelity on Durwood's part. Threatening to make her an ex-cousin, Samantha demands Serena remove the spell. Serena removes the spell making Dusty think Durwood is trying to put the moves on her and she screams. Harrison is unfroze and hears the screaming and realizes that Durwood was every bit the low life he thought. When he goes to punch him, Samantha zaps up an invisible barrier about breaking his hand. Incensed that Durwood would hurt her father, Dusty slaps him, but the barrier is gone. Dusty and her father leave in a huff, with Harrison threatening to cancel his account. Later that night though, Samantha and Durwood hear over the news that Harrison has been fired for embezzlement and so all is right with the world.

Even though it is a remake of Season One's "The Girl Reporter," I think it's rather entertaining and would give it about two and a half stars. Now were it to have been remade with Dick York, I probably would've given it less but as Dick Sargent (in my mind) is Samantha's second, less reputable husband, it doesn't seem that bad.

For one, Dusty is HOT! And how short are the dresses in this episode? For some reason I never think of her when I'm thinking of all the women that tried to get with Durwood over the years but I'm thinking it's because this episode is fairly "new" to me, meaning I haven't seen it 29,347,239,472,349 times like I have the others. She may even boot Danger out of her place as the number one hot girl to pick up on Durwood. And she's SOOOOO much better than Liza Randall who didn't even try to hide that she had the hots. True, Dusty was under a spell, but even then, she kept it relatively cool. I think it's hysterical when Durwood tells her that she can't come to the office anymore and she just falls to pieces.

And now we come to Serena, speaking of hot women. How's about that outfit at first? Skin tight and with little "peek-a-boo" holes all over it? Man! And the dress she wears is also hot. Come to think of it, aren't both of them knit? AWESOME! I do admit that this is one of the more annoying Serena appearances because of her voice, but her looks overshadow it (for me, anyway).

I thought the blue dress Samantha wore was hot, but her other outfits were ugly! And her hair was even more so. I'd almost go so far as to say this is the worst her hair has been this season.

I love it when Endora tells Samantha, "Goodbye sucker!" It was so unexpected!

MARCH 12, 1970

It was on this night ABC aired Episode #195: "Okay, Who's the Wise Witch?"

Tabitha discovers what she thinks is a new doll house for her, but is bummed out when she finds out that it's a model for her Daddy's work, a house with moveable walls, which doesn't seem too fancy for a little witch who can do it with the twitch of her nose. When Durwood and Samantha try to take it out to the car so he can take it to work for a client presentation, they find that all the doors to the house are stuck! Desperate to leave, Durwood tries the kitchen window, but it won't open either, even banging it with a hammer. When he tosses the hammer aside, he breaks the cookie jar on the counter nearby. Samantha suggests she pop him to work but when she tries, it doesn't work. Thinking there may be something wrong with her powers, she attempts to reassemble the cookie jar, which works, but when she tries to open the kitchen door it won't budge, which means everyone is trapped!

Thinking her mother might know, or be responsible for, what's going on, Samantha calls for Endora, who pops in denying anything to do with the stuck house, even giving her witches honor. When she tries to leave, she finds she can't. As the threesome thinks about it, they determine it must be a practical joke, and who but Uncle Arthur could be responsible for it? In mid call to her Uncle, Samantha realizes that if it isn't Arthur, he won't be able to pop out. Whittling down the possibilities, Samantha thinks maybe Esmeralda may have cast a spell that was having delayed effects from her last visit. She yoo-hoos for her and Esmeralda pops in wearing a robe, curlers, and a mud mask, quite excited as she was getting ready for a much-anticipated date with Ramon Verona, the salad chef at the Warlock Club. When she denies having cast any spells, Samantha breaks the bad news that she's going to have to break her date.

Meanwhile, Larry keeps calling to find out about Durwood and his whereabouts. Samantha tells him that Durwood is stuck in the house due to illness and they are waiting for the doctor to arrive. Irritated, Larry decides to drive out to check on Durwood himself as the client is getting restless.

During the wait for the possible perpetrator of the spell, Endora exchanges the living room furniture for a swing set for the children, upsetting Durwood, of course. However there is no getting rid of it with the state the house is in. At the same time, Larry shows up and Samantha tells him that they are under quarantine and finally gets rid of him after telling him the doctor has forbidden anyone to enter or leave the house.

After Larry leaves, Samantha realizes that maybe Dr. Bombay might be able to help them and she pages him. He pops in from a bull session with his new nurse and, after hearing the prognosis, zaps up his atmospheric oscillator to correctly identify his diagnosis of a vapor lock, caused by the non-use of witchcraft causing the undistributed metaphysical particles to clutter up the atmospheric continuum thereby creating a bilateral transcendental trauma. He says that the only way to get rid of the vapor lock is to cast a spell from the outside and the only way to do that is to transfer him to a flat surface, such as a photograph, and slide him under the door. Samantha takes a magic photo of him, slides him under the door, re-dimensionalizes him and he casts the spell unlocking the doors which he pushes open and with much momentum crashes into the swingset. With his job done, he pops off.

Now that Durwood can leave, Samantha thinks of an addition for Durwood's model house utilizing the swingset, in miniature. Her idea is that the roof can move too, to cover the swingset in rain. Durwood loves the idea and leaves.

Later on, he returns saying the client loved his idea and Samantha helps zaps Esmeralda to her date.

I'd give it a three star rating because I laughed so much in it! The best line of all actually comes from Durwood right after Samantha has told Dr. Bombay what is going on and Durwood says to the doc, "Diagnose THAT, bull artist!" The banter between Dr. Bombay and Endora is quite funny too, and I believe that almost all those lines never aired in the reruns because they seem new to me.

I also really enjoyed Esmeralda's appearance for once. This is how her character should've always been. I think maybe she was giving herself the beauty treatment the mortal way because she'd probably mess herself up really bad if she did it with witchcraft.

I think the vapor lock makes sense in so much as Dr. Bombay explained that all the metaphysical particles remain undisturbed causing such a lock. I always imagined that it just made all the openings stuck, but not so much that the few crevices would actually be sealed but then, if that were the case, any of the witches/warlocks would've been able to fly down the chimney like Aunt Clara always used to.

I also liked at the end when it seemed that Endora and Durwood were on real good terms with each other. And I think it's really cute when Agnes Moorehead and Liz hug.

I always wonder what happened to the atmospheric oscillator prop. It seemed to be very intricate so I can't imagine them throwing it out. Wherever it is, I want it! I think it's SO dumb when Durwood says he wishes they wouldn't call Dr. Bombay a witch doctor. It's not funny at all and when he says it here, it ruined all the witty banter that had been going on previously.

I also don't like it when Tabitha comes into the living room to swing, and not two swings in, and Samantha is telling Esmeralda to take her upstairs so she can call Dr. Bombay. Why can't Tabitha be there for that?

Were 1164 to be a real house with the garage, that window over the sink couldn't exist because it would be looking into the garage. When they were designing the sets, they should've put the stove and oven over there and the sink where the stove/oven are now because then a window would make sense.

Here are some of my favorite lines from this episode:

ENDORA: *"Durwood, have a seat. The centuries will pass by quickly."*
LARRY: *"Sam, I smell something fishy!"*
SAMANTHA: *"Oh, that must be our lunch burning! We're having boiled salmon. Gotta go Larry, love to Louise!"*
DURWOOD: *"I have a contagious disease that's about to change me into a raving maniac."*
ENDORA: *"The change will be imperceptible."*
SAMANTHA: *"Dr. Bombay, we have a peculiar problem."*
DR. BOMBAY: *"I know, but he's easy to get rid of, isn't he?"*
DR. BOMBAY: *"A-HA! Just as I suspected. Eighty over sixty."*
SAMANTHA: *"Is that bad?"*
DR. BOMBAY: *"It's terrible! Normal is three over 4/5."*
ENDORA: *"Maybe you're holding it too close to Durwood."*
DR. BOMBAY: *"Durwood is entirely irrelevant."*
ENDORA: *"I'll buy that…"*
DR. BOMBAY: *"It's not for sale! HA HA!"*

MARCH 19, 1970

It was on this night ABC aired Episode #196: "A Chance on Love" instead of "If the Shoe Pinches" which would've been a better fit for the week of St. Patrick's Day…but I digress…

While putting away the groceries, Samantha finds that the chore isn't that bad as the groceries begin to put themselves away. Well, not so much put themselves away as Serena had put them away so she could invite Samantha to the elephant races. Samantha declines the invitation as she has too much to do and soon finds out that she has even more to do than she remembered as Mrs. Corby calls to find out where she is as she is supposed to be at the Huntington Hotel selling raffle tickets going towards sending under privileged kids to camp. Realizing that her look-a-like cousin could easily double for her (with a few minor changes), she tells Mrs. Corby she'll be there. Serena isn't keen on the idea until Samantha mentions how mad Durwood would be if she were to do it. Serena zaps herself into a blonde version of herself and skedaddles to the hotel.

As it turns out, Larry is also meeting with client George Dinsdale at the hotel, and leaves before he sees "Samantha." Mr. Dinsdale walks by Sam/Serena and catches her eye. She begins flirting with him and he reciprocates in kind and invites her to lunch, where the flirting continues.

She suggests they do dinner too, but he tells her that he must go to a party that night for business. He invites her, but she's not for a business dinner at all and they make plans to meet the next day.

Later that evening at the Tate's, Mr. Dinsdale is shocked when he sees Samantha, and when he gets her alone, he asks her why she didn't tell him she was married. Of course, she hasn't a clue of what he is talking about. Durwood can't get a word in edge wise as Dinsdale is so enamored of Samantha. She soon realizes that he had met Serena earlier, and when she tries to explain that to Dinsdale, he won't hear of it. He thinks instead she is being coy and playing games with him.

During the middle of the night, Samantha calls for Serena, who pops in from another date and demands that Serena come clean to Mr. Dinsdale at their lunch. Serena agrees reluctantly and at lunch the next day, she shows up in her regular look. Still thinking that Samantha is playing games, he still won't listen to her, and she pops out before things can go any further. Incensed that "Samantha" would diss him, Mr. Dinsdale decides maybe Durwood shouldn't have his business if he can't have his wife.

Mr. Dinsdale decides to confront Samantha, who thinks that everything has been cleared up, but George just won't give up. When she tries to explain it all to him again, he repeats everything she says, and as he is acting like one, Samantha zaps him into a parrot before he can attack her any further. Just then, Durwood and Larry show up looking for George as they had heard he had asked for Durwood's address and Samantha explains she is taking care of the parrot for a friend, even though George caws that he is Dinsdale. Larry thinks they should try his hotel but the parrot keeps insisting he is Dinsdale. Realizing they'll probably never find him, Larry goes home. Durwood realizes that the parrot must be George as the parrot repeats absolutely everything. Samantha explains to him, and of course, Durwood blows up. After he's smoothed his ruffled feathers, Samantha tells him that they can fix everything as soon as she gets Serena there so that she can prove to George that there really are two Samanthas.

When Serena does show up, Samantha zaps George back and tells him that he had felt a little faint and suggests that he had wanted to change his meeting with Durwood to the house. She also introduces him to Serena and he finally believes her. As a way of apology, he tells Durwood he has the account and he takes Serena out.

A couple days later, a bewildered George shows up looking for Serena. When Durwood and Samantha ask him what's wrong, he tells them that when they had been dancing he had sang the song "Fly Me to the Moon," when suddenly he found himself on his way to the moon! When he woke up, he found himself in his hotel room three days later. Samantha tells him not to worry about it and that he may want to give up on Serena.

I really enjoy this one and would give it three stars, even though it's bits of remakes of two different episodes including "It Shouldn't Happen to a Dog" and "Which Witch is Which?" I think it works well here because it's quite believable that the same sort of situation would happen again, though I wish they would've thought up of new situations instead of going the remake route all the time.

I couldn't believe how SHORT Serena's skirt was at first, and at the last! HOLY COW! If she would've sneezed it would've been a peep show for everyone! She should've sneezed. And how about that dress at the end that laces up the middle?? And it makes me ILL thinking that DICK Michaels directed this!

And I never noticed before, but Jack Cassidy has a horrible lazy eye! This is his second, and last appearance on *Bewitched*. The first one was last season in "Samantha Goes South for a Spell." He is also David Cassidy's father.

I thought the food popping into the cupboards and the fridge was cool because we saw recognizable brands. I saw some Green Giant in there and wonder if it was by pure coincidence that Nigel popped into a Green Giant product in the *Bewitched* movie, or if they meant it as a nod to this episode. It was weird that the food popped one by one into the cupboards but then all at the same time in the fridge.

It seemed like the lobby of the Huntington Hotel and the restaurant were real places instead of just sets.

Samantha looks much better in these episodes than earlier in the season. Her clothes are much more flattering and sexy.

I was really ticked at Durwood, though, for not even listening to her explain how Dinsdale attacked her. He's too busy being worried that she broke her promise not to use witchcraft again and he's surprised that she's changed a client into an animal? Come on! This is old hat by now!

My favorite line comes from Serena after she asks Dinsdale what he has in his pocket and he ends with "...a cough drop." Serena: "I'll take the cough drop...I just got a chill!"

And how about we finally get to hear Gerald "Herbie" York SPEAK?! I wonder if he got paid extra that day?

MARCH 26, 1970

It was on this night ABC realized they'd missed out on celebrating St. Patrick's Day with a leprechaun-centered episode of *Bewitched* last week and played it this week with Episode #197: "If the Shoe Pinches."

Samantha interrupts Durwood, who was trying to come up with a slogan for Barber's Peaches, to come watch Tabitha as she plays in her

Samantha confronts the mischievous leprechaun Tim (Henry Gibson) about Durwood's new look. PHOTO COURTESY OF SHARON ORAZI

new playhouse. Tabitha pretends that she is entertaining guests by the name of Jones, making Durwood wonder if she's not just pretending. When Tabitha suggests that her parents are cramping her style, they leave off, and Tabitha serves her imaginary guests, until a lurking leprechaun named Tim O'Shanter interrupts her begging for some food. Tabitha runs into the house to get him some food and, as Tim waits, Endora pops in suggesting that he's not there to eat, he's there to do a job.

Meanwhile, Larry shows up to see how Durwood is coming along with the slogan and when Durwood tells him he's not anywhere near being done, Larry leaves. Samantha and Durwood see Tabitha taking a sandwich out to the playhouse but don't believe her when she says it's for the leprechaun. As they try to find out what's really going on, Durwood suddenly grows a long pointy nose and long pointy ears, courtesy of Tim. At first, Samantha thinks Tabitha has done it but she realizes that it must be the leprechaun and she drags him out of the playhouse and demands he return Durwood back to normal. Having done so, Tim tells them a sad story about how someone stole his magic shillelagh making it impossible for him to return home unless a witch can restore his powers. Samantha complies and Tim floats off only to land on the roof where Endora is waiting. She demands that he try harder in breaking up Samantha's marriage and sends him away.

Later in the day, Durwood finds a pair of shoes with an apology note from Tim. He goes to put them on saying that it's bad luck to refuse a gift from a leprechaun and instantly becomes lackadaisical and nonchalant about everything. Samantha knows something is up and insists he take off the shoes, but Durwood finds he can't. Just then Tim comes in to taunt. Not wanting to put up with his shhhhh-enanigans any longer, Samantha becomes invisible and sneaks up on Tim threatening him if he doesn't tell her what's going on. He claims not to know anything and that he lost his shillelagh again and came back for a bit of a drink, which Durwood is now more than happy to serve. While the two are drinking away the afternoon, Samantha retreats to the playhouse and zaps up a spell book which conveniently has a spell to control leprechauns. She finds it is best to serve it in chicken soup and invites Tim to dinner where he and she switch bowls before they begin to eat as Tim knows something is up. He finally ends up with the enchanted soup and eats it. Samantha demands he remove the shoes from Durwood's feet, which he does, and he confesses that Endora put him up to it. Samantha zaps him away and just before he leaves, he retrieves his shillelagh from Endora.

Samantha confronts Endora who admits to having Tim test Samantha's marriage. Realizing that Durwood's afternoon was wasted on the leprechaun leaving no time to think up of a slogan, and with Larry's return, Samantha suggests Endora zap a slogan into Durwood's head. She does, and it's horrible, so Samantha has Endora zap Larry into loving it.

This episode is all right in my opinion, though I don't understand about having a leprechaun do Endora's dirty work? And even more so about Durwood actually trying on those shoes? It was totally uncharacteristic.

Aside from Aunt Clara popping on the roof in "Allergic to Macedonian Dodos" and Serena popping up there in "Hippie, Hippie, Hooray," I believe this is one of the first times that scenes play prominently on the roof. I especially liked the look of the sky. It seemed like a calm summer night sky, even if this was supposed to take place in March. And as the series goes on there will be many more roof scenes. I like it though you wonder how they could do it and not have the whole neighborhood notice, especially Gladys.

My favorite line is when Tim says to Endora, "You are as full of shhhhh-enanigans as I am." It seriously sounds like he's going to say something else.

I also liked that Sam zapped in a huge spell book and that there was THAT particular "Potion to Control Leprechauns."

I also noticed that when Liz and Henry Gibson were in a scene together they were relatively the same height, but whenever Liz was in a solitary scene the camera was looking up at her to give her more height and when it was on Henry Gibson it was looking down at him to make him smaller.

I think this is one of the only episodes where you can totally see the wires when Tim is floating — very shoddy work.

Two days before, assistant director Jack Orbison passed away.

The night after the episode aired, Agnes Moorehead appeared on an Oral Roberts Easter Special doing a recitation of "The Resurrection."

APRIL 2, 1970

It was on this night ABC aired Episode #198: "Mona Sammy."

While Durwood and Samantha are reminiscing about their first date and preparing for a dinner party, Endora pops in and invites herself to dinner. As she is not a rude dinner guest, she reveals that she's brought a gift, something that has been cluttering up her closet for centuries and zaps it in under cover. Samantha unveils a painting by Leonardo Da Vinci himself! And a very familiar looking one at that as it highly resembles the Mona Lisa; however the woman in this portrait looks very much like Samantha. Durwood is shocked by it but Endora tells him there is nothing to worry about, that it's actually Samantha's Great Aunt Cornelia who looked a lot like Samantha whom "Lay-o" was mad about! She suggests it hang over the mantle to give some class to their bourgeois home and replaces it with the painting that was there. Of course, Durwood has to be a party pooper and insists that it will not hang there because he's afraid he'll have to explain it and he removes it. Just then the Tates arrive and while Durwood and Samantha greet them at the door, Endora slyly zaps the painting back to the fireplace. Larry, and especially Louise, are enchanted by the painting, and Samantha and Durwood try to pass it off as a gag gift that a friend painted but as she was insulted earlier, Endora changes the signature to that of Durwood. Louise is just thrilled wanting Durwood to do a painting of her and will not let up, especially when Larry reminds Durwood that she is the boss's wife. And so they set up a time for Durwood to come paint her.

Durwood and Samantha are furious with Endora, Durwood going so far as to say that she's worse than the Marquis De Sade, whom she was class mates with. Not wanting to put up with his insults, she vows never to return and pops off. Trying to think of a way out of it, including suicide, Samantha counters him with suggesting she cast a tiny spell on him so he can paint. He emphatically states that there will be no more witchcraft until he realizes that's his only option and relents.

The next day, they show up at the Tate's where they find that Louise has bought a gorgeous tight sparkly dress for her portrait. Samantha tells Larry that she'll play Gin with him while Durwood paints and, after he awkwardly gets everything set up, Samantha twitches to start his painting spell. Durwood paints as though he has a demon in him and Samantha blitzes Larry several times at Gin. Everything is going along great until Endora pops in outside a window that looks in on the painting. Still incensed, she zaps Durwood into giving the painting cross-eyes, a big nose, and a goofy smile. Durwood tries to notify Samantha of what is going wrong before Larry and Louise see it but he's too late and Larry gets an eyeful. He warns Louise that it's not done yet and suggests she go get everyone some coffee. He is furious with Durwood and feels he's doing it to be mean and kicks them out.

When the Stephens get home they find that Endora is still mad via a note she has left on a balloon and before they can decide what to do, they hear Louise and Larry coming up the walk. Samantha says maybe she can delete her mother's addition to the painting and Durwood lets the Tates in as Louise didn't think the painting could've been that bad. Larry promises that Durwood will never work again for any company and Louise finally gets a look at her painting, which looks just like her. She is upset now that Larry thought it so ugly and she begins crying until Samantha tells her that Larry just meant that it didn't capture her real beauty. That soothes Louise who decides that she wants a portrait of Larry done for his upcoming birthday. Durwood says definitely not and Samantha says it's because he has an allergic reaction to paint and zaps up a nervous tick for him as well as sneezing. Louise apologizes for making him go through all that for her painting and the Tates leave.

Later that night, Durwood gets to thinking about the fact that Samantha really is much older than him by centuries and what's going to happen as he gets older and she stays younger. Samantha assures him that people will be impressed that an old man has such "great ideas" to keep a young woman interested!

I actually didn't like this one as much as I used to and it's because Durwood is such an idiot! First of all, he should've been very pleased with the painting of Cornelia or Samantha or whoever he thought it was, because Endora was right—it did add a bit of class to their bourgeois establishment! If he hadn't been such a jerk about it then Endora probably wouldn't have told the Tates that he had painted it. They could've got away with just saying that they paid to get it done at some place they lost the address to. But he acted like if they even heard that Leonardo DaVinci painted it then they would automatically find out about Samantha's witchhood! And I thought he was irritating throughout the rest. I couldn't stand him singing while he was painting and Dick Sargent was totally over-acting when Endora's counter-spell take effect when he says, "Sam? Oh, Sam?" BLAH! And the sneezing was AWFUL!

But after all that, I'd say it's still worth two and a half stars. I thought Sam's hair looked great at first, I LOVED that Mona Sammy painting, which currently resides in Rebecca Asher's possession. Boy would I love to have that as part of my collection!

Kasey Rogers kept the two paintings of Louise and would have the normal one hanging up and then, as a prank at dinner parties, would switch it out for the goofy face. At the 2008 *Bewitched* Fanfare in Los Angeles, Mark Wood, Kasey's long-time companion and co-author of *The Bewitched Cookbook*, brought the two paintings to display as well as the Polaroid shots he had of Kasey that the artist took as reference for the paintings! Awesome! It's cool things that happen like that at the *Bewitched* Fanfares, so if you haven't ever been to one, pop on over to the *Bewitched* Fanfare page on Facebook to find out when the next one is.

It's too bad the idea for this episode wasn't around when Aunt Clara zapped up LAY-o so that when he saw Samantha, he would've mistaken her for Cornelia. I did like Endora's scenes, though what was up with the hotel blanket she was wearing?

Anyway, I think this is the first time this season where Dick Sargent being here really didn't thrill me. Good thing it's only happened about once which is much less than I thought it would.

The next night, *The Flying Nun* ended its three season run, much to the relief of Sally Field. The night after that, *Here Come the Brides* also ended. And on April 4, after seven seasons, *Petticoat Junction* ended.

APRIL 9, 1970

It was on this night ABC aired Episode #199: "Turn on the Old Charm."

Not impressed by the product of the Happy Heart Greeting Card Company for whom he must come up with a stellar ad campaign, Durwood asks Samantha to go with him to the movies so he can take his mind off work. She yoo-hoos for Esmeralda to come baby-sit but the ecstatic, usually nervous witch, has a date with Ramon Verona, the salad chef at the Warlock Club, which leaves just Endora as an option. When Samantha hollers for her, she is answered by a large roaring followed by Endora driving into the living room in a purple dune buggy she had been racing in the International Dune Buggy Races and won, except she was disqualified because her wheels hadn't been touching the ground. However, Durwood is furious that they are on his living room carpet and when Endora accuses him of being huffy, and he denies it, she pops off in a huff. Now, without a sitter, the couple decides to stay at home. Durwood wonders why Endora always has to be so unfriendly and Samantha tells him that there is a way to make her more friendly and that would be by use of a magical amulet. At the word "magical," Durwood stops her.

The next morning, when he looks in the bathroom mirror while getting ready, he finds Endora lurking in his mirror. Not too pleased to see his mother-in-law in the morning, especially with her laughing at him, he sprays the mirror with shaving cream. Once he wipes it off, she zaps in a can of shaving cream and sprays back at him without the protection of the mirror glass and with that, pops off. Durwood is furious and decides that maybe he should use the amulet and Samantha pops off to retrieve it.

The amulet, a peace sign with a heart inside, was used by Maurice over the centuries to get control of Endora. Samantha warns Durwood to not ever let the amulet out of his sight and even more important, not let Endora know that he has it. She calls her mother in to test it out and it obviously works when she calls him "Darrin!" (I know, right, who's that?). She apologizes for her behavior of earlier and Durwood leaves for work. After he's gone, Endora, realizing what has just happened, decides she's ill and pops off for a visit with Dr. Bombay.

At McMann and Tate, Durwood meets with the owner of Happy Heart Greeting Company, Mr. Augustus Sunshine, who is wondering why his cards aren't selling. Of course, it's because they have such outdated cheesy poems. Durwood tells him that, but Mr. Sunshine gets offended and says he feels the advertising is outdated and he withdraws his account from McMann and Tate.

That night, Durwood is happy, even with the loss of the account, because he's finally got some control over Endora. Even though it's late at night, he decides to make himself a sandwich and heads for the kitchen. Endora pops into their room to visit with Samantha to tell her that Dr. Bombay couldn't find anything wrong with her and she feels that Samantha is hiding something from her. Nervously, Samantha denies it and gets even more nervous when Endora pops out saying that she does trust Samantha.

Downstairs, Endora pops in on Durwood and he decides to use his new found power to get her to make him a sandwich. Shockingly, she tells him to make it himself and then choke on it. He realizes he left the amulet upstairs and when he goes to leave, she tells him he's not leaving and that he can beg for his sandwich, as a dog. Just before she mutates him, he yells for Samantha, who comes running with the amulet. She asks her mother to return Durwood back to his normal state, and she complies and apologizes for not making his sandwich. Samantha tells her it's all right and Endora pops off. Samantha again reminds Durwood that he's living dangerously being without the amulet.

The next day, Larry calls Durwood to tell him that he's invited Mr. Sunshine back so that they can discuss the account further and they are coming out to his house for an expensive dessert. Not having anything in the house, Durwood and Samantha decide to go shopping and call for Esmeralda. She shows up depressed as her date didn't go well and Durwood suggests that she get an amulet like the one he has. Not knowing what he means, she levitates it out of his pocket as he is leaving and once they return, she immediately pops out to try the charm on Ramon.

Endora pops in furious as she has found out what has been going on and when she asks for the amulet, Durwood finds it's gone. Samantha deduces that Esmeralda must've taken it and becomes nervous when Endora tells the both of them that she's going to punish them. And with that, she pops off to the roof where she casts a spell to cause the two to constantly bicker. The spell takes effect and the fighting begins just as Larry and Mr. Sunshine arrive. Both men are shocked at the behavior of the Stephenses and when Samantha suggests a greeting card with insults,

Mr. Sunshine becomes quite insulted and leaves. Endora pops in to check on her spell and just then Esmeralda pops in deflated that the amulet didn't work. Being under the amulet's charms, Samantha asks Endora to remove the spell and she does. Samantha explains the amulet to Esmeralda and Endora pops off and not wanting to intrude, Esmeralda does too. Durwood wonders what he'll tell Larry and Mr. Sunshine and so Samantha casts a spell to get them to come back. Once there, Samantha explains that they fought in front of him to show that in today's society not everyone communicates pleasantly, but with insults meant to be funny. Mr. Sunshine likes the idea and he says that he will branch out into funny insult cards.

I LOVE this episode and would give it three stars! I think it's totally funny and I do believe Maurice would've had the amulet in his younger days before he realized that he didn't need to use it, but only in extreme emergencies. I think that the amulet should've been something more timeless, as it was centuries old. However, I always liked that it was a peace symbol encasing a heart, representing both peace and love. It seems like something Serena would've worn.

I love it when Endora says, "Does he sound huffy to you? He sounds huffy to me." And "One more word out of you, and I'm leaving!" Durwood: "Ok." Endora: "That's the word!"

And I liked that they used the bouncing ball of light again, it's very witchy! It was previously seen in "Witches and Warlocks are my Favorite Things," "The Trial and Error of Aunt Clara," and "Samantha's Power Failure," though it was really all the same filmed scene. I noticed the lighting in this episode was witchy like it was in some of the earlier episodes.

My most favorite scene of all is when Durwood is making himself the sandwich and Endora pops in with a low, "Hi." And then he asks her to make the sandwich and she tells him to make it himself and then choke on it! I also like it when Samantha comes in and slips the amulet beneath Durwood's paw and says, "You should be ashamed of yourself!" I just like the way she says it. I thought it was cool that Durwood's doggie self is again the Rottweiler. It keeps with the rare continuity on the series as earlier this season in "Daddy Comes for a Visit" Maurice turned him into one.

I liked the insults they threw at each other, my favorite being when Samantha tells Larry "that Durwood has a perfect right. He's got a perfect left too." And also when Durwood tells her, "Me too!" Samantha: "Well, aren't you a bottomless bit of originality." If you didn't notice, the dress

Samantha is wearing has cat faces all over it amongst the stripes! Cool! And, of course, we get to see that the NY/CT area has mountains and palm trees. And we have another rooftop scene.

Also, the playhouse is still out in the back! That's cool!

This is the last time we'll see the offices of McMann and Tate this way. They get remodeled for next season, due to the fire that destroyed the sets during the break.

And lastly, I thought Agnes Moorehead looked younger in this episode than she has lately.

The next day, Paul McCartney announced the breakup of the Beatles as well as announced the release of his first solo album. Elton John's self-titled album was also released in the U.S. being the first album released in the U.S., but his second over all album. The Beatles invaded America in 1964 the same year *Bewitched* premiered.

The day after that the infamous flight of Apollo 13 was launched with astronauts Jim Lovell, Fred Haise, and Jack Swigert. Two days later, when they are in the far reaches of space, an oxygen tank explodes causing them to the abort the mission and return to Earth with all the planet waiting breathlessly to see if they will make it. In the movie starring Tom Hanks, a clip from this episode of *Bewitched* is shown when they show the televisions in the nursing home.

APRIL 16, 1970

It was on this night ABC aired the Sixth Season finale, Episode #200: "Make Love, Not Hate." Can you believe two hundred episodes have already aired with more to come?!

Anyway, Durwood and Samantha are expected for a dinner party at the Tate's to meet with new client Mr. Meiklejohn, but may have to cancel as Samantha can't get a hold of Esmeralda. When the witch maid finally shows up, she is a mess as her date with Ramon Verona went horribly bad as he started chasing after the witch in the coat check room with "legs up to here, and fake eyelashes down to there." She is in no mood to babysit and so Samantha asks her to check on Adam while she tries to find a replacement. Durwood is against Endora babysitting so Samantha suggests that she get in contact with Dr. Bombay, who may be able to cure Esmeralda of her depression. She calls for the doctor and tells him that Esmeralda might cheer up if she had a warlock take interest in her. He flatly declines and so Samantha suggests he might know a warlock that he could set Esmeralda up with. As a matter of fact he does, a chap named Norton whom he once cured of the incurable Square-Green Spots Disease (apparently Dr. Bombay never consulted with Aunt Clara about this…or maybe he did) and he pops off to find Norton.

Samantha asks Esmeralda to stay as Dr. Bombay is going to come back with a cure. While they are speaking, Dr. Bombay shows up with Norton and tells him that Esmeralda is in the kitchen and to have a peek before he declines, as Esmeralda's description doesn't sound too appealing. He looks in just as Esmeralda has faded away due to the nervousness acquired at finding out Dr. Bombay was bringing a friend. When Norton sees Samantha, he's on board and rushes in to introduce himself, just as Esmeralda fades back in. Norton is crushed that Samantha isn't Esmeralda but agrees to get to know Esmeralda. Meanwhile, Dr. Bombay goes to work concocting a love potion, which to Samantha's chagrin takes quite some time.

While waiting for Dr. Bombay, Durwood calls to tell Samantha that the dinner party has been moved to their house as Louise has a migraine headache. Shockingly, Durwood gives Samantha permission to use witchcraft to get ready and asks her to make some of her delicious clam dip. After about an hour, Dr. Bombay is finished with the potion and goes to serve it to Norton. The kitchen has become such a mess that when Samantha goes to follow him, she knocks a pan which in turn, but unknown to Samantha, knocks over the beaker containing the remaining love potion, spilling it into the clam dip. Norton drinks the potion and as it only causes love between opposite sexes, and Esmeralda has faded away again, his eyes settle on a very horrified Samantha! She begins to run away from the grossly enamored Norton and before she can get Dr. Bombay to do something, he pops out.

Durwood comes home and finds his wife running from a strange man and when he goes into the kitchen, he finds it a huge mess. When Samantha finally pops out to get away from Norton, she tells Durwood what's going on, and before they can get further into it, the doorbell rings. Larry has shown up early with the Meiklejohns who decided to not stay the night so they just drove straight from the airport. Samantha zaps the kitchen clean and when Durwood comes back to tell her about the arriving guests, he becomes the target of Esmeralda's affection after she tastes the clam dip. Samantha zaps up her evening dress only to be discovered by Norton. She requests that if he really loves her he'll behave and remain in the kitchen.

Durwood and Samantha join Larry and the Meiklejohns in the living room where the air is thick with tension from the continuing fight the

Meiklejohns are having. To soothe their feelings, Durwood suggests that they try the clam dip. Mr. Meiklejohn immediately becomes enamored of his wife, who is shocked by his affection. After she tries the clam dip, her gaze falls upon Larry, whom she can't get enough of.

Samantha and Durwood head off to the kitchen with the clam dip where Samantha calls upon Dr. Bombay to get an explanation out of him. Of course, he hasn't a notion how the potion got in the clam dip. He does offer that he can put a reverse the curse spell on the potion rather than come up with an antidote. When Samantha brings it out, Mrs. Meiklejohn can't keep herself from Larry and so Samantha offers her the spiked clam dip first. Mrs. Meiklejohn thinks Larry has been the perpetrator and she runs to her husband's arms. Seeing that the lovestruck Mr. Meiklejohn has made for a more pleasant evening, Samantha keeps him from the dip.

The next day, Durwood comes home from work and announces that Mr. Meiklejohn signed with McMann and Tate but hasn't had any other time for them as he's so in love with his wife. Samantha assures him the love potion wears off after twenty-four hours so Mr. Meiklejohn's actions have come solely from him.

I LOVE this episode and had it not been for Esmeralda and the shoddy work the special effects people did when materializing her at first (did you notice how her hat, when she was invisible, was miles higher than the hat when you could see her?) I would've given it four stars! It's hilarious and practically perfect in every way!

Dr. Bombay has the best lines though:

> SAMANTHA: *"She's had a TERRIBLE experience with Ramon Verona."*
> DR. BOMBAY: *"Ate one of his salads, eh?"*
> DR. BOMBAY: *"There's a lot less to her than meets the eye."*
> LARRY: *"Hi."*
> DR. BOMBAY: *"Evidently!"*
> DR. BOMBAY: *"I just remembered a pressing engagement with my tailor! HA HA!!"*

I would say that Charles Lane and Sarah Seegar are my favorite guest stars. Charles Lane's face was so funny when the love potion took effect.

And that scene when Dr. Bombay squeezes the lemon is a classic 'cause Bernard Fox told Herbie J Pilato that when they first shot it some juice squirted into Liz's eye. They had to reshoot because of a technical goof, which I imagine would've been the potion not falling right into the clam dip and she said, "I'll bet you can't do it again." They shot it a second time and again he squeezed some lemon in her eye and even a third time, which is what we see in the episode.

I also think it's funny that Norton is named such considering the actor's name is Cliff Norton.

I thought Samantha's black dress at the end was HOT! It looked very witchy too.

And it was dumb when Norton peeked into the kitchen and saw Samantha sitting there eating non-chalantly. Like she would've been doing that just after Esmeralda faded. But that's just a minor gripe.

This was also the last time we'd see the house decorated like it was. Everything gets a makeover next season due to the fire that will happen later this month, especially the kitchen. I'm going to be controversial right now when I say I seriously wonder if that fire wasn't purposely caused by Liz thinking that she could get out of doing the show if the set burned down?

Season Six sadly took a nose dive in the ratings for *Bewitched*, falling from #12 to #25. Even with that blow, *Bewitched* still received some accolades. At the Emmy Awards presented on June 7, 1970, Elizabeth Montgomery was nominated for "Outstanding Continued Performance by an Actress in a Leading Role in a Comedy Series" and Agnes Moorehead was nominated for "Outstanding Performance by an Actress in a Supporting Role in Comedy." Neither woman won with Liz's award going to Hope Lange for *The Ghost and Mrs. Muir* and Agnes Moorehead's going to Karen Valentine for *Room 222*.

Two days before the episode, Agnes Moorehead was a guest on *The Tonight Show with Johnny Carson*.

The following is the summer re-run schedule. The episode will be listed by number, name, and original airdate.

APRIL 22, 1970

Episode #171: "Samantha and the Beanstalk" (9/18/69)

It was also this week that the first Earth Day was held on April 22, started by Wisconsin senator Gaylord Nelson as a response to widespread global degradation. This was also the first time the ecology flag was flown to mark the day. It is a symbol we will later see on *Bewitched* in a very special place, wink, wink.

APRIL 30, 1970

Episode #172: "Samantha's Yoo-Hoo Maid" (9/25/69)

It was also on 4/28/70 that a major fire tore through the Sunset-Gower studios destroying the *Bewitched* set and most everything else, with the exception of Elizabeth Montgomery's dressing room. Luckily for the cast and crew of *Bewitched*, they had insurance which was to expire two days later. It had earlier been discussed that *Bewitched* needed to have a jolt to refresh things and, like he had done on *I Love Lucy*, William Asher decided they needed to film on location somewhere else, and that somewhere was Salem, MA, the perfect setting for a show about witches. So earlier this month, Bill Asher and Liz flew to Massachusetts to scout out locations. Now with the set needing to be rebuilt, they had the time to film elsewhere. There are pics of the wreckage on www.bewitched.net.

MAY 7, 1970

Episode #173: "Samantha's Caesar Salad" (10/2/69)

It was also on this night that NBC's *Daniel Boone* starring Fess Parker ended its six season run. It had begun the same year as *Bewitched*, in 1964.

The day before that, the horrific Kent State Shootings took place at Kent State University in Kent, Ohio when members of the Ohio National Guard opened fire on student protesters who were protesting the recent invasion into Cambodia that President Nixon had ordered on April 30. Four students were killed and nine others wounded, including one that was permanently paralyzed. This act of violence closed down many schools and universities across the country as the student bodies protested this inhumane act.

It was on May 8, 1970 that the Beatles released their final album *Let It Be*. They burst on to the American scene in 1964.

MAY 14, 1970

Episode #174: "Samantha's Curious Cravings" (10/9/69)

The next night, *Get Smart* ended its series run. It began the same night *I Dream of Jeannie* did in 1965 on NBC but for its last season ended up on CBS.

MAY 21, 1970

Episode #175: "And Something Makes Four" (October 16, 1969)

Two days later, Nydia Westerman who played Mrs. Quigley in "Samantha's Secret is Discovered" passed away. She had also been a regular on Dick York's *Going My Way* series as well as co-starred with Dick Sargent in *For Love or Money* and *The Ghost and Mr. Chicken*.

MAY 28, 1970

Episode #176: "Naming Samantha's Baby" (10/23/69)

Also on this night Erin and Diane Murphy guested on *The Art Linkletter Show*.

Two nights previously, NBC ended the five year run of *I Dream of Jeannie* by airing the final episode, #139: "My Master, the Chili King," which had originally been scheduled twice before always being pre-empted.

JUNE 4, 1970

Episode #179: "Samantha's Secret Spell" (11/13/69)

Three nights later the Emmy Awards would air but *Bewitched*, though nominated in several categories, didn't win.

JUNE 11, 1970

Episode #180: "Daddy Comes For a Visit" (11/20/69)

It was yesterday that President Nixon signed a measure lowering the voting age to eighteen years.

JUNE 18, 1970

Episode #181: "Darrin the Warlock" (11/27/69)

It was also this week that the cast and crew flew to Salem, MA to begin filming scenes for the upcoming season's Salem episodes. To learn even more about that special week please read Peter Alachi's *Salem's Summer of Sam* and *Bewitched and the Man at the Wheel* available at *www.palachi.com*.

JUNE 25, 1970

Episode #183: "You're So Agreeable" (12/11/69)

JULY 2, 1970

Episode #187: "The Phrase is Familiar" (1/15/70)

On July 4, America's Top 40 hosted by Casey Kasem began broadcasting utilizing the Billboard charts. The number one song was "The Love You Save" by the Jackson 5.

JULY 9, 1970

Episode #188: "Samantha's Secret is Discovered" (1/22/70)

Two days earlier, Chet Stratton passed away. He was seen in Season Two's "…And Then I Wrote" as Captain Corcoran.

JULY 16, 1970

Episode #189: "Tabitha's Very Own Samantha" (1/29/70)

JULY 23, 1970

Episode # 193: "Just a Kid Again" (2/26/70)

JULY 31, 1970

Episode #196: "A Chance on Love" (3/19/70)

It was also that evening Chet Huntley of NBC's news cast *The Huntley-Brinkley Report* retired after fourteen years.

AUGUST 20, 1970

Episode #190: "Super Arthur" (2/5/70)

AUGUST 27, 1970

Episode #192: "Serena Stops the Show" (2/19/70)

While everyone was getting their groove on at the Cosmos Cotillion, 600,000+ mortals were getting their groove on at the largest rock concert to date at the Isle of Wight Festival, just off the coast of England. Such performers as Jimi Hendrix, Joan Baez, The Who, and Jethro Tull were there. It should be noted that Heather Woodruff Perry, who played Durwood's Betty in the latter part of Season Three (and one of the most beautiful women inside and out), is married to the drummer of Jethro Tull.

SEPTEMBER 17, 1970

It was on this night ABC re-aired the Sixth Season Finale Episode #200: "Make Love, Not Hate" which originally aired 4/16/70. This would be the last summer re-run. ABC heavily promoted the Seventh Season with various commercials touting the show's time in Salem.

It was also on this night that *The Flip Wilson Show* premiered on NBC.

The day after this episode aired, rocker Jimi Hendrix was found dead of a drug overdose at age twenty-eight. He was the headliner at the Woodstock Festival the summer before and had just headlined at the Isle of Wight Festival this summer.

That Sunday, September 19th, one of the most prolific shows in TV history began airing on CBS, *The Mary Tyler Moore Show*, marking the return of Mary Tyler Moore to network television after five years since the end of her successful run on *The Dick Van Dyke Show*.

That Monday also marked TV history with the premiere episode of ABC's *NFL Monday Night Football*.

Season 7

SEPTEMBER 24, 1970

Tonight, *Bewitched* fans rejoiced when ABC aired the Seventh Season premiere, Episode #201: "To Go or Not to Go," after a summer of promotions touting a trip to Salem, MA, the famed witch city!

We were pleasantly surprised when Liz appeared on the screen in a bright colored top in front of a bright colored background welcoming us "to a new season of *Bewitched*, next in culluh!"

Samantha is getting breakfast in what looks somewhat like the kitchen of 1164, except that it seems much bigger, and that's only on account of it being bigger! There is also a stairway near the door to the hallway that was never there before, and you know what? The kitchen looks good in this new guise. Durwood enters seemingly distracted and totally misses Samantha's offer for breakfast. He tells her he's distracted because of a decision he has to make of taking on the Gotham Industries account, which he hasn't been given, but feels would be best in his hands. Before he can go on, Endora pops in all sunshine and daisies and Samantha tells her to go see the children while she gets Durwood off to work. Endora concedes and pops off and Samantha escorts Durwood to the door where it turns out not only did the kitchen get redone but so did the entryway, stairs, and living room! While Durwood tries to tell Samantha of what he is going to do about the Gotham account, they are interrupted by Endora shrilly singing "Buttercup" upstairs, which unnerves Durwood that his mother-in-law is in such an uncharacteristic sweet mood. After he leaves, Samantha yells for her mother, who pops downstairs and avoids the question of what her new attitude is all about. Endora relents and tells Samantha that she has a very special message for her from the High Priestess Hepzibah and she zaps it in. Samantha discovers that she has been invited to the Centennial Witches Convocation in Salem, Massachusetts. Not impressed, Samantha tells Endora that she can tell Hepzibah that she's not going to go because one, she thinks it'll be boring, and two, Durwood has too much work to do. Endora is flabbergasted that Samantha would reject the invitation and warns her that Hepzibah will not be happy. Samantha realizes she doesn't want to mess with Hepzibah but she tells her mother she'll need time to talk Durwood into it.

Meanwhile, at McMann and Tate, they seem to have got into the redecorating spirit too as Larry's office is much bigger. Durwood tells him that he thinks he's the man for the job, especially when Larry tells him that two other men are in the running. Durwood then offers to do it without a pay increase.

Later that night, Durwood is excited to tell Samantha the good news, but he's confused when she keeps offering him drinks. She finally discloses why Endora had been there earlier and he thinks that it's ridiculous she would go to a witches' convention. Endora pops in and they get into a fight about Samantha going, that is until she's had enough of Durwood and turns him into a toad and she pops off. Samantha takes Durwood up to the bath so he can have some water and she tells him that all he needs to do is apologize to Endora and let her go to Salem, so he does and Endora reverses her spell.

After he's dried off, he tells Samantha that as long as Samantha is going to go he'll join her. She tries to talk him out of it but he says that he should support her. So, much to Larry's surprise, he asks to be taken off the Gotham account the next day as he tells him that he is going to go visit Samantha's relatives in Salem.

Later on, Endora pops in to invite Samantha to go shopping with her but Samantha refuses as she's still upset over Durwood's recent bout as a frog. Endora says she changed him back and Samantha should be happy and that she'll need something for when she goes to the Convention. Samantha tells her that Durwood is going to go and Endora tells her that Hepzibah will not be happy with a mortal accompanying her. Not backing down, Samantha says Durwood will accompany her or she won't go. Endora starts counting down from ten and Samantha is startled when an arrow lands in the middle of the floor with a note attached saying that Hepzibah is going to show up for a visit! Samantha is appalled as she knows that Durwood may not survive the visit.

When she tries to explain Hepzibah to Durwood, he doesn't understand but gets the idea when strong winds blow up, the house starts rocking, and the furniture disappears and, in a show of sparks, Hepzibah, in her throne, appears with her dogs. She asks Samantha to explain herself and Samantha offers that Durwood will accompany her to Salem and Durwood demands that his furniture be returned. Hepzibah is offended by his brazenness and the fact that Samantha thinks she can go rogue by bringing a mortal to the Holy Councils. She tells them that she is through with dealing with them and that for their insolence the marriage will be dissolved at midnight! When Durwood tries to object, she banishes them to their bedroom (which has also gone through a makeover), invisible. Durwood says he will not be treated as a prisoner in his house and he goes downstairs to give Hepizbah a piece of his mind. Surprisingly, Hepzibah is impressed with his nerve and says she'll delay the decision on the marriage after she observes this first marriage between witch and "commoner." And with that she zaps in the rest of her furniture and decorations.

Stay tuned next week to find out if Samantha's marriage will survive Hepzibah's visit!

I would give this one two stars. It makes no sense that Durwood would want to go on the trip to a Witches Convention when his presence not only is not required, but not wanted! It seems to me that he's just trying to push his weight around to show who's boss, that his wife doesn't do ANYTHING without him.

I used to HATE the new decor but, quite frankly, I enjoy it the more I get older! I mean, not all of it, especially those plaid curtains in the living room, but I do like the fireplace more and I do like the blue dining room and when I build an 1164 for me I want to have that type kitchen, sans the stairs to nowhere. I wonder who's idea that was? I love that Endora even comments about the new decoration… "it's all you!"

I really like Hepzibah and I like how she talks to her dogs. I also liked that spooky music to go along with the reading of the invitation. What I didn't like was Elizabeth Montgomery's over-acting when the house apparently is rocking preparatory to Hepizbah's arrival. It's almost like Dick Sargent grabbed a hold of her to say, "Okay, we get it. The room is rocking."

I've always thought that this episode was very telling about what was REALLY going on during the entire series and gave us a clue as to why Samantha would be allowed to stay with Durwood. Hepzibah tells Endora, "We thought you told us this marriage wouldn't last!" Endora: "I'm still working on it." To me that infers that in some way everybody in the known cosmos knew the mixed marriage was going to happen and Endora asked that they just let it happen, promising that it wouldn't last. Maybe Samantha had always had a fascination with mortals, which Endora thought would pass, but unfortunately her daughter fell in love with one. And seeing that Samantha was so happy with him, she wanted to preserve that happiness yet let Hepzibah and the Witches' Council believe that she was trying to break it up, and maybe a part of her wanted that to happen but obviously, as she tells Hepzibah, there was much more to Durwood than meets the eye.

I always kind of imagined that Hepzibah and the Witches' Council, seeing Samantha's fascinations with mortals, ordered Endora to put an end to this as they couldn't have a mortal loving Queen on their hands. So Endora, in hopes of curtailing the mortal fascination, found a mortal whom she thought was the dopiest, dreariest, and most mortal mortal and arranged for the meeting in the turning doors, thinking that the love sick Samantha, who had just broken up with Rollo, would realize that she needs to find another warlock lover, but out of nowhere Samantha falls in love with this mortal specimen. Therefore, Endora tries everything she can do to make it so that Durwood would want to leave Samantha but that never happens.

But back to the episode: I love it when Endora is bowing at Hepzibah's feet and going on and says, "Oh, Mother of us all." Hepzibah: "MOTHER OF US ALL?! We are certainly not her mother!"

My favorite lines from this episode are:

> SAMANTHA: *"All right, Mother, what's it all about?"*
> ENDORA: *"How should I know? I'm not a philosopher."*

It was also on this night that ABC premiered two new series, *The Odd Couple* and *Barefoot in the Park,* which Agnes Moorehead guested on. The next night, TV history would be made when ABC aired the beloved series *The Partridge Family,* a show about a musical family who happen to live in the Kravitz's house!

OCTOBER 1, 1970

It was on this night ABC aired Episode #202: "Salem, Here We Come" sponsored by Excedrin.

The High Priestess and Empress Hepzibah is still holding court at 1164 Morning Glory Circle while she determines whether or not Samantha and Durwood's marriage should be dissolved. In her Supreme Benevolency, Hepzibah demands that everyone dress for dinner, which really gets Durwood's giblets in an uproar. When he tells Hepzibah that he is still master of the house, she tells him not while she's around and zaps up a bar with ten demerits which she commences to move one over to the other side with the warning that if he accrues all ten, HE will be dissolved! Samantha, Durwood, and Tabitha sit to dinner consisting of such delicacies as Pâté of Elephant Tail, Pickled Eye of Newt, and Hummingbird Tongue Parmesan, which Durwood at first refuses, causing him to earn another demerit, and, after he jokes about it, yet another demerit. Before he can get anymore, the doorbell rings, and who should be there but Larry wanting to go over the layouts for Gotham Industries. Hepzibah insists he stay for dinner and he obliges, loving everything until he hears what it is. Excusing himself early, he leaves for dinner at the club with Louise.

The next morning, Hepzibah pops into breakfast wondering what all this talk of "work" is and insists that she be able to observe Durwood at work. And after her breakfast of flamingo eggs once over easy, she pops on down to McMann and Tate with Samantha. Durwood is shocked to see them especially as he and Larry are meeting with the president of Gotham Industries, Mr. Ernest Hitchcock. Samantha explains that her

Samantha discusses with Hepzibah her plans for the Witches Convention.

"aunt" would like to learn more about business and when Mr. Hitchcock goes to insult her, Samantha twitches and makes him fall in love with her. Hepzibah is enchanted with him and the two decide to go to lunch.

Later on, Durwood is furious with Samantha for breaking up his business meeting but she explains she had to do it. Just then, Hepzibah pops home from her lunch with Mr. Hitchcock. Durwood blows his top and earns the rest of his demerits and Hepzibah decrees the end of the marriage and sends Durwood and Samantha to their room. Samantha tells Durwood that she'll give up her witchhood in the hopes that Hepzibah will leave their marriage alone. But Durwood tells her that even though he doesn't like her witchiness, it's part of who she is and he decides to apologize to Hepzibah. When they go downstairs they find that Mr. Hitchcock is there trying to find out where Hepzibah is going and, when Samantha reveals that Hepzibah will be traveling to Salem, Mr. Hitchcock remarks that Salem is lovely this time of year and he'd like to accompany her. Realizing that she can't have a mortal with her at a Witches Convention, Hepzibah tries to dissuade him but he won't be stopped and he even mentions that he'll be staying at the Hawthorne Hotel. And with that, he leaves. After reflecting a moment, Hepzibah decides that mortals can be endearing and that maybe she should reconsider her decision about the marriage, so she cancels the dissolvement of the marriage. Samantha then asks if Durwood can go to Salem with her and Hepzibah refuses, saying that mortals are not allowed until Samantha asks if Mr. Hitchcock is one of the witch community, and Hepzibah decrees that Durwood can go to Salem, but that she'll be watching. She returns their furniture and pops off to Salem just as Larry arrives, pleased to hear that Durwood somehow talked Mr. Hitchcock into going to Salem.

I would give this episode four stars, especially the demerits part. I would like to know how they got the bar to stick pretty much so permanently in one place. And did you notice at one point Hepzibah zaps it up and the camera goes back to Durwood who is telling her he doesn't care and then it shows her again, from further back, but the bar is gone? Sloppy!

Anyway, I like all the 'exotic' food names and especially that Larry liked them so much.

I also laugh every time Hepzibah tells Penelope "Naughty, naughty!" And my most favorite line is "Work. What is work?"

Dick Sargent is much better in this episode than usual. And didn't you think Tabitha looked like she was going to laugh saying her line about Adam making a no-no on Hepzibah? And what do you think of the new office designs? I actually kind of like it as it's much more roomy.

It's too bad Endora wasn't in this episode because Agnes Moorehead was really good friends with Caesar Romero a.k.a. Mr. Hitchcock. He's best known to TV audiences as the Joker on *Batman* and he was considered to play Maurice. That would've been awesome!

I wish that Hepzibah would've appeared at least once more, but sadly this is her last episode, though Jane Connell, who had already appeared as Queen Victoria and Mother Goose would return next season as Martha Washington.

This is also one of a few times where Samantha's stint as Queen of the Witches is mentioned. I love it when the page announces her as "ex-Queen Samantha, daughter Tabitha, and mortal."

OCTOBER 8, 1970

It was on this night ABC aired Episode #203: "The Salem Saga."

The time has finally arrived for Samantha and Durwood to fly off to Salem, MA for the Witches Convention. Endora is ready too, however, she waits for Esmeralda to arrive so she can watch the children. When she suggests that Samantha and Durwood wait so they can all fly together, Durwood says they'll just fly the mortal way, and they leave.

On the plane, Durwood settles in to read the paper and Samantha goes to rest until she notices that her mother is out on the wing of the plane, flapping her robes in the wind! Endora motions for Samantha to join her but Sam refuses. Unfortunately, Endora will not be refused and Samantha finds herself out on the wing of the plane, much to the shock of some of the passengers and one of the cute stewardesses. Endora tells her that she just wanted to tell them that Esmeralda arrived and she didn't want them to worry. Samantha tells her she doesn't want to discuss it and she'll see her in Salem and pops back onto the plane. Of course, Durwood is furious, but before he can blow his stack even further, they both hear Endora behind them telling another passenger that he has taken her seat. When he says she must be mistaken, she corrects him to say that he is mistaken and zaps him away. Samantha and Durwood are shocked, and a bit worried as to what will happen when the plane lands without him. She assures them it's all taken care of as he's already in Boston.

A little later they arrive in Boston and begin the journey up to Salem in a convertible that Endora insists on riding on the back of, much to the irritation of Durwood. When they arrive in Salem, Endora notices the signs along the streets marking the Witch Trail depicting an ugly old crone. Both witches are offended but Endora fixes it by zapping it into a blonde beautiful witch, which startles the town drunk. They continue on their way when Durwood stops in front of the Witch House, the main venue of the infamous Witch Trials, and he suggest they take the tour. Samantha tells him that they most certainly will not as that's like asking Napoleon to revisit Waterloo, that the witch trials were nothing more than mass hysteria and that no real witches were involved. Endora decides to leave them to get ready for the convention and they decide to go tour the House of the Seven Gables, the famous house from the book of the same name written by Nathaniel Hawthorne, one time resident of the house. While listening to the tour guide, Ms. Ferndale, describe the features of the house, Samantha suddenly gets a push from behind and is shocked to find that it's a bedwarmer that has hit her all by itself! She tries to hide the fact that the bedwarmer is becoming increasingly aggressive and does a good job until the tour group goes into the next room and the bedwarmer flies to the door blocking Samantha's exit. When Durwood realizes what's going on, he tries to move the bedwarmer but finds that it's much stronger than he. Ms. Ferndale sees them manhandling the bedwarmer and gets very incensed, reminding them that none of the objects in the home should be touched and she resumes the tour. Samantha tells Durwood that she is definitely not causing all this craziness and that the bedwarmer must be haunted. Durwood tells her to just tell it to leave her alone so that they can continue and he goes to join the tour group. Samantha grabs the bedwarmer and tries to reason with it only for another tour group to discover her. Insisting that she just felt nostalgic for it as it was the same one she had at the home, Samantha ushers them back out and she tells the bedwamer to knock it off and hangs it back up. But right after she leaves, the bedwarmer follows her but detours out one of the windows and floats to their car. Just after they leave, the second tour guide tells Ms. Ferndale that the bedwarmer is missing and that she last saw Samantha speaking to it. But by this time, Samantha and Durwood have begun to drive away.

On their drive back to the Hawthorne Motor Hotel, Durwood tells Samantha that he can't believe they can't do anything without her witchiness getting them in trouble. Samantha is irritated that he blames all the strange goings on on her and when they pull up to the hotel before he can go on anymore, the bedwarmer bonks him on the head, in front of the drunk, Mr. Potter.

Durwood tries to pick up the bedwarmer to take it up to their room quickly but finds that, as at the House of the Seven Gables, it won't move for him. Samantha barely grasps it and she's able to move it and they hurry up to the room.

Once in the room, Durwood demands to know what's going on and Samantha tells him that the bedwarmer must be a warlock that was transformed and wants to be released. Endora pops in and confirms what Samantha was thinking and says that it must've been done around the time of the Trials. She pops off to continue getting ready for the Convention Opening Night and when Samantha tries to zap the bedwarmer back to original form, it won't do it. Just then, there is a sharp knock at the door and they hear the police announce themselves! Durwood tries to move the bedwarmer but again is unable to until Samantha grasps it and places it in the closet. Durwood is quite nervous that they are going to be thrown in jail for bedwarmer stealing and…

…stay tuned next week for part two, "Samantha's Hot Bedwarmer"!

I love this episode! I remember when I first watched it when I was little I thought it so strange and spooky that the bedwarmer was seemingly haunted. My favorite line out of this episode is when Samantha says, "I had one just like it at the rest home."

In 2006 at the *Bewitched* Fanfare in Salem, we watched this episode on a big screen and it was amazing how many details you could see, especially realizing that Samantha's dress was covered in moons and stars!

This is the first episode that David Lawrence (now David Bloch-Mandel) appeared in. He even gets credit at the end! Even though nobody ever really likes Adam, I always did because he was a little boy that could do magic and I thought I was him. Plus, when I realized that actors played the characters and saw that his name was David, I was SURE he was me! And the birth of Adam episode aired exactly seven years to the day before I was born.

Liz's legs are really hot, especially when she's out on the airplane wing. It's a wonder with how hard the wind would be blowing that the rest of her dress wouldn't have blown up! I always try to get a wing seat just so I can imagine Endora and Samantha sitting out there. It's hysterical when Endora makes that man disappear! Did you notice Peanuts, the show's hairdresser, was sitting in the seat directly across the aisle from that one? And she's just in front of Melody and Gerald when they enter the airport.

It's so cool to have actually been to the House of the Seven Gables! I just wish they'd tried to have recreated the inside of it better. It looked nothing like that! And that Miss Ferndale, what a psycho!

There were plans to film in the Witch House but it rained that day so the plans were changed. I wonder what the scenes would've been like at the Witch House had the rain not been there? I think it's funny that when we were there, we didn't go in either, not because of rain, but because of a long day of seeing other sights.

Nancy Priddy plays one of the stewardesses. She is Christina Applegate's mother.

Salem's Mayor Samuel Zoll declared October 8, 1970 to be *Bewitched* Day in Historic Salem with the following proclamation:

"WHEREAS, Salem, Massachusetts is known throughout the world as the WITCH CITY, and WHEREAS, the image of witches and witchcraft have been tremendously enhanced by Samantha, Queen of all Witches and the "Bewitched" television program on ABC-TV, and WHEREAS, on Thursday, October 8, 1970, the historic conclave of witches meeting in historic Salem will be presented for viewing. NOW, therefore, I, Samuel E. Zoll, mayor of the City of Salem, do hereby declare and make known throughout the country that Thursday, October 8, 1970, shall be proclaimed as "Bewitched Day in Historic Salem" and I call upon all citizens to observe this occasion in a meaningful and befitting manner."

OCTOBER 15, 1970

It was on this night ABC aired Episode #204: "Samantha's Hot Bedwarmer."

Durwood and Samantha are in Salem, MA, where they have found themselves the interest of a bedwarmer from the House of the Seven Gables that Samantha thinks may be a witch/warlock that was changed at the time of the infamous Trials. As they decide what to do with the bedwarmer, they are interrupted by a knock at their hotel door from the police! Samantha, who seems to be in the good graces of the bedwarmer, hides it in the closet. With the bedwarmer safely hidden, Durwood opens the door to find two officers and Ms. Ferndale, the House of the Seven Gables tour guide, who is insistent that they reveal the whereabouts of the bedwarmer. The police remind Ms. Ferndale she was only there to identify the accused and they dismiss her. While they interrogate Durwood and Samantha, the police find that they aren't going to get a confession until suddenly the bedwarmer falls out of the closet. Seemingly caught, Samantha decides the only way out of it is to tell the truth and tells the officers that the bedwarmer followed them. Of course, the officers aren't going to believe it and they tell Durwood that he's going to go to jail and that they are taking the bedwarmer with them. Knowing that the bedwarmer won't go unless she does, Samantha picks it up and asks it to please go with them and do what they say and she sets it on the ground, standing on its handle. It suddenly jumps towards the scared officers and floats in front of them, until one of them grabs it and they leave.

Later on, at the magical grounds of the Witches Convention, Samantha finds her mother, who is preparing for the evening, to tell her that Durwood has been thrown in jail for stealing the bedwarmer. Endora couldn't care less and Samantha insists that she be able to address the Convention in an attempt to find out who changed the bedwarmer. She also promises to blackmail Endora if she doesn't let her speak by revealing to Maurice Endora's fling with Sir Walter Raleigh. Endora concedes and Samantha addresses the convocation but nobody fesses up so Samantha asks Endora to cast a spell to find the culprit. Amid sparks and fire, Endora throws her spell out to the atmospheric continuum and tells Samantha that the one they are seeking should show up in a couple minutes. With a few minutes to spare, Samantha pops back down to the jail to tell Durwood what's happening and before she can get caught by the police because of Mr. Potter, the town drunk, causing a ruckus in the cell he shares with Durwood, Samantha pops back to the Convention.

She finds that the person responsible for the bedwarmer has shown up, and it's none other than her kooky cousin Serena! She admits that

Samantha tries to persuade Newton (Noam Pitlik) that she is not Serena, his former girlfriend.

the bedwarmer is a former boyfriend, Newton, who wouldn't leave her alone, so she changed him into the bedwarmer. When Samantha asks her for the spell to change him back, Serena says she can't remember three hundred years ago so Samantha suggests Endora zap Serena back to the time of the incident so she can remember. Endora zaps Serena back to Olde Salem where she melds with her past self. She finds the Widow Patterson in the stockade accused of being a witch, and to show the witch hunters they haven't got a real witch, she zaps the stockade open, much to the disbelief of Widow Patterson.

Serena goes to her home to freshen up when Newton pops in wanting her to fly away with him. She's so not interested in him and tells him that the witch hunters have been out looking for him. He gets nervous and tries to pop out but can't as his powers (and other things, apparently) fail him when he tries. There soon comes a knock at the door from one of the witch hunters and Newton suggests that he and Serena pop out but she doesn't want to, but suggests another idea and with a zippety-zappety, he becomes the bedwarmer. She goes to answer the door and instantly she and the witch hunter fall into a mad embrace, but just as instantly, she disappears back to the Convention in the present day. Samantha is eager but Serena teases saying maybe it won't be so bad having Durwood spend awhile in jail until Samantha threatens to choke her.

With spell in hand, Samantha pops down to the jail and puts the jailer to sleep while she gets into the evidence closet and zaps Newton back to human form. He thinks she is a blonde Serena but she explains herself and tells him that in exchange for turning him back, she promised that Newton would never bug her again. Seeing that he's still in pilgrim clothing, Samantha updates his clothing and tells him they have to go to court.

In court, Samantha tells the judge that the bedwarmer wasn't an ordinary bedwarmer, which the officers reluctantly agree with. They also have bad news that the bedwarmer has gone missing, which deeply upsets Ms. Ferndale. Samantha tells the court that Newton is a specialist in bedwarmers and, as he has had eyes for Ms. Ferndale, and now she for him, he promises to duplicate the bedwarmer for her and they go off to get more acquainted and Durwood is released.

I'd give this one at least three if not MORE stars! And it's just three because Serena's voice at the Convention is irritating not to mention why aren't Maurice, Uncle Arthur, Esmeralda, and Dr. Bombay at the convention? I've always loved this episode simply because it's the first time we get to see where the convention is and we get that AWESOME witchy background music. Plus we get a ton of Sammy in her flying suit, my favorite of her flying suits.

I also LOVED that Serena had to go back to remember the spell because then we wouldn't have been treated to the cool scene of her releasing Widow Patterson from the stockade or her melding together with her Olde Salem self. Not to mention the whole line about Newton's powers not being all they should be and Serena replying, "That's not the only thing." I did, however, wonder why it was that Serena chose to zippity-zappety him into a bedwarmer when they had just barely discussed popping out. Couldn't she have just done that to him? Maybe she decided on the bedwarmer knowing that he wouldn't be able to get out of it and pester her anymore. Samantha mentions knowing Sir Walter Raleigh, which she denied in

"Marriage, Witches Style" to which Serena agreed. I wish the writers would've been more consistent.

The Police Station shown from the outside was the only shot actually filmed in Salem. Now, if I remember correctly, the building houses a law firm.

I also noticed Gerald "Herbie" York was a warlock at the convention and when we watched this one on the big screen in Salem at the 2006 *Bewitched* Fanfare, it was the first time I noticed the warlock with the polka dotted cape, which I thought was cool. I also think it's funny that when you really look at the crowd of witches/warlocks at the convention there really aren't that many.

Do you think the gold outfit Serena wears is her flying suit? I would imagine that no witch would dare show up to the convention without the proper attire on. But on the other hand, she did say she wanted to get back to the Maharajah's castle before his wives came back, so maybe that's just what she was wearing with him.

Another thing is, when Serena goes back in time, she melds with her past self, yet when Endora zaps her back to the present she disappears... so then what happened to past Serena?

Anyway, I LOVE this episode!

It was three nights before that President Nixon announced the withdrawal of forty thousand more troops from Vietnam before Christmas.

And tomorrow would be Adam's one year birthday, yet his parents are in Salem. How sad.

OCTOBER 22, 2010

Tonight Elizabeth Montgomery surprised us by switching up her greeting to say, "Hi. Stay tuned for *Bewitched*, next! In culluh!" to introduce Episode #205: "Darrin on a Pedestal" on ABC.

As if we've forgotten we're shown that we are still in Salem, MA and Durwood is nervously "to-ing and fro-ing" through their room as he feels guilty for throwing the whole Barrows Umbrella account in Larry's lap. Samantha reminds him that they are sort of on a vacation in Salem and tells him to think about all the fun they are going to have sightseeing. Just then, the phone rings and Durwood goes to answer it while Samantha finishes brushing her hair. Suddenly, a parachute floats down from the sky with a note attached, which doesn't seem to please Samantha as it's a notification of an emergency meeting of the Witches' Council where Endora is giving a special presentation on incantations past, present, and future.

Thinking that Larry would've talked Durwood into going to Boston to work on the Barrows account, Samantha finds her hopes are dashed as Durwood says he refused to leave and Samantha apologizes for not being able to go sightseeing with him. He is not bothered and says he'd rather go sightseeing alone than give into Larry, when suddenly the shrill voice of Serena is heard asking why he would go alone when she's ready, willing, and able. Suddenly, she pops in in all her green pantsuit glory in a minihelicopter that she was using to tow her kite that she was flying in the World Kite Flying Championships in India where she was disqualified for flying her kite in the helicopter. Durwood tells her to get lost, but she takes that as invitation to stick around and Samantha reminds him that he'll enjoy himself more sight-seeing if he were with someone. Durwood reluctantly agrees and he and Serena leave the hotel, where she zaps up a roadster much to the shock of Durwood, who was expecting a broom ("my broom is getting a lube job, this is a loaner") and off they go up the coast.

While driving through Gloucester, Serena's eye is caught by the Fisherman's Memorial statue and she begs for Durwood to pull over. Serena is truly smitten by the bronze sculpture of a fisherman trying to steer his ship in the face of a storm, a memorial erected to honor all the men who had died at sea. Wanting to be steered by the Fisherman, Serena incants a spell for the man to come alive, and he does. He seems to be as smitten with Serena as she is with him and Durwood is furious that one of the most famous landmarks in Massachusetts is now missing and he demands that there be a statue back on the pedestal by the time he counts to three. Serena says she will and tells him to start counting, but before he can get to three, she waves her arm and suddenly Durwood is bronzed and steering the wheel in the same position as the Fisherman was! Now that they have Durwood taken care of, Serena suggests that she and her new man fly off to be alone and she zaps them away.

Meanwhile, Larry is meeting with Mr. Barrows and finds that this account is going to be tougher than he anticipated as Mr. Barrows insists that he wants everyone to own one of his umbrellas and he won't accept anything less. Realizing that Durwood can do a better job, he suggests that they meet with Durwood.

Serena and the Fisherman end up at a beautiful castle that Serena says she whipped up to make herself comfortable while in Salem. They walk through the grounds and then begin to "catch up" on all the Fisherman has been missing while a gardener happens to be watching.

Having finished with her Witches' Council meeting, Samantha drives up the coast towards the Gloucester House restaurant, where she had told Serena and Durwood that she would meet them for lunch, when she notices the roadster parked by the Fisherman's Memorial. She pulls over to see where her cousin and husband could be when she notices that the statue looks familiar and, upon second glance, realizes with horror that it's Durwood! She's even more horrified when she hears Larry calling for her and he approaches with Mr. Barrows. They found out from the hotel clerk that Durwood was going to the Gloucester House for lunch and had pulled over when they saw Samantha at the statue. When Larry questions where Durwood is, she tells him that Durwood had already gone up to the Gloucester House and that she would meet him later and so they head up to the Gloucester House. Samantha is in a bind wondering how she is going to find her cousin, get her husband back, and entertain Larry and Mr. Barrows.

When they arrive at the restaurant, the maître'd tells them that Durwood hasn't shown up yet, so Samantha asks that Larry and Mr. Barrows sit while she excuses herself for a moment. She pops back to the Memorial and tells Durwood that she's going to do everything she can to find Serena. Realizing what Serena must've done with the real statue, she casts a spell to take her where romance can grow and ends up at Serena's castle. Not seeing the couple anywhere, she asks the gardener, who admits to having seen the girl and the fisherman, and as he draws out his story as to what they were doing, Samantha pops out back to the Gloucester House. Wouldn't you know it, Serena and the Fisherman are sitting with Larry and Mr. Barrows singing old sea shanties causing a scene and embarrassing Mr. Barrows. Samantha requests to speak to Serena aside and tells her that she would like to get Durwood back and have the Fisherman returned to his post. Serena agrees reluctantly and pops off back to the Memorial where she zaps Durwood away back to the Gloucester House. Before Mr. Barrows can get any angrier with the Fisherman, he pops back to his post. Durwood and Samantha show up just as Mr. Barrows is getting ready to leave. He tells them that he was tired of waiting after his strange day, but Samantha requests that he stay to hear Durwood's ideas which are non-existent from her. He agrees and she tells him that Durwood had decided there needed to be a campaign that would appeal more to men and that he decided to associate the umbrellas with a masculine symbol, and what better symbol than the Fisherman's Memorial. After Durwood comes up with a tagline — "Even men that go down to the sea in ships carry a Barrows Umbrella" — Mr. Barrows eagerly agrees to give the account to McMann and Tate.

Later on, Durwood and Samantha go back to the Memorial and plant an umbrella in the Fisherman's arms so that Durwood can sketch out an ad. Serena shows up looking for a thank you as she feels she is responsible for Durwood getting the account. He tells her to blow off and she takes him literally and blows up a huge wind to turn the umbrella inside out, and she pops out.

I used to really like this episode, but since I've actually been to Gloucester for some 'lobstah' (I actually just had fish sticks 'cause I'm not a seafood fan), I LOVE it! I think everything about it is great. Well, almost everything. Sammy's hair looks like crap throughout most of it and that fake smile she gives Mr. Barrows at the end when she asks him if she can tell him Durwood's ideas…what's up with that?! But for the most part, AWESOME!

The first thing I recognized from the Salem episodes when driving into Salem was the tower of the Immaculate Conception Church seen at the very first of this episode. And I found it weird that it's just down the street from the Hawthorne Hotel, which you can see at the very end of that opening scene.

We find out that Serena hasn't been to the convention on time because she was in the World Kite Flying Championship, which is a lame excuse, but I like it when she says, "I was disqualified" with her pouty face. I think she chose to go sight-seeing with Durwood just to tick him off, considering she facetiously says, "Since the invitation comes straight from the heart, I accept!"

I've always loved when Serena zapped up the Roadster and that scene totally looks like it was filmed near a restaurant was in Salem where we ate breakfast and some other meals.

The houses along Stacey Blvd (where the Fisherman's Memorial is) look just the same. Maybe a little paint job here and there, but that's cool that they look the same. One of our tour guides in Salem said she was just a little girl when they were filming scenes at the statue. Her mother owned a hair salon that was across the street from where they were filming and she was too scared to go talk to Liz because she was dressed as Serena and Serena scared her! I think that's awesome! Not that she was scared, but just to be able to have a memory like that!

Serena's castle is actually called Hammond Castle and it's located in Magnolia, not too far from Gloucester. I love the scenes shot at Hammond Castle. I love it when Serena is rubbing the Fisherman's back and he tells her lower and she says, "GLADLY!!" I also loved how the statue was one of her friends that got stoned. Hammond Castle wasn't open when I was there and so I MUST go back to Salem!

When we ate at the Gloucester House, we met the owner Michael Linquata. His father was the original owner of the restaurant. I felt so privileged to meet him and we found out he's in the episode! He and his wife are seen exiting the restaurant when Larry and Mr. Barrows are going to go in. Later on they are seen behind Serena and the Fisherman at the table totally not acting but just watching what is going on at the table. And I like it when the Fisherman says, "Chicken of the sea, that's me!"

Serena jumping to pop out was cool and did you notice that when Durwood popped in, Gerald was looking straight at him and didn't react at all?

Of course, the coolest piece of trivia about this episode is that of statue stand-in Gary Richard, who recently discovered himself in Peter Alachi's *Salem's Summer of Sam* and shared with Peter his memories as well as photos from his time on *Bewitched*, a dream all of us wish we could have had! Honestly, if you haven't purchased the *Bewitched and the Man at the Wheel* book, what are you waiting for? You can get these books from Peter's website at *www.palachi.com*.

Anyway, awesome episode!

The day before, Agnes Moorehead appeared on *The Virginian* in "Gun Quest."

OCTOBER 29, 1970

It was on this night ABC aired Episode #206: "Paul Revere Rides Again" sponsored by Oscar Mayer.

Durwood and Samantha are still in Salem and it seems as though Samantha wants to bring Salem back with her as she takes Durwood on a big shopping trip ending up with many boxed items. When they get back to their room at the Hawthorne Motor Hotel, they find that Larry has sent them a package, which turns out to be a teapot. It seems suspicious as Larry sent it special messenger and before they can have time to figure it out, they hear Esmeralda, their witch maid, greeting them, though they don't see her but for her shoes. The rest of her appears and she says that she has popped in to see if they would give permission to Tabitha to change the baby, though not by diaper — she wants to change him into something! Of course, they say no and Esmeralda says she'll pop home as Louise Tate is coming over to check on the children and she offers to take the packages home with her. Before they can object, Esmeralda disappears along with Samantha and Durwood's shopping bounty.

Samantha tells Durwood that she's planned a day of sightseeing, including the Peabody Museum and the Pioneer Village, when a phone call interrupts her itinerary recap. Durwood answers and finds its Larry wondering about the teapot, which he says is not for them but for their newest client. Reminding Larry that he's on vacation, Durwood hangs up and suggests that he and Samantha get started on their day before Larry can manage to drive up from Boston. Just as they reach the door, there is a knock and when Durwood opens it, it turns out to be Larry who really had called from the hotel lobby knowing that Durwood would try to avoid him. He advises that the new client is British Imperial Textile Mills, headed by Sir Leslie Bancroft, an avid Paul Revere enthusiast and that he would be thrilled to have an authentic Paul Revere teapot replica. Durwood still refuses Larry's invitation for lunch with he and Sir Leslie and so Larry requests his teapot back. Durwood goes to get it from the coffee table when he and Samantha are nonplussed when they remember that Esmeralda took all the packages, including the teapot, with her. Samantha says that she's put it in the hotel safe and she tells Durwood she'll pop home to get it. He insists she make sure that Louise isn't there and while Durwood and Larry go to meet Sir Leslie outside, Samantha goes into the bedroom and dials up her home on her hand mirror. The cosmic operator connects her with a saucepan hanging in the kitchen and Esmeralda answers. She confirms that the teapot is there and offers to send it back as Louise is there playing with the children. They hang up and Esmeralda casts her spell requesting that the teapot of Paul Revere return to Salem. Just then, in Samantha's hotel room, Paul Revere appears in a puff of smoke, startling Samantha. Realizing that this must be Esmeralda's work, Samantha calls her back and tells her what has happened and insists that she get Paul Revere to disappear. Esmeralda says she'll work on it. Meanwhile, Mr. Revere is quite confused and Samantha explains what has happened and where he is but he feels it's some sort of trickery by the British especially when Samantha reveals she's a witch.

Esmeralda tries to get the teapot back to Salem and for Paul Revere to disappear but when the teapot does nothing, Esmeralda complains that she's getting tired and her voice is getting hoarse. At that exact moment in Salem, in another puff of smoke, Mr. Revere's horse appears startling Samantha and Mr. Revere. Just then Durwood, Larry, and Sir Leslie enter the hotel room and Samantha requests that Mr. Revere be quiet while she greets her guests. She tells Larry that the teapot is still locked up as the hotel claims to have lost the key but Sir Leslie suggests it'll give them time to discuss the campaign. So Durwood begins to tell him his idea about a slogan announcing that "The British are Coming" in preparation for British Imperial Textiles new operations in America. Mr. Revere, who has been listening at the door, thinks Durwood is announcing a British attack and, as he did in his time, he mounts his horse and begins a ride to warn the countryside that the British are coming. Everyone is shocked and Sir Leslie is offended as it seems they are casting the British in a negative light as was done in the colonial days. Samantha chases after Mr. Revere, who is riding through Salem, when he is finally caught by the police. She goes to the police station to bail him out and finds that he's downcast as he realizes all the wonders Samantha had told him about are true. He wonders if his role in history had been worthwhile and Samantha pops himself and herself to the Paul Revere statue in Boston to show him how important he was. Just then, the teapot appears in Samantha's hands which Sam says signifies that Esmeralda's spell to get Paul back to his time is working. He recognizes that the teapot is one he had been working on the night of his famous ride and explains that it doesn't bear his mark because he was interrupted for the ride before he could set his mark on it. As thanks for her protecting him, he marks it then and just as he kisses her hand, he disappears.

Later, Samantha meets up with Durwood, Larry, and Sir Leslie in the hotel restaurant and Larry excitedly gives the teapot to Sir Leslie, who is pleased. They also find that on the back of the day's paper is an ad depicting the ride of Paul Revere but announcing that "British Imperial Textiles is Coming" and Sir Leslie loves it! Durwood and Larry are confused but Durwood realizes that Samantha must've zapped it up. As Sir Leslie looks the teapot over, he realizes that it's an original and feels he can't possibly accept it and so he gives it back to Samantha and Durwood.

This is my LEAST favorite of the Salem episodes because Liz seemed to be so bored! But that was only before Bert Convy showed up. It seemed like she was just phoning in her performance at the first but then when Paul Revere shows up, man, the sparks were flying just like when Endora cast the spell to find Serena!

And I thought her hair looked the worst it's been so far this season.

Did you notice that her dress had tiger faces scattered all through it? I thought that was cool.

I wondered how she could've managed to get so many boxes for shopping in Salem back home on the plane. I wonder if the Salem Chamber of Commerce requested that they mention something about how great the shopping is there.

Another reason that this episode is my least favorite of the Salem episodes is that there isn't one scene at the convention! You would've thought Endora, or Hepzibah (whom we haven't seen since they were at home), would've been furious!

And I'm tired of Larry interrupting everything just to get Durwood to work on yet another account! Couldn't we just have had a little more of Caesar Romero who he was supposed to be working on to get Gotham Industries? At least it would've given a chance for him and Agnes Moorehead to have a scene together.

I think that Samantha either A) should've just popped home to get the teapot. She could've done it invisibly or just popped in rather small like she and Uncle Arthur did when they were trying to find Bernie Kopell and Bunnie, or B) how hard would it have been for Samantha to cast a spell to retrieve the tea pot which Esmeralda had just took. Speaking of, when they show the coffee table where the teapot had been, the magazine was *Town & Country*. But I suppose we wouldn't have had Bert Convey show up and seeing him and Liz together was cool.

I also wonder why the police department wasn't VERY leery of Sam and Durwood considering that this was their second time being involved with them in most likely just a week's time and they're just visitors!

And can you imagine that Bert Convy had to get all dressed up as the statue for just the seconds long scenes that they used him for? Man, I would've been pissed!

A couple years later, when he and Liz were on *Password Plus* together, they didn't make one mention of having worked together on *Bewitched*, but I suppose that has no bearing on this episode. However, in the 80s, when Mr. Convy was the host of the new incarnation of *Password*, Dick Sargent was one of the players along with Art Metrano, and one of the clues was 'Elizabeth Montgomery,' at which point they all mentioned having worked on the show.

I did like the witch operator, though don't you think had Louise actually been in the kitchen, that would've been hard to explain?

The only scenes actually shot on location were of the Roger Conant statue, the police station, and the North Church. Having stayed in the Hawthorne Hotel, I can say that the rooms look nothing like is depicted here.

When Paul is riding through the park and a hippie yells "Right on," it is believed that the hippie is played by William Asher's son, Brian William Asher from his first marriage.

The next day the worst monsoon in over six years hits Vietnam killing hundreds and leaves hundreds of thousands homeless and virtually halts the continuing war.

NOVEMBER 5, 1970

It was on this night ABC aired Episode #207: "Samantha's Bad Day in Salem."

As Samantha prepares for a big meeting at the Witches Convention, she discovers Durwood hard at work on a campaign and wonders why as they are supposed to be on vacation. Durwood has told Larry that he'll rough out ideas for the Blakely account. Samantha suggests they forget about work and conventions and Durwood buys the bait and says they should just count the rest of their time in Salem as a second honeymoon. When Durwood asks how Samantha will explain her absence from the Convention, she says she'll just say she came down with a serious case of love. Just as they are about to kiss, Endora pops in saying that Samantha's excuse wouldn't be accepted as she (Endora) is the chairman and she would refuse it. And before Durwood knows it, Samantha is zapped out of his arms as Endora takes herself and Samantha to the hallowed grounds of the convention.

The agenda for that night's meeting is to install a new Resident Witch of Salem, a position created out of the wisdom of the High Priestess Hepzibah in 1692 meant to protect and preserve the image of the witch and protect those innocent people accused of being witches. When a recess is called, Samantha goes to the refreshment table and suddenly finds her eyes covered by a pair of hands, one of which has a wart on the pinky, which indicates it must be Samantha's childhood friend, Waldo. Her intuition turns out correct and she apologizes for the wart which she caused after she had changed him into a toad when they were children. He says he doesn't mind it as it reminds him of her. He tries to ask her out but she refuses reminding him that she is married, though he says it's not valid as it's to a mortal and she leaves as she has been called over by someone else. Waldo retreats to a secluded place and zaps up an exact duplicate of Samantha, in looks only as she's more Stepford Wife than Xeroxed Witch. Apparently Waldo has resorted to zapping up a fantasy Samantha since he can't have the real one and he pours his heart out to her. Just then his mother pops in reprimanding him for continuing to focus on a dream and she demands that if he is going to pine after Samantha, than he should just pursue the real one.

The next day, as Samantha prepares for another meeting of the Witches' Council and Durwood gets ready to go sight-seeing by himself, there is a knock at the door which they assume is the waiter bringing their breakfast but are shocked when the seemingly rude waiter turns out to be Larry, who had tipped the waiter off to take his place so he could come and persuade Durwood in person to come back to New York to present Mr. Blakely his ideas. Durwood reminds Larry he is on vacation and that he has no intention of leaving but to go sight-seeing in Salem. He does leave, and goes to see the statue of Nathaniel Hawthorne and Roger Conant, Salem founder, but finds that he can't enjoy himself as Larry tags along trying to beg him to come back. They end up at the House of Seven Gables where Durwood says he needs to buy some film, so Larry says he'll wait outside for him. He goes walking on the grounds behind the house and, as he nears the vineyards, he hears a man and woman talking and is startled to find it's Samantha with another man talking about how much she loves and adores him and she finds Durwood icky. Of course, it's Waldo's fake Samantha but Larry is shaken and when Durwood comes out of the shop, he apologizes to Larry and says he'll go back to New York but Larry refuses telling him that he needs to stay in Salem and they head back to the hotel for some lunch where they were to meet Samantha. Meanwhile, Waldo tells his fantasy Samantha that maybe if he met Durwood he could force himself to get rid of him.

At the hotel restaurant, Samantha meets up with Durwood and Larry and soon after, Waldo shows up. Larry about chokes on his drink and says he's not feeling well and goes up to his room. Samantha suggests Durwood go check on Larry as she knows that Waldo showing up can't be a good thing. When she asks Waldo why he's there, he tells her that he wanted to see what she saw in Durwood and he still can't see why she married him.

Up in Larry's hotel room, Durwood finds Larry very evasive and confusing and then he finally gets the real story about Larry seeing Samantha and Waldo together at the House of Seven Gables. A little surprised, Durwood returns back down stairs and happens to exit the elevator just as Samantha is going up in the elevator next to it. However, when he gets to the table, he finds "Samantha" and Waldo discussing plans to away to their rendezvous. Durwood demands an explanation but Waldo tells him to stop crowing and zaps him into a crow. Defeated once again, Durwood flies back up to his room. When Samantha gets up to their room, she can't find her husband and calls Larry to see if maybe he's there but Larry says that Durwood said he had been going back down to lunch. As she hangs up she hears a crow and goes into the bedroom to find a crow packing Durwood's things and she realizes Durwood is in their room. She tries to talk him out of packing but he won't stop until she zaps him in a cage and tells him she'll find out who it was at the Convention that night.

At the convention, Samantha pops in with the bird interrupting Endora's recitation for an April shower spell. Samantha demands her mother change Durwood back but Endora insists she didn't do it and suggests that someone else who doesn't approve of the mortal marriage did it. Furious with her witch associates, Samantha demands that whoever did it reverse their spell at once and so Waldo, from the shadows, zaps Durwood back. Instantly the gathered witches and warlocks disappear as they consider the witch grounds hallowed and now that a mortal is there…well…Durwood demands that Samantha take them back to the hotel which she does. He begins to continue packing and Samantha tells him that she deserves an explanation so he explains how Larry had seen her and Waldo at the House of Seven Gables. She insists that it wasn't her and that the person that can explain would be Waldo so she calls out for him and he appears. She demands an explanation and he concedes and tells them that as Durwood has a Samantha, so does he, and he zaps up his fantasy Samantha. A little embarrassed, Samantha tells Waldo that he needs to give up and move on. Just then, Larry walks into the room and sees "Samantha" expressing her love to Waldo, so Larry gets ready to knock Waldo out and finds himself turned into a white crested crow! Durwood wonders how they'll explain to Larry what he saw and Samantha suggest that they'll say it was Serena that was seen with Waldo and she asks Waldo to zap up a blonde Serena that looks like his fantasy Samantha. Grudgingly, Waldo accepts as he was never fond of Serena and zaps her up and returns Larry to his human form. Larry is relieved and wonders why Serena is blonde. She tells him that it's because blonds have more fun and when he goes to give her a hug his arm goes right through her. Shocked, Larry asks for a drink and Samantha suggests some Old Crow.

I've always liked this one just because of the scenes of the Convention plus Sammy is in her flying suit almost the entire time! But now that I'm older, I realize it doesn't have much to do with Salem except the small scene at the House of Seven Gables and the insert shots of "the sights of Salem." Come on, all they could show was the two statues and say that's sights?! Not to mention that Durwood and Larry weren't even there, just filmed in front of green screens.

David White was sick during this episode and you can hear it in his voice. And about Larry: he is rather annoying trying to interrupt this vacation all the damn time and then it was ridiculous for Samantha to say at the beginning, "Doesn't he know you're on vacation?" What do you think he's been doing for the past couple episodes?

Another funny part of this episode is when Durwood is changed back and then everyone leaves because they feel he has tainted hallowed ground.

Waldo seems really wimpy and not someone Samantha would've been interested in at all. George was my favorite out of her boyfriends and the only one really worthy of her. But I suppose we should keep in mind that Waldo was just a childhood friend who developed a crush on her.

One interesting tidbit from this episode is the fact that Salem really does have a Resident Witch, who lives there for the same purpose that Endora states, and that is to prevent the same witch hysteria from 1692 from happening. She's named Laurie Cabot (her website is *www.lauriecabot.com*). It's too bad they didn't just center this episode around installing the new resident witch. They should've just made it about Samantha being the new resident witch since she gave up being Queen after a year and then have her try to find a way to tell Durwood about it and finally show the witch community why she wouldn't be the best choice. That way more of the episode could've been shown at the Convention!

All in all though, I just find this episode fun.

This is the episode where we see the elevators from the lobby of the Hawthorne Hotel and we found out at the 2006 Fanfare that they are indeed the actual elevators and in forty years they haven't changed much! I thought that was really cool. I also wonder if the scenes in the restaurant were filmed there too. It doesn't seem like a familiar set.

Here is one of my favorite lines:

SAMANTHA: *"Waldo, rumor hath it that you and I were seen cavorting at the House of Seven Gables."*

I don't know why, but I just find it hysterical! That is one of my favorite *Bewitched* quotes of all time. I also laughed when Samantha is trying to find out who changed Durwood into a crow and she says, "You call yourselves witches! BULLIES!! That's what you are!"

Three days later, Renzo Cesana passed away. He played Mr. Arcarius in Episode #110: "Business, Italian Style."

NOVEMBER 12, 1970

It was on this night ABC aired the last of the Salem episodes, #208: "Samantha's Old Salem Trip."

Durwood and Samantha pop home earlier than expected from Salem when the Witches' Council orders Samantha not to be seen in public with her husband. Not wanting to concede to their irrational request, and mentioning that he wanted to leave right then, Samantha flew them home sans airplane, irritating Durwood. Having been away from their kids so long, they forget their troubles to go upstairs for a joyful reunion, but right after Durwood leaves, a witch-o-gram arrives via a flaming bolt and Esmeralda reads the message, which has come from the Witches' Council, demanding that Samantha return for the rest of the convention in sixty seconds or suffer the consequences. Worried that something bad will happen, Esmeralda casts a spell and up in Tabitha's room it apparently works, as Samantha disappears after putting Adam back in his playpen. Esmeralda is thrilled when she finds that Samantha is gone, but Durwood is furious. Things aren't as good as they appear as Endora pops in wondering where Samantha is. When she asks Esmeralda to repeat the spell, they discover that Samantha was sent back to old Salem, 17th century-witch-hanging Salem! Embarrassed at her misfire, Esmeralda fades away and Endora tells Durwood that he'll have to go back to old Salem to get Samantha back as she has lost her memory and powers. Endora would do it but she must get back to the Witches' Council to smooth their ruffled feathers. She zaps Durwood into 17th century clothing and tells him that he'll be able to restore Samantha's memory and powers by giving her a coin from the ancient tomb of Hammurabi that she must place on her forehead and, without holding it, bow three times to the East, while saying "Ahmed Talu Varsi Lupin" which means "Good Luck" in ancient Babylonian. When Durwood questions how he'll be able to get the coin to stick to her forehead without holding it, Endora tells him he'll just have to figure it out. And with that, Endora casts a spell, and in a burst of smoke, sends Durwood back.

In Old Salem, Samantha has been taken in by a kindly woman and given a job as a barmaid at Mr. Farley's bar. The townspeople are suspicious of this new girl who doesn't know who she is or where she comes from. Soon, Durwood arrives and is disappointed when she doesn't recognize him. He decides to write her a note asking her to meet him outside but when she sees it, she thinks he's being fresh and writes him back as much using his ballpoint pen. Not wanting to give up, he tells her to take the coin and do with it what he asks. Again, she thinks he's being quite forward and she smacks him causing a scene and it incites the watching suspicious crowd to throw him out of the bar for lewd behavior, which lands him in the stocks.

Later on, when Samantha goes to fetch a pail of water near the stockade, Durwood asks her if there isn't any memory of him at all but she doesn't know him at all, and when he asks for some water, she agrees to give him some and dumps her freshly drawn bucket all over his head.

Back in the bar, the judge comes in for a pint and when he sees Samantha writing with the ball point pen, he questions where she got it from and what it is. She tells him that the stranger gave it her and that she believes it's called a 'ballpoint quill' and it needs no ink. When he tries it out, he throws it down aghast as he believes it's the Devil's quill for being able to write with no ink and he accuses the stranger and Samantha of being witches and demands they be thrown in the jail where they will await trial.

In jail, Durwood finds that they are only given honey and stale bread to eat, but it's no good as the honey only makes the bread sticky. It occurs to him that if he dips the coin in honey it will stick and so he decides to try one more time with Samantha, who is in the cell across the way. He tells her that they can get out of jail using the magic coin and she is shocked to learn that he is involved with the Devil and witchcraft. He tries to throw the coin to her but it bounces off the bars to the floor. Soon after, the Judge requests that the prisoners be taken up to the Witch House for their trial and eventual sentencing. Durwood asks to pick up his coin for which the jailers laugh as they say where he's going there won't be need of money.

In the Witch House, the town is gathered and bears testimony to the strangeness of Durwood and Samantha and how they seem to be witch sympathizers. Durwood finally declares that he is ready to confess and the Judge and the crowd are pleased until he announces that it isn't he that is the witch but Samantha is and he can prove it with the coin. The Judge commands that the test be done and feeling that there is something harmless about Durwood, Samantha complies. After standing up from her third bow, Samantha's memory is restored and she is overjoyed to see Durwood. She tells the crowd that in fact she is a witch and that all the others accused were not witches and not guilty, that in fact, they are the guilty. She also makes mention of the fact that there wouldn't be a way to capture a witch who is a creature of the wind, who can transform. The Judge is not amused by her statement and says that if she were a witch she would do all those things, but she doesn't and that's because she is a cunning witch who wants to trick them. He demands that she be taken back to the jail and when the jailer grasps for her, she shocks him. For her next trick, she twitches her shackles off and then twitches Durwood's shackles off. And just to make sure that they can see that she really is a witch, she zaps a fire in the waste bin and then turns herself into a floating bucket of water and douses the fire. The crowd is shocked and the Judge is flustered and before they know it, they witness Durwood and Samantha disappear with a snap of her fingers. The Judge declares that they all go home and reflect upon the illusions they have seen which have been caused by their own witch hysteria and he declares an end to the witchcraft trials.

Back in the 20th century, Durwood wakes up the next day to find that Samantha isn't there but she soon pops in saying that she had confronted the Witches' Council and had related to them how their prejudice towards Durwood was just as bigoted as the accusers in the trials and so they reverse their mind about his appearing with her. However, they are home for good.

I LOVE this episode! It's a great way to end the whole trip and it provides a neat look at what would've happened had their really been witches at the Trials. My favorite scene is Samantha proving her powers to the court and I love it when she says, "And, now, for my next trick..." I thought it was cool that she would zap up a fire, seems like something that would've happened in the real trials. And speaking of that, according to Marilynne K. Roach's book *The Salem Witch Trials* (2002) it was recorded that in June 1688 (which was before the beginning of the Trials) that Mary Glover of Boston was accused of bewitching the Goodwin children and at her trial she admitted to witchcraft and "demonstrated here magical techniques before the court." I highly recommend that book as it gives a day by day accounting of the Trials and it's very interesting.

The only dumb part about this episode is the fact that Samantha would never in 29,374,293,423,947 years have zapped herself and Durwood home just because he said he wanted to come home right now! That's something Jeannie would've done.

I also liked when Esmeralda was reciting the spell she used. Esmeralda had a look on her face like she was quite pleased with how witty her spell was.

And that was Gerald "Herbie" York smacking Liz's arse! And notice that it was DICK Michaels which was directing this...FRESH! Which reminds me of another favorite line when Durwood tells Samantha, "Take this coin and do what I tell you."

I also thought it kind of nervy of the *Bewitched* people to reference the Devil so much in this episode, especially when they had such an uproar already about the show promoting Satanism. I liked it because it seemed like they were sticking their tongue out at all the haters.

And did you notice that when Liz does put the coin on her head when she bows her shackles are gone but when her memory comes back, so do the shackles?! SLOPPY!

I recently came across a lithograph from 1892 depicting the Trials and it shows a blonde girl at the stand zapping her shackles off and I can't help but wonder if the writer's had seen this picture and came up with the idea for this episode. I think it's awesome!

This is David Lawrence's second episode.

It was also this week that for the first time in the Vietnam War, no American casualties are reported to have happened during the week.

NOVEMBER 19, 1970

It was on this night ABC aired the first non-Salem related episode of the Seventh Season, Episode #209: "Samantha's Pet Warlock."

Having been out of town so long, Samantha finds that there needs to be some gardening done at 1164 and Durwood finds her out digging in the dirt. He would help but he has been studying about dogs all night for the new Gibbons Dog Food account. As he recounts all he has read, Endora pops in surprised that he's not racing with all the other rats, and so he leaves. She has come to visit to tell Samantha that she ran into Ashley Flynn, a warlock that Samantha used to date and before Samantha knows it, Newton, er, Ashley pops in, apparently still carrying a torch for her. Wanting to leave the two "love" birds alone, Endora pops out but Samantha isn't at all impressed. She reminds Ashley that she is married but he tells her mortal marriages don't count though he would love to meet Durwood so he can see what Samantha sees in him. She suggests that it would never happen as they run in different circles and tells Ashley to get lost, so he pops out to the roof where he decides he's gonna see what circles Durwood runs in.

At McMann and Tate, Durwood and Larry try to convince Mr. Gibbons to sign with them but he tells them that he judges people by the dog he keeps and he asks Larry about his dog. As Larry doesn't have a dog, he says as much but tells Mr. Gibbons that Durwood has one. Unbeknownst to the men, Ashley pops in invisible to watch and when Mr. Gibbons asks what kind he has, Durwood and Larry say two different breeds at the same time. Larry tries to make up for it by saying it's a mixed breed and when Mr. Gibbons asks what type of hair it has, the two men again say different things at the same time. Mr. Gibbons is perplexed but Larry tells him that Durwood's dog is quite different as it has a white spot around one eye and a dark spot around the other, with a beard. Intrigued, Mr. Gibbons asks to come see the dog and Larry says that will be OK much to Durwood's shock. They make an appointment for later and after Mr. Gibbons leaves, Durwood lays into Larry, who will not take the blame as he says if Durwood was like every other man he would've had a dog. When Durwood asks him about his not having one, Larry admits he's allergic and tells Durwood they'll just have to try and find one down at the pound. And with that, Ashley pops out.

At the pound, the worker thinks they are nuts for asking such a dog, while, in the cages, Ashley pops in and turns himself into the dog they described just as the men are led in. The worker is shocked, but no more than Larry and Durwood, but as it seems to be a bit of serendipity, they forget about it and Durwood takes Ashley the dog home.

At home, Durwood shows Samantha the dog and goes to find a blanket for the dog to sleep on. Samantha finds that the dog is very affectionate and when she sees him turn his baby food lunch into a steak, she realizes that it's not a dog at all! She realizes it must be Ashley when he won't stop being affectionate and when Durwood comes back, she tells him the truth. Ashley transforms back into his human form and tells Durwood that he wanted to meet him and now that he has, he can't see what Samantha would want to do with him. Realizing he's going to have to find another dog, Durwood gets a little upset, but Samantha tells him he doesn't need to and with a quick zap, turns Ashley back into the strange dog. With that, Durwood leaves to go buy some Gibbons Dog Burgers so he can impress the client.

Later on, Mrs. Kravitz shows up to borrow some paprika and sees that the Stephens have a new ugly dog and remarks so, causing Ashley to growl at her. Frightened, she leaves without her paprika and Samantha chides Ashley. When he begs to go outside, she thinks he wants to follow through with his attack but she won't let him out until he acts as though he will "make water" inside if she doesn't let him. She makes him promise he won't attack Mrs. Kravitz and lets him out. He rushes across the street to the Kravitz's new house, which is much bigger than their old one, and he magically knocks the door. When Mrs. Kravitz answers the door, he rushes in and delights Mr. Kravitz but Mrs. Kravitz doesn't want him in the house. Before she can catch him, he runs into the kitchen and changes into a sheep dog and then a beagle confusing and scaring Mrs. Kravitz even more. Having shown her who's boss, Ashley returns to Samantha's.

Later on, Durwood arrives back at home just as Larry and Mr. Gibbons pull up. When they come inside Samantha hasn't a clue where Ashley is until he starts howling and they find him locked in a closet. Mr. Gibbons isn't at all impressed and thinks Durwood may be abusing the dog, but Samantha assures him that Ashley loves staying in the closet and must've got locked in there by mistake. When they open the door, Ashley growls at Durwood but he says it must be because the dog is hungry and he lays down a Gibbons Dog Burger, which Ashley immediately zaps into a steak. Mr. Gibbons is shocked but Samantha tells him it was done with mirrors and that it was all done for part of the new campaign. On the fly, Durwood tells him that his idea was to shape the burgers into steaks with a rubber chew toy in the middle as the bone. Mr. Gibbons loves it and signs on immediately.

After Larry and Mr. Gibbons leave, Ashley resumes his normal shape and Endora pops in ashamed of Ashley for helping out instead of breaking up the marriage. However, Ashley makes it up to her by taking her to dinner.

I would give it only about two stars because it's just a recycle of "Man's Best Friend" from Season Two with Rodney, though I like this one much better than that one. And they not only recycle that story, but also many of the lines that Warlock George used. And what the hell is it with them using the same actor that played Newton only about four episodes earlier? They should've either got another actor or they should've just said that Newton realized what a beeyotch Miss Ferndale was, and as Serena wouldn't have anything to do with him anymore, he went for the second best thing, her look-a-like cousin Samantha.

There are only a couple of times where I liked Samantha in the pigtails, but this isn't one of them. And why didn't she change for the client? Samantha has always dressed up for the client, but here she just keeps her grub clothes on. I don't like it.

And where do you think they got that dog? I'm sure the episode idea must've come up after they found the dog. I also thought it cool that he zapped up his own steaks and such.

And the Kravitzes new house is due to *The Partridge Family* using their old house. The new house looks HUGE on the outside! But yet their kitchen looked teeny.

My favorite lines from this episode are:

SAMANTHA *(to Ashley the Dog)*: *"You wouldn't. (pause) You would!"*
DURWOOD: *"...And the name is Darrin!"*
ASHLEY: *"Then why does everyone call you 'Durwood'?"*

NOVEMBER 26, 1970

Tonight we may not have noticed that *Bewitched* was pre-empted for a Georgia college football game between the Bulldogs and Yellow Jackets. However, we were too busy digesting our big Thanksgiving feasts with our families and getting our third helping of pumpkin pie to really care.

Three nights before, CBS aired the film version of Rodgers and Hammerstein's 1955 musical *Oklahoma!* as a three hour Thanksgiving special. This was the first time the musical was aired on network television.

DECEMBER 3, 1970

It was on this night *Bewitched* returned on ABC with all new episode, #210: "Samantha's Old Man."

While putting away groceries, Samantha discovers her mother in the refrigerator dressed as the Knave of Hearts. Apparently, she has run into Samantha's old boyfriend Rollo who is hosting a costume ball to end all costume balls at the Cosmos Cotillion and has invited them to join him. Samantha refuses the invitation as she has too much housework and cooking to do. Annoyed, Endora pops out of the fridge and slams her axe into the kitchen island to drive home her point that she thinks Samantha's mortal marriage has ruined everything. Just then, Durwood comes in all gleeful about a great golf game, but soon turns his usual glum self when he sees Endora and starts throwing unkind epithets at her. When he goes to change, Endora asks again what Samantha sees in him and Samantha tells her that if she lives to be a thousand years she'll always love Durwood. Wanting to be serious, Endora asks her what's going to happen when in thirty years Durwood's dubious charms wrinkle up. Samantha tells her she'll still love him and with that Endora pops out only to pop back in at the base of the living room stairs where she casts a spell on Durwood to age him and she pops out. Durwood soon sees his reflection and roars for Samantha, who is shocked at his appearance, but not surprised at her mother. Her calls out to the cosmos for Endora go unanswered and soon Durwood becomes restless so Samantha suggests they go to a drive-in movie as they had to cancel their plans with the Tates.

At the drive-in, Samantha goes to get some snacks and wouldn't you know it, Larry and Louise are there and quite curious as to why Samantha and Durwood would cancel. Samantha says that Durwood really wasn't feeling well so she came with another friend. When they follow her back, she introduces them to Durwood's "grandfather," Grover. The Tates are pleased and run off rather suddenly and come back with Louise's Aunt Millicent, who is single, and they suggest that she join Grover for the movie. Durwood tries to fight it, but they insist.

After the movie, the Tates invite Grover and Samantha over for a visit, and as they talk, Larry decides to set Grover and Millicent up on another date the next night to a musical. Grover has no choice but to accept and when he and Samantha go home he requests that she call Endora again but Endora has left her answering service on.

The next morning, Durwood is truly worried about his looks as he has a rather important meeting with a Mr. Booker, who is only in town for a couple hours. Samantha asks if Booker has ever seen Durwood before, and when Durwood says no, she asks what difference does it make what he looks like if Booker doesn't know what he looks like, and so reluctantly Durwood goes to the meeting.

Mr. Booker is surprised at how old "young Stephens" is, but Grover tells him it's just that Larry thinks he acts so young that he gave him that nickname. Durwood starts getting nervous and excuses himself so he can call Samantha to see if she has contacted her mother yet, but is disappointed to find out she hasn't. To his horror, he finds that Larry has joined them and so when he gets back to the table, he tells the men that Durwood was at home deathly ill and so he figured he'd help his grandson out by coming to the meeting and he proceeds to present the idea, which Booker loves.

At home, Durwood tells Samantha all about getting the account and he also tells her that he will not be going out with Millicent. Just then the Tates and Millicent come knocking and Grover tells Millicent that he's not feeling well so he is going to stay home and watch TV. Louise suggests that it doesn't matter where the two seniors go just so long as they are together. Seeing that there is no way out of this, Samantha goes to get some snacks in the kitchen but changes herself into an old lady, zaps the doorbell to ring and pops out to the front door. When Larry answers it, "Samantha" storms in claiming to be Grover's wife of fifty-three years and tells him that she'll leave him if he doesn't go home. The Tates and Millicent are shocked and leave.

Samantha tries to convince Durwood that no matter how long Endora holds out, eventually she gives in, but he tells her he's not worried about that. He's been thinking of what really will happen when he does get old and Samantha stays young. She assures him that she has thought of that

Samantha and Durwood as an old couple, which disgusts Endora.

too, and that as she is a witch, she can make herself look old and she gives him a preview. Disgusted that Samantha now looks twice her age, Endora pops in furious saying that she won't stand for it. Samantha tells her that she'll remain old as long as Durwood remains old so Endora relents and changes Durwood back to his young self at the same time that Samantha goes back to her young age.

I think it's an all right episode, not one of my favorites, but I DO love that we find out that Coke is one of the official drinks of *Bewitched* (along with beer and orange juice) when we get a look in the fridge.

I always like it when Durwood tells Endora that she needs to shave.

What I think is dumb is why would Durwood think that it would be better for Samantha to go get the food at the drive-in? Like anyone would recognize him. And this is one of my favorite exchanges: Larry: "I thought Darrin had told me that you had…" Durwood: "Gone to the great beyond? That boy never gets anything right…that was my wife." The way Dick Sargent says the last part is hysterical!

I thought Dick Sargent's old man make up was good except for his bald head looked a totally different shade of skin than the rest of him, not to mention his hair looked fake. And Liz's make up always bothered me too, except when she goes to kiss him the skin around her mouth sure wrinkles up. Rolf J. Miller was nominated for Outstanding Achievement in Makeup at the Emmys for 1970 for this episode but lost to Robert Dawn for *Mission Impossible*.

The way cool part about this episode is Hope Summers, that plays Grover's wife, was in "The Rusty Heller Story" with Liz and David White on *The Untouchables*, *Rosemary's Baby* (1968) with Maurice Evans, and she was the voice of Mrs. Butterworth.

Mr. Booker was played by Ed Platt, better known to TV audiences as the Chief on *Get Smart*, which had just been cancelled the previous season. He was also in *They Came to Cordura* with Dick York in 1955, the infamous movie wherein Dick hurt his back which led to his eventual leaving *Bewitched*.

And where the heck were Tabitha and Adam through all this? My friend Sharon once remarked that, "I suppose they locked them upstairs in the closet until it all blew over. But it would have been cool to see how Tabitha reacted to Dimwit's being so old."

DECEMBER 10, 1970

It was on this night ABC aired Episode #211: "The Corsican Cousins."

Durwood comes home from playing a round of golf with Larry and client Mr. Langley, head of Bigelow Industries, to tell Samantha that they have been invited to join Mr. Langley's country club and that Samantha is going to entertain Mrs. Langley and another lady from the club's admission committee while Durwood plays golf again with Mr. Langley. Samantha is not too pleased and as they continue discussing, Durwood just about sits on Endora who has just popped in. Disgusted with his mother-in-law, Durwood goes to change and Endora relates her disgust at Samantha having been reduced to a housewife who is going to be forced into joining a country club. She suggests Samantha be more like her free spirit cousin, Serena, who doesn't give a care about country clubs or house work and she zaps up a view of what Serena is currently doing, on the TV. Serena is dancing with some handsome devils at a cosmic dance club but Samantha tells her mother that she's happy with where she is and she goes to make lunch. Frustrated, Endora tries to think of a way she can show Samantha how she is missing the good life and it dawns on her that she should cast a Corsican Brothers type spell on Samantha and Serena so that Samantha will feel what Serena does. At that moment, Serena stops dancing and her partner slaps her behind, which Samantha feels, startling her. Endora pops out and Samantha goes to call Durwood down for lunch and when he kisses her, she recoils as she felt a burning sensation caused by Serena eating something hot for an appetizer. Just then, Larry arrives with news that the ladies of the committee would like to meet Samantha straight away and have decided to come over today. All though Samantha isn't impressed, she begins laughing as Serena is being tickled. Larry is confused but leaves to go home. Durwood wonders if Samantha might be under a spell but she insists she's not and suggests they go eat their lunch.

At her lunch, Serena decides on ring-tailed pheasant causing Samantha to crave it as well though she had just made a lobster salad and she insists that they go to the store to buy some. However, when they get there, Serena has finished her lunch and quelled her craving. Seeing how erratic his wife's behavior is, Durwood decides that he must call Larry to cancel the committee ladies visit and while he goes to call Larry, Samantha suddenly starts dancing as Serena is out in the cosmos dancing with her new boyfriend. When Durwood sees this, he immediately hangs up and drags his dancing wife out to the car.

Arriving at home, Samantha stops grooving and as they walk up to the house, Mrs. Langley arrives with her friend, Mrs. Hunter, who are an hour early. Meanwhile, at the club, Serena's date sees that his wife is there and he pops out, upsetting Serena. At 1164, Samantha tries to prepare a quick appetizer for the ladies but is truly irritated with Durwood for reasons unknown. Larry shows up and gets the brunt of Serena's new hatred for males via Samantha who realizes that her canapés are burning!

At the club, Endora pops in on Serena who is crying because now she won't have anything to do that afternoon. Her tears make Samantha cry making the ladies think she's quite emotional. Endora is frustrated that Serena is spoiling her spell so she zaps up a big glass of witches joy juice for Serena, who gets drunk after a couple sips. Of course, Samantha gets drunk as well and is quite insulting to the ladies who decide to leave with a reminder that Mr. Langley will hear about this preventing McMann and Tate from getting his account. Larry is furious and he leaves too.

Later on, Endora shows up admitting that she cast a spell and she removes it. However, the damage has been done as Durwood has been fired. But all is not as bad as Durwood thinks when Larry shows up with news that Mr. Langley is being investigated for the way he became head of Bigelow Industries which means had McMann and Tate been involved with them it would've looked bad and he gives Durwood his job back.

I LOVE this episode! I think it's so funny and such a great idea! Like Endora said, "I wonder why I didn't think of this before?"

Elizabeth Montgomery reminds me very much of Carol Burnett in this episode with her comedic acting skills. Especially when she's Serena and she says, "I'd like to thank you both." 'Witch' reminds me, why wasn't Carol Burnett ever on the show? That would've been SO awesome!

I think it's very funny, especially from the audience's point of view, when Samantha says to Durwood, "You're beginning to bug me, and I don't know why." Well, we know why! It's 'cause your hubby ain't even the same guy!

I think Serena looks way hot in her outfit and I also love it when she says, "You're a rat! And that's an insult to rats!" And then, later on when Endora pops in and asks her why she's so upset and she says, "Because! Now I won't have anything to do this afternoon!" I love the way she says it.

It's also hysterical when drunk Samantha is leaning in so close to one of the ladies' faces and then just looks at her and says, "Hi."

And honestly, where the hell are Tabitha and Adam? How great would it have been to try and shield at least Tabitha from seeing her mother acting that way?

And also, ring-tailed pheasant readily available at the market? Really?!

DECEMBER 17, 1970

It was on this night ABC aired Episode #212: "Samantha's Magic Potion."

After experiencing a huge slump at work for the past several clients, Durwood begins to think that Endora has been fooling around. However, when she pops into breakfast one morning, she gives her witches' honor that she has done nothing of the sort. Samantha assures him that should be sufficient proof and he heads off to work.

At work, Larry suggests that if Durwood doesn't get out of his slump he may be out of work but will give him one last shot with the Harmon's Savings and Loan campaign and he approves of Durwood's ideas just as Mr. Mortimer, er, Harmon arrives. Durwood begins to show off his ideas (which include a grasshopper, a hippie caterpillar, and a ladybug walking into Harmon's Savings and Loan) but before he can finish Mr. Mortimer (wow! Christmas is on the mind!), I mean, Harmon gets up and walks out, saying it's too far out and cutesy. Larry promises Mr. Harmon that they will come up with something better and insists Durwood go home to come up with them.

Durwood is furious when he gets home and begins yelling for Endora, who still says she's not to blame and she pops out. Realizing that there really may be something going on, Samantha suggests they call in Dr. Bombay to diagnose Durwood with a spell and possibly find who cast it. After Samantha throws out a distress call to the atmospheric continuum, Dr. Bombay pops in wearing football gear having just tackled his nurse. He has also brought his computerized hexometer, an invention of his design to diagnose the presence of witchcraft on or about a person. The hexometer, a close cousin to an electronic keyboard, also has a line from it ending in a partial coonskin cap with a deflated balloon at the end, which he places on Durwood's head. He zaps up a candelabra and plays a mess of notes on the hexometer which cause the balloon to inflate with exhaust which will determine if magic is the cause of Durwood's woes. The exhaust is clear which indicates Durwood is filled with witchcraft, as mortal exhaust would be dirty. Dr. Bombay then says that the image of the guilty party will appear on the screen of his hexometer as he begins to play some more. However, the atmospheric continuum seems to be strangely scrambled and so there is no way of telling. Having diagnosed Durwood, Dr. Bombay pops out to make a pass at his nurse leaving Durwood still feeling at a loss.

The next morning, Samantha finds that Durwood isn't getting out of bed because he's given up as he feels he can't fight all the witchcraft. She's appalled at his lack of motivation and so she leaves him in his misery to think of a way to convince him he is wrong. She soon returns to the bedroom with what looks like a glass of orange juice but she says is a potion that will give Durwood the power to be master of any situation. Realizing what this could mean, especially where Endora is concerned, Durwood agrees. Samantha tells him he must drink the potion and recite a few words and then turn around three times. He'll know it's working when he sees himself glow purple, and he does. Feeling reenergized, he returns to work where he was supposed to be giving a different presentation to Mr. Harmon but he breaks out the bugs again. Disgusted, Mr. Harmon begins to leave but Durwood insists that he sit down and listen and when Larry tries to protest, Durwood invites him to be quiet. He continues with his presentation which includes the tagline that "Harmon's Savings and Loan there are no small investors; they are as big as you are, whoever you are." It clicks with Mr. Harmon and he immediately signs.

When he arrives at home, Durwood doesn't seem thrilled that he got the campaign and admits to Samantha that it doesn't feel right to be able to have everything you want no matter what. She admits to him that the potion she gave him was just a drink and that she did it to give him confidence and that in the future he should learn to trust in himself more.

This is one of my least favorite episodes. It not only is a remake of "The No-Harm Charm" but there are some lines taken from "A is for Aardvark" as well…it also seems like there are other episodes used here.

And Endora popping in at the end seemed so weird, as though she wasn't even there, or Sam and Durwood didn't even notice her except for Sam to say, "Stop paying attention to her, and start paying attention to me."

The only good part of the episode was Dr. Bombay, but it seemed like it was unnecessary. I did like how Samantha called him, though: "Calling all stations from Hong Kong to Pompeii! Come in, if you read me, Dr. Bombay!" Dr. Bombay: "Dr. Bombay here…" Samantha: "Nevermind your pills, forget your thermometer, come on the run with your trusty hexometer!" He does use this keyboard device again in practically every episode following though he never uses the raccoon/balloon attachment to see if there is a spell on anyone. I also liked the sound effect when he made the inflated balloon disappear — it was a combo of a magic sound effect and a balloon popping.

Other than that, this episode is DULL, DULL, DULL!

This episode was the answer to a *Jeopardy* question in 2004 when it was said "This show had Samantha giving Darrin a potion to boost his confidence."

DECEMBER 24, 1970

Tonight *Bewitched* history was made when ABC aired the last Christmas episode of the series, #213: "Sisters at Heart" sponsored by Oscar Mayer.

We were surprised to see Elizabeth Montgomery, resplendent in red, greeting us and telling us that the episode tonight was written by the Tenth Grade English class at Thomas Jefferson High School in Los Angeles and that she and her friends at Oscar Mayer feel that it's a very special episode filled with truth and love. Of course, we are quite intrigued that an episode would require such an introduction, especially for Christmas.

Tabitha is going to have her first sleep-over at her house with her new friend, Lisa, the daughter of Keith and Dorothy Wilson. Keith, who works with Durwood, is flying out to meet with a client and, as his wife is accompanying him, Lisa needed a babysitter. Samantha reminds Tabitha that she isn't to do any magic nor fly while Lisa is there and as she gets her agreement, the Wilsons and Larry arrive. After Lisa is introduced to everyone, her parents and Larry leave and Samantha suggests that she and the kids go to the park.

After being told that the show is brought to us "by Oscar Mayer, the maker of wieners, coldcuts, bacon, and a whole lot of good things" we find that the episode is indeed special, so special, in fact, that there are no 'directed by' nor 'written by' credits! Instead it just goes right into Durwood talking with Mr. Brockway, the client he is working with closely as they plan to meet about the new campaign. After Brockway hangs up, he tells his secretary, Ms. Hathaway, that he wants to make sure there are no skeletons rattling in the Stephens' closet before he commits to McMann and Tate and so he wants her to find Durwood's address so he can check up on his home life.

In 1164's kitchen, Lisa and Tabitha are coloring when Tabitha remarks that Lisa should color her character green like hers because they can't be sisters if they aren't the same color. Samantha overhears this and asks where she would come up with such an idea and Tabitha tells her at the park that another girl had heard them playing like they were sisters and they were told they couldn't be sisters because Tabitha is white and Lisa is black. She also admits that she almost did some magic to her but Samantha, who tells her the girl was wrong, also reminds her to keep the magic to herself and that she come help her with Adam. When the doorbell rings, Lisa finds that she's the only one who hears it and answers to find a shocked Mr. Brockway there. He asks her if her mommy works there or possibly her daddy and she says that her daddy works for McMann and Tate and that Tabitha is her sister. When she asks if he wants to see someone he tells her he's seen enough and leaves.

Later on, up in Tabitha's room, they are painting when Lisa accidentally spills paint all over her dress. Realizing that it would be easy to clean up with magic, Tabitha tells Lisa to close her eyes and she'll use a family secret to clean her up. Lisa complies and when she opens her eyes she finds that Tabitha is shocked and with good cause: Lisa now has white skin and blonde hair! When Lisa asks how she did it, Tabitha shows her by changing her back and admits that she is a witch. Lisa asks if Tabitha could change herself to look like Lisa and she changes her skin to brown and her hair black. The girls realize that now that they are the same colors they can be sisters, though which color should they remain as their own mothers wouldn't recognize them is still a concern. Tabitha changes back and then tells Lisa she has come up with a way that they can really be sisters.

Downstairs, Durwood tells Samantha that apparently Mr. Brockway had been over and had been turned off by whoever had answered the door, which he assumes was someone from her illustrious family. She assures him it couldn't be because all her family have gone to the 14th century for the holiday and before they can discuss it anymore, Tabitha interrupts them to show that she has made a huge mistake. When they look up the stairs, they find that Tabitha has black spots on her and Lisa has white spots on her!

The next day, Tabitha and Lisa still remain spotty and Durwood is anxious as Keith and Dorothy are going to return that day. Samantha tells him that Tabitha has been trying to turn them back but her subconscious won't let her.

Later on Larry shows up shocked that Mr. Brockway had told him he didn't want Durwood on his account because he had found him unstable. Durwood tells him that he hasn't any idea where Brockway got that idea but Larry suggests they will show him how stable he is by hosting the office Christmas party at 1164 that night!

Just before the party, Samantha tries to get rid of the spots with a spell Dr. Bombay had given her but it still doesn't work because Tabitha wants to be sisters with Lisa so much.

The party time arrives and so do Keith and Dorothy, who is quite anxious to see her daughter. Mr. Brockway arrives just as Keith walks off to mingle with his co-workers and so Dorothy answers the door with Durwood. Brockway has brought a white girl doll for Tabitha, a black girl doll for Lisa, and a panda bear for Adam as he doesn't know whose side of the family he takes after! He also congratulates Durwood and Dorothy on being so brave to be married. It occurs to Durwood why Mr. Brockway would find him unstable and tells Dorothy that Lisa must've answered the door when Brockway had come the day before and told him that Tabitha and herself were sisters. Dorothy realizes she still hasn't seen her daughter but Keith would rather introduce her to all his friends and takes her away. Durwood runs upstairs where Samantha is trying to coax Tabitha into wanting to change back and Tabitha admits that what the girl had told her in the park was really affecting her. Samantha again tells her that the girl was wrong, that two girls can be sisters who share things or ideas and that actually all men are brothers, even if they're girls. Tabitha finally sees the light and tells Lisa they'll always be sisters no matter what and she wishes them back to their normal states just as Dorothy and Keith walk in and embrace their daughter.

Meanwhile, downstairs, Larry finds out about Mr. Brockway's misunderstanding about Durwood's marriage and sets him straight. Brockway says that as Durwood isn't married to Dorothy he'll let Durwood work on his account. Shocked, Larry goes to look in the mirror to make sure it's he who is talking and tells Mr. Brockway that they don't need his multimillion dollar account. Brockway can't believe they would turn him down and as Durwood and Samantha come down the stairs they see all this. Durwood gives Samantha permission to work some magic as they hear Mr. Brockway trying to make himself look better by admitting that he has black friends; however when she twitches him into seeing everyone with black skin, including himself in the mirror, he is shocked and leaves. Larry is bewildered but feels satisfied with his decision to drop the account.

The next night, Christmas Night, the Wilsons have returned for Christmas dinner and who should show up but Mr. Brockway! He admits that he had a very restless night filled with contemplation and that he had come to apologize. He had found that he was a closet racist and that he realized that wasn't the way to be. Keith accepts his apology and as Mr. Brockway goes to leave, Samantha invites him to stay for dinner. He accepts and tells Durwood that he wishes he would take his account back but Durwood tells him business can wait until after the Christmas dinner and so they all go to enjoy the new found brotherly love.

Surprisingly, Liz shows up again saying that she hopes we all enjoyed the show as much as they all enjoyed making it and that she hopes we all have a Merry Christmas and a Happy New Year. And that's when the missing 'written by' and 'directed by' credits show up at the first of the end credits which are accompanied by a jazzy version of "Jingle Bells." The credits also show all the names of the kids in the English Class from Thomas Jefferson High and end with the last few bars of "Silent Night."

And you know what? Liz was right! It was a very special episode of *Bewitched*, the first one to tackle a real world issue head on.

I would only give this two and a half stars, maybe just two though. I used to REALLY love this episode because I thought it was so cool that it actually dealt with a real world issue, not to mention the fact that it was focused around Tabitha, and as I was young I really liked the ones about her. But as I get older, I realize how uncomfortable the episode is, especially with the corny jokes like, Larry: "Then we'll really have a white Christmas!" Keith: "Watch that!" And Samantha: "I think Mr. Brockway is dreaming of a black Christmas" and "We're having integrated turkey, white meat and dark." Maybe at the time it didn't feel as awkward because it was one of TV's first attempts at actually addressing the race issue, but now it just feels weird.

And why not have the Wilsons back again? It would've been awesome to explore further the relationship between how they felt when faced with prejudice and to lighten it up have Samantha understand because of her being part of a minority group. And heaven forbid that Tabitha ever have any friends over again! Well, I mean in a couple episodes she'll have Sidney Kravitz over but that's about it. I really liked Lisa.

However, I do think it's AWESOME that those tenth grade kids were given such a great opportunity, and that they are listed individually. The end credits start out and go for three screens with just their names.

Janee Michelle a.k.a. Gee Mercadel, who played Dorothy, goes by Sophie now and owned Sophie's Ice Cream Parlor in New Orleans. Unfortunately, the shop had to close due to Hurricane Katrina. I think she was so beautiful! And I would like to know what she thinks of the episode now.

Of course, how AWESOME was it that Liz's intro and closing were included on the DVD, even iff'n they changed the original background music? AWESOME! Plus I like that they included the "*Bewitched* back in a moment," which should've been on EVERY episode. And it's weird that if they went to all that trouble, why not just include the Oscar Mayer opening credits? Selfish, Sony, selfish!

Oh, and back to the episode, Lisa saying, "This is more fun than Disneyland" reminded me that I wish that *Bewitched* had done an episode filmed in Disneyland. How cool would that have been?! And they could've done it to where they integrated the live action with the cartoons, like *Mary Poppins*, something Liz would've LOVED! I always imagined that the story would've been something like Serena taking Tabitha to Disneyland when she finds out that Tabitha has been saving for the trip and while there Serena falls in love with one of the Princes that she sees from a poster, not a walk around, and therefore zaps him up. When Tabitha sees her do that, she zaps up all sorts of characters and it makes the news and Samantha sees and tries to get everything back to normal before Durwood finds out.

On an interview with Liz, that was included on the laser disc of *Here Comes Mr. Jordan* (1941), a movie her father Robert Montgomery starred in, she is asked which episode was her favorite and after a bit of hesitation, whether from trying to decide or trying to remember the name of the episode, she admits that the one about the polka dots that was written by the kids at Thomas Jefferson High was her favorite. I am glad we know which episode was Liz's favorite, and all though I may not really enjoy this one, it's special because it was one of her favorites.

This episode was so special in fact, that Liz went on Merv Griffin's show that week and discussed it! And we all know Liz didn't like doing interviews, so that says a lot.

An article in the December 1971 *TV Picture Life* would focus on this episode and reveal that the kids at Thomas Jefferson High were invited to the set by Liz and Bill on numerous occasions when Liz found out that *Bewitched* was their favorite show. The kids were struggling with reading and writing but after their visits to the set their teacher, Marcella Saunders, found that they improved. And this was because Bill would give them copies of the scripts so they could follow along. The students decided as a "thank you" to the Ashers, they would write a script and Liz loved it so much she got the wheels going on getting it made and had script writer Barbara Avedon help turn it into a genuine script.

The episode would win the Governor's Award from the Television Academy in 1971 as well.

I also want to mention that from here on out there are going to be a lot of "lasts" on the show as this was the last Christmas episode. It was also the last episode of 1970 to air.

The day before, Charles Ruggles passed away. He played Mr. Caldwell in Season One's "Help, Help Don't Save Me" and Aunt Clara's boyfriend Hedley Partridge in "Aunt Clara's Old Flame."

Three days after this episode aired Assistant Director Jack R. Berne passed away.

DECEMBER 31, 1970

Tonight while we were getting prepared to ring in the New Year, ABC re-aired Episode #205: "Darrin on a Pedestal" which originally aired on October 22, 1970.

The day before, Agnes Moorehead appeared on *Night Gallery* in "Certain Shadows on the Wall."

JANUARY 7, 1971

ABC pre-empted *Bewitched* for some reason which I couldn't find, though I'm sure it was for a football game.

Five nights later, January 12, 1971, CBS aired the pilot episode of *All in the Family* ringing ever so lightly the death knell for *Bewitched* as this in-your-face series that focused on real life situations inspired more real world programming and the eventual demise of *Bewitched*.

The show was so controversial for it's time that just before the airing of this episode, CBS aired this disclaimer which ended with the sound of a toilet flushing:

"The program you are about to see is *All in the Family*. It seeks to throw a humorous spotlight on our frailties, prejudices, and concerns. By making them a source of laughter we hope to show, in a mature fashion, just how absurd they are."

It's ironic that a toilet flush was used to usher in this show as it signified the beginning of degradation of TV to what we have today. Granted, I really like *All in the Family*, but this is the show from which swearing and being crass all started.

JANUARY 14, 1971

It was this night ABC aired the first episode of 1971 with the return of *Bewitched* with Episode #214: "The Mother-in-Law of the Year."

Durwood believes he's come up with the perfect campaign for Bobbins Bon-Bons by saying "Celebrate your secretary with a box of Bobbins Bon-Bons." When Endora pops in and hears it, she feels it's terrible and suggests that he say that everyone should give their mother-in-law a box on Mother-in-Law Day. However, Samantha says that can't happen because there isn't a Mother-in-Law Day but that doesn't stop Endora from believing in her idea.

At the office, when Durwood goes to present his ideas to Larry and Mr. Bobbins, Endora invisibly pops in and casts a spell wherein Durwood will speak but relate the ideas she puts in his head and he proceeds to tell them the Mother-in-Law Day idea. Mr. Bobbins loves it and decides that they can promote it on the Bobbins Sweetheart Parade on TV. Durwood is furious when he gets home and Samantha tells him it's silly for him to be mad at Endora when it looks like she's helping him out. However, she realizes it is her mother they're talking about so when Durwood leaves the room she hollers for Endora, who pops in looking innocent as a lamb.

Larry and Mr. Bobbins show up to tell Durwood how they've decided to capitalize on the Mother-in-Law Day idea. While they discuss, Endora casts another spell on Mr. Bobbins that when he hears her name, his heart will flippity-flop. The spell works and any more business is shoved aside when Endora says she is going to go home in a cab and Mr. Bobbins whisks her away. Durwood is furious, even more so when Larry tells him that they've decided to crown a Mother-in-Law of the Year at the Sweetheart Parade, and their first candidate is Endora!

Later, at home, Durwood is still seething about Endora but Samantha assures him that Endora will show up at the TV studio; however she pops in ready to go skiing with a friend named Peabody (who apparently invented thunder) and says that she has no intention of going to the TV studio and she pops out. Realizing that he'll be out a job if his mother-in-law doesn't show up, Durwood goes to call Larry to try and cancel but Samantha tells him it's much too late for that and suggests that she show up as Endora. At first he balks, but when he finds that he really will lose his job if she's not there, he concedes.

At the ABC studios, Mr. Bobbins presents "Endora" with a bouquet of roses and the director briefs her on how the commercial will go. As they prepare to start filming in about a minute, Endora shows up furious and demands to speak to Samantha. They sneak behind the set and Endora reams Samantha for trying to imitate her "when everyone knows I'm inimitable!" She also suggests that if Samantha is going to be her, she is going to be Samantha and zaps herself into Samantha's form just as the director comes looking for Endora. "Endora" goes back on set and begins filming the commercial about Bobbins Buttery Bon-Bons and as she's gushing about how great they are, "Samantha" pops in ranting about how fattening and ridiculously high priced they are. Mr. Bobbins, Larry, and Durwood are shocked but Durwood tells everyone to keep calm, that there is a surprise coming up. "Endora" refutes all claims until "Samantha" zaps herself back into Endora causing Samantha to change back into herself. When the commercial is done, Durwood says he spoke to the crew about adding the special effect and it turns out Mr. Bobbins loves it!

This one is definitely a four star episode and Elizabeth Montgomery and Agnes Moorehead should've been nominated for Emmys for their performances. Endora is especially hysterical when she walks into the living room to meet Mr. Bobbins and says, "Mercy me! I didn't know you had guests!"

I also liked seeing her sitting on the lamp in the office. We've only ever seen Samantha do that in the first Halloween episode and I think it looks cool.

I also noticed that Liz was going free as a bird in that brown top at the end.

My only complaint is that I thought we might get a little extra always cut out scene explaining just exactly who Peabody was. I have never been able to find something on the web that would tie thunder and someone named Peabody together. I also don't like it when Durwood says he has to get to the studio for the TV show and Endora says all irritated, "What TV show?!" It seems like there is a line missing, along with the two kids.

I did notice Agnes Moorehead had a lot of liver spots on her neck! I had never noticed that before either in this episode or any other and it made me think how far the cancer was probably spreading in her body.

But all in all, I really like this episode.

Around this time ABC ran a commercial touting Imogene Coca's appearance in next week's episode.

JANUARY 21, 1970

It was on this night that ABC aired Episode #215: "Mary the Good Fairy."

Just after Durwood arrives home with a big box containing a client's new product, Tabitha comes in wanting her mommy to pull a string attached to her loose tooth that Sidney Kravitz, Gladys' nephew was going to pull. However, Tabitha didn't trust him. Samantha is nervous about doing it, and possibly a little queasy, but Tabitha tells her to be brave and count to three. Before she can get to three, Durwood walks in wearing a spacesuit looking contraption startling her causing her to pull the string. Pleased that she now has something for the Good Fairy (?!), Tabitha runs across the street to tell Sidney. Durwood explains that he's wearing a new weight loss device called the Reduce-a-lator, which causes you to lose weight by letting you be in a portable sauna. He had brought it home to help him with inspiration for the new campaign.

A little while later, Tabitha runs home saying she is never going to play with Sidney again as he told her there is no such thing as the Good Fairy. Samantha reminds her that it's OK for Sidney to not believe in the Good Fairy because many mortals don't even believe in witches, and they both know that's not true.

Later that night, in a shower of magic dust, the Good Fairy flutters in on what looks like grade-school-Halloween-project sparkly wings and she tiptoes over to Tabitha's bed where she exchanges Tabitha's tooth for a coin. When she goes to leave the room, via the door, she runs into Durwood, who was up getting a glass of milk. He yells for Samantha as he realizes this must be one of Samantha's kooky friends, and he's right, as Samantha runs into the hall and exclaims with delight, "Mary!" She introduces Durwood to Mary the Good Fairy, who tells Samantha she had felt it was a witch's house, but she wasn't sure which witch. Samantha invites her to stay for a bite to eat. Mary admits that she would also like something to warm her bones and so Durwood offers her some brandy as Samantha goes to make a roast beef sandwich. Mary loves the brandy and asks for some more and immediately gets crocked. Now that she realizes she's not able to even stand up, Mary worries about who is going to collect the rest of the teeth and she nominates Samantha, who at first declines until Mary reminds her there is no one else to do it. Seeing that she has no choice, Samantha concedes and with a touch of Mary's wand, they change outfits. After quelching Durwood's resistance, Samantha goes outside to begin her flight and happens to be seen by Mrs. Kravitz, who was up because of a mosquito that was bothering Sidney. She freaks out, especially when the fake looking wings actually give Samantha flight!

After exchanging coins for teeth, Samantha flutters back in ready to give Mary back her wings, but Mary has decided that she would like to try out the mortal life and she refuses to switch! Samantha is furious but realizes that without Mary's consent, they will not be able to switch. When Durwood finds out, he's even angrier than before, but Samantha reminds him that he's the one that got Mary crocked. Just then there is a knock at the door and Samantha sees it's the Kravitzes. She goes to hide telling Durwood to tell them that Mary is her aunt. Durwood answers the door to find that Mrs. Kravitz would like for Sidney to play with Tabitha and when he tries to refuse politely by saying that Tabitha hasn't had breakfast yet, Gladys takes that as an invitation for Sidney to join in breakfast. She also wonders if Mrs. Stephens is back yet as she had seen her late in the night with the fake wings, but Durwood tells her that it must've been a mirage caused by the bright moon light. Abner agrees and they leave. When Durwood goes to speak to Mary about changing her mind, he finds that she's not in the living room anymore and he doesn't find her in the kitchen. Thinking she may have gone out back with Tabitha and Sidney, he discovers that she's not there. He tells Samantha that Mary has gone somewhere and that he must go look for her. She offers to go but he tells her she should stay in so that nobody will see her wings. Outside, he doesn't see Mary anywhere and begins to panic.

Just then, Sidney and Tabitha come in from playing startling Samantha who says that she's dressed like that as she's trying out Halloween costumes causing Sidney to think she's flipped and he tells her she's too old to go trick-or-treating. Before she knocks him with her wand, the image pauses with the announcer telling us to "stay tuned for the Return of the Good Fairy next week on *Bewitched*!"

I've actually always enjoyed these episodes about Mary, but I think it has a lot to do with the fact that Imogene Coca reminded me so much of this friend of my mother's. We used to go to her house to visit and she'd always give us ice cream and butter cookies. However, rewatching this I would give it maybe two stars, if that.

I also see that the writer, Ed Jurist, who has written FAR superior episodes, was kind of taking pot shots at the special effects people. For instance, Mrs. Kravitz tells Abner that Mrs. Stephens is wearing a short dress and fake wings. It's like the crew of *Bewitched* knew that they'd look fake so you may as well say something and get a joke out of it because suddenly Samantha is flying with her so-called fake wings. I don't think it's any excuse though. They should've tried for real looking wings and a much younger and hotter Tooth Fairy, but Liz probably didn't want to have competition.

Have any of you ever referred to the Tooth Fairy as the "Good Fairy?" The only time I've ever heard her referred to as the Good Fairy was on *Bewitched*. I remember my friend Jessica and I getting into a HUGE argument about what the Tooth Fairy wore when we were in elementary. I always imagined her in a blue sparkly dress, but Jessica insisted it was purple. It made me so mad!

And did you notice the dead flowers on the coffee table?! What the hell?

I wonder if Erin actually let Liz pull her tooth out or did they just put a fake one in?

Even though I enjoy this episode, I always view it as the defining point where Liz is starting to lose interest in being Samantha, and with the show in general, and I base this on how she acts during the scene at night when Durwood gets up to go check on things and she keeps telling him to "shoosh," even when he trips. I don't know about you, but the Samantha I know would totally get up and say, "What happened, sweetheart? Are you going to be OK?" And also at the end, when she goes to hit Sidney with her wand, what the heck?!

All that and the fact that they don't even try to hide the wires where before you'd be hard pressed to see any, leads me to believe that everyone was giving up, but no one more so than Liz. And how strange, especially right after "Mother-in-Law of the Year."

On a side note, in one of the *Sabrina the Teenage Witch* (1999) novels about the turn to the new millennium, there are a bunch of short stories in it and one of them has Sabrina taking over for the Tooth Fairy, who is described as an older lady with short reddish hair and a lacy white outfit.

And, the Reduce-a-lator outfit must've been put back in storage because about thirty years later it showed up in the *Muppets from Space* (1999) movie. The movie was produced by Sony and there is an extra wearing it at the end when everyone is waiting for a UFO to land.

My favorite line from this episode is when Mary calls Durwood "a gorgeous hunk of mortal." She must've really been sauced!

JANUARY 28, 1971

It was on this night ABC aired Episode #216: "The Good Fairy Strikes Again."

Durwood is frantic to get to work on the Reduce-a-lator campaign but can't concentrate as Mary the Good Fairy a.k.a. Tooth Fairy has gone missing leaving Samantha to do her job. Samantha suggests she'll go out to look for her, but Durwood reminds her it won't look too good for her to go out in the fairy costume. Luckily, Mary returns as she decided she needed some more brandy to warm her bones. Durwood has locked the cabinet and Samantha won't let Mary have any more until she agrees to take back on her job. Not wanting to be a burden, Mary goes out for a walk and Mrs. Kravitz sees her and asks her in to interrogate her. Seeing as how she couldn't get any more brandy from Durwood and Sam, Mary tells Mrs. Kravitz that she could use something to warm her bones. When Mary reveals who she is to Gladys, she runs off screaming to tell Abner, but when she comes back, she sees that Mary has left. Now totally sauced, Mary goes flitting down the street and gets picked up by the police and taken into jail. Gladys sees this and immediately runs over to the Stephens to tell them. She catches Samantha with a pink shawl on covering what are obviously her wings, but she can't delve into it anymore as she is reminded that Samantha's sense of privacy is bigger than her sense of curiosity.

Durwood runs down to the police station to bail Mary out, and when he comes back, his secretary calls to say that Larry and Mr. Ferber, the inventor of the Reduce-a-lator, are on their way to look at his ideas. Before the Stephenses can panic, the door rings, and Samantha runs into the den. Durwood tries to stall them but Larry insists he show them his ideas, so he goes into the den only to be surprised to find Samantha in the Reduce-a-lator. She tells them that she was going to model it for Durwood and then finds that one of the buttons, the one that turns off the sauna, has broken and she begins to cook before the gentleman tear the suit off her, shocked to find her in the white dress with wilted wings. Durwood, off the cuff, says his idea was to incorporate the Good Fairy with the slogan, "Fly now, Reduce a Later!" Oddly enough, Mr. Ferber loves it and signs McMann and Tate.

After the men leave, Samantha prepares to serve Bloody Marys and sees that Mary is irritated that the wings are so wilted. She claims she would've never let them get that way. Samantha also asks her what she should do about the kids she missed the night before, which shocks Mary. She tells Samantha she'll have to leave earlier and when Samantha goes to look at her watch, she spills her Bloody Mary causing Mary to be beside herself. Sam says she'll just throw it in the wash but Mary tells her she can't just 'warsh' it in the 'warshing' machine, that it's made from spun milkweed and has to be cleaned by flying low over a wheat field. She decides that she was doing great at the job and she can't let the name of the Good Fairy be tainted and so she agrees to switch back with Samantha. Now fitted with her wings, she asks Samantha to zap her to the nearest wheat field.

I give this one and a half stars because I LOVE that line about warshing in the warshing machine! That is one line that I remember from *Bewitched* from when I was way little! It's so funny!

I also liked when Mary was talking to the policemen and said, "Take your hands off me, you fresh young thing!" And her gallivanting down the street all drunk was really funny.

The client was rude and I can't imagine today that any client would want to go to the ad exec's house not to mention just showing up willy-nilly.

Did you notice that Abner's hair is getting longer? George Tobias must've really been into the hippie movement.

The Bloody Mary stains changed from scene to scene. They were really dark in some and really light in others and the shape of it changed.

Tabitha should've been in this one. Sharon Orazi had the idea of having her explain to Mary about how she thinks her mother works too much.

I thought it weird that Mary didn't make some sort of comment about the Bloody Mary's. That would've been a really great joke.

Three days before, Charles Manson and three female "family" members were found guilty of the Tate-LaBianca murders that happened in 1969.

And three days later, Apollo 14 launched.

FEBRUARY 4, 1971.

It was on this night that ABC aired Episode #217: "The Return of Darrin the Bold."

On a lazy Saturday afternoon Endora and Serena covertly pop in to 1164 so that Endora can ruminate about her child giving up her great and glorious heritage to end up being Durwood's live-in maid. It suddenly occurs to her that if Durwood were a warlock, he wouldn't be so against witchcraft and he might be less irritating. Serena thinks her auntie's off her rocker to think about changing Durwood into a warlock but follows her to the top of the world, where they actually have to hike because the atmosphere is much too thin for levitation, to visit the oldest and wisest warlock in the world. After waiting for him to finish smoking his hookah, he finally reveals that other than not messing with your in-laws, he does have a potion that will turn Durwood into a warlock! So, Serena and Endora fly to the ancestral grounds in Salem to enact their plan, which involves going back in time to the 14th century to administer a potion to Durwood's ancestor, Durwood the Bold, that will be enhanced with three whiskers from his beard. With much fanfare and smoke, Endora zaps Serena back to Durwood the Bold's time where she claims to have broken a wheel on her carriage and needs a place to stay for the evening. Bold is instantly smitten with her and invites her in and she asks him to help her light a fire so she can warm some medicine for a CHEST cold she is getting. When he goes to kiss her, she bites a hair out of his beard and tells him that where she's from it's a custom for a lady to pluck a hair from the man's beard to show him how much she likes him, and that if she plucks three, like WOW! He gets all excited when she plucks the third but is quite bewildered when she pours her "medicine" over him, and even more bewildered when she disappears!

Meanwhile, in the 20th century, while trimming a bush that sits between his yard and Mr. Ferguson's next door that blocks the view from the driveway, Durwood suddenly feels funny and goes into the house when Samantha asks him if he'd like some iced tea. He tells her he could really go for a beer when, shockingly, the tea turns into a beer. Durwood is irritated that Samantha would do that but she insists she didn't. While

Serena embraced by the amorous Durwood the Bold.

talking, he suggests he'd like a sandwich and one appears in his hand. Samantha thinks maybe one of her relatives is just trying to be nice to him or maybe that he is under some sort of wish spell. He wishes that she'd call for her mother so she can explain and so Samantha calls for Endora, who denies any involvement; however, when Samantha tells her all that's been going on with Durwood, she is delighted and tells them that he must've become a warlock by osmosis! Sam and Durwood are shocked and Samantha asks that they be left alone to think about it, so Endora leaves. Durwood tells Samantha that it's just not how he wants to live life, by zapping up everything he wants, and he also expresses his doubt about Endora's explanation. Samantha agrees and tells him he should probably just go back to trimming the bush to clear his head, but when he says he wished he'd never seen the bush, it disappears! He also says he needs to be in a bar thinking it all out and he immediately pops out. Samantha starts calling the bars around town to find him when Serena pops in wondering what's going on and Samantha explains that she thinks that Durwood might be thinking of leaving her. Serena expresses her sympathy but Samantha wonders why as she's never cared about Durwood before. Serena explains that recently she met someone quite like Durwood and if Samantha's Durwood is as groovy as her Durwood…which causes Samantha to realize she may have found the answer. She demands to know what is going on and Serena says if she spills the beans, Endora will zap her into the 14th century permanently! After getting the full story, Samantha pops back to the 14th century where she finds Durwood the Bold trying to have his way with one of the chamber maids, but once he sees Samantha, he thinks it's Serena with blonde hair and tries to have his way with her.

Back in the present, Durwood comes home to find the house empty when someone comes to the door. It's Mr. Ferguson who has noticed his bush is missing and he wants an explanation. Durwood says he just trimmed it a little but Ferguson shows him that it's gone and he's going to trim him a little! Realizing that he still has powers, Durwood tells Mr. Ferguson so and warns him not to mess with him.

In the 14th century, Samantha manages to pour the anti-potion on Durwood the Bold which eliminates his powers and by ripple effect, Durwood's powers. Samantha pops back and sees the front door open and is surprised to see that Durwood is about to get his block knocked off by Ferguson and so she zaps up an invisible barrier which breaks Ferguson's forceful blow, much to his surprise. Feigning his wife's call, Ferguson leaves and Samantha calls for Durwood to come in. He tells her that he's thought about it and it doesn't matter if he's a warlock or not, he loves her and that's all that matters. She is pleased but tells him that she figured out her mother's tricks and he no longer has powers, which pleases him very much.

I LOVE this episode, even more so than when Dick York played Durwood the Bold in Season Three's "A Most Unusual Wood Nymph." What's funny is that Dick York's Durwood the Bold lived in the 15th century but Dick Sargent's lives in the 14th. Maybe he's like us where we live part of our lives in the 20th century and the rest in the 21st, though it's funny that the second Durwood is playing the earlier version.

I think Endora wanted to change Durwood into a warlock because it would mean that's who he is, so why fight it? Doing it through an early ancestor would mean it was just a trait handed down, though they didn't write the episode like that and instead just had Durwood acquire the powers after Serena went back in time, when really he would've been born with the powers. But then that brings up the point that all of Durwood the Bold's descendants, including either Frank or Phyllis, would've had the powers too! What would've been cool is if it had been a two-parter involving Frank/Phyllis getting the powers (I would go with Frank) and see how everyone dealt with that. Then we could've had a great episode where Samantha's witchly identity is finally revealed to her in-laws! Of course, I'm totally thinking in terms of how time travel worked on *Back to the Future* (1985) because, if indeed Durwood the Bold got changed into a warlock, the whole course of his life would be changed possibly even negating Samantha's Durwood by virtue of maybe that maid he zapped off the face of the Earth being his great x 10 grandmother! I did like the eerie green effect that covered them when they acquired their powers.

I think Endora had Serena do it so that Endora could truthfully say it wasn't she that did it, kind of like when she had Serena put the love spell on Dusty Harrison in Season Six's "The Generation Zap." I did it find weird that Serena still had her powers 'cause I wouldn't think she's much older than Samantha. Of course, Samantha had her powers too, so it doesn't make sense.

I liked the Old Man of the Mountain scene, especially Serena saying, "I've never heard of a place that was too high to fly to!" And Burt Mustin, that played the Old Man, was eighty-six when this was filmed! In fact, according to IMDB.com, he was born the same year Marion Lorne was and in the same state, Pennsylvania! I also thought it funny when Serena asked, "What's he smoking?"

It was cool that Endora and Serena had the scene from the sacred grounds in Salem with that witchy music. And it seems they always cut out on TV when the smoke clears and Endora says, "Endora, thy gifts are infinite!" I also think it's funny after she goes through the huge list of things Serena has to do and ends it all with, "It's all so simple!"

I also liked it when Serena told Durwood the Bold that she needed her medicine because she had a CHEST cold! This episode was rather randy! And also, when she told him that he could now have anything he wanted, and he says, "Anything?!" and she smacks him only for a few seconds to pass before she throws herself all over him!

Mr. Ferguson's pits were nasty! And I think that they should've got Don Rickles to play that part. We've already seen Richard X. Slattery in a similar role when Samantha changed his grass to the fake stuff in Season Four's "How Green Was My Grass." Plus Rickles was on EVERYTHING in the 60s BUT *Bewitched*.

When the tea changes to beer, Samantha was holding a glass, however when they go to the couch it's changed into a mug. I always thought it was cool when Samantha came back from the past and threw the stein in the air and it disappeared. Liz was very good at holding still, because I used to try to do the same trick with our camera, when I was younger and you always just want to follow through with whatever you're throwing or try to catch it.

The ceiling was MUCH too high to be real in the opening scene. If the house were to be really built the ceiling to the living room would probably be where their feet were.

Anyway, LOVE LOVE LOVE this episode!

The day after this episode aired, Apollo 14 landed on the moon, the third manned moon landing since 1969. Liz was also nominated for an Emmy for Best TV Actress for Musical/Comedy for her role on *Bewitched*.

Three days later Liz appeared on *Password* with Carol Burnett.

FEBRUARY 11, 1971

Tonight ABC aired a monumental episode of *Bewitched* in Episode #217: "The House That Uncle Arthur Built."

As Samantha is straightening up the house, when she goes to fluff the couch pillows, she hears someone yelp and when she pulls it away, she finds her Uncle Arthur standing behind it. He zaps himself big so he can literally joust with Durwood, who isn't pleased to see him as they are going to have a dinner party with the Rockfields and Larry. As Durwood leaves, he asks Samantha to get rid of her uncle.

Arthur, who is dressed resplendent in a tuxedo and cape, says his new style is due to the new witch in his life, Aretha, who is soon to become Mrs. Uncle Arthur! He calls out for his love, who pops in looking like a Greek Goddess. She is quite snooty and it seems awfully odd that Arthur would be interested in her when suddenly he requests to speak to Sammy in the kitchen. When she arrives, he has a vase of flowers for her and when she smells them, she gets squirted in the face. Arthur admits that Aretha is not a fan of his practical joking and that he is having a hard time not pulling any pranks. Sammy tells him he can't go on pretending he is something he is not, but he insists he is in love with Aretha and that he'll do anything for her. When they return to the living room, Aretha suggests they discuss where they will honeymoon and Arthur offers to fly her to the moon on gossamer wings and zaps some up. This irritates Aretha, who tells him to quit clowning around so he zaps them away only to tell her that she might be happier if she would start clowning around and he zaps her into a clown costume! Furious, Aretha demands he change her back and he does after he and Sammy have had a good laugh. Aretha tells him the wedding is off and she disappears. Arthur is crushed and begins to mope.

Meanwhile, Larry is frantic to impress Mr. Rockfield of Rockfield Furniture by filling Durwood's office with some of the merchandise. However, Mr. Rockfield says he won't fall for it and that they will discuss it later at dinner.

Back at 1164, Arthur cannot get over Aretha's rejection, and after singing a little of "Laugh, Clown, Laugh" while dressed as a sad clown, he realizes that maybe he should simply get rid of his jokes all together! When Samantha goes to check on dinner, he casts a spell that his practical jokes will leave him and lodge in the walls of Sammy's house. And with that, he leaves. Coming back into the living room, Sammy finds her uncle is gone and when she calls for him, she hears her own voice echo back, and when she goes back into the kitchen to look for him, she finds a dancing skeleton in the closet. She realizes that Arthur must've left his jokes, especially when Durwood comes home and is immediately doused by water from a floating bucket of water. She promises to get Uncle Arthur to come back before dinner; however, her efforts are fruitless.

Soon, Larry and the Rockfields arrive and Mrs. Rockfield's dress is immediately blown up by a burst of air. As the night progresses, more jokes happen including Larry being punched out by a boxing glove. The Rockfields aren't the least impressed and say that it feels like they are in a fun house. Durwood nervously laughs it off and says that their home is more fun than a barrel of monkeys, which literally pops in. The mortals are definitely shocked and, furious, Durwood runs into the kitchen to find out where Arthur is. He soon pops in with Aretha and when he sees the monkeys, he can't stop laughing causing Aretha to leave once more, with no chance of returning. Arthur calls for his jokes to come back to him and the monkeys disappear to the bewilderment of the mortals. Durwood and Samantha join them again and say that it was all for a new campaign that would feature the Coney Island Fun House with the slogan "Put some fun into your decorating with Rockfield Furniture." Larry isn't impressed but Mr. Rockfield is, and that's all that matters.

This would be Uncle Arthur's last episode, and his only appearance in the Seventh Season.

I would give this two and a half stars. The funny thing about this episode (aside from Uncle Arthur) is that I always view it as though they were trying to actually out Paul Lynde via Uncle Arthur! It all starts when he tells Sammy that Aretha is going to be Mrs. Uncle Arthur. The look on Sammy's face is priceless as though she's thinking, "Yeah right!" And then later on, in the kitchen she asks him how long he's going to carry on this masquerade and then even later when she says, "Aretha is a phony and so are you for pretending to be something you're not."

Sam's hair is HORRID at the beginning, but I do like that dress! Her legs looked awesome! I remember the first time I ever saw this episode it scared the crap out of me when Mrs. Rockfield's dress flew up! Very shocking!

I wish Endora would've been in this episode. The Uncle Arthur episodes always seemed better with her in them, but that hasn't happened since Halloween Season Three.

I didn't understand why he'd want to lodge his jokes within 1164. I would figure he'd just get rid of them all together, but I guess it was all for the mild humor that happened later.

Aretha's voice IS irritating! And didn't you think she looks a lot like Marcia Cross from *Desperate Housewives*? I really liked the spell that Arthur used to call her: "Aretha, my love, I worship at your feet. Fly to my side and make it tout suite!" The actress later appeared in the original pilot for *Tabitha*, as a different character.

What's weird is, I always remembered the gossamer wings looking real, but those are almost worse than Mary's wings!

Herbie J wrote in his book that Dick Sargent and Liz were scared of the chimps, because they were old and known to get a little crazy.

I thought the slogan that Sam or Durwood came up with was dumb. "Put some fun in your house with Rockfield Furnishings." And even more cheesy, was when Rockfield says, "Stephens, you've got a good head on your shoulders!" and Sammy lays her head on his shoulders and Durwood says, "Yes, I do!" BLEH!

I noticed a lot of inconsistencies, though. First, Arthur, when he is standing on the couch, it's really quick, but when Samantha pulls away the pillow, it's actually behind him. Also, his head doesn't even come to the top of the couch, but in the long shot he's about a head taller than the back of the couch. Then, when Arthur has lodged his jokes in the house, he has nothing in his hands, there is a very quick shot of Sammy in the kitchen, and back to Arthur who suddenly has his cape and cane in his hands, which I suppose he could've magicked there but they were just sitting on the couch right next to him. It also seems like there is a brief scene missing after Durwood comes home and gets doused and Sammy says, "There's nothing I can do." It quickly cuts to her looking like she's dodging a possibly attack from Durwood, who in my opinion, got WAY too angry with Sammy for something she didn't do.

Did you notice that the skeleton in the closet (yet another jab at Arthur's light-in-the-loafers-ness) was dancing to the instrumental version of "Last Train to Clarksville" which was written by Tommy Boyce and Bobby Hart!

My favorite part of the whole episode is the "Laugh, Clown, Laugh" scene! He's so over the top and dramatic! It's hysterical!

Here are a few of my favorite lines:

> SAMANTHA: *"Oh well, in a few thousand years you will have forgotten all about her!"*
> UNCLE ARTHUR: *"I know, but what am I gonna do tonight?"*
> DURWOOD: *"Goodbye. And the next time you drop in, don't!"* (I know it's been used before, but it's more potent here considering that Arthur doesn't).
> UNCLE ARTHUR: *"Mmmm! Finger-lickin' good!"*
> SAMMY (in response to where the future Mr. and Mrs. Uncle Arthur can honeymoon): *"I know where you can go!"*
> ARTHUR: *"That's all right. We're still thinking of places."*
> MR. ROCKFIELD: *"I don't fall for that kind of bait, Tate!"*

I also liked the quick banter between Larry and Rockfield when Larry was telling him their ideas.

It was also this week that Liz appeared with friend Carol Burnett on *Password*.

FEBRUARY 18, 1971

It was on this night that ABC aired Episode #219: "Samantha and the Troll."

Samantha discovers her powers are missing when she tries to reassemble a cup Tabitha had been levitating, but let drop. While cleaning up the mess, her quite sexy cousin Serena pops in and hears from Tabitha that Samantha's powers are gone. Serena discovers it's been quite some time since Samantha's had her powers checked and she suggests a full ten thousand spell checkup that would have her gone all day. Samantha asks Serena to stay with the kids and she agrees, sending Samantha on her way. Durwood isn't happy about this at all, as he's not fond of Serena, and when Larry comes to the door, he asks her to stay out of the way.

Durwood finds out that Larry has come to pick him up to make sure that he will accept the offer to take the Berkley Hair Tonic account, which nobody wants as nobody uses hair tonic anymore. Larry thinks it's the perfect opportunity to pick up the account and he suggests that Sam and Durwood have him and the Berkleys to dinner that evening. Thinking he can get out of it with Samantha's absence, Durwood's hopes are dashed when "Samantha" walks in (who is really Serena in disguise ready to mess around).

At the office, Larry tells Durwood that the Berkleys have accepted his invitation to dinner and he wants to hear any ideas that Durwood may have. Before he can say anything, Mr. Berkley walks in and wants to hear what ideas Durwood may have. Durwood begins by saying that the sales have been slipping for the hair tonic, which Mr. Berkley doesn't want to hear, and Durwood asks that he have some time to come up with ideas to capture the youth market. Mr. Berkley says he does have time, until dinner that night, and leaves. Durwood calls Serena to see if there is any way that she can reach Samantha, but unfortunately when a witch is in for a checkup, she is incommunicado. Wanting to get back to playing with Tabitha, Serena hangs up on him.

Tabitha decides they should play hide-n-seek except there is just the two of them. Looking around Tabitha's room, Serena sees that there are plenty of players in Tabitha's toys so she zaps a Teddy Bear, a Prince doll, a panda bear, rag doll, and Fuzz to life! While playing hide-n-seek, Serena thinks she has found everyone. However, she overlooks Fuzz, who is hiding in a closet.

Soon, Durwood comes home and Serena zaps the toys back to their original form and she pops down to greet Durwood, who wants to know how dinner is coming. She assures him it'll be great as she's going to zap up the same dinner she once zapped for Henry VIII. He requests something less elaborate and she grudgingly accepts; however, as she is his wife for the day, she demands a kiss. Having no choice, he gives her a peck and asks her to be nice to the client and his wife.

Later, when the Berkleys and Larry arrive, "Samantha" is very flirty with Mr. Berkley, much to the irritation of Mrs. Berkley. "Samantha" tells them that she's become particularly interested in the new trend of developing the senses, specifically touch, at which point she grabs Mr. Berkley's hand and asks if he feels anything. Mr. Berkley asks for his wife's hand and asks her the same thing but she is not in the mood for it. He tells her she needs to be more open and that he thinks people should let themselves go, but Mrs. Berkley thinks they should just leave. Seeing how irritated Mrs. Berkley is, Durwood tells "Samantha" they should go check on dinner and she accepts but says she won't serve without a kiss, which she implies should come from Mr. Berkley. Larry demands Durwood kiss her and he does and pulls her into the kitchen. Serena tells him that she was just being nice to the client, who obviously liked it, when Samantha pops in having felt that something was wrong. Serena tells them that she was just trying to be nice and now that Durwood's in a snit she's leaving and she pops out just as Larry walks in to see what they think they are doing.

When they go back in the living room, Mrs. Berkley apologizes for how she reacted but Samantha tells her that she should've reacted as that's all part of sensitivity awareness. Seeing that his wife is now into the sensitivity awareness, Mr. Berkley asks for her hand and asks her to close her eyes and tell him what she feels. She does, but when she opens them, she sees the Fuzz scurrying behind a chair and she, along with the rest of the group, almost freak out. When Samantha comments that it's hairy, she quickly clarifies that it's Harry, an actor in a costume and Mr. Berkley decides that it must be a part of the campaign that is aimed at the longhaired hippie youth. Durwood goes along with it and says that Harry will be playing the before part in the ad. He says that the tag line will be "Why look like this when with Berkley Hair Tonic and a trip to the barber you can look like a prince!" Mr. Berkley says he can work on it but he does have the account.

I LOVE this episode! Four stars! And that's for Serena's AWESOME outfit alone! I can't believe they allowed her to wear it! I swear there were a couple times that we were going to get a wardrobe malfunction, especially when she was playing the piano!

Anyway, I'll try to talk about what else was in the episode. I guess, the cup for instance. They should've painted the strings with the green screen paint so they wouldn't show up. That was ridiculous how much you could see them! And what did Sam think she was going to accomplish by having Adam drink two cups of milk for dinner? He wouldn't even drink one! And it seemed like Samantha was irritated with Tabitha throughout the whole scene.

Have I mentioned how HOT Serena was in that boob-licious outfit? And what's even stranger was that Bill Asher was the director and not DICK Michaels!

I thought Liz made some weird movements when Samantha was about to pop out to her checkup. It looked awkward when she was blowing the kiss.

And Serena's outfit! We even get side boob when she turns around just before the opening credits!

I also liked seeing Liz playing Serena but looking like Samantha.

I thought Mr. Berkley was really weird and his wife looked WAY too old for him!

I also liked the toys coming to life. That would've been so much fun to do in real life!

But the best part of this whole episode was Serena's outfit! Man, I can't believe I haven't mentioned it before!

This is the last time we see Cousin Itt, I mean the Fuzz, but it's cool that they still had the Fuzz even two seasons after his first introduction in Season Five's "One Touch of Midas!" However, this particular costume was the one used in Season Four's "The Safe and Sane Halloween" for the goblin.

It occurred to me that it was originally intended for not only Fuzz to remain hiding but the Prince too, because Tabitha mentions that there are some toys missing when Serena zaps them back. Then at the end, when Durwood mentions his ad idea, he says that the Fuzz would be shown first and that you "can look like a Prince." I'm sure the Prince was supposed to also come out of hiding and that's how it would've been explained.

The rag doll was played by Diane Murphy, Erin's twin, who had sometimes played Tabitha in earlier seasons and was Tabitha solely in Season Five's "Samantha Fights City Hall."

And it is lame that Louise is never there. I wonder what Kasey Rogers was doing? Maybe they just didn't want to pay her. And I like thinking maybe she was just with Adam wherever he is all the time. And speaking of Adam, he makes a rare appearance; I believe his third this season!

Mr. Berkley was played by Robert Cummings who had starred in his own series *The Bob Cummings Show* from 1955-59.

Here are some of my favorite lines:

> SERENA: *"You bellowed, oh, Square One?"*
> DURWOOD: *"Just make something simple."*
> SERENA: *"How about peanut butter, straight, no jelly? Simple enough?"*
> SERENA: *"Don't you think people should love people?"*
> SERENA: *"Now he's in a snit, my feelings are hurt, and I'm leaving!"*
> SAMANTHA: *"It's hairy!"* I think it is so funny the way she said it!

FEBRUARY 25, 1971

It was on this night that ABC aired episode #220: "This Little Piggie."

One morning at breakfast, Samantha notices Durwood is sporting a rather wild tie but figures she better not mention it. However, he asks her about it and she tells him that it is a bit wild, but he tells her he was trying to keep up with the times. He tells her it's so he can meet Colonel Brigham of Colonel Brigham's Spare Ribs, his new client. He also has two jingles that he can't make up his mind about, and as he shows them to her, Endora pops in saying that his inability to make up his mind is the reason he is stuck in his mortal rut and with that, he leaves. Exasperated, Samantha tells her mother she wishes she would leave her fangs at home when she comes to visit but then she apologizes by telling her she'll go get Adam (who's that? Oh, yeah, their son) dressed so she can play with him. Endora is incensed that Samantha can't see how right she is, so she pops outside and stops Durwood, as he is backing out, to cast a spell on him that he won't be able to make up his mind. After she pops out, Mrs. Kravitz comes up wanting to know if Durwood would be interested in signing a petition about cleaning up the neighborhood garbage cans and, at first, he says he'll sign it, but then he says he won't, and tells her he can't decide so he'll think on it and he leaves for work. Confused, Mrs. Kravitz rings Samantha's door to ask her about the petition but she also mentions how confusing Durwood was and asks if he may not be feeling well. Samantha says she'll look into it and pushes Mrs. Kravitz out the door.

At the office, Larry comes in to see Durwood's ideas but finds that Durwood can't decide which one to present to Colonel Brigham. Larry also finds that Durwood's leery of his tie as it's so wild, so he decides to leave to buy a new one. When Samantha calls to check on him, Betty tells her about the tie trip and Samantha decides she better pop downtown to meet him when he comes back and she hollers for Aunt Hagatha to come babysit, as her mother seems incommunicado.

When Durwood gets back from shopping, Samantha notices he didn't get a new tie and he tells her that after the sales lady showed him all the ties he couldn't make up his mind so he just left. She tells him that she believes Endora has put a spell on him and that she's trying to contact her. Just then, Larry pops his head in to find out where Durwood is as Colonel Brigham is waiting and so after they leave, Samantha pops home.

After meeting the Colonel, Durwood is surprised to learn he's not from the south at all but from Philadelphia and he presents his first idea which is a jingle to the tune of "Pop Goes the Weasel." The Colonel likes it but Durwood seems to have reservations about it and says he wants to present his other idea, which makes the Colonel think he's unstable. When Durwood can't decide if he wants to actually present it, the Colonel gets ready to leave. Larry asks to speak to Durwood outside and tells him he isn't well and Durwood offers to go home, but maybe stay. Larry suggests the former and that he'll bring the Colonel over later to see new ideas that Durwood will come up with.

Furious, Durwood makes it home after a trying time of deciding which route to take and he hollers at Samantha, who has been trying to get a hold of her mother. She tries once more and Endora appears. Samantha demands her mother take the spell off and she does, but when Durwood threatens her with a necklace of fingers, Samantha stops him and tells her mother that she wishes she could see that Durwood isn't indecisive, that once he makes up his mind, he rarely changes it to which Endora responds that he's pigheaded. Samantha denies that but Endora says it's true and waves her hand turning Durwood's head into that of a pig! Horrified, Samantha tells her mother that it is the lowest thing she has ever done but Endora says that's not true and she zaps Durwood away telling Samantha that she placed him on the roof so the whole world can see how pig-headed he really is! Samantha runs outside and finds that her mother is right and wouldn't you know it, Larry and Colonel Brigham show up just then. When Larry asks what it is, Samantha says it's Durwood's idea for a revolving sign to go over all the restaurants and she tells him to revolve. The Colonel is intrigued and says they should go inside to discuss some more. Samantha covertly zaps in a ladder so

Durwood can get down. They go inside and she tells them that his new idea is to use "Old MacDonald Had a Farm," and she begins nervously singing about the spare ribs and has Durwood squeal at the appropriate times. Larry isn't impressed but the Colonel is, which then means Larry is, and when they ask Durwood to take off his mask, Samantha says they have a special solution to take it off and they retreat to the kitchen.

Samantha with her pig-headed husband, Durwood.

Samantha hollers for her mother to demand she remove the pig head and she reluctantly agrees, just as Larry walks in to congratulate them.

I would give this a half star. This episode is a prime (rib) example of why everybody thinks *Bewitched* is so formulaic, it's another one of them *Far Side* episodes.

The pig head is creepy beyond all belief, but a cool creepy, because it totally looks like they really got a real pig's head and used it. And it is awesome that Dick Sargent was up for having it on.

That tie was hideous and did you notice he was wearing a pin stripe shirt? I don't think Durwood has even worn one before.

A big blooper is when Durwood is backing out of the driveway when Endora pops in. Not only did Dick Sargent move when he was supposed to be frozen, but the brake lights on the car were on when the car was just supposed to be frozen in mid-backing out and then you can see them go off when he releases the brake pedal after he's unfrozen.

I'm sick of Mrs. Kravitz always having some stupid petition. I guess they thought we were tired of her borrowing a cup of sugar, but why not in this situation, just simply have her out in her yard doing work, or just taking a walk around the neighborhood? But then I guess you couldn't have the scene of Durwood disagreeing and agreeing with her.

I also noticed that Endora's hair looked totally stupid in the opening scene and the ending, which I would assume they filmed near each other, because when she pops outside and in the middle, her hair looks like it's usual classiness.

Col. Brigham was tall considering David White was 6' 1".

The only memorable line in this one is from Endora when she says, "I guess I don't get any thanks at all." Samantha: "Mother, you'll get yours."

The next evening Dick Sargent appeared on *Love, American Style* in the episode entitled "Love and the Love Potion."

MARCH 4, 1971

It was on this night that ABC aired Episode #221: "Mixed Doubles."

After reading a book entitled *Marital Unrest*, which she borrowed from Louise Tate, Samantha worries that maybe Louise is having trouble with her own marriage. The morning after she has started reading the book, and after a very restless night, Samantha is startled awake by Larry in his bedroom! What's even stranger is that Larry thinks she's Louise and when he asks her to get him breakfast, she puts him in "the deep freeze" to take a look in the mirror where she sees that she still looks and sounds like Samantha. Wondering where the real Louise must be, she zaps herself over to her house only to find Durwood referring to Louise as Samantha and Louise acting like that's normal! Not knowing what to do, Samantha hollers for her mother who pops in and after explaining it, Endora tells her that it must be a form of transfiguration, or in other words, a metaphysical molecular disturbance that is put in force by a witch. Now, as they are witches, they are immune to it, but the mortals are not. Samantha is confused and decides maybe Dr. Bombay would be able to cure them and she asks Endora to find him and with that she pops back to Larry. When she unfreezes him, he's a bit bewildered by the fact that she's dressed now and they go to breakfast where Jonathan Tate seems transfixed by Samantha, though he doesn't admit knowing why. After Larry and Jonathan leave for the day, Samantha pops back to her house to check on Louise and Durwood, who seem to be still completely unaware. Satisfied that they'll be alright, she pops back to the Tate's where Endora pops in with Dr. Bombay, who had been clowning around with his nurse. He tells Samantha to stand on her left foot, grab her right foot with her left hand while putting her right pinky on her nose, and repeat, "Willy Warlock Walked Away with Wally Walrus" while he shines a flashlight on her. She complies only to find that he just wanted to hear her recite his favorite tongue twister. However, he concurs with Endora's diagnosis and says that Samantha doesn't have it but she is a cosmic carrier and that the mortals are affected by being in contact with her. He also says that he'll have to cure Samantha, which in turn, will cure the mortals. He gives her a psychedelic harmonica and tells her to play eight bars of "Pop Goes the Cosmos," out of tune, which will then put her metaphysical particles, back in tune. She awkwardly accomplishes his suggestion and then quickly pops back to her house to check on Louise, but when Louise answers the door surprised to see "Louise" at her house, Samantha realizes that it didn't work and she tells Louise that she feels bad for not having called first and so she goes to leave. After Louise closes the door, Samantha pops back to the Tate's with the bad news. Dr. Bombay tells her the molecules must be more disturbed than he thought and that he'll have to concoct a potion which requires the marrow of the tooth of a sabre-toothed tiger, and he pops off to find some.

Later, Samantha shows up at McMann and Tate as she has missed Durwood and shocks him by kissing him. She also tells him that she knows about his witch wife because she IS his witch wife and she proves it by twitching up a row of floating ringing bells. Believing her now, she explains everything to him, and they decide that while they wait for Dr. Bombay they'll invite the Tates to dinner when hopefully Dr. Bombay will return with the potion.

That night, there is no news of Dr. Bombay and Larry starts to get aggravated when his wife doesn't seem to want to leave. Samantha asks if she can make some coffee and when she goes into the kitchen and calls for her mother, she pops in with Dr. Bombay who has the potion. After drinking it, she peeks into the living room and finds that they still think Louise is Samantha. Dr. Bombay is baffled and asks Samantha to tell him about everything that happened the night before. Samantha recalls having a dream where she was tossing and turning, and it was very breezy and in the breeze she kept hearing someone calling Louise's name. After a lame joke, Dr. Bombay says that not only were the molecules disturbed, but they were held there by a layer of dream inversion which could simply be cured by a spell which he casts over Samantha. She instantly pops into the dress Louise was wearing and goes back into the living room, where everything is back to normal.

I'd give this three stars. I think it's a very interesting premise, but like the *Bewitched* Critic said, why not have Kasey Rogers play Samantha? It would've been so awesome! And Kasey's hair looked HORRIBLE! Why would she have it that short?

The Tate's kitchen is Jeannie's kitchen, just redone. It's what it would've looked like for the Sixth Season of *I Dream of Jeannie* had they had one and it's cool that they used it again because they used it in "Hippie, Hippie, Hooray."

So we don't get to see Tabitha and Adam, but we DO get to see Jonathan! Here he is for the first time since Aunt Clara split him in two in "Accidental Twins" from Season Three. Why haven't we seen him in the mean time? And I did like that he was staring at Samantha but I wish they would've went into it more, like did he recognize that she really wasn't his mother?

I also really like the sheets on Sam and Durwood's bed. I'm always looking for some to match that. But I hate their poor man's brass headboard.

It was nice to see Dr. Bombay and what was with him hitting on Endora? That's something I was kinda bummed out about in regards to the DVDs. It seems like they cut short the scene right after Samantha pops out from the Tate's and Endora and Dr. Bombay are left on their own. You can see Dr. Bombay turning toward Endora as if to say, "Well, now that we're alone how about you and I…" I thought for sure when the DVD was released that there would be an edited out scene shown, but there's not.

I noticed that Liz seemed rather bored throughout this episode, especially with her popouts. It seemed like she was just snapping her fingers and sighing like, "How much longer do I have to do this corny crap?" Also, when she first pops back home and is standing out in the hallway and then she pops out as Louise and Durwood are coming out of the bedroom, seems to me that they definitely would've seen her.

I also liked at the end, after Samantha tells Dr. Bombay her dream and she asks him what he thinks it means, he says, "Every little breeze seems to whisper "Louise" HA HA HAH!"

Anyway, this is one of my more favorite episodes.

Here is one of my favorite lines:

> DR. BOMBAY: *"I shall have to go to Asia Minor for it, I'm no longer on speaking terms with Asia Senior!"*

In the *Bewitched* movie, Isabel and Jack recreate the first scene with the marriage book on their version of *Bewitched* just before Shirley Maclaine's TERRIBLE version of Endora pops in and Jack fittingly calls her "Rancid Fruitbag."

MARCH 11, 1971

It was on this night that ABC aired Episode #222: "Darrin Goes Ape." (I know, I again said the same thing…who is 'Darrin'?)

As the planet Icarus is passing between Venus and Jupiter, it has stilled the winds of adversity in Serena making her a veritable Sea of Tranquility, which has made her decide to bury the hatchet with Durwood, and so she pops in bringing him a gift of a portable television. Durwood and Samantha are a bit surprised but go along with it until Serena suggests he try Channel 13 for the weather report. When the weather man says that it's going to be a blizzard along the Eastern Seaboard, Durwood says that's ridiculous as there isn't a cloud in the sky. Serena tells him that he should trust the weather report as it is coming straight from THE Weather Man! Realizing that she may have zapped it up out of bat wings and eel eyes (something which no witch would ever mix), he demands she take it back. Serena is hurt and tells him that it's a gift and he shouldn't be so rude, but he doesn't care and so she pops out, insulted.

Later, after Samantha has left to go shopping with the kids, Serena pops in again and changes herself into Samantha and tells Durwood that he should reconsider Serena's gift, but he tells her that he won't have anything to do with witchcraft. She reminds him that Serena is only giving the only way she knows how, and that deep down she's really a sweet person, but he says she's really rotten. Having had enough of his thick-headedness, Serena zaps herself back into her own form and tells him that he has all the grace and gentility of a gorilla which is what he is about to become, and with a snap, he turns into one! And with that, she pops out. Furious, he starts grunting so loudly that Mrs. Kravitz hears it and is shocked when she sees that there is a gorilla in the Stephens's living room! She tries to convince Abner by dragging him over there, but in the meantime, Serena pops back in and changes Durwood back so by the time Abner is able to look in the window, he only sees Durwood. Abner heads back home leaving Gladys bewildered.

Inside, Serena asks Durwood for an apology but, of course, he won't give one and so she changes him back and pops out. Gladys is pleased, but scared, to see the gorilla again and runs back to her house to call the police. They don't believe her until they show up and see for themselves. Thinking that maybe the gorilla has escaped from Johnson's Jungle Isle, they give them a ring, but they say they aren't missing any until they hear it's most likely a male, which is what they need to breed with their female gorilla, Tilly. They come right out to 1164 and are ready to tranquilize Durwood, but he submits peacefully and they take him back to their reserve.

When Samantha comes home, she finds that Durwood isn't there, and just then Mrs. Kravitz rings the door to tell her about the gorilla, the possibility that it ate Durwood, and the fact that Johnson's Jungle Isle captured it. Samantha knows that can't be true; however, it is possible that Durwood is the gorilla as a product of Serena's revenge. When she calls out to the cosmos for Serena and threatens to report her to the Witches' Council, a banner appears saying that the Witches' Council is adjourned until after the Royal Hunt of the Gorilla. Seeing as Serena won't show up, she calls on Aunt Hagatha to babysit for a moment while she goes out to get Durwood. Before Hagatha can protest, Samantha pops out and ends up at Johnson's Jungle Isle where Tilly is trying to have her way with Durwood, who won't have his way with her. When she finds out that the gorilla really is her husband, she casts a spell to get him home and then she pops home.

Across the street, Gladys is shocked to hear the gorilla screams again and goes sneaking over to confirm, after which she phones the police. They in turn call Johnson's Jungle Isle who are shocked that the new gorilla is gone.

A little later, the police show up at 1164 again asking if Samantha is harboring a gorilla. She denies it and when they say they are going to search the premises, she forbids it, until they tell her that they are only looking after her safety. When they go to look in the den, where Mrs. Kravitz says the gorilla was, Samantha twitches him into the kitchen before they open the door. In the meantime, Johnson's Jungle Isle has shown up and sees the gorilla in the kitchen and when they open the door to do a surprise attack, the gorilla suddenly disappears. The police soon barge in and everyone is confused until they hear Mrs. Kravitz's screams of the gorilla being on the roof. Fed up with all this, Samantha calls out to the cosmos threatening to send Serena up the river Styx without a paddle if she doesn't change Durwood back. Right before the police, the Jungle men, and Mrs. Kravitz get to the front of the house, Durwood regains his human form. When the police ask him if he's seen the gorilla, he says he saw it running down the road, and so the men tell Mrs. Kravitz to go home and Johnson's Jungle Isle goes to chase down the gorilla. Suddenly, Serena pops in and when the police ask where she came from, she tells them Babylon. Thinking she's just a freaked out hippie, they set their sights to getting Durwood down from the roof, but Serena tells them not to bother and she zaps him down and she pops out. Having had enough strangeness for one day, the policemen leave.

Samantha apologizes to Durwood, who surprisingly says that he has to put up with all that because he married a witch, and a beautiful one at that.

I think this episode deserves one and a half, maybe even two stars. Herbie J Pilato designated it as "the worst episode of the series" in his book *Bewitched Forever*, but in my book "Ho Ho the Clown" or one of the ones where it's focused mainly on Durwood at work like "Your Witch is Showing" or "Instant Courtesy" is much worse than this. The gorilla suit is lame, but I suppose it was the best they could get in 1971 aside from hiring a real gorilla, which would've been awesome!

The person in the doorway as Serena when she pops in right after Samantha leaves is Melody! And I believe the reason it's her is that it made it easier to film Serena turning into Samantha 'cause you just have Melody as Serena and Liz as Sam. Then they just intercut the close-up of Liz as Serena in that scene. Paula Abdul, during promotional photo shoots for her second album *Spellbound*, looked just like Serena when she was standing in the doorway as Paula had short curly hair, and was wearing a feather boa. I think it's appropriate, then, that her album was called *Spellbound*.

I did think the gift of the TV was a bit odd, but I like that she told him to turn it to 13 because it had THE weatherman! Channel 13 in my area is Fox, and back in the day they used to be the station that would carry *Bewitched* in the afternoon. I wish they would again and I'd send them this clip and they could just substitute their weatherman for the one on Serena's set. And how strange was it that when she zapped it out they just did it off camera? I kind of liked that. And how about how far apart Durwood and Samantha were as they were going to kiss just before Serena popped in?! That was ridiculous!

I think Serena had every right to be really upset with him for refusing her gift. Here she was for the first time ever trying to be nice to him and just putting their differences aside, and he has the nerve to not only reject it, but be totally rude to her in the process? I'm sure it was something very important to her and he was rejecting it. I thought he acted like a total ass throughout this whole episode.

How about the kitchen wall just inside the door with the spice rack on it? Even when I was young, that never made sense to me. Were you to open that door and look through, you'd see straight through to the chopping block in the middle and the stove past that. But I suppose they had to do something since they were actually filming at the Ranch, though you would think for that scene they could've done it in the studio.

Abner looks disgusting and it reminded me of what a hobo he looked like a couple years later on *Tabitha*. This was his very last episode of the entire series, though Mrs. Kravitz shows up one more time.

I was also wondering why Adam was crying in the car? Maybe David Lawrence really thought he was going "bye-bye" and was sad.

Here are some of my favorite lines:

> SERENA: *"When the planet Icarus passes between Venus and Jupiter, it stills the winds of adversity in me and I become a veritable SEA of tranquility."*
> FROM THE SIGN THAT POPS IN: *"Royal Council Adjourned Until After Royal Hunt of the Gorilla."*
> THE GUY FROM JOHNSON'S JUNGLE ISLE: *"Madame, Johnson's Jungle gorillas are vegetarian!"*

Three days before, guest actress Virginia Martin, better known as Charlie Leach's wife Charmaine from Season Two's "Follow That Witch" and "The Catnapper" and Season One's "It's Magic," passed away.

MARCH 18, 1971

It was on this night that ABC aired Episode #223: "Money Happy Returns."

After a morning of swimming in their plastic pool, Tabitha asks her mother when they will get a real pool, to which Samantha replies that they'll get one when they can afford it. As Tabitha takes Adam in to dry off, Tabitha mentions how much she'd love to have a real pool. Just then Endora pops in appalled that her granddaughter was gasping for water and insists that Tabitha's wish will never come true because Durwood is too cheap. Samantha assures her that eventually it will happen and when Durwood comes downstairs she asks him to empty the pool. Not satisfied, Endora zaps a pool in right under Durwood's feet. Of course, he's furious and Samantha demands Endora zap it away.

Later, when Durwood and Larry ride into work in a cab, after Larry has left the cab, the driver notices a manila envelope and tells Durwood about it. He thinks that maybe Larry left it but when he calls Larry about it and opens it, he finds a large sum of money which he assumes is from Endora who had been insistent that he'd never make enough money for the pool. He immediately calls Samantha to tell her about it and she seems to agree. She hollers for her mother and accuses her of the money zapping, but Endora claims she didn't do it and even gives her witches' honor which leaves Samantha wondering who would've left the money...

Meanwhile, the cabbie picks up a gentleman who claims to have left the envelope and the cabbie tells him that Durwood picked it up. He drives him up to the McMann and Tate building where he shows the gentlemen Durwood, who has come down to go home. The gentlemen requests that the cabbie follow Durwood, but stay behind.

Durwood arrives at home still insistent that Endora zapped it up, but Samantha assures him she gave her witches' honor. That gets him thinking that Samantha most likely had zapped it, but even when she says she didn't, he thinks she's lying. Furious, Samantha tells him how pig-headed he is and, before she really loses her temper, she tells him she's going out for some air. Before she leaves, she zaps the money away.

Soon after she leaves, the gentleman shows up and introduces himself as Mr. Cosco and tells Durwood he knows he has the money. Sick, now that he realizes the truth, Durwood invites him in as he tries to think of a way to get Samantha back. He tries calling Louise Tate and finds that Samantha is there but Louise won't let him talk to her. When Louise tells Samantha that Durwood seemed incoherent, babbling about somebody come for the money, Samantha tells Louise she has to fly.

At home, she confronts Mr. Cosco who is getting very impatient, especially when Samantha asks him where he got the money from. Just then, Cosco's associate, Mr. Braun, shows up. They pull guns out on the Stephens when Larry shows up with some ideas for the Cushman campaign and he thinks that Durwood is trying to sign up with another agency so he offers him a raise and a $2,500 bonus to stay. Durwood accepts but asks Larry to leave. Cosco and Braun brandish their guns again but Samantha twitches them into play guns and also twitches up the sound of sirens and police calling that they want Cosco and Braun to come out with their hands up. When they get outside, nobody is there. However a cop car does pull up as they heard sirens. Samantha twitches up the money to show the cops who take Cosco and Braun in for questioning. Durwood apologizes to Samantha and also tells Larry the truth, which causes Larry to relinquish his offer, disgusting Endora.

I don't know that I'd even give it half a star. I really loathe this episode and it's mainly due to Liz's STUPID hair do! What the hell?! Peanuts and Liz should be boiled in their own pudding for doing that! Especially at the end when her curly bangs are in her face!

But aside from that, it seems that nobody but maybe Agnes Moorehead and Kasey Rogers are into their parts. Seems like everyone else is just there for the paycheck, none more than Liz.

And how about the cabbie is the guy from Johnson's Jungle Isle from just the previous episode! There is no way he could've seen that envelope.

This is one episode for proof that 1164 is in Westport as Endora says she's going to scream and shatter glass all over Westport. I was also hoping when Samantha called Durwood pigheaded she was going to zap it back on him, and it would've been cool just 'cause it's so creepy!

Gordon Jump played the cop. He would later go on to fame on *WKRP in Cincinnati* as Arthur Carlson and later as the Maytag Man in the popular commercials.

MARCH 25, 1971

It was on this night that ABC aired Episode #224: "Out of the Mouths of Babes."

While Durwood is brushing up on his putt before going out to the green on a Saturday, Larry shows up wanting him to come into the office as he just heard that Mother Flannigan Stew is leaving Sloan & Sloan Advertising looking for a new outfit, and as it will bring in lots of revenue,

Larry wants his best man on the account. Durwood tries to refuse but Larry reminds him that he's the boss, so Durwood relents while Larry goes golfing, though Samantha zaps up a storm.

Later on, Endora pops in wanting to take Tabitha to the Unicorn Handicap but Durwood won't hear of it. Endora says he's acting like a child and makes it so that his appearance matches his mentality by making him ten years old! Tired of Durwood's attitude, but pleased, Endora pops out. Samantha suggests that Durwood apologize as it will be the only way he'll get back to his adult self but, as he's so hard headed, he refuses. Just then Larry shows up and Samantha introduces the young man as Marvin, Durwood's nephew. Larry asks where Durwood is and Samantha tells him he went to the nursery for things for the garden. He says he'll just wait as he wants to run some ideas for Mother Flannigan's by him and that he'll just take a nap in the den. Meanwhile, as she doesn't want Durwood stewing at home, Samantha asks him to go play with Tabitha in the park.

When Tabitha and Durwood return, Tabitha tells her mommy that some boys at the park asked Durwood to play basketball with them and he was very good. Just then there is a knock at the door and it turns out to be a boy from the park, Herbie, who wanted to ask Marvin to join their team, especially for their big game the next day. He also smells Samantha cooking something and she tells the boys that it's Mother Flannigan's Irish Stew. Herbie invites himself to dinner but when he tastes it, he decides to go home. When Durwood tastes it, he realizes it's disgusting and he apologizes to Endora, who zaps him back. He tells Samantha that he's actually grateful that he was a kid as he would've never met Herbie who showed him the reason that the stew sales were slipping.

After Larry tastes the stew, he realizes that they are just going to have to sell it anyway, but Samantha reminds him that his integrity is at stake. Later on, Larry returns with Mr. Flannigan and Samantha suggests that Durwood have Marvin tell Mr. Flannigan that the stew is terrible. When Marvin does tell the truth, Mr. Flannigan appreciates his honesty as he recalls that he hated the stew when he was little as it was based on his mother's recipe. After Samantha changes Durwood back to normal, Mr. Flannigan laments the fact that he has so much product sitting in his warehouse but Samantha tells him that he can still use them if he makes one change, and that is to call it Mother Flannigan's Doggie Stew and label it as dog food. Larry about chokes on his drink but Mr. Flannigan likes the idea.

The next day, Herbie shows up wanting to know if Marvin is going to come play basketball just as Durwood is going to golf. Knowing that it was Herbie's help that got him the account, Durwood says he'll go get Marvin and he runs upstairs and Samantha changes him into Herbie.

I don't like this episode at all! It seems that Elizabeth Montgomery's boredom is shining brighter than ever and all with those HIDEOUS pants! Did you notice at the first when she's sitting in the chair she just looks SO bored that she can't even hold her head up in the far shots, but then when they do close-ups, she's mustered enough energy to hold her head up? I realize that it may just be Liz's acting skills, 'cause who the hell would want to see Durwood practicing golf? Especially as stupidly as he was doing it? But even then, it just seemed the whole episode was Liz just going through the motions, just like last episode.

Gene Andrusco (Marvin) grew up to be a musician and producer. He even founded a band called Adam Again. He passed away on March 20, 2000 in his sleep. Eric Scott played Herbie and would go on to play Ben Walton on *The Waltons*. I think Gene was a good choice for young Dick Sargent as I thought he looked very much like him. And it was really irritating having Dick Sargent's voice used for Marvin. It was not funny in the least, though I do like that Larry mentions it. But why not just have it like it was when Billy Mumy was Durwood (Season Two's "Junior Executive") and use his real voice? That's what would've happened had Durwood really been turned into a little boy.

I also didn't like that Endora changes him back unseen and is never heard from again the rest of the episode.

I also liked when Larry said, "SAM!"

Other than that, this episode bites.

APRIL 1, 1971

It was on this night that ABC aired Episode #225: "Samantha's Psychic Pslip."

While repapering the cupboards in the kitchen, Samantha gets a call from Durwood's mother, who is nearby, and she suggests that they go shopping even though she knows Samantha may be busy. Feeling guilty, Samantha tells her to come over, and not wanting Phyllis to see the messy kitchen, she zaps the cupboards done just as Durwood walks in. She apologizes and realizes that he has something behind his back and when she finally gets to it, he tells her it's a gift. She reads the note attached which tells her it's a reward for going above and beyond no witchcraft and she finds a blue and gold bracelet. She feels even guiltier but he tells her he understands. Soon, she starts hiccupping and with each hiccup a different bike pops in. Samantha says it's not her but she's not sure why they are popping up. Durwood gives her permission to get rid of the bikes with magic, but when her spell doesn't work, she thinks she may be ill, and she tells Durwood that she'll call for Dr. Bombay, until Phyllis shows up. Phyllis is bewildered by all the bikes in the living room and even more shocked when a unicycle pops up in front of her when she goes to go upstairs. Durwood diverts her attention to the kids upstairs, and after they leave, Samantha quietly calls for Dr. Bombay who pops in irritated that she interrupted his golf game with his nurse. Samantha tells him about the hiccups and bikes and so he begins to unpack his electronic diagnostic computer machine which he hooks up to Samantha and begins to play the information into it. When he gets the results, he tells Samantha that as she was feeling guilty for practicing witchcraft, it precipitated a crisis which manifested itself in the form of the bikes to show that she had a lack of "wheel" power. Samantha thinks that's ridiculous, but he tells her even so, it's true and he gives her a pranquilizer treatment incanting that it will eliminate all of guilt. As his job is done, Dr. Bombay pops back to his nurse.

Samantha and Phyllis get ready to go shopping. As Samantha is leaving, she hiccups, but as there aren't any bikes, she feels everything is fine and goes on. However, when Durwood closes the door, he notices that the mirror that was hanging nearby is gone. Before he can go out to flag down Samantha, Serena pops in as Samantha had asked her to come check on the kids. Durwood tells her about the mirror but she couldn't care less as it's strictly a medical condition so he asks her to call Dr. Bombay, which she reluctantly does. She also says they'll just have to wait.

Soon, Larry shows up just for a visit and is pleased to see Serena but spooked out when he just misses Serena popping up stairs. Durwood suggests maybe Larry has had too much to drink, especially when Dr. Bombay pops in right behind Larry, spooking him even more. Larry goes to lie down while Durwood explains the mirror disappearing. Dr. Bombay thinks it's not possible that the mirror has anything to do with his cure, but after recreating his incantation on the fridge, he realizes that he mentioned "eliminating all of guilt" which was interpreted by the magic as getting rid of anything gilt in gold, which the mirror was. Not knowing where Samantha and Phyllis went, Dr. Bombay zaps up his omni-directional three-dimensional vectoring cadmium shielded computer for location analysis a.k.a. the witch hunter and he starts it up so that it can search out Samantha.

Meanwhile, at the store, Samantha hiccups again causing a gold lamp and a gold necklace to disappear. The store detective sees that the necklace is gone and accuses Samantha and Phyllis of stealing it, but when they deny it, he tells them that he's going to have to take them to the office for questioning.

Back at 1164, the witch hunter stops searching and Dr. Bombay concentrates on finding Samantha.

At the store, the detective decides the best method for interrogating would be to question the women individually and so he takes Phyllis into another room just as Dr. Bombay and Durwood pop in (Durwood got caught in Bombay's jet stream). He tells Samantha that he found that he gave her the wrong cure because her problem wasn't only logical but "cycle"-logical and that she needs to stop feeling guilty about doing witchcraft so his cure will work. He gives her another dose from the pranquilizer and after she's tested her powers out, he pops out. Samantha pops Durwood home to a bewildered Larry and then shows the detective and Mrs. Stephens the necklace, which has returned, prompting the detective to apologize.

As corny as this one is, I LOVE it! I've probably watched this episode almost as many times as I've watched "Allergic to Macedonian Dodos." I would give it three stars, maybe even more!

The thing I love most about it, aside from Serena and Dr. Bombay, is that Larry shows up with no agenda what so ever, except to visit! Has he EVER done that, with the exception of when he came over to help celebrate their second anniversary? And especially here in this late season where everything has to be business for him? LOVE IT! I also like that Mrs. Stephens simply wanted to have some "fun" time with Samantha, whereas every other time she's shown up it's been to complain or make Samantha look stupid. I think they should've explained Larry's sudden showing up because I was under the impression that Durwood had said he was going to go over to Larry's to discuss something, which is why Serena showed up.

Also I love the Omni-Directional Three-Dimensional Vectoring Cadmium Shielded Computer for Location Analysis! It's groovy and would make an awesome clock! I also love it that Bernard Fox had to memorize that name and then when Durwood says, "A what?" He goes right into the whole long name again! Every witch should've had one 'cause it would saved a lot of time. But that brings up another point: ever since about "Daddy Does His Thing" we've seen that they can 'recreate' scenes in a picture or, like this episode, on the fridge to help them remember their spells. If that's the case, why didn't they do so all the times Aunt Clara, Esmeralda, or Uncle Arthur goofed up? I also love that line about the ectoplasmic vortex…Bernard Fox says it with such disgust! It's so funny!

One of my FAVORITE all time *Bewitched* scenes is when Durwood asks Serena what are they going to do in the meantime (after she's called Dr. Bombay) and she says, "We'll think of something?" and she starts giggling and then looks STRAIGHT AT HIS CROTCH and starts laughing! How risqué!

I always remember thinking how cool it would be to just hiccup a bike, especially a motorcycle and Dr. Bombay's explanation of them totally fit. I also like that Samantha says what we're all thinking "That's ridiculous!" And he replies, "Ridiculous, but true."

I thought Liz looked really pretty in this episode, especially in that green outfit. And I also thought the bracelet was pretty.

I also like Serena and Dr. Bombay popping in behind Larry. I like his absolute delight at seeing Serena and then Dr. Bombay saying, "My dear fellow, don't you signal when you turn?!" I also really like the sound effect used for Dr. Bombay popping in and out.

I think it's quite appropriate that this episode aired on April Fool's Day considering it was all about bad puns and Dr. Bombay uses the pranquilizer.

Anyway, one of my most favorite episodes!

Here are a few of my favorite lines::

DURWOOD: *"We need your help, something awful has happened!"*
SERENA: *"I know! Your mother arrived. And then something good happened — she left! Ha ha!"*
DR. BOMBAY: *"Great leaping lizards of limbo, what've I done?"*
DR. BOMBAY: *"Excellent! I haven't had a drink as good as that since Thursday."*
LARRY: *"Thursday?"*
DR. BOMBAY: *"So am I, let's have another drink…"*
LARRY: *"I've been looking all over for you and I couldn't find you everywhere!"*

Three days before, CBS aired the last new episode of *The Ed Sullivan Show*, which had been on the air since 1948!

APRIL 8, 1971

It was on this night that ABC aired Episode #226: "Samantha's Magic Mirror."

Esmeralda fades in depressed because her old boyfriend Ferdy has reappeared and wants to renew their relationship. She is very nervous as it's been over four hundred years since she dated him and, as her powers are kaput and she's older, she asks Samantha to help her look younger and more pretty. While they are discussing Esmeralda's plans, Larry shows up and so Samantha takes Esmeralda upstairs for a little witch-to-witch talk. As they are going up the stairs Esmeralda sneezes up a baby elephant which baffles Larry, who has come to hide out from a fight he's been having with Louise.

Upstairs, Samantha covers up the bedroom mirror because she wants to surprise Esmeralda with her makeover, which she is going to give her the mortal way. When she's finished, she asks Durwood to come and shower compliments on Esmeralda to give her a shot of confidence. Esmeralda comes out of the bedroom wearing a bathrobe. However, Durwood lets the compliments fly more than necessary. Esmeralda is flattered and goes back in the room to change into a dress and without her knowing, Samantha zaps the mirror to improve Esmeralda's appearance. When she pulls the cover off the mirror, Esmeralda is absolutely pleased with her makeover and can't wait to show Ferdy, who she has asked to meet her at Samantha's that afternoon. Durwood is nervous as Larry won't leave but Samantha assures him if Esmeralda can renew her love with Ferdy, she may not show up as often, and so Durwood tries to convince Larry to leave. They find Esmeralda flirting with Larry, who suggests that he and Durwood go golfing, bowling, or anything so they can get out of the house!

Later on, after Ferdy has arrived, Durwood calls from the golf course to say they are coming back, but Samantha tells him to buy another bucket of balls to keep stalling. Ferdy is pleased to see Esmeralda again, though he's not so taken by her new dolled up looks and when she suggests that they have some drinks, he asks for a scotch on the rocks. She goes to make it but he thinks that's strange and tells her to zap it, and she does; however, it's an actual Scotch on a pile of rocks! Samantha, who had been spying from the kitchen, comes in laughing saying what a marvelous sense of humor Esmeralda has. The Scotchman soon disappears and Samantha slyly zaps a scotch on the rocks in Esmeralda's hand. Ferdy zaps up a cigar and lights it with his finger as Samantha asks Esmeralda to come help her with dinner. When they leave, there is a knock at the window from a young man, who happens to be Ferdy's nephew. It turns out that Ferdy's powers are kaput, too, and so he's had his nephew there to do his zapping for him. Esmeralda comes back in and Ferdy tells her he should've brought flowers, and asks for some roses, which his nephew zaps up, complete with thorns! Just then, the police see the young man lurking at the window and when one of them ask the young man what he's doing, he disappears. Meanwhile, the phone has rang again with Durwood calling causing Samantha to lose her sight on Esmeralda, who tries to zap up a smoked salmon for dinner, but only succeeds in getting a salmon smoking a pipe. She gets nervous again and sneezes up a pair of seals and, as she's twisting Samantha's pearl necklace around her hands, it breaks. Knowing that her powers aren't any good, Esmeralda asks Ferdy to zap it back together and when he asks the necklace to go back the way it was, it materializes as a string of oysters! Ferdy admits his power loss and Esmeralda is relieved. Meanwhile, Samantha is still on the phone with Durwood, who tells her that he can't stall anymore, and she is interrupted by Ferdy and Esmeralda, who have come in to announce their engagement. They ask her to try and correct the bad zaps, and they find that the seals and salmon have disappeared, though the oyster necklace remains intact. Just then, the doorbell rings and Samantha asks if they would possibly leave as she knows it's Larry and, just as they disappear, Larry walks in with Durwood close behind. Samantha explains that Larry's just been having a bad day because of his fight with Louise. He later finds that he hadn't been able to reach her by phone all day to make up with her because the phone lines have been down.

I'd only give this one star. I have to say that I thought it was weird how Esmeralda got back into the whole sneezing thing, especially since she hasn't done that forever! And her forlorn sighs were really irritating. I do, however, like when she says that maybe she'll "turn myself into an inanimate object, like a plant, and then I can just sit in my pot and look pretty." For some reason, that line always strikes me as funny.

I did think it was weird that Ferdy is brought in and not Ramon Verona. And then, after having not seen each other in centuries, Esmeralda and Ferdy are engaged?! And I'm thinking 'Ferdy' is short for Ferdinand, but they should've had Esmeralda call him that when she was acting all prim and proper and have him remind her that he just likes to go by 'Ferdy.'

Esmeralda looked way silly with that hair and that dress, but I did think it was funny when she came down the stairs and flirted with Larry.

And I thought Ferdy's nephew totally looked like David Cassidy! In fact, I always thought it was him when I was younger.

I really liked Liz's purpley outfit. Too bad Agnes Moorehead wasn't around to enjoy it as lavender was her favorite color.

Ferdy was played by Tom Bosley, who in a few years would become better known to audiences and the Fonz as Mr. C(unningham) on *Happy Days*.

Esmeralda's reflection was played by Nancy Priddy in her second appearance on the show, the first being a stewardess earlier this season in "The Salem Saga." She would become the mother of Christina Applegate.

Three days before, Liz began a week long appearance on *Password* with Bill Bixby. He would later play Bruce Banner on TV's *The Incredible Hulk*, which Liz cited as her favorite TV show.

The next day, Charles Manson is sentenced to death. However, the next year, everyone on death row is commuted to a life sentence.

APRIL 15, 1971

It was on this night that ABC aired Episode #227: "Laugh, Clown, Laugh."

Durwood is hard at work trying to brainstorm new ideas for Mt. Rocky Mutual Insurance, a client that McMann and Tate are about to lose, when his brainstorming is interrupted by Endora riding into the living room on a camel that she had been using to play sand polo. Durwood tells Samantha to get rid of the beast, and the camel too, so Endora zaps the camel away and tells Durwood that his sense of humor is totally lacking. Irritated yet again, Durwood leaves to go eat some lunch and asks that Endora be gone by the time he's finished. Endora tells Samantha that it's disgusting that Durwood has no sense of humor, but Samantha tells her that he does, but not where she's concerned.

Later at the office, Endora pops in and casts a spell on Durwood that any time he hears a chime, he will tell jokes that will cause everyone's hair to curl. After she's popped out, Durwood's secretary, Betty, comes in to tell him about Mr. Jamison, Mt. Rocky's President, arriving, but he busts out a terrible joke about his mother-in-law. Betty cannot believe Durwood's joke and she's saved by the bell when Larry buzzes in to see where Durwood is. Durwood, realizing that he must be under a spell, tries to avoid the meeting but Larry insists he come in to meet Mr. Jamison.

Larry apologizes to Mr. Jamison, who says that Durwood seems flighty, which is not good as insurance is a serious business. As soon as Durwood enters the office, the bad jokes pour out, insulting Mr. Jamison, who decides to leave. Realizing that he can't go on like this, Durwood leaves too. At home, he lays into Samantha until the phone rings, with Larry asking that Durwood come back, as by some miracle, he was able to talk Mr. Jamison into staying. Samantha tells him that Durwood will be there soon. Soon, Endora pops in and, after Samantha requests she take the spell off, she does. Durwood tells her that she's horrible and he goes to leave. Outside, Endora freezes him and she zaps another spell on him so that anytime he hears something sad, he'll start laughing. After she pops out and unfreezes Durwood, he begins to back out, until Mrs. Kravitz stops him to tell him about her sister who is going to be having an operation. Durwood begins to chuckle and, when Mrs. Kravitz tells him it's serious, he begins to laugh out loud. Knowing that Endora has done it again, he parks and runs back inside and asks Samantha to find her mother while he goes to hide in the den. Larry calls wondering where Durwood is and Samantha tells him that he actually came back home because he's not feeling very well. Larry about loses his mind as Mr. Jamison is very annoyed with the way things are going. He tells Larry that they'll have to meet another time as he and Mrs. Jamison have to fly out. Larry offers to drive them to the airport and on the way they'll stop off at Durwood's.

Meanwhile at 1164, Mrs. Kravitz comes knocking to see how Durwood is doing as he seemed to just be full of laughter. Samantha assures her everything is fine and, when Mrs. Kravitz tells her about a terrible car accident from the other night, she hears Durwood stifling his laughter from behind the door. Samantha says it's a mice problem and asks Mrs. Kravitz not to tell another soul. Of course, Mrs. Kravitz must tell every soul and as she goes to leave, she bumps into Larry and the Jamisons. When they come in, Mrs. Jamison mentions how she has a terrible migraine which causes Durwood to go into a fit of laughter. Samantha explains that they were just laughing about Mrs. Kravitz and her keen sense of "rumor." Mrs. Jamison thinks that's funny and begins to laugh, but Mr. Jamison isn't impressed. They go to sit down to discuss the ideas Durwood had. Surprisingly, Durwood rips up his ideas and says that he has come up with a new approach to the campaign and that is to add a little laughter to your disaster. Mr. Jamison isn't having it but Mrs. Jamison thinks it's funny and, as Samantha and Durwood joke some more, Mrs. Jamison can't stop laughing. She mentions that her migraine has gone and tells her husband that he needs to lighten up and quit complaining about his bursitis. Soon, everyone is in a jovial mood and a certain joke hits Mr. Jamison the right way so that even he begins to laugh. As soon as he does, he notices that his bursitis is gone!

Later, Endora removes the spell and Durwood receives a package from Mr. Jamison with a note thanking him for showing him how to laugh. He also tells him to set down a bag that came in the package for a laugh and, when he does, it has a recording of Mr. Jamison laughing.

I don't care for this episode at all! It's very *Far Side*, with the exception of Endora not showing up at the end, though, she was supposed to according to the original script. I think everything about it is awkward, except for Endora riding in on the camel. But Durwood's "jokes" are ridiculous, and I suppose they were supposed to be, but Dick Sargent just makes it way awkward. Marcia Wallace is really awkward and, though I love him, Charles Lane plays the same client that he just played earlier in the season with the bugs in the ad ("Samantha's Magic Potion"). In fact, I always confuse these two episodes.

I thought Liz looked cute in the ponytails, but I hated all the brown she was wearing. Bleh! But it is the '70s and that's all it was: brown, avocado green, and baby poop yellow as my dad would put it.

This is the last time we see Mrs. Kravitz for the entire series. And I'm kind of glad…she's been a one trick pony lately, but it's still sad. Of course, we'll see her again on *Tabitha*, but it's just not the same.

This episode aired on Liz's thirty-eighth birthday. It's the second time an episode has aired on her birthday. The first time was Season One's "Abner Kadabra."

Here are a few of my favorite lines:

> SAMANTHA: *"Mother, how are you supposed to play polo with such a short mallet?"*
> ENDORA: *"Tall ball!"*

APRIL 22, 1971

It was on this night that ABC aired the Seventh Season finale of *Bewitched*, Episode #228: "Samantha and the Antique Doll."

Phyllis comes for a visit and brings a top for Adam and a very old cloth doll for Tabitha, a doll which her grandmother gave her as a little girl. As Samantha and Phyllis visit, they hear Adam cry and find that he wants to play with the doll. Tabitha is afraid he'll break it, but Samantha tells her that he promises not to, and to let him play with it. Adam takes it across the room and the women go back to visiting until they notice the doll floating across the room to Tabitha, who had zapped it over. Phyllis is shocked and Samantha is nervous about how she'll explain it. She asks Tabitha to take Adam to play out on the patio as she puts the doll up on a shelf. When Phyllis asks how the doll could possibly float through the air, Samantha suggests that she had been reading up on mind over matter and that it may have been Phyllis who had willed the doll to Tabitha. Phyllis surprisingly accepts that answer and tries to will the doll to herself, again. Samantha obliges and twitches it to her. Pleased with herself, Phyllis wonders why it just didn't work right away and Samantha tells her that she also read that supernatural powers have a tendency to come and go. She also promises not to tell anyone else, which Phyllis agrees with, and she decides to leave.

Later on, Phyllis arrives at home with a lot of books about supernatural powers she had got from the library and she tells Frank about her new powers. He thinks she's flipped her lid, especially when she tries to levitate an hourglass to him. She tells him that Samantha can attest to her powers and that they should go over there.

Phyllis and Frank arrive at 1164 right after Durwood has come home and Phyllis takes Samantha into the kitchen to discuss her powers some more. She tells her that she's read about some people having a familiar, a certain object that gives the person their powers, and she's decided that hers is at Samantha's house which is the reason her powers wouldn't work at home. Samantha can't believe how nuts this all is. Meanwhile, Frank is worried about Phyllis and shares this with Durwood. They don't notice Tabitha creeping down the stairs and, just as she zaps the doll to fly to her, Samantha and Phyllis enter the living room and Phyllis declares that the doll must be her familiar! She tells Frank that she can show him her powers now and she tries to levitate the doll for him, but it doesn't go anywhere. Frustrated with his wife, Frank takes Durwood with him to make a drink while Phyllis goes to study up some more on her powers. She later returns with a spell, that at first doesn't seem to work. However Samantha twitches that doll to fly, until Phyllis yells for Frank to come and see. When the doll lands, Frank shows up and tells Phyllis she's got to be crazy, but she tells him it's because he's a non-believer and an old goat. That gives Samantha the idea that the next time Phyllis says that, she'll turn Frank into a goat, which should scare Phyllis away from doing any more magic.

A little later, Phyllis confronts Frank again, who still won't believe her and so when she tells him he's as stubborn as a mule, Samantha twitches him into one. Phyllis is shocked and worried that she may not be able to change him back, but Samantha suggests they have a séance to contact Phyllis' grandmother, who people said had strange powers, for a suggestion.

They set up for the séance and soon, Samantha twitches up an apparition that tells Phyllis she shouldn't have fooled around with the powers and that the way she can get Frank back is with love and with that, the ghost disappears. Phyllis is confused, but Samantha tells her that there is no power greater than the power of love, and Durwood suggests that she tell his father that she loves him and that might bring him back. Phyllis apologizes to Frank, but reminds him that he means everything in the world to her and so, with a twitch, Samantha turns Frank back into a man and the elder Stephens embrace.

Even though it's a remake of Season One's "Abner Kadabra," this is one of my favorite episodes! True, it isn't as good "Abner Kadabra" but I think it has a lot of fine points and I would give it at least two and a half to three stars.

First of all, this is the first time that Liz (without the inclusion of Serena) seems like she's not bored this latter part of the season. She actually seems really into it, especially trying to hold back the fact that she finds Phyllis' sudden all-knowiness about the supernatural, ridiculous.

The doll should've been a porcelain doll, as being cloth it would've been in tatters had it been as old as Phyllis said. I totally loved all the levitation of the doll and the fact that it was wearing funky black shoes that reminded me of a witch. And even cooler, was the fact that Phyllis mentioned that people thought her grandmother had extra special powers.

This is the first time that Tabitha has done the crossed fingers to work magic. And I cannot believe they would dress Tabitha in such short dresses! It's wrong!

This is also the return of original Frank, Robert F. Simon! It's been since "It's Wishcraft" in Season Three since we've seen him. I like him much better than Roy Roberts and it's too bad Endora wasn't around to flirt with him some more. And it's also the last time the elder Mr. and Mrs. Stephens will appear on *Bewitched*. I wonder why the writers and the producers chose to not use the Kravitzes or the Stephenses anymore? Anyway, I like that we got the scene of Phyllis expressing her true feelings towards Frank, even if he was a jackass at the time. It made her seem more like a real character instead of the bitch we always think she is, and to which she admitted.

I liked the séance with the spooky Salem music and I thought the ghost was fun, though corny. It was voiced by Liz. I hated, though, how when Phyllis says, "It doesn't look like her?" Samantha says, "It's her spirit, not her body!" Why wouldn't a spirit of someone deceased look like their mortal body? I guess there are some that may believe that, but I definitely don't. Not to mention all the ghosts up to this point (McTavish in the episode of the same name and Uncle Willie from "Tabitha's Cranky Spell") have all looked like their mortal body.

Three days earlier, the followers of Charles Manson involved in the murders are sentenced to the gas chamber.

Two days later, five hundred thousand people in Washington, D.C. and 125,000 in San Francisco held a protest march against the Vietnam War.

The following is the summer re-run schedule. The episode will be listed by number, name, and original airdate.

APRIL 29, 1971

Episode #201, "To Go or Not to Go, That Is the Question, Part 1" (September 24, 1970)

Two days later, Glenda Farrell, who played Hortense in Season Five's "The Battle of Burning Oak" passed away.

Three days later, a Harris poll indicated that 60% of Americans are against the Vietnam War. Some of those tried to disrupt government business on this day and police and military units arrest as many as 12,000 people. Most are later released.

Two days prior, CBS cancelled *Green Acres* as part of their "rural purge" to update their programming to more urban and contemporary settings. As Pat Buttram put it, "CBS cancelled everything with a tree…" which also included *The Beverly Hillbillies*, *Hee Haw*, and *Mayberry, RFD*. The show was still garnering high ratings even after six years on the air.

MAY 6, 1971

Episode #202, "Salem, Here We Come, Part 2" (October 1, 1970)

Three nights later, *Bewitched* wins the Governor's Award at the Emmy Awards for "Sisters at Heart," Agnes Moorehead was nominated for Outstanding Performance by an Actress in a Supporting Role in a Comedy, and Rolf Miller was nominated for Outstanding Achievement in Makeup (A Single Program of a Series or a Special Program for "Samantha's Old Man").

MAY 13, 1971

Episode #203, "The Salem Saga, Part 1" (October 8, 1970)

MAY 20, 1971

Episode #204, "Samantha's Hot Bedwarmer, Part 2" (October 15, 1970)

MAY 27, 1971

Episode #206, "Paul Revere Rides Again" (October 29, 1970)

JUNE 3, 1971

Episode #207, "Samantha's Bad Day in Salem" (November 5, 1970)

JUNE 10, 1971

Episode #208, "Samantha's Old Salem Trip" (November 12, 1970)

JUNE 17, 1971

Episode #209, "Samantha's Pet Warlock" (November 19, 1970)
That same day President Nixon officially declared the U.S. War on Drugs.
The next day, Thomas Gomez, who played Garcia in Season Five's "Samantha and Darrin in Mexico City" and who also appeared with Agnes Moorehead in *The Conqueror*, passed away.

JUNE 24, 1971

Episode #211, "The Corsican Cousins" (December 10, 1970)

JULY 1, 1971

Episode #210, "Samantha's Old Man" (December 3, 1970)
The day before, Agnes Moorehead appears in *What's the Matter with Helen*.

Two days later, Jim Morrison, the lead singer of the Doors, is found dead in a bathtub in Paris. He was only twenty-seven years old. Renie Riano also passed away. She played Mrs. Granite in Season Two's "Follow That Witch" part two.

Hogan's Heroes would end its six year run on CBS on July 4. Bernard Fox was a recurring guest as the bumbling Colonel Crittenden and has cited that it was his favorite role.

Four days later, the official voting age in the U.S. is lowered from twenty-one to eighteen.

JULY 8, 1971

Episode #212, "Samantha's Magic Potion" (December 17, 1970)

Two days later the National Women's Political Caucus was formed and co-founder Gloria Steinem delivered an Address to the Women of America in which she spoke of revolution for the races and sexes, and the hope of a society that is based on humanism, where the roles of people will not be defined by their race or sex, but what they chose or earn.

JULY 15, 1971

Episode #214, "Mother-in-Law of the Year" (January 14, 1971)

JULY 22, 1971

Episode #215, "Mary the Good Fairy, Part 1" (January 21, 1971)

Three days before, the second tower of the World Trade Center is completed at 1,362 feet, making it the second tallest building in the world.

JULY 29, 1971

Episode #216, "The Good Fairy Strikes Again, Part 2" (January 28, 1971)

AUGUST 5, 1971

Episode #217, "The Return of Darrin the Bold" (February 4, 1971)

The next night, a lunar eclipse lasting one hour, forty minutes and one second was observed.

AUGUST 12, 1971

Episode #218, "The House Uncle Arthur Built" (February 11, 1971)

The day before, construction began on the Louisiana Super Dome in New Orleans.

AUGUST 19, 1971

Episode #224, "Out of the Mouths of Babes" (March 25, 1971)

AUGUST 26, 1971

Episode #226, "Samantha's Magic Mirror" (April 8, 1971)

Three days earlier, Oliver McGowan, who played Mr. Harding in Season Two's "Junior Executive," as well as Mr. Waterhouse in "The Girl with the Golden Nose" passed away.

SEPTEMBER 2, 1971

Episode #228, "Samantha and the Antique Doll" (April 22, 1971)

SEPTEMBER 9, 1971

Instead of airing a *Bewitched* rerun, ABC aired a rerun of the hour and half long pilot of *Alias Smith and Jones*. Up to this point, *Bewitched* had aired Thursday evenings, at 8:30 PM EST, but as it started to slip in the ratings, ABC began advertising that, for the Eighth Season, *Bewitched* would air Wednesdays at 8:00 PM EST beginning September 15. They would replace it with *Alias Smith and Jones*. Unfortunately, CBS also decided to start airing the Fifth Season of *The Carol Burnett Show* at the same time on Wednesday nights.

Two days before, CBS aired the last *The Beverly Hillbillies* after nine seasons as part of their rural purge.

The day after, ABC aired *That Girl* for the last time. It had been on for six seasons.

Stay tuned for the season premiere of *Bewitched*, next week!

Season 8

SEPTEMBER 15, 1971

Bewitched fans were excited for the return of our show on a new night, Wednesdays at 8:00 PM EST with Episode #229: "How Not to Lose Your Head to Henry VIII," Part One.

Elizabeth Montgomery greeted us with all new longer haired look in a brown dress inviting us "to stayed tuned for *Bewitched*" at which point she snapped her fingers and disappeared! Yet another proof that Liz really WAS a witch!

We see that we are in London, England by the visuals of Big Ben and a double decker bus. Apparently, Durwood and Samantha are on vacation in England and are getting ready to go for a tour of the Tower of London.

During the tour, while the group is stopped in a hall of paintings, Samantha's attention is captured by the painting of a nobleman on a horse, who is whispering to her! Luckily, Durwood isn't paying attention and, as the tour group moves on, Samantha stays behind and asks the nobleman, named Sir Herbert Wellingford, what's the big idea of causing a scene. He apologizes, but tells her that she's the first witch that has taken the tour in centuries and he felt she could help him. Apparently, he is a warlock who was found cheating on his wife, Malvina, and as punishment, she banished him to be stuck in the painting for a thousand years. Samantha feels that he's served enough time and zaps him out of the painting. As he's kissing her hand, Durwood returns wondering what's going on, and he's furious that she's defaced a national treasure. When they hear the tour group returning, Durwood goes to stall them while Samantha deals with Herbie. Malvina pops in furious that Samantha reversed her curse. Not thinking that Malvina would still be mad, Samantha zaps Herbie back into the painting thinking that will be the end of that. However, Malvina feels that Samantha should be punished and who better to punish her than the woman hating Henry VIII!

Samantha arrives just as the fifth wife of Henry VIII, Catherine, has lost her head, and not her temper.

After Samantha has gone back to Henry VIII's time, Durwood comes back looking for her and finds that she and Herbie are gone. Not knowing what to do, he calls Endora and explains the situation.

Back in Hampton Court, Samantha follows a traveling group of troubadours into the castle, who are there to entertain the King, who is now in a terrible mood. They find that Samantha isn't sure of who she is, or what talent she has, though she recalls playing a lute when she was little.

In the present, Durwood meets up with Endora at Herbie's painting, where she has been conversing with the Nobleman and tells Durwood that Samantha has been sent back to the year 1542 to the court of Henry VIII.

And speaking of the King, as he and his court dine, Samantha is brought in to play the lute and she begins to sing capturing the attention of the newly single King. He has the Chamberlain invite her up to sit with him at dinner. When he asks her name, she says she doesn't know, however, he's not deterred and invites her to take the late Catherine's place. Samantha respectfully declines, saying, that unlike Catherine, she'd like to retain her voice.

Back in the present, Endora tells Durwood that in order to be rescued, he'll have to go back to give Samantha a kiss, as she no longer has her memory, nor her powers. She swaps his clothes with that of the peasant's in Herbie's painting (because she thought that was more suitable for Durwood than Herbie's clothing) and, after mistakenly zapping Durwood to the time of Henry I, she brings him back and gives him a gold talisman that he can use to call on her for help by putting it between his teeth, flap his arms and quack like a duck. And with that, she zaps him back to the correct Henry's time.

Meanwhile, Samantha has found the troubadours and desires to join them, but when the King shows up to congratulate them on their great show, he sends them away and tells Samantha that he would like her to stay and that perhaps he will make her his wife. Samantha refuses as he doesn't have a great "wife expectancy." Seeing she has a strong will, he tells her he'll make her a lady-in-waiting.

How will nice little Samantha escape the clutches of Henry VIII? Stay tuned next week for Part Two of "How Not to Lose Your Head to Henry VIII!"

I would rate this at three stars. It would've got more, but Elizabeth Montgomery, for the first time ever on the series, looks old and tired. I wonder what happened during that break, between Seasons Seven and Eight, because it definitely added a lot of years to her. My goodness, she's only thirty-eight, but she looks closer to forty-eight.

Anyway, I've always liked this episode mainly for Liz singing. She looks a little smug to me, as she may have really been singing the words to Bill Asher, who was being a philanderer…"oh, never leave me, oh don't deceive me, how could you use a poor maiden so?" Maybe it was around this time that she had found out about his affairs, if she already hadn't.

I like that they specifically mention the day that Samantha was supposed to have been zapped to…well, the year (1542) and that it was on the day of Catherine's death, February 13, but it most certainly didn't look like February in Britain.

I love Malvina! She was one of the cooler guest witches. I agree with the *Bewitched* Critic that she looked like a Tim Burton character. Quite frankly, I think it would've been cool iff'n Tim Burton had directed the *Bewitched* movie.

I wish I knew if that painting of the Nobleman is real. Bob, one of the webmasters of *HarpiesBizarre.com*, said a while ago that he had seen it somewhere online and foolishly didn't save the place and now he can't find it. I've looked, too, and never found it, which I think would explain why anytime there were any changes to the painting it looked different 'cause they just didn't match the original.

And other than Ronald Long's height, I thought he made a very good Henry VIII. And did you notice that wheel of cheese? In fact that's something I've always noticed…it's almost bigger than him!

The court jester seemed really creepy to me and I wished he hadn't been in the episode at all.

I liked that Agnes Moorehead's friend Laurie Main was in the episode as the tour guide. I always think of his joke, "Be like a banana and stick with the bunch!"

I wonder if there are various other commercials out there touting the European vacation that we haven't seen other than the "Witches have strange friends…" commercial. Because I think we should've at least had a brief scene at first at home where they mention going on a vacation and Larry giving Durwood crap and then they finally go.

The opening credits were altered only by having an announcer read the name of Elizabeth Montgomery and the title of the show. This was also the first time that there wasn't sponsor openings. Also this season, Bill Asher and Liz formed a production company called Ashmont Productions, using the first syllables of their last names, and it was credited as producing the show. It was AWESOME that Sony included the Liz intro and the "Be Right Back" bumper on the DVDs! Liz actually looks happy and refreshed in the intros, yet it seems like they were filmed the same day as "Eight Year Itch Witch" which is NOT how she will act in that episode. But back to this episode…

…I should like to chalk this episode up as almost a double remake of both "Samantha Goes South for a Spell" and a little of "Samantha's Hot Bedwarmer." You will notice as the season goes on that almost half the episodes are remakes. But even if that's the case, you still get a good episode like this one.

It was also on this night that Agnes Moorehead appeared on *The Smith Family* in "The Anniversary."

Four days before, *Sabrina the Teenage Witch*, based on the Archie Comics character, debuted on CBS Saturday morning. Over on ABC,

Lidsville, *The Funky Phantom*, and *The Jackson Five*, all debuted. Two nights later *McMillan & Wife* debuted on NBC starring Rock Hudson and Susan Saint James.

SEPTEMBER 22, 1971

It was on this night that ABC aired Episode #230: "How Not to Lose Your Head to Henry VIII," Part Two.

Being a new Lady-in-Waiting to Henry VIII, Samantha is kept near the King, who requests that she play the lute and sing for him as she did when he met her. Outside in the courtyard, Durwood hears her singing and is asked by the Chamberlain to put away his horse. Durwood asks who the voice belongs to and is told the possible future wife of the King. The Chamberlain leaves to go present the King with the late Queen's jewels and Durwood sneaks in behind. He bumps into a servant bringing a pastry tray to the King and tells him that he is requested down in the kitchens and that he'll deliver the tray. After the Chamberlain has presented the jewels to the King, Durwood requests to speak to the King, privately, about the reaction of the people to the demise of the late Queen. Durwood is left alone with Samantha and he is disheartened to find that Endora was right about her not remembering him. He tells her that if he kisses her it'll all come back, but she refuses. He insists, but she yells that he un-hand her, which captures the attention of the King and Chamberlain, and before the King goes to stab Durwood, the Chamberlain stops him as he says it may inflame the people more after the events of the morning. The King agrees and demands that Durwood be taken to the dungeon.

In the dungeon, Durwood breaks out the talisman and starts flapping and quaking like a duck to call on Endora, who appears outside his cell claiming to not have any powers as she hasn't been born yet, therefore, she'll have to secure the keys with her ingenuity. She calls for the jailer and tells him that she's been asked by the King to come inspect the dungeons and she is appalled that she found Durwood with a gold talisman as he could use the chain as a weapon. As she speaks, she swings the talisman back and forth and puts the jailer into a deep sleep. She also finds that she's put Durwood to sleep and she shakes him awake and releases him from his cell with the keys.

Up in the castle, the court is having a masked ball and Endora and Durwood show up with masks. Endora finds Samantha and introduces herself as a friend of her mother's. Samantha is excited that this strange woman will know who she is, however, Endora tells her that her memory will come back if she kisses the young man that came in with her. Samantha is repulsed and tells him to leave her alone. The King notices this and is angry that Durwood escaped and says that Durwood will be beheaded. Endora stops him and tells the King that it may be more fun to have a wrestling match with Durwood for the hand of Samantha, and as the King is the Champion Wrestler of the British Isles, he agrees. Durwood is scared but Endora says that once Samantha sees that Durwood is hurt, she'll definitely give him a kiss. The match goes as planned and Durwood falls to the floor. Samantha is furious with the King and gives Durwood a kiss immediately restoring her memory. When the King sees all this, he has no time to object as Endora grabs Samantha and Durwood and in a huge wind they pop out.

Back in the present, Endora switches Durwood's clothes back and they find that Herbie has an eye for Endora, which she reciprocates by taking him home with her. Durwood is furious that the painting is now without a rider, but Samantha fixes it by zapping in a new title plate — "The Missing Horseman."

I'd give this three and a half stars, most of them going in the direction of Agnes Moorehead and, I hate to admit it, Dick Sargent. Both seemed like they were having fun and that whole scene when Durwood quacks to get Endora and then she puts him to sleep with the amulet are hysterical! And Endora telling the guard, "I am APPALLED" and her post-hypnotic suggestion are funny as well!

I did like Liz singing to Henry VIII while he's scarfing down the chicken or whatever it was. I loved her facial expressions.

I've always thought that Endora was just playing around with Durwood telling him 1) that she wasn't born yet and 2) that she didn't have her powers. I think she told him that she was powerless just to see him sweat a little and maybe for her own comfort, to see just exactly how much he'd fight for her daughter. All of us know that she's over one thousand years old (at least she admits to a thousand like Serena said in "Mrs. Stephens, Where Are You?") so her saying she wasn't born yet was just a joke, in my opinion.

Here are some of my favorite lines:

> HENRY VIII *(in reference to the jewels):* *"It'll all be yours, my Lovely."*
> SAMANTHA: *"But I've done nothing to deserve this!"*
> HENRY VIII: *"You will!"*

SAMANTHA: *"Why did he call me 'Sam?'"*

HENRY VIII: *"I don't know but for that alone we should have him beheaded!"*

ENDORA: *"Getting to Samantha is no problem but trying to convince her that you'd make a better husband than Henry VIII doesn't make too much sense. I hope I can do it without CHOKING on the words..."*

The same night, Agnes Moorehead guest starred on *Night Gallery* in an episode appropriately titled "Witches Feast."

Two days before, James Westerfield passed away. He played Mr. Farley in Episode #208: "Samantha's Old Salem Trip." He was also in *The Magnificent Ambersons* (1942) and *Since You Went Away* (1944) with Agnes Moorehead, and in *Cowboy* (1958) with Dick York.

SEPTEMBER 29, 1971

It was on this night that ABC aired Episode #231: "Samantha and the Loch Ness Monster."

Durwood and Samantha have moved their vacation to Inverness, Scotland to visit Durwood's cousin Robbie, who runs a hotel on the shores of the famous Loch Ness, famous because of the Monster that reportedly lives in it. While having a picnic on the shores of the Loch, Robbie tells them that business has been very bad because the Monster hasn't shown himself in a couple years. Durwood says the reason for that is because there is no monster but just as he says that, they are startled by a loud roaring, which is coming from a long necked, truly hideous, monster in the Loch! Both Durwood and Robbie faint, but Samantha goes up to the water's edge and, calling the Monster 'Bruce,' tells him to settle down as he's making a spectacle of himself and that she doesn't know where Serena is. She goes back to tend to her husband and his cousin who have come out of their faint after Bruce has slipped back into the water. Robbie is ecstatic and goes off to spread the news of the Monster's return.

The next day at breakfast, Robbie introduces Sam and Durwood to the Baron Von Fuchs, who has come to photograph the Monster in his mini-submarine. However, they find that his real intent is to capture the Monster so that he can get the million dollar reward that Boyd's of London is offering, and he will do it at the expense of the Monster's life. Samantha is offended and excuses herself to her room. Durwood follows her up to the room confused by her reaction until she reveals that the reason she is so upset is that the Monster is one of Serena's ex-boyfriends that she turned into a monster when he was behaving like one centuries ago. She says she'll call Serena in to reverse her spell so that Bruce won't be captured. Serena has trouble at first remembering who Bruce is, but when Samantha tells her where she is, it all comes

Serena meets up with her old boyfriend, Bruce, the Loch Ness Monster.

back and she agrees to go take a walk on the lake to find Bruce. Durwood ix-nays the lake walking and says they'll get to the middle of the lake in a boat and he and Samantha will accompany her to make sure she does her task.

When they have paddled to the middle of the lake, Serena pops below water and finds Bruce's groovy under sea pad. After drying off, she tells him that she's come to prevent his capture, but it's up to him whether he wants to become a warlock again. He agrees and she changes him back, much to his delight. He also tells her he has a little toast for her that he's been rehearsing for when he would meet up with her again. It starts out sweet but when he gets to the end, he zaps her legs into a mermaid tail! Exacting his revenge, Bruce pops out to find a witch to get cozy with after all that time.

Up on the surface, Durwood wonders what is taking so long until he is interrupted by a holler, and when they look out in the distance, they see Serena swimming at super-fast speed toward them. She asks for help getting into the boat and they are shocked to see that she has a fish tail! Serena suggests they get her back to the hotel so that they can think of something to do to get her out of her predicament, and Samantha zaps them back.

Back in the hotel, Serena is moping and Samantha decides that she'll just have to zap Bruce in, and does so, taking him from the tango contest he was in. He is tickled to see Serena so put out and he tells her that it'll take about forty years for him to forgive her, so until then he'll get back to his tango. Before Samantha can zap him back, they hear Robbie coming in and they cover Serena's tail. He tells them that there are news crews coming in from all over and that it's going to provide the most advertising the Loch has had in years. After he shares the news, he runs off and Samantha decides that she'll play to Bruce's ego by saying that maybe Serena the Mermaid can take the place of the Loch Ness Monster. Bruce thinks that's ridiculous, but as Serena excitedly talks up her new show, he realizes she may be right. He admits that he wasn't much of a warlock in the first place, and so he zaps Serena's legs back and she zaps him back to the lake in his monster form.

Later on, Durwood and Samantha are on the edge of the lake again when a ruffled Baron comes tromping up out of the water, having been attacked by Bruce.

It's hard to rate this episode unless I do it in sections, because it's actually one of my favorites. So for acting: maybe two and a half stars, script:

two, and props: probably zero, if that! The guy who made the monster suit should be shot and boiled in his own pudding! And Bill Asher should also be boiled in pudding for allowing it to happen in the first place! Had they never heard of Jim Henson? Of course, Jim was two years deep into *Sesame Street* at the time, but still! And that mermaid tail...holy cow! It looks like they picked it up at K-mart on the Halloween clearance rack. But that monster is embarrassing.

Anyway, Liz looks like literal hell at the first of the episode: her hair looks like fine straw and what the hell is with her not wearing a bra?! Liz said during the filming of the opening scene, she was smoking and an ash fell on her blouse, starting it on fire, and as she was about to take it off when she realized the whole crew was looking at her and she would've been naked, so she just patted it out. What was she thinking?!

Cousin Robbie is irritating! It's stupid that Durwood would have a cousin so Scottish. His hair also looks very unkempt, but I guess that's the '70s for you.

The scene up in the Inn room where Samantha is sitting with her face on her hands seems to be a good indication of how Liz was feeling about the whole thing, and WOWSA at that dress! She looked pretty good in those scenes. But she just seemed bored and then Serena pops in and it's like Liz is a whole new woman, rejuvenated and ready to rock. I also liked her greeting to Durwood — "Hello talk, dark, and NOTHING!"

I've also noticed that when Melody is playing Sam, her hair is much more flat and greasy looking.

I think Serena's walking under water scene is really cool. When I was younger, I was shocked that she could stay under water so long, but seeing it now, I realize Liz wasn't really under water. I wonder though, why doesn't Brucie's groovy little undersea pad fill up with water when he opens the hatch?

Steve Franken (Bruce) mentioned that this was his favorite role on *Bewitched* at the 2008 *Bewitched* Fanfare which made me happy as it's my favorite of his episodes. This would also be his last episode.

I noticed a "new" scene that seems to never be shown on TV and that's when they have the Mermaid Serena back at the Inn and Samantha asks her to try and remember the spell Bruce used and she says: "Witch Serena, sweet and frail, I'd like to grab you by the t..."

And it seemed like the Bernie Kopell had just pulled out his old Siegfried schtick to play the Baron Von Fuchs, but it was still funny. And I kept thinking, when his character was introduced, of the Beatles' "Yellow Submarine!"

All in all, I guess it's really a bad episode, but I love it because it's so CORNY I could die! That line from Serena was an impromptu line from Liz, which I would say sums up how she feels about this whole last season. I'm glad Bill Asher kept it in.

> SERENA: *"You really should see a skin doctor."*
> BRUCE: *"I happen to have a little witch in the neighborhood who cares a great deal about me."*
> SERENA: *"Ohhh...how is your mother?"*

Two days later, Walt Disney World opened its doors in Orlando, Florida.

OCTOBER 6, 1971

It was on this night that ABC aired Episode #232: "Samantha's Not-So-Leaning Tower of Pisa."

Durwood and Samantha have moved their work vacation to Pisa, Italy, where their villa has a nice view of the famous Leaning Tower. While they are admiring it, they hear the phone ringing, however, it's not the phone, but the lamp! Esmeralda has called from home using a spell she cast on the phone, but of course, it went awry. Soon the connection fails, and as Samantha tries to call her back on the actual phone, Durwood shows her that it's pointless as Esmeralda has shown up in the villa! She tells them that Hagatha is watching the children now and Esmeralda had wanted to tell them about the vase she broke when trying to putting out the curtains that a dinosaur had caught on fire! When Samantha asks how that possibly could've happened, Esmeralda tells her that Tabitha and her friend Dinah were arguing and Esmeralda told Tabitha not to make Dinah sore—get it, dinasaur? Esmeralda had used a vase full of water to put out the curtains and the vase slipped. Samantha dismisses it as an accident and Esmeralda says that Pisa is the last place she'd want to go as she is the one responsible for the leaning of the Tower! She had been dating the architect of the Tower, Bonano Pisano, and she said he was quite angry when it all happened. Before Durwood can get all bent out of shape, he drags Samantha out on the patio to tell her to get Esmeralda back home. But as Esmeralda is so depressed, Samantha doesn't think she'll be much use in watching the kids and asks Durwood if Esmeralda can stay until she feels better. Before he can object, he hears Larry come in with the client, Count Bracini. He is shocked to see Esmeralda but Count Bracini is smitten with her (really?!) and when he asks her to accompany him on a tour of the sites, she gets nervous and begins to fade. Luckily, Samantha diverts the Count to the patio to tell him how much she loves his olive oil and Durwood draws Larry's attention away to explain Esmeralda's presence. Soon, Esmeralda fades back in and the group go out to visit the Tower, however, they all decide to just do lunch instead.

Liz goofing off with Alice Ghostley during the filming of this episode.

Back at the villa, Samantha is ecstatic that Esmeralda has found someone so smitten by her, especially since the Count asks Esmeralda out on a date for that evening. Esmeralda is pleased too, however, she still feels bad about the tower. Meanwhile, Larry is upset that the Count has no time to discuss the new campaign and so Durwood suggests while they pass time waiting for the Count to drop off Esmerlda off later that evening, they can find something to watch on TV. When Samantha leaves Esmeralda by herself for a moment, the nervous witch decides she'll right her wrong and casts a spell to set the tower straight. Amid a bunch of shaking, the tower does right itself just as Samantha catches her doing it. Furious that Esmeralda has essentially ruined a national treasure, she insists that Esmeralda undo it. Esmeralda can't understand why everyone would rather have it lean but she also doesn't remember how she got it to lean in the first place.

Soon, the country is an uproar about the tower righting itself and Durwood and Larry's TV movie is interrupted for a news report. Larry is sick knowing that the trouble with the tower will now occupy the Count's time. Durwood demands an explanation as he knows it had to be witchcraft, but Samantha tells him that he'll need to occupy Larry while she works on Esmeralda. Wracking her brain, Esmeralda can't remember what the spell was though she admits she had brought Bonano his lunch. It occurs to Samantha that if they fly back to that time, Esmeralda would be more prone to remember, so after zapping herself and Esmeralda into period clothing, she takes them back to that day. They find Bonano in the midst of plastering the inner walls and when Esmeralda tells him she forgot his lunch, he requests that she get him a tower sandwich with lean meat. Esmeralda casts a spell for "one tower, and make it lean!" Of course, the Tower obliges, and when it's finished its leaning with a shower of rocks, Samantha takes them back to the present.

The Count shows up to break off his date with Esmeralda as he is going to fly to Rome to discuss what damages may have been done to the Tower, but when Larry shows him the corrected Tower, thinking it will persuade him to stay, the Count says it's even more important that he leave to find out what damage all that movement may have caused the Tower.

A little later, the Count returns with the good news that the Tower has been found to be stronger than ever and he invites the group to his place to celebrate.

This one is painful! Any time someone tells me how much they hate *Bewitched*, I always think it's because they must've just watched this one and are basing their opinion of the show on it. And why isn't called "Esmeralda's Not-So-Leaning Tower of Pisa?" Did Liz possibly insist that everything be about her? Or were the writers just lazy and figured the show is about Samantha so the tower may as well be hers? Same thing goes for last episode which should've been titled "Serena and the Loch Ness Monster" or just "Warlock Bruce of Loch Ness Fame" or something like that.

Anyway, back to this episode…I think Liz looks much better than she has in the previous episodes this season. I like the curl to her hair and I do like her outfits, but they are not age appropriate. She looks groovy, but she's a mother of three and doesn't need to look groovy. But, my goodness, attitude! She actually seems like she was going to hit Esmeralda, and a couple times, she did with her elbow! But, really, do we blame her? I do not think Esmeralda has been any more irritating than she is in this episode what with all her groans and her weird "I-have-to-poop-and-it-hurts" faces. And what in the HELL does Count Bracini see in her? He's probably crazy, which explains the walking stick he carries around, yet never leans on.

And the fade-ins/outs are truly horrible. It's like they didn't even care to try and match it, they were just hurrying through as fast as they could, which they probably were on account of how tense it must've felt on the set with Liz and Bill Asher, who surprisingly has directed all these Europe episodes. I'm wondering if Liz is bra-less just to piss him off because she's being so blatant about trying to put herself out there with all the other men on the set? I wish she were around to tell the story. Honestly, one of the questions I would've asked her is to describe her mood and feelings during the last season and maybe show her some clips from these Eighth Season episodes and ask her about those specific times.

We should've known from the very first scene this was going to be a horrible episode what with Liz's stupid line about "if you lean this way everything else looks like it's leaning." It almost felt like an impromptu line that, to me, conveys that Liz wasn't even focused on the task at hand.

I don't even want to talk about the cardboard tower. How in the world could they have felt that was a good idea?! And yet there are fans that INSIST the Eighth Season had the biggest budget of all and that the quality of the show hadn't waned in the least. If the budget was the biggest, ALL of it was being funneled to Liz's bank account and her Louis Vitton purses and not to the sets, the writers nor the props department.

I will have to say that I did think it was cool that they somehow placed the interior tower set on some sort of platform that could rock, because didn't it really look like the floor was tilting? Of course, the walls looked like they were going to tear because they were just paper but it was kind of cool. I thought the whole sandwich thing was absolutely stupid. They should've said she made it lean some other way, like possibly zapping up a non-fire breathing dinosaur that leaned against the tower or something.

That scene outside with the whole crew and Liz and David White in sunglasses was new to me and it made me sad because, anytime I've seen Liz in sunglasses, it was during the later 70s or other times where she seemed to be pissed off, so I guess this where it all started.

I didn't understand her lame joke about "Hello Esmeralda, arrivederci Roma." What did that have to do with anything, especially considering they stayed in Pisa/Rome for the next episode?

Anyway, the whole situation with Liz's attitude, the writers, and the sets is just ill-making considering what a bright shining example of a superb show this once was. Super fan Sharon Orazi pointed out that there are so many quotes from this episode that sum up the demise of this show:

> ESMERALDA: *"I did it, I'm cured!"*
> SAMANTHA: *"You're cured, but I'm SICK!"* (As are we all…)
> COUNT BRACINI: *"Who knows how the Tower is suffering as the result of these changes?"* (Who knows how the audience is suffering as a result of these changes?)
> SAMANTHA: *"It doesn't look like it's suffering to me."* (Oh, but it IS, Sam…)
> LARRY: *"Not half as much as I am."* (I hear ya, Larry…)

OCTOBER 13, 1971

It was on this night that ABC aired Episode #233: "Bewitched, Bothered, and Baldoni."

When Durwood has a business appointment in Rome, Samantha decides to accompany him so that after the meeting, they can get in a little site seeing and they go to a museum where they see beautiful statues of Venus and Adonis. They break off from the group and as they are admiring a collection of dolls, they discover that Endora is one of the dolls! She claims that the children had wanted spaghetti so she thought she would get them authentic Italian spaghetti and that she would kiss their parents for them, though she balks at Durwood. He decides that it's time for him to leave for his meeting and so he leaves them, but Endora notices that his head turns when a beautiful woman happens by him. Knowing her mother has an ulterior motive, Samantha demands to know what it is and Endora tells her that she wanted to watch over Durwood as he is in the romantic city of Rome where he would most definitely be tempted by the beautiful women. Samantha thinks that's ridiculous and takes her leave. Wanting to prove her point, Endora decides that she'll tempt Durwood with a woman that is truly irresistible and she brings to life the statue of Venus and replaces the missing statue with a covered sheet. After zapping Venus into modern clothes, Endora tells her what she would like her to do.

Later, while Durwood is sitting at an outdoor café, Venus pops in when he goes to pick up a fork that had magically slipped off the table. Durwood is immediately smitten and Vanessa (what Venus calls herself) asks if he would like to accompany her on a tour of the non-tourist Rome. Durwood says he has a business meeting but he can't resist her and so they spend the afternoon together.

Back at the villa, Larry barges in wondering where Durwood was as he didn't show up to the meeting. Samantha isn't sure until Durwood comes in saying that he met an Italian and as the client, Mr. Baldoni, and his wife were going to be staying with them in their villa, he felt it would be OK to miss the meeting. He also says that Vanessa is need of employment and suggests that she become their maid, even though the villa has a staff of four. Durwood says that he's already invited her and retrieves her from outside. When she comes in, Larry is immediately smitten and forgets his anger towards Durwood as he can't take his eyes off Vanessa. Samantha reluctantly tells Vanessa she can stay and help with the housekeeping and gives her an apron to put on. Knowing that her mother must have something to do with Vanessa's effect on the men, she hollers for Endora who sends a note on a flaming bolt telling her that she told her mother knows best. Just then Durwood comes in wanting to know if Samantha is irritated with him but she tells him no, that she's more irritated with her mother but she is interrupted when Vanessa knocks on the door asking to show them how she looks in the apron. Samantha asks her to come in and about faints when she sees that Vanessa is wearing JUST the apron! She asks Vanessa to go put on more clothes and then asks Durwood if he can't see that there is something definitely wrong with Vanessa. Of course, Durwood is in so much pleasurable shock, he can't think straight.

That evening the Baldonis arrive and when Vanessa enters the room, Mr. Baldoni falls under her spell, much to the irritation of his wife. A phone call soon comes in for him and it's not good news. It was from the Director of the National Museum for which Baldoni is on the Board of Trustees and they have just discovered that the statue of Venus has been stolen! Samantha realizes who Vanessa is now and Vanessa confirms it with a knowing look. Samantha runs up to her room and calls on Endora again but Endora only sends another reminder that she knows best. When Durwood shows up, Samantha tells him what's going on and she says that she needs to make a quick trip to Rome to solve the problem.

Samantha smiles at the soon-to-be living statue of Adonis.

She ends up at the museum and brings the statue of Adonis to life and, after updating his clothing, she zaps them back to the Villa. When Venus sees Adonis, whom Samantha introduces as Alberto, she is immediately in love with him again. Mrs. Baldoni is also in love which causes Mr. Baldoni to be quite jealous and they get in an argument. While Larry tries to calm the Baldonis, Samantha drags the lovers out to the patio and calls on her mother, who finally shows up. The two witches zap the lovers back into stone however, they are now holding hands. Samantha is upset but Endora reminds her that everyone will just chalk it up to one more miracle in the enchanted city of Rome and she zaps them back to the museum.

This one is much better than the previous episode, but I'd go only about a two and a half stars and that's 'cause they're using the same old sets (did you notice the museum was actually the Tower of London from the Henry VIII episodes?) and a little bit of the same bit from last episode where the client is involved with the crazy goings on a la Mr. Baldoni just happening to be on the board of directors for the museum just like Count Bracini was involved with the Tower of Pisa. Plus there are two scenes involving hair being totally different that should not have happened if they were truly paying attention. When Sammy zaps Adonis to life, he has no chest hair whatsoever, which I've always thought was weird considering one always thinks of men in the 70s flaunting their chest hair with their unbuttoned shirts and gold necklaces, but then again, he was supposed to be a statue, so it made sense. Well, what do you know, when they get back to the Villa he's suddenly sprouted a full chest of hair! Which means they probably filmed the Villa scenes first and then decided he should be clean shaven for the statue zapping scene. The other that I've ALWAYS noticed is at the end when Sammy and Endora are out on the patio. I've always loved Liz's wavy long hair in this episode when suddenly it goes to straight and blah in her close ups!

Liz seemed to have a lot more energy and seemed to really enjoy herself probably 'cause she FINALLY got a male co-star that was truly handsome and worthy of Bill Asher's jealousy, not to mention he was half naked for part of it. But then again she didn't truly "win" because Bill had the GORGEOUS Francine York pretty much naked! I'm surprised they got away with it, but PLEASED they got away with it because it was awesome and funny! I love it when Liz says, "When I said go put on an apron, I didn't mean JUST an apron. Please go out and change… BACKWARDS!" I thought Francine York looked very much like a red-headed Barbara Eden. Now that would've been awesome! Of course, Liz would've never allowed it, but still. I also liked Vanessa's look when Mr. Baldoni has found out about the disappearance of the Venus statue and she looks at Liz like, "yeah, that's me."

Did you notice just how BIG that cook was compared to Liz? Like four or five times her size! I'll bet when the actress that played the cook saw that scene she wanted to die!

According to Shemp over at *HarpiesBizarre.com*, "Almost all the real European film footage was originally filmed for the James A. FitzPatrick TravelTalk short subjects released by MGM in the 1930s/40s. (The FitzPatrick shorts are frequent fare on TCM.)"

I really liked the Baldonis, especially Mrs. Baldoni. She was funny.

I didn't like that the statues were left holding hands even if Endora said, "What's one more mystery in the enchanted city of Rome?" It would've just been too much for the mortals to handle. I'd like to think that Samantha just popped over to the museum and zapped them back to their original positions, though she acted like she wouldn't have been able to.

Dick Sargent did a fairly good job of acting like he was totally smitten with Vanessa. It made the scenes with him and her all the more funny knowing he WAS trying to act!

Of course, poor little Adam was AGAIN without parents for what would've been his second birthday.

Two days later Agnes Moorehead guest starred in the TV movie *Marriage: Year One*.

OCTOBER 20, 1971

It was on this night that ABC aired Episode #234: "Paris, Witches Style."

Now having business in Paris with Europa Tours, Samantha tells Durwood that it might be a good idea if they make a small trip back to London to visit her father as he'll be furious that Samantha didn't pay him a visit. Durwood tells her as he's leaving to go pick up some items from the printers that they'll visit him when they go back to London at the end of their trip. After he leaves, Endora pops in with the bad news that Maurice had shown up at Samantha's and was furious to find out that Samantha and Durwood hadn't come to visit him. She also says that Maurice is on his way to share his anger and, no sooner has she spoken it than Samantha sees the black smoke of her father cruising through the air straight for her hotel room! Maurice is indeed furious and accuses Durwood of being the reason that they didn't come to visit. He then busts out into an appropriate Shakespearean soliloquy. Meanwhile, Endora signals to Samantha to pay attention to the door and in walks Durwood, though Endora tells Samantha it's just a dummy Durwood, though not too different from the real thing. When Maurice sees the dummy Durwood, he stops but before he can lay into Durwood, Dummy Durwood tells Maurice what a pleasure it is to see him and that he's hearbroken over

Endora tries to stand up for Samantha to Maurice, who is hurt that Samantha didn't come to visit him.

Maurice spoiling the surprise. When Maurice asks what it is, Dummy Durwood tells him that he had commissioned a work from Pablo Picasso, a portrait of Maurice which he unveils. Maurice is impressed, though still mad. After Endora zaps the painting to hang over the mantle, Maurice asks to speak to Dummy Durwood alone so he can talk some sense into him. They go into the other room and Maurice tells him that his apologies are very demeaning and though he did have nerve not to come visit, he needn't make a fool of himself in the process. Dummy Durwood agrees but as Samantha listens in, she tells Endora that it's just too much and that they need to get Dummy Durwood out of there. Endora zaps him with hiccups and so Maurice offers to go get him a glass of water. After he leaves, the Dummy Durwood disappears. However, the real Durwood shows up and when he asks when Maurice got there, Maurice realizes there is something fishy. He asks how long Durwood has been there and when Durwood gets tired of the game he admits that he just arrived and that after he and Samantha had seen the sights of Paris, they were going to come visit. Now knowing the truth, Maurice tells Durwood that as he wants to see the sights he'll arrange it and immediately zaps Durwood away. Scared of what her father has done with her husband, Samantha demands to know where he is and Maurice zaps up a pair of binoculars and directs her to the window. When she looks out she is horrified to see Durwood stuck up towards the top of the Eiffel Tower! Samantha pleads with her father to bring him back but Maurice says he won't until Durwood has learned his lesson. Soon enough though, Durwood comes storming in, as he was rescued, and tells Maurice that he will not be bullied around. Maurice tells him that it takes courage, though he goes about breaking the lamps in the room with his anger and when he continues on his rant, he goes to look into a mirror that he's about to break. Discreetly, Endora zaps Durwood into a bust of Napoleon and puts him in the corner by the window. When Maurice turns around and sees Durwood is gone, he knows that Endora has done something with him and wants to know what. Endora claims she didn't do anything but Maurice says he'll find him and as he goes searching around the room, he suddenly turns toward the bust and bursts it into pieces! Samantha is horrified that her husband is now fallen apart and pleads with Maurice to return him back to one piece. Maurice half-heartedly attempts but it's of no use until Endora threatens to move back in with him. He goes to make another attempt and tells Durwood to pull himself together and simple as that, the pieces come flying back together and the bust turns back into Durwood.

Soon, Mr. Saigon of Europa Tours shows up as they are making plans to go to Maxim's for a celebration dinner but Durwood says that they'll have to postpone dinner. Mr. Saigon isn't impressed by Durwood's picture at the top of the Eiffel Tower, however, Maurice suggests its perfect advertising if they show an American Tourist hanging at the top of the Tower with the slogan "Europa Tours. Towers Above Them All." Mr. Saigon loves it and leaves the family so they can get ready for dinner.

I actually really enjoy this episode, even if it is a direct rip-off of "Just One Happy Family." I'd give it at least two stars. Liz looks better in this episode than she has in all the rest up to this point. And she actually seems to be in a better mood and Agnes Moorehead and Maurice Evans give great performances!

Speaking of Maurice Evans, this is the first time we've seen him since the middle of Season Six when he gave Durwood the magic watch. I really like Maurice.

Really, my only qualm with Samantha in this episode is that she pulls a total Jeannie when she sends the postcards to the kids. Really, she's going to pull that magic stuff right in that small cab for Gerald/Herbie to hear? And all though it does seem like Maurice's entrance at 1164 was reused, I don't believe it was because his car is usually driven by Herbie, but this time it's driving itself on account of Herbie getting another driving gig in "Paris." They should've shown Endora and Maurice's discussion at the house. I had hoped on the DVDs we'd get that scene.

I LOVE Maurice's smoky entrance into the "Paris" hotel! It showed that the special effects people were trying to broaden their horizons by experimenting with different effects. Unfortunately, when the smoke is supposed to be off in the distance, part of its tail whips around in front of the curtains and even more unfortunately, when the camera pulls back the smoke comes with it, but it was a good attempt. And it totally seems like the inspiration for the way the Death-Eaters in Harry Potter flew around in clouds of black smoke.

I rather like the Picasso Maurice! I wonder who has it now? I think it was a perfect choice because Picasso was the "in" thing at the time and Maurice definitely would've wanted one, especially one of himself, to stroke his ego. I'm sure Endora knew that Maurice would be so blinded by the gesture he wouldn't of even thought of the fact that how WOULD Picasso know what he looks like? It was lame, though, that Endora zapped it to the mantle as though Maurice was going to stay there. It would be interesting to know if Picasso did see this episode.

I think Maurice reciting Shakespeare is hysterical this time around… "Has not a father eyes? If you tickle us, do we not laugh?"

I would think that Durwood would've been thrown in jail for having "attempted" to climb the Eiffel Tower especially 'cause he's a dirty American.

Maurice blowing up the lamps totally scared me when it first happened. And, in contrast to "Just One Happy Family," Maurice Evans doesn't even flinch when it happens.

And I've always loved the scenes around Durwood getting turned into the bust. I love it when Maurice passes by it and then turns around, salutes, and says, "Mon General." I always thought it cool when the busted up pieces moved trying to get back together. I liked that they didn't JUST do the old tired reverse the film.

The end scene is just plain stupid. It's like they realized, "Oh, dammit! We forgot to include the scene with the client!" Why not just leave the client out of the whole thing?

According to the filming schedules, this is the last of the Europe episodes to be filmed though there is one more to be shown. They also filmed all of Maurice's three episodes from this season in a row. I think that Liz looks better and acts better here because Maurice Evans is there. I think they were close and he probably provided a safe haven for her what with Bill Asher cavorting and all. Her being happy about Maurice Evans being there could be the reason that she looks so happy in those introductions as she's wearing the same brown dress that she wears at the end of this episode, but maybe I'm just reading into it.

Here are some of my favorite lines:

> ENDORA: *"Why not just say thank you for the gift?"*
> MAURICE: *"It's very hard to be gracious when you've worked yourself into a rage!"*
> DUMMY DURWOOD: *"I ordered a halo but Pablo must've forgot."*
> MAURICE: *"It's all very well to appreciate your parents, but you mustn't tear yourself down in the process."*
> MAURICE: *"Arise, thou miserable mortal, arise!"*
> SAMANTHA: *"Never mind the editorial comments!"*
> MAURICE: *"I've tried, I've tried, devil knows I've tried!...tis better to have tried and lost, than never to have tried at all."*

The day before, Agnes Moorehead guest starred in the TV movie *Suddenly Single*.

OCTOBER 27, 1971

It was on this night that ABC aired the last of the Europe episodes with Episode #235: "The Ghost Who Made a Spectre of Himself." And as it was about ghosts, it was quite appropriate for Halloween.

For the last leg of the European trip, Samantha and Durwood end up back in England, ready to head home as Durwood has given the Regal Silverware account to Larry. However, during packing, Larry shows up with Louise and tells the Stephenses that he has booked a weekend at the Duke of Whitzett's castle where they can relax and then on Monday, Larry and Durwood can meet with Regal Silverware. Durwood reminds Larry that they are going home but Larry won't hear of it and so they stay.

After arriving at the castle, they take a tour which ends with the hall of the ancestral portraits, including the black sheep of the family, Harry the Eighth Duke of Whitzett, who died in mortal combat after Lady Windemere's husband found her with Harry. While they are looking at the portraits, Samantha notices that one of the suits of armor that she was standing nearby has suddenly put its hand on her shoulder! She brushes it off, just chalking it up to an unusual, and possibly haunted, circumstance especially since they are told that Harry haunts the castle.

That night everyone is woken up by a spooky howling that Larry says is just done for the tourists. Meanwhile, Samantha can't sleep so she says she is going to go to the library to read. On her way there, she happens to find the ghost howling in a room, shaking his chains. She startles him and asks him to be quiet. He's surprised that she's not afraid of him but she tells him that it's because she's a witch. The ghost, who happens to be Harry, doesn't believe it until she levitates an axe off the wall to fall on the floor and then back up. The ever amorous Harry suggests that they fool around, however, Samantha reminds him that he's transparent, and she's married. She suggests he find a lady ghost and she heads back to bed where Durwood grabs her by the head and plants a huge kiss on her and won't let go. She realizes that it's not Durwood, but Harry, and she demands he leave Durwood's body! Harry refuses until he gets a kiss. She refuses and leaves. Larry and Louise hear the two fighting and come out to see what's going on. Samantha tells them that they just had a little disagreement but things are better now, but Louise can see that it's not, so she suggests Samantha stay with her and Larry stay with Durwood.

The next morning, Durwood and Larry greet them in the dining hall where Durwood apologizes, but Samantha doesn't accept causing Larry and Louise to worry. However, Samantha knows Harry is still inhabiting her husband's body and he has no intention of leaving. When the Duke comes to tell them about breakfast, he apologizes about the ghost and mentions how he's surprised the ghost doesn't get tired. Harry reminds him it's impossible for a ghost to get tired and when the Duke responds that it's nothing to get worked up about, especially over a stupid ghost, Harry gets belligerent. The Duke leaves and Larry asks Durwood why he's getting so upset, but Harry says he is going to go cool off out on the patio. Samantha goes to talk to him, but Louise tells her she will. When she is outside with him, Durwood starts making advances and asks her to go to the gardener's cottage with him. Realizing that Durwood mustn't be well, she comes back in and Samantha goes out to take care of the situation. She drags Durwood/Harry into the library and tells him that she's done dealing with him and that the only way Harry is going divert his attention from her is with a real live lady ghost, and so she zaps up Lady Windemere's ghost. Harry is quite pleased and steps out of Durwood's body and he and the Lady walk off into the afterlife. Just then Larry and Louise come in as Larry wants to teach Durwood a lesson about picking up on his wife, but Durwood is saved by the Duke coming in to announce breakfast. Samantha twitches her necklace to fall off and asks Durwood to help her put it back on while the others leave for breakfast. She tells him all about the ghost and how she thinks that they will explain Durwood's behavior. At breakfast, Samantha tells Larry and Louise that Durwood's plan seemed to have work and that was to make Larry see how overworked he was on the vacation. And with tempers settled, they settle into their kidney pie breakfast (blech!).

I'd give this episode two stars. Liz truly has a horrible attitude throughout this whole episode! My only guess is that she was acting in defiance to Bill Asher's possible fooling around/flirting with Francine York as "Bewitched, Bothered and Baldoni" finished filming just the week before.

For Louise to be Samantha's best friend, I thought it repulsive when Louise enters the room, Samantha doesn't even budge to give her a hug or anything. And to me it seemed like Kasey Rogers was expecting it and it didn't happen. Then later on, after Sam and the ghost have been fighting and Louise knocks on the door and asks if she can come in, Sam looks so disgusted and rolls her eyes, whereas if this same situation had happened in earlier seasons, Sam would've looked like she had just pricked herself, but in worry about how she was going to explain things.

The photos of Harry and Lady Windemere are laughable to say the least! You can totally tell they're photos and not paintings.

Kasey Rogers looks absolutely fabulous so for her to always be covered up is ridiculous but I definitely don't mind Liz being in the short nighties all the time.

There were two lines that could be taken multiple ways that were WAY funny. The first was:

SAMANTHA: *"If it's in Larry's lap, what is it doing in your mind?"*

And then this made me think that maybe Samantha FINALLY (after three years) realized that her husband was actually different:

HARRY VIA DURWOOD: *"Is that any way to treat your dear, beloved husband?"*
SAMANTHA: *"Yes, especially when you're not my dear, beloved husband!"*

That scene in the library, when Samantha levitates the axe, was new to me. I liked it.

The whole deal of being at the castle felt like a re-hash of movies that were done during the mid 60s, particularly *Munster, Go Home* (1966).

And Harry using "ducky" all the time irritated me! And how's about they were going to be served a hot breakfast at 11 O'CLOCK?! Good hell! I would be FAMISHED by then! Screw having a hot breakfast, just give me a crumpet or something!

I always wondered how it was that Harry could make his shackles disappear. He should've just asked Samantha to do it but, of course, we're in the Eighth Season and nobody cares anymore.

Anyway, I'm certainly glad this is the last of the "Europe" episodes. Here are some of my favorite lines:

LOUISE: *"That certainly is a ghost with a lot of spirit."*
LARRY: *"Louise, you're not at your best when you try humor."*
SAMANTHA: *"Lots of people don't believe in ghosts."*
HARRY: *"But they're quite wro-o-o-ng!"*
SAMANTHA: *"So are you-u-u-u."*

Three days later, on Halloween, Agnes Moorehead guest starred on *The Wonderful World of Disney* in "The Strange Monster of Strawberry Cove," Part One.

NOVEMBER 3, 1971

It was on this night that ABC aired Episode #236: "TV or Not TV."

While Tabitha and Adam are watching *Steamboat Bill* and the Punch and Judy puppet show sketch on the show, Tabitha notices that Adam is copying Punch's punching style as he starts hitting her. She thinks it's terrible that Punch would hit Judy and she decides to tell him, so she pops on over to the studio. Meanwhile, Durwood is watching the show, as he is in charge of the advertising for it, and about chokes when he sees Tabitha pop into the show. Tabitha tells Punch that she doesn't think it's very nice that he's so mean to Judy and she zaps up away his club. The director and the rest of the crew of the show are quite puzzled as to where this girl came from but go with it as it's a live production. Durwood calls Samantha and demands to know what Tabitha is doing on TV causing her to be ill thinking of what Tabitha could've possibly be doing and she goes into the den to tell Tabitha to get back pronto. Tabitha appears and tells her mommy that she didn't do anything to hurt anyone and asks why it is that Samantha sometimes does magic. Samantha tells her it's only to correct a catastrophe that Uncle Arthur or Esmeralda caused.

Over at McMann and Tate, Larry bursts in wanting to know who the girl was as the client, Mr. Silverton, had just called and was quite impressed with the girl and wants her back. Durwood says the producer just picked her out of the audience and they'd probably never find her again.

At home, Durwood gives Samantha an unjustified talking to about Tabitha until he is interrupted by Larry and kooky Mr. Silverton showing up. Mr. Silverton, a toy manufacturer, insists that everyone pull a pull string on his lapel in order to talk to him. They have come to tell Durwood their idea to find the mystery girl that has captured the hearts of people in TV land and whoever identifies her would be given a substantial cash prize. Before they can go any further, Tabitha comes down to give her parents a good night kiss and Mr. Silverton is thrilled knowing that Tabitha is the mystery girl. He asks Tabitha if she'd like to be the star of his TV show. She says she'd love to but Samantha tells her that they'll discuss it in the morning. Mr. Silverton wonders why Durwood would keep it a secret, and he says he came up with the idea so soon before the show that he didn't have time to audition any girls, so he decided to use Tabitha. Larry says Tabitha will be at the studio the next day, but Mr. Silverton insists everyone know that he's against nepotism, even for his own daughter being on his show, even though she's a fine actress. When Larry says he'll see Durwood the next day for auditions for a new girl, Mr. Silverton says there won't be auditions because Tabitha is it as his sense of profit is stronger than his sense of nepotism.

The next morning Samantha tells Durwood that Tabitha's star will be eclipsed before it even shines just as soon as she thinks of how it will be done. After Durwood leaves for work, Samantha casts a spell to find where the Silvertons dwell so that she can make sure that Mr. Silverton's daughter, Robin, gets the gig.

She appears invisibly at the Silvertons just as Mrs. Silverton is telling her husband that she is going to take Robin to the zoo, the museum, and then a movie. However, after he leaves, Samantha zaps Mrs. Silverton into deciding that instead she'll take Robin down to the TV studio.

At the studio, Tabitha soon becomes tired of the grind of television work and tells Samantha that she wants to quit. Samantha tells her she can't quit, however, she can make it so they let her go and she suggests that Tabitha flub her lines. Tabitha flubs perfectly, however, it drives the director nuts and just then Mrs. Silverton and Robin arrive. Samantha twitches Mr. Silverton into suggesting that Robin take over and she does a great job relieving Tabitha of her star duties.

I'd give this one and a half stars, maybe even less. It seems like the pacing in this one is really jerky and just weird. I liked that necklace Sam was wearing, but the dress was blah. And I really like that her hair looked better. That's on account of (with the exception of "Serena's Richcraft") this was the first episode filmed of the Eighth Season.

I noticed when Samantha is making the peanut butter jelly sandwiches that she puts the jelly on the peanut butter and that is silly! You'd mess up the knife, especially if you had to get more! But maybe we can chalk it up to one of those mortal things she just never got the hang of.

Did you notice Adam's shoes? They look like total girly shoes! And how's about the fact that in 1971 they had a 'CULLUH' TV in the den?! Durwood must've been really raking in the dough. And why can't the kids watch TV in the living room on the bigger TV?

Mr. Silverton is one of the most irritating clients ever! What's with having to pull his string to have him talk? Who the hell thought that little bit up? And it irritated me to no end to see him always look at Larry for encouragement.

The Silvertons looked much too old to be Kathy Richard's parents. And if you weren't aware, Kathy would grow up and become the mother of Paris Hilton! You can tell her how much you loved her performance in this episode on Twitter (*@KathyHilton*).

I liked that they harkened back to the GREAT old days of *Bewitched* by having Samantha sit atop a table lamp. I also liked the music they played while she was doing it. It seems to me that she hasn't been lamp sitting since that first time in the Halloween episode. And it was a great way to show off her legs.

I love how Diego says practically the same line, in the same way that he did in "Nobody's Perfect": "Wait 'til my analyst hears about this!"

It's getting so OLD for Durwood to blame Samantha for everything everyone else does concerning magic. And how about him saying "YOUR daughter is on television." What a jerk!

I did think Adam looked really cute and sweet! I just wish he hadn't been wearing those girl shoes!

I also thought it was funny that Mr. Silverton told his wife that Tabitha was such a pro at making the audience believe that she was talking to real people when she was just talking to puppets, as though she was the first to ever do it. Apparently, and this is ironic him being a toy sales man and all, he had never watched *Sesame Street* with Robin, when that show had been on the air for two years by this time and was a HUGE SUCCESS! And it was successful because they had managed to capture that magic of people interacting with puppets. And speaking of *Sesame Street*, whenever I watched this episode when I was younger, I always wished Tabitha had popped herself into the show and gave a talkin' to to Oscar about him being so mean to Big Bird.

Also, that scene towards the beginning when Durwood pours himself two drinks was funny on account of how much they drink and now he's doubled it up.

Anyway, I think from here on out the episodes get better...hopefully... it's so sad that the last year Liz had to have such seeming disdain for everything.

Three days later Agnes Moorehead guest starred on *The Wonderful World of Disney* in "The Strange Monster of Strawberry Cove," Part Two.

NOVEMBER 10, 1971

It was on this night that ABC aired Episode #237: "A Plague on Maurice and Samantha."

Samantha discovers that her powers are shot and becomes quite worried when she can't even levitate a bowl of flowers. She is pleased when her mother pops in, but when she suggests they call Dr. Bombay, Samantha says he's already been there and gave her a checkup with his his computerized hexameter and couldn't find a solitary thing wrong with her. However, he does say that it is a result of her mortal marriage and Endora becomes enraged, causing a windstorm to blow in. Endora wonders if Durwood knows, and Samantha confirms that he does but that he also pointed out that millions of people get along without witchcraft so maybe Samantha can adjust to it. Endora says that's all good and well for them, and she may even learn to live with it, but she cannot vouch for Durwood's continued existence when Maurice finds out, which he will sooner or later. Just then they hear trumpeting and see three trumpeters walk through the wall and when they turn around, their tunics say,

"Daddy is Coming." Samantha suggests maybe they can hide her loss of powers by having Endora covertly perform any magic for Samantha that Maurice may request. Soon, Maurice arrives in his chauffeured vehicle and says he had just come to visit to shower his daughter with his love. When he asks how Adam is progressing with his powers, he recalls how Samantha used to turn herself into a polka-dotted unicorn when she was a child and tells her how he'd love to see it again. With a look to Endora, Samantha soon turns into a polka-dotted unicorn. Maurice says that it doesn't look quite right and before he and Endora can discuss it anymore, Durwood shows up. When he asks if Samantha happened to get her powers back, Maurice is shocked and Endora changes Samantha back. Samantha hesitantly tells her father about the loss of her powers due to her mortal marriage. Maurice is furious and tells Durwood that when they first met Maurice had wanted to turn him into a leaping lizard and now it was going to come true. However, when Maurice throws his spell, nothing happens! Everyone is confused, when suddenly Dr. Bombay pops in wearing a contamination suit. He tells Samantha that his computerized hexameter was wrong and that he's isolated the bug that she has, a rare disease called Peri-Meri Dictamitus, which he is working on the cure, though he's not sure how long he'll be. He also warns everyone not to kiss Samantha as it's transferrable and everyone realizes that Maurice kissed Samantha upon his arrival. With that, Dr. Bombay pops off to work on the cure.

The next morning, when Durwood comes down to breakfast, he mentions how Maurice is upstairs still shaving with a razor causing Samantha, and especially Endora, to be ill at the thought of him having to lower himself to that mundane task. Maurice soon arrives quite impressed with how the shave felt and when he smells breakfast cooking, he's quite intrigued by the combination of ham and eggs. Endora is beside herself and goes to lie down. Seeing as Durwood is going to work, and the state he is in, Maurice invites himself to join Durwood at work. Durwood refuses until Maurice comes back with a sword he happened to bring with him, so Durwood relents.

After Maurice and Durwood have left for work, Samantha and Endora bide the time waiting for Dr. Bombay, who soon arrives with the ingredients for the anti-toxin which must be filled at the Apothecary's, who insists that the patient come to retrieve them so he can validate Bombay's diagnosis. And so Samantha goes and finds that the Apothecary only wanted to validate his libido and tells her that he'll get the ingredients in exchange for a kiss. Samantha isn't that easy and, after a bit of a chase, the old Apothecary finally sits down. Feeling bad for him, Samantha gives him a peck on the nose and he goes to fill the prescription.

At McMann and Tate, Durwood gives Maurice a pad of paper to write down his ideas for possible slogans for Benson's Chili Con Carne. When Maurice asks to have some, Durwood says it isn't necessary, but Maurice insists he can't write about the chili until he's eaten it and so Durwood asks the secretary to go get some. They soon meet with Mr. Benson, who isn't at all impressed with Durwood's ideas, but Maurice shares his ideas saying that he absolutely loved the product. Mr. Benson is quite impressed with Maurice's ideas and hires Durwood because of his father-in-law. In the middle of their meeting, Samantha shows up with the medicine and to retrieve her father.

Back at 1164, Maurice gets ready to leave and requests Samantha keep practicing her witchcraft. Durwood objects, but Maurice tells him he'll be watching and before Maurice can get any angrier, Samantha asks Durwood to help her in the kitchen. Maurice says his goodbyes to Endora and their one time romance seems to be rekindled. Soon, Endora comes into the kitchen furious because Maurice had kissed her without taking the potion and now she has lost her powers! But soon, Maurice pops in saying he was just joking and tells her he saved half the potion for her. After she has drunk it, he suggests they go have dinner on the Milky Way and they pop out.

I LOVE this episode and would totally give it four stars, even compared with the rest of the series. I think it's funny throughout and I think everyone has great energy, even Liz. Those ponytails are weird, but it's a nice change from her dull drab hair that she's going to have the rest of the season.

I love all of Maurice's Shakespearean soliloquies. He seems to be in rare form and like Endora said, "A Danish ham." My favorite is when he's going on and Samantha is trying to tell him she's sorry and she desperately says, "I said I was sorry!"

It's absolutely brilliant to have Maurice, probably the most powerful of all warlocks and witches, to lose his powers. Watching this the first time centuries ago, it was quite shocking! I wish, however, that when he was telling Durwood that his first instinct upon meeting him was to turn him into a leaping lizard, he would've said something about how when he first met him he disintegrated him and now regrets the decision of having reintegrated him. Of course, maybe he's speaking about the first time he met Dick Sargent's Durwood.

I really liked Samantha's hair the next morning when she's cooking "just ham and eggs." I also wish they would've shown Durwood teaching Maurice how to shave. One of my all-time favorite scenes is after Durwood tells Endora and Samantha that is what he has done and they are both absolutely mortified and Samantha says, "The THOUGHT of Daddy having to use a razor!" and, of course, Endora's, "Ill-making, it's just ill-making!" I also think it's funny how Maurice says, "Dora, have you gone completely batty?" The THOUGHT of anyone calling Endora "Dora" is ill-making! Except in this case, it's cute 'cause we know how much they really love each other.

I liked the siren used for the impending arrival of Dr. Bombay. They should've used it more often. And I also like that line about "lucky for me, she's not a fellow!"

I always liked the Apothecary…he's very un-PC, but I think his scenes are funny, though it's kind of got old.

I HATE how Dick Sargent, whenever he's presenting a new campaign, has a shaky voice and NO confidence whatsoever, whereas Dick York, no matter how silly the campaign, said it with enthusiasm and gusto.

I wish that they would've shown Maurice kissing Endora at the end. They just about do it and then the scene switches to the kitchen. And when Endora pops in and tells Sam and Durwood that she now has the bug, it is HYSTERICAL the way Dick Sargent laughs about it! It almost makes up for Dick Sargent's lack of confidence mentioned previously. And how's about Maurice patting her waist before they leave?! WOO WOO!

So, really, this is the last time Maurice Evans was on *Bewitched* as this is the last episode he filmed but, he does have just one more episode. It's too bad he wasn't around for most of the season 'cause Liz seems to be in such a better mood with him around.

Here are some of my favorite lines:

YORICK: *"COUGH! COUGH!" (pop out)*
MAURICE: *"Alas, poor Yorick, he isn't well."*
ENDORA: *"Durwood, like the rest of you your timing is atrocious!"*
MAURICE *(to Durwood's secretary):* *"What comes under the heading of "anything"?"*

Two days later President Nixon sets February 1, 1972 as the date for the removal of another 45,000 troops from Vietnam.

NOVEMBER 17, 1971

It was on this night that ABC aired Episode #238: "Hansel and Gretel in Samanthaland."

Samantha has to break off a reading of *Hansel and Gretel* to Tabitha and Adam so she can rescue her cheese puffs from burning, which she had been making for dinner with the Tates. When Tabitha asks what happens next, Samantha tells her she's old enough to finish reading to her brother and, after Samantha leaves, Tabitha reads that the children's stomachs were growling from hunger and she decides to cheer them up and zaps the photo alive. The children mention how hungry they are making Tabitha feel bad for them and so she zaps them out of the book and invites them to eat at her house. They smell the cheese puffs, which makes their mouths water, and so Tabitha zaps up the freshly baked puffs to her room, bewildering her parents who had both just seen them sitting out. Hansel and Gretel mention that their father, who was out in the forest cutting wood, will not let them stay, so Tabitha says she'll go find him to tell him and convince him. She pops into the book and zaps the leg of lamb that her mother was making to fly up to them and she heads out into the woods. Meanwhile, Samantha is shocked when the leg of lamb she just checked on, floats out of the oven up the kitchen stairs and she decides to follow it. She is even more shocked to find that her daughter has been exchanged for two children who look an awful lot like Hansel and Gretel! Gretel tells her that Tabitha went into the book just as Durwood gets upstairs as the Tates have arrived. Apprehensively, Samantha tells him about Tabitha and the story and also the fact that it may not be safe for Tabitha to be in the book because of the witch, and so she pops into the book to find Tabitha.

In the forest Samantha soon happens upon a gingerbread candy house and can't help but take a bite off a shingle, but when it snaps, the owner of the house, a wicked old Witch comes out wanting to know who is nibbling at her house. Samantha introduces herself and asks if the Witch has seen a little girl named Tabitha. The Witch says she doesn't know any girls but Gretel, whom she was expecting, and sends Samantha on her way. After Samantha has left, and with an evil cackle, the Witch steals into her home where she has Tabitha locked in a prison. She tells her that she's going to fatten her up to make a nice Tabitha pie, but Tabitha demands she be let out or she'll do magic to her. The Witch tells her that all storybook witches are stronger than real witches and when Tabitha tries some magic, she finds that the Witch may be right.

Soon, Larry and Louise arrive and are amused by Hansel and Gretel, who Durwood says are part of a play that Samantha is going to be putting on in a month. When he goes to get some bouillon for a drink, Hansel and Gretel decide to go find some more food and leave. Durwood returns and is horrified to find that the children are gone and he excuses himself to go look for them.

Meanwhile, in the storybook forest, Samantha runs into the Woodcutter's Cottage and his cranky wife who thinks that the Woodcutter has been having some hanky-panky with "the mean, nasty, ugly old witch" in the wood. Samantha assures her that no such thing has gone on and that she's only looking for her daughter. The Woodcutter's wife says she hasn't seen her and that maybe she's off in the other direction where the Witch is supposed to live, but Samantha tells her the Witch told her she hadn't seen her. It occurs to Samantha that you should never trust storybook witches and she runs off into the woods. When she gets to the Witch's house, the Witch comes out wanting to know who is nibbling at her house, but Samantha tells her she knows that the Witch knows where Tabitha is. The Witch denies it and Samantha tells her that she's going to be in trouble as she is a real witch and she turns the Witch's staff into a snake. The Witch pleads for her staff back but Samantha changes into a wand. When the Witch still refuses to tell her of Tabitha's whereabouts, Samantha changes her into a Fairy Godmother and says she'll stay like that until she admits to where the girl is. The Witch consents and Samantha changes her back. They go into the house and after telling Tabitha that she's going to be in trouble, Samantha zaps herself and Tabitha back home.

In the real world, the police have shown up with the children just as Samantha comes downstairs. She thanks the officers and assures the children that they can go with the police as they'll be going home very soon. After the officers leave with a fake address Samantha has given them, she zaps the children up to Tabitha's room leaving the policemen in a tizzy.

Samantha tells the Tates that she had just been having trouble with Tabitha which is why she had been gone all evening though she finds that she's going to have to find a way out of the play she's apparently directing.

I wouldn't go higher than maybe three stars, and that's only 'cause I got to watch part of it with Billie Hayes (the Witch) at the 2008 *Bewitched* Fanfare. Before then, I would've gave it maybe one. I'll never forget watching it with her either. It was so sweet!

I've never liked this episode because I think the kid who plays Hansel is CREEPY with his painted on eye brows and the fact that a cheese puff acts better than he does. And I HATE his line of "Witches are toothless old HAY-GS." BLEH! By the way, he was one of the Trick-or-Treaters, from Dick Sargent's Halloween episode, that actually called Elizabeth Montgomery "Mommy." Plus it's just a remake of the much better "Samantha and the Beanstalk."

However, I do think Liz looks way hot in this episode and I love her elephant belt. And Bobo Lewis (the Woodcutter's wife) is hysterical, as is Billie Hayes. I have to admit, before meeting her, she was part of the reason I didn't like the episode 'cause I just thought she was too manic but I can see that it was just great acting on her part. I also think I didn't like her because I HATED *H.R. PuffnStuff* and remembered her from that.

I noticed Sam putting the cheese puffs in the bottom of the oven with the leg of lamb already in there. That doesn't make any sense. And how about when the oven door opens, how LOUD it is? I'm surprised the whole set didn't collapse when that happened. I think where those stairs in the kitchen to nowhere lead is most likely to a trap door in the hallway floor right before Tabitha's bedroom door, which seems like a very dangerous place to put a door. I hate it.

And the ending is just horrible! It's another reason I've always disliked this episode. First of all, why tell Louise and Larry that Sam is directing a play? Why not just say that Hansel and Gretel just were playing around in costumes their mother had made them rather than dig yourself deeper by saying that the play is going to be in a month?! What happens in a month from now? You just say it got cancelled just because? And Liz's face in the very end shot…she looks so irritated at the whole thing and really quite bitchy.

I do like that Larry and Louise are here for no other purpose than to just hang out. It's refreshing.

Here are some of my favorite lines:

WITCH: *"Waddya want, mister?"*
SAMANTHA: *"You need to get those glasses checked."*
WITCH: *"Say, I need to get these glasses checked!"*
HANSEL: *"But you don't know Papa."*
TABITHA: *"He doesn't know me!"*

NOVEMBER 24, 1971

Bewitched was pre-empted so ABC could air a special presentation of *South Pacific* (1958). Two days before, Walter Sande passed away. He played Giddings in Episode #128: "Hippie, Hippie, Hooray." He was also in *Citizen Kane* (1941) with Agnes Moorehead.

DECEMBER 1, 1971

It was on this night that ABC returned with an all new episode of *Bewitched*, Episode #239: "The Warlock in the Gray Flannel Suit."

Endora pops in to invite Samantha and Durwood to her cousin Panda's wedding in Hong Kong, as Samantha and Panda were close as children. Durwood says that as they just got back from Europe, work has been piling up in the office, so there is no way that he can leave. And as Samantha doesn't want to go without him, she asks Endora to give her regrets to Panda. Insulted, Endora zaps Samantha into a prison outfit and a jail cell as she feels that Durwood keeps Samantha a prisoner there, but Samantha assures her that she is deciding not to go to the wedding on her own. After springing Samantha, Endora pops out to end up on the roof where she calls on Warlock Alonzo, someone she apparently hasn't seen in quite some time as he is now a dirty hippie. She tells him of her trouble with Durwood and tells him that since the job is keeping them from going to Panda's wedding, she wants Alonzo to unjob Durwood as she has promised not to meddle in her daughter's life. On threat of roasting like a marshmallow in an open volcano, Alonzo accepts.

A little while later at the office, as Durwood and Larry are discussing the new Monticello Carpet account, Betty interrupts them to tell them that there is a weird man out in the waiting room who refuses to leave and she's kind of scared of him. When they go out there, they find Alonzo sitting barefoot atop his chopper bike. He says that he has come to get a job with McMann and Tate as he has some new ideas he'd like to share. Before Larry can throw him out, he freezes everyone and, with the ankh necklace he is wearing, he casts a spell on Larry to like anything he says. After unfreezing them, Larry invites Alonzo into his office to talk with him. Alonzo says that he is in tune with the universal vibrations that will help him to revolutionize the advertising world and he wanted to share that with McMann and Tate. Durwood is not buying any of this but under influence of the spell, Larry drinks it in and asks Alonzo to come up with ideas for the Monticello Carpet account. While Alonzo goes off into the corner to meditate, Durwood draws Larry aside, but finds he can't get through to him. Soon, Alonzo leaves from standing on his head to tell them that he has come up with something so in tune with the human pulsations of mankind that they are going to feel it in their whole being, and he soon scribbles out his ideas, which turn out to be the beautiful words "Flurpity Flurp!" Durwood is astonished that Alonzo could come up with such drivel, however, Larry is sold! He tells Alonzo that's a great start and to come up with some more. Once again, Durwood tries to show Larry the error of his ways, but Larry won't hear of it and is absolutely tickled when Alonzo comes up with another idea where a blank page is only interrupted by the Monticello Carpets logo in the corner in very tiny print. Larry loves it and tells Alonzo he'll be presenting his ideas to Mr. Cushman, head of Monticello Carpets, that afternoon. Fed up with all this craziness, Durwood phones Samantha and tells her he thinks her mother has been fooling around and asks her to find Endora. After they hang up, Samantha finds that her mother is not too easy to find.

Later on, Durwood can't take anymore and he goes to drown his sorrows at the bar when Samantha pops in telling him that she has been unsuccessful at finding Endora. Durwood tells her that Larry had suggested he open his own office if he didn't like how Larry ran things and Samantha tells him that would be a great idea as Alonzo's spell was only for Larry to like his ideas, but not to fire Durwood. Durwood realizes there is an empty office across from McMann and Tate, and so with Samantha's offer of a little witchly wifecraft, they go over to the offices to set things up. Soon, Larry shows up wanting to know what they are doing, and Durwood tells him that he's set up shop across the hall. Larry can't believe he could've set up anything so fast but with a few quick zaps, Samantha fills the new offices with ritzy furniture. Larry is bewildered but his worry soon disappears when Mr. Cushman shows up for their meeting. He is intrigued by Durwood's new agency but says that he'll fulfill his meeting with McMann and Tate and then possibly flow over afterward. Samantha decides she'll need to keep watch on Alonzo and zaps herself into her flying suit and pops into Larry's office, invisibly.

Mr. Cushman is not at all impressed with Alonzo and his far out ideas and so Alonzo goes to give him an ankh zap but is stopped when Samantha zaps the ankh with a jolt. He realizes there is a witch watching them and he takes the spell off Larry and leaves. Larry realizes that he may have lost the account and tries to say that Durwood had let Alonzo in but Samantha twists his words into saying that Durwood had actually wanted to stop Alonzo and so Mr. Cushman leaves. When he sees the original ideas Durwood has, he wants to sign up with him.

Later that night, as Samantha and Durwood are celebrating his success, Larry shows up to snoop and is insulted that Durwood would take advantage of him in a weak state. Samantha suggests Durwood forgive and forget but zaps Larry into giving Durwood his job back as well as making him a partner. However, because Larry's greed is so powerful, he tells Durwood that his partnership will happen one day when he's proven himself.

I think it's absolutely hysterical! It's one of my favorites and I definitely give it four stars!

It's sort of *Far Side*-ish but I think it works because Bernie Kopell and David White have such enthusiasm in their roles that you can't help but love it. Alonzo is one of my most favorite characters. I love his far out attitude and his groovy clothes. Everything he says is hysterical! "Panda's getting married? Ugh! Who's the unlucky dude?" I wonder if the real Panda Cushman, Liz's cousin, was getting married again? Plus I like that the client's last name is Cushman. I wish we could see what Panda looks like today and if she still looks like Liz.

I always laugh hysterically when Larry asks why Alonzo chose McMann and Tate and he says, "I've seen your ideas, daddy. Ugh!" And especially during his spell:

> *Tail of newt and eye of bat* *STOMP*
> *this is where the spell is at!*
> *Because I know it's what he'd hate,*
> *all I say appeals to Tate!*

I also like that he uses the ankh to cast the spell. Seems like it gives it more oomphs and amphs.

I think David White should've got some award for his acting in this one. His enthusiasm is hysterical!

And how couldn't you love the buildup and reveal of the two greatest words ever: FLURPITY FLURP! It's the sound of bare feet on a Monticello Carpet and it's in tune with the human pulsations and universal vibrations! Alonzo having his chopper all those floors up isn't believable unless they have a freight elevator he used.

I liked that we finally get to see Durwood be fine with Sam's "wifely witchcraft." I know we've seen him be lenient before but it's been a long time. I also liked the furniture zapping but that French furniture doesn't make any sense.

I also wish that if Samantha is going to be invisible in her flying suit, that they would've made her see through like they do sometimes. But it's still cool to see her in it and floating in the air. I also don't like Endora's new suit, but it's good to see her in it again. It HAS been a long time.

I think it's funny when Alonzo says, "I got a bad vibe. There's a witch in here!" But it is a chintzy way to end it.

But all in all, I LOVE this episode!

Here are some of my favorite lines:

> ENDORA: *"Alonzo! You look perfectly disreputable!"*
> ALONZO: *"Why thank you! I'm just doing my thing."*

Plus all the other quotes I mentioned earlier.

Two days before, Agnes Moorehead guested on *Laugh-In* in a sketch called "The Mad World of Villains." The next day the movie *Brian's Song* is aired as the ABC-TV Movie of the Week and utilized the living room set of 1164. Starring James Caan, it also co-starred *Bewitched* guest stars including Jack Warden (Mr. Barker from "It Shouldn't Happen to a Dog") and David Huddleston (Mr. Flannigan from "Out of the Mouths of Babes").

DECEMBER 8, 1971

It was on this night that ABC aired Episode #240: "The Eight Year Itch Witch."

When Samantha goes to get the milk out of the fridge, she is surprised to find a photo of a bikini-clad girl. She's even more surprised when she finds another in the bread bin and realizes her mother must be up to something, and she's right as Endora pops in claiming to have found the photos in Durwood's briefcase. Samantha assures her that beautiful women are just tools of the ad trade. She also says that she's very much in love even after eight years and that they are going to celebrate the anniversary of their first date. Endora is disgusted and pops off but, from nowhere, agrees to babysit that night.

Endora ends up on a cloud and calls for her familiar, a Siamese cat named Ophelia, to come help her catch a rat named Durwood.

At the office, Durwood and Larry discuss how they are having trouble finding the new face of TomKat Tractors with Mr. Burkholder, the account holder, when suddenly a gorgeous statuesque woman named

Ophelia enters saying she had heard they were looking for someone to model. Mr. Burkholder is smitten and so they immediately sign Ophelia on and get to work on the photo shoot. Mr. Burkholder invites Ophelia to go to the Annual Sales Convention in Albany that night to show her off but she insists that Durwood join them as he calms her nerves. Durwood tries to decline but Larry insists for the good of his job that he go.

Later, as Durwood is getting ready to leave, he apologizes to Samantha, who tells him they'll celebrate the next night. After he's left, Endora pops in sure that Durwood is off to Albany to fool around but Samantha assures her it isn't so.

After the convention, Durwood says he is going to book a late flight out and calls Samantha to tell her that he'll be home for a late dinner. However, Ophelia calls Durwood's room and acts as the airline operator to tell him that the airport is all socked in with fog so there are no flights leaving. Dejected, Durwood calls Samantha to tell her the bad news. Samantha accepts it and is annoyed when her mother pops in to taunt her.

Back in Albany, Ophelia asks Durwood if she can borrow some ice as her room hasn't any, and when he lets her in, she closes the door putting the do-not-disturb sign out. Larry soon arrives, intrigued by Durwood's little dalliance and he tries to put the moves on Ophelia. She soon puts Larry to sleep and tries to get snuggly with Durwood.

Meanwhile, at 1164, Endora pops back in with a clear weather report from Albany. Samantha still believes Durwood and says that she'll get Hagatha to come babysit while she and Endora pop over to Albany. When they get there, they find Ophelia zapping Larry asleep again and zapping Durwood to fall in love with her. Samantha freezes Durwood and pops in to find out what Ophelia is up to. Ophelia admits that she's only doing Endora's bidding but Samantha tells her that she can trust Durwood if Ophelia doesn't pull anymore tricks. She pops out unfreezing Durwood but Ophelia can't help herself and zaps him again. Samantha blocks her and wakes up Larry, who Ophelia again puts to sleep. Samantha interrupts again saying that there is no point in going on and she zaps Durwood back to normal and pops out. Ophelia finally gives up as Durwood says he is just going to go ride the fog out at the airport and so, as she's left behind with Larry, she goes to flirt with him but Samantha pops in again to say that Louise is a very dear friend and she zaps Larry into wanting to leave, too.

Back at home, Durwood is shocked to find that Endora is issuing an apology to him that the whole world can see when Samantha shows him the sky writing out their backdoor that says, "I, Endora, promise never to bother What's-His-Name again."

I wouldn't go higher than one star. This is the episode that, for me, encapsulates the fact that EVERYBODY involved with the show has given up! Shall I list them and the reasons? OK!

1. The writers. Like has, and will be done, this season, this is simply a rehash of not one, but two episodes, that were much better in their original forms ("It Takes One to Know One" and "Ling Ling" both from Season One). I cannot understand how when Ruth Brooks Flippen was given the job of writing an episode, she simply cut and pasted the script from those other two writers and Bill Asher and Elizabeth Montgomery were OK with it…well, I can understand Liz 'cause at this point she didn't care anyway.

2. The set decorators and filmographers. There's just so much that is wrong in this episode starting with the obvious wires holding up the cotton clouds. Not only can you see all of them, but nobody even cared to try and situate Endora's flying suit around them! You can see where the material bunches up around the wires, something which I don't think has happened before. Then, on the set when they are shooting Ophelia, you can totally see the kitchen wallpaper behind Mr. Burkholder! And it's not just a little bit, it's practically one whole wall! And lastly, as if Durwood and Samantha's bedroom set isn't getting enough use doubling for Tabitha's room, it is now also Durwood's hotel room! SLOPPY! SLOPPY! SLOPPY!

3. Elizabeth Montgomery. Speaking of sloppy, Liz, who has for the past couple episodes looked really good, suddenly is hippy chick again going braless and quite frankly, she didn't need to even wear that red Supergirl top as you can see EVERYTHING! This wouldn't be a problem except for when you're watching with conservative people (i.e. my mom) and it's just embarrassing. It also conveys that Liz has simply given up…maybe she thought it would draw all the attention away from HOT Julie Newmar, and it did to a degree, but I don't think in a good way. I HATE her up do! One of the best attributes Liz has is her beautiful hair, and what does she do but pin it all up on her head, and not in a very good way at all. I still like the elephant belt, though. But also sloppy is her acting. She's reverted back to the rolling eyes and just no enthusiasm that she had in most of the Europe episodes. And it's probably 'cause she realized she's just doing a redo of better episodes from a much better time in her life when her husband most likely wasn't cheating on her and she was just starting her new family.

So now for the stuff I did like: that would pretty much be Julie Newmar. I like that they used her for a Cat Girl. I'll bet all the *Batman* fans were thrilled to see her in a cat woman role. And she is super sexy! I also liked Endora and Samantha appearing see-through, which is what should've been done last episode.

I watched this episode with my cousin Tracey, who knows *Bewitched* somewhat on account of my having lived with him for a long time, and he actually said, "Did nobody on *Bewitched* care at this time?" He was surprised they weren't all just reading from their scripts and just walking on and off screen when they were supposed to be popping in and out. It's sad that our show has come to this.

DECEMBER 15, 1971

It was on this night that ABC aired Episode #241: "Three Men and a Witch on a Horse."

When Endora finds out that Durwood had refused a tip on the daily double for the horse races, she says that it's because he's too afraid to take a chance. She also thinks that means he'll always be stuck on his treadmill but Samantha won't hear of it and leaves to go do the morning chores. As Durwood has just left, Endora pops out to the driveway and freezes him, casting a spell on him that infects him with the gambling bug and the desire to go to Tabitha's room for the daily double. She disappears and he runs up stairs not knowing what to expect, but when he finds Tabitha playing, he asks her to choose the horses in the race. She tells him she doesn't understand and leaves to go to play with Adam. He's startled by the rocking horse that asks him if he would like the inside track on the horse races and asks him to get on his back. Awkwardly, Durwood complies, and the horse gives him the name of two horses. Just then Samantha finds him and asks what he is doing and, when he tells her, she realizes her mother is up to something. Durwood leaves and Samantha calls for Tabitha to ask her if Grandmama had done anything funny when visiting earlier. When Tabitha mentions that Endora made her rocking horse talk, Samantha's suspicions are confirmed.

Later on, Durwood arrives late for business luncheon with Larry and Mr. Spengler as he stopped at an off track betting station. He offers the men a piece of the action, but they refuse and are intrigued when Durwood wins over $800 on a $20 bet. Durwood tells them his source is at home and before Larry can refuse, Mr. Spengler says he'd be interested in making a small bet.

At home, Samantha finally gets Endora, who tells her that Durwood just won all the money. Samantha is furious that she would fix the races, but Endora assures her she didn't fix the races, she just did a little predicting. Samantha reminds her that it's against witch ethics to predict anything and asks her mother to remove the spell before Durwood gets home, however, he suddenly walks through the door with Larry and Mr. Spengler. Endora pops out and Samantha thinks everything is OK until Durwood goes up stairs and the hobby horse is still spouting off horse names, particularly Count of Valor. After he leaves, Endora pops in petting the horse with the comment, "You win some, you lose some!"

When Samantha hears who he is going to pick, she finds that Count of Valor is only predicted as the winner if you hold the newspaper upside down, but she can't talk Durwood out of betting, and things get worse when Durwood bets $200 a piece for Larry and Mr. Spengler. He suggests that they go to watch the race at the off-track betting station so they'll be closer to their money. After they leave, Samantha hollers for her mother and finds out that Endora changed her spell so that Durwood would lose, which will even him out from his earlier winnings, but she worries about Larry and Mr. Spengler losing. She asks Endora to babysit while she goes to encourage Count of Valor to win with a little people sense. She pops down to the track and zaps Count of Valor into a human so she can talk to him. Samantha tells him that he should be ashamed of himself for not winning, but he tells her that it's because he feels that if he keeps losing his owners are going to put him out to pasture. Soon their discussion is interrupted by the horse groom, who tells Samantha that if the Count doesn't win this race, he is going to the glue factory! This puts a jolt in the horse, who starts acting very nervous, surprising the groom, who says that's the most action he's ever seen from him.

Samantha soon shows up to the off-track betting station to find Durwood and watch the races. As the race begins, Count of Valor is in last place, which makes Larry and Mr. Spengler think they've been had and they give up their bets. After they leave, however, the horse soon starts speeding up and wins at the last second, bringing him $4,000!

Later, Durwood finds out about Endora's spell and is mad that his winnings came from witchcraft. Samantha suggests he donate it to charity which will in turn make Endora mad. Larry shows up and admits that Mr. Spengler found out about the winning horse and has some story that he didn't understand racetrack jargon and would like his money restored. However, Samantha and Durwood can see that Larry wants his money too and so in the best interest of preserving a beautiful friendship and his job, Samantha suggests Durwood comply.

I'd go with one star. What's amazing is that Elizabeth Montgomery told Herbie J Pilato this was one of her favorite episodes! And you can sort of tell with the way she was so excited during the race scene and the way she interacted with the horse. I do have to say, though, that I enjoy this episode WAY more than Season Two's "The Horse's Mouth."

I think Liz looks way hot, even in that loud mini-skirt. At least she wasn't wearing knee-highs…that was left to Tabitha to do.

I also noticed a "new" scene in this one and that's where Sam asks Tabitha to call for Grandmama for her. I thought it was funny and cute.

Dick Sargent riding that hobby horse was creepy to me…just didn't like it.

And the human-horse reminded me a LOT of Don Knotts…in fact, that would've been awesome to have Don Knotts play him!

The horse wrangler was played by Scatman Crothers. He's a jazz musician and actor. Did you notice how brilliant white his teeth were? Too bad Liz couldn't have had her teeth as white.

Anyway, I think it's a very dull episode.

I also noticed that Liz stood with her one arm all the way behind her back almost the whole episode.

And, of course, this is the perfect example of a *Far Side* episode.

Though they weren't aware of it, the next day the cast and crew of *Bewitched* finished filming the last episode #254: "The Truth, Nothing But the Truth, So Help Me, Sam" before they left for Christmas break. The episode would air the following March.

The following evening Agnes Moorehead guested on *Love, American Style* in "Love and the Single Girl."

DECEMBER 22, 1971

It was on this night that ABC re-aired Episode #215: "Sisters at Heart" with a new introduction from Liz. This was her favorite episode of the series.

DECEMBER 29, 1971

It was on this night that ABC aired Episode #242: "Adam, Warlock or Washout," the last episode of 1971.

While getting the milk out of the fridge, Samantha is surprised to find Endora in it telling her it's an emergency! Samantha zaps the sound of the doorbell and says she'll go answer it and when she gets to the living room, she pops out into the fridge. Endora wants to know why Durwood is still home as he was supposed to be playing golf so that the testing committee can come to test Adam's powers. She suggests that Samantha get rid of Durwood for the day especially since Maurice is also coming for the testing, which Samantha is nervous about as Adam hasn't shown the least inclination towards witchcraft. After Samantha pops out, she tells Durwood, who she had just asked to stay home with the family, that maybe he should go play golf. Her lame excuses don't faze him when Endora pops in asking why he isn't out playing a set of golf. It suddenly becomes apparent as to why they want him gone as they hear the sound of Maurice's impending arrival. Upon hearing that, Durwood agrees that he should go play golf as Samantha and Endora go into the living room where they see Maurice being brought into the living room on a chair held by four beautiful women. After his greetings and dismissing his litter, Maurice wants to know when the rest of the committee is going to be there. Samantha tells him that she's not sure and suggests maybe he wouldn't want to wait around especially since she knows he won't be pleased that Adam may not have any powers. Maurice tells her he wouldn't miss the test and that he thinks Adam should have some advance testing and he goes up to Adam's room (which looks an awful lot like Tabitha's old room, redone). He tries to show Adam how to levitate a toy but Adam acts like he hasn't a clue what his Grandpapa is talking about. Maurice realizes that because of Adam's unfortunate lineage, he may need an assist from him and so he endows him with some of his own powers.

Meanwhile, the members of the testing committee, Grimalda and Enchantra, arrive just as Maurice comes downstairs with Adam. Endora zaps in the testing furniture and equipment. For the first test, Enchantra zaps up a red ball and asks Adam to levitate it to him, however, he says he can't. The women are shocked but Maurice says it's because they are testing him on too elementary a level and suggests they ask him to fly. They think he's much too young to fly, but Maurice says that as Adam is his grandson, it should be an easy task. Samantha and Endora are suspicious but when they ask Adam to fly, he says he would like to and he soon begins to fly around the room. The women are impressed, with the exception of Endora, who thinks something is going on. Maurice is satisfied that Adam has proven himself, and so leaves to referee a race. After he leaves, Adam asks his mommy where Daddy is and when she tells him he's golfing, Adam wishes his daddy were there. Soon, Durwood pops in mid swing quite shocked at not only appearing there but at the presence of the other witches.

Samantha soon explains what is going on and Durwood is furious and he tries to tell the women to leave. However, Adam interrupts him asking him if he wants to see him fly. Durwood says no and tells Adam to get up to his room, which he does by popping out. Furious that his son is apparently a warlock, Durwood hollers for Adam to come back and Samantha suggests Adam take the stairs. After Adam has left, Durwood asks that the witches leave but Endora tells him that they haven't given their decision about Adam. They tell Samantha and Durwood that as Adam is living in such a dubious environment with hardly any witchcraft practiced, they think he should be removed so that he can get proper training and that he'll be returned in twenty or thirty years! Samantha and Durwood are appalled, and when Durwood goes on a rant, Enchantra changes his voice into a dog bark. Seeing that she's outnumbered, Samantha calls for her father and when he finds out what is going on, he admits that Adam was only able to fly because of his assistance. He also admits that Adam shows no propensity for witchcraft. He also suggests that maybe Adam does have his own powers but, as he would never be allowed to use them, he would've never been able to develop them. Samantha asks Enchantra to restore Durwood's voice on condition that he keep his cool and Maurice calls for Adam, who pops down with a conch shell. Maurice uses the shell as part of his spell to return Adam to normal and then asks Samantha to show him how to levitate it. Samantha gets Durwood's halfhearted approval and shows Adam what to do by floating the shell back and forth. She asks him to try and, when Adam looks sheepishly at his father, Durwood gives him approval and soon the shell flies from Samantha to Adam. Everyone is ecstatic, but for Durwood, however, Samantha tells him it's just like watching Adam take his first baby steps. Enchantra and Grimalda leave and, as the family is saying their goodbyes, Adam mentions that he'd like a drink of milk and zaps one in. Durwood isn't too happy about his son's new found talent for magic, and Samantha says she'll have a talk with him about it later and asks him to take it into the kitchen. Endora and Maurice soon leave and just as Durwood is going to hug Samantha she pops out. She soon comes in from the kitchen with Adam and says that maybe she'll have her little talk with him now.

I LOVE this episode and would totally give it four stars! I think everyone is in top form and Liz seems to really enjoy herself. Of course, that's 'cause Maurice Evans was there in his last appearance on the show.

The scene around the table was sweet. It makes them seem like a real family.

I also like the scenes in the fridge though this time there wasn't a Coke bottle like there was in "Samantha's Secret Spell." It was probably on one of the lower shelves. I did notice at one point Endora's hand disappeared half way because of the blue screen.

The music that's played when Maurice arrives is the same that is used on *I Dream of Jeannie* when some member of royalty from Baghdad showed up. And did you notice the gray hair of his servants? And does Maurice have a dead flying rat on his turban? I love when he tells Enchantra "how do you keep your girlish figure?" But I think that both those women are wearing way too much makeup. Quite frankly, Agnes Moorehead's makeup looked rather thick and, in the opening scene, I thought she looked rather ill. I also thought Grimalda looked like a man in drag so it's way funny when Maurice says to her, "You look ravishing!" It is odd that the two aunts would be dressed in Victorian clothes but if you think about it, it's even odder that any witches would choose to fly around in automobiles! But I like it!

All though Adam's room seems to really be Tabitha's old room in blue disguise, the back wall doesn't extend as far as Tabitha's room did because there used to be shelves on either side of the window box. I also didn't like that they would give him tile in his room. I always loved seeing Adam fly! David Lawrence still remembers that and his mother was scared when he was doing it. Herbie J also said that when the twins filmed this episode, they both were sick. I think it's cute though when he's flying during the test and he keeps saying, "Hi Mommy!"

I think all the test tubes and all provide a great atmosphere, though the set up that was used when Tabitha's powers were tested was much more basic.

That scene with Tabitha and Maurice on the stairs seems to be a new one. I think it's funny how Tabitha tells him his voice is loud.

One of my most favorite scenes is when Sam and Durwood are in the den when he's going off about all the witches in the house, he hands the golf club to her and she just about beats the hell out of him with it! Oh, I wish she would've done it!

I like seeing Adam being able to pop in and out too! When I was younger I always associated myself with Adam, especially 'cause I saw that he was played by a kid named David and even more so when I found his birth episode aired on my birthday (Oct 16) in 1969.

I also think it's a very sweet scene between Samantha and Adam when she teaches him how to levitate the seashell and, I don't know why, but I love that they used the shell. It seems like Samantha is so proud of him and is really pleased to be teaching him how to use his magic.

Of course, this episode is the last episode to be aired in ABC primetime on July 1, 1972, and I think it makes a very good series ending because of finding out Adam has powers. But nobody seemed to notice that as everyone always seems to question if Adam had powers, that is when they even know who Adam is. I wonder if everybody tuned out after they had seen Maurice give him powers or maybe they just didn't even tune in at all.

Anyway, I love this episode! Here are some of my favorite lines:

> ENDORA: *"Well, Maurice, you're certainly a hit with the ladies... of the geriatric set."*
> MAURICE: *"How comforting to know you still care."*
> ENDORA: *"You see, Samantha's husband, that mortal LAME BRAIN, absolutely forbids the use of witchcraft in this house!"*
> ENCHANTRA: *"No!"*
> ENDORA: *"Yes!"*
> GRIMALDA: *"No!"*
> ENDORA: *"YES!"*
> ENCHANTRA: *"NO!"*
> ENDORA: *"Why do you keep saying 'no' when I tell you 'yes'??!"*

JANUARY 5, 1972

It was on this night that ABC aired Episode #243: "Samantha's Magic Sitter."

As Durwood and Samantha get ready for a business dinner, Esmeralda pops in on them embarrassed as she's caught Durwood in just his boxers and so she pops down stairs to fix herself some eggs. Before Durwood can ask why she is there, they hear screaming from downstairs and, when they arrive down there, they find Esmeralda's legs dangling from the chimney, where she is stuck. After being freed and cleaned up, Esmeralda sees that they are going out and thinks it's lucky that she's shown up so she can babysit, but Samantha tells her that they asked Aunt Hagatha to babysit. Esmeralda is deflated and says she's going to change herself into a punching bag as she'll then be useful. Samantha assures her that they really do want her, they just decided on Hagatha for that night. Just then Larry arrives with the bad news that the client, Mr. Norton, and his wife had to cancel their dinner because their sitter conked out. However, as Esmeralda has just been told that she's the Stephenses favorite sitter, she offers her services. Samantha tries to dissuade her but Larry won't hear of it, and so he calls the Nortons.

At the dinner, Mrs. Norton worries about the capability of Esmeralda with their son, Ralph, but Samantha assures her she has nothing to worry about. Mr. Norton says it's more likely that Esmeralda would have to worry about Ralph.

Over at the Norton's, Esmeralda finds that Mr. Norton may be right as Ralph keeps shooting toy arrows at her while she tries to read to him. When she goes to put the book away, Ralph goes to squirt her with a water gun, but she sees him and makes it squirt him! He wonders how it happened and she says that it was by magic. He tells her that there isn't any such thing as magic, but she insists there is and she tries to make his toy mountain lion's tail wag. When it doesn't happen, she tries a spell and ends up with a black bear in the room! Ralphie is pleased, if not a little scared, and so Esmeralda nervously speaks another spell and the bear disappears. However, she doesn't notice that she's also managed to turn the toy mountain lion into a real one! Ralphie asks how Esmeralda is able to do that and she tells him it's because she's a witch and he admits that he would like for her to sit with him all the time.

Later on, the Nortons and the Stephens arrive and the Nortons are impressed that Esmeralda could get Ralphie to sleep. However, Samantha is not impressed when she sees the lion cub walk down the stairs and she covertly zaps it away. She suggests that she, Durwood, and Esmeralda leave as she's tired and when they get outside, she shows them the lion cub. Durwood is furious with Esmeralda and Samantha turns the lion cub into a toy and they leave it on the doorstep.

The next day, Mrs. Norton shows up at Samantha's with Ralphie, who has a black eye. Mrs. Norton says he got it from being beat up after telling the kids at school about the animals appearing and disappearing and how his babysitter is a witch. Mrs. Norton says that Esmeralda must've done something terrible to have Ralphie believe in all that nonsense and she assures Samantha that Mr. Norton will no longer be doing business with her husband and she leaves. Soon after, Durwood calls to tell her about Mr. Norton cancelling his account because of Ralphie's situation but it occurs to Samantha that maybe there is a way to prove to the Nortons that Ralphie wasn't really telling stories.

When Durwood gets home, Samantha tells him that she has planned a party for Ralphie, Tabitha, Adam, the Nortons, and Larry where Esmeralda will perform mortal magic tricks with a little assist from her faulty magic so that the Nortons will see that Ralphie just saw some very convincing magic. At first, Mrs. Norton is astonished that Samantha would have the nerve to call her but Samantha twitches her into accepting.

The party soon starts and Esmeralda tries to do some tricks but, as she fouls up the mortal tricks, she inadvertently zaps up some rats and when she says what a silly goose she is, a goose pops in. The Nortons are surprised by the great magic show but when Esmeralda casts a spell to get rid of it, she does but also manages to change Mr. Norton into a monkey! Mrs. Norton is shocked and Samantha gets Esmeralda to change him back. Mrs. Norton asks Esmeralda how she did it but Esmeralda has no clue. Samantha tells Mrs. Norton that just as she, Larry, and the children saw the trick, Ralphie saw the tricks from the night he was babysat so maybe Mrs. Norton should believe him. Mrs. Norton apologizes and Mr. Norton signs back on.

I would give this one star. The original with Aunt Clara ("There's No Witch Like an Old Witch") was infinitesimally better. Plus this episode is so WEIRD! Before I begin with why I think it's so weird, I must say that this is my "lost" episode. It was the last "new" episode of the series I saw. It took me forever to catch this one. So when I saw all the weirdness of it, it was truly a mind blower.

1. *That opening scene with the nose ring.* It was funny but so out of character for Samantha. Plus the risqué-ness of having Esmeralda pop in while he's getting dressed was weird. And she never said why she was there, yet Sam tells Durwood, "You heard her. She said her flaps were flipping when they should've been flapping."

2. *The camera shot of the fireplace after Esmeralda gets unstuck.* I don't ever remember seeing a shot like that where the camera was shooting from the stairs as well as magic being filmed from anything but a close-up (Sam cleaning up Esmeralda). Weird, but at the same time, cool!

3. *Everyone referring to Esmeralda as "Aunt."* I almost think that Larry referred to her that way to ease Mrs. Norton's mind. Where I think it went wrong was when Samantha responded casually by referring to Esmeralda as "Aunt" when I think the line should've been said emphasizing the word "aunt" in a sarcastic way which would've acknowledged that Samantha knew what Larry was trying to do but at the same time made sure everyone knew that Esmeralda is not the aunt.

4. *Sam's cloak.* When the hell did Samantha get a cloak?! And more importantly, how did she manage to get away with wearing it outside with Durwood's total disdain for anything that resembles witchcraft? I think the cloak is awesome but just so weird in the context of the show.

5. *The turning of the cub into the toy.* You mean to tell me she can do that to the lion cub, but she couldn't do that to the toy elephant from Season Three's "A Gazebo Never Forgets?" Like my fellow *Bewitched* fan Sharon

said, "I want my money back!" I mean it makes sense but only if they'd utilized that rule the whole series.

   6. *And lastly, the utilization of a real bear.* It's weird only in the fact that a real bear wasn't used in "The Safe and Sane Halloween." I LOVED that they used it and it even looked like Alice Ghostley really was in the shot being filmed with it close by.

   I also wonder why not only Louise wasn't at the party but why didn't Jonathan come with his Dad? One of the guests at the party was Diane Murphy, Erin's twin sister who also originally played Tabitha.

   The spells that were used were strange too but kind of fun.

   I also liked the actress that played Mrs. Norton. She should have been used as a witch. I wish however that at least once Don Rickles would've been used in one of Richard X. Slattery's roles. *Bewitched* is probably the only '60s sitcoms that Rickles didn't guest on.

   I totally forgot to mention the fact that Liz was totally 'nippular' in that brown dress! I don't know how she could've felt comfortable like that. But I did think she looked very pretty in this episode.

   All in all a weird episode.

   The day before, the first scientific hand held calculator is introduced for a price of $395.

   The same day as the episode aired, President Nixon orders the development of a space shuttle program.

   It was also around this time that a couple commercials with Liz were aired where she talked about switching nights from Wednesday to Saturdays, "our new niche!"

JANUARY 15, 1972

   As *Bewitched* was floundering in the ratings, it was moved to Saturdays at 8:00 PM against CBS's powerhouse *All in the Family*, to essentially put it out of its misery. The first episode on this new night was Episode #244: "Samantha is Earthbound."

   Durwood notices Samantha doesn't seem too thrilled about volunteering for Mrs. Prescott's Charity Bazaar, however, she tells him that that isn't it at all, but that she just has an acute case of the 'blahs.' When she tries to bring his breakfast to him, she about falls on the floor and says that she just feels very heavy and, when Durwood tries to lift her, he about breaks his back as she seems to weigh a ton! She asks him to take her into the living room so she can lie down and, when she's only been on the couch but a moment, it suddenly crashes through the floor. Seeing that she's obviously ill, Samantha yells for Dr. Bombay. He soon appears, irritated that they interrupted his delivery of a set of quintuplets, though it wasn't their birthday. When she describes that she now is quite heavy, he asks to be able to check her out when standing up. As Durwood and he struggle to bring her over next to the couch, the floor suddenly gives way below them. After shoring the floor with a spell, Dr. Bombay zaps in a scale and has Durwood drag Samantha over to it where they find that she weighs over 500 pounds! Dr. Bombay says that it's not her weight but a fluctuation in gravity, a condition peculiar to witches and warlocks called Gravititus Inflammitus. Not trusting his diagnoses, as they've been burned in the past, Samantha and Durwood request a second opinion, so Dr. Bombay zaps in his computerized hexameter, which confirms that he was right. He zaps in a potion that Samantha drinks while he works a spell. Samantha soon finds that she's not so heavy and that she feels much better but, just as Durwood is thanking the doctor, Samantha finds her feet leaving the floor as now she's suddenly lighter than air! Dr. Bombay apologizes and says that he'll have to go find an antidote for the antidote and leaves. Meanwhile, Durwood fishes his wife from the ceiling and just gets her to the floor in a tight grasp when they see Mrs. Prescott peeping through their front window, where there aren't any curtains as they have been taken to the cleaners. Durwood walks Samantha over to the door and they find that Mrs. Prescott has come to pick up Samantha for the bazaar. Durwood tells her that he has decided to join Samantha at the bazaar, though it's for a ladies fashion show, and they'll just go together. He also realizes that he's going to have to bail out on a golf date with Mr. Prescott, one of McMann and Tate's new clients, of Prescott Shoes.

At the bazaar, Mrs. Prescott puts Samantha at a booth to sell bolts of material, which is perfect for a Samantha-weight as they weigh heavy, especially when Mrs. Prescott asks Durwood to come help with something. When one of the ladies wants to buy the particular bolt that Samantha is holding, Sam tries to talk her out of it but the woman becomes incensed and asks Mrs. Prescott to come over. Mrs. Prescott insists Samantha give it up and so when the women take the bolt and prepare to exchange the item for money, Samantha floats away and ends up in a tree. Durwood soon returns and is shocked that Samantha is now tree sitting and she asks him to come up to help her down. When he gets in the tree, Mrs. Prescott notices them and is furious that they are fooling around and things get more awkward when Mr. Prescott shows up offended that Durwood ditched their golf game for a fashion show.

Mr. Prescott suggests that if Durwood doesn't get down from the tree right away, especially since Samantha is supposed to be getting ready for the fashion show, he will not have his account. Durwood and Samantha struggle getting down and it occurs to Samantha that she can save the account as part of her turn on the catwalk. Durwood goes to help her change and, when the fashion show starts, he asks Mrs. Prescott if he can take over the mic. He asks everyone to imagine an Egyptian slave girl going to the river for some water and that this doesn't seem to be a chore at all as she seemingly floats down to the river. The audience and Mr. Prescott are astounded as Samantha barely touches the ground, which is due to her carrying a somewhat heavy vase. Durwood says that it's for a new ad campaign for Prescott Shoes, that "with Prescott Shoes you don't walk, you float."

A little later, Samantha and Durwood get home and find Dr. Bombay waiting for them with another potion. Before Samantha can take it, Mr. Prescott rings the doorbell, and Durwood doesn't know what to do with Samantha, especially since he's sneezed and let her go. She tells Durwood to go answer it and she'll take care of the rest. Mr. Prescott is astonished that he's seen Samantha floating but, when he looks again, he sees she's on a ladder. Durwood tells him that they were testing out the invisible wires at home to make sure they worked and, after Samantha takes the potion she finds that she is cured, however, Dr. Bombay begins to float. She says that she took the wires off herself to put on Dr. Bombay which Durwood says was to see if the campaign for men's shoes would work the same.

I would give this one two and a half stars. It's one of my favorites of the Eighth Season just because, to me, it made total sense that if Samantha never used her powers to fly around than she would be grounded, and of course, since Dr. Bombay can't ever diagnose something correctly the first time, his cure would make her float. And that right there is why they ask for a second opinion, though I didn't understand why they would accept it from one of his diagnosing machines. Why not call in Dr. Agraphor?

All though it is Dick Sargent carrying Samantha into the living room, it is Melody he's carrying 'cause her hair is always flatter and straighter than Liz's and, when she's lying on the couch, for the brief minute you see her face it looks like Melody. I also liked the couch sinking into the floor, however, for the floor to give way simply because she weighs 518 pounds would make me think they really DID need to have their floors shored! Also, did you notice the square of carpet move beneath Dr. Bombay's feet when he and Durwood are trying to get Samantha off the couch?

I think it would've been more along the lines of Samantha feeling like crap to simply have her in her bathrobe with messy hair, but I think she looked hot in the sweater-skirt combo.

It seemed the wires were really invisible except during the fashion show which makes the lines about "If you saw them, they wouldn't be invisible! Ha ha" even funnier. It's also funny how Liz says it and the look on her face.

I liked Samantha's fashion show dress. I cannot believe how they didn't even try to hide the wires but have that whole conversation about them being invisible! But I suppose at this point, they didn't care as up to now, *Bewitched* was on the same time as *The Carol Burnett Show*. I guarantee had I been alive then, I wouldn't have been able to watch *Bewitched* because my family would've been watching Carol's show. Heck, I would've chose Carol's show! And, then, as of this episode, *Bewitched* moved to Saturday nights directly opposite *All in the Family*, the new hit show! So it's no wonder the ratings dropped! *Bewitched* had no chance being an old show against such great new shows.

> DURWOOD: *"Sam, you weigh over 500 lbs!"*
> SAMANTHA: *"Yeah, but Sweetheart, that's with all my clothes on!"*
> DURWOOD: *"What do we do now?"*
> DR. BOMBAY: *"I have a previous engagement, but I might suggest you take her out to the park and fly her like a kite!"*

And this scene was totally new to me (and I'm surprised by how blatant it was!):

> MR. PRESCOTT: *"That's a pretty squirrelly couple."*
> MRS. PRESCOTT: *"It's called 'love,' Wilbur!"*
> WILBUR: *"Why's he holding her like that?"*
> ELMA: *"That's also called 'love', Wilbur!"*
> WILBUR: *"He's going to help her dress?!"*
> ELMA: *"'Love', Wilbur!"*
> WILBUR: *"'Sex', Elma!"*

The night before, *Sanford and Son* premiered on NBC.

Three days later George Mitchell (Andre) passed away. He played Announcer in Episode #90: "Soapbox Derby." He was also a regular in the *Dark Shadows* series.

JANUARY 22, 1972

It was on this night that ABC aired Episode #245: "Serena's Richcraft."

Just before Larry and prospective client Harrison Wolcott of Wolcott Towers arrive to pick Durwood up for a business meeting, Serena shows up at 1164 quite put out. Samantha finds that Serena was caught fooling around with the Contessa Piranha's fiancée, Otto, and so when she wasn't looking, Piranha zapped away all of Serena's powers and zapped her to the middle of the freeway! Samantha asks Durwood if Serena can stay with them until her powers are restored, but of course, he's against it. However, he can't argue long as they all hear a helicopter that sounds very close and when they go outside, they find that it's Larry and Mr. Wolcott who have come to take Durwood to survey the site of the newest tower and to discuss possible business. After the helicopter flies off to the distant Connecticut mountains (?!), Serena mentions that she would like to start something with Mr. Wolcott. Samantha assures her that Mr. Wolcott is strictly business, but Serena takes it as a challenge.

After the helicopter tour, the men return and Serena gets her flirt on with Harrison. She almost blows her cover when she tells him how much she enjoyed his hotel in San Francisco, but he tells her there isn't any way she could've stayed there as it burned down over fifty years ago. Durwood is irritated when he sees that Harrison won't pay him or Larry any attention to discuss the campaign and he asks to speak to Samantha in the kitchen. He tells her she needs to get rid of Serena before they lose the account, however, Serena walks in and says that she and Harrison have a date for a trip on his yacht which they are about to leave for.

On the yacht, Serena is impressed by Harrison's 'richcraft' as he has copies of famous paintings on the craft, as the originals would've been damaged by the salt air (however he has the originals at home) and she impresses him with her knowledge of wines.

Three days pass and Harrison isn't heard from because he's spent all his time with Serena, which worries Larry and Durwood. Samantha tells Durwood she's decided that the way they'll get Harrison back is that for their next date, she is going to zap herself into Serena and put her cousin the deep freeze so that she can make the dinner date and break up with Harrison.

At the dinner, Harrison proves to be harder to break up with than she thought but "Serena" tells him that it was just a meaningless fling and, when Harrison turns away to call a waiter, she disappears.

At home, Samantha zaps up the Contessa Pirhana and asks her how many fiancées she currently has on tap and when the Contessa loses count,

Samantha asks her if any of them are Otto. Contessa admits she forgave him and so Samantha zaps the frozen Serena downstairs and asks the Contessa to forgive Serena. She says she'll only do it if Serena is remorseful and so Samantha unfreezes Serena, who is furious. Larry, Durwood, and Mr. Wolcott arrive and before Serena can work her charms on him again, Samantha zaps Harrison into falling for the Contessa. She is smitten and quickly accepts when Harrison asks her for a dinner date that night that would include dancing, merrymaking, and etcetera. Samantha says she'd like to speak to Serena in the kitchen and, as she drags her in there, Serena grabs the Contessa. In the kitchen, Serena apologizes to the Contessa, who gives her her powers back and she quickly leaves to go with Harrison.

The next day, Harrison arrives wanting to apologize to Serena and tells Durwood that the account is his. They ask how his date with the Contessa went and he says it ended very strangely as they were dancing in the moonlight and he began to softly sing "Fly Me to the Moon" to her when suddenly, he found himself flying to the moon!

Even with Serena and the star power of Peter Lawford, I think this one is dull. I'd only give it about two stars. And I ALWAYS confuse this one with "A Chance on Love" with Jack Cassidy so I get confused when Jack Cassidy doesn't show up in the helicopter or Peter Lawford isn't over at the Tate's when he picks up on Samantha.

This episode was filmed at the end of the Seventh Season but kept back until now. I wonder why they kept it so long? You can tell it's from earlier because Samantha's hair is a bit bigger and not as long.

Liz looked like crap almost the entire episode! Those frumpy sweaters and her awful hair! But the good thing was it seemed that she was in much better spirits and was actually into it, almost like Maurice Evans was there.

That scene on the yacht with Serena naming all the portraits was new to me. And I liked when she said that Van Gogh ATTACKED the canvas!

I liked that Serena was now obsessed with rich people. It's just like she said, "There's not much difference between WITCH-craft and RICH-craft...except maybe you fly a little slower." I've always thought of the witches and warlocks as being the elite of society, so as she didn't have her powers any longer, she just went with the next best thing.

I also liked the Contessa Pirhana. I love it when she tells Peter Lawford that they can go out for an evening of dancing, merrymaking, etcetera and Serena says, "Etcetera!"

Liz and Peter Lawford appeared on the later version of *Password* in 1971. Those episodes, I guess, are "lost." I wonder if they mentioned him being on *Bewitched* or if it aired the same week as this?

This episode also always reminds me of the day Liz died. And that's 'cause *Extra*, in their bit about her death, used many clips from this episode including the one where Samantha is on the phone at the beginning and says, "You're kidding!" I had never seen the episode before then.

The day before, the first *Star Trek* Convention was held in New York's Statler-Hilton Hotel. It had only been off the air a little less than three years. The first *Bewitched* convention happened a little less than THIRTY years after *Bewitched* ended. It was an intimate affair at the home of fan Andrea White in Sparks, Nevada in August of 2000.

JANUARY 29, 1972

It was on this night that ABC aired Episode #246: "Samantha on Thin Ice."

Tabitha is excited when she's invited to her friend Janice London's ice skating birthday party, but Samantha reminds her that she doesn't know how to skate. Endora is appalled that Tabitha can't ice skate, as when Samantha was quite young she took lessons in the morning and won the Cosmic Ice Capades in the evening. Durwood says that it didn't count because she learned by witchcraft and that Tabitha will learn the mortal way, at a mortal rink, with a mortal instructor. He says that witches always result to witchcraft when anything impossible is presented to them, which Samantha takes offense to, and she offers to take lessons with Tabitha to prove him wrong.

At the skating rink, Tabitha finds that she cannot stay up on the skates and Samantha find she can't stay on the skates either as the skating instructor picks her up and twirls her around the ice. While Samantha is otherwise occupied, Tabitha makes her way off the ice into the stands where Endora pops in to see how things are going. Tabitha admits not very well and Endora is hurt when she sees Tabitha try to go out again only to fall down immediately. Not abiding by the hurt and embarrassment that would come to Tabitha, Endora casts a spell making Tabitha into a champion skater. Tabitha does all manner of tricks on the ice much to the delight of the instructor, and the horror of Samantha.

When they get home, Tabitha tells her Daddy that they kept their promises not to use magic and she goes upstairs to play with Adam leaving Durwood impressed. Later that evening, Samantha admits that she and Tabitha were having a guilty conscience but, before she can say why, the doorbell rings. They find Billy "Blades" Bookholzer, the Dean of American Figure Skating, winner of five Olympic gold medals, and a laundry list of other skating accomplishments, at their door. He virtually skates into their living room and tells them that he had received a call from the skating instructor telling him of the amazing talent that

Samantha and the ice skating instructor (Bob Paul) are in shock when they see Tabitha skating like a pro.

Tabitha had and, as he lived nearby, Blades wanted to check this claim out himself as he wants to have a prodigy in the Olympics. He requests that they bring Tabitha to the rink the next day so he can see her skate. Samantha and Durwood refuse, but Blades thinks it's un-American and insists they bring her or he promises he will never give up on trying to get them to change their minds and he leaves. Samantha has Durwood guess why Tabitha is so good, and he gets it on the first try.

The next morning, Samantha tries to butter Durwood up with a fancy breakfast so he won't be as mad when they go to the rink later on. However, her attempt fails as he's still in a snit about Tabitha's impending fame as a young skater.

At the skating rink, Tabitha proves that Endora's spell is gone as she can't stay up on the ice at all. The instructor is shocked, and a little scared as his reputation is on the line since Blades hasn't shown up yet. Samantha and Durwood are pleased until they see Tabitha get up and begin to do jumps and backward skating. Seeing that Tabitha just had a slow start, the instructor goes to fetch Blades and Samantha begins to search the stands for Endora, whom she soon finds and demands join them on the floor. Samantha explains that Tabitha is about to be put in the Olympics which will occupy all her time which means no time for her Grandmama. Not wanting that, Endora removes her spell and Tabitha immediately falls down.

Soon Blades and the instructor return and Blades is not amused when Tabitha can't remain on her feet. Furious that his time has been wasted, he tells Samantha that Tabitha is a klutz which angers Endora and, as the instructor follows Blades off the rink, she makes both of them fall down.

I would only give this one star. I actually like "Samantha and the Keyboard" much better than this one. I think Samantha looks anorexic in her skating outfit and her hair looks messy. Plus I don't like thinking about the rumor about Nancy Fox and Bill Asher cavorting. Wish we could confirm it. However, I believe I had heard that she was the girl in the American flag looking outfit.

Bob Paul looked very creepy to me, however, I think that's on his account of his porn-stache which was popular in the '70s. He was actually a champion Olympic gold medal winner in 1960 for Canada and was the flag bearer at those Olympics. He decided to become an actor and appeared on *Bewitched* and some other show and thought it was too much and became an instructor to Peggy Fleming. He just passed away in January 2011.

I loved Endora's pea-shooter too. Very psychedelic!

Blades was ridiculous and I HATED how he skated into their living room. It was very cartoony, but I suppose that›s what we can expect for the last season.

I loved the last scene when Endora makes Blades and the instructor fall down. And even more so, when she did it to Durwood! And I thought Samantha looked like she was getting ready to go rob a bank with that ski cap on!

I wonder if that ice skating rink is still open and where it was?

Here are some of my favorite lines:

SAMANTHA: *"Holy Hans Brinker!"*
SAMANTHA: *"I learned my lesson somewhere else."*

The night before, Agnes Moorehead appeared on *Love, American Style* in "Love and the Anxious Mother."

FEBRUARY 5, 1972

It was on this night that ABC aired Episode #247: "Serena's Youth Pill."

While Serena is babysitting for Samantha, but more like sunbathing for herself, Larry comes over to return Durwood's putter and is pleased to find the sexy vixen alone. Serena immediately begins flirting with him and asks him to stick around to sing and dance and "putter" around. He tells her that she better beware 'cause she's going to turn him into the red devil of yesteryear, to which she responds she could really do it and she tells him she has a Vitamin V pill that will put the spring of life back into him. He's a bit apprehensive but when he sees that she'll be offended, he relents and takes it. She starts getting friendlier with him, but Larry keeps his cool, thanks her for the pill and leaves.

By the time he gets home, Larry's once brilliant white hair is now flaming red, which shocks Louise. Larry realizes that Serena must've been telling the truth about her Vitamin V pill. It then occurs to him that her pill could be worth millions and he immediately heads out to Durwood and Samantha's again.

Meanwhile, Samantha and Durwood have returned and are shocked to find that the only magic Serena pulled was to zap up a Guernsey to milk for the kids. Soon, Larry shows up and they realize Serena forgot to tell them about her V pill. Durwood refuses to have Samantha call on Serena and so Larry leaves. Still fuming over Serena's hijinks, Durwood mentions that not only did Larry's hair look different but he acted and looked much younger.

The next morning, Serena pops in and admits that she slipped Larry a sort of a youth pill that would reverse his age by five, ten, or more years. Samantha is furious as that pill has never been tried out on mortals before and she demands that Serena contact Dr. Bombay for a cure and so Serena pops out.

A little later, a distressed Louise shows up worried about how Larry has been acting as he took her for a nice candle light dinner and dancing and when they got home, she was very tired and he called her a party poop. She also said that he tried finding *The Jack Paar Show* on TV. Samantha suggests Durwood get to the office as it's obvious Larry is getting very young. He's disturbed to find that Larry has gone so far back in time that he's reached the point of his first meeting with Durwood. As they speak, Larry mentions that if Durwood is still with the firm at the end of the '60s and has proven himself, he will be made a first vice-president. Realizing that this could be his ticket in, Durwood asks Larry to write down his offer and sign it.

After speaking to Samantha to find out if Serena has shown up yet, Durwood is startled when Samantha pops in. When he goes to introduce her to Larry, they find that Larry is now a bright eyed young man whose last memory was playing ice hockey. Samantha tells him that he must've been hit in the head by a puck which caused him to lose his memory and she offers to take him home so he can recover. By the time they get to the door, Larry has turned into a boy and is scared as to why he's there in clothes that are much too big. Avoiding much contact with Louise, who was sitting, Samantha takes Larry upstairs after hearing Serena say she has returned. She talks the suspicious Master Tate into drinking the medicine and promises to take him home after a nap.

Downstairs, they find Louise and Serena conversing and when Samantha asks Serena how long the "plant grower" takes to work, she is told almost immediately. Soon, a befuddled gray haired Larry comes downstairs to the delight of his wife. He also finds that he won't make millions on Serena's pill and she leaves.

As the Tates and Stephenses celebrate Larry's recovery, Durwood shows him the note about making him a Vice-President but Larry denies ever having written it.

I think this episode is excellent, especially for being an Eighth Season episode and I would give it three stars. I think it was awesome to see Liz in a swimsuit again! We haven't seen that since way back in Season One's "And Something Makes Three..." I also think Liz (as Serena) and David White had tons of energy and I really like it when they have scenes where they flirt. However, Liz as Samantha was totally devoid of any energy and her skin looked totally greazzy.

I think the only other time we see the outside of the Tate's house is in the Second Season episode where Durwood wishes that he were Larry for one day ("Double Tate"). We see it when Larry comes to the door and Samantha keeps zapping him outside.

I also think Louise looked great and I think it's a shame that Louise wasn't on the show more, especially considering she's supposed to be Samantha's best friend. This would be the last time that Louise appears on the show.

I LOVE Serena's aqua swirly outfit...it's really hot! I can't believe we're to the point where there will be no more Serena, as this is her last episode.

This is one of two episodes this season that wasn't directed by Bill Asher or DICK Michaels (it was directed by E.W. Swackhamer) and as a matter of fact, it was filmed just after the "Thin Ice" episode which I think would account for Liz looking so pissed and tired. She was probably having a hell of a time knowing that Bill was allegedly fooling around with Nancy Fox.

I also think that the company that produces Viagara should've totally used the clip of Serena's explanation of Vitamin V in their ads.

Here are some of my favorite lines:

> SERENA: *"We'll drink and dance and...putter around!"*
> DURWOOD: *"How could you do such a terrible thing?!"*
> SERENA: *"Well, the children were upstairs playing at the time and there wasn't anything else to do."*
> LARRY: *"What is it?"*
> SERENA: *"Vitamin V!"*
> LARRY: *"V?"*
> SERENA: *"For Va-Va-VOOM!"*
> LARRY: *"Vitamin?"*
> SERENA: *"Vitamin...PLUS!"*
> SERENA: *"That pill's a fast worker!"*
> LARRY: *"Really?"*
> SERENA: *"So am I."*
> DURWOOD: *"Now Larry, about that pill — "*
> LARRY: *"Oh, so you've met McMann..."*

Two days later Ottola Nesmith passed away. She played Enchantra in Episode #95: "The Trial and Error of Aunt Clara." She was also in *The Story of Three Loves* with Agnes Moorehead.

FEBRUARY 12, 1972

It was on this night that ABC aired Episode #248: "Tabitha's First Day of School."

Samantha and Durwood receive a visit by Maude Hickman, of the Board of Education, as the Board has found that they have a child of school age who is not enrolled in school. Caught by surprise, Samantha tells Mrs. Hickman that she has been tutoring Tabitha at home. Mrs. Hickman questions Samantha's credentials and insists that as she isn't qualified to teach, they must enroll Tabitha in school at once or she'll report them to the authorities. Furious, Samantha reluctantly agrees and, as Mrs. Hickman leaves, Samantha twitches a devil's tail on her only to remove it moments later at Durwood's insistence.

Later on, Samantha takes Tabitha to school to enroll her and before they enter Mrs. Peabody's class, Samantha has Tabitha promise not to use witchcraft of any kind. Tabitha agrees and they enter the class, even though it's almost over. Mrs. Peabody has Tabitha join the Terrarium Group where they keep the lizards and frogs for Activities Period. Samantha requests if she could stay for this first day, but Mrs. Peabody insists that Tabitha will be fine and insists she leave. However, they are interrupted by the sound of Tabitha being bullied by problem child Charlton Rollnick, Jr. Mrs. Peabody instructs him to take a seat and then returns to getting Samantha to leave. She introduces Tabitha to the class and to Samantha and asks the class to say "goodbye" to Mrs. Stephens. Samantha leaves and Mrs. Peabody finds Tabitha a seat, which happens to be right in front of Charlton, who had taken a frog from the terrarium and put it in her desk. As Mrs. Peabody goes to read to them, she hears a frog croaking and finds that it's coming from Tabitha's desk. Annoyed, she tells Tabitha to return the frog to its place. Tabitha complies and when she goes back to her seat, Charlton pulls on her braids causing her to yell out. Mrs. Peabody reprimands Tabitha and is surprised to find Samantha has returned. She asks if everything is all right, and Mrs. Peabody tells her that Tabitha just isn't used to the classroom environment and so Samantha leaves, however, she stays just outside the door and when she sees Charlton go to pull Tabitha's braids again, she twitches them to shock him. Done with all the interruptions,

Mrs. Peabody tells Charlton that he will remain after school the next day for detention.

When school lets out, Charlton confronts Tabitha telling her that it's her fault he's going to have to do detention and grabs her by the arm. She tells him to let go but he won't and he asks her what she's going to do. She tells him he's hurting her, but he insists he wouldn't hurt a fly. Done with his bullying, Tabitha tells him he may not hurt flies but he's going to enjoy eating them and she zaps him into a bullfrog! Just then, Mrs. Peabody comes out and thinks Tabitha has again taken the frog from the terrarium and demands she put him back. Tabitha tries to tell her it's not the same frog but Mrs. Peabody won't hear of it and she goes on reprimanding Tabitha. When the teacher has her back to Tabitha, she goes to retrieve Charlton and realizes she's not sure which frog he is and so she just takes one.

At home, Tabitha tries to change Charlton back but it doesn't work and when Samantha sees what she's doing, she realizes that Tabitha must've changed the bully into a frog. Tabitha admits it and tells her mother what happened and Samantha realizes Tabitha must've brought home the wrong frog. She calls Charlton's mother to make her aware of the whereabouts of her son and before she can refuse, Mrs. Rollnick says she'll be over to pick him up as he's going to be late for his piano lesson. After getting off the phone, Samantha takes the frog with her and pops back to the school. Just as she retrieves the right frog, the janitor walks in wanting to know what Samantha is doing. Not having time to be bothered, Samantha pops out right in front of him.

Samantha pops in just as Mrs. Rollnick arrives. Samantha has Durwood stall Mrs. Rollnick while she takes the frog out to Tabitha. She changes him back but finds that he still croaks but, with one more zap, Tabitha restores his voice. Mrs. Rollnick is furious with Charlton but Samantha tells her that maybe what Charlton needs in order to stop being a bully is a little love and understanding.

I'd give it three stars. It's one of my favorites. Liz doesn't seem as pissed off and she looks way hot through the whole thing, though she needs to dye her roots. And Erin seemed to be able to act much better. And Nita Talbot is a riot! How about her legs and that short dress?! Yet she's always standing jaunty…way funny! I love it when she rolls her eyes after she hangs up with Samantha as she's taking the curlers out of her hair. But I gotta say that I always thought she probably beat Charlton all the time. He totally reminds me of the kids at school whom we knew that their parents beat them and also neglected them. I also don't believe that Mrs.

Rollnick was being serious about canceling his piano lesson and taking him out for ice cream. I think she was putting on airs with Samantha and pretty much beat the living hell out of him once they got home.

I also thought Samantha had no right getting up in Mrs. Hickman's face about keeping Tabitha at home. True, Mrs. Hickman shouldn't have been so snotty but at the same time I would think that the board of education would want to know why a child is not going to the public school. I also thought Durwood should've stood up for Samantha and said something…seemed like he really was two-dimensional in this episode and therefore faded into the background.

I thought the Snoopy drawing looked like it could've been done by someone Robert Asher's age. It is weird that there were all those corrections on it.

I think Maudie Prickett was a good choice for the teacher even though it's kind of lame that she already played the nursery school teacher ("I Don't Want to be a Toad…"). I also remember at least one teacher like her when I was in kindergarten. I also liked that she was reading them *Alice in Wonderland*. That would've been an AWESOME book for Tabitha to zap herself into, even cooler to have had Agnes Moorehead play the Red Queen like she did in the TV movie.

I wonder why Samantha didn't just pop into the class room when she went to exchange the frogs. Seemed like she wanted to be mean to the janitor, but that scene is always one of my favorites. I like to see her flaunting her powers.

Erin said this wasn't one of her favorites. I'm wondering if it was because that kid that played Charlton really pulled on her hair and it hurt. She did say, though, that she got to take home one of the toads after filming.

Here are some of my favorite lines:

> SAMANTHA: *"Well, I had to get it off my chest!"*
> DURWOOD: *"Now will you kindly get it off her…?"*
> DURWOOD: *"How was school?"*
> TABITHA: *"Oh, it's still there."*
> MRS. ROLLNICK: *"Bah-king at his mutha like a dawg?"*

FEBRUARY 19, 1972

It was on this night that ABC aired Episode #249: "George Washington Zapped Here," Part One.

Tabitha decides to take part of her father's George Washington memorabilia collection to school for show-n-tell, comprised of a button from one of his coats and a buckle from his shoe. But Samantha tells her they are much too valuable to take to school and tells her instead she can take a book with a picture of Washington and tell the class that her daddy collects Washington relics. After Samantha leaves, Esmeralda comes in to make the beds and finds that Tabitha isn't too happy about bringing the book to school. She agrees and tells Tabitha that if she promises to bring them back right after school, she'll zap the buckle and button out of the picture and return them when Tabitha is done. Tabitha agrees and when Esmeralda casts her spell, she does get what she wants, however they are attached to the man himself!

After Tabitha leaves for school, Samantha and Durwood's breakfast is interrupted by the sound of George Washington's voice. Samantha insists Durwood go to work while she finds out what's going on. When she gets to Tabitha's room, she is shocked to find the Founding Father and she realizes that he's there because of Esmeralda and she insists that Esmeralda work on returning him to the past. As Samantha explains to Durwood who is upstairs, Esmeralda and George come downstairs as he is wondering where he is and how he came to be there. Samantha tells him that he is in the 20th century, which he doesn't believe though he admits the room is filled with contraptions and devices he has never seen before. He says that he is going to go for a walk to clear his head, but Samantha suggests he stay and sit down so she can explain. She reveals that she is a witch and so is Esmeralda and that he has arrived there by witchcraft. He doesn't believe her until she asks him for another explanation. Resigned to the fact that he is in fact in the 20th century, George asks how the thirteen colonies fair and Samantha tells him that they are now fifty states and they show him how he has been honored on the dollar bill. Just then Larry calls wondering where Durwood is and so he rushes off with the admonition that Samantha make sure George doesn't leave her sight until Esmeralda figures out her spell.

After Durwood leaves, Samantha shows George what else has changed since his lifetime and he decides he must sit down as he is too stimulated by all this new information. He asks for a cup of tea and when she goes to make it, he decides to go out on the walk to clear his head. When Samantha comes back, she's horrified to find he's left out the front door, which is wide open. She goes to search for him and bumps into her neighbor mowing his lawn. She asks him if he had seen George Washington pass by and he admits he did, that George was taking in the neighborhood and so he had suggested he go for a walk in the park.

In the park, George has found protestors of the war and after speaking with the people, he realizes that all though there have been many advancements, it seems that the people have forgotten the original principles of the Constitution. He soon gathers a big crowd which attracts the attention of the police. An officer asks to see George's permit for a rally but George says he has the right to gather people in assembly to assert their rights. Samantha

Samantha catches up with George Washington (Will Geer) in the park.

soon shows up and claims that George is her uncle but George refuses to go with her and threatens the officer with his sword. The officer says that now as he's been threatened, he's going to have to book George into jail.

At the court, the bailiff says that there will be a court hearing in a week but that George can be released on $2,000 bail.

After arriving back at home, George admits his displeasure at the

Samantha accompanies George Washington to the police station.

apparent lack of respect for the Constitution and feels that the American people should know his story. Samantha reminds him that as she is a witch and part of a silent minority, she would like to remain that way. He excuses himself to go to the den for tea and contemplation. Durwood and Samantha go into the kitchen to find Esmeralda working on the spell and Samantha gives her some tea to take into George. They soon hear a crash and when they get into the den, they see George fading away as Esmeralda has remembered the spell. Durwood actually congratulates her and he and Samantha go into the living room to rest from their stressful day.

As Esmeralda is cleaning up the mess from the tea, she finds that George left his shoes behind and when she tries to send them back, she ends up bringing not only George back, but Martha Washington, his wife, as well!

Stay tuned for the further adventures of George Washington, next week on *Bewitched!*

I'd only give it about half star. Will Geer bugs me so much in the way he speaks. It's like a rickety old robot and what the hell was up with him, when he's looking at the TV, he lifts up his right leg as though he's going to fart or something? Anyway, I thought the Ben Franklin episodes were boring and these George Washington ones were even more so especially 'cause they're a remake of all ready boring ones.

I also think that were Durwood really a George Washington collector, he would've let his adversity towards witchcraft be negated by the thrill of actually meeting George Washington. It would've been much funnier to see him fawning all over him and Samantha being relieved that he's not all pissed off about it or have Durwood try to prevent Esmeralda from remembering the spell.

Also, when Durwood says he pulled some strings, he seemed REALLY uncomfortable about how he "pulled" those "strings." What the hell did he do? He honestly had shifty eyes when he said it.

I think Washington's outfit would've made more sense if we had seen that he was wearing the same thing for the portrait he was zapped out of...it looks too dressy.

I think it would be cool iff'n you happened to come across one of those particular bills used in the episode.

It's ironic that Dick Wilson's first appearance on *Bewitched*, at the beginning of "A Change of Face," he's not drunk and in his last appearance he's not drunk, yet almost all the ones in between he is.

Also, besides "Samantha's Good News," this is the only episode where Samantha uses absolutely no witchcraft. Too bad Durwood didn't notice but I suppose he was too busy "pulling strings."

This one and its second part were the second to last episodes to be filmed, by the way. I'm so sad that we're coming up on the end of the series.

The night before, Dick Sargent guest starred on *Love, American Style* in "Love and Lovers' Lane."

The same night as this episode, Sammy Davis, Jr. appeared as himself on *All in the Family* and elicited one of the longest laughs in TV history after kissing Archie Bunker on the cheek.

FEBRUARY 26, 1972

It was on this night that ABC aired Episode #250: "George Washington Zapped Here," Part Two.

Samantha and Durwood are shocked to find that the recently departed (from their home and time) George Washington has returned with his wife Martha Washington as a result of Esmeralda's goof-up. The President and his wife are actually quite pleased to be back as George didn't want to sully his reputation by missing his hearing. He has also told Martha all about the wonders of the 20th century and after Durwood has insulted Esmeralda, who disappears, Samantha shows Martha the great steps forward in the kitchen.

The next morning, Samantha hasn't had any luck finding Esmeralda until Durwood asks her to try one more time. Esmeralda pops in from Pluto where she had been brooding and admits that she has remembered the spell but Durwood and Samantha tell her to wait until after the hearing.

As Durwood and Samantha join the Washingtons for breakfast, Larry shows up to pick Durwood up so they can go over ideas for the Whirlaway Washing Machine account. Samantha suggests Larry just go without Durwood as he hasn't had breakfast, but Larry invites himself in for coffee while he waits. He is surprised by the Washingtons, who are still dressed in period clothing, but Samantha introduces them as her aunt and uncle. Uncomfortable with Larry finding out any more, Durwood says they should leave and, as they near the door, he tells Larry that George was a history professor who majored in George Washington and unfortunately went a little mad. This gives Larry the brilliant idea to slap the name of "Washington" on a Whirlaway Washing Machine and before Durwood can object, Larry returns to the dining room and offers George the opportunity to advertise. George accepts and he joins Durwood and Larry for their drive into the city.

At the offices of Mr. Jamison, president of Whirlaway Washing Machines, Larry presents George Washington, which thrills Mr. Jamison who had a relative that was in the platoon that George had led in war. George recalls that this particular man was a deserter and a coward which angers Mr. Jamison. Larry calms Mr. Jamison telling him that it's obvious that George is an eccentric and that the idea of having George Washington as part of the campaign is an excellent idea. He relents and lets George read the copy for the ads but George is confused as to why he would sell machines that he has had no experience with and even more so when he finds that all the various models of washing machines are the same. This infuriates Mr. Jamison who takes his account from McMann and Tate.

Later on in the Judge's chambers, Officer Crandall tells the Judge about his attack by George. Samantha asks if she can say something and presents as evidence the sword which is just a ceremonial sword that couldn't cut through butter. However, Officer Crandall says that he could've used the hilt of the sword to hit him on the head. George stands to defend himself and says that he was just exercising his ability to free speech and assembly. The officer mentions that he still didn't have a permit. The Judge asks George to identify who he really is and George maintains that he really is who he says he is and the Judge makes a point that no matter who he says he is, the safety of the officer was just being watched over. Samantha speaks up and says that George had no malicious intent, he was just protecting his beliefs in the Constitution and that his being there had just served to remind the people about what George Washington stood for. The Judge agrees and dismisses the case and has George sign for his sword.

At home, George and Martha express their desire to leave, so Samantha calls Esmeralda in who works her original spell backwards therefore sending George and Martha back. Right after they have faded out, the doorbell rings revealing the Judge, who seems to be in a panic looking for George. He shows them a book with a copy of a letter from George Washington to James Madison and the receipt George had signed and mentions that the court clerk, who is a collector of George Washington memorabilia, verified it as authentic so the Judge wanted to speak to George and find out how he did it.

This one is a definite clunker...really, the only good part is at the very end just before the fade out to the credits when you can see Dick Sargent goose Elizabeth Montgomery and she looks like she was about to rip his face off.

I hate all this talk on *Bewitched* of, "You're going to use my face for a commercial venture?" Who cares?! And again, Will Geer, when he's reading the lines for the commercial does it in such a way that cannot be duplicated, nor should it be.

Liz seems truly pissed off at the entire world, her hair really is flat and unfortunately her boobs look the same way, yet again without a bra. It also seems like everyone is yelling at everyone else, with the exception of Jane Connell, who like the *Bewitched* Critic said, apparently missed the memo that nobody cares anymore.

I think it's ironic how when Martha and Sam are talking about how the smell of sun dried linens will soon be in a box, it is now, with dryer sheets.

This was the second to last episode to be filmed before the end of the series and, if this is any indication of how it would've been had they continued on, then I'm glad they stopped.

It's the last time Esmeralda appears. What a waste of Alice Ghostley's talents on that character. And I HATED when she's reversing the spell and Durwood stops her by saying, "What is she doing?!" Sam: "She's reversing time by reversing the spell!" Durwood: "Well, can't she say it to herself?" What in the hell?! He goes on and on about wanting her to send George Washington back and then when she does it, he doesn't like how she does it?!

And another thing…really, the whole judiciary system in NY are George Washington collectors? Give me a break! It's just ill-making that a show that was once so brilliant and creative swung to the very end of the spectrum to pretty much be an embarrassment. I think for the most part, all those mortals that say they don't like the show are keeping episodes like this in mind considering Dick Sargent's years seems to be re-run more than Dick York's were.

MARCH 4, 1972

It was on this night that ABC aired Episode #251: "School Days, School Daze."

Endora pops in when she hears that Tabitha has started school at Towners Elementary, especially as it's a mortal school. She tells Samantha she is vehemently opposed to it but Samantha tells her that no matter, Tabitha will still be going to the mortal school. Insulted, Endora disappears and pops in on Tabitha, who isn't very happy as she is going to take a test to see if she can skip to the second grade. She is scared as she hasn't ever taken a test, but Endora assures her she will do well and puts her under the deep freeze while she casts a spell giving her all the knowledge in the world. After casting the spell, she unfreezes Tabitha, wishes her luck and Endora disappears.

At the school, Mrs. Peabody gives Tabitha the instructions and waits out in the hall with Samantha as she says that the test will be about twenty minutes. But moments later, Tabitha comes out claiming to be finished. Mrs. Peabody and Samantha are sure Tabitha is mistaken but when Mrs. Peabody checks the answers, she finds that Tabitha answered every question right. Samantha realizes that Tabitha must've had "tutoring" from her Grandmama but Mrs. Peabody insists there isn't any way to prepare for a test like this. Thinking that Tabitha must be a child prodigy, Mrs. Peabody insists that she introduce Tabitha to the school principal, Mr. Roland.

In the Principal's Office, Mr. Roland thinks that there must be some kind of trick going on as Tabitha is able to add up large sums quickly, but

Mrs. Peabody assures him it's no trick. When he asks Tabitha to explain to him the Theory of Relativity, she does so just like a textbook. His doubts are squashed when Tabitha identifies a recreation of the Mona Lisa by a lesser known artist that he has a print of. Mr. Roland tells Samantha that he thinks that Tabitha should skip more than the first grade but Samantha says she won't have it and that Tabitha will just skip to the second grade.

At home, Samantha calls on her mother and demands she remove the spell, though Endora does so with regret. Later on, Mrs. Peabody shows up saying that she is writing an article for the *Scholastic Monthly* about Tabitha and she barges in looking for her. Samantha tells her that Tabitha is out on the patio playing with her brother and reminds her that she didn't want Tabitha's abilities exploited and she invites Mrs. Peabody to leave. Outside, Mrs. Peabody decides to sneak to the backyard so she can speak with Tabitha. When she gets to the gate she sees Tabitha and Adam playing ball and is shocked when she sees Tabitha wiggle her fingers towards the ball and makes it bounce midair to her. She's even more shocked when Tabitha changes a quaint castle of building blocks into a model castle. Mrs. Peabody comes into the backyard and asks Tabitha how she did all those things, but Tabitha tells her she can't tell, however, Adam tells her that Tabitha is a witch. Dismissing the little boy, Mrs. Peabody says there are no such thing as witches. Just then Samantha comes out on the patio, furious that Mrs. Peabody is trespassing and she sends the children inside. Mrs. Peabody tells her what she saw and that she thinks that Tabitha and Samantha must be from outer space and if so, the FBI must find out. Samantha tells her it's not true and that if she is going to snitch, she may as well have her facts straight. She reiterates that she is a witch but Mrs. Peabody thinks she's lying and so Samantha tells her that she is barking up the wrong tree and twitches her up into the nearest tree. After she repeats her statement about being a witch, Samantha twitches Mrs. Peabody down, who admits she believes her. Samantha tells her that she'll tell her everything and when Mrs. Peabody asks for a pencil, Samantha twitches one up. Feeling faint, Mrs. Peabody asks for water and Samantha zaps some up which is too much for Mrs. Peabody to take and she runs off.

Mrs. Peabody ends up back at the school and tells Mr. Roland of her marvelous experience but of course he doesn't believe it. She suggests he come with her back to the Stephens so he can see for himself and so to get her off his back, he agrees.

Meanwhile, Durwood has come home and Samantha decides to reveal what has happened during the day and before he can really lose his cool, the doorbell rings. Samantha finds Mrs. Peabody and Mr. Roland, who is quite embarrassed. She invites them in and asks Durwood to help her get some drinks for them in the kitchen. Durwood wonders what Samantha is up to, but she tells him to just follow her lead and she zaps up a traveling trunk behind the couch. Back in the living room, Samantha tells them that she is indeed a witch and that her husband is a mortal. She also does a little magic for them by zapping up a drink for Durwood but when Mr. Roland goes to examine it, he finds that it's attached to a rubber band. Samantha asks if they would like to see another trick and she goes to fetch one out of the trunk. Mr. Roland and Mrs. Peabody see that the trunk has "The Witches. America's Foremost Magicians" printed on it and Samantha tells them that they used to have a traveling act. Mrs. Peabody wants to know how the events of earlier in the afternoon were accomplished and Samantha tells her that it really was magic. Mr. Roland feels that he's had proof enough of Mrs. Peabody's instability and tells them that they won't have to worry about her sneaking in again.

I would give this a four star rating because this script was truly original, pretty much the last original script of the season and series! Which meant that Liz was happier, which meant everyone was happier. I also noticed that Durwood didn't seem to be in this one much.

This one has always been a favorite and it's because I LOVE the scene where Samantha confronts Mrs. Peabody in the backyard and says, "Let me put it another way: You are barking up the wrong tree!" ZONK! Sam had every right to accuse her of snooping because Mrs. Peabody just walked right on into the house and WAS snooping! I'd have been pissed as hell if I had told her she wasn't welcome only to find her out in MY backyard talking to MY children! I'd have done much worse than simply zapping her into a tree! I do think its lame that Mrs. Peabody accused Samantha of being from outer space but I WOULD think someone was a witch iff'n I suddenly found myself in a tree! There is no magician that could pull that trick in broad daylight. I did like Mrs. Peabody's line about "Imagine! Someday this house will be a shrine!" How prophetic!

I always thought it made no sense that they aired this episode after the bullfrog episode but it was actually filmed before that one…at the same time though, the bullfrog episode has her being introduced to the class, whereas that probably should've taken place in this episode.

Towners Elementary came from the area around Patterson, NY where Liz spent much of her time. It's weird that they would change it. I did like that they dropped the names of *Time* and *Life* magazines. I didn't catch the name of the magazine Samantha was reading and when the camera zoomed in on her, she rolled up the corner as though she didn't want us to see.

The principal, Charles Lane, is my favorite of the guest actors. He's always so good! And as a little side note, he and Maudie Prickett played Maxwell Smart's Uncle and Aunt in an episode from *Get Smart*'s first season, I believe. I like it when Mrs. Peabody tries to show him how Samantha twitched her nose. She did a horrible job trying to recreate it but it was funny!

Adam should've been the one to zap up the castle. One simple little spell like that would've solidified in everyone's mind that he was a warlock but then again, at this point, everyone was watching *All in the Family*.

I think Agnes Moorehead looks totally ill in this episode, especially when she's up in Tabitha's room. I'm wondering if this is the episode where Agnes mentions that she had called in sick and somebody called her up and told her she had better show up or she would be fired? This story is mentioned in Charles Tranberg's excellent biography of Agnes entitled *I Love the Illusion* (2005). In chapter 15, Quint Benedetti, Agnes' friend and travelling companion, says that she was almost let go. He said that she was suffering from bouts of the flu and one day was so ill she could barely move so she had Quint call in for her. Minutes after he called the phone rang and he gave it to her and she later told him that she had been told, "either you come in or you will be put on suspension." So she went in and told the unnamed director, "Here I am! Are you satisfied?" She worked that day but she got sicker and was finally granted time off. It also says that Liz and Dick sent her flowers and a note saying how much they missed her. In looking at the filming schedule and seeing how she did look on film, I'm guessing the episode Quint is referring to, iff'n his story is correct, is "Samantha on Thin Ice" because that one finished filming 9/30/71 and the next episode she was in that was filmed was "School Days, School Daze" that didn't finish filming until 11/4/71. In between that time there were only two other episodes which finished filming and there was a two week stretch where none were done making me think that the whole show shut down to wait for her.

MARCH 11, 1972

It was on this night that ABC aired Episode #252: "A Good Turn Never Goes Unpunished."

Durwood spends all night coming up with ideas for the Benson Mattress account but he feels that his ideas are lacking. When Samantha sees them, she says that maybe they just need a different approach and she sketches out a few additions, which are perfect. Happy that he has a solid approach to the account, Durwood begins to get ready for work, but pauses as he realizes that Samantha may have used witchcraft to come up with the ideas. She insists they were just merely ideas but he still says he can't be too sure and he leaves. Endora pops in irritating Samantha even more, especially since Endora thinks that Durwood wouldn't be able to make it without Samantha. Before they can get any further into it, Endora pops out.

At the office, Durwood meets with Larry and Mr. Benson, and finds that his original ideas are just not what Mr. Benson would like. Before Mr. Benson can leave, Durwood infers that he has some variations on his ideas but he hedges and says that they just aren't ready yet and so Mr. Benson, seeing that Durwood is tired what with all his yawning, tells the gentleman that they can call him when they are ready.

At home, Durwood and Samantha discuss his failure at the office and she assures him again that she didn't use magic, but he still seems to believe that she did use magic. He insults her age, which is several hundred years because of being a witch, which leads to a big argument. Seeing that Durwood is being the pig-head her mother always said he was, Samantha tells him that if she's going to be saddled with the name, she may as well play the game and she becomes invisible. Even when they get ready for bed, Samantha is still invisible and when Durwood tries to get her to calm down, she zaps him to the couch for the night.

The next morning, Samantha is still sticking to her invisible guns at breakfast and she uses Tabitha as a mouthpiece to argue with Durwood. After he leaves for work, Samantha returns to visibility and explains to Tabitha about how silly adult arguments are.

Later on, while doing the dishes, Samantha finds that the dishes are suddenly gone and her mother appears inviting her to join her on Cloud Nine with the children but Samantha refuses. She insists that Durwood was right and she should've just minded her business. Endora offers the invitation again and pops out.

At the office, Durwood finds that Larry has been going through Samantha's additions and he loves them and he insists that they share them with Mr. Benson, who agreed to give them another shot. Durwood tells him that they shouldn't show them to Mr. Benson as he would be powerless to refuse them and as they argue, Mr. Benson walks in. Once they have settled down, Larry shows Mr. Benson the ideas and to Durwood's shock, Mr. Benson isn't impressed. It finally dawns on him that Samantha was telling the truth and without further ado, he excuses himself to go home to apologize.

Meanwhile, Endora has popped in on Samantha and convinces her that a trip to Cloud Nine would do her good, especially since Tabitha is at school and Esmeralda has taken Adam to the park. Cloud Nine is absolutely serene and beautiful, especially as there isn't any smog up in the heavens. Down on Earth, Durwood arrives home and calls out to Samantha. She hears him and his apology and she flies down to be with him. He continues to apologize and she accepts and wonders why he changed his mind. He tells her about Benson and how he didn't care for her ideas. She takes it that it proved that he was wrong but that he also thought she was guilty until proven innocent. He sidesteps all that telling her that he loves her. She agrees and says that it's ridiculous that they'd lose sleep over some dumb account. A light bulb goes off in Durwood's head and he tells her that she inspired a new idea and that he must tell Benson before it's too late.

Later on, Durwood returns with the good news that Benson loved the idea and so the account is theirs.

I would give this a one and a half star rating. From here on out they totally just dust off some First (in this case, "Help, Help, Don't Save Me") or Second Season scripts, change some names and voila! A whole "new" episode! Actually, for this one they integrated some of "To Twitch or Not to Twitch" from Season Four when they have that whole scene about "Just how well did you know Socrates?" Except, here both Dick Sargent and Liz recite their lines like robots, whereas in "To Twitch…" it was funny. It really is irritating for Durwood to automatically assume Sam is using witchcraft for the ideas and even more so when Samantha tells Endora that she's going to apologize to Durwood and tell him that he was right and she was wrong! Are you freaking kidding me?! I did like seeing Liz draw again. I like her style and I wish I had a drawing of hers.

And how's about her nightie?! I think that's the slinkiest one she's worn so far!

I do like this episode, however, on account of the invisible Samantha scene. It seemed like the special effects department was really trying to do something new. I thought her holding the book and all seemed TOO natural. It really seemed like there was somebody in the bed 'cause you could totally see her breathing by the movement of the indent and all and, when she zaps Durwood out of bed, the sheets actually FALL! If you compare it to the couple other times she zapped Dick York's Durwood out of bed, you'll notice that when he disappears the sheets are just suddenly flat. But then, with all the attention they paid to that scene they totally let everything else slip. When Sam reappears after taking the flowers to change them (which I thought was a stupid excuse to move the flowers, she should've said she was going to go water them) they didn't even try to match up the film. And the same thing goes for when Samantha pops out from Cloud 9. Endora was sitting up and when Sam pops out she's reclining…sloppy SLOPPY work. And did you notice that when invisible Sam is eating the bacon and toast the film is reversed? Whatever for?

And where was Adam at breakfast? Especially when he's mentioned later on as being at the park with Esmeralda? This is also Erin's last episode.

I liked seeing Samantha in her flying suit again. I do like the scene on Cloud 9 even if the lettering in the clouds is corny. However, I do not believe any witch would be reclining on patio recliners up there, they'd simply be reclining on the clouds.

And then, I have never noticed until the DVDs, that in Endora's last scene her right eye makeup is all smeared to the effect of making it look like she's got a black eye! I wonder iff'n they shot it and didn't tell her because they simply didn't care to take the time to fix and re-shoot. I'll bet she was pissed when she saw it, iff'n she ever did.

This is the second of two episodes this season that wasn't directed by either William Asher or DICK Michaels. This one was by Ernest Losso, who happened to be the casting director from Seasons Five and Six and associate producer on "Sisters at Heart."

MARCH 18, 1972

It was on this night that ABC aired Episode #253: "Samantha's Witchcraft Blows a Fuse."

While dining at Ah Fong's, Samantha and Durwood are treated to Mr. Fong's special creation called the Heavenly Himalayan that contains secret ingredients, but for one—the Himalayan Cinnamon Stick. The drink is quite good but Samantha finds it going to her head very quickly and she soon is plastered, which is odd as she is a witch and they don't get plastered, so Durwood takes her home.

At home, Aunt Hagatha is surprised that they've returned early and even more surprised that Samantha is drunk and she offers to call Dr. Bombay. However, the drunkenness seems to have worn off so Samantha tells her to wait to call the doctor and she goes to try out her powers by levitating a lamp. Things go well until it crashes mid-flight and, as they think about what to do, Samantha suddenly finds vertical red stripes on her face! Durwood insists Hagatha call for Dr. Bombay. After calling out to the cosmos, Hagatha, Samantha, and Durwood are surprised when Dr. Bombay's nurse pops in. She tells them that the Doctor is out but she'll relay the message and she pops out. Before they can wonder where the Doctor is, he pops in having been trying out his new wrestling mat on his new nurse. Samantha shows him the stripes and tells him about her loss of powers. When he asks if she has been anywhere near the Himalayas, and she tells him no, Durwood realizes their drink had the Himalayan Cinnamon Stick in it. Dr. Bombay says that is the exact cause for Samantha's condition as eons ago the Tibetan monks that lived in the Himalayans cross-polinated a rare herb with the cinnamon sticks to drive the witches out of there, and it worked. If it isn't cured within eight hours, the effect will be permanent, so he zaps in his ultra-vascular self-denominating power tricloscope with, of course, the super duper predictor attachment to get the antidote. After writing down the ingredients, Dr. Bombay gives the list to Hagatha to fill with the Apothecary, but she won't have anything to do with him. She gives it to Samantha and tells her she'll zap her there and Dr. Bombay leaves.

Later, Samantha pops in on the Apothecary, who is very pleased to see her, even with her stripes. He goes to fill the prescription and, after giving her a chase around his store, he finally tells her he'll give her everything for a kiss and so she gives him a peck on the nose and he zaps her back.

While waiting for Samantha, Durwood suddenly bumps into Dr. Bombay, who has popped back in as he realizes that he forgot one ingredient—the tail feather of a dodo bird. And before Durwood can argue with him about the impossibility of finding a dodo bird alive, Dr. Bombay pops out. Soon, Samantha pops in and Durwood shares the bad news with her. She remembers that Endora had given Tabitha a cosmos coloring book for her last birthday and it may have had a picture of a dodo bird in it, so she suggests Hagatha pop upstairs, find the picture and zap it out of the book. She complies and soon comes running down the stairs, screaming, as the huge dodo is chasing her! Hagatha tells Durwood he'll have to try to obtain the tail feather and before he can get near the bird, it runs outside and somehow manages to fly up to the roof. Durwood gets the ladder out and climbs up on the roof and just as he about falls, he grabs onto the dodo's tail and falls off. However, as he had some hold on the tail, his fall was broken and he has the feather. Hagatha zaps the bird back in the book and Samantha stirs the potion and tries it however, nothing happens except that she gets horizontal red stripes! Hagatha calls for Dr. Bombay who pops in surprised that Samantha hasn't taken the potion. She angrily tells him she has and he reviews the potion and mentions the Himalayan Cinnamon Stick. Samantha tells him he never mentioned that part, but he insists he did as it provides the necessary anti-toxins. Before Samantha can get any angrier, Dr. Bombay pops off. Durwood realizes that it's getting close to the eighth hour and that the only place that would have the cinnamon stick would be Ah Fong's, which is closed so he gathers up his courage and goes to break into the restaurant. He is caught by the police and posts bail and hurries home. Samantha mixes the potion once more and drinks it and soon her stripes disappear.

I would totally give it four stars…JUST KIDDING! More like a half star. I remember this episode from when I was little and I think it was one of the first ones I ever recorded because I've seen it 23,947,239,472,934, 723,472,394,723,947 times and practically have it memorized because I thought Dr. Bombay was so funny. In fact, I'd have to say this is where my love of Dr. Bombay came from, but in comparing it to the rest of the series, they should've titled this "The One Where *Bewitched* Blows a Fuse." First of all, it's a retread of about THREE episodes, the main one being "Take Two Aspirin and a Half a Pint of Porpoise Milk" where Sam got Square Green Spots Disease, which is much more imaginative and believable. But then they've retread on a stripey disease because she had bright green stripes in "Out of Synch, Out of Mind" and then, of course, "Allergic to Macedonian Dodos." It seems like it was honestly a cut and paste job with those scripts. Actually, now that I think about it, FOUR scripts because there is one of the more recent episodes where practically the same scene at the Apothecary's takes place. It is one of the worst episodes of the series but I still think "Birdies, Bogeys and Baxter" is my least favorite. It's golf and BORING! At least this one has some funny moments.

If Tammy Grimes, the creator's original choice for Samantha, saw this episode, she probably thanked her lucky stars she said no. We should thank our lucky stars that she DID turn down *Bewitched* because her voice is so irritating and, having seen snippets of *The Tammy Grimes Show*, I doubt *Bewitched* would've lasted past five episodes.

I like the Apothecary. I think he's funny and I do think it's funny him chasing Sam just because it's funny that he thinks he's still "got it."

A couple years ago I looked up the actor Benson Fong because I found it strange that they would name the restaurant after him and found that it's because Benson Fong actually owned the restaurant chain Ah Fong's! There were several in Hollywood including the original on Vine Street and on Sunset. I don't think they are around anymore because as of his death in 1987, there was only one left open. But it seemed business was booming in 1971 so I'm wondering iff'n Liz or Bill Asher really liked the place and decided to feature it on *Bewitched*. And how do you like that Sam and Durwood are waiting for Louise and Larry, making us think we'll see Louise and then it just doesn't happen. You'd think that they'd be right over to see what's wrong with Samantha. I also wonder if Ah Fong's really had the Heavenly Himalayan drink. And why would Samantha wear that UGLY outfit to a business dinner? That's something you'd just wear in everyday living, if at all.

Drunk Samantha always reminds me of Carol Burnett…it seems like she sounds just like one of her characters, so it's funny. It was cool to see Reta Shaw again as Aunt Hagatha, a role which she started in. But you could totally tell without looking at the script comparisons that Endora was supposed to be in this episode. I've always loved Nurse Often! She's hot and funny and I love it when she's asked, "Where's Dr. Bombay?" Nurse Often: "Bomb's away! That's what I call him for short, "Bomb." Samantha: "And what — and I'll be afraid I asked — does he call you?" Nurse Often: "Often, he call me often." Hagatha: "Now look here, Miss Often!"

I also like Dr. Bombay's long name for his machine—the Ultra Vascular Self-Denominating Power Tricloscope with, of course, the Super Duper Predictor Attachment. I also like that he adds the toasted cheese on rye at the end and Hagatha says, "Toasted cheese?!" Dr. Bombay: "Yes, that's for me. I'm starved!" And then a little later…Apothecary: "Toasted Cheese on Rye?!" Samantha: "That's for Dr. Bombay. He's hungry." I did think it was dumb that he had all those ingredients all ready in a blue liquid. You would think if he all ready had the ingredients mixed, that they would've included the Himalayan Cinnamon Stick and the Dodo bird's tail feather.

You can totally tell Liz has had it…I'm surprised she agreed to even film this script, what with all her cries of, "NOW WHAT" being so infused with desperation and irritation. And then later, when she practically bites Dr. Bombay's head off, "YOU DID NOT mention ANYTHING about the HIMALAYAN CINNAMON STICK!!!!!" I thought her head was going to explode! And she also practically bit Durwood's head off when he asks her what they are going to do now and she says, "HOW should I know?!"

I noticed the backdrops too and I hate the LONG scene of Durwood chasing the Dodo bird. If anything, they should've had one of the policeman be a bird expert and recognize that bird as a Dodo bird or something.

I also think it's dumb how Durwood stops chasing the bird to stop Sam from following him because "I can probably explain the bird but how would I ever explain you" only for Sam to later just simply say, "My husband wanted to see how I looked in stripes."

And if they're going to break out the old Dodo bird costume why not have Tabitha in the episode excited that Bobby the Bird is back and have her simply ask him if she can have a tail feather after Durwood's been trying to chase him? It would've been funny to see the bird simply turn to her to let her pluck one. Oh, but I forgot, none of the writers at this point are caring.

It is sad that *Bewitched* has come to this. And I'm sure this is one of the episodes *Bewitched* haters think of when they say how stupid the show is.

HAGATHA: *"NOW should I call Dr. Bombay or are you STILL in your mortal SNIT?"*
NURSE OFTEN: *"Now I have to get back. I'm his receptionist. I'm VERY receptive!"*
SAMANTHA: *"Dr. Bombay, we do not find your personal peccadillos the least bit amusing!"*
DR. BOMBAY: *"Oooh! You peeked!"*
DR. BOMBAY: *"We start with eye of condor, powdered snakeskin, fig newts..."*
DURWOOD: *"Fig NEWTS?"*
DR. BOMBAY: *"That's the way the cookie crumbles! Ha-ha! One pint of unicorn milk — nonfat — and a toasted cheese sandwich on rye."*
HAGATHA: *"Toasted cheese?"*
DR. BOMBAY: *"That's for me, I'm starved!"*
Hagatha: *"A dodo bird? Why, they're extinct!"*
DR. BOMBAY: *"Not only that, there haven't been any around for millions of years!"*
DR. BOMBAY: *"Samantha, you haven't taken the potion."*
SAMANTHA: *"Yes I have, and I'm running out of patience!"*
DR. BOMBAY: *"You and me both..."*
MR. FONG: *"Night after night, I stayed after work, mixing this form-oo-la with that, like a witch over her cauldron."*
SAMANTHA: *"And you certainly came up with a bewitching brew! And heady too!"*
APOTHECARY: *"I started out as a friendly neighborhood druggist but I couldn't find a friendly neighborhood."*

MARCH 25, 1972

All though we were unaware of it at the time, *Bewitched* history was made when ABC aired the final episode of the series, Episode #254: "The Truth, Nothing But the Truth, So Help Me, Sam."

Durwood finds Samantha gardening out in the backyard in the morning, dirty almost everywhere on her body, but he tells her he doesn't mind. She offers to clean up to make him breakfast, but he declines as he has a meeting at the office. He also tells her that he is going to pick up a surprise for her that he bought simply because he loves her and he leaves. Endora pops in, sickened at the baloney she believes Durwood is spouting off. She insists that mortals always tell lies as the truth hurts them too much, but Samantha says that isn't at all the truth. Before Endora can go any further, she says she has an appointment she had forgot about and she disappears.

At the office, Durwood arrives at the same time Endora pops in, invisibly, and he goes to show Secretary Betty the surprise he bought for Samantha, a unicorn pin, as unicorns are Samantha's favorite animal. Just then Endora freezes them and casts a truth spell on the pin, that whoever comes within close proximity of it, they will be forced to tell the truth. Endora unfreezes them and as Betty approaches she tells Durwood how beautiful the pin is and how she wishes she were married to a man so thoughtful as Durwood. When she goes to leave, she realizes she has been very forward, but Durwood assures her that he didn't mind and under the influence of the pin, tells her how sexy and tight her dress is. Betty is shocked and when Durwood tries to approach her to apologize, she falls under the pin's spell and tells him that she wore it specifically for him so that he would notice her. Soon, Larry buzzes in wondering if Durwood has started work on the Cora May Dress account, but Durwood hasn't and he goes to tell Larry that he just hasn't had the time, but when he gets on the phone, he truthfully reveals that he thinks the product isn't worth it and so he couldn't come up with any enthusiasm for it. Larry shows up in the office wondering if Durwood has flipped his rocker but when he gets close to the pin, he admits that he gave it to Durwood as he didn't want anything to do with it either. Larry tells Durwood that all though he understands why Durwood doesn't want to work on it, he had better come up with something for the dinner with the client that night.

When Durwood gets home, he finds that Samantha has her hair up in curlers and he tries to dodge a kiss. She wonders what he's doing, and he admits that he didn't want to get a curler in the eye and that all men find women who have hardware in their hair very unattractive. Samantha tells him he's being unattractive just as Endora pops in wondering why Samantha isn't pleased with the truth that he's apparently sharing. She also tells them that she had heard their discussing the dinner party with the Franklins and insinuates that she may want to show up for dinner. Durwood refuses and so Endora pops off.

Later that night, the Franklins and Larry arrive for dinner and the conversation becomes centered on Cora May Franklin, who tells them that she worked her way up the corporate ladder. Mrs. Franklin also tells them that she has come up with a great idea for her dress account which is, "Confucious say, "Don't be messy-wessy, try a Cora May Dressy-wessy." "The men are shocked at her conviction in saying something so ridiculous, and when Samantha, who is wearing the unicorn pin, passes by with hors d'ouevers, Durwood tells Cora May how ridiculous it is. Larry is horrified until he gets near Samantha and tells Durwood he agrees. Samantha is shocked and tries to say that Durwood and Larry are joking around with her as they do with every client they like. She accepts that and goes on about her climbing the ladder to her success story, however, Samantha sits next to the usually reserved Mr. Franklin, who tells his wife that she is lying and that, as matter of fact, the reason she got anywhere was because her father owned the company and had given her money to get out of the house. Realizing that something witchly is going on, Samantha excuses herself to the kitchen where she tries to get her mother to appear but to no avail. When she goes back into the living room, Samantha is shocked by how forward Mr. Franklin is with his wife, who is more shocked than everyone else. Soon, everyone begins arguing with everyone else, with Samantha in the middle and it soon ends with everyone leaving before dinner is even served.

The next morning, when Durwood wakes up, he finds that Samantha finally got a hold of Endora, who admitted to putting a truth spell on the unicorn pin. Just then Larry shows up to say that he was up all night trying to talk to Mr. and Mrs. Franklin and he expects Durwood to apologize. Samantha thinks that no apology is necessary and that they can get along without one. Larry threatens to get along at the office without Durwood, but when Samantha stands near him, the pin works it's magic and Larry admits he couldn't get along without Durwood. He also admits that Mrs. Franklin had called him that morning and told him that she and her husband had patched things up and they definitely wanted McMann and Tate to handle their advertising. After he leaves, Samantha marvels at how well the pin worked and she and Durwood embrace with words of love.

I can't believe this is how they would let the series end with a reheated version of a much superior episode ("Speak the Truth"). *Bewitched* is SO deserving of much more! I wonder how it all went down with the ending. It's been said by William Asher that Liz just said she didn't want to do it anymore. Obviously it was a surprise that it ended because Agnes Moorehead said so (she got a letter) and I think Erin said that her mother got a phone call saying it was ended. This episode finished filming on 12/16/71 when they went on Christmas break and iff'n they had followed previous schedules, they would've come back about mid to late January and filmed at least four more. So I would think there had to have been more scripts. And this episode was directed by Bill Asher, which I find fitting for the end of the series. I wonder if both Liz and Bill knew before they got to this episode that she wasn't coming back but they kept it to themselves? And knowing how Liz was with her friends and associates from earlier in her life where she just cut them off when moving on, I'm sure she did the same thing here and definitely wouldn't have called anyone.

There was speculation that Liz and DICK Michaels were having an affair which lead to the split up of the Ashers, however, it's well known that Bill was philandering well before. Their divorce would happen in 1973. I wonder if Liz quitting was a mixture of her not wanting to be with Bill anymore, getting tired of the retread of scripts, and just outright seeing that the show hadn't a chance where it was scheduled? Anyway, it's sad.

The episode isn't as bad as you think it's going to be. It does seem like everyone has energy, even Liz, and maybe that's just cause they knew Christmas break was coming and just the general feeling in the air. It does seem to capture some of the original magic the series once had until you realize that you've already heard all these lines before.

The episode begins with a closeup on Liz's rear, particularly a patch on her pocket. Until recently, I always thought that patch was the US flag on account of the crappy quality of the prints from TV. However, it is the ecology flag and I think that somehow being ecologically aware should've been put in the episode, maybe by having the client having something to do with that. I was shocked to the very marrow of my bones to see that on *HarpiesBizarre.com* one of the original scripts had Samantha saying of Endora, "And what she knows best is how to be a pain in the @ss."! Of course it was changed to "And what she knows best is how to be difficult." I can't believe they would've tried that, but I suppose they were trying to compete with *All in the Family*.

The unicorn pin is actually a hippocampus (half horse/half fish) but with a single horn making it a "unicorn" according to Durwood. I actually like it but it seems like cheating on Durwood's part to say it's a unicorn when it's not. And it looks dumb pinned to the middle of Liz's chest. Another dumb part is how shocked the sex-retary is when Durwood tells her the unicorn is Samantha's favorite animal. Nobody would be shocked…they would think it's cute that someone has a mythical beast as their favorite animal while the viewing audience would think it's funny cause we know that in the context of this show, they're not mythical. Of course, I did like Endora lamp-sitting again…seemed like her flying suit was again different, like the collar was much bigger. And Agnes Moorehead's voice seemed rather deep in that scene, like she had a cold or something. And I always remember the sex-retary mentioning how she has been with her boyfriend eight years and still not married. She started going out with him when Durwood and Samantha got married! That's a long damn time!

The jumper suit was totally wrong for this occasion but any other time I would've liked it minus the pin. I hated Samantha's "Oh brother" and "Oh no" throughout most of the episode. Seemed like it was merely Liz relating her displeasure with the whole thing.

And it is dumb that Louise is not at the party and yet again, Tabitha and Adam aren't mentioned.

The vacuum salesman was a totally new scene to me and I really liked it because every time I've seen this episode it cuts straight from the office to Durwood suddenly giving Samantha the cautious kiss.

And even though it's not a true series finale, Samantha kind of makes it so when at the end she laughs and says she wishes that Endora were there because she just loves happy endings and then the ending is Samantha and Durwood professing their love for each other, even if it was in a kinda corny way.

Way back on Broph's *Bewitched* Board in 2000 I posted my idea about a series finale:

My idea would be that it turns out that Endora and the Witches' Council planned Samantha's meeting with Durwood knowing that Samantha was into the mortal scene and they wanted to show her what a yutz a mortal love would be but Samantha really fell in love with him which was not expected. So the whole eight years was Endora trying to break it up at the bidding of the Council. The Council requests the presence of Durwood and Sam and, through a series of flashbacks, they show why their marriage should remain. Of course they would showcase all the great moments from the series. It would've been much better than 'The Truth, Nothing but the Truth, so Help Me Sam."

I didn't mention in my original posting but the episode would begin by Endora saying that the Witches' Council really has had it with the marriage, and they are not only mad at Samantha but Endora too who had promised to break it up and that now they really are going to dissolve the marriage unless it can be proven why it should remain intact. It would've been even cooler if Dick York had been brought back for this last episode and have the episode begin with Dick Sargent. He, Sam, and Endora are zapped in front of the Witches Council where the flashbacks begin showing both Dick Sargent years and Dick York years, having the Council say that they would like to speak to Samantha alone and have them zap him (Dick York now) home only for him to go for a drink downtown and then for a walk while he wonders what the Council is going to decide and at the crack of thunder he ducks into the nearest store, which happens to be the same one where he and Samantha met and where he bumps into her again now, she having just returned from the Council with an official proclamation of the approval of their marriage. They kiss and rejoice and then the original announcer comes over while all this is happening and says, "And so the red-blooded American boy and the typical American girl, who happened to be a witch, found that love conquers all and they lived happily ever after."

But of course, I was born about twenty years too late.

The day before, the big screen classic *The Godfather* made its debut.

The following is the summer re-run schedule. The episode will be listed by number, name, and original airdate.

APRIL 1, 1972

Episode #229: "How Not to Lose Your Head to King Henry VIII, Part 1" (September 15, 1971)

APRIL 8, 1972

Episode #230: "How Not to Lose Your Head to King Henry VIII, Part 2" (September 22, 1971)

Four days later Harry Ackerman, the show's producer, sends a letter to Agnes Moorehead and presumably the rest of the cast, saying that there will not be any new episodes of *Bewitched* made.

APRIL 15, 1972

Episode #231: "Samantha and the Loch Ness Monster" (September 29, 1971)

APRIL 22, 1972

Episode #232: "Samantha's Not-So-Leaning Tower of Pisa" (October 6, 1971)

APRIL 29, 1972

Episode #233: "Bewitched, Bothered and Baldoni" (October 13, 1971)

MAY 6, 1972

Episode #234: "Paris, Witches' Style" (October 20, 1971)

MAY 13, 1972

Episode #235: "The Ghost Who Made a Spectre of Himself" (October 27, 1971)

MAY 20, 1972

Episode #236, "TV or Not TV" (November 3, 1971)

MAY 27, 1972

Episode #237, "A Plague on Maurice and Samantha" (November 10, 1971)

JUNE 3, 1972

Episode #238, "Hansel and Gretel in Samanthaland" (November 17, 1971)

JUNE 10, 1972

Episode #245, "Serena's Richcraft" (January 22, 1972)

JUNE 24, 1972

Episode #252, "A Good Turn Never Goes Unpunished" (March 11, 1972)

JULY 1, 1972

Episode #242, "Adam, Warlock or Washout?" (December 29, 1971) This would be the last time *Bewitched* was aired in ABC primetime.

Afterword

All though there wouldn't be any new episodes of *Bewitched*, the magic wouldn't end there. Four years later, ABC would try to recapture the original magic in a spin-off *Tabitha* focused on Samantha and Durwood's daughter. However, Tabitha (Lisa Hartman) was now in her early twenties, living in Los Angeles, working at KTLA with her mortal OLDER brother Adam. The show lasted a surprising thirteen episodes and towards the end of its run, was actually becoming good. Tabitha was getting involved with her hunky co-worker Paul (Robert Urich) and was learning to deal with her kooky Aunt Minerva (Karen Morrow). Elizabeth Montgomery, Dick York, and Dick Sargent didn't have any part of the show but cast regulars Sandra Gould and a long haired and bearded George Tobias reprised their roles as Gladys and Abner Kravitz who come to visit, twice. Bernard Fox also popped in as the witch doctor Dr. Bombay, twice. There were many *Bewitched* fans that were furious and confused that Tabitha, who should only have been about twelve, was now ten years older and they voiced their concerns to Liz who responded to every one of their letters saying she had nothing to do with it.

In 1977 Hanna Barbera produced a Saturday morning cartoon special called *Adam and Tabitha and the Clown Family*, which had the Stephens children joining a circus.

Elizabeth Montgomery went on to become a TV movie queen starring in more than twenty highly rated movies, the most popular being her dramatic turn as the accused axe-murderess Lizzie Borden in *The Legend of Lizzie Borden* (1975). In the '80s Liz secretly filmed commercials in Japan for some cookie products where she was seen twitching her nose and performing magic. Sadly, she passed away on May 18, 1995 after being diagnosed with colon cancer.

Agnes Moorehead was ill with cancer towards the end of the series and, after appearing in her one woman show and a turn in the play *Gigli*, she passed away on April 30, 1974.

Dick York had felt like he could've returned to *Bewitched* had he had the summer of '69 to recuperate, though he was still very ill. He would make a few guest appearances on shows like *Simon & Simon* and ended up being bankrupt at the end of his life due to his charitable ways. Though he was in less than ideal circumstances because of his finances and health, Dick kept a positive attitude. He passed away on February 20, 1992 from complications due to emphysema.

Dick Sargent continued acting in various guest spots on such shows as *The Dukes of Hazzard* and *Family Ties*. Witchcraft was still in his life as he ended up playing the father of a teenage witch in the '80s cult hit movie *Teen Witch* (with *Bewitched* co-stars Shelley Berman and Marcia Wallace). In 1989 Dick was diagnosed with prostate cancer and soon after he revealed his homosexuality when a tabloid threatened to reveal it. He joined his witch-wife, Elizabeth Montgomery, to be the Grand Marshal of the 1992 Los Angeles Gay Pride Parade. Sadly, Dick succumbed to the cancer on July 9, 1994.

Erin Murphy turned down a role on *The Waltons* after *Bewitched* to go to Girl Scout Camp and through her teens appeared in many commercials. As an adult, Erin has taken on the role of casting agent, fashion stylist, reality show guru appearing on such shows *Hulk Hogan's Celebrity Championship Wrestling*. She is married to a man named, get this, Darren, and has six boys! You can contact her on Twitter at @Erin_Murphy.

Beginning in the mid-80s, Hollywood started doing movie remakes of TV shows and *Bewitched* was discussed. Many scripts were written and many people were attached but they all fell to the wayside, until about 2003 when Nora Ephron was chosen to write the script which she wrote with Nicole Kidman in mind for the lead role. As Nicole was such a big *Bewitched* fan growing up, and considering she was always compared to Elizabeth Montgomery, she accepted the role. Jim Carrey was also asked to play the part of Durwood however, once he met with Nora and saw that the script wasn't a direct remake, he dropped out and popular comedian Will Ferrell, riding high on the success of *Elf* (2003), was signed on with his writing partner, Adam McKay. With a June 24, 2005 opening set, Sony began promoting the movie by starting to release the original series on DVD and TV Land, which aired the series, announced and unveiled the next in their line of TV Land Landmark statues with Elizabeth Montgomery as Samantha riding a broom across a crescent moon to be erected in the Witch City, Salem, MA. The statue caused an uproar among some Salem residents who felt it was disrespectful to the victims of the Salem Trials to honor an imaginary witch, however, the majority of Salem residents were pleased that America's favorite TV witch was returning to Salem thirty-five years after her original visit. On June 15, 2005, a rainy day, the statue was unveiled in Lappin Park to a crowd of hundreds. Attending were Erin Murphy, Bernard Fox, Kasey Rogers, and William Asher. The movie premiered nine days later and, because of the terrible script, it bombed at the box office.

Even forty years since the last new episode of *Bewitched* aired, the show is still as popular as ever. It has never left the airwaves due to reruns and in some cities one would be able to watch the show at least four times a day! All eight seasons are available on DVD from Sony Pictures Home Entertainment, though fans hope that Sony will revisit the series with the restoration of the sponsor openings, cast commercials, and show promos with a Complete Series boxed set. As of this writing, CBS has ordered a pilot script from Sony for a re-boot of the series.

Beginning in 2001 with a small group of fans that gathered in Reno, Nevada, the gatherings have continued almost every year since and have evolved into what is called the *Bewitched* Fanfare where fans gather mainly in Los Angeles and sometimes in Salem to meet other fans and celebrate the magic of our favorite show. Mark Simpson a.k.a The *Bewitched* Collector is the organizer of the Fanfare and has been able to introduce us to such *Bewitched* alumni as Steve Franken, Billie Hayes, Art Metrano, Bobby Hart, Heather Woodruff-Perry, Ron Masak, and stars Erin Murphy, Kasey Rogers, and Bernard Fox, and director William Asher! The Fanfares have even gathered at 1164 Morning Glory Circle at the WB Ranch on three occasions over the years and the 2006 Fanfare in Salem was featured on the Canadian TV show *FANatical*, along with the collections of Mark Simpson (known as the *Bewitched* Collector) and author Gina Meyers (*The Magic of Bewitched Trivia and More, The Magic of Bewitched Cookbook*). If you would like to join us at the Fanfares in the future, you can find the *Bewitched* Fanfare page on Facebook or contact Mark Simpson at *bewitchedcollector@gmail.com*. However, if you would only like to discuss the show with other fans, you can also join us over at *www.harpiesbizarre.com*, the website where this book began.

Index

'68 Comeback Special 388
"Darrin" 21-27, 29-30, 50, 52, 63, 78, 80, 126, 140, 236, 250, 301, 365, 368, 418, 439, 445-446, 476, 499, 518, 561, 564, 568, 598
...And Debbie Makes Six 336
60 Minutes 362
1164 Morning Glory Circle 26, 27, 31, 35, 39, 50, 55, 58, 91-92, 98, 102, 119, 123, 126, 133, 160, 172-174, 177-178, 209, 212, 217, 223, 227, 229, 232, 234, 238-239, 248, 249, 251, 253, 258, 281, 304, 317, 335, 341, 348-349, 356, 363, 387, 411, 414, 417, 464, 479, 485, 490, 503, 509, 531, 533-534, 558, 566, 569-570, 581, 586-587, 599, 600, 603, 607, 612, 614, 641, 650, 658-659, 674, 711
Abdul, Paula 11, 600
Abigail Adams Cosmetics 330
Academy Awards 18, 87, 573
Ackerman, Harry 706
Adam and Tabitha and the Clown Family 709
Adam-12 429
Adams, Don 357
Addams Family, The 24
Adonis/Alberto 634, 636-637
Africa 228
Agnew, Spiro 359, 407
Agraphor, Dr. 267-268, 672
Akron, Ohio 229-230
Al (bartender) 325
Alabama 76, 78, 80
Alachi, Peter 526, 547
Albert (uncle) 177-178, 184, 189, 330
Albertson, Mabel 54
Alden, John 303
Aldrin, Buzz 442
Alexander, Jackie 448

Alford, Vi 78
Ali, Muhammed 105
Alias Smith and Jones 619
Alice in Wonderland 684
Alice in Wonderland, Disney's 347
Alice Through the Looking Glass 211, 496
All in the Family 574, 670, 673, 688, 694, 704
All My Children 486
Alonzo 655-658
Alpha 347-348
Ambassador Hotel 358
Amelia 399-400
American Cinema Editors Award 204
Ames, Leon 499
Ames, Roxie 59-60
Ames, Wally 71-72
Anders, William A. 398
Anderson Jr., James 359
Andrews, Edward 155, 423, 459
Andrusco, Gene 605
Andy Griffith Show, The 18
Angel Falls 68
Angel, Mr. 355
Anita 463-464
Ansara, Michael 203
Anton, Dr. 453-455
Antony and Cleopatra 194
Apollo I 239
Apollo VII 368
Apollo VIII 398
Apollo XI 442
Apollo XII 471
Apollo XIII 521
Apollo XIV 581, 585
Apothecary (Postlethwaite) 465, 468, 483, 485, 649-651, 698-701

Applegate, Christina 539, 611
Aragon, Carlos 438
Archie Comedy Hour, The 448
Arden, Eve 154
Aretha 586-587
Armstrong, Neil 442
Arnold, Jeanne 189
Arnold, Phil 355
Art Linkletter Show, The 526
Artful Dodger 486, 488
Arthur, Uncle 82, 126-128, 205-207, 209-210, 277, 351-353, 370, 379-380, 386-388, 411-412, 419, 424-427, 430, 434, 437, 463-464, 474, 491, 495-497, 508, 542, 550, 585-588, 608, 646
Asher Guitars 328
Asher, Brian William 550
Asher, Rebecca Elizabeth 50, 426, 441, 517
Asher, Robert Deverell 126, 684
Asher Jr., William 37, 245, 328
Asher, William/Bill 9, 24, 27, 37, 59, 64, 82, 102, 113, 119, 126, 131, 173, 175, 183, 255, 328, 357, 379, 396, 400, 427, 431, 445, 456, 525, 550, 573, 591, 622-623, 629, 630, 633, 637, 642, 644, 660, 678, 681, 697, 700, 704, 711
Ashmont Productions 623
Asmiov, Isaac 429
Athens 413
Atlantic City 324, 376
Aubert 163-165
Aunt Jenny 364-366
Aunt Renee's Raisin Nut Nibbles (cookies) 420
Australia 392,
Autobiography of Benjamin Franklin, The 222
Avedon, Barbara 573
B'Nai B'rith'sHuman Relations Award 221
Back to the Future 203, 584
Baddeley, Hermione 311
Baer, Parley 170
Baez, Joan 442, 527
Baine, Gary & Louise 84
Baine, Mrs. 84
Baker, Mr. and Mrs. 341-342
Baker, Sarah 46, 47, 433
Baldoni, Mr. and Mrs. 635, 637
Baldwin, Linton H. 104, 105
Baldwin, Mr. (Baldwin Blankets) 255-256

Ball, Lucille 155, 357
Ballad of Andy Crocker, The 471
Bancroft, Sir Leslie 548-549
Barber's Peaches 51
Barefoot in the Park 534
Barker, Rex (Barker's Baby Food) 108-111, 658
Barkley, Mr. 174-177
Barrows, Mr. (Barrows Umbrellas) 544-547
Bartenbach, Mr. and Mrs. (Bartenback Beauty Products) 461-462
Barton Industries 381-382
Bates, Irving 503-505
Bathroom 108, 133, 138, 294, 518, 532
Batman 52, 236, 338, 536, 660
Baxter, Mr. and Mrs. 289
Beach Boys, The 183
Beacham, Abigail 432-433
Beams, Mr. 413, 415
Bean, Alan 471
Bean, Judge 189, 240-241
Beatles, The 17, 113, 126, 213, 218, 271, 293, 307, 383, 451, 521, 525, 629
Beaulieu, Priscilla 270
Bedknobs and Broomsticks 213
Begg, Jim 158
Bell, Book, and Candle 174
Belnap, Janette Clark 298
Benedetti, Quint 694
Benjamin, Richard 357
Benson, Mr. (Benson's Chili Con Carne) 650
Benson, Mr. (Benson Mattress) 695-696
Bentley, Mrs. 386
Berkley, Mr. (Berkley Baby Foods) 456-457
Berkley, Mr. and Mrs. (Berkley Hair Tonic) 589-592
Berkley, University of CA 28, 50, 97, 103
Berman, Shelley 37, 710
Bermuda 260, 286-287
Berne, Jack R. 573
Bertha 35-37, 82, 198, 311
Betty (secretary)145, 147-148, 176, 186, 245, 253, 255, 257-260, 282, 354, 472
Beverly Hillbillies, The 18, 47, 442, 616, 619
Bewitched and the Man at the Wheel 526, 547
Bewitched Baby Bottle 293, 494
Bewitched Book, The 151
Bewitched Collector, The 402, 494, 711
Bewitched Comic book 85, 112, 162
Bewitched Cookbook, The 517

INDEX 715

Bewitched Critic, The 10, 294, 408, 475, 597, 622, 690
Bewitched Day in Historic Salem 539-540
Bewitched Fanfare 10, 74, 173, 175-176, 259, 350, 426, 502, 517, 539, 543, 554, 629, 653, 711
Bewitched Forever 10, 111, 131, 254, 396, 431, 485, 600
Bewitched Fun & Activity Book 45, 85
Bewitched movie 128, 131, 148, 188, 497, 512, 598, 623, 710
Bewitched novelization 85, 111
Bewitched puzzles 85
Bewitched Storybook 64, 85
Bewitched.net 10, 525
Bigelow Industries 565-566
Bigelow, Mr. 285
Billie 119
Bixby, Bill 611
Black Bart 419
Black Eyed Peas 252
Blake, Madge 416
Blakely, Mr. 551-552
Bliss Jr., Mr. (Bliss Pharmaceutical) 469, 472
Bliss Sr., Mr. 469, 471-472
Blodgett, Franklyn 413-416
Blue Beard 337
Bob Cummings Show, The 592
Bob Hope Presents the Chrysler Theater 172
Bobbins, Mr. (Bobbins Bon-Bons) 574-576
Bold, Darrin the 201, 203-204, 581-585
Bombay, Dr. 9, 173, 189, 267-270, 286, 288, 294-295, 299-302, 366, 392-395, 407-408, 434, 453, 455, 464, 473, 483-485, 495-497, 503-505, 508-510, 518-519, 521-523, 542, 567-568, 570, 596-598, 606-608, 648-649, 651, 671-673, 680, 697-701, 709
Bonanza 18, 27, 112
Bonaparte, Napoleon 13, 204, 264, 379-381, 453, 537, 640
Booker, Mr. 562, 564
Bookholzer, Billy "Blades" 677-679
Borman, Frank 398
Bosley, Tom 611
Boston 220, 225, 242, 411, 537, 544, 548-549, 557
Boyce & Hart 500-502, 588
Bracini, Count 630-633
Braddock, Mr. (Braddock Sports) 498-499

Bradley, Mr. 380
Brady Bunch, The 50, 134, 443, 451
Braun Cologne 416-417
Braun, Mr. 603
Breeze Shampoo 500
Brian's Song 658
Brigham, Colonel (Colonel Brigham's Spare Ribs) 592-593, 595
Brinkman, Mr. 35-37, 462
British Imperial Textile Mills 548-549
Brocken, Merle 143-144, 334
Brockway, Mr. 569-572
Broph's *Bewitched* Board 705
Bruce 626-630
Brunhilde 363-366
Buck (manager) 425-426
Bueno 437-438
Buffy 242-243
Bullifant, Joyce 102
Bunny 173, 463-465, 496
Burch, Mrs. 389-391
Burke's Law 87
Burkett, Colonel 348-349
Burkholder, Mr. 658-660
Burnet, Carol 366, 566, 585, 588, 700
Burning Oak Country Club 421-423
Burning Tree Country Club 423
Burns, Marshall (Marshmallow) 33-34
Butch Cassidy and the Sundance Kid 450
Butler, Rance 364-366
Byles, Bobby 443
Caan, James 658
Cabot, Laurie 554
Cabot, Sebastian 357
Caesar, Julius 204, 451-453
Caldwell Soup 31-32
Caldwell, Jimmy 84
Caldwell, Mr. and Mrs. 84
Callahan, Bo 318-319
Campbell Sporting Goods 409
Campbell, Ruthie 503-505
Campbell, Walden R. 409-410
Canada 72, 678
Candid Camera 344
Canfield, Mary Grace 175
Capp, Al 440
Carlotta 370-372
Carradine, John 189
Carrey, Jim 42, 148, 710

Carter, Hazel 308-309
Carter, Tommy 160
Cashman, Chick 500, 502
Cassidy, David 365, 512, 611
Cassidy, Jack 365, 512, 675
Castro, Fidel 124
Cavanaugh, John C. 101-103
Cesana, Renzo 554
Chaffee, Roger 239
Chair, walking 219-221, 276-277
Chappel, Roy 310-312
Charday, Evelyn 451-453
Charlie (lumberjack) 396
Charlie and the Chocolate Factory 59
Charlie Brown Christmas, A 146
Charlie, Prince 329-331
Charlie, the doorman 297
Charone, Irwin 163
Chase, Bob 277, 279
Chef Romani Foods 280-281
Chesney, Diana 148, 189
Chevrolet 25, 27, 31, 35, 40, 45, 50, 55, 59, 64, 68, 72, 76, 81, 85, 90, 97, 103, 119, 124, 128, 134, 138, 143, 146, 149, 152, 158, 161, 165, 170, 207-208, 230, 246, 250, 361, 404
Chi, Greta 72
Chicago 65, 162, 250, 296-297, 340, 359, 366, 467, 481-482, 495
Chicago Tribune 112
Chimpanzee 117-119, 402-403, 416-418, 587
Church of Jesus Christ of Latter-Day Saints, The 34
Churchill, Winston 68
Citizen Kane 655
Civil War, The 87, 95, 136
Clairol 483
Clara, Aunt 35, 37, 52-54, 66, 82-85, 117-118, 121-123, 127, 129-131, 134-136, 138, 141-143, 158-159, 174, 175, 189, 195-201, 212-213, 221-229, 237-242, 250-252, 262-264, 277, 293-297, 299, 301-304, 315-317, 329, 331-333, 345-350, 355, 357, 380, 439, 497, 509, 514, 517, 522, 573, 597, 608, 669
Clarissa 382-383
Claus, Santa 55-58, 313-315, 478-480
Cleopatra 452
Clown, Ho Ho the 233-234
Club Bimbo 342
Clyde, Shirley 28, 102

Coach Gribben 34
Coca, Imogene 576, 578
Cochrane, Captain 137, 138
Collins, Michael 442
Columbia House 10, 222, 402
Columbia University 353
Connell, Jane 536, 690
Conqueror, The 355, 617
Conrad, Charles 471
Convy, Bert 549-550
Cooper, Gary 228
Cooper, Jackie 408
Cora May Dresses 702
Corby, Mrs. 510
Corden, Henry 203
Cornelia, Great Aunt 515, 517
Corporation for Public Broadcasting 298, 468
Cosby Show, The 14
Cosco, Mr. 602-603
Cosgrove, Mr. and Mrs. 219-221
Cosmo (hairdresser) 406
Cosmos Cotillion 500-501, 527, 561
Count of Valor 662
Countess Margaret's Cosmetics 64
Court Martial of Billy Mitchell, The 355
Cousins, Michael and Michelle 10
Cousteau, Jacques Eve 369
Cowboy 626
Crandall, Officer 689
Crazy in Alabama 47
Cronkite, Walter 343, 442
Crothers, Scatman 663
Cummings, Robert 592
Cunningham, Mr. 246-247
Cushman, Amanda "Panda" 158, 372, 455, 655, 657
Cushman, Julius 156-158
Cushman, Mr. 656-657
Custer 312
Daily, Bill 58
Dallyrand 165-166
Daly, Jonathan 70
Dan, Diaper 210-211
Daniel Boone 158, 222, 244, 525
Darin, Bobby 336
Dark Shadows 272, 673
Dave 22, 73-76, 99, 120-121, 154, 186, 325, 326
Davis Jr., Sammy 688

INDEX

Davis, Paul 90, 183, 259, 332
Days of Our Lives 136, 502
DeHaviland, Olivia 55
Delightful Day Nursery School 389
Democratic National Convention 359, 366
Denney, Dodo 386
Detroit 82, 235, 272
Devlin, Toni 182-183
Dick Van Dyke Show, The 18, 161, 171, 183, 187, 386, 528
Dillaway, Horace 177-178
Dinsdale, George 510-511
Disney, Walt 18, 32, 225, 290, 311, 347
Disneyland 427, 572-573
Dodo Bird 299-302, 418, 698, 700-701
Don Rickles Show, The 396
Donkey ears 291-292
Donna Reed Show, The 170
Doohan, James 144
Doors, The 232, 280, 617
Doris Day Show, The 362
Dozier, William 329
Dreyfus, Richard 181
Duke of Whitzett 642-644
Duke, Patty 119
Dukes of Hazzard, The 710
Dundee's Bar 159-160
Dunn, William 177-178
Durfees, Mr. and Mrs. (Durfees Dog Food) 407-408
Dylan, Bob 113-114
Eastwood, Frank 255
eBay 85
Ed Sullivan Show, The 280, 608
Eden, Barbara 119, 203, 473, 637
Edgar (cousin) 106-108
Edgar (Gladys' nephew) 167, 169
Edwards, Gerald 367
Egypt 69, 403
Eisenhower, Dwight D. 429
Elephant (including pink polka-dotted) 142, 225, 227-229, 238, 510, 534, 609, 669
Elf 710
Ellington, Governor 270
Elspeth, Nanny 310-312
Emmy Award 78, 90, 112, 128, 163, 179, 183, 244, 301, 350, 357, 440-441, 524, 526, 564, 576, 585, 616

Enchantra, Aunt 148, 189, 197, 199, 220, 239-242, 276, 664-667, 682
Endora 13, 21, 26-27, 29-32, 40-47, 50, 58, 62-70, 72-78, 81-82, 85-87, 91-92, 95, 97-99, 101-107, 117-121, 124, 126-129, 132-134, 136, 138-142, 145-148, 153-156, 158-159, 161-163, 165, 167-169, 172-174, 178-180, 182-185, 187, 193-194, 197-198, 202-211, 215-218, 220-221, 231-237, 239-250, 253-261, 267-270, 275, 277, 279-289, 292, 298-302, 305-311, 315, 317-325, 329-331, 335, 337-338, 340, 350, 353-354, 361-362, 365-375, 377-378, 380, 388, 396-399, 404, 406-411, 417-428, 430-436, 438-439, 445-450, 456-462, 464-468, 475-478, 481-482, 486-487, 489-492, 497-498, 505-510, 513-521, 531-534, 536-541, 543, 549, 551, 553-555, 558, 560-568, 574-576, 581, 583-585, 587, 592-593, 595-598, 602-605, 611-613, 615, 621-622, 624-626, 634-642, 648-651, 655-656, 658-667, 676, 678-679, 691-692, 695-698, 700, 702-706
England 141, 331-333, 380, 527, 621, 642
Ephron, Nora 42, 188, 710
Esmeralda (mortal maid) 152, 450
Esmeralda (witch maid) 315, 448-452, 456, 467, 473-475, 478, 480, 483, 485, 493, 508-509, 518-524, 537, 542, 547-550, 555, 557, 608-611, 630-634, 646, 667-669, 685, 687-691, 696-697
Europa Tours 638, 640
Evans, Douglas 340
Evans, Maurice 9, 45, 345, 430, 460, 470, 564, 640-642, 651, 665, 675
Extra 676
EZ Way Rent-a-Cars 385
Fallon, Jimmy 282
Family Affair 357
Family Guy 410
Family Ties 710
Fanatical 711
FAO Schwartz *Bewitched* doll 315
Far Side, The 398, 478, 595, 613, 657, 663
Farley the monkey 279
Farley, Mr. 555, 626
Farnsworth, Bob 256
Farnsworth, Clyde 220
Farrell, Glenda 616
Farrinini, Maestro 367

Fat Albert and the Cosby Kids 368
Fauntleroy, Little Lord 311, 370
Faust 197
Faye, Herbie 158
Feather Touch Electric Typewriters 91
Feldon, Barbara 357
Fell, Norman 216
Ferber, Mr. 580
Ferdy 609-611
Fergus the Frog 265-267, 415
Ferguson, Mr. 582-583, 585
Ferndale, Ms. 537-540, 542, 560
Ferrell, Will 710
Fiedler, John 266
Field, Sally 518
Fisherman's Memorial 544-546
Flannigan, Mr. 604, 658
Fleming, Peggy 678
Fleur, Janine 45, 46
Flintstones, The 131, 203, 388
Flip Wilson Show, The 527
Flippen, Ruth Brooks 245, 660
Flipper 265
Fluffy 112
Flying Nun, The 236, 277, 357, 518
Flying suit 31-32, 56, 91, 93, 177, 240, 242-244, 281-282, 314, 324-325, 370, 372, 427, 439, 462-463, 491, 542-543, 553, 656, 658, 660, 697, 705
Flynn, Ashley 558-561
Flynn, Mr. 416-417
Fonda, Henry 356
Fong, Benson 699-700
Fong, Mr. (Ah Fong's Restaurant) 697, 701
For Love or Money 526
Foray, June 169
Foreman, Joey 234
Foster, Donald 481
Foster, June 28, 102
Foster, Shirley 100, 102
Fox, Bernard 9, 173, 174, 189, 269, 270, 523, 607-608, 617, 709, 711
Fox, Nancy 678, 681
Foxworth, Robert 451
France 42, 121, 134, 191, 209, 292, 332, 379, 430
Franken, Steve 175, 227-229, 349-350, 437, 629, 711
Franklin Electronics 221

Franklin, Aretha 246
Franklin, Benjamin 13, 194, 198, 204, 221-225, 379, 453, 688
Franklin, Cora May and Mr. 703
Frazer, Elizabeth 148
Frazer, Robert E. 77, 78, 481
Frazier and Colton 466
Freud, Dr. Sigmund 215-216
Friends 74, 140
Funky Phantom, The 624
Fuzz, The 405-406, 489-591
Garcia, Raul 438, 617
Gardener, Joe 10, 112
Garland, Judy 441
Garson, Greer 172
Gautier, Dick 164
Geer, Will 686, 688, 690
Genesis, Book of 398
Gentry, Heidi and Laura 158
George (warlock) 91-93, 220, 554, 560
Georgia 234, 561
Gerace, Adam 357
Germany 358
Gertrude 50-52
Get Smart 119, 357, 428, 440, 465, 525, 564, 694
Ghost 89, 331-333, 341-342, 615-616, 642-645
Ghost and Mr. Chicken, The 158, 355, 526
Ghost and Mrs. Muir, The 440, 524
Ghostley, Alice 9, 152, 158, 206, 315, 450, 631, 670, 691
Giant, the 447-448
Giant's wife 447, 457
Gibbons, Mr. (Gibbons Dog Food) 558-560
Gibson, Henry 513, 515
Giddings, Mr. 327-329, 655
Gidget 119
Gigli 709
Gilby and Associates 469
Gilligan's Island 24, 259, 277
Girl Talk 114
Girl with Broom 194, 207, 229
Glendon, J.T. 163
Gloucester House Restaurant 544-545, 547
Gloucester, MA 544-547
Glover, Mary 557
Goblin 290-292, 591
Godfather, The 706

INDEX

Godfrey, Charlie 64, 65
Going My Way 526
Golden Girls, The 151
Golden Globe Awards 55, 72, 246, 418
Golden Laurel Awards 28, 55, 124, 208
Golf 117-118, 128, 289-290, 324, 363, 373-374, 398, 421, 445, 474-475, 483, 498, 503, 561, 565, 604-606, 609, 664, 666, 671, 699
Gomez, Thomas 617
Gone with the Wind 366
Good Fairy, Mary the 577-581, 587
Goose, Mother 473-475, 536
Gorshin, Frank 336
Gotham Industries 531-532, 534-535, 550
Gould, Sandra 95, 158, 206, 223, 230, 304, 335, 357, 709
Governor's Award 573, 616
Graduate, The 315
Grange, Mrs. 55, 58, 297
Green Acres 616
Green Giant 512
Green stripes 294-95, 699
Greenwich Village 441
Gregg, Julie 171
Gregory, Dick 440
Gregson, Mr. 305-307
Gremlin 290-292
Griffin, Merv 573
Griffith, Melanie 47
Grimalda 664-667
Grimes, Tammy 191, 699
Grissom, Gus 239
Gruber, Louis 187-188
Gunsmoke 259
Gurney, Mrs. 386
H. R. Puffnstuff 654
Hafner, Dr. 422
Hagatha, Aunt 197-199, 239, 240-242, 311, 382, 422-423, 436, 470, 493, 593, 599, 630, 659, 667, 697-701
Hagman, Larry 119
Hair 290, 355
Haise, Fred 521
Hallmark Channel 345,
Hallmark ornament 218
Hammond Castle 546
Hampton, Mr. (Hampton Motors) 449-450
Hanks, Tom 521
Hanley, Bridget 216

Hanley's Department Store 405, 503
Hansel and Gretel 652-654
Hansen, Elaine 392, 394, 397
Happy Days 611
Happy Heart Greeting Card Company 518-519
Hard Day's Night, A 293
Harding, Mr. 139-140, 618
Harmon, Mr. (Harmon's Savings and Loan) 567-568
Harold, Harold 81-82, 128
Harper Honey 145
Harper, Charlie & Daphne 248-249
Harper, Mrs. 399
HarpiesBizarre.com 10, 14, 357, 392, 406, 423, 440, 623, 638, 704, 711
Harriet, Aunt 340-341
Harris, Jonathan 368
Harrison, Dusty 505-507, 584
Harrison, Mr. 506
Harry Potter 198, 641
Harry, Eighth Duke of Whitzett 643-645
Hartman, Lisa 331, 709
Hascomb, Mr. and Mrs. (Hascomb Drugs) 377-378
Haskell, Mr. 427-428
Hathaway, Ms. 569
Hawaii 242
Hawaii 5-0 359, 362
Hawkins (butler) 313-314
Hawkins, District Attorney 223-224
Hawkins, Mr. 226-229
Hawthorne Hotel 536, 538, 546-547 550, 554
Hawthorne, Nathaniel 537, 552
Haydn, Richard 347
Hayes, Billie 653-654, 711
He & She 357
Hee Haw 616
Heidi 381
Helen (cousin) 329-330
Henderson, Mr. 341
Hendrix, Henri 442, 527
Henry (cousin) 70, 232, 434-436
Henry VIII 337, 449, 590, 621-626
Henson, Jim 301, 409, 629
Hepzibah, High Priestess 372, 531-536, 550-551
Herbert (uncle) 147
Herbie 604-605

Here Come the Brides 362, 518
Here Comes Mr. Jordan 573
Here's Lucy 362
HHH 344
Hickman, Maude 189, 682, 684
Hillgreen Coffee 505
Hilton, Kathy Richards & Paris 647
Hine, Al 85, 111
Hinkley Jr., Joseph (Hinkley's Department Store) 435-437
Hitchcock, Ernest 535-536
Hogan's Heroes 357, 617
Hogersdorf, Leon 356
Hollywood Forever Cemetary 410
Hollywood Palace, The 168, 199, 218, 457
Hollywood Squares 208
Hollywood Talent Scouts 172
Hong Kong 469, 568, 655
Hope, Bob 336, 355
Hornbeck, Mr. 268-269
Hot Wheels 359
Hotchkiss, Mr. and Mrs. 147-148
House of the Seven Gables 537-540, 552-553
How the Grinch Stole Christmas 225
How to Stuff a Wild Bikini 113
Howard University 340
Hubert, Humphrey 185, 359, 366, 376
Huckster Club 354
Huddleston, David 658
Hudson, Rock 624
Hulk Hogan's Celebrity Championship Wrestling 710
Human Equation, The 413
Humphrey, Hubert 185, 359, 366, 376
Hunter, Henry 189
Hunter, Mrs. 565-566
Hunters Club Ball 310
Huntington Hotel 510, 512
Huntley, Chet 527
Huntley-Brinkley Report, The 527
Hush…Hush, Sweet Charlotte 55, 72, 124
I Dream of Jeannie 58, 76, 119, 155, 180, 203, 207, 213, 216, 220, 228, 246, 248, 270, 293, 319, 322, 362, 381, 407, 423, 429, 468, 473, 525-526, 557, 597, 641, 666
I Love Lucy 24, 175, 400, 427, 525
I Love the Illusion 694
I Married a Witch 58, 174
Icarus 370-371, 598, 601

Ideal Samantha doll 85, 119, 279
Ideal Tabatha doll 196
Illinois Meat Packers 466
Immaculate Conception Church 546
Incredible Hulk, The 611
Indian, American 137, 138
Ingels, Marty 211
Inherit the Wind 270
Inverness, Scotland 626
Ireland 170, 201
Isle of Wight Festival 527
It's the Great Pumpkin, Charlie Brown 210
Italy 280-281, 332, 630
Jack 446-447
Jack and the Beanstalk 446
Jack o'Lantern 290-292
Jack Paar Show, The 680
Jackman, Ralph 466-467
Jackson 5 457, 526
Jackson Five, The 624
James, Luther 477
Jamison, Mr. (Whirlaway Washing Machines) 689
Jamison, Mr. 611-613
Japan 146, 231, 481-482, 709
Jeopardy 151, 568
Jethro Tull 527
Jewel of the East 70-71
Joe's Bar and Grill 276
John Gary Show, The 372
John, Elton 521
Johnny Belinda 245
Johnny Cool 24, 158
Johnson, Lyndon 17, 40, 61, 80, 103, 113, 271, 295, 298, 302, 307, 342, 347, 376
Johnson's Jungle Isle 599-601, 603
Jones, Brian 441
Jones, Lenard and Louise 10
Jones, Tracey 10, 661
Joplin, Janis 442
Juke 370-372
Julia 362
Julian, Arthur 162, 213, 247
Jump, Gordon 603
Jungle Book, The 225, 290
Jurist, Ed 334-335, 578
Kabaker, Miss 171
Kansas City Chiefs 234
Karloff, Boris 225

INDEX

Kasem, Casey 526
Kattan, Chris 282
Keith, Brian 357
Kellaway, Cecil 58
Kelton, Nurse 153-154
Kennedy (Onasis), Jacqueline 23, 372
Kennedy Jr, John F 17, 24, 40, 255
Kennedy, Robert 338, 358
Kent State University shootings 525
Kenya 413
Kermit 50-52
Kidman, Nicole 710
Kimberly, A.J. 210-211
King Jr, Dr. Martin Luther 14, 17, 32, 78, 82, 183, 262, 343, 358
Kingsley Potato Chips 149
Knight, Don 189
Knotts, Don 158, 663
Kodak 376, 378, 392
Kopell, Bernie 428, 465, 491, 550, 629, 657
Kovak, Joking Joe 159-160
Kovak, Nancy 24, 402
Kramer, Dr. 214-215
Kravitz, Abner 25, 27, 29-30, 58, 61, 76, 80, 85-86, 88-90, 93, 95-97, 102, 118, 124, 130, 141-143, 156, 157, 159, 165, 167, 174, 188, 230, 253, 265-266, 283, 304, 308-309, 344-345, 348, 355-356, 361, 431, 483, 484, 486, 577-580, 599, 601, 709
Kravitz, Flash 229-230
Kravitz, Gladys 25, 27-30, 58, 60, 76, 85-90, 93, 95-97, 102, 117-118, 124-126, 129-130, 141-143, 156-160, 167, 169, 174-175, 187-188, 205-207, 209, 213, 223, 225, 229-230, 238, 253, 266, 291-292, 304, 309, 344, 350, 355, 356, 395, 431, 478, 497, 515, 576-577, 579, 599, 709
Kravitz, Harriet 174-175, 178, 181
Kravitz, Sidney 478, 480, 494, 572, 576-579
KSTU Fox13 9, 601
La Bella Donna 252-254
La-Choy Dragon 301
Lancer 473
Land of the Giants 362
Lane, Charles 148, 158, 314, 477, 523, 613, 694
Lange, Hope 440, 524
Langley, Mr. and Mrs. 565-566
Lassie 34

Lauriecabot.com 554
Lawford, Peter 675-676
Lawrence (Bloch-Mandel), David 465, 487, 539, 558, 601, 666
Lawrence (Mandel), Greg 465
Layton, Lila 428
Leach, Charlie 174-178, 182-183, 228, 236, 601
Leach, Charmaine 177, 182-183, 601
Leary, Timothy 440
Legend of Lizzie Borden, The 709
Lennon, John 213, 440
Leonov, Aleksi 80
Leprechaun 170, 204, 292, 362, 513-515
Lewis, Bobo 404, 447, 457, 654
Liar, Liar 148
Lidsville 624
Life magazine 693
Ling Ling 71-72, 347
Linquata, Michael 547
Liston, Sonny 105
Liuzzo, Viola 82
Live a Little, Love a Little 376
Loch Ness Monster 626-628
Lockhart, June 34
London 124-125, 621, 626, 637-638
Long, Ronald 448, 623
Lorne, Marion 9, 37, 54, 83, 85, 131, 142, 199, 213, 222, 315, 350, 355, 357, 584
Los Angeles Times 112
Losso, Ernest 697
Lost in Space 58, 336, 368
Lousiana Super Dome 618
Love is a Many Splendored Thing 280
Love, American Style 486, 595, 663, 679, 688
Lovelace, Mr. 415
Lovell, Jim 398, 521
Lucy Show, The 338, 357
Lupino, Ida 64
Lynde, Paul 82, 128, 199, 208, 319, 427, 587
MacElroy, Mr. (MacElroy Shoes) 212-213
Maclaine, Shirley 598
Maclane, Mr. and Mrs. 335
Madden, Dave 236
Maddox, Lester 234
Magic of Bewitched Cookbook, The 711
Magic of Bewitched Trivia and More, The 711
Magical Mystery Tour 307
Magnificent Ambersons, The 626

Main, Laurie 189, 623
Malcom 363-364, 366
Malet, Arthur 189
Mallory, Ed 102
Malmgren, Shelley 10
Malvina 621-622
Man from U.N.C.L.E., The 27
Manson, Charles 442, 581, 611, 616
Mantle, Mickey 344
Mardis Gras 235-236
Mariner 4 (spacecraft) 112
Marines, U.S. 76, 359, 372
Mario (cousin) 69
Mario's Restaurant 103-105, 355
Markham, Mr. 352-353
Marriage: Year One 638
Marshall, Margaret 65
Marshall, Thurgood 271, 273
Martin, Virginia 601
Marushka, Madame (Madame Marushka's Cosmetics) 260-261
Mary 35-37, 416, 470
Mary Poppins 18, 24, 37, 45, 87, 154, 213, 310-311, 573
Mary Tyler Moore Show, The 528
Masak, Ron 425-426, 711
Mathers, Jimmy 34
Mattel 359
Maurice 43-45, 50, 124-126, 198-200, 206, 241-242, 277, 311, 345, 371, 412, 419, 429-434, 456-460, 468-473, 518, 520, 536, 540, 542, 638-642, 648-651, 664-667, 675
Max (bartender) 256
Mayberry, RFD 618
Mayflower, The 422-423
Mays, Willie 209-210, 434
McAllister, Professor 404-406
McBain, Charles and Alice 150-151
McCain, John 293
McCarthy, Eugene 358, 366
McCormick, Maureen 50, 134
McDevitt, Ruth 412
McGowan, Oliver 618
McKay, Adam 710
McKinley, J. Edward 158, 277, 477
McMann, Howard 354, 498-499
McMann and Tate 23, 38, 48, 63, 104-105, 108, 111, 132, 139, 150, 152, 162, 164, 170, 172, 183, 186, 210, 217, 219, 220, 226, 228, 238, 252-253, 256, 260, 277, 279, 285, 289, 296-297, 306, 308, 313, 316-318, 320, 322, 324, 345-346, 350, 353, 377-378, 382, 385, 396-397, 404, 407, 416, 421, 438, 455, 466, 469, 476, 492, 498, 519, 521, 523, 531, 535, 545, 558, 566, 569, 570, 580, 596, 602, 611, 646, 650, 655-657, 671, 689, 703
McMillan & Wife 624
McNamara, Robert 307
McQueen, Steve 402, 434
McTavish, Kevin 331-333
Meet Me in Las Vegas 355
Meiklejohn, Mr. and Mrs. 521-523
Metrano, Art 502, 550, 711
Mexico 176-177, 193, 233, 355, 437-439
Meyers, Gina 711
Miami 178-180, 359, 482
Michael 55-58, 149, 504
Michaels, DICK 379, 412, 512, 557, 591, 681, 697, 704
Michelle, Janee (Gee Mercadel) 572
Mike Douglas Show, The 270, 319, 322, 357
Mike Douglas Show, The 357
Miller, Marvin 111, 131
Miller, Rolf J. 564, 616
Millhowser, Gretchen & Michael 339
Millicent, Aunt 562-563
Mills, Johnny & Mr. 229-230
Milwaukee, MN 271
Miranda (cousin) 145
Mishimoto, Kensu 345-347
Miss Jasmine 45-47
Mission Impossible 564
Mitchell, George 673
Mod Squad, The 362
Mona Lisa, The 316, 515, 692
Monaco 298, 420
Monchet, Henri 246-247
Monkees, The 342, 502
Monkey 118, 279, 296-297, 325, 401-404, 418, 586-587, 669
Monroe, Johann Sebastian 367-368
Monster (Liza's boyfriend) 39-40
Montdrako, Lord Clyde 310-311
Montgomery, Elizabeth /Liz/Lizzie 9, 13, 19, 24, 27-28, 32, 37, 45, 47, 49-50, 54, 66, 72, 78, 82-83, 85, 87, 90, 92, 95, 102, 108, 111, 113, 118-119, 126, 131, 148, 155, 158, 162, 166-167, 173, 177-178, 183, 185, 189, 193-

INDEX

194, 196, 199, 203, 208, 213, 216, 218, 229-230, 232, 242, 245-246, 248, 254-255, 265, 267, 271, 281, 284, 288, 289, 293, 295, 298, 305, 312, 314, 328-329, 335, 350, 355, 357, 363, 366, 368, 372, 374, 379-380, 386, 388, 394, 396, 404, 406, 408, 416, 418, 423, 426, 429, 434, 439-441, 445, 447-448, 450-452, 455-457, 459-460, 462, 464, 482-483, 485, 487, 491, 494, 502, 505, 509, 515, 524-525, 531, 533, 539, 543, 546, 549-550, 557-558, 564, 566, 569, 571-573, 576, 578-579, 585, 587-588, 591, 600, 603, 605, 608, 611, 613, 615-616, 621-623, 625, 629-631, 633-634, 637-638, 640, 642, 644, 648, 650-651, 654, 657, 660, 663, 665, 670, 672-673, 675, 676, 680-681, 683, 690, 693-694, 696, 700, 704-705, 709-710
Montgomery, Robert 24, 45, 573
Monticello Carpet 655-656
Moon Landing 14, 17, 232, 437, 442, 471, 585
Moonthatch Inn 375-376
Moore, Joanna 249
Moore, Mary Tyler 183, 528
Moorehead, Agnes/Aggie 9, 19, 24, 30, 45, 55, 72, 78, 87, 114, 124, 170, 172, 180, 183, 189-190, 202, 208, 211, 213, 218, 221, 230, 232, 234, 236, 244-245, 259, 264, 267, 270, 281, 301, 312, 315, 319, 322, 326, 335-336, 355, 357, 359, 372, 379, 396, 407, 440-441, 462, 471, 473, 482, 487, 491, 509, 515, 521, 524, 534, 536, 547, 550, 574, 576, 603, 611, 616-617, 623, 625-626, 638, 640, 642, 645, 648, 655, 658, 663, 666, 679, 682, 684, 694, 704-706, 709
Morgan, Mr. 250-252
Morning Glory Circle Welcome Wagon Committee 28-29, 61, 102
Morrison, Jim 280, 617
Morrow, Karen 709
Mortimer, Jesse (Mortimer Instant Soup) 312-315, 567
Morton, Mr. (Morton Milk) 237-238
Mosler, H.B. 383-386
Mother Flannigan's Irish Stew 603-604
Movie Stars magazine 448
Mr. Blackwell Presents 190, 270
Mr. Ed 162
Mr. Roger's Neighborhood 333
Mrs. Sundance 451

Mt. Rocky Mutual Insurance 611
Mumy, Billy 58, 140, 605
Munster, Go Home 189, 645
Munsters, The 24, 181, 189, 482
Muppets from Space 579
Muppets, The 409, 579
Murphy, Diane 194, 196, 206, 385, 441, 526, 591, 670
Murphy, Erin 9, 194, 196, 199, 206, 218, 279, 292, 293, 295, 335, 385, 392, 441, 488, 494, 526, 578, 591, 670, 683-684, 697, 704, 710-711
"Old MacDonald Had a Farm" 293, 594
Muskie, Edmund 359
Mustin, Burt 158, 584
Mutz, Kimberly 10
My Favorite Martian 18
My Lai Massacre 338
Nabors, Jim 336
Name of the Game, The 440
Naomi 152, 450
NASA 17, 231-232, 239, 347, 368, 440, 471
Nassau 23, 231
Nelson, Barry 267
Nelson, Gaylord 524
Nero 286
Nesmith, Ottola 682
Neumann, Dorothy 255
New Jersey 271
New Orleans 235-236, 364-366, 572, 618
New York 76, 113, 125, 161, 179, 182, 194, 257, 262, 265, 315, 353, 381, 435, 442, 552, 676
New York Mets 455, 457, 487
New York Times 112
Newlarkin, Adam 121-123
Newman, Paul 450
Newmar, Julie 660
Newton 541-542, 558, 560
NFL Monday Night Football 528
Nick-at-Nite 9, 151, 194
Nickerson, Mr. and Mrs. 492, 494
Nielsen Ratings 357
Night Gallery 574, 626
Niles-Munster, Mary Jane 287-288
Nixon, Richard 359, 376, 379, 407, 525-526, 543, 617, 651, 670
Nobel Peace Prize 32
Noel, Chris 51

North Church 550
Norton 522, 524
Norton, Cliff 158, 189, 409, 524
Norton, Mr. and Mrs. 667-670
Norton, Ralph 668-669
O'Brian, Brian 170
O'Connor, Donald 336
O'Hara, Frank 362
O'Neal, Ryan 249
O'Riley, "Danger" 90-93, 433, 492, 507
O'Riley, Priscilla "Pleasure" 79-80, 90, 232, 433, 456
O'Shanter, Tim 513-515
O'Toole, Gerry 201-204
Ocky 212-213, 331-333, 345-347 439
Odd Couple, The 534
Oklahoma 236
Oklahoma! 561
Old Testament 213
Oliver Twist 486
Omega National Bank 350, 352
Onassis, Aristotle 372
One Life to Live 358
Ono, Yoko 213, 440
Ophelia 658-660
Orazi, Sharon 10, 102, 351, 409, 435, 439, 446, 454, 474, 513, 564, 581, 634, 669-670
Orbison, Jack 515
Orlando, Florida 630
Orvis 347-350
Oscar Mayer 547, 569, 572
Oswald, Lee Harvey 232
Otis, Leslie 399
Our World 271
Outcasts, The 440
Owen, Reginald 213, 347
Palachi.com 526, 547
Panda (cousin) 655
Parenthia 347, 349
Paris 40-42, 47, 119, 126, 163, 317, 361, 380, 617, 638, 640, 641
Parker, Fess 525
Parkinson, Mr. 217
Parkside Rest Home 490
Parsons, Ms. 411-412
Partridge Family, The 211, 365, 417, 534, 560
Partridge, Hedley 141, 142, 241, 573
Passamore, Dr. 136-138
Password 267, 550, 585, 588, 611, 676

Password Plus 550
Patterson, New York 230, 693
Patterson, Widow 541-542
Paul II, Pope John 68
Paul VI, Pope 126
Paul, Bob 677-678
Peabody Museum 548
Peabody, Mrs. 682-683, 691-694
Peanuts (hairdresser) 384, 386, 404, 406, 456, 462, 539, 603
Pearce, Alice 27, 90, 97, 138, 158, 161, 165, 166, 169, 175, 183, 188, 206, 259, 304, 332, 450, 457
Pennybaker, Cynthia & Ed 244-245
Perfect Pizza 104, 105
Perkins, Ted 415
Perry, Barbara 386
Petticoat Junction 18, 518
Peyton Place 171
Phineas 303-304
Phipps, Professor Poindexter 486, 488
Phoebe the Frog 266-267
Picasso, Pablo 639, 641
Pickering, Mr. 71
Pie 39-40, 284, 293-294, 399, 482, 644, 652
Pierce, Captain John 423
Pierce, Franklin 223, 379
Pierce, Mayson 9
Pierce, William 423
Pilato, Herbie J 10, 111, 131, 151, 166, 254, 396, 431, 485, 523, 600, 663
Pillsbury Dough Boy 136
Pink Floyd 272
Pioneer Village 548
Pirhana, Contessa 674-675
Pisano, Bonano 630, 632
Pitlik, Noam 541
Planet of the Apes 345
Platt, Ed 564
Plymouth 302, 379
Poe, Edgar Allan 91
Potter, Mr. 537-538, 541
Powell, Richard 504
Prentiss, Paula 357
Prescott, Mr. and Mrs. (Prescott Shoes) 670-673
Presley, Elvis 270, 376, 388, 443
Preston, Robert 172
Prickett, Maudie 131, 391, 684, 694

Priddy, Nancy 539, 611
Priest, Pat 189, 457, 485, 505
Prince Pepe 280
Pritchfield, Mr. 316-317
Private Navy of Sgt. O'Harrell, The 355
Prune Valley Retirement Village 322, 325
Pulp Fiction 502
Punch and Judy 645
Quaker Oats 21, 28, 33, 38, 42, 47, 52, 61, 66, 70, 74, 78, 82, 87, 93, 96, 100, 106, 117, 121, 126, 132, 136, 141, 145, 148, 152, 155, 159, 162-163, 167, 172, 207, 244, 366, 485
Queen of the Witches 275-277, 282, 284, 331, 376, 533, 536, 539, 554
Queen Victoria 13, 204, 250-252, 453, 536
Quigley, Mrs. 490-491, 526
Quinn, Teddy 340, 385
Rafkin, Alan 59
Ralph 329-330
Rand, Dolly 165-166
Randall, Liza 38-39, 507
Randall, Tony 112
Rat Patrol, The 322
Raven, The 91
Ray, James Earl 358
Reactor Mach II 235
Reagan, Ronald 213
Red, Rufus the 201, 203-204
Reddington, Leatrice and Ray 10, 151
Reddington, Pam 298
Redford, Robert 450
Redmond, Marge 357
Reduce-a-lator 576, 579-580
Reed, Paul 227-228
Regal Silverware 642
Rembrandt 194, 248
Republican National Convention 359
Rerun Show, The 180, 465
Revere, Paul 122-123, 548-549
Reynolds, Debbie 170, 336
Rheinhouse, Dr. 490, 492
Riano, Renie 617
Richard, Gary 547
Rickles, Don 335, 585, 670
Riddle, Nelson 336
Riggs, Travis 10
Rightmire, Osgood 172-174, 270
Roach, Marilynne K. 557
Robbie (cousin)189, 626, 628-629

Robbins, Mr. (Robbins Baby Food) 174, 176
Roberts, Roy 295, 333, 615
Robinson, Jay 452
Robinson, Mr. 170
Robinson, Mrs. 290-291
Rock, Chris 180
Rockeford, J. Earl & Mrs. 421-423
Rockfields, Mr. and Mrs. (Rockfield Furniture) 585-586
Rockwell, George Lincoln 272
Rocky and Bullwinkle 169
Rodney 180-181, 560
Roger Conant statue 550, 552
Rogers, Kasey 74, 196, 246, 499, 517, 591, 597, 603, 644, 711
Rohn, Jennifer 10
Rohrbach, Mr. 275-277
Roland, Mr. 691-693
Rolling Stones 441, 447
Rollnick Jr., Charlton 682-684
Rollnick, Mrs. 683
Rollo 317-319, 534, 561
Romani, Mr. 280-281
Rome 120, 286, 401, 632, 634-638
Romero, Caesar 536, 550
Room 222 443, 524
Rooney, Mickey 222
Rooney, Tim 222
Rosemary's Baby 564
Roses, Black Peruvian 129-131
Rotisserie, The 413
Rowan and Martin's Laugh-In 326, 440, 658
Ruby, Jack 232
Rudolph, the Red-Nosed Reindeer 50
Ruggles, Charles 573
Sabrina the Teenage Witch (1971) 623
Sabrina the Teenage Witch (1996) 579
Saigon, Mr. 640
Saint James, Susan 440, 624
Saks, Sol 31
Salem 13-14, 73-74, 121, 190, 246, 277, 423, 426, 525-527, 531-532, 534, 536, 537, 539-544, 546-555, 557, 581, 585, 611, 616-617, 626, 710-711
Salem Witch Trials, The 557
Salem's Summer of Sam 526, 547
Salvation Army 489
Samantha and Endora board game 85
Samantha paper doll 85, 103

San Francisco 234, 265, 616, 674
Sande, Walter 655
Sanford and Son 673
Sanford, Isabel 365
Sargent, Dick 9, 64, 112, 119, 158, 172, 180, 191, 197, 199, 204, 244, 292, 321-322, 355, 359, 376, 423, 429-430, 439, 440, 450, 455, 470, 475, 481-482, 486, 488, 499, 507, 517, 526, 533, 536, 550, 564, 584, 587, 595, 605, 613, 625, 638, 650-651, 654, 663, 672, 688, 690-691, 696, 706, 709-710
Saturday Night Live 282, 502
Saunders Soups 265
Saunders, Marcella 573
Saunders, Mr. 265-266
Save Most market 385
Schallert, William 455
Scibetta, Joe 403
Scooby Doo, Where Are You? 448
Scott, Eric 605
Scranton, Mr. 226-227
Screen Gems 9, 119, 208, 211, 408
Screen Stories 155, 368
Scully, Vin 232
Sebastian, Adrienne (Adrienne Sebastian Cosmetics)396-397
Seegar, Sara 297
Seesaw Girl and Me, The 430
Serena 95, 153-154, 158, 277, 282-284, 297-298, 326-329, 363-365, 372-376, 379, 400-404, 411-416, 424-426, 442, 455, 458, 466, 482, 493-494, 500-502, 505-507, 510-512, 514, 520, 541-547, 549, 553, 560, 565-566, 573, 581-585, 589-592, 598-601, 606-608, 615, 625-630, 647, 674-675, 679-681
Sesame Street 14, 468, 477, 629, 648
Shakespeare, William 336, 433, 437, 468, 639, 641, 650
Sharp, Mr. and Mrs. 336-338
Shaw, Reta 37, 158, 198, 311, 423, 700
Shea Stadium 113, 455
Sheldrake, Mr. (Sheldrake Sausages) 235-236
Shelley Shoes 106-107
Shemp 638
Shotwell, Mr. 476-477
Siamese cat 65-66, 70-72, 658
Silverton, Lester & Mrs. 646-648
Silverton, Robin 646-648
Simian, Harry 417

Simon & Simon 222, 710
Simon, Robert F. 54, 312, 615
Simpson, Mark 10, 26, 29, 33, 36, 38, 41, 43, 49, 51, 57, 62, 83, 109, 396, 494, 711
Simpsons, The 14
Since You Went Away 626
Singing Nun, The 170, 208
Sirhan Sirhan 358
Slattery, Richard X. 585, 670
Sleeping Beauty 329-330
Slocum, Mr. 354
Smith Family, The 623
Smith, Howard 322
Smothers Brothers Comedy Hour, The 242
Smothers, Dick 340
Snow White and the Seven Dwarfs 32
Snow, Jack 435
Solow, Mr. (Solow Toy Company) 233-234
Sommers, H.P. 486-489
Sommers, J.P. 320
Sommers, Sheila 23-24, 320-322, 324-325, 362, 402
Sony Home Entertainment 10, 14, 225, 267, 362-363, 406, 572, 579, 623, 710-711
Sorrells, Robert 166
Sorrento's 404
Sound of Music, The (stage musical) 76
South Pacific 655
Soviet Union 239
Spengler, Mr. 661-662
Springer Pet Food 296, 327-328
Springer, Miss 397
Springer, Mr. and Mrs. 296-297
Square Green Spots Disease 129-130, 175, 295, 522, 699
St. Louis, MO 185
Staley, Joan 158
Standish, Miles 303-304
Stanton, General 344
Star Trek 144, 244, 440, 676
Steinem, Gloria 618
Stengel, Casey 114
Stephens, Adam 194, 434, 459-460, 462, 464-465, 468, 470, 473, 481, 487, 489, 492-494, 521, 536, 539, 543, 555, 564, 566, 569, 571, 591-592, 597, 601-602, 613-614, 638, 645, 647-649, 652, 661, 664-668, 676, 692, 694, 696-697, 705

INDEX

Stephens, Frank 53-54, 66-68, 159, 161, 257-259, 293-295, 331, 333, 391, 418-421, 458-460, 474-475, 489-490, 584, 614-615
Stephens, Phyllis 53-54, 66-68, 79, 90, 161-162, 257-259, 293-294, 331-333, 339, 381, 383, 388-389, 391, 398, 399, 411-412, 418-421, 446-447, 474-475, 458-460, 474, 489-492, 584, 605-607, 613-616
Stephens, Tabatha/Tabitha 151, 153-162, 167-169, 175, 178, 189, 193-200, 204-206, 210-212, 215, 221, 225-227, 229, 233-234, 236, 240-241, 244, 248, 255-259, 261, 263, 265, 275-280, 282, 284, 286, 290-293, 295-299, 301-303, 305, 310, 314-315, 322, 326-327, 329-331, 333-334, 337-341, 340, 344-345, 347, 350, 352-353, 362-363, 365, 366-368, 372-375, 381-383, 385-386, 388-392, 395, 399, 404, 408-409, 411, 416-420, 423-424, 426, 430-436, 439, 445-447, 450-451, 453, 457, 459, 462-463, 466, 473-474, 478-481, 483-484, 486, 488-489, 492-494, 503-504, 507, 509, 513-514, 534, 536, 547, 555, 564, 566, 569-573, 576-578, 581, 587, 589, 591, 597, 601-602, 604, 613-616, 630, 645-648, 652-654, 660-661, 663-664, 666, 668, 670, 676-678, 682-685, 691-692, 694-696, 698, 701, 705, 709
Stern Chemicals 178
Steve Allen Show, The 359
Stewart, Dale 10
Stone, Frazer, Moreheim, Cooper, Cooper and Washburn 476
Stratton, Chet 527
Stymie card game 85
Suddenly Single 642
Summers, Hope 158, 564
Sunset-Gower Studio 525
Sunshine, Augustus 519-520
Super Bowl 234
Super Soapy Soap 226
Superman 496, 312
Susan 51-52
Susie Bruisie doll 313-314
Swackhamer, E.W. 216, 681
Swenson, Thor "Thunderbolt" 79-80
Swigert, Jack 521
Sylvester, A.J. 463-464
Tabitha 331, 709
Tahiti 381

Taj-mahal 186, 275, 277
Talbot, Nita 357, 683
Tammy Grimes Show, The 191, 194, 197, 199, 699
Tarantino, Quentin 502
Tate, Jonathan 124-125, 145, 198, 199-201, 228, 464, 596-597, 670
Tate, Larry 31-32, 35-37, 39-43, 45-48, 50, 64-65, 69, 71, 73, 75, 91-96, 98, 104-108, 111, 117, 119-120, 124-125, 132-134, 136, 139-140, 143, 145-151, 160, 162-163, 171-172, 174, 178-179, 184-186, 195-197, 200, 210, 212, 214, 216-221, 223, 226-227, 232-238, 240, 244-248, 250-253, 255-256, 260-266, 268-270, 277-281, 283-285, 287-292, 295-297, 305-308, 310-314, 316-317, 319-321, 323-325, 327-330, 333, 337-338, 340-343, 345-347, 350, 352, 354, 361, 374, 377-378, 380, 382-383, 386-388, 394, 396-397, 400-401, 403, 407-410, 416-417, 421, 437-439, 445, 449-457, 461-463, 466-472, 476-477, 479-482, 486-487, 489, 492, 494-496, 498-502, 506, 508, 510-511, 513-516, 519-520, 522-523, 531-532, 534-536, 543-545, 547-554, 558-560, 562, 564-572, 574-575, 580, 585-590, 592-597, 602-612, 623, 630-632, 634-635, 637, 642-647, 653-659, 661-662, 667-669, 674-675, 679-681, 685, 689, 695, 700, 702-703
Tate, Louise 40, 47-48, 50, 63, 74-75, 93-96, 111, 125, 143, 145-146, 152, 162-163, 171-172, 174, 186, 195-197, 199-200, 210, 214-216, 220-221, 237-238, 245, 247, 262-266, 282, 291, 296-297, 306, 319, 327-328, 330, 340-341, 386, 388, 464, 479-481, 483, 494, 499, 510, 515-517, 522, 534, 547-548, 550, 562, 591, 595-598, 602, 609-610, 642-645, 653-654, 659, 670, 679-681, 700, 705
Tate, Sharon 442
Taylor, Amy 389-391
Teen Witch 710
Tennessee 270, 343
That Girl 277, 357, 619
That's Life 406
They Came to Cordura 228, 564
This Proud Land 171
Thomas Jefferson High School 569, 572-573
Thomas, Dave 471
Thomas, Marlo 357

Thomas, Melody 49, 502, 539, 600, 629, 672
Thompson, Elizabeth 452
Three's Company 216
Thriller 189, 255
Tibet 182, 247, 698
Ticheba, Queen of the Witches 275-276, 412
Tiffin, Pamela 172
Time Magazine 171, 693
Timothy, Heather Pierce 9, 218, 298
Tinker Bell Diapers 381-382
Tippet's Toy Store 146, 154
Tobias, George 27, 97, 580, 709
Tobin, Dan 171, 232, 246, 267
Tom and Jerry 124
TomKat Tractors 658
Tommy (the orphan) 55-58, 334
Tommy 291-292
Tonight Show with Johnny Carson, The 524
Top Pop 495-496
Top Tiger cologne 451
Tournament of Roses Parade 232
Town & Country magazine 550
Towners Elementary 691, 693
Toy Soldier 277-279
Tracy, Spencer 270
Tranberg, Charles 10, 694
Traynor, Mr. 396-397
Truth God 147, 185
Tucker, Evelyn 416-417
Tugwell, Captain 348-349
Turgeon, Mr. 162-163
Tuttle, Lurene 158
TV Guide 10, 47, 151, 178, 271, 329, 410, 429, 437, 445, 473, 499
TV Land 10, 246, 710
TV Picture Life 573
Tweety 70-72
Udall, Stewart 185
UFO 347, 350, 579
UNICEF 427, 428, 460-462
United Cosmetics 182
United Kingdom 239, 272
Untouchables, The 564
Urich, Robert 709
Valentine, Karen 524
Valley of the Dolls 442
Van Gogh, Vincent 298, 675
Van Millwood, John 433-434
Vanita, Clio 400-404

Vaughn, Robert 27
Venus (planet) 88, 498, 598, 601
Venus/Vanessa 634-638
Vernon, Irene 174, 196
Verona, Ramon 508, 518, 521, 523, 610
Vic's *Bewitched* Page 10, 208
Vietnam War 14, 17, 76, 113, 169, 183, 262, 265, 290, 293, 295, 307, 322, 338, 340, 353, 366, 372, 376, 543, 551, 558, 616, 651
Vino Vanita 400, 403
Violet (Northern Girl) 137
Virginian, The 547
Voland, Herb 297
Von Fuchs, Baron 626, 628-629
Voyagers! 222
W, Agent 344
Waldo 551-554
Wallace, Marcia 613, 710
Walt Disney World 630
Walters, Gus 165-166
Walters, Mr. and Mrs. Bill 318-319
Waltons, The 605, 710
Warbell, Jay (Warbell Dress) 252, 254
Warbell, Terry 171, 252-254
Warden, Jack 658
Warlock Club 124-125, 508, 518
Warner Bros. Studio Ranch 27, 50, 140, 293, 396, 432, 480, 601, 711
Washburn, Mr. 476-477
Washington, D.C. 272, 290, 340, 616
Washington, George 13, 204, 684-690
Washington, Martha 536, 687, 689-690
Waterhouse Account 186
Watson, Debbie 189
Watts Riots 113
Wayne, Carol 173, 465
Wayne, Fredd 222
Wayne, Nina 173
Webley Foods 320-321
Wellingford, Sir Herbert 621-622, 625
Wendle, Leroy 325
Wendy's Old Fashioned Hamburgers 471
West, Adam 52
Westerfield, James 626
Westerman, Nydia 158, 526
Westport 75, 153, 178, 230, 503, 505, 603
What's the Matter with Helen 617
Whirlaway Washing Machines 689
White, Andrea 676

White, David 163, 200, 279, 335, 345, 380, 396, 397, 410, 445, 474, 482, 554, 564, 595, 634, 657, 681
White, Edward Higgins 239
Whittle Agency 237
Whittle, Mr. 237-238
Whitzett, Gideon 69, 70, 435, 437, 499
Who, The 442
Wicked Witch 652-653
Wild Wild West 244
Wilkerson, Mr. 260
Williams, Matthew 367-368
Willie (uncle) 341-342, 616
Willow Street Park 383
Willy Wonka and the Chocolate Factory 386
Wilson, Dick 99, 136, 158, 234, 277, 688
Wilson, Keith & Dorothy 569-572
Wilson, Lisa 569-572
Wilson, Ms. 404-406
Windemere, Lady 643-644
Winters, Roland 354
Witch House 537, 539, 556
Witches' Council, The 372-373, 375-376, 423-424, 426-428, 432-433, 457, 490, 533, 543-544, 552, 555, 557, 599, 601, 705-706
Who's Been Sleeping in My Bed? 148
Witches' Nursery School 340
Witching Hour, The 386
Wizard of Oz, The 36, 437, 462
WKRP in Cincinatti 603

Wolcott, Harrison (Wolcott Towers) 674-675
Wolfe Brothers Department Stores 69
Wonderful World of Disney, The 645, 648
Wood, Mark 517
Woodcutter's Wife 653
Woodruff-Perry, Heather 255, 257, 259, 527, 711
Woodstock Music and Arts Festival 442, 527
World Trade Center 618
Wright, Ed 100-102
Xanadu, Shah of 398
York, Dick 9, 24, 42, 47, 66, 70, 80, 103, 108, 113, 121, 128, 131, 146, 155, 171, 179, 193, 197, 204, 228, 230, 252, 259-270, 277, 281, 290, 305, 309, 330, 333, 335, 342, 357, 368, 372, 376, 379, 388, 396-399, 406, 408, 410, 412, 415, 418, 421-423, 426, 430-432, 437, 439, 442, 445-446, 460, 470, 482, 499, 506, 526, 564, 584, 626, 651, 691, 696, 706, 709-710
York, Francine 637, 644
York, Gerald "Herbie" 512, 539, 543, 547, 557, 641
Young, Gig 439
Young, Julie 168
Young Runaways, The 359
Zeno 59-61
Zip-Zip 66, 72
Zoll, Mayor Samuel 539
Zoom detergent 380

Bear Manor Media

Classic Cinema.
Timeless TV.
Retro Radio.

WWW.BEARMANORMEDIA.COM

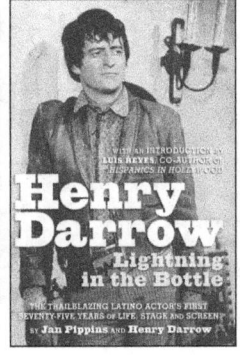

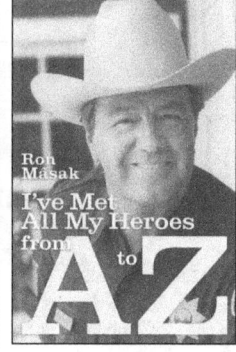

www.ingramcontent.com/pod-product-compliance
Lightning Source LLC
Chambersburg PA
CBHW071229300426
44116CB00008B/968